MODELS OF WORKING

Mechanisms of Active Maintenance and Executive Control

Edited by

AKIRA MIYAKE AND PRITI SHAH

CAMBRIDGE
UNIVERSITY PRESS

PUBLISHED BY THE PRESS SYNDICATE OF THE UNIVERSITY OF CAMBRIDGE
The Pitt Building, Trumpington Street, Cambridge, United Kingdom

CAMBRIDGE UNIVERSITY PRESS
The Edinburgh Building, Cambridge CB2 2RU, UK   http://www.cup.cam.ac.uk
40 West 20th Street, New York, NY 10011-4211, USA   http://www.cup.org
10 Stamford Road, Oakleigh, Melbourne 3166, Australia

First published 1999

Printed in the United States of America

Typeface Stone Serif 9/12 pt.   *System* QuarkXpress™   [HT]

A catalog record for this book is available from the British Library.

Library of Congress Cataloging-in-Publication Data

Models of working memory : mechanisms of active maintenance and
executive control / edited by Akira Miyake, Priti Shah.
p.   cm.
Includes bibliographical references and indexes.
ISBN 0-521-58325-X. – ISBN 0-521-58721-2 (pbk.)
1. Short-term memory.   I. Miyake, Akira, 1966– .   II. Shah,
Priti, 1968– .
BF378.S54M63 1999
153.1´3 – dc21   98–35134
                                                           CIP

ISBN 0 521 58325 X hardback
ISBN 0 521 58721 2 paperback

Contents

Contributors

Alan D. Baddeley
Department of Psychology
University of Bristol
8 Woodland Road
Bristol BS8 1TN
United Kingdom
e-mail: Alan.Baddeley@bristol.ac.uk

Philip J. Barnard
Medical Research Council Cognition and Brain Sciences Unit
15 Chaucer Road
Cambridge CB2 2EF
United Kingdom
e-mail: philip.barnard@mrc-cbu.cam.ac.uk

Todd S. Braver
Department of Psychology
Washington University
St. Louis, MO 63130-4899
e-mail: tbraver@artsci.wustl.edu

Jonathan D. Cohen
Department of Psychology
Princeton University
Princeton, NJ 08544
e-mail: jdc@princeton.edu

Nelson Cowan
Department of Psychology
210 McAlester Hall
University of Missouri
Columbia, MO 65211
e-mail: psycowan@showme.missouri.edu

Peter F. Delaney
Department of Psychology
Florida State University
Tallahassee, FL 32306-1270
e-mail: delaney@psy.fsu.edu

Randall W. Engle
School of Psychology
Georgia Institute of Technology
Atlanta, GA 30332-0170
e-mail: randall.engle@psych.gatech.edu

K. Anders Ericsson
Department of Psychology
Florida State University
Tallahassee, FL 32306-1270
e-mail: ericsson@psy.fsu.edu

Alice F. Healy
Department of Psychology
University of Colorado at Boulder
Campus Box 345
Boulder, CO 80309-0345
e-mail: ahealy@psych.colorado.edu

Mary Hegarty
Department of Psychology
University of California, Santa Barbara
Santa Barbara, CA 93106
e-mail: hegarty@psych.ucsb.edu

Michael J. Kane
Department of Psychology
Georgia State University
University Plaza
Atlanta, GA 30303
e-mail: mkane@gsu.edu

David E. Kieras
Artificial Intelligence Laboratory
Department of Electrical Engineering and Computer Science
University of Michigan
Advanced Technology Laboratory Building
1101 Beal Avenue
Ann Arbor, MI 48109-2110
e-mail: kieras@eecs.umich.edu

Walter Kintsch
Department of Psychology
University of Colorado at Boulder
Campus Box 345
Boulder, CO 80309-0345
e-mail: wkintsch@clipr.colorado.edu

Christian Lebiere
Department of Psychology
Carnegie Mellon University
Pittsburgh, PA 15213-3890
e-mail: cl+@cmu.edu

Richard L. Lewis
Department of Computer and Information Science
Center for Cognitive Science
Ohio State University
2015 Neil Avenue Mall
Columbus, OH 43210
e-mail: rick@cis.ohio-state.edu

Robert H. Logie
Department of Psychology
University of Aberdeen
Kings College
Aberdeen, AB24 2UB
Scotland, United Kingdom
e-mail: r.logie@abdn.ac.uk

Marsha C. Lovett
Department of Psychology
Carnegie Mellon University
Pittsburgh, PA 15213-3890
e-mail: lovett+@cmu.edu

David E. Meyer
Department of Psychology
University of Michigan
525 East University
Ann Arbor, MI 48109-1109
e-mail: demeyer@umich.edu

Akira Miyake
Department of Psychology
University of Colorado at Boulder
Campus Box 345
Boulder, CO 80309-0345
e-mail: miyake@psych.colorado.edu

Shane Mueller
Department of Psychology
University of Michigan
525 East University
Ann Arbor, MI 48109-1109
e-mail: smueller@umich.edu

Randall C. O'Reilly
Department of Psychology
University of Colorado at Boulder
Campus Box 345
Boulder, CO 80309-0345
e-mail: oreilly@psych.colorado.edu

Bruce F. Pennington
Department of Psychology
University of Denver
2155 S. Race Street
Denver, CO 80210-4633
e-mail: bpenning@nova.psy.du.edu

Lynne M. Reder
Department of Psychology
Carnegie Mellon University
Pittsburgh, PA 15213-3890
e-mail: reder@cmu.edu

Timothy A. Salthouse
School of Psychology
Georgia Institute of Technology
Atlanta, GA 30332-0170
e-mail: tim.salthouse@psych.gatech.edu

Walter Schneider
LRDC
3939 O'Hara St.
University of Pittsburgh
Pittsburgh, PA 15260
e-mail: wws+@pitt.edu

Travis Seymour
Department of Psychology
University of Michigan
525 East University
Ann Arbor, MI 48109-1109
e-mail: nogard@umich.edu

Priti Shah
Department of Psychology
University of Memphis
Campus Box 526400
Memphis, TN 38152-6400
e-mail: pshah@memphis.edu

Stephen W. Tuholski
Department of Psychology
Southern Illinois University at Edwardsville
Edwardsville, IL 62026
e-mail: stuhols@siue.edu

Richard M. Young
Department of Psychology
University of Hertfordshire
Hatfield
Herts AL10 9AB
United Kingdom
e-mail: R.M.Young@herts.ac.uk

In memory of my father

A.M.

For my parents

P.S.

Preface

Without doubt, working memory is one of the "hottest" topics in cognitive psychology and cognitive neuroscience. Since the publication of Baddeley's (1986) landmark book, several monographs and edited volumes that explore various aspects of working memory have been published (e.g., Gathercole, 1996; Gathercole & Baddeley, 1993; Logie, 1995; Logie & Gilhooly, 1998; Richardson, Engle, Hasher, Logie, Stoltzfus, & Zacks, 1996; Vallar & Shallice, 1990). Also, at least four journals have published a special issue on this topic (*International Journal of Behavioral Development*, 1994; see also de Ribaupierre & Hitch, 1994; *Memory & Cognition*, 1993; *Neuropsychology*, 1994; *Quarterly Journal of Experimental Psychology*, 1996), and another is also planning to publish a special section in 2000 (*Journal of Experimental Psychology: General*). In July of 1994 – 20 years after the publication of the seminal article on working memory that defined the field (Baddeley & Hitch, 1974) – an international conference specifically dedicated to working memory was held in Cambridge, UK, bringing together more than 200 researchers from across the world.

Working memory is also one of the most intensively studied areas in a new emerging field of study, cognitive neuroscience. Reflecting the dramatic surge of interest in neuroimaging studies of working memory, two general science magazines (*Science* and *Scientific American*) recently published articles that report the state of the art of research inquiry into the neural basis of working memory (Beardsley, 1997; Wickelgren, 1997). Working memory research has also made important advances on the theoretical front, producing a number of well-developed models of working memory that are quite diverse in their theoretical scope and emphasis (e.g., Anderson, Reder, & Lebiere, 1996; Baddeley, 1986; Barnard, 1985; Cowan, 1988; Ericsson & Kintsch, 1995; Just & Carpenter, 1992; Schneider & Detweiler, 1987).

We believe that the field has made significant progress during the past 25 years and has reached a critical point at which detailed comparisons of different theoretical proposals are not only possible but would be tremendously beneficial for further theoretical development of working memory research. The central rationale behind this volume is to provide such a forum for systematic comparisons of existing models and theories of working memory.

This strong theoretical focus reflects a current need in the field. Whereas existing models of working memory each provide a sophisticated account of certain aspects of working memory processes and functions, different models have different theoretical emphases and tend to leave some other aspects of working memory relatively unspecified. Although such differences in scope and emphasis are quite natural and not necessarily bad, they could have some negative consequences on working memory research by serving as a source of misunderstanding and confusion and making detailed empirical and theoretical evaluations of different theoretical proposals a rather difficult task.

The main goal of this volume is to alleviate this problem and encourage communication among different working memory researchers by focusing on detailed comparisons of current working memory models. This volume attempts to fulfill this goal by asking leading working memory theorists in the field to address the same set of theoretical issues and questions that have been guiding recent research in this area. These designated questions, to be explained and motivated in Chapter 1 (see Table 1.1), are broad in scope and concern the nature, functions, and structure of working memory as well as its biological implementation. By explicitly asking each contributor to address a common set of important (and often controversial) issues and questions, we thought we might be able to better elucidate the commonalities and differences among different working memory models that may not necessarily have been clear and/or may not have been fully appreciated before.

It is probably important to point out here our bias in the selection of the working memory models represented in this volume. Our main focus was to include models or theoretical frameworks that are broad enough in their scope that they can provide principled answers to the designated questions. We believe that working memory is not an isolated cognitive component that operates independently of other aspects of cognition and, hence, that a complete understanding of working memory requires considering it within a broader context of a cognitive architecture. The models included in this volume, thus, are often more than just models of working memory and have a lot to say about the overall architecture of human cognition.

This emphasis on the breadth of theoretical scope means that some important models or theoretical approaches that focus primarily on some specific aspects of working memory are not included in this volume. For example, we decided not to include a number of well-developed computational models of phonological short-term memory documented in the literature, primarily because these computational models cannot provide a basis for many (if not all) of the wide-ranging designated questions, although they are impressive in their details and precision. We refer readers interested in these models to the Gathercole (1996) volume. For a similar reason, we were also not able to represent in this volume interesting conceptions and theoretical proposals that are derived primarily from empirical research on one specific aspect of working memory, such as the nature of working memory involved in sentence comprehension and the neural/cellular basis of object and spatial working memory.

Even though we focus on models and theoretical frameworks with a broader scope, we probably have missed some important models of working memory. One such model is Just and Carpenter's, originally outlined in their 1992 article. They were invited to contribute a chapter to this volume, but, unfortunately, they decided not to contribute a chapter partly because of previous commitments and partly because of considerable changes in their views since 1992 as a result of their recent work on functional neuroimaging.

Despite these provisos, we believe that this volume nonetheless represents a wide range of influential theoretical perspectives on working memory and that the contributors have done an excellent job of fleshing out their current theoretical views. As editors, however, we attempted to make sure that this book is more than simply a collection of excellent chapters describing different theoretical perspectives. The editing process implemented a number of mechanisms that would ensure that the 13 chapters are tightly integrated with one another in such a way that readers will have a good idea of how these models of working memory are related to one another.

First, as we mentioned, the chapters in this volume addressed the same set of theoretical questions, which not only serve as recurring themes that run through the entire volume, but also provide a basis for systematic comparisons across different models of working memory represented in this volume (Chapters 2 to 11). Although the contributors differ in the way they addressed the eight designated questions (some directly tackle them one by one, whereas others address them within the context of describing their own model and relevant empirical research), they nonetheless addressed all the questions in some way or other. These designated questions are also the main focus of the remaining three chapters in this volume. The introductory chapter (Chapter 1) outlines the eight designated theoretical questions and their significance in working memory research. The discussion chapter (Chapter 12) revisits the designated questions one by one, compares and contrasts the answers provided by each chapter, and evaluates how well the models as a whole addressed each theoretical issue. Finally, the concluding chapter (Chapter 13) points out some commonalities that seem to be emerging across the 10 models and lists some of the unresolved theoretical issues for each of the designated questions.

Second, the editing process provided ample opportunities for the contributors to exchange their opinions and relate their own perspectives to other theorists' perspectives. After the first drafts of the chapters were in, all the contributors got together at the University of Colorado, Boulder, campus for a four-day companion symposium entitled "Models of Working Memory" (July 10–13, 1997) to present the ideas developed in their respective chapters, exchange their viewpoints, and comment on each other's answers to the eight designated questions. We believe this volume is all the better for the active interactions we had at the symposium. The symposium was particularly informative in making us realize that, although there are certainly some differences in opinion, these seemingly different models of working memory indeed have a lot in common. Thus, the ensuing revision process (each chapter was revised at least twice) was designed to make sure that this volume, as a whole, reflects this sense of emerging unity across different models. Specifically, we asked each chapter author to briefly refer to other models in this volume whenever they express similar (and sometimes contrasting) ideas or viewpoints. To facilitate this cross-referencing process, we made the drafts of different chapters available on a protected web site so that the contributors could refresh their memory about the theoretical claims of other models and also check the accuracy of their cross-references. As a result, the chapters in this volume include extensive, insightful cross-references to other chapters, which we believe give readers a good sense of how different models relate to one another even before they read the final integrative chapters (Chapters 12 and 13).

Third, we also incorporated a number of features that we believe might help readers understand and remember the theoretical positions of different models and, possibly, do their own in-depth comparisons of the models in this volume. For example, each chapter that describes a specific model of working memory (Chapters 2 to 11) starts with a brief abstract that points out the five central features of that model. Also, each theory chapter contains a table that concisely summarizes the model's answers to each of the eight designated theoretical questions. We believe that this "Five Central Features of the Theory" abstract and the summary table in each chapter together provide a good overview of what that model is like. These features also serve as a useful memory aid – we ourselves went back to these summary tables many times to refresh our memories when we were in the process of preparing and editing Chapters 1, 12, and 13. Moreover, the subject index was specifically designed to facilitate the comparison and evaluation of each chapter's answers to the eight designated questions.

Finally, we tried to make this volume as accessible as possible to student readers by soliciting reviews of chapter drafts from graduate students as well as active working memory researchers who did not contribute to this volume. Specifically, we gave drafts of the chapters to several graduate students in cognitive psychology or cognitive neuroscience who were not particularly familiar with the models described in the assigned chapters and asked them to identify the sections that were not clear and needed further explanation. We believe that these comments from student reviewers as well as expert reviewers helped make the complex theoretical ideas and proposals accessible to readers of this volume.

Although neither of us had any prior experience in editing a book, we are quite pleased with the final product. It is our hope that this volume will serve not only as a milestone that documents recent theoretical progress in working memory research but also as a thought-provoking guidebook that could trigger whole new lines of active research projects and more precise and comprehensive models of working memory.

REFERENCES

Anderson, J. R., Reder, L. M., & Lebiere, C. (1996). Working memory: Activation limitations on retrieval. *Cognitive Psychology, 30,* 221–256.

Baddeley, A. D. (1986). *Working memory*. New York: Oxford University Press.

Baddeley, A. D., & Hitch, G. J. (1974). Working memory. In G. H. Bower (Ed.), *The psychology of learning and motivation: Advances in research and theory* (Vol. 8, pp. 47–89). New York: Academic Press.

Barnard, P. J. (1985). Interacting cognitive subsystems: A psycholinguistic approach to short-term memory. In A. W. Young (Ed.), *Progress in the psychology of language* (Vol. 2, pp. 197–258). London: Erlbaum.

Beardsley, T. (1997). The machinery of thought. *Scientific American, 277* (August), 78–83.

Cowan, N. (1988). Evolving conceptions of memory storage, selective attention, and their mutual constraints within the human information processing system. *Psychological Bulletin, 104*, 163–191.

de Ribaupierre, A., & Hitch, G. J. (1994). *The development of working memory*. Hove, UK: Erlbaum.

Ericsson, K. A., & Kintsch, W. (1995). Long-term working memory. *Psychological Review, 102*, 211–245.

Gathercole, S. E. (1996). *Models of short-term memory*. Hove, UK: Psychology Press.

Gathercole, S. E., & Baddeley, A. D. (1993). *Working memory and language*. Hillsdale, NJ: Erlbaum.

Just, M. A., & Carpenter, P. A. (1992). A capacity theory of comprehension: Individual differences in working memory. *Psychological Review, 99*, 122–149.

Logie, R. H. (1995). *Visuo-spatial working memory*. Hove, UK: Erlbaum.

Logie, R. H., & Gilhooly, K. J. (Eds.). (1998). *Working memory and thinking*. Hove, UK: Psychology Press.

Richardson, J. T. E., Engle, R. W., Hasher, L., Logie, R. H., Stoltzfus, E. R., & Zacks, R. T. (Eds.). (1996). *Working memory and human cognition*. New York: Oxford University Press.

Schneider, W., & Detweiler, M. (1987). A connectionist/control architecture for working memory. In G. H. Bower (Ed.), *The psychology of learning and motivation* (Vol. 21, pp. 53–119). New York: Academic Press.

Vallar, G., & Shallice, T. (1990). *Neuropsychological impairments of short-term memory*. New York: Cambridge University Press.

Wickelgren, I. (1997). Getting a grasp on working memory. *Science, 275*, 1580–1582.

Ode on Working Memory

There once was a box called short-term store
Whose function was storage and nothing more.
But along came Alan Baddeley
Whose subjects dual-tasked madly
And WM replaced STS forevermore.

For those who've been living in caves
Working memory is a system with slaves.
They are independent buffers
So that neither one suffers
When doing verbal memory with visual maze.

While storage is the job of each little slave
The central executive says how we behave.
From up in the prefrontal lobes
It activates and controls all nodes
Through a dopamine system acting as gates.

The unanswered questions on WM abound
Despite numerous studies whose findings are sound.
What's needed right now
Is for us to see how
We can put all these data on common ground.

JANICE KEENAN

Acknowledgments

We owe thanks to many people, institutions, and organizations, who all contributed to make this a better book.

First, we would like to acknowledge granting agencies that supported our research on working memory, executive functions, and higher-level visuospatial cognition during the editing of this book. Akira Miyake was supported by grants from the James S. McDonnell Foundation (Cognitive Rehabilitation Program) and National Science Foundation (IBN-9873492). Priti Shah was supported by fellowships from the James S. McDonnell Foundation (Cognitive Studies in Educational Practice Program) and the National Academy of Education (Spencer Postdoctoral Fellowships), as well as grants from the Office of Naval Research (N00014-98-1-0350 and N00014-98-1-0812).

In addition, we would like to acknowledge the contributions of different organizations and individuals that provided invaluable support for a companion symposium held in July 1997 at the University of Colorado, Boulder. The symposium provided a forum for the cross-fertilization of ideas, and we believe that this symposium helped make this book coherent as a whole. We would especially like to acknowledge the contribution of the Office of Naval Research (N00014-97-1-0547), particularly Helen Gigley, our program officer, and Susan Chipman, for their financial support for this project and their participation in the symposium. In addition, the Institute of Cognitive Science (ICS) and the Council on Research and Creative Work (CRCW), both at the University of Colorado, generously provided additional financial support for which we are very grateful. Thanks also go to Martha Polson and Toni Wettlaufer at ICS as well as graduate students at the University of Colorado, who provided valuable help in different aspects of symposium planning.

Although they did not contribute chapters to this volume, Meredyth Daneman and Marcel Just both presented their latest research and theoretical ideas at the symposium. Their participation enriched the discussion and, hence, the ideas presented in this volume. We thank them for coming to Boulder.

We would also like to thank many people who contributed to this volume by reviewing one or more chapters. Several working memory researchers provided detailed theoretical comments, including Prahlad Gupta, Dan Kimberg, Satoru Saito, Sashank Varma, and especially Andy Conway. Several others provided very helpful comments about the content as well as the readability of chapters from a student's perspective, including Mike Emerson, Naomi

Friedman, Alan Sanfey, Eric Schumacher, Tor Wager, and Mike Wolfe. We appreciate all of their help in making the chapters in this book theoretically more rigorous as well as clearer and more readable.

Several people provided assistance in preparing the final book. We would like to thank Amy Howerter and Mike Emerson for their help in putting together the index for this volume. We would also like to thank Alex Witzki for designing and implementing the web page for the chapter contributors, which was crucial for cross-referencing of chapters to occur. In addition, Ilavenil Subbiah created the cover design representing the "juggler" metaphor of working memory, and we thank her for her artistic contribution. We are also grateful to Janice Keenan for writing the poem "Ode to Working Memory," which nicely captures the main purpose of this book, and graciously allowing us to print it here. Finally, Debbie Aguiar provided an enormous amount of clerical and technical assistance for all phases of this project, and we are truly grateful to her.

A number of our colleagues provided support and advice throughout the editing of the book and the planning of the companion symposium. In particular, we are very happy to acknowledge the kindness of Reid Hastie, Walter Kintsch, and Peter Polson at the University of Colorado. We would also like to thank Jim Hoeffner for support, advice, and lots of encouragement.

Of course, this book would not have been complete without the help of the capable staff of Cambridge University Press. We would like to thank Julia Hough, our editor, who has guided us through all stages of the project. Thanks also go to Bill Grundy, Kelly Hamilton, Janis Bolster, Genevieve Scandone, and other members of the editorial and production staff for their careful and efficient work.

Finally, we owe an enormous debt of gratitude to the contributors to this volume, who went beyond the call of duty. They agreed to a rather unusual set of specifications for their chapters, including addressing the same set of theoretical questions and writing abstracts that describe the "Five Central Features" of their theories. In addition, they worked within very limited time schedules and kindly revised their drafts multiple times so that they could incorporate cross-references to the other chapters in this volume. Most of all, the contributors have been enormously supportive of the goals of this endeavor. For all of that and more, we thank you.

1   Models of Working Memory

An Introduction

PRITI SHAH AND AKIRA MIYAKE

Working memory plays an essential role in complex cognition. Everyday cognitive tasks – such as reading a newspaper article, calculating the appropriate amount to tip in a restaurant, mentally rearranging furniture in one's living room to create space for a new sofa, and comparing and contrasting various attributes of different apartments to decide which to rent – often involve multiple steps with intermediate results that need to be kept in mind temporarily to accomplish the task at hand successfully. "Working memory" is the theoretical construct that has come to be used in cognitive psychology to refer to the system or mechanism underlying the maintenance of task-relevant information during the performance of a cognitive task (Baddeley & Hitch, 1974; Daneman & Carpenter, 1980). As reflected by the fact that it has been labeled "the hub of cognition" (Haberlandt, 1997, p. 212) and proclaimed as "perhaps the most significant achievement of human mental evolution" (Goldman-Rakic, 1992, p. 111), it is a central construct in cognitive psychology and, more recently, cognitive neuroscience.

Despite the familiarity of the term, however, it is not easy to figure out what working memory really is. To begin with, the term *working memory* is used in quite different senses by different communities of researchers. In the behavioral neuroscience and animal behavior fields, for example, the term is associated with the radial arm maze paradigm. In this paradigm, a hungry animal (usually a rat) is placed in a multipronged maze and searches for food located at the end of each arm. If the animal has a good "working memory" and can remember which arms it has already visited, it should not return to those arms because the food there is already gone. Thus, in this context, working memory has a specific operational definition different from that generally used by cognitive psychologists: "the ability of an animal to keep track of its location in space by remembering where it has been" (Olton, 1977, p. 82; see Gagliardo, Mazzotto, & Divac, 1997, for a recent study of "working memory" in this sense).

The confusion remains even within the discipline of cognitive psychology. First of all, there is not always a clear-cut distinction between working mem-

We thank Andrew Conway, Peter Delaney, Arthur Graesser, Reid Hastie, Janice Keenan, Daniel Kimberg, Peter Polson, Satoru Saito, and Sashank Varma for reading an earlier version of this chapter and giving us useful comments and suggestions.

ory and the still prevalent concept of "short-term memory" or STM (Brainerd & Kingma, 1985; Engle, Tuholski, Laughlin, & Conway, in press; Klapp, Marshburn, & Lester, 1983; see also a collection of articles in the March, 1993, issue of *Memory & Cognition* on STM). Textbooks, in particular, often contradict one another and are sometimes even internally inconsistent in their discussion of the distinction between STM and working memory. Adding to the confusion is that a number of different metaphors are used to refer to working memory and to highlight different characteristics of the concept, including the "box" or "place" metaphor, the "workspace" or "blackboard" metaphor, the "mental energy" or "resources" metaphor, and the "juggling" metaphor.

To make things even worse, the working memory literature is filled with seemingly contradictory claims. For example, some articles emphasize the unitary nature of working memory (e.g., Engle, Cantor, & Carullo, 1992), whereas others focus on its non-unitary nature and argue for a more domain-specific view of working memory (e.g., Daneman & Tardif, 1987). Some articles put forth a theory in which individual differences in working memory capacity are conceptualized in terms of variation in the total amount of mental resources available (e.g., Just & Carpenter, 1992), whereas others claim that long-term knowledge and skills provide a better account of individual differences in working memory (e.g., Ericsson & Kintsch, 1995). The common practice of capitalizing on differences in viewpoints is understandable in terms of the sociology of science, but it is not always clear from these articles whether such different conceptualizations are fundamentally incompatible or merely reflect differences in emphasis.

A variety of models and theories proposed earlier reflect such diverse – and one might say, disparate – perspectives on the nature, structure, and functions of working memory (e.g., Anderson, Reder, & Lebiere, 1996; Baddeley, 1986; Barnard, 1985; Cowan, 1988; Ericsson & Kintsch, 1995; Just & Carpenter, 1992; Schneider & Detweiler, 1987). Attempts to figure out what characteristics working memory has and how it is organized by carefully reading these theoretical articles sometimes leave one even more confused than before. We ourselves experienced this frustration prior to editing this volume and would imagine that our frustration might be somewhat analogous to what Eysenck (1986) once felt about various psychometric theories of intelligence: "Discussions concerning the theory, nature, and measurement of intelligence historically have resulted more in disagreement than in agreement, more in smoke than in illumination" (p. 1). Many people might agree that this quote would continue to make sense if the phrase *working memory* were substituted for the word *intelligence*. Indeed, this suspicion has been confirmed by one embarrassing question repeatedly raised by different colleagues and students of ours, all aware of different conceptions of working memory: "What is working memory, anyway?"

We believe that the time has come to take a step toward clarifying this confusing state of affairs in the field. In this volume, we tackle this challenge by systematically comparing existing influential models and theories of working memory. As a casual skimming of the subsequent chapters (Chapters 2 to 11) makes clear, the models included in this volume represent a wide range of theoretical perspectives that, on the surface, look quite different from one another. Our primary goal is to closely examine how these different models characterize working memory and elucidate some commonalities among them – commonalities that may help us better define and understand working memory.

The specific approach we decided to adopt for this purpose is to ask each theorist to address the same set of important (and often controversial) theoretical questions that have been guiding working memory research. This "common-question" approach to theory comparison has rarely been used in cognitive psychology. To the best of our knowledge, the only book that has explicitly used this approach is a volume edited by Baumgartner and Payr (1995), entitled *Speaking Minds: Interviews with Twenty Eminent Cognitive Scientists*. In that volume, Baumgartner and Payr interviewed leading cognitive scientists and asked them the same set of theoretical questions such as, "Do you think the Turing Test is a useful test (or idea)?" We found their approach quite effective in elucidating the commonalities and differences of various researchers' opinions because the shared questions provide a useful common ground against which different theorists' ideas can be compared and contrasted. Because existing models of working memory differ radically in their scope and focus, we thought that, without such shared questions, it might be difficult to compare seemingly disparate models and identify their commonalities.

WHY THEORY COMPARISON? In our view, systematically comparing and contrasting different models of working memory in terms of the common set of designated questions has several important merits that are worth pointing out in addition to the ones mentioned above. First, systematic issue-by-issue comparisons help clarify common misconceptions or misinterpretations of different models of working memory. Theoretical articles often provide detailed specifications of some aspects of a model, but give cursory or no treatment to other aspects of the model. Although there is nothing inherently wrong with this common practice, it invites a lot of guessing on the part of readers about various issues, sometimes leading to confusion and even wrong interpretations.[1] Asking different theorists to address all major aspects of working memory may reduce the confusion and misinterpretations.

---

[1] For example, one common misinterpretation prevalent in the literature is that Just and Carpenter's (1992) model assumes a unitary, domain-general notion of working memory. The model described in the 1992 paper included only one "resource pool," but it only reflected the fact that the model was restricted to the domain of language comprehension. Just and Carpenter themselves had a more domain-specific view of working memory, assuming at least a distinction between language and visuospatial working memory. Another common misinterpretation concerns the processing capabilities of the visuospatial sketchpad system in Baddeley's (1986) model. Although Baddeley himself has consistently argued that it can actively manipulate mental images, some researchers have portrayed Baddeley's sketchpad system as a pure storage buffer without any processing capability.

Second, systematic issue-by-issue comparisons can also crystallize which seemingly conflicting theoretical claims are indeed mutually incompatible (rather than merely complementary) and, hence, must be resolved in future research. The identification of mutually incompatible claims not only sharpens the focus of research, but also provides an important basis for rigorous tests of competing ideas by way of "competitive argumentation" (VanLehn, Brown, & Greeno, 1984) – pitting competing models (or alternative versions of a single model) *directly* against one another to analyze and clarify theoretical issues often left implicit. VanLehn et al. clearly articulate the importance of this approach:

> To show that some constraint is crucial is to show that it is *necessary* in order for the theory to meet some criteria of adequacy. To show that it is *sufficient* is not enough. . . . [W]hen there are two theories, one claiming that principle X is sufficient and another claiming that a different, incompatible principle Y, is sufficient, sufficiency itself is no longer persuasive. One must somehow show that X is better than Y. Indeed, this sort of competitive argumentation is the only realistic alternative to necessity arguments (VanLehn et al., 1984, p. 240).

Last but not least, unification is always an aim of science, as Newell (1990) pointed out in his book *Unified Theories of Cognition*. Identifying which seemingly conflicting theoretical claims are in fact complementary could help unify or synthesize different models, possibly leading to a unified theory of working memory. As the broad range of the eight designated questions we discuss in the next section indicates (see Table 1.1), the key theoretical issues in current working memory research interface many (if not all) aspects of cognitive psychology. To borrow Haberlandt's (1997) expression, the study of working memory is essentially "a microcosm of the field of cognition" (p. 213). Thus, systematic comparisons of different models of working memory may even contribute strongly to the development of unified theories of cognition.

The Eight Designated Theoretical Questions for This Volume

The eight designated theoretical questions that provide a basis for the theoretical comparisons offered in this volume are listed in Table 1.1. They touch on all major theoretical issues of central importance to working memory research, including those that are currently highly controversial (particularly, Questions 3 and 4). We motivate the eight designated questions below, one by one, by discussing their importance in working memory research and providing a brief historical review. In addition, we offer some guidelines that might help readers in their endeavor of comparing and evaluating the models presented in this volume.

Table 1.1. The Eight Designated Questions for This Volume

(1) Basic Mechanisms and Representations in Working Memory
How is information encoded into and maintained in working memory? What is the retrieval mechanism? Also, how is information represented in working memory? Is the representation format for different types of information (e.g., verbal or visuospatial information) the same or different?

(2) The Control and Regulation of Working Memory
How is the information in working memory controlled and regulated? What determines which information is stored and which is ignored? Is the control and regulation of working memory handled by a central control structure (e.g., the central executive)? If so, what are the functions of the control structure? If your model does not postulate a central control structure, how do the control and regulation of information emerge?

(3) The Unitary Versus Non-Unitary Nature of Working Memory
Is working memory a unitary construct, or does it consist of multiple separable subsystems? If the latter is the case, then what are the subsystems of working memory and how do they interact with one another? What evidence or theoretical considerations justify your view?

(4) The Nature of Working Memory Limitations
What are the mechanisms that constrain the capacity of working memory (e.g., a limited supply of activation, processing speed, decay, inhibition, interference, skills)? If your model postulates multiple subsystems within working memory, does the same set of constraining mechanisms apply to each subsystem? What evidence or theoretical considerations have motivated the postulation of those capacity-constraining mechanisms?

(5) The Role of Working Memory in Complex Cognitive Activities
How is working memory implicated in the performance of complex cognitive tasks, such as language comprehension, spatial thinking, mental arithmetic, and reasoning and problem solving? What complex cognitive phenomena have you examined from the perspective of your model, and, according to your analysis, what role(s) does working memory play in these tasks? How does your model account for the performance limitations associated with these tasks?

(6) The Relationship of Working Memory to Long-Term Memory and Knowledge
What is the relationship between working memory and declarative long-term memory? Are they structurally separate entities? Or is working memory simply an activated portion of long-term memory? How do they interact with each other? How does working memory also relate to procedural skills? How might working memory limitations or functions be influenced by learning and practice?

continued

Table 1.1,   continued

(7) **The Relationship of Working Memory to Attention and Consciousness**
What is the relationship between working memory and attention? Do these terms refer to the same construct? Or are they somehow separate from each other (either partially or completely)? If so, what differentiates them, and how do they interact with each other? Also, how does working memory relate to consciousness or awareness?

(8) **The Biological Implementation of Working Memory**
How does your model relate to various neuroscience findings on working memory (e.g., studies of brain-damaged patients, neuroimaging data, electrophysiological measures, animal studies)? How might your view of working memory be implemented in the brain?

Question 1: Basic Mechanisms and Representations in Working Memory

How is information encoded into and maintained in working memory? What is the retrieval mechanism? Also, how is information represented in working memory? Is the representation format for different types of information (e.g., verbal or visuospatial information) the same or different?

The traditional view of human memory (e.g., Atkinson & Shiffrin, 1968; Waugh & Norman, 1965) offers an elegant account of the basic mechanisms (encoding, maintenance, and retrieval) and representations in working memory or, rather, STM. According to this view, there are a number of structurally separate components or stores through which information is transferred. A subset of the information in the sensory registers is chosen for later processing via *selective attention* and is transferred into a short-term store (STS) (encoding). The information in the STS is considered fragile and decays quickly, so *rehearsal* is necessary to keep it within the STS (maintenance) and to transfer it to a more durable long-term store (LTS). The information in the STS is assumed to be accessible relatively quickly and effortlessly (retrieval), but there may be a slight slowdown of retrieval speed as a function of the number of items within the STS (Sternberg, 1966). Once lost from the STS, information cannot be retrieved unless it is encoded in the LTS. Retrieval from the LTS, however, is generally considered a slower and more effortful process than that from the STS.

As for the representation issue, the traditional view emphasizes speech-based codes (i.e., acoustic, phonological, or verbal) as the predominant memory code in STM, as reflected in the fact that most of the STM experiments in the 1960s and 1970s were done using verbal materials, despite the fact that Atkinson and Shiffrin (1968) themselves explicitly acknowledged the possibility of other STM codes (e.g., visual, spatial). The emphasis on speech-based codes in STM is contrasted with meaning-based (semantic) codes considered dominant in LTM.

This traditional view is simple and intuitively makes sense, but the story is too simplistic. It could be argued that the overall framework of the "modal" model is defensible (Healy & McNamara, 1996; Pashler & Carrier, 1996), but the basic mechanisms and representations of the model need to be modified, qualified, or elaborated further, given the recent empirical and theoretical advances in the field, particularly those associated with working memory research. The first question, thus, asked each contributor to outline his or her current view of the encoding, maintenance, and retrieval mechanisms as well as the nature of the representational codes in working memory.

Although all 10 theory chapters in this volume (Chapters 2 to 11) address the basic mechanism and representation issue, the types of answers they provide and the manners in which they answer this question vary considerably. Indeed, of all the eight questions, answers to the first question seem to be the most difficult to discern, perhaps because it is such a basic issue that, with the exception of Cowan (Chapter 3), the question is answered in an implicit, highly distributed fashion. Even though some chapters have a section dedicated to it, the arguments relevant to the basic mechanism and representation issue tend to be made in many different places throughout the chapter. Moreover, the chapters describing computational models tend to answer this question by outlining the overall architecture and the basic assumptions of their respective models. Although most of their descriptions have important implications for the issue of basic mechanisms and representations, those descriptions are not always directly cast in terms of the concepts we used in formulating this first question (i.e., encoding, maintenance, retrieval, and representational format). Thus, readers interested in comparing and contrasting the answers to Question 1 should keep these provisos in mind when they go through the chapters in this volume.

Question 2: The Control and Regulation of Working Memory

How is the information in working memory controlled and regulated? What determines which information is stored and which is ignored? Is the control and regulation of working memory handled by a central control structure (e.g., the central executive)? If so, what are the functions of the control structure? If your model does not postulate a central control structure, how do the control and regulation of information emerge?

From the beginning of modern working memory (or STM) research, the issue of control and regulation has been considered of central importance. Indeed, the notion of "control processes" was already present in Atkinson and Shiffrin's (1968) modal model of human memory. The control processes in that model, however, were limited to those involved in pure memorization, such as rehearsal, coding, and search strategies. In contrast to the traditional,

storage-oriented notion of STM, working memory is considered a more processing-oriented construct and is sometimes conceptualized as the "workspace" or "blackboard" of the mind in which the active processing and
temporary storage of task-relevant information dynamically take place. Such
a view of working memory necessitates a more sophisticated account of control mechanisms that go beyond simple memorization strategies. In addition,
there is an increasingly popular view of working memory as consisting of
multiple subsystems. This view requires a satisfactory explanation of how
these different subsystems are regulated so that working memory as a whole
functions smoothly. The second designated question, therefore, asked the
contributors to specify the mechanisms of control and regulation.

The classic answer to this "control and regulation" question is to postulate
a central control structure like the central executive, as Baddeley and Hitch
(1974) did in their influential multicomponent model. As often pointed out by
critics, however, this approach has the danger of implicating a mysterious little "homunculus" inside working memory. In addition, as Baddeley (1986)
himself admitted, the central executive may have become almost synonymous
with a theoretical "ragbag" for all functions not attributable to the peripheral
slave systems (i.e., the phonological loop and the visuospatial sketchpad).

Donald (1991) vividly described these problems associated with the notion
of the central executive: "The 'central executive' is a hypothetical entity that
sits atop the mountain of working memory and attention like some gigantic
Buddha, an inscrutable, immaterial, omnipresent homunculus, at whose busy
desk the buck stops every time memory and attention theorists run out of
alternatives" (p. 327). The challenge, therefore, is to more precisely specify
the mechanisms underlying the control and regulation of information in
working memory without postulating an explicit homunculus-like entity.

The chapters in this volume provide interesting answers to this formidable
challenge. As we discuss in more detail in the concluding chapter (Miyake &
Shah, Chapter 13), the general approaches to the control and regulation issue
represented in this volume range from specifying the subcomponents or subfunctions of a "central executive," through relying on regulatory mechanisms
inherent in the underlying computational architecture, to conceptualizing
control and regulation as an emergent property (i.e., a natural consequence of
dynamic interactions among different subsystems). Readers might be interested in speculating on how well these models as a whole manage to address
the "homunculus" or "ragbag" problem, a focus of the commentary provided
in Chapter 12 by Kintsch, Healy, Hegarty, Pennington, and Salthouse.

Question 3: The Unitary Versus Non-Unitary Nature of Working Memory

*Is working memory a unitary construct, or does it consist of multiple separable
subsystems? If the latter is the case, then what are the subsystems of working*

memory and how do they interact with one another? What evidence or theoretical considerations justify your view?

The issue of whether working memory is unitary or non-unitary has been a source of controversy in the working memory literature. Some researchers have emphasized the unitary nature of working memory (e.g., Anderson et al., 1996; Engle et al., 1992; Kyllonen & Christal, 1990), whereas others have emphasized its non-unitary nature (e.g., Daneman & Tardif, 1987; Martin, 1993; Monsell, 1984; Shah & Miyake, 1996). Within the non-unitary camp, different researchers fractionate working memory in different ways, and there has been little consensus as to the number of subsystems and the nature of each subsystem. Some researchers, for example, are relatively conservative, proposing only a few domain-specific subsystems such as those for verbal and visuospatial storage or processing (e.g., Baddeley, 1986), whereas others postulate other subsystems or types of codes or representations, such as auditory, motor, lexical, semantic, syntactic, and so on (e.g., Barnard, 1985; Martin, 1993; Schneider & Detweiler, 1987). Some accounts go even further, postulating separable subsystems at a much finer level of analysis. One study of aphasic language comprehension, for example, argues for the independence of processing resources for computing a verb's thematic representations and those for computing the syntactic trace-antecedent relations (Shapiro, Gordon, Hack, & Killackey, 1993). The third designated question, thus, asked the contributors to discuss their current thoughts on the unitary or non-unitary nature of working memory.

This controversy has an interesting historical parallel in the domains of intelligence and attention.[2] In the case of intelligence, the Spearman–Thurston controversy is well known. Spearman (1904) argued that a single entity called *general intelligence* or *g* (conceptualized by Spearman as neurologically based "power" or "energy") underlies intellectual performances of various types, whereas Thurston (1938) argued that seven independent primary abilities can explain intellectual functioning well without postulating a general factor. Guilford (1967) went even further than Thurston, postulating 120 distinct ability factors in his "Structure of Intellect" model. Indeed, Eysenck's (1986) remark quoted earlier illustrates how radically different these psychometric theories looked from one another. Analogously, the "unitary versus non-unitary" debate also surrounded the resource (or capacity) theories of attention, some theorists

---

[2] The similarity of the unitary vs. non-unitary debate in intelligence and attention research is perhaps no coincidence. The factor analysis technique, used to develop psychometric theories of intelligence, and the analysis of performance-operating characteristics (POC), used to specify resource theories of attention, share some underlying commonalities (Heuer, 1985).

proposing a unitary view (e.g., Kahneman, 1973) and others a non-unitary view (e.g., Navon & Gopher, 1979; Wickens, 1984).[3]

At first glance, the answers to the question of the unitary versus non-unitary nature of working memory provided in this volume appear rather disparate. Some models strongly emphasize the unitary characteristics of working memory (e.g., Engle, Kane, & Tuholski, Chapter 4; Lovett, Reder, & Lebiere, Chapter 5), whereas others argue for a non-unitary position (e.g., Baddeley & Logie, Chapter 2; Barnard, Chapter 9; Schneider, Chapter 10). However, we would like to invite interested readers to evaluate if those seemingly different answers are fundamentally incompatible. The answer we offer in the final two chapters of this volume (Kintsch et al., Chapter 12; Miyake & Shah, Chapter 13) is "no." Whereas there are clearly some unresolved issues (see Chapter 13), we argue that a global consensus seems to be emerging and that some sort of synthesis may even be near.

Question 4: The Nature of Working Memory Limitations

What are the mechanisms that constrain the capacity of working memory (e.g., a limited supply of activation, processing speed, decay, inhibition, interference, skills)? If your model postulates multiple subsystems within working memory, does the same set of constraining mechanisms apply to each subsystem? What evidence or theoretical considerations have motivated the postulation of those capacity-constraining mechanisms?

The fourth designated question concerns the hallmark characteristic of working memory, identified and studied for over a century – the severe limitations in its capacity (e.g., Jacobs, 1887; James, 1890). In his classic book, William James (1890) stated that, unlike the virtually unlimited amount of knowledge that can be stored in a person's "secondary memory," only a small amount of information can be kept conscious at any one time in one's "primary memory." Moreover, the early scientific work reviewed by James suggests that there was much interest in the 1800s in just how much information can be temporarily maintained and for how long.

Despite the wide consensus on the existence of capacity limits in working memory, there has been little consensus, since the beginning, on the underlying mechanisms responsible for these limitations. For example, James (1890)

---

[3] Of course, this unitary vs. non-unitary debate still continues in both intelligence and attention research, but in a new direction. In intelligence research, the notion of g is still popular (Dennis & Tapsfield, 1996; Jensen, 1998), but modern versions of the non-unitary perspective that explicitly deny the necessity of postulating g also abound (e.g., Gardner, 1983/1993; see also Ceci, 1990/1996, for a detailed critique of g). In attention research, although the seemingly unitary characteristic of attention is noted by many researchers (e.g., Engle et al., Chapter 4; Lovett et al., Chapter 5), different ways of fractionating attention into different components or aspects have also been strongly advocated recently (e.g., Allport, 1993; Pashler, 1997; Posner & Raichle, 1994).

himself described a limitation in the absolute amount of information that can be maintained, whereas Hebb (1949) later described the limitation in terms of the amount of time that reverberatory circuits of neurons (so-called cell assemblies) can remain activated.

Undoubtedly, however, the best-known account of working memory limitations is George Miller's (1956) proposal of capacity limits, in which he argued that people are able to keep track of a "magic number 7 plus or minus 2" chunks of information. Perhaps influenced by the implication of Miller's analysis that most or all limits on mental processes could be attributed to a single source, subsequent proposals on the nature of working memory limitations tended to draw dichotomies between pairs or general classes of mechanisms. The most famous dichotomy is the one between "decay" and "interference" accounts of the forgetting mechanism in STM. Numerous studies have been conducted to resolve this still ongoing debate (Baddeley & Logie, Chapter 2; Cowan, Chapter 3).

More recently, explorations of the nature of working memory limitations have focused on the sources of individual and/or age-related differences in working memory capacity. Although it is generally agreed that there is a substantial individual or age-related variation in the amount of information one can keep track of simultaneously, the specific factor assumed to underlie the variation is different from proposal to proposal, including the total amount of activation resources available to the system (Engle et al., 1992; Just & Carpenter, 1992), processing speed (Salthouse, 1996), efficiency of inhibitory mechanisms (Stoltzfus, Hasher, & Zacks, 1996), and domain-specific knowledge and skills (Ericsson & Kintsch, 1995).

Here again, a popular research strategy seems to be dichotomization. These different accounts are typically pitted against each other in a pairwise fashion, and only one account is usually favored for the sake of "parsimony." In particular, the debate between the camp that emphasizes a basic cognitive mechanism as the primary source (i.e., the total amount of resources, processing speed, and inhibition) and the camp that emphasizes an experience-based or practice-based factor (i.e., knowledge and skills) is reminiscent of the (in)famous nature versus nurture debate, another intriguing parallel to intelligence research.

Given this situation, it is perhaps not surprising that the chapters in this volume propose many different underlying mechanisms for working memory limitations. Some models even propose that working memory limitations may be an emergent property (Young & Lewis, Chapter 7; Barnard, Chapter 9; Schneider, Chapter 10; O'Reilly, Braver, & Cohen, Chapter 11). As Kintsch et al. summarize in Chapter 12 (see Table 12.1), the specific capacity-limiting factors mentioned in this volume are quite diverse and, at this microlevel of analysis, there seems to be no general consensus among the answers to this fourth designated question. As is the case with the unitary versus non-unitary issue, however, we are optimistic that the field may already be moving toward a resolution of this controversial issue regarding the nature of working memory limitations (see Miyake & Shah, Chapter 13). We invite readers to evaluate whether the answers given to this question indeed share some commonality that goes beyond the seemingly disparate capacity-limiting mechanisms advocated by each model.

Question 5: The Role of Working Memory in Complex Cognitive Activities

How is working memory implicated in the performance of complex cognitive tasks, such as language comprehension, spatial thinking, mental arithmetic, and reasoning and problem solving? What complex cognitive phenomena have you examined from the perspective of your model, and, according to your analysis, what role(s) does working memory play in these tasks? How does your model account for the performance limitations associated with these tasks?

One of the major driving forces behind the theoretical transition from STM to working memory was the realization that the memory models developed to account for STM phenomena cannot necessarily illuminate the kinds of temporary memory involved in the performance of complex cognitive tasks (Baddeley & Hitch, 1974; Reitman, 1970). Indeed, one could reasonably argue that working memory is a theoretical concept developed to bring studies of memory into closer alignment with studies of cognition. The fifth question, thus, asked the contributors to outline how their respective models represent this rapprochement between memory and cognition and how working memory is implicated in the performance of complex cognitive tasks.

This issue has typically been addressed in three complementary ways, all of which have been successful in demonstrating the importance of working memory in the performance of a variety of complex cognitive tasks. One popular approach, frequently used in the United Kingdom in the context of Baddeley's (1986) model of working memory, is to conduct experiments using the so-called dual-task interference paradigm. In this paradigm, a cognitive task of interest is performed by itself and with a secondary task considered to tap primarily one of the subcomponents of working memory.[4] If the secondary task disrupts the performance of the primary cognitive task when compared to the control condition, then it is usually inferred that the sub-

---

[4] In the case of the phonological loop, the secondary task typically used is articulatory suppression (repeatedly articulating familiar syllables, words, or phrases, such as "the, the, the . . ." or "one, two, three"). In the case of the visuospatial sketchpad, a spatial tapping task (sequentially tapping four corners of a square with a finger) is often used, particularly when a primary task is considered to implicate the maintenance of spatial (as opposed to purely visual) information. In the case of the central executive, the secondary task often used is a random generation task, which involves the oral generation of a random sequence of numbers or letters.

component tapped by the secondary task is involved in the performance of the primary cognitive task. This approach has successfully been used to specify whether a given cognitive task implicates a given subcomponent of working memory (Baddeley & Logie, Chapter 2).

Another approach, particularly popular in North America, has been to examine the role of working memory in complex cognitive tasks from the perspective of individual differences, using various working memory span tasks (such as reading, operation, and spatial spans) as a research tool (Daneman & Carpenter, 1980; Engle et al., 1992; Salthouse & Babcock, 1991; Shah & Miyake, 1996). These span tasks are designed to resemble the working memory demands during the performance of complex cognitive tasks by placing simultaneous demands on both processing and storage. This individual differences approach usually specifies the role of working memory in complex cognition either by correlating participants' performance on these span tasks with that on other target tasks or by classifying the participants into different groups on the basis of their performance on the span tasks and examining how these groups differ in their performance of complex cognitive tasks.

The third, most recent approach is to develop computational models that simulate the effects of individual differences and/or working memory load on participants' performance on various cognitive tasks. Previous examples of this approach include the models of sentence comprehension (Just & Carpenter, 1992), discourse comprehension (Goldman & Varma, 1995), mental algebra (Anderson et al., 1996), reasoning and problem solving (Just, Carpenter, & Hemphill, 1996), and human–computer interaction (Byrne & Bovair, 1997; Huguenard, Lerch, Junker, Patz, & Kass, 1997).

The 10 theory chapters in this volume, as a whole, discuss an impressively wide range of complex cognitive tasks, ranging from immediate serial recall of words (Kieras, Meyer, Mueller, & Seymour, Chapter 6) through syllogistic reasoning (Baddeley & Logie, Chapter 2) to human–computer interaction (Young & Lewis, Chapter 7). All three approaches outlined above are represented in the contributors' answers to this fifth question, but the recent studies discussed in the chapters incorporate some interesting new twists. We briefly mention a few examples here.

Although the dual-task methodology is usually used to demonstrate whether or not a certain subcomponent is implicated in a given cognitive task, Baddeley and Logie (Chapter 2) discuss several recent studies in which the dual-task methodology was successfully used to specify exactly what role a specific subcomponent plays in the performance of the target task. Engle et al. (Chapter 4) present their new individual differences work (Engle et al., in press), in which they go beyond simple correlational analyses by using a sophisticated latent variable technique to address what factors are driving the correlation between working memory spans and complex cognitive tasks. As for the computational modeling approach, Lovett et al. (Chapter 5) discuss work in which they go beyond the common practice of simulating aggregated group-level data (e.g., high-span vs. low-span participants) and predict participants' performance across multiple tasks on an individual-by-individual basis by manipulating a simple parameter.

In addition to these exciting new developments in the typical approach to studying the role of working memory in complex cognitive tasks, the chapters in this volume consider two relatively new directions. Some chapters (most notably, Ericsson & Delaney, Chapter 8), for example, argue for the necessity of extending the three approaches to include studies of how experts or skilled individuals maintain task-relevant information during the performance of familiar tasks. In addition, some chapters also argue for the importance of understanding how different areas of the brain are implicated in working memory (e.g., O'Reilly et al., Chapter 11). Thus, taken together, the answers to the fifth question presented in this volume delineate a useful overview of the state-of-the-art research that deepens our understanding of the role of working memory in complex cognitive tasks.

Question 6: The Relationship of Working Memory to Long-Term Memory and Knowledge

What is the relationship between working memory and declarative long-term memory? Are they structurally separate entities? Or is working memory simply an activated portion of long-term memory? How do they interact with each other? How does working memory also relate to procedural skills? How might working memory limitations or functions be influenced by learning and practice?

On the basis of the well-known serial position effects (i.e., the primacy and recency effects in free recall) and some neuropsychological dissociations (as demonstrated by such patients as HM), early information-processing models of memory assumed a structural distinction between STM (or working memory) and LTM (e.g., Atkinson & Shiffrin, 1968; Broadbent, 1958; Waugh & Norman, 1965). Moreover, these models considered STM a gateway or stepping stone to a more permanent LTM,[5] proposing that information that is either rehearsed, attended to, or organized properly in STS is transferred to an LTS. In contrast to this structural view of human memory, an alternative view emphasized the continuity between working memory and LTM and proposed that working memory can be considered an activated portion of LTM representations (Norman, 1968). This more continuous view gained some popularity in cognitive psychology (Anderson, 1983; Cowan, 1988), as empirical data that challenged the interpretations of the hallmark empirical findings for the

---

[5] James (1890) expressed this "gateway" idea more than a century ago, arguing that, for information to be in a retrievable "after-memory," it must have reached some state in our primary memory by having been active for a minimal period of time (see also Hebb, 1949, for a similar idea).

structural view – the serial position effects and the neuropsychological disso-ciations – started to accumulate (for a review of the evidence against the struc-tural view, see Crowder, 1982, 1993). The sixth question, thus, asked the contributors to outline their current take on the nature of the distinction between working memory and LTM.

Another issue raised by Question 6 concerns the role of long-term knowl-edge and skills in the performance of working memory tasks. Historically, much STM research followed the Ebbinghaus tradition, using stimulus mate-rials and experimental paradigms that were not particularly meaningful or familiar to participants. However, as more researchers started to examine peo-ple's temporary memory performance using tasks more familiar and more meaningful to them, such as chess positions (Chase & Simon, 1973) and restaurant orders (Ericsson & Polson, 1988), the role of long-term knowledge and skills in STM or working memory tasks became more obvious. Even the signature task for STM research, the serial recall of digit sequences, was not an exception in this regard: Individuals could be trained to use their existing long-term knowledge to strategically encode the digit sequence to enhance later retrieval (Chase & Ericsson, 1981). Moreover, developmental studies highlighted the strong impact of content knowledge on temporary memory by demonstrating that knowledgeable children can outperform less knowl-edgeable adults in the children's domains of expertise, such as chess (Chi, 1978) and soccer (Schneider, Körkel, & Weinert, 1989) (for more details, see Ericsson & Delaney, Chapter 8).

The important question, then, is what implications the effects of long-term knowledge and skills have for models of working memory. Ericsson and Kintsch (1995) recently proposed the notion of "long-term working memory" (LT-WM) to account for such phenomena, arguing that long-term knowledge can be used to supplement the severely limited capacity of what they called "short-term working memory" (ST-WM). They also put forth a provocative claim that individual differences in long-term knowledge and skills may be able to provide a complete, parsimonious account of individual differences in working memory performance, without postulating any systematic differ-ences in the capacity of ST-WM per se (e.g., the total amount of activation available, as proposed by Just & Carpenter, 1992). This claim is controversial because it could essentially be interpreted as arguing for an extreme "nurture" view of individual differences in working memory capacity, if we revert back to the parallelism to intelligence research. The second part of the sixth ques-tion, thus, asked the contributors to express their theoretical position on the role of long-term knowledge and skills in working memory performance.

The chapters in this volume provide interesting answers to both of the the-oretical issues regarding the relationship between working memory and LTM. Although there are some important differences, readers will undoubtedly notice that the answers to this sixth question reveal a surprisingly high degree of consensus among the contributors (see Miyake & Shah, Chapter 13, for a detailed discussion of the nature of the general agreement). Briefly put, the chapters highlight the necessity to go beyond the traditional structural distinction assumed in the classic information-processing models of human memory (e.g., Atkinson & Shiffrin, 1968; Waugh & Norman, 1965). As for the role of LTM in working memory performance, several chapters explicitly discuss Ericsson and Kintsch's (1995) LT-WM proposal and some even point out analogous mechanisms present in their own models (Baddeley & Logie, Chapter 2; Cowan, Chapter 3; Young & Lewis, Chapter 7; O'Reilly et al., Chapter 11; see in particular Cowan's proposal of "virtual short-term memory" in Chapter 3). Ericsson himself offers an interesting synthesis of the working memory analog of the nature versus nurture controversy (Ericsson & Delaney, Chapter 8).

Question 7: The Relationship of Working Memory to Attention and Consciousness

What is the relationship between working memory and attention? Do these terms refer to the same construct? Or are they somehow separate from each other (either partially or completely)? If so, what differentiates them, and how do they interact with each other? Also, how does working memory relate to consciousness or awareness?

Perhaps because there are clear limitations in the amount of information one can attend to or be conscious of, as well as in the amount of information that can be maintained in working memory, it is widely acknowledged that the constructs of working memory (or STM), attention, and consciousness are related to one another. Indeed, these constructs are sometimes used almost interchangeably. Atkinson and Shiffrin (1971) expressed a view that essentially equates STM to the content of consciousness: "In our thinking we tend to equate the short-term store with 'consciousness,' that is, the thoughts and information of which we are currently aware can be considered part of the contents of the short-term store" (p. 83). Similarly, Baddeley (1993) once remarked that working memory may actually be better construed as "working attention." Despite the apparent close interrelationship among working memory, attention, and consciousness, many researchers draw some distinctions among them or propose a subset or overlapping relation (e.g., Baars, 1997a; Cowan, 1988). The seventh question, thus, asked the contributors to speculate on the question of how working memory is related to the concepts of attention and consciousness or conscious awareness.

Traditional models of human memory characterized attention as a filtering mechanism that limits the amount of information entering or remaining in a memory store (Atkinson & Shiffrin, 1968; Broadbent, 1958). In these conceptions, temporary memory and attention were considered distinct, associated with separate functions. This distinction was blurred, however, as the notion of "processing resources," originally proposed within the context of resource theories of attention (Kahneman, 1973; Navon & Gopher, 1979; Wickens, 1984), gained some popularity and was eventually incorporated into models of working memory (Baddeley & Hitch, 1974; Just & Carpenter, 1992). In addition, Baddeley's (1986, 1993) emphasis on the control functions of the central executive and, more specifically, his proposal that Norman and Shallice's (1986) Supervisory Attentional System (SAS) may be considered a model of the central executive might have also contributed to the blurring of the distinction between the notions of working memory and attention.

Just as working memory and attention have been considered related, the idea that there is an intimate link between working memory and consciousness also has a long history. For example, William James (1890) cited many of his contemporaries or predecessors who noted the inextricable link between primary memory and consciousness (e.g., Richet's remark, "Without memory no conscious sensation, without memory no consciousness"). More recent specific proposals about the relation between working memory and consciousness seem to center around the view reflected in the previous quote from Atkinson and Shiffrin (1971), namely that the contents of working memory are what we are conscious of at the moment. Although this view seems prevalent (e.g., Moscovitch & Umiltà, 1990), another view expressed by several researchers is that, to be aware of something, that something must be in working memory, but that not everything in working memory can be consciously experienced – only elements in working memory under the "focus of attention" or a "spotlight" can (e.g., Cowan, 1988). Baars's (1997b) Global Workspace theory, which argues for the "theater" metaphor of consciousness, expresses this viewpoint particularly clearly:

[In the Global Workspace theory,] conscious contents are limited to a brightly lit spot of attention onstage, while the rest of the stage corresponds to immediate working memory. Behind the scenes are executive processes, including a director, and a great variety of contextual operators that shape conscious experience without themselves becoming conscious. In the audience are a vast array of intelligent unconscious mechanisms. . . . Elements of working memory – on stage, but not in the spotlight of attention – are also unconscious (Baars, 1997b, p. 43).

The answers to this seventh designated question extend the previous accounts of the relationship between attention and working memory in exciting new ways. Just to give an example, Engle et al. (Chapter 4) put forth an intriguing proposal that working memory essentially amounts to STM plus what they call "controlled attention," thereby arguing for a clear separation between the storage and (attentional) control functions of working memory (see Baddeley & Logie, Chapter 2, for a similar claim and O'Reilly et al., Chapter 11, for an opposing claim). Although most chapters provide interesting discussions of the relationship between attention and working memory, this is one area where we feel that there is not yet a general point of agreement. In Chapter 13, we will discuss how we might go about developing a more comprehensive account of how working memory and attention inter-act. As for the relationship between working memory and consciousness, most chapters in this volume acknowledge a close relationship between the two, but their accounts do not go much beyond the previous accounts we outlined earlier, even though the models in this volume have a theoretical scope broad enough to serve as a basis for exploring how working memory and consciousness relate to each other.

Question 8: The Biological Implementation of Working Memory

How does your model relate to various neuroscience findings on working memory (e.g., studies of brain-damaged patients, neuroimaging data, electrophysiological measures, animal studies)? How might your view of working memory be implemented in the brain?

Cognitive neuroscience has made remarkable progress in the understanding of the biological and neural basis of cognition during this "decade of the brain" (Gazzaniga, 1995; Gazzaniga, Ivry, & Mangun, 1998; Rugg, 1997). This new emerging field pursues the question of how the brain enables complex perceptual and cognitive processes, using a variety of research methodologies. These methodologies include (but are not necessarily limited to) (a) behavioral studies of brain-damaged patients (sometimes called "cognitive neuropsychology"); (b) neuroimaging (e.g., positron emission tomography [PET]; functional magnetic resonance imaging [fMRI]); (c) electrophysiological recordings from humans (e.g., event-related brain potentials [ERP]); (d) animal studies (e.g., lesioning, single-cell recordings, etc.); and (e) computational modeling of neurophysiological or neuropsychological phenomena (e.g., connectionist simulation).

Working memory is one of the major foci of current cognitive neuroscience research, and the progress and its impact on cognitive psychology have been impressive (for a recent overview, see Beardsley, 1997; Smith & Jonides, 1997; Wickelgren, 1997). This volume might have focused a great deal more on the purely cognitive aspects of working memory if it had been edited several years ago, but comprehensive models of working memory can no longer ignore the insights and constraints offered by rich cognitive neuroscience findings. Thus, the final designated question asked the contributors to discuss how their respective models can accommodate (or at least relate to) recent cognitive neuroscience findings. The question also asked them to speculate about how their respective views of working memory might be actually implemented in the brain.

Although the surge of interest in the neural basis of working memory is a quite recent phenomenon, the important role of the prefrontal cortex (PFC) in working memory, emphasized in several chapters of this volume (most notably, Engle et al., Chapter 4; O'Reilly et al., Chapter 11), has long been anticipated. In their influential book *Plans and the Structure of Behavior*, Miller,

Galanter, and Pribram (1960) not only used the term "working memory" for the first time (Richardson, 1996), but also speculated that "[the] most forward portion of the primate frontal lobe appears to us to serve as a 'working memory' where Plans can be retained temporarily when they are being formed, or transformed, or executed" (Miller et al., 1960, p. 207). Recent cognitive neuroscience studies seem to confirm the involvement of PFC during working memory performance (see Fuster, 1997, for a comprehensive review of the PFC anatomy and functions). In particular, existing evidence seems to be converging on the view that various areas of the brain work together, perhaps orchestrated by PFC, to produce working memory phenomena (Wickelgren, 1997), a view that also seems to be generally endorsed by the chapters in this volume.

Although incorporating biological-level mechanisms is the primary concern of only two models in this volume (Schneider, Chapter 10; O'Reilly et al., Chapter 11), other contributors also offer extensive discussions of how their respective models can accommodate some of the recent neuroscience findings on working memory. The range of cognitive neuroscience evidence discussed in this volume is impressive, covering all five major approaches to cognitive neuroscience we listed above: neuropsychological dissociations (Baddeley & Logie, Chapter 2), neuroimaging (Schneider, Chapter 10; O'Reilly et al., Chapter 11), ERP (Cowan, Chapter 3), single-cell recordings from nonhuman primates (Engle et al., Chapter 4; O'Reilly et al., Chapter 11), and computational modeling (Lovett et al., Chapter 5; Schneider, Chapter 10; O'Reilly et al., Chapter 11). Thus, this volume as a whole serves as an up-to-date review of recent cognitive neuroscience research on working memory.

Organization of This Volume

Following this introductory chapter, the subsequent chapters (Chapters 2 to 11) present 10 different models of working memory. Figure 1.1 provides a schematic summary of the models presented in this volume, including the chapter number, the names of the contributors, and the name of the model. The figure also indicates some information about the perceived relatedness or compatibility of the 10 models; pairs of models that were informally judged to be closely related or highly compatible at a global level by the contributors to this volume are connected by the links on the left-hand side of the figure.[6] Note that these links are intended to serve only as a rough guideline of which

---

[6] The informal ratings were collected at the end of the companion symposium (July 10–13, 1997) on which this volume is based. The contributors to this volume (one questionnaire per chapter) were asked to rate the compatibility among different models in a pairwise fashion on an 11-point scale, ranging from 0 (totally incompatible) to 10 (totally compatible). The links included on the left-hand side of the figure shows the pairs of models that received an average rating of 6.0 or above and, hence, were judged to be relatively compatible with each other in some way by the contributors of this volume.

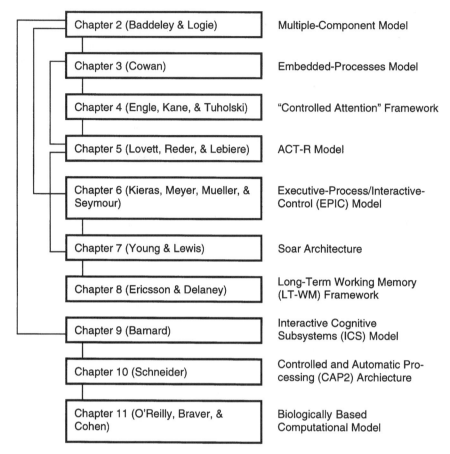

Figure 1.1. A schematic summary of the models included in this volume and their interrelationships. The name that is used to refer to the model, theory, or framework in this volume is included in the figure, as well as the chapter number and the names of the authors. The additional links, provided on the left-hand side of the figure, connect the models that were informally judged to be highly related or compatible by the chapter contributors (see footnote 6 for more details on the basis for these links).

models are particularly similar to one another. As the rich set of cross-references included in the chapters of this volume makes clear, the models that are not connected to one another in Figure 1.1 often share some important common features or ideas as well.

The first four models (Chapters 2 to 5) are closely related to one another because they emphasize a close relationship between attention and working memory. The presentation of the models begins with Baddeley and Logie's (Chapter 2) discussion of the well-known multiple component model of working memory (or "working attention," Baddeley, 1993). Although the

Baddeley–Logie model maintains the original tripartite structure proposed by Baddeley and Hitch (1974), it has undergone a number of important changes, particularly in regard to specifying the functions of the central executive. Chapter 2 documents these changes.

Chapter 3 presents Cowan's Embedded-Processes Model, a broad-scope information processing framework originally developed to synthesize a vast array of empirical findings on attention and memory (Cowan, 1988). Although it is not a model of working memory per se, it can serve as a basis for detailed, empirically well-supported answers to the eight designated questions.

In Chapter 4, Engle, Kane, and Tuholski describe their new theoretical perspective on working memory, which could be called the "controlled attention" framework. Recent cognitive neuroscience findings on the role of PFC in executive control and attentional processes provided an inspiration for this framework, and Engle et al. discuss an interesting series of studies to illustrate the important role of "controlled attention" in working memory and complex cognition.

Chapter 5 presents Lovett, Reder, and Lebiere's ACT-R model of working memory (Anderson, 1993; Anderson & Lebiere, 1998; Anderson et al., 1996). Their conceptualization of working memory is similar to Just and Carpenter's (1992) model in a number of respects, but the characterization of working-memory limitations in ACT-R is different in that it postulates an attentional limit (i.e., how much information one can simultaneously attend to) by limiting the total amount of "source activation" (rather than the total amount of activation available to the system).

The ACT-R chapter is also the first of the three (Chapters 5 to 7) that are based on symbolic computational architectures. The focus of Chapter 6 is the Executive-Process/Interactive-Control (EPIC) architecture, developed by Kieras, Meyer, and their colleagues (e.g., Meyer & Kieras, 1997). EPIC is unique in its well-developed interface with perceptual and motor processes and its strong emphasis on strategic executive control of behavior. In Chapter 6, Kieras, Meyer, Mueller, and Seymour discuss this EPIC framework within the context of its application to one of the signature working memory tasks, the immediate serial recall of words.

Chapter 7 discusses working memory from the perspective of Soar (Laird, Newell, & Rosenbaum, 1987), a cognitive architecture that Newell (1990) presented as a candidate unified theory of cognition in his book. In this chapter, Young and Lewis provide interesting answers to one common criticism of the Soar architecture, namely that its working memory is too big as a theory of human cognition because virtually no constraints are placed on it (e.g., Carlson & Detweiler, 1992; Lewandowsky, 1992).

Soar's functional account of working memory emphasizes the important role of learning, knowledge, and skills and, in that sense, has a strong resemblance to Ericsson and Kintsch's (1995) LT-WM account. In Chapter 8, Ericsson and Delaney elaborate this LT-WM framework and argue for extend-

ing the scope of working memory research to encompass temporary maintenance of information in not just unfamiliar, lab-based tasks, but also skilled
everyday activities.

Chapters 9 and 10 are closely related to each other in that both propose a
distributed framework in which working memory emerges from multiple subsystems interacting with one another over a network. In Chapter 9, Barnard
outlines the Interactive Cognitive Subsystems (ICS) architecture, which
started as a psycholinguistic model of STM (Barnard, 1985), but has since
been refined and applied to a wider range of phenomena, including
human–computer interaction and normal and pathological cognitive-affective processing. Although strikingly different from the Baddeley–Logie model
(Chapter 2) on the surface, it is highly compatible with their model (as
reflected in the link between these two models in Figure 1.1) in that the three
subcomponents of the Baddeley–Logie model (i.e., the phonological loop, the
visuospatial sketchpad, and the central executive) can be nicely mapped onto
the ICS framework.

The focus of Chapter 10 is Schneider's Controlled and Automatic
Processing (CAP2) architecture, which has been strongly influenced by
research in learning and skill acquisition as well as in cognitive neuroscience.
Like the ICS architecture, the CAP2 system was originally presented as a
model of working memory (Schneider & Detweiler, 1987), but is indeed a general cognitive architecture that can account for a wide range of cognitive performance. In Chapter 10, Schneider offers his latest account of this
connectionist architecture that features hierarchically organized executive
control mechanisms.

Schneider's (Chapter 10) emphasis on the neural basis of working memory
provides a nice transition to the last model of this volume, O'Reilly, Braver,
and Cohen's biologically based model of working memory (Chapter 11).
O'Reilly et al.'s connectionist framework represents an attempt to start developing an explicit computational model of working memory and executive
control that is biologically plausible and is firmly rooted in the principles of
cognitive processing in the brain. Although the novel framework outlined in
this chapter is not yet implemented in its entirety, it brings studies of working
memory into closer alignment with our rapidly expanding knowledge of its
underlying biological and neural basis.

This volume concludes with two integrative chapters (Chapters 12 and 13)
whose goal is to put these 10 different models of working memory into perspective. Chapter 12, written by the researchers who served as discussants at a
companion symposium that was held in July 1997 (Kintsch, Healy, Hegarty,
Pennington, & Salthouse), provides issue-by-issue analyses and evaluations of
the 10 models' answers to the eight designated questions outlined in this
chapter.

Whereas the focus of Chapter 12 is the evaluation of the *current* status of
the models, the primary focus of our final chapter (Miyake & Shah, Chapter

13) is the *future* of working memory models and research. In this final chapter, we go back to the original motivation for this volume mentioned at the beginning of this chapter (i.e., addressing the "What is working memory, anyway?" question). Based on our reading of Chapters 2 to 11, we offer six common themes or points of general consensus that we believe unify the 10 seemingly disparate models of working memory and, hence, jointly define what working memory really is. We then present our analysis of the major unresolved theoretical issues for each of the eight designated questions and also point out some other promising future directions that are not covered in this volume, but that we believe may become increasingly important in the future.

In summary, this volume offers detailed, systematic comparisons of 10 influential models of working memory by asking each contributor to address the same set of important theoretical questions. Our primary goal is to elucidate the commonalities and differences among these models to better define and understand working memory. Although the final two chapters (Chapters 12 and 13) provide detailed discussions of what commonalities and differences exist among the 10 models, we would like to emphasize here that they are nothing but our opinions, our reflections on what we have learned from this issue-by-issue comparison. Thus, we hereby urge readers to compare and contrast the models in this volume and to draw their own conclusions about the current status and future directions of the field.

REFERENCES

Allport, A. (1993). Attention and control: Have we been asking the wrong questions? A critical review of twenty-five years. In D. E. Meyer & S. M. Kornblum (Eds.), *Attention and performance XIV: Synergies in experimental psychology, artificial intelligence, and cognitive neuroscience* (pp. 183–218). Cambridge, MA: MIT Press.

Anderson, J. R. (1983). *Architecture of cognition*. Cambridge, MA: Harvard University Press.

Anderson, J. R. (1993). *Rules of the mind*. Hillsdale, NJ: Erlbaum.

Anderson, J. R., & Lebiere, C. (1998). *The atomic components of thought*. Mahwah, NJ: Erlbaum.

Anderson, J. R., Reder, L. M., & Lebiere, C. (1996). Working memory: Activation limitations on retrieval. *Cognitive Psychology, 30,* 221–256.

Atkinson, R. C., & Shiffrin, R. M. (1968). Human memory: A proposed system and its control processes. In K. W. Spence & J. T. Spence (Eds.), *The psychology of learning and motivation: Advances in research and theory* (Vol. 2, pp. 89–195). New York: Academic Press.

Atkinson, R. C., & Shiffrin, R. M. (1971). The control of short-term memory. *Scientific American, 225,* 82–90.

Baars, B. J. (1997a). Some essential differences between consciousness and attention, perception, and working memory. *Consciousness and Cognition, 6,* 363–371.

Baars, B. J. (1997b). *In the theater of consciousness: The workspace of the mind.* New York: Oxford University Press.

Baddeley, A. D. (1986). *Working memory.* New York: Oxford University Press.

Baddeley, A. D. (1993). Working memory or working attention? In A. D. Baddeley & L. Weiskrantz (Eds.), *Attention: Selection, awareness, and control. A tribute to Donald Broadbent* (pp. 152–170). New York: Oxford University Press.

Baddeley, A. D., & Hitch, G. J. (1974). Working memory. In G. H. Bower (Ed.), *The psychology of learning and motivation: Advances in research and theory* (Vol. 8, pp. 47–89). New York: Academic Press.

Barnard, P. J. (1985). Interacting cognitive subsystems: A psycholinguistic approach to short-term memory. In A. W. Young (Ed.), *Progress in the psychology of language* (Vol. 2, pp. 197–258). London: Erlbaum.

Baumgartner, P., & Payr, S. (1995). *Speaking minds: Interviews with twenty eminent cognitive scientists.* Princeton, NJ: Princeton University Press.

Beardsley, T. (1997). The machinery of thought. *Scientific American, 277,* 78–83.

Brainerd, C. J., & Kingma, J. (1985). On the independence of short-term memory and working memory in cognitive development. *Cognitive Psychology 17,* 210–247.

Broadbent, D. E. (1958). *Perception and communication.* New York: Pergamon Press.

Byrne, M. D., & Bovair, S. (1997). A working memory model of a common procedural error. *Cognitive Science, 21,* 31–62.

Carlson, R. A., & Detweiler, M. (1992). A unified theory for psychologists? *Behavioral and Brain Sciences, 15,* 440.

Ceci, S. J. (1990/1996). *On intelligence: A bioecological treatise on intellectual development.* Cambridge, MA: Harvard University Press.

Chase, W. G., & Ericsson, K. A. (1981). Skilled memory. In J. R. Anderson (Ed.), *Cognitive skills and their acquisition* (pp. 141–189). Hillsdale, NJ: Erlbaum.

Chase, W. G., & Simon, H. A. (1973). The mind's eye in chess. In W. G. Chase (Ed.), *Visual information processing* (pp. 215–281). New York: Academic Press.

Chi, M. T. H. (1978). Knowledge structures and memory development. In R. S. Siegler (Ed.), *Children's thinking: What develops?* Hillsdale, NJ: Erlbaum.

Cowan, N. (1988). Evolving conceptions of memory storage, selective attention, and their mutual constraints within the human information processing system. *Psychological Bulletin, 104,* 163–191.

Crowder, R. G. (1982). The demise of short-term memory. *Acta Psychologica, 50,* 291–323.

Crowder, R. G. (1993). Short-term memory: Where do we stand? *Memory & Cognition, 21,* 142–145.

Daneman, M., & Carpenter, P. A. (1980). Individual differences in working memory and reading. *Journal of Verbal Learning and Verbal Behavior, 19,* 450–466.

Daneman, M., & Tardif, T. (1987). Working memory and reading skill reexamined. In M. Coltheart (Ed.), *Attention and performance XII: The psychology of reading* (pp. 491–508). Hillsdale, NJ: Erlbaum.

Dennis, I., & Tapsfield, P. (Eds.). (1996). *Human abilities: Their nature and measurement.* Mahwah, NJ: Erlbaum.

Donald, M. (1991). *Origins of the modern mind: Three stages in the evolution of culture and cognition.* Cambridge, MA: Harvard University Press.

Engle, R. W., Cantor, J., & Carullo, J. J. (1992). Individual differences in working memory and comprehension: A test of four hypotheses. *Journal of Experimental Psychology: Learning, Memory, and Cognition, 18,* 972–992.

Engle, R. W., Tuholski, S. W., Laughlin, J. E., & Conway, A. R. A. (in press). Working memory, short-term memory, and general fluid intelligence: A latent variable approach. *Journal of Experimental Psychology: General.*

Ericsson, K. A., & Kintsch, W. (1995). Long-term working memory. *Psychological Review, 102,* 211–245.

Ericsson, K. A., & Polson, P. G. (1988). A cognitive analysis of exceptional memory for restaurant orders. In M. T. H. Chi, R. Glaser, & M. J. Farr (Eds.), *The nature of expertise* (pp. 23–70). Hillsdale, NJ: Erlbaum.

Eysenck, H. J. (1986). The theory of intelligence and the psychophysiology of cognition. In R. J. Sternberg (Ed.), *Advances in the psychology of human intelligence* (Vol. 3, pp. 1–34). Hillsdale, NJ: Erlbaum.

Fuster, J. M. (1997). *The prefrontal cortex: Anatomy, physiology, and neuropsychology of the frontal lobe* (3rd ed.). Philadelphia: Lippincott–Raven.

Gagliardo, A., Mazzotto, M., & Divac, I. (1997). Memory of radial maze behavior in pigeons after ablations of the presumed equivalent of mammalian prefrontal cortex. *Behavioral Neuroscience, 111,* 968–975.

Gardner, H. (1983/1993). *Frames of mind: The theory of multiple intelligences.* New York: Basic Books.

Gazzaniga, M. S. (Ed.). (1995). *The cognitive neuroscience.* Cambridge, MA: MIT Press.

Gazzaniga, M. S., Ivry, R. B., & Mangun, G. R. (1998). *Cognitive neuroscience: The biology of the mind.* New York: Norton.

Goldman, S. R., & Varma, S. (1995). CAPping the Construction-Integration model of discourse comprehension. In C. A. Weaver, S. Mannes, & C. R. Fletcher (Eds.), *Discourse comprehension: Essays in honor of Walter Kintsch* (pp. 337–358). Hillsdale, NJ: Erlbaum.

Goldman-Rakic, P. S. (1992). Working memory and the mind. *Scientific American, 267,* 110–117.

Guilford, J. P. (1967). *The nature of human intelligence.* New York: McGraw-Hill.

Haberlandt, K. (1997). *Cognitive psychology* (2nd ed.). Boston: Allyn & Bacon.

Healy, A. F., & McNamara, D. S. (1996). Verbal learning and memory: Does the modal model still work? *Annual Review of Psychology, 47,* 143–172.

Hebb, D. O. (1949). *The organization of behavior.* New York: Wiley.

Heuer, H. (1985). Some points of contact between models of central capacity and factor-analytic models. *Acta Psychologica, 60,* 135–155.

Huguenard, B. R., Lerch, F. J., Junker, B. W., Patz, R. J., & Kass, R. E. (1997). Working-memory failure in phone-based interaction. *ACM Transactions on Computer–Human Interaction, 4,* 67–102.

Jacobs, J. (1887). Experiments on "prehension." *Mind, 12,* 75–79.

James, W. (1890). *Principles of psychology.* New York: Holt.

Jensen, A. R. (1998). *The g factor: The science of mental ability.* Westport, CT: Praeger.

Just, M. A., & Carpenter, P. A. (1992). A capacity theory of comprehension: Individual differences in working memory. *Psychological Review, 99,* 122–149.

Just, M. A., Carpenter, P. A., & Hemphill, D. D. (1996). Constraints on processing capacity: Architectural or implementational? In D. M. Steier & T. M. Mitchell (Eds.), *Mind matters: A tribute to Allen Newell* (pp. 141–178). Mahwah, NJ: Erlbaum.

Kahneman, D. (1973). *Attention and effort.* Englewood Cliffs, NJ: Prentice Hall.

Klapp, S. T., Marshburn, E. A., & Lester, P. T. (1983). Short-term memory does not involve the "working memory" of information processing: The demise of a common assumption. *Journal of Experimental Psychology: General, 112,* 240–264.

Kyllonen, P. C., & Christal, R. E. (1990). Reasoning ability is (little more than) working-memory capacity?! *Intelligence, 14,* 389–433.

Laird, J. E., Newell, A., & Rosenbloom, P. S. (1987). Soar: An architecture for general intelligence. *Artificial Intelligence, 33,* 1–64.

Lewandowsky, S. (1992). Unified cognitive theory: Having one's apple pie and eating it. *Behavioral and Brain Sciences, 15,* 449–450.

Martin, R. C. (1993). Short-term memory and sentence processing: Evidence from neuropsychology. *Memory & Cognition, 21,* 176–183.

Meyer, D. E., & Kieras, D. E. (1997). A computational theory of executive cognitive processes and multiple-task performance: I. Basic mechanisms, *Psychological Review, 104,* 3–65.

Miller, G. A. (1956). The magical number seven, plus or minus two: Some limits on our capacity for processing information. *Psychological Review, 63,* 81–97.

Miller, G. A., Galanter, E., & Pribram, K. H. (1960). *Plans and the structure of behavior.* New York: Holt, Rinehart, and Winston.

Monsell, S. (1984). Components of working memory underlying verbal skills: A `distributed capacities' view—A tutorial review. In H. Bouma & D. G. Bouwhuis (Eds.), *Attention and performance X* (pp. 327–350). Hillsdale, NJ: Erlbaum.

Moscovitch, M., & Umiltà, C. (1990). Modularity and neuropsychology: Modules and central processes in attention and memory. In M. F. Schwartz (Ed.), *Modular deficits in Alzheimer-type dementia* (pp. 1–59). Cambridge, MA: MIT Press.

Navon, D., & Gopher, D. (1979). On the economy of the human processing system. *Psychological Review, 86,* 214–255.

Newell, A. (1990). *Unified theories of cognition.* Cambridge, MA: Harvard University Press.

Norman, D. A. (1968). Toward a theory of memory and attention. *Psychological Review, 75,* 522–536.

Norman, D. A., & Shallice, T. (1986). Attention to action: Willed and automatic control of behavior. In R. J. Davidson, G. E. Schwartz, & D. Shapiro (Eds.), *Consciousness and self-regulation: Advances in research and theory* (Vol. 4, pp. 1–18). New York: Plenum Press.

Olton, D. S. (1977). Spatial memory. *Scientific American, 236,* 82–98.

Pashler, H. E. (1997). *The psychology of attention.* Cambridge, MA: MIT Press.

Pashler, H. E., & Carrier, M. (1996). Structures, processes, and the flow of information. In E. L. Bjork & R. A. Bjork (Eds.), *Memory* (pp. 3–29). San Diego, CA: Academic Press.

Posner, M. I., & Raichle, M. E. (1994). *Images of mind.* New York: Scientific American Library.

Reitman, W. (1970). What does it take to remember? In D. A. Norman (Eds.), *Models of human memory* (pp. 469–509). New York: Academic Press.

Richardson, J. T. E. (1996). Evolving concepts of working memory. In J. T. E. Richardson, R. W. Engle, L. Hasher, R. H. Logie, E. R. Stoltzfus, & R. T. Zacks (Eds.), *Working memory and human cognition* (pp. 3–30). New York: Oxford University Press.

Rugg, M. D. (Ed.). (1997). *Cognitive neuroscience.* Cambridge, MA: MIT Press.

Salthouse, T. A. (1996). The processing-speed theory of adult age differences in cognition. *Psychological Review, 103*, 403–428.

Salthouse, T. A., & Babcock, R. L. (1991). Decomposing adult age differences in working memory. *Developmental Psychology, 27*, 763–776.

Schneider, W., & Detweiler, M. (1987). A connectionist/control architecture for working memory. In G. H. Bower (Ed.), *The psychology of learning and motivation* (Vol. 21, pp. 53–119). New York: Academic Press.

Schneider, W., Körkel, J., & Weinert, F. E. (1989). Domain-specific knowledge and memory performance: A comparison of high- and low-aptitude children. *Journal of Educational Psychology, 81*, 306–312.

Shah, P., & Miyake, A. (1996). The separability of working memory resources for spatial thinking and language processing: An individual differences approach. *Journal of Experimental Psychology: General, 125*, 4–27.

Shapiro, L. P., Gordon, B., Hack, N., & Killackey, J. (1993). Verb-argument structure processing in complex sentences in Broca's and Wernicke's aphasia. *Brain and Language, 45*, 423–447.

Smith, E. E., & Jonides, J. (1997). Working memory: A view from neuroimaging. *Cognitive Psychology, 33*, 5–42.

Spearman, C. (1904). General intelligence, objectively determined and measured. *American Journal of Psychology, 15*, 201–293.

Sternberg, S. (1966). High speed scanning in human memory. *Science 153*, 652–654.

Stoltzfus, E. R., Hasher, L., & Zacks, R. T. (1996). Working memory and aging: Current status of the inhibitory view. In J. T. E. Richardson, R. W. Engle, L. Hasher, R. H. Logie, E. R. Stoltzfus, & R. T. Zacks (Eds.), *Working memory and human cognition* (pp. 66–88). New York: Oxford University Press.

Thurston, L. L. (1938). *Primary mental abilities*. Chicago: University of Chicago Press.

VanLehn, K., Brown, J. S., & Greeno, J. (1984). Competitive argumentation in computational theories of cognition. In W. Kintsch, J. R. Miller, & P. G. Polson (Eds.), *Methods and tactics in cognitive science* (pp. 235–262). Hillsdale, NJ: Erlbaum.

Waugh, N. C., & Norman, D. A. (1965). Primary memory. *Psychological Review, 72*, 89–104.

Wickelgren, I. (1997). Getting a grasp on working memory. *Science 275*, 1580–1582.

Wickens, C. D. (1984). Processing resources in attention. In R. Parasuraman & R. Davies (Eds.), *Varieties of attention* (pp. 63–101). New York: Academic Press.

2 Working Memory

The Multiple-Component Model

ALAN D. BADDELEY AND ROBERT H. LOGIE

FIVE CENTRAL FEATURES OF THE MODEL

(1) According to our view, working memory comprises multiple specialized components of cognition that allow humans to comprehend and mentally represent their immediate environment, to retain information about their immediate past experience, to support the acquisition of new knowledge, to solve problems, and to formulate, relate, and act on current goals.

(2) These specialized components include both a supervisory system (the central executive) and specialized temporary memory systems, including a phonologically based store (the phonological loop) and a visuospatial store (the visuospatial sketchpad).

(3) The two specialized, temporary memory systems are used to actively maintain memory traces that overlap with those involved in perception via rehearsal mechanisms involved in speech production for the phonological loop and, possibly, preparations for action or image generation for the visuospatial sketchpad.

(4) The central executive is involved in the control and regulation of the working memory system. It is considered to play various executive functions, such as coordinating the two slave systems, focusing and switching attention, and activating representations within long-term memory, but it is not involved in temporary storage. The central executive in principle may not be a unitary construct, and this issue is a main focus of current research within this framework.

(5) This model is derived empirically from studies of healthy adults and children and of brain-damaged individuals, using a range of experimental methodologies. The model offers a useful framework to account for a wide range of empirical findings on working memory.

There is broad agreement among the contributors to this volume that working memory refers to aspects of on-line cognition – the moment-to-moment monitoring, processing, and maintenance of information both in laboratory tasks and in everyday cognition. Our own definition of working memory is that it comprises those functional components of cognition that allow

Working Memory

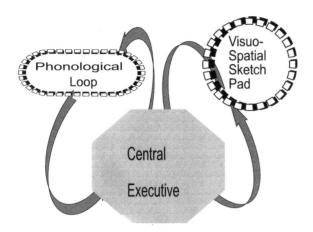

Figure 2.1. A schematic diagram of a multiple-component model of working memory (derived from Baddeley & Hitch, 1974).

humans to comprehend and mentally represent their immediate environment, to retain information about their immediate past experience, to support the acquisition of new knowledge, to solve problems, and to formulate, relate, and act on current goals.

Our theoretical approach has developed in the framework of working memory comprising multiple specialized subcomponents of cognition. The exact nature of these components is considered an empirical question, rather than something that forms an a priori assumption of the model. The original model proposed by Baddeley and Hitch (1974), shown schematically in Figure 2.1, comprises a *central executive* controlling mechanism and two subsidiary or "slave" systems, called the *phonological loop* and the *visuospatial sketchpad*, which are specialized for the processing and temporary maintenance of material within a particular domain (i.e., verbally coded information and visual and/or spatial information, respectively).

In this chapter, we outline our responses to each of the eight designated questions from the perspective of this model. The responses are generally organized according to the original scheme set by the editors (Shah & Miyake, Chapter 1, this volume). In writing the chapter, however, we became aware that our responses to some of the questions could be best answered within a single section, using the same arguments and evidence. Therefore, we have combined our discussion of the non-unitary nature of our model with that of basic mechanisms and representation, although the material relevant to both of these questions crops up throughout the chapter. Our response to the question on biological implementation of working memory is also provided throughout the chapter and illustrated with concrete examples in relevant sections. Table 2.1 presents a brief summary of our answers to each question.

Basic Mechanisms and Representations in Working Memory and the Unitary Versus Non-Unitary Nature of Working Memory

As the above overview indicates, our model of working memory is inherently non-unitary in nature. It comprises multiple specialized components, including the central executive and the two slave systems. The evidence supporting

Table 2.1. *Summary Responses to the Eight Questions from the Perspective of the Multiple-Component Model of Working Memory*

(1) **Basic Mechanisms and Representation in Working Memory**
The multiple-component model consists of a central executive controller and two subsidiary systems specialized respectively for temporary storage of phonologically based material (the phonological loop) and of visuospatial material (the visuospatial sketchpad). The characteristics of these systems have been derived largely from empirical investigations. The phonological loop is further fractionated into a passive, phonological store and an active rehearsal system, whereas the visuospatial sketchpad has recently been fractionated into a passive visual cache and an active spatially based rehearsal system called the inner scribe.

(2) **The Control and Regulation of Working Memory**
The central executive offers the mechanism for control processes in working memory, including the coordination of the subsidiary memory systems, the control of encoding and retrieval strategies, the switching of attention, and the mental manipulation of material held in the slave systems (Baddeley, 1996). The central executive itself, however, is not equipped with the supplementary storage capacity. The detailed nature of the processes attributed to the central executive are derived empirically. The organization of these processes remains an open question and is the subject of ongoing empirical exploration.

(3) **The Unitary Versus Non-Unitary Nature of Working Memory**
Our model has an inherently non-unitary nature in that it comprises several specialized components, which can be further fractionated if such fractionation is adequately justified empirically. Even the central executive in principle may not be a unitary construct, but this is the subject of current work in this framework.

(4) **The Nature of Working Memory Limitations**
The components each have constraints commensurate with the specialist function that each provides, and these constraints may arise from capacity for activation or from capacity for rehearsal, or from capacity for complexity

of material, or from the extent to which they are supported by acquired strategies and prior knowledge.

(5) **The Role of Working Memory in Complex Cognitive Activities**
Our model offers a coherent account of the role of working memory in different domains of complex cognition, such as language comprehension, counting and mental arithmetic, syllogistic reasoning, and dynamic perceptuomotor control. All these complex cognitive tasks rely on a range of cognitive resources, and the multiple-component model and the associated dual-task methodology offer a fruitful framework for exploration of such tasks.

(6) **The Relationship of Working Memory to Long-Term Memory and Knowledge**
Temporary memory is influenced by information from long-term knowledge as well as the operation of the components of working memory. Although some have viewed working memory as an activated portion of long-term memory, such a view is probably an unhelpful oversimplification. We believe instead that working memory and long-term memory comprise two functionally separable cognitive systems. More specifically, a major role for working memory is retrieval of stored long-term knowledge relevant to the tasks in hand, the manipulation and recombination of material allowing the interpretation of novel stimuli, and the discovery of novel information or the solution to problems. Working memory also plays a major role in encoding into long-term memory the outcome of its operations.

(7) **The Relationship of Working Memory to Attention and Consciousness**
The central executive is thought to play an important role in the control of attention, although it is becoming clear that attentional control is not a unitary function, and the central executive is not the only system to contribute. The work of Norman and Shallice (1986) and, more recently, Posner (1995), has been used as a possible framework for the role of the central executive in attentional control. The executive does appear to offer a plausible account for some aspects of attention switching and of dividing attention. Our model also provides a useful way to study conscious awareness and its relation to working memory (Baddeley & Andrade, 1998).

(8) **The Biological Implementation of Working Memory**
The development of our model has relied in part on detailed studies of brain-damaged patients, and these studies have offered insights into the possible aspects of brain organization linked to the components of working memory. More recently, these neuropsychological studies have been supplemented by a range of neuroimaging techniques (Smith & Jonides, 1997). The lower part of the left parietal lobe appears to be associated with verbal short-term memory tasks, while the right posterior parietal lobe appears to be one of several anatomical locations linked with visuospatial working memory tasks. Some of the executive functions have been linked to the frontal lobes, although many tasks thought to involve the central executive may involve other areas of the brain as well.

the separability of these subcomponents of working memory is abundant, ranging from the selective interference effects found in normal adults in dual-task paradigms (e.g., Baddeley, 1986; Logie, 1995), through the patterns of selective sparing and impairments in brain-damaged patients (e.g., Della Sala & Logie, 1993), to the differential rates of developmental changes (or "developmental fractionation") observed among children (e.g., Hitch, 1990). We will discuss relevant findings supporting this multiple-component framework throughout this chapter.

Each of these components of working memory can be further fractionated if such fractionation is adequately justified empirically. Since the proposal of the original model, the phonological loop has been fractionated into a passive *phonological store* and an active *rehearsal process*. The phonological store represents material in a phonological code, which decays with time, whereas the rehearsal process serves to refresh the decaying representations in the phonological store, a distinction that is supported not only by experimental and neuropsychological findings (e.g., Baddeley, 1986) but more recently by neuroimaging data as well (e.g., Smith & Jonides, 1997). Similarly, the visuospatial sketchpad has recently been fractionated by one of us into a passive *visual cache* and an active spatially based system called the *inner scribe* (Logie, 1995). The evidence supporting this distinction will be reviewed shortly. As we will argue later in the "Control and Regulation of Working Memory" section, the central executive may also, in principle, not be a unitary construct, and a fractionation into different subcomponents or subprocesses is probably necessary (Baddeley, 1996).

With respect to the rehearsal mechanism for the two slave systems, we assume that memory traces can be set up, using processes that overlap with those involved in perception, and can be actively maintained using processes related to those involved in action or response production. In the case of the phonological loop, these processes are assumed to involve aspects of the systems necessary for speech perception and for assembling speech output programs. In the case of the visuospatial sketchpad, the nature of the rehearsal mechanism is less clear, although one of us has argued that preparation for actions, handled by the inner scribe, might subserve maintenance functions for spatially based information, whereas some aspects of image generation might support visual retention (Logie, 1995). Immediate memory performance is a joint function of these two subprocesses of storage and rehearsal. However, whereas we assume that initial activation is essential for working memory performance, active rehearsal is regarded as an optional means of enhancing performance, and hence is not obligatory (Logie, Della Sala, Laiacona, Chalmers, & Wynn, 1996).

The Nature of Working Memory Limitations

The subcomponents of our model are thought to have constraints commensurate with the specialist functions that each provides. In each case, however, we tend to have assumed a structure or set of structures that depends on activation, with both the amount and duration of activation being limited. In this section, we review some relevant evidence on this issue for each of the two slave systems.

Limitations in the Phonological Loop

We assume that individual differences in the phonological loop capacity reflect the amount of memory activation available, partly as a result of genetic factors. In addition, some variation in memory activation may result following brain damage. For example, patients with impaired verbal short-term memory (STM) appear to be able to encode material quite normally, in the sense of perceiving words and sentences, but the trace of such perceptual processing does not persist, indicating a lack either of adequate activation or of maintenance. Such patients, however, often have a normal capacity for speech production (Vallar & Baddeley, 1984), suggesting that the principal problem is not one of response production and, hence, probably not of incapacity to rehearse.

In addition to the limits on degree of activation, we also assume that subjects may differ in their rehearsal capacity. In the case of the phonological loop, this capacity appears to reflect one's ability to set up and run speech output programs, but does not require that such programs be explicitly realized through articulatory output. Our reason for this assumption is that dysarthric patients who have lost the capacity to control their peripheral speech musculature nonetheless show normal rehearsal patterns (Baddeley & Wilson, 1985; Della Sala, Logie, Marchetti, & Wynn, 1991), whereas dyspraxic patients who have lost the capacity to set up the appropriate speech motor programs have difficulty in rehearsing (Caplan, Rochon, & Waters, 1992).

A related issue that has evoked considerable research concerns the developmental changes in the phonological loop capacity. Nicolson (1981) first demonstrated a close association between an age-related increase in memory span and increase in speed of articulation, leading to an extensive series of studies exploring the possibility that the development of span can be entirely attributed to faster rehearsal (e.g., Hulme, Thomson, Muir, & Lawrence, 1984). Although this hypothesis initially appeared to fit the data remarkably well, subsequent research has suggested that this view is probably an oversimplification, with rehearsal in young children being qualitatively different from that found in older children and adults (see Gathercole & Hitch, 1993, for a review).

In the case of adults, one of the principal means of studying verbal rehearsal has been through the word length effect, whereby memory span is a direct function of the spoken length of the to-be-recalled items (Baddeley, Thomson, & Buchanan, 1975). In these initial studies, subjects were instructed to respond in writing and to limit their response to the first three letters of each word, so as to equate the amount of output interference. In studies where this precaution is not taken, an additional major factor is the increased delay engendered by the spoken recall of longer words, a point amply demonstrated by Cowan et al. (1992). The word length effect, however, is not entirely due to output delay because the effect is still present (albeit smaller) when performance is measured by a probe technique (Henry, 1991) or a recognition procedure (Baddeley & Wilson, 1985; Della Sala et al., 1991).

What then is our current position on word length and rehearsal? We still believe that rehearsal operates in real time and that longer items will take longer to rehearse, allowing more forgetting to occur. We accept, however, that, under standard conditions, performance will reflect both rehearsal and output delay effects. In short, we stand by the proposed phenomena of real-time rehearsal and trace decay, but acknowledge that the contribution of various factors to the word length effect may well vary depending upon the circumstances (Logie et al., 1996).

TRACE DECAY OR OUTPUT INTERFERENCE? As Cowan, Wood, Nugent, and Treisman (1997) have pointed out, the differential output delay engendered by recalling words differing in length could represent either spontaneous fading of the memory trace or interference from the intervening material. Baddeley et al. (1975) attempted to test this issue by comparing the recall of words that were matched for number of phonemes, but differed in spoken duration, contrasting long-duration words (such as *Friday* and *harpoon*) with shorter-duration ones (such as *bishop* and *wicket*). They observed that words with longer duration led to poorer performance. Cowan et al. (1997) challenged this conclusion, arguing that the longer-duration words have stresses on both syllables, whereas the shorter-duration words have only one stress. In a rather complex study in which subjects were trained to vary the pronunciation of monosyllabic and disyllabic words on instruction and were required to recall in reverse order, they report evidence of both a negative effect of duration and a positive effect of complexity (see Cowan, Chapter 3, this volume, for more detailed discussions of this study). There appears to be disagreement among the authors as to the interpretation of these results, with Cowan wishing to continue to support a trace decay assumption, whereas Treisman argues for an interference interpretation. It should be noted, however, that this interference interpretation is a rather unusual one in that it appears to assume that similarity does not influence interference, but duration does.

Evidence that the word length effect is not specifically an output interference phenomenon comes from an earlier study by Baddeley and Hull (1979), in which seven-digit sequences were followed by either a prefix that the subject had to speak before recalling or by a stimulus suffix that required no response. The prefix/suffix ranged in length from one to five syllables. The results showed a clear effect of length, which was broadly equivalent whether the subject was required to speak the item or merely listen to it. It is important to note that the effect in question operates throughout the list. This effect thus differs from the standard suffix effect, which impairs recall of the last item.

Baddeley (1986, pp. 94–95) presents further evidence for a decay interpretation of this through-list suffix effect. In this study, subjects were presented with sequences of nine digits and required to recall by writing the sequence on either the left- or right-hand side of their response sheet. The instruction "left" or "right" was always presented immediately after the last digit, resulting in a brief delay during which the instruction was processed. In a second condition, the instruction was again given, but subjects were informed that the instructions would always alternate "left, right, left, right," and so on, making the information redundant. Subjects' recall performance showed a consistent advantage when the prefix was redundant over when the instruction information had to be processed. Such a result, however, left at least one alternative to the temporal delay hypothesis, namely that forgetting occurred because of interference from the requirement to process the response instruction, not from decay during the temporal delay per se. These two hypotheses were tested in a further experiment in which the instruction was presented between the eighth and ninth digits, allowing the response decision to be made *before* the last digit and hence removing the delay, but still exposing retention of eight of the nine digits to potential interference. The informational disruption hypothesis thus predicts substantial interference, whereas the temporal delay hypothesis would predict that the difference between the two conditions would vanish. The results matched the latter prediction, hence supporting the hypothesis that forgetting occurs because of the temporal delay. Thus, like Cowan (Chapter 3, this volume), we continue to assume trace decay, but would accept that its detailed nature and time course remain to be explored.

Limitations in the Visuospatial Sketchpad

Measures of visuospatial working memory have focused on memory for spatial movement and for visual patterns. The thrust of much of the evidence now available points to the dissociation between a capacity for retaining visual patterns (the visual cache; Logie, 1995) and that for retaining sequences of movements (the inner scribe). For example, a number of dual-task studies demonstrated a disruptive effect of concurrent movements on the retention of spatial patterns (Baddeley & Lieberman, 1980; Logie, Zucco, & Baddeley, 1990; Smyth & Pendleton, 1989) as well as a disruptive effect of concurrent or interpolated viewing of irrelevant, changing visual material on the retention of visual information (Logie, 1986; Quinn & McConnell, 1996). Logie and Marchetti (1991) demonstrated this double dissociation in a single study, showing that retention of spatial patterns, but not visual information (shades of color), was disrupted by arm movements during a retention interval, whereas retention of visual information, but not spatial patterns, was disrupted by a visual interference task interpolated between presentation and retrieval. Further evidence comes from a recent developmental study (Logie & Pearson, 1997). In this study, children aged 5, 8, and 11 were tested on their memory span for recognition and recall of square matrix patterns and of movements to a series of targets (the Corsi blocks test). Within each age group, the span measures for patterns correlated poorly with span for movements. Furthermore, while performance on both types of task improved with age, span for patterns improved much more rapidly across age than did span for movement sequences. Such developmental fractionation indicates that the capacity of these subsystems develops at different rates.

Given that there is an empirically based case for separate subcomponents within the visuospatial sketchpad, this visual versus spatial distinction then raises the issue as to what constrains the capacity of each subsystem. Although the precise nature of the mechanisms underlying the capacity limitations for spatial and visual information is not clear yet, recent work has revealed some important factors that contribute to the capacity limits of each subsystem.

As for the spatial subcomponent (or the inner scribe), we know that retention of movement or of paths between objects and locations does not depend on visual perceptual input. The relative physical location of objects can be determined by hearing, by touch, or by arm movement as well as by vision, and few would dispute that the blind can have spatial representations (Kerr, 1983; Vecchi, Monticellai, & Cornoldi, 1995). We also know that memory for movement sequences can be affected by complexity, such as dimensionality. Cornoldi, Cortesi, and Preti (1991), for example, asked subjects to imagine paths through two-dimensional (e.g., 5×5 squares) and three-dimensional (e.g., $3 \times 3 \times 3$ blocks) square matrices. Most subjects found the three-dimensional matrix more difficult than the two-dimensional one, despite the fact that the total number of squares or blocks is approximately the same in each case. However, the detailed characteristics of the limitations on memory for movement sequences have yet to be explored fully.

As for the visual subcomponent (or the visual cache), one important capacity-constraining factor seems to be the visual similarity of to-be-maintained items. For example, Hitch, Halliday, Schaafstal, and Schraagen (1988) found visual confusion errors occurring in young children's recognition memory. The children in these studies were shown a series of pictures, some of which were visually similar to one another (such as a brush, a rake, and a pen), while other items were visually distinct (such as a pig, a ball, and a pen). Five-year-old children showed poorer recognition memory for items from the visually similar set. With older children, the effect of visual similarity also appeared, but only if they were required to suppress verbalization (via concurrent articulation of well-known words or syllables, such as "the, the, the. . .") and thereby forced to rely more heavily on visual rather than verbal codes (Hitch, Woodin, & Baker, 1989). Analogous visual similarity effects for familiar letter or digit stimuli have also been found among adults, both in healthy normals under articulatory suppression conditions (Walker, Hitch, & Duroe, 1993) and in patients with severe phonological loop impairments, such as Patient KF

(Shallice & Warrington, 1970), whose memory span errors in visual presentation tended to be visual in nature. Furthermore, using visually complex Chinese characters that were not familiar to their subjects and thereby forcing them to rely on visual codes, Hue and Ericsson (1988) found visual similarity effects in the immediate recall of these Chinese characters. These studies all support the idea that visual similarity between the items being retained in this system leads to a reduction in capacity. This visual similarity effect (as well as an analogous phonological similarity effect associated with the phonological loop; Conrad, 1964) is essentially equivalent to the notion of similarity-based interference discussed by Young and Lewis (Chapter 7, this volume).

Another capacity-limiting factor for visual pattern memory may be the number of items. For example, Phillips and Christie (1977) and, more recently, Walker et al. (1993) reported a one-item recency effect in recognition memory for a sequence of square matrix patterns or random block patterns. Similarly, Broadbent and Broadbent (1981) showed analogous recency effects for abstract wallpaper patterns or sets of irregular abstract line drawings. This kind of evidence points to the suggestion that visual temporary memory may be able to hold only a single pattern, but the visual complexity of the pattern or the similarity of the pattern elements to one another may constitute additional limitations on the capacity of the system.

The Control and Regulation of Working Memory

As with the original Baddeley and Hitch (1974) model, we continue to assume that working memory is controlled by a central executive. The concept of the central executive, however, has undergone a number of significant changes over the past 20 years. In particular, the original model assumed that the central executive comprised a pool of general-purpose processing capacity that could be used to support either control processes or supplementary storage. We have subsequently abandoned the assumption that the central executive itself stores information, proposing instead that any increase in total storage capacity beyond that of a given slave system is achieved by accessing either long-term memory (LTM) or other subsystems (for a similar proposal, see Ericsson & Delaney, Chapter 8, this volume). There are a number of reasons for this change, some theoretically driven and others empirically driven.

From a theoretical viewpoint, we were unhappy about giving the central executive the capacity to supplement and, hence, mimic the capacities of the slave systems or indeed in principle any other memory system. We felt that this practice would make the central executive system simply too powerful and too flexible to be productively investigated. As some chapters of this volume propose (Cowan, Chapter 3; Engle, Kane, & Tuholski, Chapter 4), separating out control and storage processes seemed to offer a better chance for making progress.

From an empirical viewpoint, the motivation for revising our initial assumptions reflects growing evidence that working memory can utilize temporary storage in systems other than the two slave systems. One obvious example is the recency effect, which we have suggested represents the priming of representations in LTM, a relatively automatic process, coupled with a specific and active retrieval strategy (Baddeley & Hitch, 1977, 1993). We suspect that this process can extend well beyond the priming of individual lexical items up to the activation of relatively high-level semantic structures such as complex schemata. An interesting source of evidence for such a view comes from the observation that certain densely amnesic but otherwise intact patients are nevertheless capable of demonstrating excellent immediate recall of a prose passage, coupled with an almost complete absence of delayed recall (Wilson & Baddeley, 1988). We assume that this capability reflects the process of comprehension, whereby schemata are activated and maintained by the central executive. In a normal subject, this would lead to encoding and storage in LTM, whereas in a profoundly amnesic patient, once activation by the central executive is removed, performance rapidly declines. A similar and much more articulated view of this issue was proposed by Ericsson and Kintsch (1995) (see Ericsson & Delaney, Chapter 8, this volume).

Another empirical reason for not giving the central executive a supplementary storage capacity comes from our recent work involving the processing and storage demands associated with the performance of complex working memory tasks (Logie & Duff, 1996). One widely used verbal measure, Daneman and Carpenter's (1980) reading span task, for example, requires subjects to read a series of sentences and maintain the final word of each for later recall (see Engle et al., Chapter 4, this volume, for further discussions on working memory spans). In general, Daneman and Carpenter (1980) suggest that this recall measure of the sentence final words reflects the operation of executive processes in working memory, rather than or besides the functioning of the slave systems like the phonological loop alone. The underlying assumption, then, is that as memory demands increase, there is less capacity available for processing and vice versa.

One possible alternative view is that the working memory measure involves not only on-line processing and control but also short-term verbal memory, and that these cognitive demands are supported by separate components of working memory (i.e., the central executive and the phonological loop, respectively). Supporting this alternative view, Engle et al. (Chapter 4, this volume) report an elegant analysis of the partial correlations arising from putative different components of the task, suggesting that temporary storage (handled by the phonological loop) and controlled attention (handled by the central executive) each make semiindependent contributions to individual variations in the performance of complex fluid intelligence tasks.

In our recent work (Logie & Duff, 1996), we have attempted to examine more closely the possible separate cognitive demands of processing and stor-

age. In particular, we have examined the extent to which increasing processing demands results in poorer performance on the storage elements of the
task. In one of the experiments, subjects were given a processing task, a storage task, and a processing-and-storage task. The processing task required a
verification of a series of simple sums within a 10-s period. Subjects were first
given a two-sum trial (e.g., $9 + 6 = 15$ or $5 + 8 = 12$), where each sum was presented for 5 s. Following correct verification of both sums, three sums were
presented for 3.33 s each, followed by four sums (2.5 s each), and so on, until
subjects were no longer able correctly to verify all of the sums presented in
the 10-s period. In the storage task, these same subjects were tested for immediate serial recall span for sequences of unrelated words. The subjects were
then required to perform both the processing and storage elements of the task
with each verification sum shown along with an unrelated word. The main
results of the study were that a demanding storage task had virtually no
impact on the capacity for arithmetic verification and also that a demanding
verification task had little effect on span for words. Three other experiments
using similar procedures showed similar patterns of results, offering little support for the view that processing and storage demands compete for a single
resource. A more plausible explanation is that the words were retained in a
temporary verbal store such as the phonological loop, while the executive was
involved in conducting the verification task.

Is the Central Executive Merely a Homunculus?

One problem with postulating a control structure like the central executive
is that such a model simply postulates a homunculus, a little person who
makes all the awkward decisions in some unspecified way and, hence, that it
adds nothing in explanatory value. This general issue is discussed in detail
elsewhere (Baddeley, 1996; Baddeley & Della Sala, 1996) and, hence, the arguments will be summarized only briefly.

Our previous research has focused primarily on the structure and the functions of the two slave systems (Baddeley, 1986; Logie, 1995), which were considered more tractable than the central executive. We believe that this
research strategy has already proved its value in terms of the progress made in
understanding both the phonological loop and the visuospatial sketchpad.
We fully accept, however, that it is not satisfactory to simply leave the central
executive as a useful ragbag to contain all the phenomena that cannot be
readily accounted for otherwise. In an attempt to make progress, we began a
few years ago to postulate some of the processes that would have to be performed by any adequate central executive.

One of these processes concerns the capacity to control and coordinate the
two slave systems. We devised a series of tasks in which a slave system and the
central executive were used independently and in combination. For example,
we found that the dual-task condition produced particularly marked decrements in patients suffering from Alzheimer's disease (Baddeley, Bressi, Della

Sala, Logie, & Spinnler, 1991; Baddeley, Logie, Bressi, Della Sala, & Spinnler, 1986) and in a specific subsample of patients with frontal lobe damage (Baddeley, Della Sala, Papagno, & Spinnler, 1997). We have subsequently begun to postulate a number of other executive functions, including the capacity to focus attention, to switch attention, and to activate representations within LTM (see Baddeley, 1996, for more detailed discussions on these executive functions).

We do not regard these as the only functions that are served by the central executive. We leave open to empirical investigation the question of whether they are indeed separate functions or might possibly reflect different operations of a smaller number of underlying control processes. We also leave open the possibility that many such subprocesses might reflect the amount of some common capacity such as excitation or inhibition. Finally, we can at present see no reason for taking a strong view on whether the central executive will ultimately prove to be a system within which a range of equally important control processes interact in a quasiautonomous way, with overall control forming an emergent feature, or whether there is a hierarchy of such processes with one dominant controller. In short, we leave open to investigation the question of whether the central executive resembles an organization run by a single chairperson or one governed by the collective wisdom of a committee of equals (see Barnard, Chapter 9, this volume, for a conception of this latter view of the central executive).

Clearly, for anyone wishing to simulate the working memory model, our extreme lack of specification must be a source of frustration. We feel, however, that simply making a guess on all the points discussed would have a vanishingly small chance of producing an accurate model of working memory. In addition, the formulation we propose has the major advantage of setting out a series of empirically tractable questions, the answers to which are likely to be of direct relevance to any adequate model of executive control.

The Role of Working Memory in Complex Cognitive Activities

As is clear from our discussion so far and also from other chapters of this volume, working memory plays a crucial role for complex cognitive activities such as language comprehension, mental arithmetic, and reasoning. All these cognitive activities require the moment-to-moment monitoring, processing, and maintenance of task-relevant information, which, as we argued in the last section, are supported by different components of working memory. Therefore, as will become clear shortly, any complex cognitive tasks, regardless of content domain, require the involvement of multiple components of working memory and the dynamic coordination of activities among them. The specific studies we review in this section also help to specify the precise role that each component plays in each specific complex cognitive task.

Language Comprehension

There has been considerable investigation into the role of working memory in this area (see Gathercole & Baddeley, 1993, for a more detailed review). The phonological loop might reasonably be considered to form a major bottleneck in the process of spoken language comprehension. Such a view was, for example, proposed by Clark and Clark (1977), who assumed that the syntactic analysis of a sentence required it to be held in verbal STM. This view would predict that the comprehension limits of a patient with an STM deficit would be set by the length of sentence that could be held in memory (typically, a 6-word sentence for such patients). In general, this is not the case, however. STM patients typically show only relatively minor comprehension problems, unless they are required to process sentences for which comprehension depends upon retaining the surface structure of the beginning of the sentence across many intervening words (see Vallar & Shallice, 1990, for a review).

A broadly similar picture emerges from studies of the role of the phonological loop in comprehension by normal subjects, as reflected in studies using techniques such as articulatory suppression to disrupt the operation of the phonological loop. Both articulatory suppression and phonological similarity do impair performance on certain types of reading task, particularly those involving detection of errors of word order (Baddeley, Eldridge, & Lewis, 1981), but the effects on comprehension per se appear to be relatively slight. It remains possible that there may be certain situations or types of material for which phonological coding is particularly important (possibly for the kind of prose that appears in legal documents, where the precise word order is important and the semantics obscure), but, to the best of our knowledge, even this has not yet been demonstrated.

There has been considerably less work on the role of the visuospatial sketchpad in comprehension. It seems possible, however, that reading may well depend on the capacity to hold and maintain some form of visuospatial framework. Brooks (1967), for example, showed that the act of reading may interfere with the temporary storage of imaged material, presumably through the operation of the sketchpad. Similarly, Eddy and Glass (1981) demonstrated that reading while attempting to verify high-imagery sentences resulted in poorer performance than when subjects listened to those same sentences. Some comprehension tasks may also depend on the setting up of some form of visuospatial representation, again involving the sketchpad. Haenggi, Kintsch, and Gernsbacher (1995), for example, demonstrated that the construction of spatial mental models from text might depend on visuospatial capacity.

As suggested earlier, we assume that the central executive plays an important role in comprehension (Gathercole & Baddeley, 1993). The executive is assumed to activate representations in LTM extending up from individual words and concepts to complex schemata. In a normal subject, the internal representation or model constructed by the central executive will result in the registration of that representation in long-term episodic memory, a process that does not adequately occur in the case of amnesic patients. We assume that the capacity to comprehend a particular passage will be determined both by the existing representations in LTM and by the capacity of the central executive to activate and combine such representations into a coherent mental model, which can then be consolidated into LTM (see O'Reilly, Braver, & Cohen, Chapter 11, this volume, for a similar proposal). Consistent with this view, an intelligent but densely amnesic patient can comprehend but not store a complex passage (Wilson & Baddeley, 1988), whereas patients with Alzheimer's disease who demonstrate an impairment in executive processes cannot even create the initial representation, performing poorly on both immediate and delayed recall.

Counting and Mental Arithmetic

Despite the fact that much of basic arithmetic skill involves automatic access to solutions of well-practiced arithmetic operations, recent studies convincingly demonstrate that working memory plays important roles in both counting and mental arithmetic.

COUNTING. The existing evidence suggests that, in addition to knowledge of the counting sequence and counting heuristics, counting requires temporary storage of the running total. This keeping track of the running total seems to be handled by the phonological loop (Hitch, 1978; Logie & Baddeley, 1987). For example, in a study by Nairne and Healy (1983), participants were required to orally count backwards. Errors in this relatively simple task were rare, but one type of systematic error concerned subjects' omitting numbers with repeated digits (e.g., *88, 66*). The authors demonstrated that such repeated digit errors were based on phonological confusions between repetition of the decade prefix (*eighty, sixty*) and the second digit (*eight, six*), suggesting the involvement of the phonological loop (particularly, the phonological store) in counting. In some of our own studies (Logie & Baddeley, 1987), we examined counting of items in stimulus arrays or of event sequences, using the articulatory suppression technique. The stimulus arrays comprised from 1 to 25 dots presented at random positions on a computer screen, with subjects counting the number of dots as rapidly and as accurately as possible. The event sequence task involved counting the number of occasions on which a square appeared, at irregular intervals (400 to 900 ms), in the center of a computer screen. For both array counting and event counting, concurrent articulatory suppression resulted in a substantial number of errors, and the number of errors increased as the number of items or events increased. Counting performance, however, was not disrupted simply by the requirement to carry out any secondary task, because concurrent hand tapping failed to disrupt performance. These results strongly support the idea that the phonological loop is a highly plausible candidate for keeping track of a running total in counting. In addition to the phonological loop, the central executive may also play an important role in counting under certain circumstances, as Engle et al. (Chapter 4, this volume) report in their chapter.

MENTAL ARITHMETIC. Mental arithmetic is a complex skill that seems to require different components of working memory (Ashcraft, 1995; Logie, Gilhooly, & Wynn, 1994). More specifically, it appears to rely on temporary storage of partial solutions (primarily, the phonological loop function) as well as the application of algorithms for calculation and estimation (primarily, the central executive function).

In a recent study (Logie et al., 1994), for example, we used a dual-task methodology to examine the role of the phonological loop in mental arithmetic. We used cumulative addition of a series of two-digit numbers (e.g., 13 + 18 + 24 + 17 + 48 + 33 = ?) in this study, a task that was unlikely to be highly practiced and, hence, required subjects to keep track of the cumulative totals until responding with a final total. The results indicated that, with both auditory and visual presentation of the numbers, articulatory suppression as well as irrelevant background speech resulted in a substantial increase in the number of errors, whereas concurrent tapping did not. This pattern of results strongly points to a key role for the phonological loop in mental arithmetic.

An interesting finding from this study that illuminates the role of the central executive was that, whereas we observed a significant increase in the number of error totals with articulatory suppression, participants could still generate reasonable approximations: The mean error responses were within 6% of the correct total. This relatively intact approximation ability suggests that participants had a means to circumvent some of the disruptive effects of articulatory suppression or irrelevant speech. In the case of mental arithmetic, this means that there may be learned strategies that draw on well-learned sums. For example, the correct total for the sum 18 + 19 + 23 may not be available immediately, but the total for 20 + 20 + 20 is likely to be. Therefore, participants could guess that the answer to the former sum would be close to 60 without having to precisely keep track of running totals. As such, one suggestion is that the central executive is responsible for selecting and implementing such calculation heuristics.

To investigate this possible role of the central executive, we used a secondary task thought to disrupt strategy deployment, namely oral random generation (Baddeley, 1966a). This task involves subjects repeating aloud a series of letters of the alphabet selected in as random a fashion as possible. The cognitive demands of this task are thought to stem from the need to keep track of the frequency with which individual letters of the alphabet have been generated and to inhibit the production of well-learned or stereotyped sequences such as a-b-c-d-e. This inhibition of what are thought to be largely automatic processes is considered a form of executive or supervisory function. (Note that this task also disrupts the functioning of the phonological loop because of the continuous production of verbal outputs.) The effects of concurrent random generation on mental arithmetic are clear-cut. Random generation resulted in mean error rates of around 40%, and a number of participants even found it impossible to perform mental arithmetic at the same time. Moreover, error responses were poorer approximations to the correct totals than was found with articulatory suppression and irrelevant speech.

Taken together, these results point to the idea that mental arithmetic relies on the phonological loop for temporary storage, possibly that of partial solutions, and subvocal rehearsal of running totals. It also relies on the central executive for access and execution of computational algorithms or heuristics.

Syllogistic Reasoning

Syllogistic reasoning comprises the presentation of two related statements that are assumed to be true, for example, *All baritones are singers; all singers are human.* The subject's task is to determine what conclusion, if any, can be drawn from relating the two statements (Answer: *All baritones are human*). There is a large range of such syllogistic argument combinations with variation in the quantifiers (e.g., *all, none, some*) and the inclusion of negatives (e.g. *Some tenors are not men; all tenors are human*; Answer: *Some humans are not men*). This last example is rarely solved correctly, particularly when the syllogistic arguments are presented in an abstract form (e.g., *Some B are not A; all B are C. Therefore?*). The question, then, is why some problems are harder than others and how working memory might be implicated in the solving of these syllogistic reasoning problems (see Young & Lewis, Chapter 7, this volume, for a discussion of an alternative perspective on the role of working memory in syllogistic reasoning).

Johnson-Laird (1983; Johnson-Laird & Byrne, 1991) has argued that some forms of syllogistic reasoning require the formation of two or more mental models and that additional mental models place additional demands on working memory, resulting in slower or less accurate conclusions. Alternative explanations suggest that most participants do not follow the rules of formal logic in performing these tasks and instead adopt heuristics that result in above-chance performance. The *atmosphere hypothesis* (Woodworth & Sells, 1935), for example, postulates that participants derive their conclusion from the quantifiers in the two initial statements or premises (e.g., including the quantifier "some" in the conclusion if one or both premises contain "some"). Alternatively, the *matching hypothesis* (Wetherick, 1989) postulates that subjects are thought to generate a conclusion that is similar to the more conservative of the two premises.

Crucial to our current discussion is that the mental model hypothesis predicts a heavy demand on working memory (particularly for those problems that require the construction of multiple models), whereas both the atmosphere and matching hypotheses predict a low demand on working memory for the selection and implementation of heuristics aimed at producing an acceptable level of performance. Therefore, while the mental model hypothesis predicts a significant impact of concurrent tasks on reasoning performance, the other two hypotheses predict little such impact. Moreover, if there are any participants who do happen to perform above the level expected for the atmosphere or matching hypothesis, then it is likely that they are generating mental models and would be more prone to disruption from secondary tasks.

In a series of studies, we have investigated these predictions regarding the effects of concurrent tasks, most notably articulatory suppression and random generation (Gilhooly, Logie, Wetherick, & Wynn, 1993). Performance in single-task conditions fitted most closely with the predictions of the matching hypothesis, and this result also held when syllogistic reasoning was combined with articulatory suppression, which caused no disruption in reasoning performance. However, concurrent random generation did result in a significant drop in reasoning performance, although the absolute drop in performance was quite small, and the performance level remained well above chance. That is, working memory appeared to play only a minor role in performance of syllogistic reasoning tasks for many subjects.

This finding, however, was most likely due to the fact that most subjects did not reason logically and therefore did not place heavy demands on working memory. The small effect of random generation points to some role of executive processes in the implementation of the matching heuristic that appeared to be adopted by most subjects. In more recent, as yet unpublished studies (Gilhooly, Logie, & Wynn, 1998), we have explored the effects on dual-task performance of individuals who have been trained on syllogistic reasoning. Subjects were given extensive practice with different forms of the task, and their performance was later tested on a new set of problems. Most of the participants successfully improved their performance, and subsets of participants who performed particularly well or particularly poorly (but well above chance) completed both single- and dual-task conditions. Those subjects who performed poorly were largely unaffected by the secondary tasks. However, those subjects who had produced the highest scores following training were especially vulnerable to the disruptive effects of random generation. That is, the training seemed to have resulted in better performance at the expense of an additional load on the executive resources of working memory. These results are reminiscent of the recent observation (Rosen & Engle, 1997) that high-working-memory-span subjects tended to show a clearer decrement following a concurrent load than low-span subjects in a demanding memory retrieval task that required the involvement of the central executive or controlled attention.

Dynamic Cognition and Complex Perceptuomotor Control

The multiple component model of working memory has also been found to be useful in studying the cognitive effects of training in complex dynamic tasks. We used dual-task procedures to investigate the cognitive resources involved in a complex computer game known as Space Fortress (Logie, Baddeley, Mane, Donchin, & Sheptak, 1989). The game involved a high level of perceptuomotor control of a "space ship," which was maneuvered around a computer screen using a joystick. The game also involved accurate timing of responses, a verbal STM load, and the development of long-term and short-term strategies. Space Fortress required around 10 h of practice to reach a reasonable level of performance. The general aim of this research was to determine whether the Space Fortress task could be fruitfully split into a number of subcomponent skills and to examine the changes in demands on working memory following extensive training (25 h or more). We used a range of secondary tasks each thought to draw on specific components of working memory.

Early in training, we observed that game performance was equally impaired by concurrent verbal tasks and by concurrent visuospatial tasks, each of which involved heavy demands on temporary storage and a small degree of processing (Brooks, 1967). In contrast, concurrent repeated and alternate tapping of the feet had very little effect on performance. When the participants had reached a much higher level of expertise on the game, a rather different pattern of dual-task disruption emerged. Instead of across-the-board impairment, the concurrent visuospatial tasks disrupted only those game parameters that were linked to perceptuomotor control, while the verbal secondary tasks impaired parameters linked with verbal STM. Moreover, the tapping task, which previously had shown little effect when players were less experienced, appeared to cause considerable disruption of game performance. This disruption arose from poor motor control of the joystick and other motor responses required for game performance.

These results seem to suggest that the general cognitive load was very high in the early stages of the game, while motor control was poorly deployed. As a result, any secondary cognitive load was sufficient to disrupt performance. However, with the acquisition of expertise came the use of specialized rather than general purpose resources and greater demands on more finely tuned perceptuomotor control. Such a change in working memory demands is perfectly in line with Ackerman's (1988) theory of complex skill acquisition, which postulates that as one's skill level increases, the primary factor that constrains performance changes from general fluid intelligence through domain-specific perceptual speed to psychomotor abilities.

This work (Logie et al., 1989) represents one of the few attempts to use working memory in complex dynamic environments and, because initial work on this topic proved promising, it is an area that merits significantly more attention.

Summary

The studies we reviewed in this section clearly demonstrate that complex cognitive tasks rely on a range of cognitive resources and implicate multiple components of working memory. They also highlight the utility of the multiple-component model and the associated dual-task methodology as a basis for cognitive task analyses.

The Relationship of Working Memory to Long-Term Memory and Knowledge

As we have already made clear, we assume that one important feature of the central executive is to activate and integrate representations in LTM. In this respect, our views have a good deal in common with Ericsson's proposal of long-term working memory (Ericsson & Delaney, Chapter 8, this volume; Ericsson & Kintsch, 1995) and Cowan's proposal of virtual STM (Cowan, Chapter 3, this volume). Does this then mean that working memory is simply the currently activated portion of LTM? Although we believe that such a formulation is defensible and has the attraction of apparent conceptual simplicity, we regard it as an unhelpful oversimplification and believe that working memory and LTM comprise two functionally separable cognitive systems. Below, we characterize the relationship between the two memory systems and provide illustrative evidence for the separability of each of the slave systems from LTM.

The Phonological Loop

There is considerable evidence that long-term knowledge has an influence on the performance of verbal STM tasks. For example, memory span for familiar words is longer than for nonsense syllables, and memory span for words in sentences is longer (15–16) than for unrelated words (5–6) (Baddeley, Vallar, & Wilson, 1987). In addition, nonwords that approximate English result in better immediate recall than those that do not (e.g., Gathercole & Baddeley, 1989), and familiarizing subjects with nonwords increases serial recall capacity (Hulme, Maughan, & Brown, 1991). Furthermore, as discussed in the chapter by Ericsson and Delaney (Chapter 8, this volume), the superior memory performance that often underpins expert performance is typically based on the temporary utilization of gradually acquired schemata.

One apparently simple interpretation of this wide range of data is to propose something like a pandemonium model (Selfridge, 1959) in which acoustic information is encoded and processed through a series of levels, beginning with isolated speech sounds, moving up to phonemes, then syllables, which in turn may map onto sublexical and lexical units. Where appropriate, these may activate higher level syntactic and semantic structures, which in turn may be categorized in terms of semantic schemata. The level at which the encoding stops will be determined by the capacity of the system to provide useful and meaningful chunks (Miller, 1956). In the case of complex nonwords, these chunks are likely to be sublexical units, with letter sequences approximating to the native language of the subject offering a greater capacity for chunking than would be possible with less familiar phonetic sequences (Gathercole, 1995). In the case of words, the already existing lexical representations will help performance, but where the same set of unrelated words is used repeatedly, as in the typical memory span procedure, the capacity to form meaningful chunks will be minimal; moreover, lexical priming is likely to offer little help in storing serial order, forcing the subject to depend upon phonological cues and minimizing any effects of semantic similarity within the set (Baddeley, 1966b). However, when the material allows semantic and syntactic links to be readily formed between the items, either by selecting combinations of nouns and adjectives that are readily compatible (Baddeley & Ecob, 1970) or by using material that approximates to the sentential structure of English (Miller & Selfridge, 1950), subjects will extend the amount of material held by incorporating more items in each individual chunk (Miller, 1956). Thus, the available evidence suggests that STM performance reflects the activation of those long-term representations involved in perceiving and comprehending spoken language.

There is also considerable evidence that the phonological loop has an influence on long-term phonological learning. For example, patients with STM deficits have major impairments in the capacity for new phonological learning (Baddeley, Papagno, & Vallar, 1988), and normal subjects show impairment in new phonological learning if performing concurrent tasks that interfere with the phonological loop (Papagno, Valentine, & Baddeley, 1991). Such learning, involving the modification and development of existing phonological representations, appears to be crucial in natural language acquisition, suggesting an important role for the phonological loop (see Baddeley, Gathercole, & Papagno, 1998).

Therefore, any adequate model of human memory must be capable of explaining not only how long-term phonological representations serve to enhance immediate memory performance, but also how new phonological structures may be created on the basis of the long-term phonological knowledge. In our view, a model in which working memory is merely the activation of LTM representations cannot adequately support the learning of new phonological structures, hence failing on the first criterion.

Consider the phonological processing stages of the pandemonium model outlined above. Let us assume, first of all, that this model adapts to a long-term "diet" of heard speech by developing representations that are characteristic of the language experienced, resulting in the capacity to detect readily the characteristic phonemes of that language. Furthermore, at a somewhat higher level within the same system, frequent clusters of phonemes also set up networks that optimize the detection of syllables and, at an even higher level within the hierarchy, words. Such a system would have the advantage of being well attuned to detecting the common linguistic entities of the language, but would have the disadvantage of being likely to fail to respond accurately to unfamiliar sound sequences because it would try to interpret the new sound in terms of its existing structure. Thus, new items might be "misheard" as familiar items, something that would make it difficult to add new words, or indeed the names of new people, to the existing system. One way around this problem would be to have a *second* system that is much less influenced by past experience, but is capable of interacting with and gradually modifying the more durable long-term phonological system. This idea has a good deal in common with the proposal made by Hinton and Plaut (1987) about the utility of neural network systems with both slow and fast weights. The slow weights provide a durable long-term basis, while the fast weights provide a rapid and flexible learning system that is linked to the slow system but not dominated by it. The slow and fast weight systems might in principle either operate within the same structure or represent separate but strongly communicating structures (for a similar proposal, see Schneider, Chapter 10, this volume). Regardless of their precise realization, however, we propose that the slow and fast components may be considered functionally separate systems corresponding to long-term learning and temporary maintenance.

A second argument in favor of separate systems is that if the phonological loop is simply the activation of part of the speech system, then patients with a major STM deficit should have major speech-perception problems. Though it is often the case that patients with STM deficits will have some language problems, the classic cases on which the literature rests typically have either minimal and subtle language deficits (Shallice & Warrington, 1970), or, as in the case of PV (Vallar & Baddeley, 1984), no apparent deficit. It is also the case that patients with major language-processing deficits may nevertheless have a far better memory performance than the classic STM case (Baddeley & Wilson, 1993).

Hence, although we believe that the phonological loop uses much of the same system as is involved in speech perception and production, we would maintain that it represents a supplementary system that is specialized for the temporary maintenance of sound-based information (Baddeley et al., 1998). We accept that this system is influenced by existing phonological knowledge, but suggest that it must be sufficiently independent of that knowledge so that it can represent novel experiences with minimal distortion.

The Visual Cache and the Inner Scribe

Turning to the visuospatial sketchpad, we can formulate an analogous argument. As the phonological loop has been linked with, but seen as distinct from, the speech system, so the visual and spatial components of working memory have been linked with the visual imagery system and with the representation and planning of movement. As discussed earlier in this chapter, some of the relevant evidence comes from studies where subjects are required to retain a sequence of movements to targets (Logie & Marchetti, 1991), body movements generated by the experimenter (Smyth & Pendleton, 1989), or an imaged matrix (Baddeley & Lieberman, 1980; Logie et al., 1990). Recall performance on such tasks is impaired by asking subjects concurrently to tap a series of keys laid out on a table or to move their arm to follow a moving target. A number of studies also provide evidence that visual imagery and the processing and retention of visually presented information share cognitive resources (Logie, 1986: Logie et al., 1990; Quinn & McConnell, 1996).

Although the precise relationship between visuospatial working memory and visual imagery is still a matter of debate (Cornoldi, Logie, Brandimonte, Kaufmann, & Reisberg, 1996; Logie, 1995; Reisberg & Logie, 1993), the visual and spatial components of working memory do not seem to be synonymous with the imagery system. First, there is a case report of a patient who shows a clear dissociation between visuospatial working memory and mental imagery (Morton & Morris, 1995). More specifically, this patient (MG) performed poorly on typical mental imagery tasks involving mental transformation (e.g., mental rotation, mental scanning), whereas her performance on the temporary maintenance of visual and spatial information in working memory was essentially intact. This dissociation suggests that the visuospatial working memory system and the imagery system are not identical. Second, concurrent spatial tapping or arm movement, which is considered to disrupt the functioning of the visuospatial sketchpad, may or may not disrupt the performance of mental imagery tasks, depending on the nature of the imagery task (Pearson, Logie, & Green, 1996; Salway & Logie, 1995). Specifically, the necessity of temporary visuospatial storage of the image seems to be an important factor, again suggesting that imagery and temporary visuospatial storage are not synonymous.

Regardless of the nature of the relationship, it is generally agreed that both imagery and visuospatial temporary memory tasks involve activated long-term stored knowledge, coupled with information extracted from the sensory properties of the stimulus array. However, there is a body of evidence that points to visual and spatial working memory being identifiable, functionally separate cognitive functions, rather than reflecting the sum total of currently activated components of long-term knowledge. One of us (Logie, 1995) has argued that the visual and spatial knowledge that is activated has privileged access to, respectively, the visual (the visual cache) and spatial (the inner scribe) components of working memory, but that these systems are functionally separate. A schematic diagram of this view of visuospatial working memory is shown in Figure 2.2.

Other researchers have argued that images are interpreted within a particular frame of reference (Chambers & Reisberg, 1985, 1992), although there remains a debate as to the ease with which images can be reinterpreted without external stimulus support such as a picture (Brandimonte & Gerbino, 1993; Cornoldi et al., 1996). The idea is that the physical picture is divorced from the interpretation placed on the mental representation of the depicted material. Therefore, looking at an ambiguous picture on different occasions

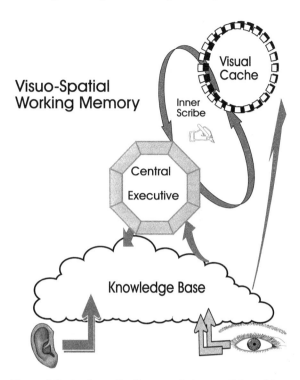

Figure 2.2. A schematic diagram of visuospatial working memory (derived from Logie, 1995).

allows for different interpretations to be formed on each occasion, and the reinterpretation of the mental image is facilitated by physical stimulus support (Chambers & Reisberg, 1985, 1992; Pearson et al., 1996). Reexamining the mental image without such stimulus support present simply reinforces the previous interpretation derived from the frame of reference for the image. Therefore, to be able to reinterpret the stored mental image, some sort of covert stimulus support is necessary, and we believe that the visual cache and the inner scribe may provide such support, enabling rehearsal and allowing novel interpretations to be applied to the current image (Cornoldi et al., 1996; Reisberg & Logie, 1993). In the context of the present chapter, the conclusion is that activated stored knowledge is transferred to the visuospatial components and the central executive of working memory. This information is then incorporated within the generated and manipulated representations supported by working memory components.

Data from patients with hemispatial neglect present complementary evidence for the functional separation of temporary maintenance of visuospatial information and stored imaginal knowledge. These patients appear to ignore half of their visual field, of objects and of their body space, most commonly on the left (for a review, see Bisiach, 1993). Interestingly, a number of neglect patients have recently been reported as having an additional difficulty with reporting from memory details of the imaged left half of familiar scenes such as buildings in a town square or the interior of their home (e.g., Bisiach & Luzzatti, 1978). It is even the case that a small number of patients appear to have difficulty with reporting details from memory, but not from perception (Guariglia, Padovani, Pantano, & Pizzamiglio, 1993; Beschin, Cocchini, Della Sala, & Logie, 1997). These patients can readily describe a scene with their eyes open, but omit details on the left when asked to describe that same scene after they close their eyes or to describe a familiar town square from a particular vantage point. However, these patients do not appear to have lost their memory of the square, because when asked to describe it from the opposite vantage point, they report details that are now on the imagined right and that were omitted. Such evidence points to a clear separation between the stored knowledge base, which appears to be intact, and the mental representation and manipulation of visual and spatial information in working memory.

Summary

In this section, we argued that LTM and working memory are closely related and that both systems may play a role in complex verbal and visuospatial tasks. However, we also argued that working memory cannot merely be an activated portion of LTM, because the two systems must serve different functions under certain situations (e.g., learning novel phonological information or reinterpreting visual images). Data from brain-damaged patients (with STM deficits and hemispatial neglect) provide further evidence that LTM and working memory must be functionally separate systems.

The Relationship of Working Memory to Attention and Consciousness

Although we would certainly not wish to identify working memory with attention, we do believe that the two concepts are closely related. The central executive is typically regarded as an attentional system (e.g., Cowan, Chapter 3; Engle et al., Chapter 4, this volume), and one might well use the general term *attention* to refer to the control processes that operate throughout the working memory system. Indeed, as one of us has previously suggested (Baddeley, 1993a), the use of the term *working memory*, rather than *working attention*, reflects the fact that we initially approached the system through its mnemonic capacities rather than its control mechanisms. Had we approached the same system from an attentional viewpoint, it would have been equally appropriate to label it "working attention."

It is important to point out, however, that the concept of attention itself is not unitary. Posner (1995), for example, distinguishes three separate attentional systems concerned respectively with orienting, alertness, and high-level attention, each represented by a separate anatomical substrate. It is clear that the control processes involved in the central executive are also complex and are likely to have substantial overlap with aspects of the more established approaches to the study of attention. Our own work has been strongly influenced by the attentional literature, particularly by the work of Norman and Shallice (1986), which contributed to our initial formulation of the central executive. Our more recent approaches, however, are beginning to reflect some of the work stemming from Posner's framework (e.g., Duncan, 1995; Robertson, Ward, Ridgeway, & Nimmo-Smith, 1994). As Engle et al. (Chapter 4, this volume) argue, we also expect the study of attention and of control processes in working memory to continue to interact productively.

As for the relationship between working memory and consciousness, one of us (Baddeley, 1993b) has argued that conscious awareness is a means of maintaining and coordinating information from a number of sources, including the present, specific episodes from the past, and projections as to the future and that working memory mediates this dynamic coordination. More specifically, working memory allows the organism to reflect on the available options and choose a particular action or strategy, rather than being driven by the sheer weight of past experience (for more detailed discussions, see Baddeley, 1993b, 1997). Although this view is highly speculative, it provides a way to empirically examine how working memory is related to conscious awareness. In a recent dual-task study, for example, Teasdale et al. (1995) demonstrated that the production of stimulus-independent thoughts – streams of thoughts and images unrelated to immediate sensory input – depends on the central executive. Another study also suggests that working memory might be related to the phenomenological experience of the vividness of visual imagery (Andrade, Kavanagh, & Baddeley, 1997; Baddeley & Andrade, 1998). Although more detailed exploration is certainly necessary, our model provides a useful framework to study consciousness and its relation to working memory.

The Biological Implementation of Working Memory

As will be clear from our discussion thus far, the development of our model of working memory has relied in part on detailed studies of brain-damaged patients. These studies have offered significant insight into the possible aspects of brain organization that might be linked to the operation of the various components of working memory. We have referred throughout the chapter to the studies of brain-damaged patients. There have in addition been a number of recent studies that have explored the use of neuroimaging techniques in normal subjects as they undertake working memory tasks.

The Phonological Loop

In the case of the phonological loop, Della Sala and Logie (1993) summarize the lesion sites for a number of patients with verbal short-term memory

deficits who have been described by various researchers in the published literature. In 17 out of the 18 patients listed, the lesion was in the left hemisphere,
with the 18th patient having more diffuse brain damage. For those patients,
the lesions were primarily in the lower part of the parietal lobe close to the
junction with the upper part of the posterior temporal lobe. This same general
area has been confirmed as the locus of the lesion in group studies of patients
with poor digit span (e.g., Warrington, James, & Maciejewski, 1986). More
sophisticated localization techniques have identified the supra-marginal
gyrus as the area most commonly damaged in cases of verbal STM impairment (e.g., Warrington, Logue, & Pratt, 1971).

It is of course possible that evidence linking impairment with areas in a
damaged brain does not necessarily reflect the areas that support the same
cognitive functions in the healthy brain. This particular issue is addressed
neatly by more recent studies that have adopted measures of activity in the
brains of healthy subjects. A number of studies have used positron emission
tomography (PET) during the performance of various working memory tasks
(Paulesu, Frith, & Frackowiak, 1993; Salmon et al., 1996). The data are broadly
consistent in showing activity in the lower left supra-marginal gyrus during
short-term verbal memory tasks, giving evidence that converges with the
finding from brain-damaged patients.

The Visuospatial Sketchpad

The neuropsychological data corpus for visuospatial sketchpad is not as
well endowed as its verbal counterpart. At a gross level, it appears that right
hemisphere lesions are more commonly associated with visuospatial memory
deficits (e.g., De Renzi & Nichelli, 1975). As to more specific anatomical local-
izations, there seems to be no clear consensus (see Della Sala & Logie, 1993,
for more details). Note that there appears to be a clear distinction between the
lesion sites associated with visuospatial working memory deficits and those
linked with visual imagery deficits. In the latter case, some of the brain-damaged data seem to point to areas in the left hemisphere (Farah, 1984), while
evidence from studies of representational neglect (e.g., Bisiach & Luzzatti,
1978; Beschin et al., 1997) and studies of lesions in monkeys (see Stein, 1992,
for a review) link impairments in visuospatial representation with damage to
the right posterior, parietal cortex.

PET studies of the normal brain have also implicated activity in the right
hemisphere with visuospatial working memory tasks, although which areas
are active within that hemisphere seems to depend on the nature of the task.
Jonides et al. (1993) and Mellet, Tzourino, Denis, and Mazoyer (1995)
reported activity in the occipital and parietal areas along with some activity in
the prefrontal cortex and premotor areas during visuospatial imagery tasks.
Kosslyn et al. (1993) have reported additional activity in the primary visual
areas of the occipital lobe. However, Mellet et al. (1995) noted that the primary visual areas were involved only when their imagery task also involved

some visual perceptual input. Courtney, Ungerleider, Keil, and Haxby (1996) have further reported that tasks involving visual working memory appear to generate activity in a range of areas excluding the right parietal lobe, whereas a spatial working memory task was associated with activity in the superior and inferior parietal cortex. They conclude that visual and spatial working memory are handled by different areas of the cortex, a finding consistent with our suggestion that these two functions of working memory are relatively independent (Logie, 1995).

The Central Executive

As one of us (Baddeley, 1986) argued earlier, executive or supervisory processes associated with the central executive seem to be closely linked to the prefrontal cortex, although it may not be the only brain area that supports the executive control of behavior. One particularly illuminating recent finding on the role of the prefrontal cortex in executive function is that performing a language task (i.e., semantic judgment) and a visuospatial task (i.e., mental rotation) simultaneously may require the contribution of the additional area of the brain – the prefrontal cortex – that is not necessarily implicated in the performance of individual component tasks (D'Esposito et al., 1995). The study has also shown that this intriguing finding is not merely a simple artefact of task difficulty or effort. Although more research is necessary, this result provides an initial promising step toward examining the neural basis of specific executive processes. A more detailed review of the role of prefrontal cortex in executive or supervisory processes are presented in Della Sala and Logie (in press) and also in the Engle et al. (Chapter 4, this volume) chapter.

Summary

Clearly the biological correlates of the various subcomponents in working memory remain to be fully explored. The data from neuroimaging studies and from brain-damaged patients, however, converge with the behavioral data in healthy subjects in supporting a multiple-component model (see Smith & Jonides, 1997, for a more detailed review of neuroimaging evidence supporting the multiple-component model of working memory).

REFERENCES

Ackerman, P. L. (1988). Determinants of individual differences during skill acquisition: Cognitive abilities and information processing. *Journal of Experimental Psychology: General, 117,* 288–318.

Andrade, J., Kavanagh, D., & Baddeley, A. D. (1997). Eye-movements and visual imagery: A working memory approach to the treatment of post-traumatic stress disorder. *British Journal of Clinical Psychology, 36,* 209–223.

Ashcraft, M. H. (1995). Cognitive psychology and simple arithmetic: A review and summary of new directions. *Mathematical Cognition, 1,* 3–34.

Baddeley, A. D. (1966a). The capacity for generating information by randomization. *Quarterly Journal of Experimental Psychology, 18,* 119–130.

Baddeley, A. D. (1966b). Short-term memory for word sequences as a function of acoustic, semantic, and formal similarity. *Quarterly Journal of Experimental Psychology, 18,* 362–365.

Baddeley, A. D. (1986). *Working memory.* New York: Oxford University Press.

Baddeley, A. D. (1993a). Working memory or working attention? In A. D. Baddeley & L. Weiskrantz (Eds.), *Attention: Selection, awareness, and control: A tribute to Donald Broadbent.* Oxford, UK: Oxford University Press.

Baddeley, A. D. (1993b). Working memory and conscious awareness. In A. Collins, S. E. Gathercole, M. A. Conway, & P. E. Morris (Eds.), *Theories of memory* (pp. 11–28). Hove, UK: Erlbaum.

Baddeley, A. D. (1996). Exploring the central executive. *Quarterly Journal of Experimental Psychology, 49A,* 5–28.

Baddeley, A. D. (1997). *Human memory: Theory and practice* (Rev. ed.). Hove, UK: Psychology Press.

Baddeley, A. D., & Andrade, J. (1998). Working memory and consciousness: An empirical approach. In M. A. Conway, S. E. Gathercole, & C. Cornoldi (Eds.), *Theories of memory II* (pp. 1–23). Hove, UK: Psychology Press.

Baddeley, A. D., Bressi, S., Della Sala, S., Logie, R. H., & Spinnler, H. (1991). The decline of working memory in Alzheimer's disease: A longitudinal study. *Brain, 114,* 2521–2542.

Baddeley, A. D., & Della Sala, S. (1996). Working memory and executive control. *Philosophical Transactions of the Royal Society of London B, 351,* 1397–1404.

Baddeley, A. D., Della Sala, S., Papagno, C., & Spinnler, H. (1997). Dual task performance in dysexecutive and nondysexecutive patients with a frontal lesion. *Neuropsychology, 11,* 187–194.

Baddeley, A. D., & Ecob, J. R. (1970). Simultaneous acoustic and semantic coding in short-term memory. *Nature, 227,* 228–229.

Baddeley, A. D., Eldridge, M., & Lewis, V. (1981). The role of subvocalisation in reading. *Quarterly Journal of Experimental Psychology, 33A,* 439–454.

Baddeley, A. D., Gathercole, S. E., & Papagno, C. (1998). The phonological loop as a language learning device. *Psychological Review, 105,* 158–173.

Baddeley, A. D., & Hitch, G. J. (1974). Working memory. In G. H. Bower (Ed.), *The psychology of learning and motivation: Advances in research and theory* (Vol. 8, pp. 47–89). New York: Academic Press.

Baddeley, A. D., & Hitch, G. J. (1977). Recency re-examined. In S. Donic (Ed.), *Attention and performance* (Vol. 6, pp. 647–667). Hillsdale, NJ: Erlbaum.

Baddeley, A. D., & Hitch, G. J. (1993). The recency effect: Implicit learning with explicit retrieval. *Memory & Cognition, 21,* 146–155.

Baddeley, A., & Hull, A. (1979). Prefix and suffix effects: Do they have a common basis? *Journal of Verbal Learning and Verbal Behaviour, 18,* 129–140.

Baddeley, A. D., & Lieberman, K. (1980). Spatial working memory. In R. S. Nickerson (Ed.), *Attention and performance VIII* (pp. 521–539). Hillsdale, NJ: Erlbaum.

Baddeley, A., Logie, R., Bressi, S., Della Sala, S., & Spinnler, H. (1986). Senile dementia and working memory. *Quarterly Journal of Experimental Psychology, 38A,* 603–618.

Baddeley, A. D., Papagno, C., & Vallar, G. (1988). When long-term learning depends on short-term storage. *Journal of Memory and Language, 27,* 586–595.

Baddeley, A. D., Thomson, N., & Buchanan, M. (1975). Word length and the structure of short-term memory. *Journal of Verbal Learning and Verbal Behavior, 14,* 575–589.

Baddeley, A. D., Vallar, G., & Wilson, B. (1987). Sentence comprehension and phonological memory: Some neuropsychological evidence. In M. Coltheart (Ed.), *Attention and performance XII: The psychology of reading* (pp. 509–529). London: Erlbaum.

Baddeley, A. D., & Wilson, B. (1985). Phonological coding and short-term memory in patients without speech. *Journal of Verbal Learning and Verbal Behavior, 24,* 490–502.

Baddeley, A. D., & Wilson, B. (1993). A case of word deafness with preserved span: Implications for the structure and function of working memory. *Cortex, 29,* 741–748.

Beschin, N., Cocchini, G., Della Sala, S., & Logie, R. H. (1997). What the eyes perceive, the brain ignores: A case of pure unilateral representational neglect. *Cortex, 33,* 3–26.

Bisiach, E. (1993). Mental representation in unilateral neglect and related disorders: The twentieth Bartlett memorial lecture. *Quarterly Journal of Experimental Psychology, 46A,* 435–461.

Bisiach, E., & Luzzatti, C. (1978). Unilateral neglect of representational space. *Cortex, 14,* 129–133.

Brandimonte, M., & Gerbino, W. (1993). Mental image reversal and verbal recoding: When ducks become rabbits. *Memory & Cognition, 21,* 23–33.

Broadbent, D. E., & Broadbent, M. H. P. (1981). Recency effects in visual memory. *Quarterly Journal of Experimental Psychology, 33A,* 1–15.

Brooks, L. R. (1967). The suppression of visualisation by reading. *Quarterly Journal of Experimental Psychology, 19,* 289–299.

Caplan, D., Rochon, E., & Waters, G. S. (1992). Articulatory and phonological determinants of word length effects in span tasks. *Quarterly Journal of Experimental Psychology, 45A,* 177–192.

Chambers, D., & Reisberg, D. (1985). Can mental images be ambiguous? *Journal of Experimental Psychology: Human Perception and Performance, 11,* 317–328.

Chambers, D., & Reisberg, D. (1992). What an image depicts depends on what an image means. *Cognitive Psychology, 24,* 145–174.

Clark, H. H., & Clark, E. V. (1977). *Psychology and language.* New York: Harcourt Brace Jovanovich.

Conrad, R. (1964). Acoustic confusions in immediate memory. *British Journal of Psychology, 55,* 75–84.

Cornoldi, C., Cortesi, A., & Preti, D. (1991). Individual differences in the capacity limitations of visuospatial short-term memory: Research on sighted and totally congenitally blind people. *Memory & Cognition, 19,* 459–468.

Cornoldi, C., Logie, R. H., Brandimonte, M. A., Kaufmann, G., & Reisberg, D. (Eds.). (1996). *Stretching the imagination: Representation and transformation in mental imagery.* New York: Oxford University Press.

Courtney, S. M., Ungerleider, L. G., Keil, K., & Haxby, J. V. (1996). Object and spatial visual working memory activate separate neural systems in human cortex. *Cerebral Cortex, 6,* 39–49.

Cowan, N., Day, L., Saults, J. S., Keller, T. A., Johnson, T., & Flores, L. (1992). The role of verbal output time in the effects of word length on immediate memory. *Journal of Memory and Language, 31,* 1–17.

Cowan, N., Wood, N. L., Nugent, L. D., & Treisman, M. (1997). There are two word-length effects in verbal short-term memory: Opposed effects of duration and complexity. *Psychological Science, 8,* 290–295.

Daneman, M., & Carpenter, P. A. (1980). Individual differences in working memory and reading. *Journal of Verbal Learning and Verbal Behavior, 19,* 450–466.

Della Sala, S., & Logie, R. H. (1993). When working memory does not work: The role of working memory in neuropsychology. In F. Boller, & H. Spinnler (Eds.), *Handbook of neuropsychology* (Vol. 8, pp. 1–63). Amsterdam: Elsevier.

Della Sala, S. & Logie, R. H. (1998). Dualism down the drain: Thinking in the brain. In K. J. Gilhooly & R. H. Logie (Eds.), *Thinking in working memory* (pp. 44–66). Hove, UK: Psychology Press.

Della Sala, S., Logie, R. H., Marchetti, C., & Wynn, V. (1991). Case studies in working memory: A case for single cases? *Cortex, 27,* 169–191.

De Renzi, E., & Nichelli, P. (1975). Verbal and nonverbal short term memory impairment following hemispheric damage. *Cortex, 11,* 341–353.

D'Esposito, M., Detre, J. A., Alsop, D. C., Shin, R. K., Atlas, S., & Grossman, M. (1995). The neural basis of the central executive system of working memory. *Nature, 378,* 279–281.

Duncan, J. (1995). Attention, intelligence and the frontal lobes. In M. Gazzaniga (Ed.), *The cognitive neurosciences* (pp. 721–733). Cambridge, MA: MIT Press.

Eddy, J. K., & Glass, A. L. (1981). Reading and listening to high and low imagery sentences. *Journal of Verbal Learning and Verbal Behavior, 20,* 333–345.

Ericsson, K., & Kintsch, W. (1995). Long-term working memory. *Psychological Review, 102,* 211–245.

Farah, M. J. (1984). The neurological basis of mental imagery: A componential analysis. *Cognition, 18,* 245–272.

Gathercole, S. E. (1995). Is nonword repetition a test of phonological memory or long-term knowledge? It all depends on the nonwords. *Memory & Cognition, 23,* 83–94.

Gathercole, S., & Baddeley, A. D. (1989). Evaluation of the role of phonological STM in the development of vocabulary in children: A longitudinal study. *Journal of Memory and Language, 28,* 200–213.

Gathercole, S., & Baddeley, A. D. (1993). *Working memory and language.* Hove, UK: Erlbaum.

Gathercole, S. E., & Hitch, G. (1993). Developmental changes in short-term memory: A revised working memory perspective. In A. Collins, S. E. Gathercole, M. A. Conway, & P. E. Morris (Eds.), *Theories of memory* (pp. 189–209). Hove, UK: Erlbaum.

Gilhooly, K. J., Logie, R. H., Wetherick, N. E., & Wynn, V. (1993). Working memory and strategies in syllogistic reasoning tasks. *Memory & Cognition, 21,* 115–124.

Gilhooly, K. J., Logie, R. H., & Wynn, V. (1998). *Syllogistic reasoning tasks, working memory, and skill.* Manuscript submitted for publication.

Guariglia, C., Padovani, A., Pantano, P., & Pizzamiglio, L. (1993). Unilateral neglect restricted to visual imagery. *Nature, 364,* 235–237.

Haenggi, D., Kintsch, W., & Gernsbacher, M. A. (1995). Spatial situation models and text comprehension. *Discourse Processes, 19,* 173–199.

Henry, L. A. (1991). The effects of word length and phonemic similarity in young children's short-term memory. *Quarterly Journal of Experimental Psychology, 43A,* 35–52.

Hinton, G. E., & Plaut, D. C. (1987). Using fast weights to deblur old memories. *Proceedings of the Ninth Annual Conference of the Cognitive Science Society* (pp. 177–186). Hillsadale, NJ: Erlbaum.

Hitch, G. J. (1978). The role of short-term working memory in mental arithmetic. *Cognitive Psychology, 10,* 302–323.

Hitch, G. J. (1990). Developmental fractionation of working memory. In G. Vallar, & T. Shallice (Eds.), *Neuropsychological impairments of short-term memory* (pp. 221–246). Cambridge, UK: Cambridge University Press

Hitch, G. J., Halliday, M. S., Schaafstal, A. M., & Schraagen, J. M. C. (1988). Visual working memory in young children. *Memory & Cognition, 16,* 120–132.

Hitch, G. J., Woodin, M. E., & Baker, S. (1989). Visual and phonological components of working memory in children. *Memory & Cognition, 17,* 175–185.

Hue, C., & Ericsson, J. R. (1988). Short-term memory for Chinese characters and radicals. *Memory & Cognition, 16,* 196–205.

Hulme, C., Maughan, S., & Brown, G. D. A. (1991). Memory for familiar and unfamiliar words: Evidence for a long-term memory contribution to short-term memory span. *Journal of Memory and Language, 30,* 685–701.

Hulme, C., Thomson, N., Muir, C., & Lawrence, A. (1984). Speech rate and the development of short-term memory span. *Journal of Experimental Child Psychology, 38,* 241–253.

Johnson-Laird, P. N. (1983). *Mental models.* Cambridge, MA: Harvard University Press.

Johnson-Laird, P. N., & Byrne, R. (1991). *Deduction.* Hove, UK: Erlbaum.

Jonides, J., Smith, E. E., Koeppe, R. A., Awh, E., Minoshima, S., & Mintun, M. A. (1993). Spatial working memory in humans as revealed by PET. *Nature, 363,* 623–625.

Kerr, N. (1983). The role of vision in visual imagery experiments: Evidence from the congenitally blind. *Journal of Experimental Psychology: General, 112,* 265–277.

Kosslyn, S. M., Alpert, N. M., Thomson, W. L., Maljkovic, V., Weise, S. B., Chabris, C. F., Hamilton, S. E., Rauch, S. L., & Buonanno, S. F. (1993). Visual mental imagery activates topographically organized visual cortex: PET investigations. *Journal of Cognitive Neuroscience, 5,* 263–267.

Logie, R. H. (1986). Visuo-spatial processing in working memory. *Quarterly Journal of Experimental Psychology, 38A,* 229–247.

Logie, R. H. (1995). *Visuo-spatial working memory.* Hove, UK: Erlbaum.

Logie, R. H., & Baddeley, A. D. (1987). Cognitive processes in counting. *Journal of Experimental Psychology, 13,* 310–326.

Logie, R. H., Baddeley, A. D., Mane, A., Donchin, E., & Sheptak, R. (1989). Working memory and the analysis of a complex skill by secondary task methodology. *Acta Psychologica, 71,* 53–87.

Logie, R. H., Della Sala, S., Laiacona, M., Chalmers, P., & Wynn, V. (1996). Group aggregates and individual reliability: The case of verbal short-term memory. *Memory & Cognition, 24,* 305–321.

Logie, R. H., & Duff, S. C. (1996). *Processing and storage in working memory: Multiple components?* Poster presented at the annual meeting of the Psychonomics Society, Chicago, IL.

Logie, R. H., Gilhooly, K. J., & Wynn, V. (1994). Counting on working memory in mental arithmetic. *Memory & Cognition, 22,* 395–410.

Logie, R. H., & Marchetti, C. (1991). Visuo-spatial working memory: Visual, spatial or central executive? In R. H. Logie & M. Denis (Eds.), *Mental images in human cognition* (pp. 105–115). Amsterdam: Elsevier.

Logie, R. H., & Pearson, D. G. (1997). The inner eye and the inner scribe of visuo-spatial working memory: Evidence from developmental fractionation. *European Journal of Cognitive Psychology, 9*, 241–257.

Logie, R. H., Zucco, G., & Baddeley, A. D. (1990). Interference with visual short-term memory. *Acta Psychologica, 75*, 55–74.

Mellet, E., Tzourio, N., Denis, M., & Mazoyer, B. (1995). A positron emission tomography study of visual and mental spatial exploration. *Journal of Cognitive Neuroscience, 7*, 433–445.

Miller, G. A. (1956). The magical number seven, plus or minus two: Some limits on our capacity for processing information. *Psychological Review, 63*, 81–97.

Miller, G. A., & Selfridge, J. A. (1950). Verbal context and the recall of meaningful material. *American Journal of Psychology, 63*, 176–185.

Morton, N., & Morris, R. G. (1995). Image transformation dissociated from visuospatial working memory. *Cognitive Neuropsychology, 12*, 767–791.

Nairne, J. S., & Healy, A. F. (1983). Counting backwards produces systematic errors. *Journal of Experimental Psychology: General, 112*, 37–40.

Nicolson, R. (1981). The relationship between memory span and processing speed. In M. P. Friedman, J. P. Das, & N. O'Connor (Eds.), *Intelligence and learning*. New York: Plenum.

Norman, D., & Shallice, T. (1986). Attention to action: Willed and automatic control of behavior. In R. J. Davidson, G. E. Schwartz, & D. E. Shapiro (Eds.), *Consciousness and self-regulation: Advances in research and theory* (Vol. 4, pp. 1–18). New York: Plenum.

Papagno, C., Valentine, T., & Baddeley, A. D. (1991). Phonological short-term memory and foreign-language vocabulary learning. *Journal of Memory & Language, 30*, 331–347.

Paulesu, E., Frith, C. D., & Frackowiak, R. S. J. (1993). The neural correlates of the verbal component of working memory. *Nature, 362*, 342–345.

Pearson, D. G., Logie, R. H., & Green, C. (1996). Mental manipulation, visual working memory, and executive processes. *Psychologische Beträge, 38*, 324–342.

Phillips, W. A., & Christie, D. F. M. (1977). Interference with visualization. *Quarterly Journal of Experimental Psychology, 29*, 637–650.

Posner, M. (1995). Attention in cognitive neuroscience: An overview. In M. Gazzaniga (Ed.), *The cognitive neurosciences* (pp. 615–624). Cambridge, MA: MIT Press.

Quinn, J. G., & McConnell, J. (1996). Irrelevant pictures in visual working memory. *Quarterly Journal of Experimental Psychology, 49A*, 200–215.

Reisberg, D., & Logie, R. H. (1993). The ins and outs of visual working memory: Overcoming the limits on learning from imagery. In M. Intons-Peterson, B. Roskos-Ewoldsen, & R. Anderson (Eds.), *Imagery, creativity, and discovery: A cognitive approach* (pp. 39–76). Amsterdam: Elsevier.

Robertson, I. H., Ward, T., Ridgeway, V., & Nimmo-Smith, I. (1994). *The test of everyday attention*. Bury St. Edmunds, UK: Thames Valley Test Company.

Rosen, V. M., & Engle, R. W. (1997). The role of working memory capacity in retrieval. *Journal of Experimental Psychology: General, 126*, 211–227.

Salmon, E., Van der Linden, M., Collette, F., Delfiore, G., Maquet, P., Degueldre, C., Luxen, A., & Franck, G. (1996). Regional brain activity during working memory tasks. *Brain, 119,* 1617–1625.

Salway, A. F. S., & Logie, R. H. (1995). Visuo-spatial working memory, movement control and executive demands. *British Journal of Psychology, 86,* 253–269.

Selfridge, O. (1959). Pandemonium: A paradigm for learning. In *Symposium on the mechanization of thought processes.* London: H. M. Stationery Office.

Shallice, T., & Warrington, E. K. (1970). Independent functioning of verbal memory stores: A neuropsychological study. *Quarterly Journal of Experimental Psychology, 22,* 261–273.

Smith, E. E., & Jonides, J. (1997). Working memory: A view from neuroimaging. *Cognitive Psychology, 33,* 5–42.

Smyth, M. M., & Pendleton, L. R. (1989). Working memory for movements. *Quarterly Journal of Experimental Psychology, 41A,* 235–250.

Stein, J. F. (1992). The representation of egocentric space in the posterior parietal cortex. *Behavioral and Brain Sciences, 15,* 691–700.

Teasdale, J. D., Dritschel, B. H., Taylor, M. J., Proctor, L., Lloyd, C. A., Nimmo-Smith, I., & Baddeley, A. D. (1995). Stimulus-independent thought depends on central executive resources. *Memory & Cognition, 23,* 551–559.

Vallar, G., & Baddeley, A. D. (1984). Fractionation of working memory: Neuropsychological evidence for a phonological short-term store. *Journal of Verbal Learning and Verbal Behavior, 23,* 151–161.

Vallar, G., & Shallice, T. (Eds.). (1990). *Neuropsychological impairments of short-term memory.* Cambridge, UK: Cambridge University Press.

Vecchi, T., Monticellai, M. L., & Cornoldi, C. (1995). Visuo-spatial working memory: Structures and variables affecting a capacity measure. *Neuropsychologia, 33,* 1549–1564.

Walker, P., Hitch, G. J., & Duroe, A. (1993). The effect of visual similarity on short-term memory for spatial location: Implications for the capacity of visual short-term memory. *Acta Psychologica, 83,* 203–224.

Warrington, E. K., James, M., & Maciejewski, C. (1986). The WAIS as a lateralising and localising diagnostic instrument: A study of 656 patients with unilateral cerebral lesions. *Neuropsychologia, 24,* 223–239.

Warrington, E. K., Logue, V., & Pratt, R. T. C. (1971). The anatomical localization of selective impairment of auditory verbal short-term memory. *Neuropsychologia, 9,* 377–387.

Wetherick, N. E. (1989). Psychology and syllogistic reasoning. *Philosophical Psychology, 2,* 111–124.

Wilson, B., & Baddeley, A. D. (1988). Semantic, episodic, and autobiographical memory in a post-meningitic patient. *Brain and Cognition, 8,* 31–46.

Woodworth, R. J., & Sells, S. B. (1935). An atmosphere effect in formal syllogistic reasoning. *Journal of Experimental Psychology, 18,* 451–460.

3   An Embedded-Processes Model of Working Memory

NELSON COWAN

FIVE CENTRAL FEATURES OF THE APPROACH

The embedded-processes model of working memory relies upon the following five principles, which emphasize links between memory and attention.

(1) Working memory information comes from hierarchically arranged faculties comprising: (a) long-term memory, (b) the subset of long-term memory that is currently activated, and (c) the subset of activated memory that is in the focus of attention and awareness.

(2) Different processing limits apply to different faculties. The focus of attention is basically capacity limited, whereas activation is time limited. The various limits are especially important under nonoptimal conditions, such as interference between items with similar features.

(3) The focus of attention is controlled conjointly by voluntary processes (a central executive system) and involuntary processes (the attentional orienting system).

(4) Stimuli with physical features that have remained relatively unchanged over time and are of no key importance to the individual still activate some features in memory, but they do not elicit awareness (i.e., there is habituation of orienting).

(5) Awareness influences processing. In perception it increases the number of features encoded, and in memory it allows new episodic representations to be available for explicit recall.

Two prior integrative reviews of information processing, an article (Cowan, 1988) and a book (Cowan, 1995), describe a view that will serve as my basis for discussing working memory. According to this view, working memory refers to cognitive processes that retain information in an unusually accessible state, suitable for carrying out any task with a mental component. The task may be language comprehension or production, problem solving, decision making, or other thought. Most such tasks require that certain information be kept in mind. For example, in language comprehension, if the first word is totally for-

This work was supported by NIH grant R01 HD-21338.

gotten by the time the second or third word is perceived, one is in bad shape. The mnemonic functions preserving information that can be used to do the necessary work collectively make up working memory. This is a functional definition in that any processing mechanisms contributing to the desired outcome, which is the temporary availability of information, are said to participate in the working memory system. In contrast, some researchers appear to prefer to define working memory according to the mechanisms themselves (e.g., Engle, Kane, & Tuholski, Chapter 4, this volume; Schneider, Chapter 10, this volume). Though my framework has much in common with those of these researchers, a functional definition of working memory seems more likely to encourage a consideration of diverse relevant mechanisms.

The boundaries of this definition are fuzzy. If the process holding information to be used in a mental task also holds information irrelevant to the task (mistakenly or unavoidably), then this irrelevant information still might be said to be in working memory. The same is true if an entire process is invoked without the task being facilitated at all (e.g., if a subject tried to use verbal rehearsal to assist in the recollection of a meaningless shape, but to no avail).

Figure 3.1, reproduced from Cowan (1988), suggests the components of working memory that form an "embedded processes" model. The large rectangle represents all of the information in long-term memory. The jagged shape represents that subset of memory in a temporarily heightened state of activation. The small circle represents the information in the current focus of attention or conscious awareness. That information is assumed to be a subset of the activated information because it is presumably not possible to attend to information without activating it. However, the converse is not true. Many studies suggest that it is possible to activate information automatically, outside of the focus of attention and awareness (e.g., Balota, 1983; Marcel, 1983; Wood & Cowan, 1995), though it still is a matter of debate exactly how much information, and what types, can be activated automatically (Cowan, 1995; Holender, 1986). At least the information in the focus of attention, and possibly all of the activated information, can result in new links between concurrent or consecutive activated elements, forming new composites that are entered into long-term memory (e.g., in learning new words or remembering new episodes).

Some theories of working memory equate it to the focus of attention and awareness (similar to the "primary memory" concept of James, 1890) and some equate it to the sum of activated information (similar to the activated cell assembly notion of Hebb, 1949). Often, the distinction between activation and awareness is left unclear, but I argue that the distinction is important and that working memory must involve both, and some long-term memory information as well.

Cowan (1988, 1995), like James (1890), considered "attention" and "awareness" to be coextensive, at least within neurologically intact individuals. Attention was seen as an enhancement of the processing of some information to the exclusion of other, concurrently available information. This

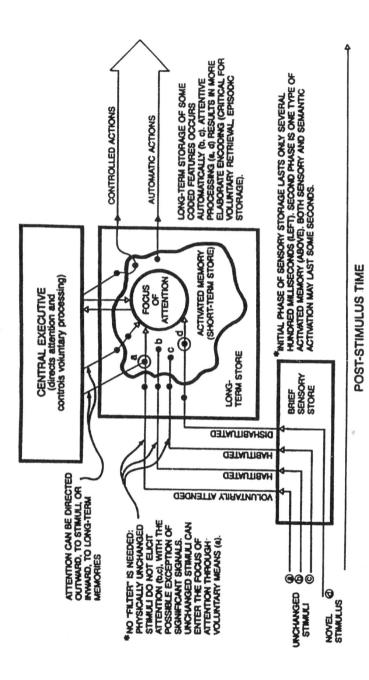

Figure 3.1. The Cowan (1988) model. Reprinted with permission of the American Psychological Association from Cowan (1988, p. 180, Figure 1). Copyright © 1988 by the American Psychological Association.

effect of attention was viewed as cutting across processing domains and tasks. For example, switching lanes on a highway probably is attention demanding in that it restricts diverse types of information processing, such as those involved in conversation or ongoing thought. In contrast, navigating the vehicle automatically according to well-learned geographical cues probably would not be considered attention demanding, even if it resulted in the failure to use other potentially available visual cues, unless it more generally restricted the ongoing stream of thought and voluntary actions. In this conception of attention, processing termed "automatic attending" (Shiffrin & Schneider, 1977), the automatically preferred processing of cues that have been well-learned, would not be considered attention demanding.

Although some activation of memory occurs for all stimuli, the sets of features of items entering the focus of attention are activated more completely than the sets corresponding to items out of the focus. An important item presented in an ignored channel while awareness is directed elsewhere, such as one's own name in an unattended voice, activates some features of the memory representation automatically. If these activated features are sufficient, they recruit attention to this channel, which then results in a more complete encoding. As shown in Figure 3.1, it is assumed that the allocation of attention is controlled jointly by (a) the automatic recruitment of attention to especially noticeable events (e.g., loud noises or bright lights, changes in physical properties of background stimulation, and sometimes signals that are of especially high personal relevance) and (b) voluntary, effort-demanding processes directed by the central executive (defined operationally as the collection of mental processes that can be modified by instructions or incentives).

Finally, it may be possible for attention to be directed away from particular features in memory rather than toward them. This inhibition of information in memory is something that many investigators have discussed lately (e.g., Conway & Engle, 1994; Gernsbacher, 1993; Hasher & Zacks, 1988). When I refer to activation and attention, I mean relative amounts, presumably including below-baseline amounts of activation for inhibited stimuli. Engle, Conway, Tuholski, and Shisler (1995) showed that inhibition appears to use the same resources as attentive processing in working memory, by demonstrating that negative priming was eliminated by a sufficiently large memory load (3 to 4 words, but not 1 to 2 words).

All three of the memory components (activation, the focus of attention and awareness, and long-term memory) contribute to working memory. The information in the current focus is the most readily accessible information in working memory. Information that is activated, but not to the point of conscious awareness, also can be retrieved reliably, albeit with slightly more of a delay. For example, when a subject searches through recently presented items to determine if a probe item was present among them (Sternberg, 1966), it is presumably this activated memory that must be searched. Finally, an item that is not even in an activated state still can be thought of as in working memory according to the foregoing definition, if there are cues in working memory that point to the item and raise the likelihood that it could be retrieved if necessary. This point will be addressed in the section on the relation of working memory to long-term memory (see also Cowan, 1995; Ericsson & Delaney, Chapter 8, this volume).

The theoretical model depicted in Figure 3.1 is not intended as a detailed description of processing that can be used to predict performance quantitatively. That would require many arbitrary assumptions to which I do not wish to be committed at present. Instead, the model is intended as a simple summary and organization of what I actually believe about attention and memory. It does incorporate a few common, key assumptions that I see as high priorities for research (e.g., assumptions that temporary memory activation outside of awareness exists, that the habituation of orienting serves as an attentional filter, and that there is a central attentional resource).

In the model there also is an attempt to reach a very general level of analysis. In doing so, many potential distinctions between processes are not discussed, but they are not denied either. For example, verbal and pictorial codes are very different and may be represented in separate parts of the brain and differing properties (e.g., the suitability for temporal versus spatial recall), but both are considered to be portions of long-term memory that can be activated in an analogous manner and that may well have similar temporal parameters of activation and decay. Covert verbal articulation and mental imagery are two processes that are very different, but both can be represented as learned routines that can be elicited through commands issued by the central executive to assist in a task. It is my belief that there is a gain in clarity from sometimes ignoring differences between particular materials, modalities, and codes to think about the system as a whole. Also, we could not be sure at this point about which domain distinctions would be most fundamental.

My tentative answers to the designated questions (summarized in Table 3.1) will be illustrated with results from my own recent research, to clarify how one might address the questions from this viewpoint and where it leads.

Basic Mechanisms and Representations in Working Memory

These include mechanisms of encoding, representation, maintenance, and retrieval of information, to be addressed in turn.

Encoding

A stimulus presumably activates features of memory, and the composite of activated features forms the encoding of the stimulus used in working memory. However, the activation of features is only partial if the stimulus is unattended to when it is presented. Under these circumstances, physical features are more likely to be represented than are semantic features. If the stimulus (or its sensory afterimage) are attended to, then more features corresponding to the stimulus will be activated. A more extensive activation of features also results in a more stable memory representation.

The emphasis on multiple codes for a stimulus seems present also in Baddeley and Logie (Chapter 2, this volume), Engle et al. (Chapter 4, this volume), and Schneider (Chapter 10, this volume). However, those investigators stress abstract codes such as the phonological code (derived from either spoken or visual language stimuli) and the semantic code (derived from any potentially meaningful stimulus). I emphasize the importance of these codes also, but I may place more emphasis on sensory codes available only for a specific modality of input. One must consider all available codes to understand how items are preserved in working memory.

A study by Cowan, Lichty, and Grove (1990) illustrates the generation of multiple codes. They examined the memory of consonant–vowel syllables (*bee, dee, gee, bih, dih, gih, beh, deh,* and *geh*) that were presented one at a time, at irregular intervals of 2 to 13 s, and were to be ignored while the subject was busy silently reading a novel. Once in a while, the reading task would be interrupted by a recall signal light; then the subject was to put down the book

---

Table 3.1. *Embedded-Processes Model: Brief Summary of Answers to the Eight Designated Questions*

(1) Basic Mechanisms and Representations in Working Memory
The model (Figure 3.1) was described by Cowan (1988, 1995). Working memory is a complex construct involving all information accessed for a task, including (a) memory in the focus of attention, (b) memory out of the focus but nevertheless temporarily activated, and (c) inactive elements of memory with sufficiently pertinent retrieval cues. The organization is embedded, with active memory as a subset of long-term memory and the focus of attention as a subset of active memory.

(2) The Control and Regulation of Working Memory
Operationally defined, the "central executive" is the set of processes influenced by instructions or incentives. The direction of the attentional focus is controlled jointly by (a) the central executive and (b) automatic recruitment of attention to physically changed stimuli or, occasionally, stimuli with special significance to the subject (Wood & Cowan, 1995). When the stimuli are unchanged, habituation of the attentional orienting response occurs, making it easier for the central executive to control the attentional focus.

(3) The Unitary Versus Non-Unitary Nature of Working Memory
The concept of "activated memory" subsumes activation that is sensory and abstract and that is based on any modality and any form of representation. In this sense, the model is unitary. (It is acknowledged that forms of representa-

continued

Table 3.1, continued

tion have different consequences for processing, but they all may be included under the rule that interference occurs between representations that are similar.) The model is less unitary than models that do not include activation outside of attention.

(4) The Nature of Working Memory Limitations

Each aspect of working memory has some limit. The evidence from various types of stimulus and coding modalities suggests that there is a time limit in the activation of memory, with activation fading within about 10 to 20 s unless it is reactivated (Cowan et al., 1990, 1994, 1997). In contrast, the focus of attention is limited by its capacity rather than by time. It appears to be limited to very few (3 to 5) unrelated items, though chunking and structure can raise the effective limit.

(5) The Role of Working Memory in Complex Cognitive Activities

People will obtain the information needed for complex tasks from any source available. Thus, information will be held in the focus of attention when that is possible, and more information may be kept active in memory, outside of the focus, when the capacity of the focus is exceeded. For example, rehearsal may serve to recirculate items into the focus, reactivating them. Long-term memory may also be used if relevant information can be retrieved.

(6) The Relationship of Working Memory to Long-Term Memory and Knowledge

Information in long-term memory is activated when it is to be used in a task. If it isn't possible for all of the necessary information to be activated, additional long-term memory information sometimes can be retrieved as necessary. Often, though, for success in a task, certain pieces of information must be activated concurrently to be combined. New combinations of information can be formed within active memory, which then may become part of long-term memory.

(7) The Relationship of Working Memory to Attention and Consciousness

Working memory includes the focus of attention, which holds the information of which the person is conscious (in neurologically intact individuals, though attention and consciousness can be dissociated in split-brain patients). However, working memory also includes activated memory outside of attention or conscious awareness.

(8) The Biological Implementation of Working Memory

Cowan et al. (1993) demonstrated memory activation using mismatch negativity responses within auditory event-related potentials. The mismatch negativity was shown to result when a deviant tone differed from a repeating standard tone, but only if the standard's representation was active when the deviant was presented. Cowan (1995) suggested biological underpinnings of the major aspects of the model (see Figure 3.9). For example, the inferior parietal areas were suggested as critical in representing the focus of attention.

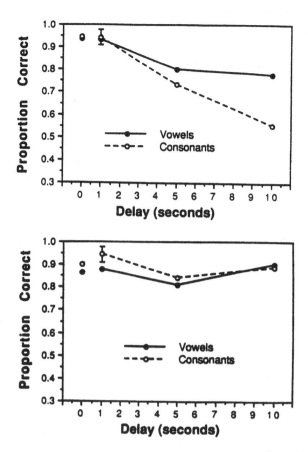

Figure 3.2. Memory for consonants and vowels within syllables presented in an auditory manner that was ignored (top panel) or monitored for occurrences of the syllable "dih" (bottom panel) during a silent reading task. Reprinted with permission of the American Psychological Association from Cowan, Lichty, and Grove (1990, p. 260, Figure 1, and p. 263, Figure 3). Copyright © 1990 by the American Psychological Association.

and identify the last syllable presented, and write a sentence about what was happening in the reading. The recall signal could come 1, 5, or 10 s after the last syllable. Finally, there was a comprehension test on the reading.

Figure 3.2 (top panel) shows the speech memory result, scored separately for the consonants and vowels. Consonant recall dropped quickly across retention intervals, but the acoustically simpler vowels were better preserved across retention intervals. Another experiment showed that this difference between consonants and vowels was not just a matter of phoneme order within a syllable; a consonant advantage was not obtained when the stimuli were vowel–consonant syllables. Reading comprehension in these experiments was no worse than for a control group that did not receive sounds while reading. The results suggest that speech information was activated automatically but that the acoustically more complex consonant information did not last as long in memory as the acoustically simpler vowel information.

In another experiment of Cowan et al. (1990), attention was divided between reading and listening. The stimuli were as in the first experiment, but the subject had the added task of pressing a button whenever the sound "dih" was heard. (Reading comprehension was hurt only slightly, but subjects found this dual task much more difficult than in the other experiments in the series.) The results under these divided attention conditions are as shown in Figure 3.2 (bottom panel). The consonant/vowel difference no longer appeared, and performance no longer was lost rapidly across retention intervals. Under these conditions, encoding was enhanced enough to produce a longer-lasting memory representation. If the speech representation that was formed with the help of attention was categorical rather than simply acoustical in nature, that could explain why performance in this experiment was equally good for consonants and vowels despite their difference in acoustic complexity. Thus, attention can change the nature of perceptual encoding dramatically.

In a final experiment of Cowan et al. (1990), subjects whispered the reading instead of reading silently, and the whispering response was recorded to allow an on-line indication of attention. A break in audible reading throughout either the 1-s period before or the 1-s period after the onset of the target syllable was considered as potential evidence of an attention shift toward that syllable. In 83% of the trials there was no such evidence of attention-shifting, and in those trials performance looked like the overall results. In the other 17% of the trials, in which there was a break in whispered reading at a critical time, the results were different. Consistent with the speculation that attention sometimes shifted toward the spoken syllable, the consonant–vowel difference was much smaller in these trials, with performance levels at a 1-s retention interval for the consonants (93% correct) being much higher than in the trials with no evidence of attention shifts (70% correct). These results reinforce the conclusion that attention enhances the encoding process and may be necessary for a categorical level of coding.

Some well-known research suggests that some semantic processing can occur automatically, but it is not clear to what extent. For example, Moray (1959) found that although people can fully attend to only one channel of information at a time, they notice their names spoken in an unattended channel when questioned about it several minutes later (Moray, 1959). However, Moray performed this experiment only on a preliminary basis and the actual finding was that 4 of 12 subjects noticed their names. Surprisingly, we found no replications of the effect in the literature. In response, Wood and Cowan (1995) replicated the effect with a better-controlled method and more subjects. The percentage of subjects who noticed their names (34%)

was quite similar to what Moray found, and an on-line measure of attention shifting (errors and pauses in shadowing or repetition of information in an attended message) yielded no evidence that subjects who noticed their names had been shifting attention beforehand to the ear in which the name occurred. A dramatic shift of attention occurred afterward, as shown in Figure 3.3. This result suggests that semantic encoding of unattended information is limited in its extent. Otherwise, an item as salient as the subject's own name should have occurred more frequently. Articles proposing that a more complete semantic encoding takes place without awareness have been criticized by Cowan (1988, 1995), Wood, Stadler, and Cowan (1997), and Holender (1986), among others.

Representation

The basic principles of encoding, maintenance, and retrieval could be similar no matter what the form of the representation of an item. Although there is extensive evidence that phonological short-term retention is impeded by competing phonological activity (articulatory suppression) whereas visuospatial short-term retention is impeded by competing spatial activity (Baddeley, 1986; Baddeley & Logie, Chapter 2, this volume), these phenomena could be subsumed under the principle that representations in memory are degraded by similar representations. A peculiarity in Baddeley's (1986) formulation that Cowan (1988) aimed to address is that Baddeley focused on two possible storage types and generally neglected others, such as the storage of nonverbal sounds or tactile sensations. Also, if various types of storage all have similar properties, then these similarities may be important, not just the differences between them.

At least some aspects of representation do seem similar across modalities. Cowan (1988) pointed out that in each modality (including at least vision, audition, and tactile senses), the ability to compare two slightly different stimuli declines rapidly as a function of the time between the two stimuli across about 10 to 20 s. Also, in each modality, it seems that the greatest interference comes from additional similar stimuli in that modality. The same appears true for types of internal code or representation (e.g., spatial or phonological coding). Interference comes from similar coding of subsequent stimuli (e.g., see Nairne, 1990; Cowan & Saults, 1995). Thus, similar decay properties over time and modality- or code-specific interference appear to characterize various types of temporarily activated memory.

Within this view, Baddeley's (1986) phonological loop and visuospatial sketchpad are just two varieties of memory activation, along with the processes that can be used to reactivate this memory (e.g., rehearsal or visualization). These reactivation routines are initiated by the central executive, although they can become to some extent automatized. Thus, as children grow older the amount of attention they need to carry out rehearsal decreases (Guttentag, 1984).

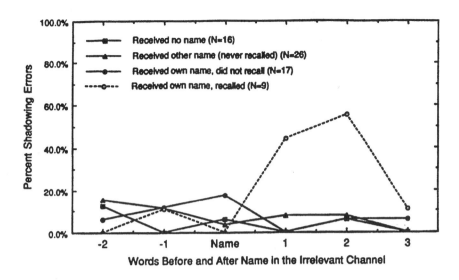

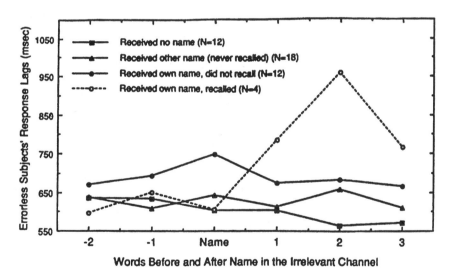

Figure 3.3. Performance in a shadowing task before and after the subject's name is presented in the ignored channel. Top panel, errors in shadowing; bottom panel, response lags within errorless responses. Reprinted with permission of the American Psychological Association from Wood and Cowan (1995, p. 258, Figure 1, and p. 259, Figure 2). Copyright © 1995 by the American Psychological Association.

The properties of the representation depend partly on the modality and physical properties of the stimulus and partly on the recoding of the stimulus. For example, phonological coding of visual materials (Conrad, 1964) presumably takes place because this coding is best suited to serial recall, whereas a visuospatial code seems best suited for following directions to a location. For a printed word, orthographic, phonological, and semantic codes may coexist in memory (Cowan & Saults, 1995).

The interference between different kinds of codes is limited. Take, for example, the interference between auditory sensory and auditory imagery codes. On the one hand, it is clear that people can use auditory imagery processes to construct sensory-like codes (Crowder, 1989). On the other hand, this auditory imagery is not interchangeable with a truly sensory memory record. Keller, Cowan, and Saults (1995) presented two tones to be compared, separated by a 0.5-s or a 10-s silent interval. During the longer intervals, subjects had to rehearse either a short tone series or short melody silently, or were permitted to spend the time rehearsing the first tone in the pair. Either type of filler task produced performance that was worse than in the rehearsal condition, as shown in Figure 3.4. Thus, auditory imagery constructed in the distracting tasks does not have exactly the same function as auditory sensory memory formed from an actual stimulus.

Maintenance

The form of maintenance depends on the aspect of working memory being considered and its limits that must be overcome. The most conventional meaning of maintenance is finding a way to continue *activating* items in memory. For example, Baddeley's (1986) model highlights verbal rehearsal as a means to reactivate items in a phonological store (see also Baddeley & Logie, Chapter 2, this volume). In the present view, keeping an item in the focus of attention would serve a similar function. Central executive processes may carry out particular operations that reactivate items in memory as a by-product. For example, Cowan (1992) proposed that the process of searching through a set of items can help to reactivate them. The items may be recirculated through the focus of attention.

These suggestions about the effect of a search on activation were inspired by measurements of the duration of elements within spoken responses in a memory-span task administered to 4-year-old children (Cowan, 1992). If all children have a similar persistence of information in memory (e.g., the approximately 2-s period proposed by Baddeley, 1986) and it cannot be altered, then that memory persistence should limit the potential duration of a list-recall response. Consequently, differences between individuals in the proportion recalled would be related to differences in the rate of pronunciation of the items within the fixed recall period. Contrary to this prediction, Cowan (1992) found that as the list length increased, the durations of silent periods between the words in the response increased markedly. (In contrast, the dura-

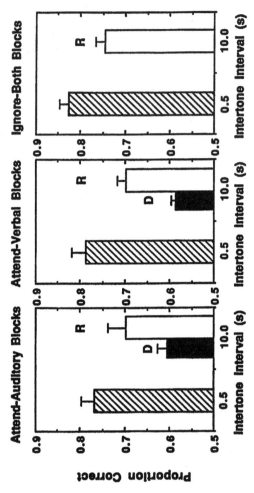

Figure 3.4. Tone comparison performance in several conditions. D = distraction during 10-s intertone intervals, R = rehearsal of the first tone during those intervals. Reprinted with permission of the American Psychological Association from Keller, Cowan, & Saults (1995, p. 642, Figure 3). Copyright © 1995 by the American Psychological Association.

tions of words did not change.) When one looked at the length of utterances in the span-length responses of various children, it turned out that the rates of production were similar; those who recalled more items did so in a response that lasted longer, with the duration of the recall response increasing by about 1 s for each word in the list. This suggested that the mental processing occurring during recall (primarily in the inter-item pauses) may have helped to reactivate the memories, allowing that longer response period.

The relevant activity that children carried out during inter-item pauses could be a mental search for the correct item to repeat next, rather than, say, verbal rehearsal. As each item is examined in the search, it may briefly enter the focus of attention and become reactivated. One clue that it is not a verbal rehearsal process taking place during these pauses is that they are unaffected by word length (Cowan, 1992; Cowan, Keller et al., 1994), which also is the case in memory scanning procedures (Chase, 1977; Clifton & Tash, 1973).

A subsequent study (Cowan et al., 1998) showed that subjects' ability to articulate quickly (estimating rehearsal speed?) and the durations of inter-word pauses in the memory span responses (estimating the speed of memory search processes?) did not correlate with each other at all, even though both of them produced moderate correlations with memory span (about .4). With multiple measures of each type of speed, the two types picked up different portions of the span variance and together accounted for a large portion of variance in a latent-variable model. The model explained about 60% of the total span variance and 87% of the age-related span variance on the basis of these two types of speed. Perhaps both speeds are important because memory decay can occur during either memory search or covert rehearsal.

Thus, various maintenance processes may work together or in sequence. In a trip to the store, one might encode the shopping list according to some meaningful scheme, rehearse the list several times, attend to key parts of it, mentally search for the item to acquire next, reconstruct part of the list from long-term memory, and so on. Recall ability may depend upon the success of the various processes.

Retrieval

Within the present model, retrieval means entering the correct items into the focus of attention. If an item is in the focus at the moment when it is needed, it probably can be recalled. Retrieval from activated memory and retrieval from long-term memory differ in important ways. Long-term memory has a richer information structure to rely upon. Also, retrieval from long-term memory is time limited only for practical reasons (e.g., the response period allowed on a recall trial in an experiment, or the amount of time one has to think of an acquaintance's name and introduce him or her to another person when it is expected socially). Retrieval from activated memory must occur quickly because the memory will not stay activated long. If the activated memory representation has disappeared, retrieval of the same information from long-term memory is still possible only if a sufficient episodic memory trace has been stored. Thus, retrieval processes must race against forgetting from activated memory. There also are tall hurdles in the race, in the form of interference among activated items.

Baddeley's (1986) working memory model is similar in principle to the current one, but the actual influences on retrieval seem more complex than he noted. In his description of memory span, a particular person can recall about as much from a particular stimulus set as he or she can pronounce in about 2 s. The theoretical explanation that Baddeley offered is that the speed at which one can pronounce the items estimates the rate of covert rehearsal. Both age and word length were said to affect rehearsal speed. Cowan, Keller, et al. (1994) found, however, that they work differently. The timing of spoken responses of children 4 and 8 years of age for lists of short (monosyllabic) or long (multisyllabic) words was measured. Better recall occurred for older children and shorter words, as expected. However, these variables resulted in different patterns of response timing. The word length (number of syllables) was found to alter the duration of words in the spoken responses, but not the duration of the silent periods. Conversely, the age of subjects altered the silent periods, but not the duration of words in the responses. Figure 3.5 shows aspects of the timing of correct responses to span-length lists. In preparatory intervals (top panel) there was only an effect of age, whereas in word durations (bottom panel) there was only an effect of stimulus word length. Interword pauses, not shown, revealed no effect in span-length lists, but they showed an age effect when examined for comparable list lengths at each age (mean = .38 s at age 4 versus .23 s at age 8). The response timing pattern suggests that the age and word length effects on span have different mechanisms. Both may arise only partly from covert rehearsal effects. The age effect may operate partly by influencing the speed of covert search processes during retrieval, whereas the word-length effect may operate partly by influencing the rate of overt pronunciation in recall (see Cowan et al., 1992). The efficiency of all such processes may contribute to span.

The Control and Regulation of Working Memory

In the present model, regulation of working memory amounts to the control of the focus of attention by the central executive. This control also is one way that information in memory can be activated; items in the focus become activated. However, the amount of information that can remain activated at one time is greater than the amount that would fit in the focus of attention (see also Engle et al., Chapter 4, this volume).

The model of Cowan (1988, 1995) has addressed the question of how voluntary and involuntary mechanisms work together to determine the focus of attention. The necessary background is as follows. Research on selective attention showed that it is easier to attend to one of several channels if they are

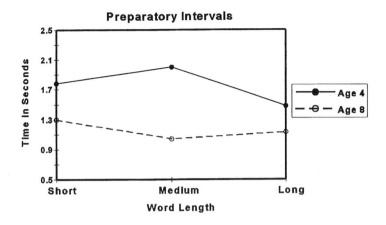

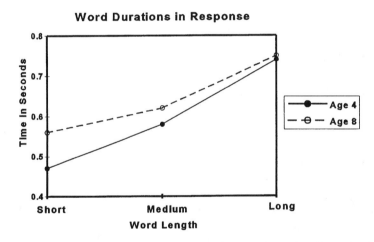

Figure 3.5. The timing of performance in correct responses to span-length lists in a word span task with short, medium, or long words. Top panel, preparatory intervals; bottom panel, word durations in the response. Adapted with permission of Academic Press, from Cowan, Keller et al. (1994). Interword pauses described in text but not shown in the figure.

distinguished by physical characteristics than if they are distinguished only by semantic characteristics (e.g., Broadbent, 1958; Johnston & Heinz, 1978). However, subsequent research showed that some of the semantic information is processed also (e.g., Gray & Wedderburn, 1960; Moray, 1959). Such findings led A. M. Treisman (1964) to adopt an "attenuating filter" theory of attention in which all information enters the processing system, but with attenuated processing of the unattended information and more complete processing of the attended information.

Cowan (1988, 1995) proposed a mechanism of control that serves a purpose similar to Treisman's (1964) notion of an attenuating filter, but with the mechanism of attenuation specified. Rather than unattended stimuli being filtered out, all stimuli activate some elements of memory, but this process is enhanced for attended stimuli (or for stimuli that recruit attention). The attention-recruiting mechanism is based on Sokolov's (1963) work on the orienting response and its habituation. The orienting response is a composite of physiological and behavioral responses, including temporarily reduced muscular activity, slowing of the heart rate, and increased sensitivity to incoming stimulation. It can be elicited when a new stimulus is presented, when the physical properties of a repeating stimulus are changed, or when a particularly significant stimulus is presented (Cowan, 1995; Öhman, 1979). However, when a stimulus is repeated with no change, habituation of the orienting response occurs. Sokolov's explanation was that a neural model of the stimulus is built up through repeated exposure. New stimuli are compared to the neural model, and an orienting response occurs only if there is a discrepancy.

The orienting response and its habituation are used in the model of Cowan (1988) to take the place of a selective filter or attenuator, as shown in Figure 3.1. All stimuli activate features in memory. However, attention is recruited to a stimulus through the orienting response only if the conditions are right. Therefore, if a subject wishes to ignore a repeated stimulus, he or she easily can do so; yet, some (mostly physical) features corresponding to the stimulus still will be activated in memory and compared to the neural model. Most complex semantic features of unattended stimuli will not be automatically processed and therefore are not available to be compared to the neural model (which itself may include attended features).

There are instances in which one needs to attend to a repeated stimulus. This can be done with input from the central executive, though only with effort. Thus, the focus of attention is controlled by the voluntary processes and automatic attentional recruitment together. Supporting this notion, Waters, McDonald, and Koresko (1977) had subjects carry out math problems, sometimes in the presence of auditory interference consisting of an audiotape of spoken mathematical terms ("plus," "equals," "three," etc.). Some of the subjects were allowed to hear the distracting audiotape beforehand, whereas others heard only control tones or nothing beforehand. Pre-exposure to the mathematical speech reduced the amount of distraction early in the session, as measured both by a reduction in errors and a physiological measure of the orienting response (skin resistance). There is also a recent finding of habituation and dishabituation to the disruptive effects of speech and office noise (Banbury & Berry, 1997).

In sum, the orienting mechanism and its habituation allow an effortless mode of attention in which some processing of the unattended information takes place. The central executive uses effortful processes to help direct the control of attention. The effortless and effortful influences operate together. Presumably, if the physical properties of stimulation lead the subject toward the target object of attention (e.g., listening to an exciting lecturer in a quiet room) much less effort is needed for paying attention than when the physical properties lead away from the target object (e.g., listening to a lecture delivered in a monotonous voice over the cries of an infant in the room or a nearby siren).

Unitary Versus Non-Unitary Nature of Working Memory

The present model is unitary in some ways and non-unitary in others. The model seems more unitary than Baddeley's (1986) model, which makes a sharper distinction between phonological and visuospatial sources of information (see Baddeley & Logie, Chapter 2, this volume). Clearly, these types of information are quite different from one another, but different codes may be processed according to the same principles. It is not denied here that two items that require the same type of coding can interfere with one another more than two items that require different coding. However, coding distinctions other than phonological versus visuospatial may be equally important. The present view seems more unitary in this consideration. However, both models seem less unitary than that of Just and Carpenter (1992) or Lovett, Reder, and Lebiere (Chapter 5, this volume). Those models do not distinguish between activation and attention, which are discussed as if coextensive. Automatic activation apparently is outside the scope of their models. Like Baddeley's (1986) model, the present one postulates both a passive storage component and an active processing component. The modeling difference may hinge on whether one believes in the importance of automatic activation in working memory tasks.

It seems clear that all of the information reproduced in a simple memory span task could not result from the items in the focus of attention. It seems unlikely that, say, seven items could be held in attention at once. Therefore, in addition to attended information, one needs activated sources outside of attention and/or supplementary help from long-term memory. Thus, the present model includes several components and is not fully unitary.

The Nature of Working Memory Limitations

This question is probably critical in distinguishing between theories of working memory. In principle, there are at least two ways that a type of memory can be limited: in its capacity to hold information at any one time, and in the time for which information can be held. Both of these limitations are proposed, for different aspects of working memory (Cowan, 1995), with a time limit of memory activation and a capacity limit of the focus of attention. The time limit in activation is found also in the models of Baddeley (1986) and Baddeley and Logie (Chapter 2, this volume), Schneider (Chapter 10, this volume), and O'Reilly, Braver, and Cohen (Chapter 11, this volume), as well as in many older theoretical approaches (e.g., Broadbent, 1958), though I will argue that it is still difficult to obtain incontrovertible evidence for the time limit. The capacity limit of the focus of attention forms the basis of many approaches to working memory, including those of Engle et al. (Chapter 4, this volume) and Lovett et al. (Chapter 5, this volume), with some other researchers probably also being sympathetic (e.g., Young & Lewis, Chapter 7; Schneider, Chapter 10; O'Reilly et al., Chapter 11, this volume). It goes back to James (1890). Just and Carpenter (1992) use a similar limit but call it "activation," in contrast to the present terminology.

My approach appears to differ most from several investigators who seem more interested in constraints on processing arising from limitations in the available knowledge, its structure, or how it can be used (Young & Lewis, Chapter 7; Ericsson & Delaney, Chapter 8, this volume), or in how multiple tasks can be coordinated through the use of strategies (Kieras, Meyer, Mueller, & Seymour, Chapter 6; Barnard, Chapter 9, this volume). These additional limits are not denied here, either. The theories differ primarily in where one looks first for working memory limits in a particular task. Is the default hypothesis one of retention and capacity limitations, or one of strategic processing limitations? No one knows, but in my work (and below) the potential retention and capacity limitations are emphasized more.

Limitations of Activated Memory

The existence of limits on activated memory is critical for the present view. If there were no such limits, then activated memory would not really exist as a separate entity and could just as easily be conceived as simply the most easily retrievable items in memory, based on the current contextual cues.

CAPACITY LIMIT? Cowan (1988, 1995) suggested that the amount of activation that could take place at one time could be limitless. In contrast, Cantor and Engle (1993) argued that it is limited, based on their finding of larger fan effects in participants with a lower working memory span. They suggested that low-span participants have less activation to be shared among the learned examples, and therefore that their activation is spread thinner than high-span subjects when it must be shared among more than one item in an association fan. However, in a memory search task, Conway and Engle (1994) found that changes in response time as a function of set size were affected by working memory span only if each target item was used in sets of more than one size. The findings of Cantor and Engle were reinterpreted as resulting from high-span participants' greater ability to inhibit associated information that was irrelevant on a particular trial, not from the greater availability of activation in these participants. There is no known limit to the amount of activation, it appears.

TIME LIMIT? The other possible limitation of activated memory is that it decays. As time goes on, some of the activated features in memory cease to be activated, making the temporary representation of an item more and more vague until it disappears completely. Memory decay is a very common assumption. Baddeley (1986) assumed that activated elements in a phonological memory store decay in about 2 s, which is supposed to account for the fact that memory span is limited to the number of items that can be repeated in about that period. Many studies have been conducted in which two identical or slightly different tones or vowels are to be compared on each trial, and these studies have shown that performance declines as the time between sounds increases across about 10 to 30 s (see Cowan, 1984, 1995). Similar time estimates have come from studies of memory for several letters in the presence of a distracting task (e.g., Peterson & Peterson, 1959) and of the decline in the recency effect in list recall across a distracting period (e.g., Glanzer & Cunitz, 1966). The difference between these findings and the 2-s estimate of Baddeley (1986) could result from a number of differences among procedures in the required responses or sources of interference.

There has appeared, however, a body of research seriously challenging the notion that there is any kind of dependence on the passage of time per se. There was an article by Keppel and Underwood (1962) questioning the basis of forgetting in the procedure of Peterson and Peterson (1959). The latter found retention of consonant trigrams that declined steadily during a distracting task (counting backward by 3), with the performance reaching an asymptotically low level by 18 s. However, Keppel and Underwood found that this effect of the duration of distraction was not present in the first couple of trials, and emerged only after that. Their conclusion was that proactive interference from previous lists has to build up before the effect can be obtained.

Theoretically, there are two ways to interpret this finding of Keppel and Underwood (1962). One way is according to a theory in which there is no such thing as memory decay; there is a common or "unitary" set of memory principles that are supposed to apply to memory phenomena on any time scale (McGeoch, 1932; Crowder, 1993). According to this type of theory, in the Peterson and Peterson (1959) procedure the effect of the distracting task is to allow the temporal context to change. Shortly after the presentation of a trigram, it seems distinct from all of the others. However, after a long distractor task, the temporal distinctiveness of the final trigram is lost because the past few trigrams are now relatively close together compared to the retention interval.

According to an alternative interpretation, though, short- and long-term memory work together in this task (Cowan, 1988). The effect of the distracting task is presumably that it allows memory to decay. However, even when that decay has taken place, subjects will be able to retrieve the last trigram on the basis of a long-term memory representation, unless the proactive interference from previous trials is sufficient to prevent long-term retrieval. That presumably is what happens after a few trials.

A key claim of the unitary memory theory is that it is relative, not absolute, amounts of time that result in memory loss. More evidence for that claim came from a finding termed the "long-term recency effect." Prior studies had found that the recency effect (enhanced recall of items at the end of a list) was eliminated if a long (e.g., 20-s) distracting period was placed between the list and the recall period (e.g., Glanzer & Cunitz, 1966). However, in studies of the long-term recency effect (e.g., Bjork & Whitten, 1974), distracting periods are placed not only after the list, but also before the list and between items, a method usually termed the "continuous-distractor procedure." Under those circumstances, a recency effect is obtained even though the list-final distracting task should have been long enough to allow any activated memory to decay. The results follow a "ratio rule": performance is better when the ratio between the interpresentation interval and the retention interval is larger. The ratio is relatively large for the last few items in ordinary immediate recall and in the continuous-distractor procedure, but not for the last few items in delayed recall (uninterrupted presentation with a post-list distraction period). An explanation is that the recency effect reflects the special temporal distinctiveness of the last item or so when the time of recall is much closer to the end of the list than it is to previous list items, as is the case in the conditions in which the recency effect is obtained. Other research shows that several other effects usually taken as indicative of short-term memory also can be obtained in the continuous-distractor procedure (see Cowan, 1995, for a review).

A number of investigators have been looking for signs of similarities between recall in the ordinary procedure and the continuous-distractor procedure. However, it has been much less common to look for possible differences between these procedures, a strategy that potentially could reconfirm the concept of memory decay. Recently, we have pursued that strategy. Though several of the effects that had been taken as signatures of short-term memory and its decay have been compromised by the continuous-distractor results, one effect that has not been so compromised is the word-length effect. Cowan, Wood, and Borne (1994) examined this effect in the ordinary, immediate recall procedure and the continuous- (or "through-list") distractor procedure. Backward recall was used so that the words that could be rehearsed for the longest time were not the same as the ones to be recalled first, allowing rehearsal versus output delay mechanisms of the word-length effect to be distinguished. Word length was manipulated separately in the first and second halves of the list. The short words were monosyllabic, the long words trisyllabic.

The results are shown in Figure 3.6. In immediate recall, there was an advantage for lists in which the words to be recalled early on were short rather than long, replicating a previous finding (Cowan et al., 1992) and suggesting that items are forgotten during the time in which other items are recalled.

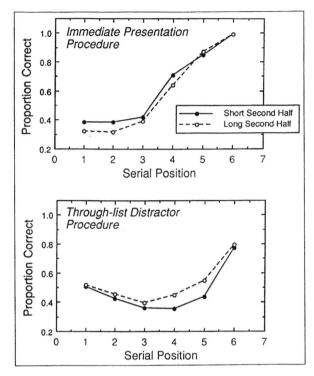

Figure 3.6. Performance on a backward span task for lists with short versus long words in the first half-list. Top panel, immediate recall; bottom panel, through-list distractor recall. Reprinted with permission of Cambridge University Press from Cowan, Wood, and Borne (1994, p. 105, Figure 1). Copyright © 1994 by Cambridge University Press.

However, in through-list (continuous) distractor recall, there actually was a long-word advantage, which might be attributed to the greater number of phonological cues in long-term memory. Thus, unlike other effects for which the immediate and continuous distractor procedures have been compared, the word length effect was not at all similar in the two procedures. Clearly, then, the word length effect may be particularly important in confirming the idea of the decay of activated memory.

However, the word length results have been criticized recently. The effect could result from the greater complexity, rather than the greater duration, of longer words. It is difficult to match sets of shorter and longer words on all potentially relevant phonemic features. On a suggestion by M. Treisman, an experiment was conducted by Cowan, Wood, Nugent, and Treisman (1997) to overcome this difficulty. One- and two-syllable, printed words were used, but the syllable number was not the only basis of word length. In addition, words were to be pronounced more quickly or slowly, as cued by a row of asterisks

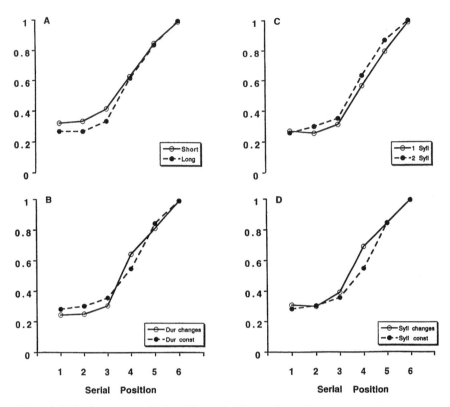

Figure 3.7. Performance in backward span for lists with words pronounced short versus long throughout (panel A), lists split according to word duration (panel B), lists with monosyllabic versus disyllabic words throughout (panel C), and lists split according to number of syllables (panel D). Reprinted with permission of Cambridge University Press from Cowan, Wood, Nugent, and Treisman (1997, Figure 2). Copyright © 1997 by Cambridge University Press.

that grew longer for either 300 ms or 600 ms. The same pronunciation duration cue appeared before a particular item at the time of presentation of the list and at the time of spoken recall. Recall was, once more, in the backward order. Figure 3.7 summarizes the most important results of this study. There was an advantage for words that were pronounced more quickly (panel A). The decay theory would predict this on the grounds that when words are pronounced more quickly, there is less time for forgetting to occur. There also was an unexpected advantage for disyllabic words over monosyllabic words, perhaps because the disyllabic words provide more phonological cues (panel C). This shows that word complexity is not the basis of the ordinary short-word advantage. The bottom panels (B and D) show that there were additional effects of splitting the list in terms of either duration or complexity.

As Treisman pointed out within our collaborative paper (Cowan et al., 1997), it still cannot be taken as proven that the word-length effect demonstrates the existence and importance of memory decay. The problem is that the longer-duration pronunciations expose subjects to their own speech for a longer time, and therefore the total amount of interfering content still is greater for words produced in the longer fashion. However, several previous investigators have obtained results with verbal stimuli that also seem to indicate the existence of verbal memory decay (Conrad & Hille, 1958; Reitman, 1974; Watkins, Watkins, Craik, & Mazuryk, 1973; Wingfield & Byrnes, 1972). Also, Cowan, Saults, and Nugent (1997) found separate roles of absolute and relative time in two-tone discriminations. Nevertheless, the concept of decay remains controversial in cognitive psychology (Crowder, 1993; Neath & Nairne, 1995) in light of potential nondecay accounts, and further evidence on the role of decay is still needed.

In sum, the notion of activation seems to depend on its temporal limitations, without which the activation would just appear to be a part of long-term memory with no special status except that it matches the current context well. This analysis of the meaning of the activation concept may explain, among other things, why decay plays a prominent role within the theory of Baddeley (1986). Although this is a difficult issue to examine, I have cited tentative evidence that memory activation is time limited.

Limitations in the Focus of Attention

CAPACITY LIMIT? Less controversial than the limits in activation discussed above, there is a limit to how many unrelated items can be in the focus of attention or awareness at any given time (James, 1890; Broadbent, 1958). It may be that people can focus on at most one general scheme (or several?) at a particular moment, not on many unrelated items or schemes.

A dissenting voice might be found in the late-filter theory of attention (e.g., Deutsch & Deutsch, 1963). According to that kind of view, the limit in attention is how much one can respond to at a particular time, not how much one can perceive or apprehend. Another dissenting view might be found in the multiple resources approach (e.g., Wickens, 1984), in which the idea of a central processing capacity limit is replaced with limits for specific types of material, with the total capacity depending on how dissimilar the streams of information are in various ways. However, it is not absolutely clear to me how, according to these alternative approaches, the behavioral aspects of attention and phenomenological aspects of awareness are supposed to be related to one another. Note that the suggestion that there is a central processing capacity (or attention) limit does not mean that there cannot also be more specific resource limits, such as a limit in verbal or spatial processing.

One of the simplest demonstrations of limits in attention comes from research on dichotic listening (e.g., Broadbent, 1958). Suppose that prose in a male voice is presented in one of the subject's ears and prose in a female voice is presented in the other ear. The subject will find it impossible to comprehend the meanings of both messages at once, even though both messages are acoustically clear. This is an easy demonstration to carry out. However, one might object that the limit could be in the language comprehension apparatus and not in the ability to hold multiple sources of information in mind once they have been comprehended.

A finding seemingly counter to the conclusion that attentional capacity is limited is that people can be trained to do two complex tasks at the same time (Hirst, Spelke, Reaves, Caharack, & Neisser, 1980). However, Cowan (1995) offered an extensive critique, suggesting that attention-switching or automaticity may well underlie such feats.

Most of the literature on capacity limits does require simultaneous perception of multiple channels, or multiple simultaneous responses. It is difficult to avoid the input and output requirements so as to examine the limits in what can be held in the focus of attention per se. Here one might think of limits in short-term memory (Miller, 1956) or in the size of the memory set within search tasks (Shiffrin & Schneider, 1977; Sternberg, 1966). However, these types of task might overestimate how much can be held in the focus of attention. In them, information might be kept active (e.g., through covert rehearsal) with only a small amount of the information actually residing in the focus of attention at one time. Nevertheless, these types of procedure at least do seem to indicate that there is some upper bound on the focus of attention.

There is, however, a seemingly "magical number" 4 ± 1. Derived measures of short-term memory in the immediate recall of verbal lists, designed to eliminate contributions of long-term memory, generally have suggested that no more than about 4 unconnected items can be kept in mind at one time (see Watkins, 1974). Converging evidence on this comes from a number of research domains. (a) A number of related phenomena were pointed out by Broadbent (1975), such as the limit in the number of items that occur in a cluster in free recall and the limit for obtaining perfect immediate memory performance. (b) On each trial within an experiment by Halford, Maybery, and Bain (1988) a memory list did or did not have marked similarities to the previous list. Proactive interference effects on search time were obtained with relatively long memory lists, but not with lists of 4 or fewer items. (c) In the classic research by Sperling (1960), a partial report cue was used to indicate to subjects which row of a briefly viewed, multicharacter array to report. When the partial report cue delay was short, subjects seemed to have access to most or all of the items in the array, which presumably were saved temporarily in an unanalyzed sensory form. However, with or without the cue, there also was a limit in the absolute number of items that could be reported on a particular trial. At most about 4 items could be reported, the "whole report" limit. One explanation for this limit is that only about 4 items can be drawn from sensory memory to the focus of awareness on a particular trial. A similar limit on whole report was observed using spatiotemporal arrays in the auditory modality (Darwin, Turvey, & Crowder, 1972). (d) In research on subitizing (e.g., Trick & Pylyshyn, 1993) subjects are to count sets of small items such as dots. With 1 to 4 items, normal adult response times increase at the rate of about 40 to 120 ms per additional item, whereas starting with the fifth item, response times increase at the rate of 250 to 350 ms per item. This discontinuity has led to the notion that a "subitizing" or apprehension of the first 4 items takes place in parallel, with a deliberate, serial counting process necessary only with numbers larger than about 4. It could be argued that the subitized items are in the focus of attention at the same time. (e) In a recently developed, "multiobject tracking" procedure, many dots are presented on the computer screen at once. Several of the dots begin to flash on and off, and then cease flashing. All of the dots then begin to wander around the screen for a period of time and then come to a halt. The task is to identify the final resting locations of the dots that had been flashing. In this task, it is found that only about 4 dots can be tracked at one time; if a larger number of dots flash, their locations are not correctly tracked. Finally, (f) Fisher (1984) developed a model of consistently mapped search that included a limit in the number of comparisons that could be made at one time. Subjects examined a series of rapidly presented character arrays and searched for the single digit "5." The ability to detect this target depended on both the presentation duration of each array and the number of items in each array. In the mathematical model of performance, based on Erlang's Loss Formula, characters in the visual array enter the information-processing system in parallel for comparison with the target in memory, and if a comparison channel is unavailable at the time of arrival then that particular comparison is not made and the stimulus item is lost from the system. The model provided a very good fit to the data, with the best fit for each individual occurring with 3 to 5 comparison channels.

There are numerous other procedures that yield seemingly similar results. Research is needed to determine the extent to which these diverse procedures are tapping the same mental faculty, and the extent to which their convergent findings are merely coincidental. Until a common mechanism can be unambiguously identified (e.g., some structural or functional limit in the capacity of the focus of attention), we can only be haunted by the integer plus or minus 1. However, the procedures leading to this constant do seem to me to be more numerous even than the number 7 plus or minus 2 that haunted Miller (1956) and could well reflect a limit in what can enter the focus of awareness. The limit may or may not be a discrete integer value and probably applies only to the number of unconnected units or chunks (Miller, 1956), with grouping and chunking processes resulting in a larger effective limit.

TIME LIMIT? The only time limit in attention that is apparent is that reflected in the research on vigilance (e.g., Davies & Parasuraman, 1982). That research suggests that it is impossible to maintain maximal attention on an object indefinitely because the state of alertness wanes (e.g., after $1/2$ hour).

The Role of Working Memory in Complex Cognitive Activities

In the present view (cf. Cowan, 1988, 1995), a distinction is to be drawn between the fundamental mechanisms of working memory and the performance on a task. The idea of working memory is simply that the information needed to do a task must be made especially accessible temporarily; often, for a creative task, several pieces of information must be active concurrently so that they can be combined. Thus, I agree with Baars's (1988) view of working memory as a global workspace within which information is integrated rather than held in isolated bundles. However, the mechanisms through which information can become accessible vary widely. Some of the necessary information may be in the focus of attention; some may be in an especially active state, ready to enter the focus as needed; and some may simply have the appropriate contextual coding in long-term memory that allows it to be made available quickly.

Thus, there is no single, separate theoretical entity that I would call working memory; that is a practical, task-oriented label. What are potentially more meaningful in a theoretical sense are the basic mechanisms proposed to underlie this complex system, including activation of memory, the contents of an attentional process, and the contextual organization of memory.

A further important question is what types of information become active or become the focus of attention in complex tasks. My assumption is that multiple types of features become active. However, the focus of attention will prolong this activation for some types of features more than others. Studies of language comprehension in normal and brain-damaged patients clearly show that language is retained in primarily a phonological form only if the language is challenging or complex, in which case the correct syntactic and lexical analysis may not become immediately clear to the listener or reader (e.g., Caplan & Waters, 1990; Martin, 1993). Thus, attention may be focused so as to select, from among the available types of representation, the ones affording the most efficiency and usefulness given a limited attentional capacity.

The Relation of Working Memory to Long-Term Memory and Knowledge

At any moment there is assumed to be a currently active subset of long-term memory, and the focus of attention is assumed to be a subset of that activated information. This attentional focus and the activated memory both play a role in working memory. Both Ericsson and Delaney (Chapter 8, this volume) and Cowan (1995, chapter 4) suggested that items in long-term memory that are strongly associated with the subject's current situation can be accessed easily and function much as if they were held in an activated form. Cowan (1995, chapter 4) called this use of long-term memory as if it were part of short-term memory "virtual" (as opposed to actual) short-term memory, and

Ericsson and Kintsch (1995) called it "long-term working memory." For complex tasks, Ericsson and Delaney (Chapter 8, this volume) describe the processes of long-term working memory in much more detail. However, long-term memory plays a role even in ordinary memory span tasks. Spans are higher for word stimuli than for nonsense word stimuli, the only difference between them being a long-term memory representation available for the words (Hulme, Maughan, & Brown, 1991). Cowan's (1995) "virtual short-term memory" concept was developed to account for such findings and for list-recall results that mimic short-term memory results, but over periods of time so long that they could not actually involve short-term memory mechanisms (e.g., Bjork & Whitten, 1974).

Despite this proposed use of long-term memory, the concept of memory activation is included in the present model given the existing evidence (e.g., Figure 3.6). Also, for success in some tasks, it may be necessary for several pieces of information to be activated concurrently, not just available in long-term memory. For example, it may well be that the structure of an English sentence can be adequately understood only if the subject and verb are active in memory at the same time.

Finally, there is one important qualification of the statement that working memory contains activated elements of long-term memory. Most stimulus situations in life include novel combinations of familiar features. In memory the elements are activated independently, but the particular links between those elements are often novel. The current combination of elements may, however, be stored as a new long-term memory trace. Declarative memories are said to be encoded only with the presence of attention, whereas procedural memories might be encoded more automatically, provided that sufficient attention is devoted to the task to allow the relevant stimulus features to be processed (Cowan, 1995).

The Relationship of Working Memory to Attention and Consciousness

I assume that, in neurally intact individuals, the information in the focus of attention is the same information that the person is aware of, which is also the same information to which a central capacity limit applies (Cowan, 1988, 1995). (See my definition of attention in the introduction.) One type of evidence for this assumption is the close relation between measures of attention shifting to an event in a task-irrelevant channel and subsequent measures of memory of that event (Wood & Cowan, 1995; see Figure 3.3). Activated memory outside of awareness also can count as part of working memory because that information is more readily available to influence task performance than information that is not activated. Presumably, most of the 7 ± 2 chunks of information that people can remember (or whatever the actual limit is) are activated but still are outside the focus of attention at any one moment, given the more severely limited capacity of awareness observed in a number of situations (see above). Covert rehearsal may serve to reactivate information by recirculating it through the focus of attention.

The Biological Implementation of Working Memory

Two main aspects of the biological implementation of the present model merit consideration. First, some psychophysiological research is relevant to the functioning of working memory. Second, other research on lesions and neuroimaging is relevant to the neuroanatomical representation of working memory. These aspects will be addressed in turn.

Psychophysiological Investigations of Working Memory Function

The model of working memory of Cowan (1988) was used by Cowan, Winkler, Teder, and Näätänen (1993) to generate hypotheses about event-related potentials (ERPs). The topic of research was the mismatch negativity (MMN) and its interpretation. The MMN is obtained by repeating an auditory stimulus presentation and then changing the stimulus in some discriminable way. The changed or "deviant" stimuli produce an average waveform that at a certain point becomes more negative than the average waveform produced by the standard stimuli (for a review see Ritter, Deacon, Gomes, Javitt, & Vaughan, 1995). This negative-going difference wave can be obtained for any discriminable acoustic change, even if the subject carries out a different task and ignores the auditory stimuli when they are presented. However, the MMN occurs only if the standard and deviant sounds occur within about 10 s of one another (Mäntysalo & Näätänen, 1987; Sams, Hari, Rif, & Knuutila, 1993). The interpretation has been that a short-lived sensory representation of the standard is compared to the deviant, and the MMN results from a process in which these stimuli are compared and found to differ. This process cannot take place if the sensory representation of the standard has decayed away before the deviant is presented.

One anomaly of this account is that it appeared from various studies that multiple presentations of the standard were necessary before a deviant would produce the MMN. That should not be the case if the standard representation is purely a temporary representation of the last stimulus and is not influenced by the past history of stimulation. A more sophisticated concept of the sensory representation was needed.

Such a concept can be derived from the model in Figure 3.1. According to this model, a repeated presentation of the standard tone should produce a long-term memory representation of that tone. The long-term representation then could be in an active state (likely if the last standard tone occurred about 10 s ago or less) or an inactive state (likely if the last standard tone occurred much prior to that). It was proposed that the MMN would occur only if (a) an adequate representation of the standard tone existed, and (b) that representation was in an active state when the deviant tone was presented.

Cowan et al. (1993) examined this account by presenting trains of nine tones with 610 ms onset-to-onset intervals within a train and silent periods of 11 to 15 s between trains. The tones in each train were all the same except that one deviant could occur, in Serial Positions 1, 2, 4, 6, or 8 within a train. The MMN was examined by comparing ERPs for the deviants in a particular serial position to ERPs for standard tones in the same serial position within trains that had no deviants up to that serial position. There were two kinds of sequences: "constant-standard" sequences in which the standard tone frequency was the same in each train, and "roving-standard" sequences in which a new standard tone was used in each train. In either case, if a deviant occurred it was 7/6 the frequency of the standard tones in its train.

The results beautifully matched the theory. Several standards are needed for the construction of a representation of that tone. In the roving-standard condition, that representation had to be built up for each train anew. Accordingly, there was no MMN for deviants in Serial Positions 1 or 2 within the train, but there was an MMN for deviants later in the train. In the constant-standard condition, however, a long-term memory representation of the standard tone could be built up across trains. However, the intertrain interval would render that representation inactive, so a single reminder presentation would be needed to reactivate the standard tone representation. As this line of reasoning predicts, the MMN did not occur with the deviant in Serial Position 1, but it did occur with the deviant in Serial Position 2 or later. (For a Position 2 deviant, the Position 1 standard was assumed to reactivate the representation.) The magnitude of the MMN in each condition is shown in Figure 3.8. It shows that a deviant in the second serial position elicited an MMN in the constant-standard condition (because the first serial position standard could reactivate the previous standard representation) but not in the roving-standard condition (because the standard was new with the first serial position stimulus). This research thus helps to confirm the theory's emphasis on the concept of the activation of long-term memory as a factor in working memory.

Another main emphasis of the theory is on the habituation and dis-habituation of the orienting response as mechanisms regulating the entry of information into the focus of attention automatically. Some of the psycho-physiological research on habituation of the orienting response helped to provide the basis of the theory in the first place, showing that the orienting response occurs when there is a change in the basic properties of the stimuli or the appearance of an especially significant stimulus (e.g., Gati & Ben-Shakhar, 1990; Öhman, 1979; Waters et al., 1977).

One aspect of the theoretical rationale is especially important in understanding a broad range of behavioral and psychophysiological evidence on what causes an orienting response. Features of the stimuli that have been extracted from the environment can be added to the neural model that is used in a comparison with subsequent stimuli. However, features that have not been extracted obviously cannot contribute. More features will be

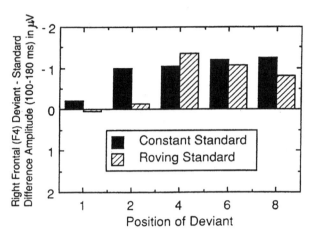

Figure 3.8. Magnitude of the mismatch negativity response in auditory event-related potentials, for constant- and roving-standard conditions with the deviant at various serial positions within a train. Reprinted by permission of the American Psychological Association from Cowan, Winkler, Teder, and Näätänen (1993, p. 915, Figure 3). Copyright © 1993 by the American Psychological Association.

extracted for attended stimuli than for unattended stimuli, and therefore the orienting processes will differ. For example, if an unattended speech channel switches from a discussion of beans to a discussion of flowers, with no change in the physical properties of the channel, no orienting response would be expected. If the channel is attended, the semantic change would be encoded and an orienting response would be expected. The orienting-response literature appears to bear out this difference.

Neuroanatomical Investigations of Working Memory

Cowan (1995, pp. 249–272) ventured to suggest what areas or systems of the brain appear to be involved in each aspect of the model from Cowan (1988), based on literature that is largely beyond the scope of the present chapter. A diagram briefly summarizes the proposals (Figure 3.9). Most of them should be taken as hypotheses to help guide further investigations. Such conjectures may be important because there have been few attempts to synthesize neurological findings related to a broad spectrum of information-processing mechanisms. (1) In electrophysiological and neuroimaging studies related to *sensory memory*, activity in modality-specific cortical areas has been observed; (2) *activated memory* is assumed to be mediated by diverse areas of association cortex, as they appear to become active not only with sensory input but also with the mental imagery and retrieval (e.g., temporal association cortex for auditory imagery); (3) *automatic long-term storage* was tentatively assumed to conform to the proceduralist view in which the brain areas

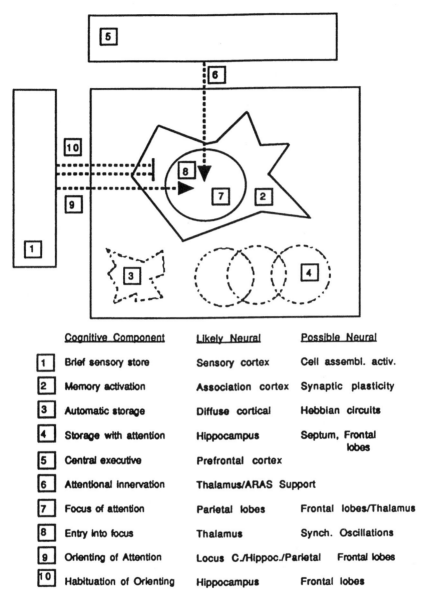

Figure 3.9. Suggestions of areas in the brain underlying various components of the model. Reprinted by permission of Oxford University Press from Cowan (1995, p. 250, Figure 8.1). Copyright © 1995 by Oxford University Press.

active in the original processing of a stimulus or event (often distributed across many areas of the brain) are also involved in the storage of the information related to the event; (4) *attention-related long-term storage* was assumed to take place also in diverse cortical areas, but with the additional critical involvement of the hippocampus and surrounding brain areas, resulting in a much more accessible memory record; (5) the *central executive* was strongly linked to the prefrontal cortex on the basis of neurological deficits and neuroimaging results; (6) based largely on the neuroanatomical organization of the brain, it was suggested that the *innervation or source of attentional activity* flows through the thalamus with the support of the ascending reticular activating system (ARAS); (7) it was suggested that the *focus of attention or awareness* critically involves areas of the parietal lobes, which receive signals from the frontal lobes, the ARAS, and the various sensory systems (the basis for this assumption being that deficits in awareness arise primarily from parietal damage, as opposed to deficits in control, which arise primarily from frontal damage); (8) *entry of information into the focus of attention or awareness* was said to occur via the thalamus, with the possibility that there are synchronous oscillations of various areas representing features of the attended object; and (9) the *orienting of attention* was said to involve the locus ceruleus among other areas, as shown in physiological research, whereas (10) its *habituation* requires the formation of a neural model built up with the help of various cortical areas and hippocampal involvement; with hippocampal damage, habituation of orienting appears to be impaired.

Below I will discuss just two especially critical assumptions in further detail: those related to memory activation (Conjecture 2) and the focus of attention and awareness (Conjecture 7).

MEMORY ACTIVATION. The "memory activation" concept subsumes activities for various modalities and codes, in various parts of the brain. The point of discussing them together under the term *activation* is to acknowledge that these types of activity may be fundamentally similar in their mode of operation in the brain. For example, Cowan (1988) discussed similarities in the time scales for a literal sensory afterimage of the stimulus (about 200 to 300 ms) and for a secondary, more processed sensory representation (about 20 to 30 s) in the auditory, visual, and tactile modalities, and potentially in all modalities.

The areas of the brain involved in perceiving stimuli are assumed to be the same as, or adjacent to, the areas containing the activated representations of the stimuli. The link between perception and activated memory already seems clear in the case of auditory sensory information. Thus, magnetoencephalographic studies indicate temporary changes in the auditory cortex concurrent with auditory sensory memory and its decay (Hari, Kaila, Katila, Tuomisto, & Varpula, 1982; Lü, Williamson, & Kaufman, 1992; Sams et al., 1993), and damage to the temporal cortex has been shown to produce a loss of auditory information in monkeys that is much more rapid and severe than normal (Colombo, D'Amato, Rodman, & Gross, 1990). Perceived, remembered, or imagined features of a particular stimulus all may activate neurons in similar areas of the brain (e.g., Farah, 1988), although truly sensory features in working memory are not fully interchangeable with remembered or imagined features (e.g., Keller et al., 1995). In recent work, there are leads helping to distinguish automatic activation from working-memory processes that require attention (e.g., Miller & Desimone, 1994).

THE FOCUS OF ATTENTION AND AWARENESS. One of the key issues of our time is the neural representation of the focus of attention and awareness. There have been a number of proposals about this, and it is clear that the attentional system encompasses much of the brain (including frontal, parietal, and thalamic areas among others). However, a more specific and difficult challenge will be to differentiate this system into subsystems; for example, those subserving (a) central executive functioning, (b) attention switching and attention maintenance, and (c) the focus of attention or seat of awareness.

One popular view is that the frontal lobes mediate consciousness. However, I do not see how to reconcile it with the neurological evidence that frontal brain damage does not generally result in a loss of awareness, but rather in an impairment of central executive functions such as the maintenance of attention and the instigation, control, organization, planning, and execution of complex activities directed toward a goal. Cowan (1995, pp. 257–261) reviewed evidence that deficits of awareness are more characteristic of inferior parietal lobe damage (e.g., see Schacter, 1989). The parietal areas are typically involved, for example, in cases of anosognosia, in which the patient may be partly paralyzed but denies having any deficit, and in cases of unilateral neglect. Its involvement in attention mechanisms has been studied mostly with visual stimuli, but is not limited to that modality. The inferior parietal lobe and surrounding areas also are qualified for the "focus of attention" role in that they (in particular, Area 7 along with the adjoining Area Tpt of the temporal lobe) are thought by some researchers to be involved in the integration of data from all of the senses together, and perhaps uniquely so (e.g., Hyvärinen, 1982). Thus, there is reason to suspect that these areas (and parts of the thalamus that innervate them) may play a large role in the seat of awareness as opposed to its control.

Research on the parietal lobes has helped to make the point that not all processing is accompanied by conscious awareness of the processed information. In one striking example, Volpe, Ledoux, and Gazzaniga (1979) studied the ability of four patients with right parietal lobe tumors to (a) identify objects in the left and right hemifields and (b) compare objects across hemifields. These patients could make same–different comparisons between the objects in the two hemifields very well (88–100% correct, mean = 93%), but still they were generally unable to identify the objects in the left hemifield (0–48% correct, mean = 18%). For example, one subject correctly responded "different," and when then asked, "what exactly?" responded, "a comb and I don't know what the other was." The parietal lobe damage appears to have affected awareness of the objects without having affected the processing needed for the same–different comparison.

Attention and awareness generally coincide in the normal individual, but they are not logically inseparable. If the left and right parietal lobes are prevented from exchanging signals, as in split-brain individuals (who do not have intact corpus collosums), awareness should be divided in two; and that is the case. However, if attention were the same as awareness, then the attentional capacity also should be divided in two, or at least limited separately in each hemisphere. That, however, is not what is found. Instead, a central capacity limit remains even though awareness is divided into two separated entities. Holtzman and Gazzaniga (1982) found that perceptual tasks in the left and right hemispheres of split-brain patients share processing capacity even though the hemispheres are unaware of each other's tasks. This suggests that attentional capacity and awareness are not logically the same thing, though they work as an integral system normally. There may be a system involving the frontal lobes and thalamic centers that innervates the parietal lobes and determines attentional capacity, whereas the parietal lobe itself is more heavily involved in awareness.

It is important to ask what impact neuroscientific research could have on the present theoretical view. There is a lot of potentially relevant, though as yet indecisive, recent research on the frontal and parietal lobes (e.g., see Beardsley, 1997; Buckner, 1996). Such neuroimaging research theoretically could result in a confirmation, clarification, modification, or disconfirmation of the view espoused by Cowan (1995). A neuroimaging result that simply indicated a dissociation not present in Cowan (1995) is capable of clarifying or modifying the functional theoretical view, but not disconfirming it. For example, the finding that different areas of the prefrontal cortex are involved in different working memory tasks, or that attention and awareness can be dissociated neurally, would not disconfirm the theory, but it might refine it. What would be injurious to the model would be an organization or *alignment* of processes different from the expected one. For example, according to the model, the central executive does not maintain its own duplicate representation of the items in working memory, but instead causes the relevant representations (which exist elsewhere in the brain) to be in the focus of awareness. If it were found that the central executive actually has its own duplicate representation, that would go against the theory. Assuming that certain areas of the prefrontal areas correspond to central executive processes, it should not be found that these areas remain active in a successfully completed working memory trial in the absence of any involvement of other areas in the brain that presumably would contain the memory representation. Moreover, in cases of unattended information held temporarily in a sensory form, the sensory areas but not the frontal lobes should be involved in the task (though the frontal lobes might be busy with other tasks). Thus, the biological implementation is of potential relevance to the cognitive level of modeling.

Concluding Observations

The concept of working memory is central to cognitive psychology because it is assumed to be the vehicle for the retrieval of all information that is needed to carry out a particular task. As such, it is unlikely to be limited to one mechanism; people are likely to use any processing mechanisms at their disposal to come up with the needed information. The use of several mechanisms usually is less taxing than the reliance on any one mechanism. Cowan (1988, 1995) described a processing framework based on the premise that memory activation mechanisms, attentional and executive mechanisms, and long-term retrieval mechanisms all work together in processing to form an effective working memory system. There are still many unknowns, but the modeling framework is designed to organize the knowns and encourage direct tests of some fundamental, unproven assumptions.

REFERENCES

Baars, B. J. (1988). *A cognitive theory of consciousness.* New York: Cambridge University Press.

Baddeley, A. D. (1986). *Working memory.* New York: Oxford University Press.

Balota, D. A. (1983). Automatic semantic activation and episodic memory encoding. *Journal of Verbal Learning and Verbal Behavior, 22,* 88–104.

Banbury, S., & Berry, D. C. (1997). Habituation and dishabituation to speech and office noise. *Journal of Experimental Psychology: Applied, 3,* 181–195.

Beardsley, T. (1997, August). The machinery of thought. *Scientific American, 277,* 78–83.

Bjork, R. A., & Whitten, W. B. (1974). Recency-sensitive retrieval processes in long-term free recall. *Cognitive Psychology, 6,* 173–189.

Broadbent, D. E. (1958). *Perception and communication.* London: Pergamon Press.

Broadbent, D. E. (1975). The magic number seven after fifteen years. In A. Kennedy & A. Wilkes (Eds.), *Studies in long-term memory* (pp. 3–18). New York: Wiley.

Buckner, R. L. (1996). Beyond HERA: Contributions of specific prefrontal brain areas to long-term memory retrieval. *Psychonomic Bulletin & Review, 3,* 149–158.

Cantor, J., & Engle, R. W. (1993). Working memory capacity as long-term memory activation: An individual differences approach. *Journal of Experimental Psychology: Learning, Memory, & Cognition, 19,* 1101–1114.

Caplan, D., & Waters, G. S. (1990). Short-term memory and language comprehension: A critical review of the neuropsychological literature. In G. Vallar & T. Shallice (Eds.), *Neuropsychological impairments of short-term memory* (pp. 337–389). New York: Cambridge University Press.

Chase, W. G. (1977). Does memory scanning involve implicit speech? In S. Dornic (Ed.), *Attention and performance VI* (pp. 607–628). Hillsdale, NJ: Erlbaum.

Clifton, C., & Tash, J. (1973). Effect of syllabic word length on memory-search rate. *Journal of Experimental Psychology, 99,* 231–235.

Colombo, M., D'Amato, M. R., Rodman, H. R., & Gross, C. G. (1990). Auditory association cortex lesions impair auditory short-term memory in monkeys. *Science, 246,* 336–338.

Conrad, R. (1964). Acoustic confusion in immediate memory. *British Journal of Psychology, 55,* 75–84.

Conrad, R., & Hille, B. A. (1958). The decay theory of immediate memory and paced recall. *Canadian Journal of Psychology, 12,* 1–6.

Conway, A. R. A., & Engle, R. W. (1994). Working memory and retrieval: A resource-dependent inhibition model. *Journal of Experimental Psychology: General, 123,* 354–373.

Cowan, N. (1984). On short and long auditory stores. *Psychological Bulletin, 96,* 341–370.

Cowan, N. (1988). Evolving conceptions of memory storage, selective attention, and their mutual constraints within the human information processing system. *Psychological Bulletin, 104,* 163–191.

Cowan, N. (1992). Verbal memory span and the timing of spoken recall. *Journal of Memory and Language, 31,* 668–684.

Cowan, N. (1995). *Attention and memory: An integrated framework.* New York: Oxford University Press.

Cowan, N., Day, L., Saults, J. S., Keller, T. A., Johnson, T., & Flores, L. (1992). The role of verbal output time in the effects of word length on immediate memory. *Journal of Memory and Language, 31,* 1–17.

Cowan, N., Keller, T. A., Hulme, C., Roodenrys, S., McDougall, S., & Rack, J. (1994). Verbal memory span in children: Speech timing clues to the mechanisms underlying age and word length effects. *Journal of Memory and Language, 33,* 234–250.

Cowan, N., Lichty, W., & Grove, T. R. (1990). Properties of memory for unattended spoken syllables. *Journal of Experimental Psychology: Learning, Memory, & Cognition, 16,* 258–269.

Cowan, N., & Saults, J. S. (1995). Memory for speech. In H. Winitz (Ed.), *Human communication and its disorders* (Vol. 4). Timonium, MD: York Press.

Cowan, N., Saults, J. S., & Nugent, L. D. (1997). The role of absolute and relative amounts of time in forgetting within immediate memory: The case of tone pitch comparisons. *Psychonomic Bulletin & Review., 4,* 393–397.

Cowan, N., Winkler, I., Teder, W., & Näätänen, R. (1993). Memory prerequisites of the mismatch negativity in the auditory event-related potential (ERP). *Journal of Experimental Psychology: Learning, Memory, and Cognition, 19,* 909–921.

Cowan, N., Wood, N. L., & Borne, D. N. (1994). Reconfirmation of the short-term storage concept. *Psychological Science, 5,* 103–106.

Cowan, N., Wood, N. L., Nugent, L. D. & Treisman, M. (1997). There are two word length effects in verbal short-term memory: Opposed effects of duration and complexity. *Psychological Science, 8,* 290–295.

Cowan, N., Wood, N. L., Wood, P. K., Keller, T. A., Nugent, L. D., & Keller, C. V. (1998). Two separate verbal processing rates contributing to short-term memory span. *Journal of Experimental Psychology: General., 127,* 141–160.

Crowder, R. G. (1989). Imagery for musical timbre. *Journal of Experimental Psychology: Human Perception and Performance, 15,* 472–478.

Crowder, R. G. (1993). Short-term memory: Where do we stand? *Memory & Cognition*, *21*, 142–145.

Darwin, C. J., Turvey, M. T., & Crowder, R. G. (1972). An auditory analogue of the Sperling partial report procedure: Evidence for brief auditory storage. *Cognitive Psychology*, *3*, 255–267.

Davies, D. R., & Parasuraman, R. (1982). *The psychology of vigilance*. New York: Academic Press.

Deutsch, J. A., & Deutsch, D. (1963). Attention: Some theoretical considerations. *Psychological Review*, *70*, 80–90.

Engle, R. W., Conway, A. R. A., Tuholski, S. W., & Shisler, R. J. (1995). A resource account of inhibition. *Psychological Science*, *6*, 122–125.

Ericsson, K. A., & Kintsch, W. (1995). Long-term working memory. *Psychological Review*, *102*, 211–245.

Farah, M. J. (1988). Is visual imagery really visual? Overlooked evidence from neuropsychology. *Psychological Review*, *95*, 307–317.

Fisher, D. L. (1984). Central capacity limits in consistent mapping, visual search tasks: Four channels or more? *Cognitive Psychology*, *16*, 449–484.

Gati, I., & Ben-Shakhar, G. (1990). Novelty and significance in orientation and habituation: A feature-matching approach. *Journal of Experimental Psychology: General*, *119*, 251–263.

Gernsbacher, M. A. (1993). Less skilled readers have less efficient suppression mechanisms. *Psychological Science*, *4*, 294–298.

Glanzer, M., & Cunitz, A. R. (1966). Two storage mechanisms in free recall. *Journal of Verbal Learning and Verbal Behavior*, *5*, 351–360.

Gray, J. A., & Wedderburn, A. A. I. (1960). Grouping strategies with simultaneous stimuli. *Quarterly Journal of Experimental Psychology*, *12*, 180–184.

Guttentag, R. E. (1984). The mental effort requirement of cumulative rehearsal: A developmental study. *Journal of Experimental Child Psychology*, *37*, 92–106.

Halford, G. S., Maybery, M. T., & Bain, J. D. (1988). Set-size effects in primary memory: An age-related capacity limitation? *Memory & Cognition*, *16*, 480–487.

Hari, R., Kaila, K., Katila, T., Tuomisto, T., & Varpula, T. (1982). Interstimulus interval dependence of the auditory vertex response and its magnetic counterpart: Implications for their neural generation. *Electroencephalography and Clinical Neurophysiology*, *54*, 561–569.

Hasher, L., & Zacks, R. T. (1988). Working memory, comprehension, and aging: A review and a new view. In G. H. Bower (Ed.), *The psychology of learning and motivation* (Vol. 22, pp. 193–225). New York: Academic Press.

Hebb, D. O. (1949). *Organization of behavior*. New York: Wiley.

Hirst, W., Spelke, E. S., Reaves, C. C., Caharack, G., & Neisser, U. (1980). Dividing attention without alternation or automaticity. *Journal of Experimental Psychology: General*, *109*, 98–117.

Holender, D. (1986). Semantic activation without conscious identification in dichotic listening, parafoveal vision, and visual masking: A survey and appraisal. *Behavioral and Brain Sciences*, *9*, 1–66.

Holtzman, J. D., & Gazzaniga, M. S. (1982). Dual task interactions due exclusively to limits in processing resources. *Science*, *218*, 1325–1327.

Hulme, C., Maughan, S., & Brown, G. D. A. (1991). Memory for familiar and unfamiliar words: Evidence for a long-term memory contribution to short-term memory span. *Journal of Memory and Language*, *30*, 685–701.

Hyvärinen, J. (1982). *The parietal cortex of monkey and man.* Berlin: Springer-Verlag.

James, W. (1890). *The principles of psychology.* New York: Henry Holt.

Johnston, W. A., & Heinz, S. P. (1978). Flexibility and capacity demands of attention. *Journal of Experimental Psychology: General, 107,* 420–435.

Just, M. A., & Carpenter, P. A. (1992). A capacity theory of comprehension: Individual differences in working memory. *Psychological Review, 99,* 122–149.

Keller, T. A., Cowan, N., & Saults, J. S. (1995). Can auditory memory for tone pitch be rehearsed? *Journal of Experimental Psychology: Learning, Memory, and Cognition, 21,* 635–645.

Keppel, G., & Underwood, B. J. (1962). Proactive inhibition in short-term retention of single items. *Journal of Verbal Learning and Verbal Behavior, 1,* 153–161.

Lü, Z.-L., Williamson, S. J., & Kaufman, L. (1992). Physiological measures predict behavioral lifetime of human auditory sensory memory. *Science, 258,* 1668–1670.

Mäntysalo, S., & Näätänen, R. (1987). The duration of a neuronal trace of an auditory stimulus as indicated by event-related potentials. *Biological Psychology, 24,* 183–195.

Marcel, A. J. (1983). Conscious and unconscious perception: Experiments on visual masking and word recognition. *Cognitive Psychology, 15,* 197–237.

Martin, R. C. (1993). Short-term memory and sentence processing: Evidence from neuropsychology. *Memory & Cognition, 21,* 176–183.

McGeoch, J. A. (1932). Forgetting and the law of disuse. *Psychological Review, 39,* 352–370.

Miller, E. K., & Desimone, R. (1994). Parallel neuronal mechanisms for short-term memory. *Science, 263,* 520–522.

Miller, G. A. (1956). The magical number seven, plus or minus two: Some limits on our capacity for processing information. *Psychological Review, 63,* 81–97.

Moray, N. (1959). Attention in dichotic listening: Affective cues and the influence of instructions. *Quarterly Journal of Experimental Psychology, 11,* 56–60.

Nairne, J. S. (1990). A feature model of immediate memory. *Memory & Cognition, 18,* 251–269.

Neath, I., & Nairne, J. S. (1995). Word-length effects in immediate memory: Overwriting trace decay. *Psychonomic Bulletin & Review, 2,* 429–441.

Öhman, A. (1979). The orienting response, attention, and learning: An information-processing perspective. In H. K. Kimmel, E. H. Van Olst, & J. F. Orlebeke (Eds.), *The orienting reflex in humans* (pp. 443–471). Hillsdale, NJ: Erlbaum.

Peterson, L. R. & Peterson, M. J. (1959). Short-term retention of individual verbal items. *Journal of Experimental Psychology, 58,* 193–198.

Reitman, J. S. (1974). Without surreptitious rehearsal, information in short-term memory decays. *Journal of Verbal Learning and Verbal Behavior, 13,* 365–377.

Ritter, W., Deacon, D., Gomes, H., Javitt, D. C., & Vaughan, H. G., Jr. (1995). The mismatch negativity of event-related potentials as a probe of transient auditory memory: A review. *Ear and Hearing, 16,* 52–67.

Sams, M., Hari, R., Rif, J., & Knuutila, J. (1993). The human auditory sensory memory trace persists about 10 sec: Neuromagnetic evidence. *Journal of Cognitive Neuroscience, 5,* 363–370.

Schacter, D. L. (1989). On the relation between memory and consciousness: Dissociable interactions and conscious experience. In H. L. Roediger & F. I. M. Craik (Eds.), *Varieties of memory and consciousness: Essays in Honor of Endel Tulving* (pp. 355–389). Hillsdale, NJ: Erlbaum.

Shiffrin, R. M., & Schneider, W. (1977). Controlled and automatic human information processing: II. Perceptual learning, automatic attending, and a general theory. *Psychological Review, 84,* 127–190.

Sokolov, E. N. (1963). *Perception and the conditioned reflex.* New York: Pergamon Press.

Sperling, G. (1960). The information available in brief visual presentations. *Psychological Monographs, 74* (Whole No. 498).

Sternberg, S. (1966). High-speed scanning in human memory. *Science, 153,* 652–654.

Treisman, A. M. (1964). Selective attention in man. *British Medical Bulletin, 20,* 12–16.

Trick, L. M., & Pylyshyn, Z. W. (1993). What enumeration studies can show us about spatial attention: Evidence for limited capacity preattentive processing. *Journal of Experimental Psychology: Human Perception and Performance, 19,* 331–351.

Volpe, B. T., Ledoux, J. E., & Gazzaniga, M. S. (1979). Information processing of visual stimuli in an "extinguished" field. *Nature, 282,* 722–724.

Waters, W. F., McDonald, D. G., & Koresko, R. L. (1977). Habituation of the orienting response: A gating mechanism subserving selective attention. *Psychophysiology, 14,* 228–236.

Watkins, M. J. (1974). Concept and measurement of primary memory. *Psychological Bulletin, 81,* 695–711.

Watkins, M. J., Watkins, O. C., Craik, F. I. M., & Mazuryk, G. (1973). Effect of nonverbal distraction of short-term storage. *Journal of Experimental Psychology, 101,* 296–300.

Wickens, C. D. (1984). Processing resources in attention. In R. Parasuraman & D. R. Davies (Eds.), *Varieties of attention* (pp. 63–102). New York: Academic Press.

Wingfield, A., & Byrnes, D. L. (1972). Decay of information in short-term memory. *Science, 176,* 690–692.

Wood, N., & Cowan, N. (1995). The cocktail party phenomenon revisited: How frequent are attention shifts to one's name in an irrelevant auditory channel? *Journal of Experimental Psychology: Learning, Memory, and Cognition, 21,* 255–260.

Wood, N. L., Stadler, M. A., & Cowan, N. (1997). Is there implicit memory without attention? A re-examination of task demands in Eich's (1984) procedure. *Memory & Cognition, 25,* 772–779.

4 Individual Differences in Working Memory Capacity and What They Tell Us About Controlled Attention, General Fluid Intelligence, and Functions of the Prefrontal Cortex

RANDALL W. ENGLE, MICHAEL J. KANE, AND
STEPHEN W. TUHOLSKI

FIVE CENTRAL FEATURES OF THE THEORY

Working memory is a system consisting of those long-term memory traces active above threshold, the procedures and skills necessary to achieve and maintain that activation, and limited-capacity, controlled attention. The specific features of our model include:

(1) Domain-free, limited-capacity controlled attention.

(2) Domain-specific codes and maintenance (phonological loop and visuospatial sketchpad are two examples but the potential number of such codes is large).

(3) Individual differences in both 1 and 2, but individual differences in capacity for controlled processing are general and possibly the mechanism for general fluid intelligence. Although people can, with practice and expertise, circumvent the abiding limitations of controlled attention in quite specific situations, the limitations reemerge in novel situations and even in the domain of expertise if the situation calls for controlled processing.

(4) Limited-capacity, controlled processing is required for maintaining temporary goals in the face of distraction and interference and for blocking, gating, and/or suppressing distracting events.

(5) The dorsolateral prefrontal cortex (PFC) and associated structures mediate the controlled processing functions of working memory. We also argue that individual differences in controlled processing represent differences in functioning of the PFC.

This work was supported by Grants F49620–93–1–0336 and F49620–97–1–0041 from the Air Force Office of Scientific Research and RO1–HD27490–01A1 from the National Institute of Child Health and Human Development.

A number of intellectual influences have served to shape our thinking about working memory (WM) and its evolution as a construct separate from that of short-term memory (STM). In thinking about the nature of these constructs, both behavioral and biological, we need always be mindful of the tasks that we use to measure them. It is important to understand that tasks vary in validity as measures for their putative constructs. Further, there is no such thing as a pure measure of any construct, including short-term and working memory. This chapter will describe an attempt by our lab to determine construct validity for short-term and working memory measures.

Another influence is an approach to developmental psychology often called "neo-Piagetian," although the ideas can easily be traced back to Baldwin (1894), one of Piaget's early influences. Baldwin and others argued that memory span tasks reflect ability to maintain attention, a fundamental aspect of intellectual abilities, both for the developing human and across individuals at given stages of development (Case, 1985; Pascual-Leone & Baillargeon, 1994; Piaget, 1926). At least in studies with normal adults, however, simple digit and word span tasks do not consistently and reliably predict such mainstays of higher-level cognition as reading or listening comprehension (Perfetti & Lesgold, 1977).

Daneman and Carpenter (1980) developed a span measure called the reading span task that correlated reasonably well with language comprehension measures. Subjects read (or listened to) a list of 2 to 6 sentences. Afterward, the subject recalled the last word of each sentence. This critical measure, the number of sentence-final words recalled, is, on the face of it, very much like a simple word span task. Turner and Engle (1989) developed a similar task in which the subject solved a string of arithmetic operations and then read aloud a word that followed the string. After a series of such operation–word strings, the subject recalled the words.

Both the reading span task and the operation span task are really dual tasks that require the subject to do something (read a sentence or solve an operation string) and, separately and interleaved with this task, to keep track of an evolving and growing list of words. These span tasks, and others developed since, apparently reflect some ability that is fundamentally important to higher-level cognition because measures of working memory capacity reliably predict performance in a wide variety of real-world cognitive tasks. Significant relationships with measures of working memory capacity have been reported for reading comprehension (Daneman & Carpenter, 1980, 1983), language comprehension (King & Just, 1991; MacDonald, Just, & Carpenter, 1992), learning to spell (Ormrod & Cochran, 1988), following directions (Engle, Carullo, & Collins, 1991), vocabulary learning (Daneman & Green, 1986), notetaking (Kiewra & Benton, 1988), writing (Benton Kraft, Glover, & Plake, 1984), reasoning (Kyllonen & Christal, 1990), and complex learning (Kyllonen & Stephens, 1990; Shute, 1991).

Two questions have guided our work over the past 10 years. The first is "What accounts for individual differences on measures of working memory capacity?" More specifically, "What is measured by the complex tasks that is *also* important to higher-level cognitive tasks?" The second question is "What do results of studies on individual differences in WM capacity tell us about the nature of working memory in general?" Our attempts to answer these questions have used a combination of both regression studies and experimental or ANOVA-based studies using extreme groups. The extreme groups are individuals who score in the upper (high WM) and lower (low WM) quartile on a variety of working memory capacity tasks such as the reading span and operation span tasks.

We think of "working memory" as a system consisting of (a) a store in the form of long-term memory traces active above threshold, (b) processes for achieving and maintaining that activation, and (c) controlled attention. However, when we refer to "working memory capacity," we mean the capacity of just one element of the system: controlled attention. We do not mean the entire working memory system, but rather the capabilities of the limited-capacity attention mechanism which Baddeley and Hitch (1974; see also Baddeley & Logie, Chapter 2, this volume) called the central executive. Thus, we assume that "working memory capacity" is not really about storage or memory per se, but about *the capacity for controlled, sustained attention in the face of interference or distraction.* This is conceptually similar to what Norman and Shallice (1986) called the Supervisory Attentional System and is related to what Posner and Snyder (1975) and Schneider and Shiffrin (1977) referred to as controlled attention. The central executive is also likely related to the anterior attention system proposed by Posner and Peterson (1990; see also Gevins, Smith, McEvoy, & Yu, 1997).

We have proposed that individual differences on measures of working memory capacity primarily reflect differences in capability for controlled processing and, thus, will be reflected only in situations that either encourage or demand controlled attention (Conway & Engle, 1994; Engle, Conway, Tuholski, & Shisler, 1995; Rosen & Engle, 1997). Such situations include (a) when task goals may be lost unless they are actively maintained in working memory; (b) when actions competing for responding or response preparation must be scheduled; (c) when conflict among actions must be resolved to prevent error; (d) when there is value in maintaining some task information in the face of distraction and interference; (e) when there is value in suppressing or inhibiting information irrelevant to the task; (f) when error monitoring and correction are controlled and effortful; and (g) when controlled, planful search of memory is necessary or useful.

Our proposal, then, is that working memory capacity reflects the ability to apply activation to memory representations, to either bring them into focus or maintain them in focus, particularly in the face of interference or distraction. We have also argued recently that controlled processing capability is necessary in the case of suppression to either dampen activation of representations or otherwise remove them from focus (Engle et al., 1995). This attention capability is domain free and therefore individual differences in this capability will reveal themselves in a wide variety of tasks. We have also argued (Engle & Oransky, 1999; Kane & Engle, 1998) that differences in working memory capacity correspond to individual differences in the functioning of the prefrontal cortex.

But do the different tasks we refer to as measures of working memory capacity really reflect the same underlying construct? Further, do such tasks measure something different from traditional short-term memory tasks and, if so, what distinguishes them? Engle, Tuholski, Laughlin, and Conway (in press) addressed these questions in a recent study directed at Cowan's (1995; see also Chapter 3, this volume) distinction between short-term memory and working memory and the relationship of these constructs to general fluid intelligence (gF). Cowan considers short-term memory a subset of working memory. Short-term memory is a simple storage component meaning those memory units active above some ambient baseline, whereas the term "working memory" refers to a system consisting of that storage component as well as an attention component. This view is consistent with Baddeley and Hitch's (1974) original model, except the concept of short-term memory is retained and viewed as consistent with the slave systems (the phonological loop and the visuospatial sketchpad). Thus, Cowan's view is that working memory consists of the contents of short-term memory plus controlled attention.

Engle et al. (in press) performed an analysis of the unique and shared variance in tasks thought to reflect STM and WM, the underlying factor structure of that variance, and the extent to which a theory of the two constructs is supported by structural models of the variance in the tasks. Figure 4.1 shows a schematic of a measurement model based on those constructs. Controlled attention can be used to achieve activation of long-term traces through controlled retrieval, to maintain activation through various means, or to dampen activation through inhibition. Short-term memory consists of those traces active above threshold, with loss of activation caused by decay and/or inhibition. The short-term traces could be primarily in the form of phonological features or visual features or, indeed, many other features; however, the traces obey the same principles of forgetting, interference, and so on, regardless of format. Some very small number of those traces receive increased activation through attention resulting from salience to the current task goal or from endogenous activation resulting from emotional salience.

Cowan defined short-term memory as a subset of working memory. Thus, at a conceptual level, variance shared between pure working memory tasks and pure short-term memory tasks should reflect the short-term component. The variance left over (or residual) in working memory tasks after removal of the variance shared by the two tasks should reflect the controlled attention or

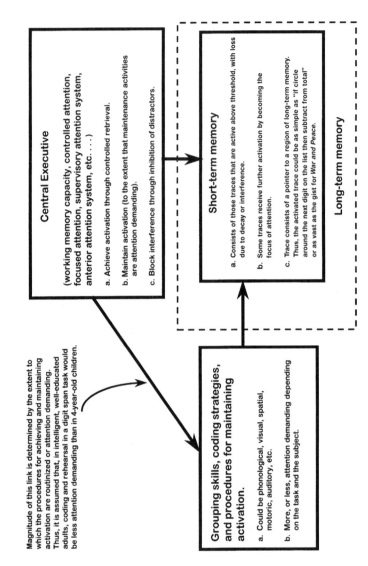

Figure 4.1. A measurement model of the relationship among long-term memory, short-term memory, and the central executive.

Relationship of Components of Working Memory System

Any given WM or STM task reflects all components to some extent

Central Executive

(working memory capacity, controlled attention, focused attention, supervisory attention system, anterior attention system, etc. . . .)

a. Achieve activation through controlled retrieval.

b. Maintain activation (to the extent that maintenance activities are attention demanding).

c. Block interference through inhibition of distractors.

Magnitude of this link is determined by the extent to which the procedures for achieving and maintaining activation are routinized or attention demanding. Thus, it is assumed that, in intelligent, well-educated adults, coding and rehearsal in a digit span task would be less attention demanding than in 4-year-old children.

Grouping skills, coding strategies, and procedures for maintaining activation.

a. Could be phonological, visual, spatial, motoric, auditory, etc.

b. More, or less, attention demanding depending on the task and the subject.

Short-term memory

a. Consists of those traces that are active above threshold, with loss due to decay or interference.

b. Some traces receive further activation by becoming the focus of attention.

c. Trace consists of a pointer to a region of long-term memory. Thus, the activated trace could be as simple as "if circle around the next digit on the list then subtract from total" or as vast as the gist for *War and Peace*.

Long-term memory

central executive component of working memory. However, variance could be shared between short-term memory and working memory tasks at several other levels as well depending on (a) the specific mental procedures, skills, and strategies used to achieve and maintain activation and (b) the specific materials used in the tasks. For example, if both WM and STM tasks used digits in a serial recall task, then individual differences in perceptual grouping or chunking skills, skill at phonological coding, and speed of phonological rehearsal would all contribute to shared variance between the WM and STM tasks. Likewise, skill at imaginal coding and speed of manipulating visual and spatial images would contribute to shared variance to the extent that both types of tasks make use of visual/spatial materials and require similar mental procedures. However, to the extent that STM and WM tasks require *different* procedures, there would be unique variance in each task associated with individual differences in the domain-specific skills and abilities.

Another point at which variance would be shared between the two types of tasks is the extent to which they both rely on controlled attention. To the extent that the different mental procedures do *not* rely on limited-capacity, controlled attention, the shared variance would depend on whether the two tasks shared specific materials or procedures. However, if the procedures required for the STM and WM tasks both require controlled processing, they would tap variance common to the central executive. That would be true even if the materials used in the two types of tasks were from different domains and the procedures required different coding strategies. Thus, there are no "pure" STM or WM tasks. Tasks are graded in the extent to which they are a "good" STM or WM task depending on the overlap in the task content or materials, in the procedures used to perform the task, and on the extent to which the tasks require controlled processing.

We (Kane & Engle, 1998) and others (cf. Duncan, 1995) have made the argument that the construct of working memory capacity is isomorphic with the capacity for controlled processing, which has a strong relationship to general fluid intelligence or *gF*. Fluid intelligence refers to the ability to solve novel problems and is putatively nonverbal and relatively culture free (Horn & Cattell, 1967). The Raven's Standard Progressive Matrices (Raven, Court & Raven, 1977) and the Cattell Culture Fair Test (Institute for Personality and Ability Testing, 1973) were used as our *gF* measures. Both tests consist of visual patterns and the choice of a pattern that would complete the larger target pattern or that would fit a sequence of patterns.

We tested 133 subjects on a variety of tasks that logic and research had led us to believe would be good working memory tasks. These included reading span, operation span, and counting span (a form of the task used by Case, Kurland, and Goldberg, 1982, but modified to require controlled counting). We also used tasks we thought would be good short-term memory tasks including forward-word span with dissimilar words, forward-word span with similar (rhyming) words, and backward-word span with dissimilar words. We also tested all subjects on full versions of the Ravens and Cattell Culture Fair tests.[1]

One question was whether all the memory tasks reflected a single construct or whether a two-factor model (i.e., STM and WM) was necessary. A second question was whether, at the latent variable level, after variance common to WM and STM was removed, the WM residual variance (which should reflect controlled attention) would correlate with the residual for gF, and, whether the STM residual would also correlate with the gF. Of course, the STM residual should not correlate with the gF residual if it reflects only error as our logical analysis would suggest.

Confirmatory factor analysis/structural equation modeling was performed on the three tasks we thought would be good STM tasks and the three we thought would be good WM tasks. The goodness-of-fit results showed that the two-factor model was a significantly better fit than the single-factor model. Thus, the model required a separate construct for working memory capacity and for short-term memory even though the two constructs were strongly related. The next question was whether the two constructs showed any relationship to general fluid intelligence (gF) as indexed by the Ravens and Cattell Culture Fair tests. The analysis showed that the model required a strong connection between the working memory latent variable and general fluid intelligence but did not require a connection between short-term memory and gF.

If our arguments about the relationship among the constructs of working memory, capacity for controlled attention, and gF are correct, then we should be able to test whether controlled attention is related to general fluid intelligence. Starting with all the variance in complex working memory measures, we should be able to remove that variance owing to domain-specific materials and procedures. The residual variance in WM, after removal of the variance common to STM, should reflect the capacity for controlled processing. The WM residual should, therefore, strongly relate to the construct general fluid intelligence. Thus, the line of logic is as follows: (a) complex span tasks of working memory capacity reflect the construct short-term memory *plus* the construct controlled attention; (b) the construct controlled attention has a strong relationship with the construct general fluid intelligence; (c) there is little or no relationship between the construct short-term memory and the construct general fluid intelligence. Therefore, if, at the latent-variable level, we partial out the variance common to the constructs working memory and short-term memory, we would expect the residual variance in working memory capacity to reflect controlled attention. This method of removing com-

[1] Several other tasks were also used, including the ABCD and Continuous Opposites tasks from the CAM4 battery (Kyllonen & Christal, 1990), keeping track task (Yntema, 1963), the primacy and recency portion of immediate free recall, and the random generation task. Scores were obtained on Verbal and Quantitative Scholastic Aptitude Test but those variables are not discussed here.

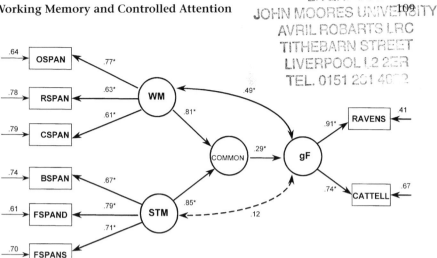

Figure 4.2. Path model with the variance common to STM and WM removed as common and the relationships among the various constructs. The curved lines represent correlations between the construct gF and the residual for STM and WM.

mon variance to see what connections need to be there above and beyond the common factor has been used by Salthouse and his colleagues very effectively to demonstrate the variables important to cognitive declines that occur with aging (Salthouse, 1991). The results of our common-factor analysis are shown in Figure 4.2. The arrows leading to the rectangles reflect the residual variance, and the numbers associated with the arrows between rectangles and circles reflect the standardized regression coefficient between the task (rectangle) and the latent variable. Solid lines reflect a significant link and dotted lines reflect a nonsignificant link. The numbers associated with the two curved lines reflect correlations between the residuals of the STM and WM latent variables after the variance common to the two latent variables is removed.

When the variance common to the STM and WM latent variables is removed, the correlation between the residual of WM and *gF*, which should reflect capacity for controlled attention, is sizable and highly significant. The link between the STM residual and *gF*, which should be entirely error, was, in fact, not significant. This finding is even more impressive if we consider that, despite the fact that STM and WM latent variables are highly correlated, this analysis shows them to be quite separable. Another note about the analysis is that earlier we argued that even the STM tasks would covary with the WM tasks to the extent that controlled processing was necessary. Thus, the analysis depicted in Figure 4.2 actually is a conservative estimate of the correlation between the construct for controlled attention and *gF* because the common factor, which does also have a significant link to *gF*, removes the portion of that variance common to the STM tasks.

The Engle et al. (in press) latent-variable study yields two important conclusions: (a) working memory and short-term memory are highly related but separable constructs, and (b) when we partial out the variance common to STM and WM, the link between the residual of WM and gF, which should theoretically be controlled attention, is high and highly significant. This lends support to the idea that the component of the working memory tasks that is important to higher-order functioning is controlled attention.

As we said earlier, the reading span and operation span are really dual tasks and so should tap the subject's capability to sustain, divide, or switch attention between these task components. One component can be thought of as a processing task, reading the sentence, or solving the arithmetic string, and the other can be thought of as a storage task, recalling the gradually lengthening list of words or digits. One possible alternative reason that these tasks correlate with higher-order measures of cognition is that individuals differ in skill on the processing component as a result of experience; this processing efficiency frees up resources to be used to rehearse the items in the storage task.[2] Engle, Cantor, and Carullo (1992) measured the time it took subjects to perform the processing component of the reading span and operation span tasks. They then used these times as measures of processing efficiency and/or the extent to which subjects traded off time on the processing component for time on the storage component. The processing-skill explanation of the relationship between WM measures and measures of higher-order cognition suggests that when the measure of processing time is partialed out of the relationship between complex span and reading ability, the correlation should significantly decrease if not disappear. However, Engle et al. showed that partialing out the processing-time measure led to *no* decrease in the correlation between span and the Verbal Scholastic Aptitude Test.

A study by Conway and Engle (1996) approached this same issue differently. Instead of statistically controlling for processing skill, they attempted to equate, across subjects, the processing demands of the span task. The logic was quite simple. If the relationship between the WM measure and reading comprehension is a result of trade-off between the processing and storage components, then when the difficulty of the processing component is equated, the correlation between the span measure and reading comprehension should disappear. On the other hand, if the correlation between the WM measure and comprehension is a result of a controlled attention capability above and beyond the trade-off, then equating subjects on the difficulty of the processing task should have no effect on the correlation. Conway and Engle pretested subjects on operations of the type used in the operation span task but differing greatly along a dimension of difficulty. The pretest determined the point on the difficulty dimension at which each subject solved

---

[2] It should be noted that this makes the storage component even more like the short-term memory latent variable in the Engle, Tuholski, Laughlin, and Conway analysis.

operations accurately 75%, 85%, and 95% of the time. Each subject then received an operation–word span task in which the sets of operations were created specifically for that subject. One set was created separately at each of the 75%, 85%, and 95% levels, specifically for each subject. One question was whether the correlation between the operation span score and reading comprehension would disappear since the procedure equated the processing skill component. The second was whether the correlations between the resulting span scores and reading comprehension would differ as the processing component of the span test varied in difficulty from 75% to 95% accuracy. The answer to both questions was a resounding NO. The correlation between the span score and Verbal Scholastic Aptitude test for the easy 95% condition was .62 and for the difficult 75% condition the correlation was .54. This compares to a correlation of .59 for the same sample of subjects on an operation span test in which all subjects receive the same set of operations. Conway and Engle also measured the time each subject took to perform the operation-processing component in the various tasks and statistically removed this solution time from the aforementioned correlations. The effects were virtually identical, with a partial correlation of .60 for the easy condition and .52 for the difficult condition. Clearly, skill on the processing component had no bearing on the significant and high correlation between this measure of working memory capacity and a measure of reading ability.

These findings show, quite convincingly, that the correlation between measures of working memory capacity and higher-order cognitive tasks is *not* a result of skill in the specific processing components of the WM tasks. These findings are hard to reconcile with the views of Ericsson and Delaney (Chapter 8, this volume) and O'Reilly, Braver, and Cohen (Chapter 11, this volume) that individual differences in WM capacity represent differences in skill resulting from experience. The findings do support our view that the critical feature of the tasks accounting for the correlations with higher-order cognition is some aspect of controlled attention, and that it represents a rather abiding characteristic of the individual.

We have recently completed two longitudinal studies with young children that further support this conclusion. In one study, children were given a series of WM tasks and an age-appropriate listening-comprehension test at ages 3.5, 4.5, and 5.5. The memory measures for each year predicted the subsequent year's comprehension scores; however, the comprehension scores for each year did *not* predict the subsequent year's memory measures. Moreover, the WM scores at age 3.5 accounted for 27.5% of the variance in comprehension at 5.5. Interestingly, the WM scores were better predictors of comprehension at age 5.5 than at 3.5 or 4.5, suggesting that controlled attention is not as important for comprehension at younger ages but becomes more important by age 5.5.

A second longitudinal study investigated the relationship between working memory capacity and inhibition in children. Adele Diamond and her

colleagues (Gerstadt, Hong, & Diamond, 1994) have argued that development of the ability to inhibit or suppress prepotent or predisposed behaviors
corresponds with the development of the frontal lobes. They performed a
study in which children were shown pictures of the moon and stars and were
required to say "day" and a picture of a sun and were required to say "night."
Though the children could perform the task initially, performance deterio-
rated over the 16 trials. Performance improved over the ages at which the
frontal lobes are thought to be completing their development. The conclusion was that maturation of the frontal lobes was necessary to inhibit the
prepotent response and allow performance of the lower-strength response
instead. In our second longitudinal study, children were tested on measures
of WM capacity and a "Stroop-like" test in which they were shown line drawings of a traditional mother (long skirt, hair in bun, etc.) and asked to call it
"dad" and a drawing of an adult male (pants, facial hair, etc.) and asked to
call it "mom." Scores on the WM tasks measured at age 3.5 predicted Stroop
accuracy 2 years later (with correlations ranging from .34 to .40; span scores
given at the same age as the Stroop task correlated with Stroop from .33 to
.38). These studies suggest that relatively simple measures, which we argue
reflect capacity for controlled attention, are valid measures for very young
children and that they reflect an abiding ability important to higher-level
cognition.

Working Memory, General Fluid Intelligence, and Controlled Attention

The behavioral evidence discussed thus far certainly suggests that individual
differences in working memory and in general fluid intelligence are significantly related to one another and that they probably do not depend on differences in general knowledge or specific procedural skills. Our discussion of
latent-variable results and individual-differences work on WM tasks themselves tentatively suggests that controlled attention capabilities lie at the
heart of individual differences in working memory capacity. We briefly review
some further evidence below. We will then focus our discussion on a recent
set of studies from our lab that explicitly ties together WM capacity, general
fluid intelligence, and controlled-attention constructs.

   The evidence that people who differ on indices of working memory show
systematic differences in other controlled attention measures may be found
from studies of both perceptual and memory interference. In perceptual interference tasks, subjects typically must identify visual target stimuli that appear
simultaneously amidst salient visual distractors. In memory interference
tasks, subjects are required to recall some subset of previously presented information while disregarding similar prior information. In both classes of tasks,
attention must be selectively directed toward some information sources
(external or internal) and away from others. In both classes of tasks, high-

span subjects outperform low-span subjects. For example, in a perceptual interference task (negative priming), high-span subjects appear to inhibit visual distractors during selection whereas low spans do not (Conway, Tuholski, Shisler, & Engle, 1998).

Furthermore, on selective-attention tasks involving memory distraction, low spans experience more proactive and retroactive interference than do high spans (Conway & Engle, 1994; Kane & Engle, 1997; Rosen & Engle, 1998). In verbal fluency tasks, where subjects generate exemplars from a category such as "animals," low spans recall few exemplars compared to high spans. This is particularly true across long retrieval periods where competition (distraction) from already-recalled, high-probability exemplars should be high (Rosen & Engle, 1997). Finally, performance on interference and attention-switching tasks is severely disrupted by the imposition of a simultaneous working memory load – that is, by a divided attention requirement (Engle et al., 1995; Kane & Engle, 1997; Law, Morrin, & Pellegrino, 1995; Roberts, Hager, & Heron, 1994).

Furthermore, people who differ in psychometric intelligence also show differences in controlled attention capabilities that are similar to those seen across subjects who differ in working memory. For example, correlations between gF and controlled-visual-search tasks are high under *variably mapped conditions*, where specific stimuli may appear as targets or distractors across trials and so *automaticity is unlikely* to develop. Correlations between gF and visual search are low, however, under *consistently mapped conditions*, where specific stimuli appear only as targets or as distractors, and so *automaticity is likely* to develop (e.g., Ackerman, 1988). Thus, performance under controlled processing, as opposed to automatic processing, correlates with psychometric gF. Furthermore, individuals with low scores on psychometric gF tests are more disrupted by perceptual distractors than are those who score high on gF tests (e.g., Blanco & Alvarez, 1994; Witkin & Goodenough, 1981). Low-gF individuals have more difficulty initiating shifts of attention from one stimulus location or modality to another when the shifting rules must be maintained in working memory (e.g., Duncan, 1995; Duncan, Emslie, Williams, Johnson, & Freer, 1996). Finally, scores on tests of psychometric gF predict the ability to divide attention among simultaneous tasks or among competing stimuli, with high-gF individuals being the more effective "timesharers" (e.g., Hunt, 1980; Morrin, Law, & Pellegrino, 1994; Pellegrino, Hunt, & Yee, 1989; Stankov, 1983).

Thus, individuals with poor working memory capabilities, and those of lower psychometric intelligence, do indeed show similar patterns of performance to each other. When tasks demand that subjects selectively focus attention amidst external or internal sources of distraction, or that subjects shift attention according to memorized rules, or that subjects divide their attention between different stimuli or tasks, working memory capacity and psychometric gF scores are good predictors of performance.

But do we have any direct support for this idea that capability for controlled processing is the critical element common to the working memory tasks, tests of general fluid intelligence, and tests of higher-order functions such as reading comprehension? A recent set of studies performed by Tuholski (1997) might provide that support. He used a speeded-counting task that, though quite ancient (Jevons, 1871), was recently repopularized by Trick and Pylyshyn (1993). The task requires the subject to simply count from 1 to n presented objects as quickly as possible. The time to count objects is a nonlinear function of the number of objects with the slope of the function nearly flat over the first 3 to 4 objects but rising steeply from 4 to n. The argument is that subjects retrieve the number of objects from 1 to 4 automatically (i.e., they subitize) and as a single pattern. However, counting the number of objects of number 4 and higher requires controlled processing, hence the steeper slope of the counting time function (Trick & Pylyshyn, 1993). Tuholski reasoned that, if high and low working memory capacity subjects differ in their capacity for controlled attention, that difference should be reflected in the time to count from 4 to n objects but not in the time to subitize from 1 to 4 objects. Further, if controlled attention is related to general fluid intelligence, the slope of the counting function for more than 4 objects should correlate with a measure of gF. An independent prediction is that high and low WM subjects might differ in the size of the pattern they could subitize, with high spans possibly able to pick up a larger number of objects in the initial encoding than are low WM subjects. If that were true, then we should see the flat subitizing function extending over more targets for high WM subjects than for low WM subjects.

Tuholski (1997) tested 60 subjects who had been previously tested on the operation span task and the Cattell Culture Fair test. For the counting task, 1 to 12 vertical yellow bars were arranged randomly on a computer screen and the subject counted them silently, as quickly as possible without sacrificing accuracy, and then gave an oral response of the total, which activated a speech trigger. The 15 subjects who scored in the upper quartile on the operation span task were selected as high WM subjects and the 15 scoring in the bottom quartile were selected as the low WM subjects. The size of the subitizing range was determined by doing a series of incremental analyses that tested linear and quadratic trends as the number of targets increased from 1 to n. The subitizing span was indicated when the quadratic trend became significant. Thus, if the quadratic trend was not significant over the range 1 to 3 but was significant over the range 1 to 4, this indicated the subject had subitized 3 objects but not 4. This analysis showed that high WM subjects had a subitizing span of 3.35 and low WM subjects had a subitizing span of 3.25, quite remarkably similar and refuting the possibility that high and low WM individuals differed in the size of the initial pattern they were able to perceive. As shown in Figure 4.3, the slope over the subitizing range, presumed to reflect automatic processing, was flat and not different for the two groups. However,

Counting time as a function of # targets

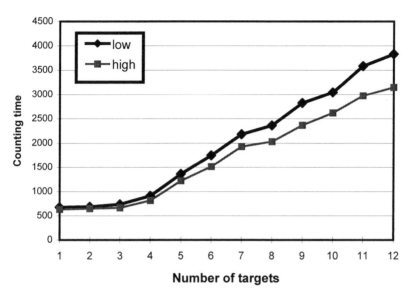

Figure 4.3. Counting time as a function of number of targets in the Tuholski study.

high and low WM subjects did differ dramatically over the counting range presumed to require controlled attention.

Tuholski then looked at correlations among the slope of counting time over the range 4 to 12, the slope of the subitizing function, operation span, and the Cattell Culture Fair test for all 60 subjects. First, the correlation between operation span and Cattell was .52, a strong correlation between a measure of working memory capacity and a nonverbal test of spatial reasoning and general fluid intelligence. The slope of the counting function correlated with both operation span (–.32) and with the Cattell measure of gF (–.26) but the subitizing slope correlated with neither.

Why do high and low WM subjects differ in counting time from 4 to 12? What is it that requires controlled attention? We think that the difficult part in counting beyond the subitizing range is keeping track of what you have already counted and that high WM subjects are better able to keep active the tags that indicate an object has been counted. In other words, this is another example of a task that puts a premium on maintaining a representation in an active and easily accessible state and individuals with greater capability for controlled processing are better able to do that.

In a second study, Tuholski did a manipulation that should lead to controlled counting even over the subitizing range. He included distractors that either shared physical features (orientation or color) with the targets, the *con-*

junctive condition, or distractors that did not share physical features with targets, the *disjunctive* condition. This manipulation, following the work of Treisman and Gelade (1980), should cause controlled counting even over the subitizing range in the conjunctive condition but not in the disjunctive condition. The results were clear that high and low WM subjects differed even in the counting of 1 to 3 objects in the conjunctive condition but not in the disjunctive condition. The correlation analysis showed that, in the disjunctive condition, the slope of the counting range correlated with the measure of WM capacity and the measure of *gF* but the slope over the subitizing range did not. In the conjunctive condition, however, the slope of the counting range and the slope over the subitizing range both correlated with the WM and *gF* measures.

In these two studies, Tuholski (1997) has provided support for the idea that controlled processing is one of the critical elements of measures of working memory capacity. The task used in these studies does not involve recall of words or digits, and it does not involve reading or performing mathematical operations. It involves simple counting, one of the first procedures we learn as children. Nevertheless, over the two studies, it took low WM subjects nearly 700 ms longer to count 12 objects than it did high WM subjects! The results also provide additional support for the idea that capability for controlled attention is the important connection between working memory capacity and general fluid intelligence.

Both the latent-variable study by Engle et al. (in press) and the Tuholski (1997) studies with counting showed that measures of working memory capacity, all based on processing and/or storage of verbal material, strongly correlated with tests of spatial reasoning and general fluid intelligence. These findings support our argument that controlled attention capability, as assessed by the measures of working memory capacity, is domain free and general.

Working Memory, *gF*, and the "Front of the Mind"

To what can we attribute these individual differences in WM capacity, controlled attention, and general fluid intelligence? A diverse body of research suggests some specific neurobiological substrates to working memory, controlled attention, and general fluid intelligence. Before reviewing this evidence, however, let us first briefly note that biological explanations of behavioral phenomena do not necessitate genetic causes. Even the biological substrates of cognitive individual differences must be shaped by both environmental and genetic factors.

Generally speaking, the research regarding working memory and controlled attention has pointed to the prefrontal cortex (PFC), and more specifically to the dorsolateral region of the PFC (areas 9, 10, and 46 of Brodmann and Walker in humans and macaques), as critical to many working memory and controlled-attention capabilities. The research has used methods such as surgery and/or single-cell recording with nonhuman primates, cognitive testing of human patients with brain damage, and cognitive testing of healthy humans under various brain-imaging techniques. Each one of these methods has inherent limitations, and the PFC is clearly a heterogeneous region both structurally and functionally. Nevertheless, we believe that the confluence from the various methods provides an emerging story of working memory and PFC functioning (for recent reviews see Duncan, 1995; Goldman-Rakic, 1987; Pennington, 1994; see also O'Reilly et al., Chapter 11, this volume).

We first discuss experiments that demonstrate the role of the PFC in working memory functions associated with tasks that require simultaneous (or alternating) storage and processing of information. Next, we review findings that suggest PFC involvement in more "classic" controlled-attention tasks, such as those requiring the maintenance, focusing, or shifting of attention. Finally, we consider evidence that the PFC is critical to tasks that most effectively tap general fluid intelligence or *gF*.

Working Memory and the PFC

With macaques, working memory research has focused on so-called delay tasks (such as *delayed response, delayed alternation,* and *delayed matching-to-sample*). On each trial, a stimulus (an object or stimulus location) is briefly presented and is then removed from view for some delay duration. Following the delay, the monkey must recognize the stimulus from among distractors. The stimuli are typically chosen from a small pool and tested repeatedly across trials, which would create a high potential for proactive interference. Monkeys with surgical lesions to dorsolateral PFC, or with temporary "lesions" from cortical cooling or electrical stimulation, show chance levels of recall on these delay tasks. Deterioration in performance is found even with delays of only a few seconds (e.g., Fuster & Bauer, 1974; Jacobsen, 1936; Mishkin & Pribram, 1955, 1956).

Several brain areas that are anatomically connected with the dorsolateral PFC also appear to be important to delay-task performance. For example, lesions to certain parietal, hippocampal, and subcortical regions produce deficits that mirror those produced by PFC lesions (e.g., Koch & Fuster, 1989; Kojima & Goldman-Rakic, 1982, 1984; Watanabe & Niki, 1985). Such findings make sense, because these structures are significantly interconnected with the PFC. Further, as we argued above, there are no such tasks as "pure" WM and STM tasks and, thus, no complex cognitive task is likely to rely on a single brain region in isolation. Delay-task performance thus appears to involve integrated neural networks that operate together to retain information across temporal delays.

One might be wary of our reference to these delay tasks as working memory tasks. After all, on the surface they appear to have more in common with human short-term memory tasks, for they seem to require only information

storage, and not much simultaneous processing. However, these tasks typically demand that the monkey's attention be drawn away from the to-be-
recalled information during the delay either by placing a physical barrier
between the subject and the stimuli, by requiring subjects' eyes to remain
fixed at a neutral location, or by requiring subjects to extend their hand
toward a neutral stimulus. Thus, just as in span tasks inspired by the Baddeley
and Hitch (1974) model, these delay tasks require subjects to remember stimuli to which they are only intermittently permitted to attend.

This point is made all the more clear by an experiment by Malmo (1942)
that demonstrated that macaques with large PFC lesions showed delay-task
deficits *only* when the testing chamber remained brightly lit during the delay.
When the chamber was darkened during the delay, thus reducing visible distractions, no deficits were evident. *It appears, then, that the PFC is critical to
maintaining the memorial activation of information across shifts in attention.*

The delays used in human research are typically longer than those used
with nonhuman primates (i.e., 10 to 20 s). Nevertheless, humans with PFC
damage show more forgetting in delay tasks than do healthy subjects or control patients with comparable damage to posterior brain areas (Chorover &
Cole, 1966; Verin et al., 1993).

Imaging studies with healthy human subjects indicate that working memory tasks elicit significant increases in dorsolateral PFC activity compared to
non–working memory tasks. For example, in PET studies using short-term
memory tasks that merely require subjects to retain information across short
delays, there is limited evidence of frontal lobe activation. Where activation
has been observed, it was not centered in the dorsolateral PFC, but in more
ventral areas such as Broca's area and/or in premotor cortex and supplementary motor area (e.g., Dupont et al., 1993; Smith, Jonides, & Koeppe, 1996).

In contrast, other imaging studies that required subjects to retain information across longer delays, or to shift attention between storage and processing
functions, such as in the "*N*-back" task, did show PFC activation. In the *N*-
back task subjects must monitor a long sequence of visual or auditory stimuli
and continuously report the stimulus that occurred *n* (1 to 3) stimuli ago in
the sequence. Such tasks clearly involve more information storage and processing than do short-delay tasks, and so it is no surprise that significant dorsolateral PFC activation is seen during the performance of these tasks (e.g.,
Cohen et al., 1994).

In sum, evidence from a variety of tasks and subject populations clearly
shows that PFC lesions cause considerable difficulties on working memory
tests, and that PFC structures increase their activity while the subject is performing working memory tests but not during short-term memory tests. The
existing data suggest that the dorsolateral PFC, and regions to which it is networked, are critical to working memory functions, that is in behavioral tasks
that require retention of information across shifts of attention. Therefore, we
think it is reasonable to contemplate the possibility that individual differ-

ences in working memory capacity among normal individuals are mediated through individual differences in PFC functioning.

Controlled Attention and the PFC

Attention is complex and multidimensional, and so it may be naive to presume that all controlled processing is accomplished by a single brain region. Indeed, the neuroscience of attention has suggested broad networks of cortical and subcortical regions that participate in various attentional functions (e.g., Posner & Peterson, 1990). But, though current theories may not all agree on the precise function of the PFC, most theories would suggest it has an integral role in controlled attention. Below we briefly review the empirical evidence for PFC involvement in maintenance, focusing, and shifting attention, most of which includes human studies using neuropsychological testing or imaging.

Regarding attention maintenance, experiments with brain-damaged humans have shown that patients with PFC lesions show marked difficulty with vigilance tasks. On those tasks that require subjects to maintain attention to long series of stimuli while in search of rare targets, patients with PFC damage miss more targets and commit more false alarms than do control patients (e.g., Salmaso & Denes, 1982; Wilkins, Shallice, & McCarthy, 1987). In visual and auditory detection tasks with healthy humans, PFC areas (along with some parietal areas) show increased activation compared to baseline conditions (Cohen et al., 1988; Pardo, Fox, & Raichle, 1991). Furthermore, PFC activation changes are also seen during habituation. Here, one might expect that if the PFC is critical to attention maintenance, then its role (and hence its activation) should decrease as a habituated context demands less and less attention. Indeed, this appears to be the case. Warach et al. (1992) found decreased PFC (and inferior parietal) blood flow across three 14-min rest periods in which the testing context became less novel. No changes in blood flow were evident in temporal, occipital, or superior parietal areas across these rest periods.

As in the working memory and intelligence literatures, the PFC's selective attention functions may be measured in perceptual and memory interference tasks. In perceptual interference tasks, nonhuman primates with PFC lesions clearly demonstrate increased perceptual distractibility. They are often hyperactive in brightly lit, but not in dimly lit, environments (e.g., Isaac & DeVito, 1958; Settlage, Zable, & Harlow, 1948), and they have difficulty performing previously learned visual discrimination tasks when visual or auditory distractors are presented simultaneously with the target stimuli (Grueniger & Pribram, 1969).

Humans with PFC damage also show a heightened susceptibility to perceptual distractors, but it may only be evident when a simultaneous memory load is also imposed. For example, PFC damage reliably impairs performance in the classic Stroop (1935) color–word interference task only in discrete-trial procedures with a random sequence of trials on which some color–word combinations match and some mismatch (e.g., Vendrell et al., 1995). It is also under these same Stroop conditions that PFC areas show evidence of activation in imaging studies with healthy subjects (e.g., Bench et al., 1993). In contrast, if patients perform the Stroop task in which all color–word combinations either match or mismatch within a block, PFC-lesions sometimes do (Perret, 1974; Richer et al., 1993), but often do not, lead to significant deficits (e.g., Ahola, Vikki, & Servo, 1991; Butters, Kaszniak, Glisky, Eslinger, & Schacter, 1994; Shallice & Burgess, 1991). It thus appears that PFC involvement in Stroop performance will be found consistently only when the task demands must be constantly maintained in working memory (see Richer et al., 1993).

Memory interference paradigms also suggest that the PFC is important to the control of selective attention. In proactive interference tasks, in which subjects must recall only the most recent of a series of memory lists, patients with PFC damage have difficulty in limiting recall to the target list. Frontal-lesion patients recall fewer target words as the successive lists proceed, and they make more intrusion errors from prior lists than do controls (e.g., Freedman & Cermak, 1986; Parkin, Leng, & Stanhope, 1988; Van der Linden, Bruyer, Roland, & Schils, 1993). Imaging data also point to the PFC as crucial to interference resistance, because dorsolateral and anterior PFC areas show increased activity in healthy subjects when they attempt to recall words under high-interference conditions but not under low-interference conditions (Uhl et al., 1990; Uhl, Podreka, & Deecke, 1994).

Finally, increased interference susceptibility may be inferred from the performance of PFC-lesioned patients in verbal fluency tasks. When subjects are asked to recall category exemplars for periods of longer than 5 min, patients with PFC lesions recall fewer instances than do patients with nonfrontal lesions (e.g., Milner, 1964; Pendleton, Heaton, Lehman, & Hulihan, 1982; Perret, 1974). The longer recall period likely places a premium on controlled, effortful search and increases the interference from previously recalled items (Rosen & Engle, 1997). Additionally, imaging studies show significant left-PFC activation in healthy adults during long-duration fluency tests (e.g., Cuenod et al., 1995; Frith, Friston, Liddle, & Frackowiak, 1991). However, when recall periods are 2 min or less, recall can likely occur more on the basis of automatic spreading activation and PFC lesions appear to have little effect on recall (e.g., Joanette & Goulet, 1986; Newcombe, 1969; Shallice & Burgess, 1991).

Research on attention shifting has also implicated the PFC in attentional control. Some of the "evidence," however, is based more in clinical folklore than in fact. For example, the Wisconsin Card Sorting Test (Berg, 1948; Grant & Berg, 1948) and the Trail Making Tests (Armitage, 1946) are two neuropsychological tests that are widely believed to tap attentional-shifting capabilities and to be sensitive to frontal lobe damage (for reviews see Reitan & Wolfson,

1994, 1995). In fact, whereas some studies show Wisconsin Card Sorting Test deficits in patients with PFC injury (e.g., Drewe, 1974; Milner, 1963; Nelson, 1976), many others do not (e.g., Anderson, Damasio, Jones, & Tranel, 1991; Grafman, Jones, & Salazar, 1990; Shallice & Burgess, 1991). Furthermore, no studies to date indicate substantial Trail Making Test deficits for frontal-lesion patients compared to nonfrontal-lesion patients (e.g., Reitan & Wolfson, 1995; Shallice & Burgess, 1991). Clearly, any conclusions about the role of the PFC in attention shifting should not be based on findings from these tests.

However, there is limited evidence from other tests that are conceptually related to the Wisconsin Card Sorting Test that PFC damage impairs performance when attention must be shifted away from a previously learned discrimination in favor of a new discrimination. These findings suggest that simpler measures of attention shifting may be selectively sensitive to PFC lesions (e.g., Delis, Squire, Bihrle, & Massman, 1992; Harlow & Dagnon, 1943; Owen, Roberts, Polkey, Sahakian, & Robbins, 1991). In addition, an oral version of the Trail Making Test, in which the subject must count aloud an alternating progression of letters and numbers, and so must also *maintain the last reported letters and numbers in working memory*, appears to discriminate PFC-lesioned subjects from nonfrontal-lesioned subjects (Ricker, Axelrod, & Houtler, 1996). Finally, tasks in which subjects must switch their visual attention from one spatial location to another on demand (and in opposition to a salient cue) indicate that patients with PFC damage perform more poorly than do patients with nonfrontal damage (e.g., Duncan et al., 1996; Pierrot-Deseilligny, Rivaud, Gaymard, & Agid, 1991).

A growing body of work using varied methodologies and subject populations thus supports the notion that the PFC is an important structure to the functioning of attention. As inferred from patients with PFC damage, and from imaging studies with healthy subjects, the PFC is an active participant in attention maintenance, selection, and shifting. Again, it seems plausible that individual differences in these attention functions among normal, healthy individuals are mediated by individual differences in PFC functioning.

General Intelligence and the PFC

If working memory and controlled attention rely on intact PFC functioning, then the behavioral research we described earlier surely suggests that general intelligence should also depend heavily on PFC structures. Indeed, patients with PFC damage show problems with complex, everyday cognitive activities (e.g., Lezak, 1983; Luria, 1966; Shallice & Burgess, 1991). It may be surprising, then, that clinical and experimental reports indicate that PFC injury has little effect on intelligence as defined by conventional psychometric IQ tests (e.g., Ackerly, 1937; Hebb, 1945; Hebb & Penfield, 1940). Duncan (1995) attempted to resolve this paradox by arguing that broad IQ test batteries assess crystallized knowledge as well as general fluid intelligence whereas novel reasoning tests such as the Raven's Progressive Matrices or the Cattell

Culture Fair have very high *gF* loadings (e.g., Carroll, 1993; Snow, Kyllonen, & Marshalek, 1984). WAIS-R subtests such as Vocabulary and Information, for example, more accurately reflect *gF* at the time of learning, and not necessarily at the time of testing. Averaging across high-*gF* and low-*gF* subtests in conventional IQ tests may thus dilute any real effect that PFC lesions have on *gF*.

To test this idea, Duncan, Burgess, and Emslie (1995) matched three patients with frontal lobe lesions (of mixed etiologies) to healthy controls on age and on their overall WAIS or WAIS-R scores, with these scores ranging from 126 to 130. These subjects were then administered the Cattell Culture Fair test, as a measure of *gF*. All of the frontal-lesion patients showed a significant drop in "intelligence" (22–38 points) from their WAIS to their Cattell scores. In contrast, their matched controls showed *equivalent or higher* Cattell scores than WAIS scores. Moreover, the Culture Fair IQs of the frontal-lesion patients were significantly lower (by 23 to 60 points, or 3 standard deviations) than those of their controls. Finally, a group of 5 patients with posterior cortex damage, with significantly lower WAIS or WAIS-R scores than the other subject groups, showed IQ patterns similar to those of the control subjects. Although these findings involved few subjects and therefore demand replication, they do provide rather striking preliminary evidence that the PFC is significantly involved in the performance of tasks that load highly onto psychometric *gF*.

These clinical data are consistent with a recent imaging study with healthy adults (Prabhakaran, Smith, Desmond, Glover, & Gabrieli, 1997; see also Risberg, Maximilian, & Prohovnik, 1977). Seven subjects solved Raven's Progressive Matrices problems while undergoing fMRI scans. Activation patterns were compared across different subtypes of Raven's problems: those that required only figural reasoning and those that additionally required more abstract analytical reasoning. Figural reasoning activated the right dorsolateral PFC (and some networked posterior areas). However, analytical reasoning activated dorsolateral PFC bilaterally (as well as other PFC areas and posterior areas bilaterally). Thus, when the task required more general, less-specialized reasoning, greater bilateral PFC activation was observed.

The intelligence findings reviewed earlier, in concert with those concerning working memory/attention, then, converge to tell a consistent story. *The PFC may be the critical brain structure mediating functions of, and individual differences in, working memory, controlled attention, and general intelligence in normal, healthy individuals.*

Speculations, Suggestions, and Conclusions

Do individual differences in working memory, attention, and general intelligence arise from individual differences in PFC functioning? In this chapter we first discussed correlational and experimental studies indicating that working memory and general intelligence constructs are intimately linked – if not isomorphic. We then reviewed neuropsychological evidence suggesting that working memory, attention, and *gF* are all subserved by the PFC and the various posterior regions to which it is networked.

It is therefore very tempting to conclude that individual differences in working memory/controlled attention and general intelligence are mediated strictly by individual differences in PFC functioning or efficiency. We must be careful, however, because in the absence of other supporting evidence, the fact that PFC damage causes working memory/attention dysfunction does not *necessarily* dictate that working memory/attention dysfunction reflects PFC damage (or differences). This result could instead reflect the fact that the PFC is heavily interconnected to other important processing regions. For example, research with macaques shows that specific lesions to posterior or subcortical brain areas to which the PFC is networked produce PFC-lesion-like syndromes in delay task performance. Likewise, human neuropsychological research indicates that damage to some posterior brain areas (or widely diffuse brain damage) elicits PFC-lesion-like impairments on some working memory and attention tasks. Finally, we know from human brain-imaging studies that some posterior brain areas anatomically connected to the PFC are highly activated during the performance of working memory, attention, and psychometric *gF* tasks.

Such findings do not rule out the importance of the PFC to working memory/attention and *gF*, or to individual and group differences therein. Rather, the PFC is not *uniquely* important to these, or probably to any other functions. The PFC appears to be a necessary brain structure in the emergence of working memory/attention behaviors, but is not the only important structure for these functions (see also O'Reilly et al., Chapter 11, this volume). Thus, individual or group differences that are observed in working memory/attention capabilities *may* reflect specific differences in PFC functioning. But we need to be cautious and point out the possibility that they reflect discrete differences in posterior cortical areas or, indeed, diffuse variations across many brain regions. An interesting question for further research, then, is whether imaging techniques suggest individual differences in brain structure or volume to be more pronounced in anterior than in posterior cortex. If there is more variation across frontal areas than across parietal or temporal areas, this would tentatively support the notion that individual differences in working memory/attention and *gF* arise from individual variations in frontal lobe functioning.

We also suggest that further behavioral work be aimed at the generality of working memory and controlled attention. We find the evidence for a unitary working memory/attention system to be compelling. We have reviewed findings in which widely varying working memory and *gF* tests predict a broad range of attentional capabilities and in which PFC lesions impair performance on a vast array of working memory and controlled-attention tests. We also offer the following findings as further support for a unitary working memory/attention system, at least insofar as working memory's executive functions are concerned:

1. Working memory test scores correlate significantly with higher-order ability scores even when the broad domains of these predictor and criterion tests do not match (e.g., working memory tests with numerical stimuli and mathematical processing requirements correlate with language comprehension tests; see Crawford & Stankov, 1983; Daneman & Merikle, 1996; Engle et al., 1992; Kyllonen & Christal, 1990; Law et al., 1995; Woltz, 1988).
2. Although working memory tasks and higher-order ability tasks may correlate more strongly when their domains match than when they do not (e.g., Daneman & Merikle, 1996; Daneman & Tardif, 1987; Jurden, 1995; Shah & Miyake, 1996), the lower correlations seen for mismatching domains tend to be driven by the domain of the *to-be-stored information* in the working memory test, and not by the domain of the background processing task (see also Engle et al., 1992; Turner & Engle, 1989). Thus, the short-term memory requirements of the span task seem to have rather limited cross-domain predictive validity, whereas the concurrent processing requirements – or the central executive functions – appear to predict performance independently of the problem domains.
3. Delayed-memory tests with visual-object, visuospatial, haptic, or cross-modal stimuli elicit similar deficits in PFC-lesioned macaques (e.g., Fuster & Bauer, 1974; Quintana & Fuster, 1993). Working memory tasks with either object or spatial stimuli may evoke similar bilateral brain activation patterns in healthy adult humans (e.g., Braver et al., 1997; Smith et al., 1996).
4. Different subregions of the lateral PFC are networked to different posterior areas, and these posterior areas generally process different types of information (i.e., macaque principal sulcus cells are connected to posterior parietal cortex that is specialized for spatial processing; inferior convexity cells are networked with temporal cortex that is specialized for object processing). However, anatomical links between these different lateral-PFC areas may allow coordination of their activity (e.g., Barbas & Pandya, 1991; Pandya & Barnes, 1987). In addition, a small number of cells in each of these lateral subareas respond to the stimulus domain generally reserved for the other lateral subarea (e.g., Funahashi, Bruce, & Goldman-Rakic, 1989; Kubota, Tonoike, & Mikami, 1980; Wilson, O'Schalaidhe, & Goldman-Rakic, 1993). Moreover, in a single delayed-memory test demanding that both object and spatial information be maintained, Rao, Rainer, and Miller (1997) found that a majority of delay-sensitive PFC cells responded *equally* to object and spatial stimuli. Further, these "what-and-where" cells were distributed equally across principal sulcus ("*where*") areas and inferior convexity ("*what*") areas.

There is clearly empirical support for a unitary working memory. In truth, however, the working memory/attention system is probably neither entirely unitary nor entirely separable into domain-specific systems. Instead, we suggest that working memory/attention may be organized similarly to intelligence (e.g., Carroll, 1993; Kyllonen, 1996; Snow et al., 1984), that is, as a hierarchical structure with a general domain-free factor overarching several subordinate domain-specific factors. Just as in intelligence research, general working memory factors appear to account for too much variance to be ignored. However, in some studies (e.g., Shah & Miyake, 1996), significant variance is left to be explained beyond that accounted for by a general factor. We suggest that the behavioral, neuropsychological, and neuroanatomical evidence supports such a hierarchical view of working memory/attention. The specific factors correspond primarily to the domain of to-be-stored information, but the general factor transcends the domain of processing. Our answers to the eight questions posed by the editors of this volume reflect that view (see Table 4.1).

Table 4.1. *The Eight Great Questions*

---

(1) **Basic Mechanisms and Representations in Working Memory**
Encodings and representations are as varied as the formats for perception, emotion, and thought. Maintenance is through exogenous activation from focus of attention, of which rehearsal is one form. However, some knowledge units achieve activation through endogenous emotional salience or as a result of a goal that has reinforcement or emotional salience. Retrieval results from automatic spreading activation but can be supported and guided by planned, effortful search – which is controlled.

(2) **The Control and Regulation of Working Memory**
The particular units that are active above threshold (i.e., STM) are a result of a variety of factors including the recency with which they were activated, importance of the unit to the task goal, etc. Some units may have a salience tag, which leads to some thoughts coming to consciousness regardless of the immediate task goal. These units typically have a strong emotional color to them. Except for such endogenous activation, maintaining the contents of working memory, particularly in the face of automatically elicited thoughts such as those just mentioned, requires controlled attention.

(3) **The Unitary versus Non-Unitary Nature of Working Memory**
The myriad representational formats, controlled attention, and the procedures and skills for maintaining activation constitute a system. What we have called working memory capacity or capacity for sustaining attention is not just unitary but is domain free.

continued

Table 4.1, continued

(4) The Nature of Working Memory Limitations

Much, if not all, retrieval is automatic in nature, but controlled processing is necessary to deal with the results of that retrieval. Procedural skills for manipulating language and spatial/visual representations certainly differ across individuals as does episodic and semantic knowledge. Thus, people will differ in knowledge and the skills for manipulating that knowledge. However, people also differ in their capacity for sustaining, maintaining, and shifting attention. This leads to differences in the ability to maintain and to inhibit or suppress activation. The difference in working memory capacity or controlled attention is isomorphic with general fluid intelligence.

(5) The Role of Working Memory in Complex Cognitive Activities

Individual-differences studies have implicated working memory or controlled-attention capacity in nearly every activity on this list. However, individuals can differ in these tasks because of differences in PFC-mediated controlled processing and/or differences in the procedural skill and knowledge necessary to perform the task.

(6) The Relationship of Working Memory to Long-Term Memory and Knowledge

Working memory is a system consisting of LTM units activated above threshold plus controlled attention. The limitations on controlled processing capability can, at least to some extent, be circumvented by expert knowledge and practice on the task. However, even slight changes in the task demands can lead to reemergence of the limitations.

(7) The Relationship of Working Memory to Attention and Consciousness

WM = STM (activated portion of LTM) + controlled attention.

(8) The Biological Implementation of Working Memory

There is considerable evidence supporting the role of the dorsolateral prefrontal cortex of the frontal lobes in the functions of controlled attention, primarily maintenance and suppression. It is also likely the case that the anterior attention system proposed by Posner and Peterson (1990) is involved in these functions. Further, we believe that the patterns of performance we observe between high and low working memory capacity subjects is strikingly similar to differences in psychometric general fluid intelligence and to the differences between intact normals and patients with prefrontal damage. The so-called slave systems would be mediated by the structures appropriate to the domain. Thus, the speech-based coding would be mediated speech centers in the brain.

REFERENCES

Ackerly, S. (1937). Instinctive, emotional and mental changes following prefrontal lobe extirpation. *American Journal of Psychiatry, 92,* 717–729.

Ackerman, P. L. (1988). Determinants of individual differences during skill acquisition: Cognitive abilities and information processing. *Journal of Experimental Psychology: General, 3,* 288–318.

Ahola, K., Vilkki, J., & Servo, A. (1996). Frontal tests do not detect frontal infarctions after ruptured intracranial aneurysm. *Brain and Cognition, 31,* 1–16.

Anderson, S. W., Damasio, H., Jones, R. D., & Tranel, D. (1991). Wisconsin Card Sorting Test performance as a measure of frontal lobe damage. *Journal of Clinical and Experimental Neuropsychology, 13,* 909–922.

Armitage, S. G. (1946). An analysis of certain psychological tests used for the evaluation of brain injury. *Psychological Monographs, 60* (Whole No. 277).

Baddeley, A. D., & Hitch, G. J. (1974). Working memory. In G. H. Bower (Ed.), *The psychology of learning and motivation: Advances in research and theory* (Vol. 8, pp. 47–89). New York: Academic Press.

Baldwin, J. M. (1894). *Mental development in the child and the race.* New York: Macmillan.

Barbas, H., & Pandya, D. N. (1991). Patterns of connections of the prefrontal cortex in the rhesus monkey associated with cortical architecture. In H. S. Levin, H. M. Eisenberg, & A. L. Benton (Eds.), *Frontal lobe function and dysfunction* (pp. 35–58). Oxford: Oxford University Press.

Bench, C. J., Frith, C. D., Grasby, P. M., Friston, K. J., Paulesu, E., Frackowiak, R. S. J., & Dolan, R. J. (1993). Investigations of the functional anatomy of attention using the Stroop test. *Neuropsychologia, 31,* 907–922.

Benton, S. L., Kraft, R. G., Glover, J. A., & Plake, B. S. (1984). Cognitive capacity differences among writers. *Journal of Educational Psychology 76,* 820–834.

Berg, E. A. (1948). A simple objective technique for measuring flexibility in thinking. *Journal of General Psychology, 39,* 15–22.

Blanco, M. J., & Alvarez, A. A. (1994). Psychometric intelligence and visual focused attention: Relationships in nonsearch tasks. *Intelligence, 18,* 77–106.

Braver, T. S., Cohen, J. D., Nystrom, L. E., Jonides, J., Smith, E. E., & Noll, D. C. (1997). A parametric study of prefrontal cortex involvement in human working memory. *NeuroImage, 5,* 49–62.

Butters, M. A., Kaszniak, A. W., Glisky, E. L., Eslinger, P. J., & Schacter, D. L. (1994). Recency discrimination deficits in frontal lobe patients. *Neuropsychology, 8,* 343–353.

Carroll, J. B. (1993). *Human cognitive abilities: A survey of factor-analytic studies.* New York: Cambridge University Press.

Case, R. (1985). *Intellectual development.* Orlando, FL: Academic Press.

Case, R., Kurland, M. D., & Goldberg, J. (1982). Operational efficiency and the growth of short-term memory span. *Journal of Experimental Child Psychology, 33,* 386–404.

Chorover, S. L., & Cole, M. (1966). Delayed alternation performance in patients with cerebral lesions. *Neuropsychologia, 4,* 1–7.

Cohen, J. D., Forman, S. D., Braver, T. S., Casey, B. J., Servan-Schreiber, D., & Noll, D. C. (1994). Activation of the prefrontal cortex in a nonspatial working memory task with functional MRI. *Human Brain Mapping, 1,* 293–304.

Cohen, R. M., Semple, W. E., Gross, M., Holcomb, H. H., Dowling, M. S., & Nordahl, T. E. (1988). Functional localization of sustained attention: Comparison to sensory stimulation in the absence of instruction. *Neuropsychiatry, Neuropsychology, and Behavioral Neurology, 1,* 3–20.

Conway, A. R. A., & Engle, R. W. (1994). Working memory and retrieval: A resource-dependent inhibition model. *Journal of Experimental Psychology: General, 123,* 354–373.

Conway, A. R. A., & Engle, R. W. (1996). Individual differences in working memory capacity: More evidence for a general capacity theory. *Memory, 4,* 577–590.

Conway, A. R. A., Tuholski, S. W., Shisler, R. J., & Engle, R. W. (1998). *The effect of memory load on negative priming: An individual differences investigation.* Manuscript submitted for publication.

Cowan, N. (1995). *Attention and memory: An integrated framework.* New York: Oxford University Press.

Crawford, J. D., & Stankov, L. (1983). Fluid and crystallized intelligence and primacy/recency components of short-term memory. *Intelligence, 7,* 227–252.

Cuenod, C. A., Bookheimer, S. Y., Hertz-Pannier, L., Zeffiro, T. A., Theodore, W. H., & Le Bihan, D. (1995). Functional MRI during word generation, using conventional equipment: A potential tool for language localization in the clinical environment. *Neurology, 45,* 1821–1827.

Daneman, M., & Carpenter, P. A. (1980). Individual differences in working memory and reading. *Journal of Verbal Learning and Verbal Behavior, 19,* 450–466.

Daneman, M., & Carpenter, P. A. (1983). Individual differences in integrating information between and within sentences. *Journal of Experimental Psychology: Learning, Memory and Cognition, 9,* 561–584.

Daneman, M., & Green, I. (1986). Individual differences in comprehending and producing words in context. *Journal of Memory and Language, 25,* 1–18.

Daneman, M., & Merikle, P. M. (1996). Working memory and language comprehension: A meta-analysis. *Psychonomic Bulletin & Review, 3,* 422–433.

Daneman, M., & Tardif, T. (1987). Working memory and reading skill reexamined. In M. Coltheart (Ed.), *Attention and performance XII: The psychology of reading* (pp. 491–508). Hove, UK: Erlbaum.

Delis, D. C., Squire, L. R., Bihrle, A., & Massman, P. (1992). Componential analysis of problem-solving ability: Performance of patients with frontal lobe damage and amnesic patients on a new sorting test. *Neuropsychologia, 30,* 683–697.

Drewe, E. A. (1974). The effect of type and area of brain lesion on Wisconsin Card Sorting Test performance. *Cortex, 10,* 159–170.

Duncan, J. (1995). Attention, intelligence and the frontal lobes. In M. S. Gazzaniga (Ed.), *The cognitive neurosciences* (pp. 721–733). Cambridge, MA: MIT Press.

Duncan, J., Burgess, P., & Emslie, H. (1995). Fluid intelligence after frontal lobe lesions. *Neuropsychologia, 33,* 261–268.

Duncan, J., Emslie, H., Williams, P., Johnson, R., & Freer, C. (1996). Intelligence and the frontal lobe: The organization of goal-directed behavior. *Cognitive Psychology, 30,* 257–303.

Dupont, P., Orban, G. A., Vogels, R., Bormans, G., Nuyts, J., Schiepers, C., De Roo, M., & Mortelmans, L. (1993). Different perceptual tasks performed with the same visual stimulus attribute activate different regions of the human brain: A positron emission tomography study. *Proceedings of the National Academy of Sciences, USA, 90,* 10927–10931.

Engle, R. W., Cantor, J., & Carullo, J. J. (1992). Individual differences in working memory and comprehension: A test of four hypotheses. *Journal of Experimental Psychology: Learning, Memory, and Cognition, 18,* 972–992.

Engle, R. W., Carullo, J. J., & Collins, K. W. (1991). Individual differences in working memory for comprehension and following directions. *Journal of Educational Research, 84,* 253–262.

Engle, R. W., Conway, A. R. A., Tuholski, S. W., & Shisler, R. J. (1995). A resource account of inhibition. *Psychological Science, 6,* 122–125.

Engle, R. W., & Oransky, N. (1999). The evolution from short-term to working memory: Multi-store to dynamic models of temporary storage. In R. J. Sternberg (Ed.), *The nature of cognition.* Cambridge, MA: MIT Press.

Engle, R. W., Tuholski, S. W., Laughlin, J. E., & Conway, A. R. A. (in press). Working memory, short-term memory, and general fluid intelligence: A latent variable approach. *Journal of Experimental Psychology: General.*

Freedman, M., & Cermak, L. S. (1986). Semantic encoding deficits in frontal lobe disease and amnesia. *Brain and Cognition, 5,* 108–114.

Frith, C. D., Friston, K. J., Liddle, P. F., & Frackowiak, R. S. J. (1991). A PET study of word finding. *Neuropsychologia, 29,* 1137–1148.

Funahashi, S., Bruce, C. J., & Goldman-Rakic, P. S. (1989). Mnemonic coding of visual space in the monkey's dorsolateral prefrontal cortex. *Journal of Neurophysiology, 61,* 331–349.

Fuster, J. M., & Bauer, R. H. (1974). Visual short-term memory deficit from hypothermia of frontal cortex. *Brain Research, 81,* 393–400.

Gerstadt, C. L., Hong, Y. J., & Diamond, A. (1994). The relationship between cognition and action: Performance of children $3^{1}/_{2}$–7 years old on a Stroop-like day-night test. *Cognition, 53,* 129–153.

Gevins, A., Smith, M. E., McEvoy, L., & Yu, D. (1997). High-resolution EEG mapping of cortical activation related to working memory: Effects of task difficulty, type of processing, and practice. *Cerebral Cortex, 7,* 374–385.

Goldman-Rakic, P. S. (1987). Circuitry of primate prefrontal cortex and regulation of behavior by representational memory. In F. Plum (Ed.), *Handbook of physiology – The nervous system* (Vol. 5, pp. 373–417). Bethesda, MD: American Physiological Society.

Grafman, J., Jones, B., & Salazar, A. (1990). Wisconsin Card Sorting Test performance based on location and size of neuroanatomical lesion in Vietnam veterans with penetrating head injury. *Perceptual and Motor Skills, 71,* 1120–1122.

Grant, A. D., & Berg, E. A. (1948). A behavioral analysis of degree of reinforcement and ease of shifting to new responses in a Weigl-type card-sorting problem. *Journal of Experimental Psychology, 38,* 404–411.

Grueniger, W. E., & Pribram, K. H. (1969). Effects of spatial and nonspatial distractors on performance latency of monkeys with frontal lesions. *Journal of Comparative and Physiological Psychology, 68,* 203–209.

Harlow, H. F., & Dagnon, J. (1943). Problem solution by monkeys following bilateral removal of the prefrontal areas: I. The discrimination and discrimination-reversal problems. *Journal of Experimental Psychology, 32,* 351–356.

Hebb, D. O. (1945). Man's frontal lobes: A critical review. *Archives of Neurology and Psychiatry, 54,* 10–24.

Hebb, D. O., & Penfield, W. (1940). Human behavior after extensive bilateral removal from the frontal lobes. *Archives of Neurology and Psychiatry, 44,* 421–438.

Horn, J. L., & Cattell, R. B. (1967). Age differences in fluid and crystallized intelligence. *Acta Psychologica, 26,* 107–129.

Hunt, E. (1980). Intelligence as an information processing concept. *British Journal of Psychology, 71,* 449–474.

Institute for Personality and Ability Testing. (1973). *Measuring intelligence with the Culture Fair Tests.* Champaign, IL: The Institute for Personality and Ability Testing.

Isaac, W., & DeVito, J. (1958). Effect of sensory stimulation on the activity of normal and prefrontal-lobectomized monkeys. *Journal of Comparative and Physiological Psychology, 51,* 172–174.

Jacobsen, C. F. (1936). Studies of cerebral function in primates: I. The functions of the frontal association area in monkeys. *Comparative Psychology Monographs, 13,* 1–68.

Jevons, W. (1871). The power of numerical discrimination. *Nature, 3,* 281–282.

Joanette, Y., & Goulet, P. (1986). Criterion-specific reduction of verbal fluency in right brain-damaged right-handers. *Neuropsychologia, 24,* 875–879.

Jurden, F. H. (1995). Individual differences in working memory and complex cognition. *Journal of Educational Psychology, 87,* 93–102.

Kane, M. J., & Engle, R. W. (1997, May). *Working memory, divided attention, and proactive interference.* Paper presented at the annual meeting of the Midwestern Psychological Association, Chicago, IL.

Kane, M. J., & Engle, R. W. (1998). Full frontal fluidity: Working memory capacity, controlled attention, intelligence, and the prefrontal cortex. (Unpublished manuscript).

Kiewra, K. A., & Benton, S. L. (1988). The relationship between information processing ability and notetaking. *Contemporary Educational Psychology, 13,* 33–44.

King, J., & Just, M. A. (1991). Individual differences in syntactic processing: The role of working memory. *Journal of Memory and Language, 30,* 580–602.

Koch, K. W., & Fuster, J. M. (1989). Unit activity in monkey parietal cortex related to haptic perception and temporary memory. *Experimental Brain Research, 76,* 292–306.

Kojima, S., & Goldman-Rakic, P. S. (1982). Delay-related activity of prefrontal neurons in rhesus monkeys performing delayed response. *Brain Research, 248,* 43–49.

Kojima, S., & Goldman-Rakic, P. S. (1984). Functional analysis of spatially discriminative neurons in prefrontal cortex of rhesus monkeys. *Brain Research, 291,* 229–240.

Kubota, K., Tonoike, M., & Mikami, A. (1980). Neuronal activity in the monkey dorsolateral prefrontal cortex during a discrimination task with delay. *Brain Research, 183,* 29–42.

Kyllonen, P. C. (1996). Is working memory capacity Spearman's *g*? In I. Dennis & P. Tapsfield (Eds.), *Human abilities: Their nature and measurement* (pp. 49–75). Mahwah, NJ: Erlbaum.

Kyllonen, P. C., & Christal, R. E. (1990). Reasoning ability is (little more than) working-memory capacity?! *Intelligence, 14,* 389–433.

Kyllonen, P. C., & Stephens, D. L. (1990). Cognitive abilities as determinants of success in acquiring logic skill. *Learning and Individual Differences, 2,* 129–150.

Law, D. J., Morrin, K. A., & Pellegrino, J. W. (1995). Training effects and working memory contributions to skill acquisition in a complex coordination task. *Learning and Individual Differences, 7,* 207–234.

Lezak, M. D. (1983). *Neuropsychological assessment.* New York: Oxford University Press.

Luria, A. R. (1966). *Higher cortical functions in man.* New York: Basic Books.

MacDonald, M. C., Just, M. A., & Carpenter, P. A. (1992). Working memory constraints on the processing of syntactic ambiguity. *Cognitive Psychology, 24,* 56–98.

Malmo, R. B. (1942). Interference factors in delayed response in monkeys after removal of frontal lobes. *Journal of Neurophysiology, 5,* 295–308.

Milner, B. (1963). Effects of different brain lesions on card sorting. *Archives of Neurology, 9,* 90–100.

Milner, B. (1964). Some effects of frontal lobectomy in man. In J. M. Warren & K. Akert (Eds.), *The frontal granular cortex and behavior* (pp. 313–334). New York: McGraw-Hill.

Mishkin, M., & Pribram, K. H. (1955). Analysis of the effects of frontal lesions in monkeys: I. Variations of delayed alternation. *Journal of Comparative and Physiological Psychology, 48,* 492–495.

Mishkin, M., & Pribram, K. H. (1956). Analysis of the effects of frontal lesions in monkeys: II. Variations of delayed response. *Journal of Comparative and Physiological Psychology, 49,* 36–45.

Morrin, K. A., Law, D. J., & Pellegrino, J. W. (1994). Structural modeling of information coordination abilities: An evaluation of the Yee, Hunt, and Pellegrino model. *Intelligence, 19,* 117–144.

Nelson, H. E. (1976). A modified card sorting test sensitive to frontal lobe defects. *Cortex, 12,* 313–324.

Newcombe, F. (1969). *Missile wounds of the brain: A study of psychological deficits.* Oxford: Oxford University Press.

Norman, D. A., & Shallice, T. (1986). Attention to action: Willed and automatic control of behavior. In R. J. Davidson, G. E. Schwartz, & D. Shapiro (Eds.), *Consciousness and self-regulation* (Vol. 4, pp. 1–18). New York: Plenum Press.

Ormrod, J. E., & Cochran, K. F. (1988). Relationship of verbal ability and working memory to spelling achievement and learning to spell. *Reading Research and Instruction, 28,* 33–43.

Owen, A. M., Roberts, A. C., Polkey, C. E., Sahakian, B. J., & Robbins, T. W. (1991). Extra-dimensional versus intra-dimensional set shifting performance following frontal lobe excisions, temporal lobe excisions or amygdalo-hippocampectomy in man. *Neuropsychologia, 29,* 993–1006.

Pandya, D. N., & Barnes, D. L. (1987). Architecture and connections of the frontal lobe. In E. Perecman (Ed.), *The frontal lobes revisited* (pp. 41–72). New York: IRBN Press.

Pardo, J. V., Fox, P. T., & Raichle, M. E. (1991). Localization of a human system for sustained attention by positron emission tomography. *Nature, 349,* 61–64.

Parkin, A. J., Leng, N. R. C., & Stanhope, N. (1988). Memory impairment following ruptured aneurysm of the anterior communicating artery. *Brain and Cognition, 7,* 231–243.

Pascual-Leone, J., & Baillargeon, R. (1994). Developmental measurement of mental attention. *International Journal of Behavioral Development, 17,* 161–200.

Pellegrino, J. W., Hunt, E. B., & Yee, P. L. (1989). Assessment and modeling of information coordination abilities. In R. Kanfer, P. L. Ackerman, & R. Cudeck (Eds.), *Abilities, motivation, and methodology* (pp. 175–202). Hillsdale, NJ: Erlbaum.

Pendleton, M. G., Heaton, R. K., Lehman, R. A., & Hulihan, D. (1982). Diagnostic utility of the Thurstone Word Fluency Test in neuropsychological evaluations. *Journal of Clinical Neuropsychology, 4*, 307–317.

Pennington, B. F. (1994). The working memory function of the prefrontal cortices. In M. M. Haith, J. B. Bensen, R. J. Roberts, & B. F. Pennington (Eds.), *The development of future-oriented processes*. Chicago: University of Chicago Press.

Perfetti, C. A., & Lesgold, A. M. (1977). Discourse comprehension and sources of individual differences. In M. A. Just & P. A. Carpenter (Eds.), *Cognitive processes in comprehension*. Hillsdale, NJ: Erlbaum.

Perret, E. (1974). The left frontal lobe of man and the suppression of habitual responses in verbal categorical behavior. *Neuropsychologia, 12*, 323–330.

Piaget, J. (1926). *The language and thought of the child*. New York: Routledge & Kegan Paul.

Pierrot-Deseilligny, C., Rivaud, S., Gaymard, B., & Agid, Y. (1991). Cortical control of reflexive visually-guided saccades. *Brain, 114*, 1473–1485.

Posner, M. I., & Peterson, S. E. (1990). The attention system of the human brain. *Annual Review of Neuroscience, 13*, 25–42.

Posner, M. I., & Snyder, C. R. R. (1975). Attention & cognitive control. In R. Solso (Ed.), *Information processing and cognition: The Loyola Symposium* (pp. 55–85). Hillsdale, NJ: Erlbaum.

Prabhakaran, V., Smith, J. A. L., Desmond, J. E., Glover, G. H., & Gabrieli, J. D. E. (1997). Neural substrates of fluid reasoning: An fMRI study of neocortical activation during performance of the Raven's Progressive Matrices Test. *Cognitive Psychology, 33*, 43–63.

Quintana, J., & Fuster, J. M. (1993). Spatial and temporal factors in the role of prefrontal and parietal cortex in visuomotor integration. *Cerebral Cortex, 3*, 122–132.

Rao, S. C., Rainer, G., & Miller, E. K. (1997). Integration of what and where in the primate prefrontal cortex. *Science, 276*, 821–824.

Raven, J. C., Court, J. H., & Raven, J. (1977). *Standard progressive matrices*. London: H. K. Lewis & Co.

Reitan, R. M., & Wolfson, D. (1994). A selective and critical review of neuropsychological deficits and the frontal lobes. *Neuropsychology Review, 4*, 161–197.

Reitan, R. M., & Wolfson, D. (1995). Category test and Trail Making Test as measures of frontal lobe functions. *The Clinical Neuropsychologist, 9*, 50–56.

Richer, F., Decary, A., Lapierre, M. F., Rouleau, I., Bouvier, G., & Saint-Hilaire, J. M. (1993). Target detection deficits in frontal lobectomy. *Brain and Cognition, 21*, 203–211.

Ricker, J. H., Axelrod, B. N., & Houtler, B. D. (1996). Clinical validation of the Oral Trail Making Test. *Neuropsychiatry, Neuropsychology, and Behavioral Neurology, 9*, 50–53.

Risberg, J., Maximilian, A. V., & Prohovnik, I. (1977). Changes of cortical activity patterns during habituation to a reasoning test. *Neuropsychologia, 15*, 793–798.

Roberts, R. J., Jr., Hager, L. D., & Heron, C. (1994). Prefrontal cognitive processes: Working memory and inhibition in the antisaccade task. *Journal of Experimental Psychology: General, 123*, 374–393.

Rosen, V. M., & Engle, R. W. (1998). Working memory capacity and suppression. *Journal of Memory and Language, 39*, 418–436.

Rosen, V. M., & Engle, R. W. (1997). The role of working memory capacity in retrieval. *Journal of Experimental Psychology: General, 126*, 211–227.

Salmaso, D., & Denes, G. (1982). Role of the frontal lobes on an attention task: A signal detection analysis. *Perceptual and Motor Skills, 54*, 1147–1150.

Salthouse, T. A. (1991). *Theoretical perspectives on cognitive aging.* Hillsdale, NJ: Erlbaum

Schneider, W., & Shiffrin, R. M. (1977). Controlled and automatic human information processing. I. Detection, search, and attention. *Psychological Review, 84*, 1–66.

Settlage, P., Zable, M., & Harlow, H. F. (1948). Problem solution by monkeys following bilateral removal of the prefrontal areas: VI. Performance on tests requiring contradictory reactions to similar and to identical stimuli. *Journal of Experimental Psychology, 38*, 50–65.

Shah, P., & Miyake, A. (1996). The separability of working memory resources for spatial thinking and language processing: An individual differences approach. *Journal of Experimental Psychology: General, 125*, 4–27.

Shallice, T., & Burgess, P. W. (1991). Deficits in strategy application following frontal lobe damage in man. *Brain, 114*, 727–741.

Shute, V. J. (1991). Who is likely to acquire programming skills? *Journal of Educational Computing Research, 7*, 1–24.

Smith, E. E., Jonides, J., & Koeppe, R. A. (1996). Dissociating verbal and spatial working memory using PET. *Cerebral Cortex, 6*, 11–20.

Snow, R. E., Kyllonen, P. C., & Marshalek, B. (1984). The topography of ability and learning correlations. In R. J. Sternberg (Ed.), *Advances in the psychology of human intelligence* (Vol. 2, pp. 47–103). Hillsdale, NJ: Erlbaum.

Stankov, L. (1983). Attention and intelligence. *Journal of Educational Psychology, 75*, 471–490.

Stroop, J. R. (1935). Studies of interference in serial verbal reactions. *Journal of Experimental Psychology, 18*, 643–662.

Treisman, A. M., & Gelade, G. (1980). A feature-integration theory of attention. *Cognitive Psychology, 12*, 97–136.

Trick, L. M., & Pylyshyn, Z. W. (1993). What enumeration studies can show us about spatial attention: Evidence for limited capacity preattentive processing. *Journal of Experimental Psychology: Human Perception and Performance, 19*, 331–351.

Tuholski, S. W. (1997). *Examining the relationships among attentional resources, working memory, and fluid intelligence.* Unpublished doctoral dissertation, University of South Carolina, Columbia, SC.

Turner, M. L., & Engle, R. W. (1989). Is working memory capacity task dependent? *Journal of Memory and Language, 28*, 127–154.

Uhl, F., Franzen, P., Serles, W., Lange, W., Lindinger, G., & Deecke, L. (1990). Anterior frontal cortex and the effect of proactive interference in paired associate learning: A DC potential study. *Journal of Cognitive Neuroscience, 2*, 373–382.

Uhl, F., Podreka, I., & Deecke, L. (1994). Anterior frontal cortex and the effect of proactive interference in word pair learning – Results of Brain-SPECT. *Neuropsychologia, 32*, 241–247.

Van der Linden, M., Bruyer, R., Roland, J., & Schils, J. P. (1993). Proactive interference in patients with amnesia resulting from anterior communicating artery aneurysm. *Journal of Clinical and Experimental Neuropsychology, 15*, 525–536.

Vendrell, P., Junque, C., Pujol, J., Jurado, M. A., Molet, J., & Grafman, J. (1995). The role of prefrontal regions in the Stroop task. *Neuropsychologia, 33,* 341–362.

Verin, M., Partiot, A., Pillon, B., Malapani, C., Agid, Y., & Dubois, B. (1993). Delayed response tasks and prefrontal lesions in man – Evidence for self generated patterns of behaviour with poor environmental modulation. *Neuropsychologia, 31,* 1379–1396.

Warach, S., Gur, R. C., Gur, R. E., Skolnick, B. E., Obrist, W. D., & Reivich, M. (1992). Decreases in frontal and parietal lobe regional cerebral blood flow related to habituation. *Journal of Cerebral Blood Flow and Metabolism, 12,* 546–553.

Watanabe, T., & Niki, H. (1985). Hippocampal unit activity and delayed response in the monkey. *Brain Research, 325,* 241–254.

Wilkins, A. J., Shallice, T., & McCarthy, R. (1987). Frontal lesions and sustained attention. *Neuropsychologia, 25,* 359–365.

Wilson, F. A. W., O'Scalaidhe, S. P., & Goldman-Rakic, P. S. (1993). Dissociation of object and spatial processing domains in primate prefrontal cortex. *Science, 260,* 1955–1958.

Witkin, H. A., & Goodenough, D. R. (1981). *Cognitive styles: Essence and origins.* New York: International Universities Press.

Woltz, D. J. (1988). An investigation of the role of working memory in procedural skill acquisition. *Journal of Experimental Psychology: General, 117,* 319–331.

Yntema, D. B. (1963). Keeping track of several things at once. *Human Factors, 5,* 7–17.

5 Modeling Working Memory in a Unified Architecture

An ACT-R Perspective

MARSHA C. LOVETT, LYNNE M. REDER, AND
CHRISTIAN LEBIERE

FIVE CENTRAL FEATURES OF THE MODEL

We describe a model of working memory that is developed within the ACT-R cognitive architecture. Some of its main features are derived from the basic features of ACT-R:

(1) Processing depends on the current goal of the system.

(2) The accessibility of declarative and procedural knowledge varies with experience.

In addition, the following features are important to working memory in particular:

(3) There is a limited attentional resource, focused on the current goal, that increases the accessibility of goal-relevant knowledge relative to other knowledge.

(4) In more complex and memory-demanding tasks, this limited resource is spread more thinly thus impairing retrieval of goal-relevant items.

(5) The "capacity" of this attentional resource may vary from person to person, influencing the ability to access goal-relevant information across domains.

In performing almost any cognitive task, one must engage *working memory* to maintain and retrieve information during processing. For example, in mental arithmetic (e.g., multiplying large numbers without pencil and paper), one must hold intermediate results in memory while solving the problem. Similarly, in sentence processing, one must maintain various syntactic and

We would like to thank John Anderson, Mike Byrne, Andrew Conway, Sott Filipino, and all of the symposium participants for helpful comments. The work presented here was funded by Grant F49620-97-1-0054 from the Air Force Office of Scientific Research, and also supported in part by Grant N00014-95-1-0223 from the Office of Naval Research and Grant 1R01 MH52808-01 from the National Institutes of Mental Health.

semantic structures until subsequent processing reveals their roles. Because working memory is involved in so many tasks, studying its characteristics and its impact on cognitive processes is critical to gaining a deeper understanding of how people perform cognitive tasks in general.

Past research highlights two important results, each of which demonstrates that working memory modulates task performance. First, when the working memory demands of a task increase (either by increasing the number of items in a "pure" memory task or by increasing the difficulty of concurrent processing in a dual-task situation), errors and latencies tend to increase (e.g., Anderson, Reder, & Lebiere, 1996; Baddeley, 1986; Caplan, Rochon, & Waters, 1992). Second, groups of subjects who have been separately identified as having "low" or "high" working memory capacity exhibit different degrees of sensitivity to increases in working memory load (e.g., Engle, 1994; Just & Carpenter, 1992). Together, these results suggest a view of working memory as a cognitive resource that (a) can be allocated to enable the maintenance and processing of information, (b) is inherently limited, and (c) differs in supply across individuals.

Within this view, however, there are still multiple ways for working memory to be implemented. Computational modeling has therefore contributed greatly to this field because it requires that the working memory mechanisms posited by a given theory be specified in a rigorous (programmable) way. The resulting model provides a detailed account of how such mechanisms interact and yields quantitative predictions that can be compared with observed data. This makes possible the systematic comparison of models representing different theories. Computational models are also particularly appropriate for studying individual differences in working memory because they enable researchers to maintain the basic structure of their theory while perturbing a particular "individual difference" component. The different patterns of results that such a variablized model exhibits can be compared with the different patterns of results displayed across subjects performing the same task. Thus, computational models can be evaluated not only according to how well they fit aggregate data but according to how well they account for the observed differences among people.

Our approach to the study of working memory involves developing computational models of a few different working memory tasks and comparing model predictions to performance data – at both the aggregate and individual levels. We see several advantages to our approach. First, we obtain predictions from a running computer simulation. This offers quantitative predictions along several dimensions (e.g., latencies, percent correct, patterns of errors). Second, we evaluate each model by comparing its predictions to aggregate and individual subject data. The latter is particularly important because of the systematic subject-to-subject variation in working memory capacity that has been observed (e.g., Cantor & Engle, 1993; Daneman & Carpenter, 1980; Waters & Caplan, 1996). Third, we model several tasks, all using the same theory of working memory developed within the ACT-R framework (Anderson, 1993). This is important for testing whether a single theory can cover the variety of tasks in which working memory plays a role. This final point reflects the fact that our work is embedded within a unified cognitive architecture (cf. Newell, 1982), as are some other working memory theories (Kieras, Meyer, Mueller, & Seymour, Chapter 6, this volume; Young & Lewis, Chapter 7, this volume).

In this chapter, we describe the basic features of the ACT-R theory and relate them to several working memory issues (the designated questions). We present an ACT-R model that predicts working memory results at the aggregate level and then go on to report our work in progress – developing ACT-R models of *individual's* working memory performance. We summarize some of the encouraging results we have obtained thus far and discuss their implications for future work.

The ACT-R Theory

The ACT-R theory of cognition specifies a fixed computational architecture that applies to all cognitive tasks. Within this architecture one can develop ACT-R models for different tasks. The main difference among ACT-R models is not in their way of processing information but in the initial knowledge with which they are endowed. This initial knowledge includes the facts and skills that are relevant to the task being modeled and that are presumed to be known by the subject population being studied. For example, a model of elementary school students solving arithmetic problems would only represent certain arithmetic facts (e.g., 3 + 4 = 7) and skills (e.g., how to carry a digit). Regardless of the content of this initial knowledge, ACT-R assumes the same performance and learning mechanisms for all tasks. Specifically, knowledge is always learned, deployed, interfered with, and decayed in the same way. These mechanisms are implemented in a simulation program that can be used to generate a set of theoretical predictions for a given task model. The interested reader is invited to visit the ACT-R home page (at http://act.psy.cmu.edu/) to learn more about developing ACT-R models. Before describing ACT-R's mechanisms, we provide an overview of how knowledge is represented in the system.

Symbolic Components of ACT-R

ACT-R is a hybrid system with symbolic and subsymbolic aspects. Knowledge is represented symbolically, whereas the processes acting on knowledge occur at a subsymbolic level. In this section, we describe the two symbolic representations in ACT-R. Declarative knowledge (for facts) is represented as a network of interconnected *nodes,* and procedural knowledge (for skills) is represented as a set of *productions.* Figure 5.1a depicts a node representing the fact 3 + 4 = 7. This node is labeled "Addition-fact$_i$" and is linked to

(a)

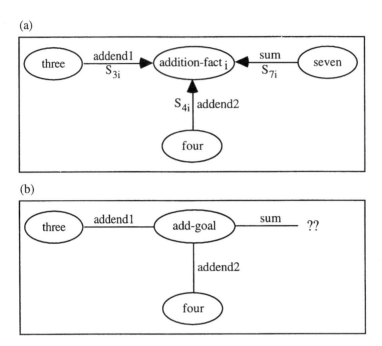

(b)

Figure 5.1. (a) A declarative node representing the fact "3 + 4 = 7." (b) A node representation of the goal to add 3 + 4.

"three," "four," and "seven," which comprise the fact's first addend, second addend, and sum, respectively. The links in Figure 5.1a vary in strength (S_{ji}), indicating the strength of the relationship between connected concepts – nodes that frequently occur together will have high associative strengths. Separate from declarative knowledge is the set of all productions held by the system. Each production represents a contingency for action. A production takes the form IF <condition>, THEN <action>. Here, <condition> specifies the circumstances under which the production is relevant, and <action> specifies a possible action to be taken. Table 5.1 presents a production for retrieving the sum in an arithmetic problem.

   The processing of declarative and procedural knowledge in ACT-R is primarily driven by the *current goal* of the system (e.g., finding the sum of three plus four). The current goal contains the information in the focus of attention and uses a declarative node structure (Figure 5.1b). Its contents are either established by previous processing (e.g., when one part of a problem is solved, attention is switched to another part) or by stimuli in the environment (e.g., upon hearing a loud noise, the focus of attention may switch to process the sound). Figure 5.2 sketches the cycle of processing. First, the goal acts as a filter to select only those productions relevant to its current

Table 5.1. *Sample Production for Arithmetic Retrieval*
IF   the current goal is to add $a + b$ when no sum has been computed and an addition fact stating that the sum of $a + b$ is c can be retrieved THEN   update current goal's sum to be c

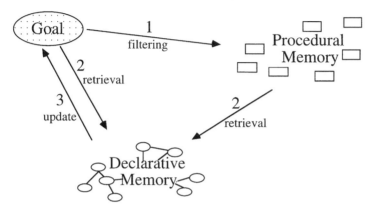

Figure 5.2. The role of the current goal in ACT-R's processing cycle: (1) It acts as a filter on procedural memory so that only goal-relevant productions are available. (2) Along with the selected production, the goal (via its links to declarative memory) makes some nodes more accessible than others. (3) Once a declarative node is retrieved, information from that node is used to update the current goal.

state. For example, the production in Table 5.1 is relevant to the goal in Figure 5.1b because both specify adding two numbers when no sum has been computed. Of the productions offering such a match to the current goal, the production with the highest expected utility (estimated from past use) is selected for continued processing. (See Lovett & Anderson, 1996, for more details on this selection mechanism and how it enables the successful modeling of various problem-solving data.) Second, the retrieval specified by the selected production is attempted. This retrieval is influenced by both the current goal (via its connections to declarative memory) and the selected production (via the retrieval pattern specified in its condition). In the addition example, an addition fact involving "three" and "four" is retrieved because the current goal includes "three" and "four" and the Retrieve-Sum production specifies retrieving an addition fact. Third, the contents of the retrieved node are used to update the current goal according to the production's action specification, for example, if "3 + 4 = 7" is retrieved, "seven" is added to the current goal's "sum" link. Then, the cycle of processing is reinitiated with the modified goal.

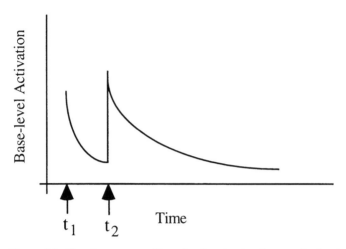

Figure 5.3. The time course of base-level activation for a node that is created at time t_1 and later accessed at time t_2 (see Equation 1).

Subsymbolic Processing in ACT-R

The above processing cycle describes performance at a symbolic level. Learning and other performance mechanisms, however, are defined in terms of processes at the subsymbolic level. Here, we focus on the subsymbolic mechanisms acting on declarative knowledge because they are most relevant to working memory.

For declarative knowledge, *activation* is the main unit of "currency" for learning and processing. Each node has a certain base-level activation that influences its accessibility. Specifically, when a fact is first learned (stored as a new node), it is endowed with an initial activation. Each time that fact is accessed (retrieved), it receives a boost to its base-level activation (learning). However, each of these "boosts" decreases as a power function of time (forgetting). Figure 5.3 shows how base-level activation changes with time for a node that was created at time t_1 and later accessed at time t_2. The ACT-R function for base-level activation of node i is

$$B_i = \log\left(\Sigma t_k^{-d}\right), \tag{1}$$

where t_k is the time lag since the kth access of node i and d is the decay rate. A node's base-level activation reflects that node's prior history of use. Because this prior history of use is a good index of future likelihood of use, the system is adaptive: Nodes that have high activation (high past use) are both more likely to be needed and more accessible.

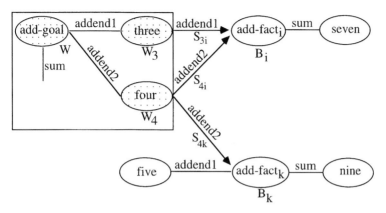

Figure 5.4. The goal (dotted) and declarative nodes for an arithmetic task (adding three plus four). The goal's source activation W is divided between the goal nodes "three" and "four" and then is spread along the arrows to addition facts in declarative memory.

Base-level activation represents a node's overall accessibility but does not account for any effects of the current context. In ACT-R, the current goal represents a person's focus of attention and thus drives context effects. The goal propagates "attentional" activation to declarative memory, raising the accessibility of some nodes relative to others. For example, Figure 5.4 shows the current goal (dotted) propagating activation along the arrow-links to related nodes in declarative memory. Specifically, the goal's attentional activation, or *source activation W*, is divided among the goal nodes "three" and "four," and then these shares (W_3 and W_4) are each spread among neighboring nodes in declarative memory. The amount of source activation received by neighbor node i from goal node j is the product of W_j (the source activation from goal node j) and S_{ji} (the strength of the link between goal node j and neighbor node i). A node that is connected to the goal by more than one link receives source activation along all those links. For instance, in Figure 5.4, "add-fact$_i$" receives $W_3 \cdot S_{3i} + W_4 \cdot S_{4i}$ units of source activation. The *total activation* of declarative node i, then, is the sum of its base-level activation and its received source activation:

$$A_i = B_i + \Sigma_j \, W_j \cdot S_{ji}. \tag{2}$$

The main implication of this equation is that both past use of a fact and its relevance to the current goal jointly determine that fact's accessibility. Familiar facts will be more accessible than unfamiliar facts because of their difference in use, and contextually relevant facts will be more accessible than irrelevant facts because of their difference in association to the current goal. These activation mechanisms have been used to model many memory experiments successfully (Anderson & Matessa, 1997).

In summary, ACT-R claims that when people focus their attention on the current goal, they are directing additional activation to declarative memory elements that are related to that goal. Source activation spreads from each goal node in proportion to the strength of association between that node and various declarative nodes. Declarative nodes also differ in terms of base-level activation, which is determined by their past history of use. One way of conceiving ACT-R's distinction between base-level activation and source activation is that the former represents the activation of each node without any context effects and the latter represents a kind of attentional activation that gets dynamically applied to particular nodes based on the current context.

Performance Functions for Declarative Retrieval

The latency T_i for retrieving node i is a function of total activation A_i. Specifically,

$$T_i = Fe^{-A_i}, \qquad (3)$$

where F is a time-scaling factor. An important implication of Equation 3 is that there is a cost for accessing a declarative node; the lower the node's activation, the greater the time taken to retrieve it. To generate ACT-R's prediction for the time to take a certain observable step, we add all the *retrieval times* (Equation 3) and *action times* for the productions leading up to that step. (The default action time is 50 ms; productions that involve motor actions have longer action times.) Thus, ACT-R predicts longer latencies on average for steps requiring longer production sequences and/or the retrieval of less activated declarative nodes.

To handle nodes with very low activation, ACT-R posits a retrieval threshold below which nodes will not be retrieved. (One can think of this threshold as a fixed waiting time; if a node is not retrieved within that time, the retrieval attempt is aborted.) Of the nodes with above-threshold activation, it would be natural for the maximally activated node to be retrieved. However, ACT-R recognizes that there may be noise in the system, so noise is added to each node's total activation, and then the node with the highest "noisy" activation is selected. The following equation describes the behavior of a system with this noisy selection process:

$$P\,(\text{retrieve}_i) = e^{\,A_i/s}/\Sigma_j e^{\,A_j/s} \qquad (4)$$

where the denominator sums over all nodes competing to be retrieved and s represents the level of activation noise.[1] This equation states that the lower a node's total activation relative to competing nodes, the lower its chance of being retrieved.

---

[1] This noise is approximately Gaussian, centered at 0, and with spread parameter s. The retrieval threshold is included as one of the "competing nodes" in Equation 4 to reflect the fact that a node's "noisy" activation must be greater than its competitors' and the retrieval threshold in order to be retrieved.

The probability of declarative node i *not* being retrieved – an error of omission – is just the complement of Equation 4. Errors of commission (when an incorrect node is retrieved) are produced by a mechanism known as partial matching. This mechanism allows a node to be retrieved even if it does not exactly match the production's retrieval condition. Such a node competes based on a reduced total activation, A_i':

$$A_i' = A_i - M, \qquad (5)$$

where M represents a mismatch penalty. This penalty is a measure of the "psychological distance" between node i and the node described in the production's retrieval condition.[2] It produces a bias against retrieving nontarget nodes. Nevertheless, with activation noise, nodes that are slightly dissimilar to the production's specification may be retrieved, especially if their total activation is high enough to compensate for the mismatch penalty.

In summary, both latency and probability of retrieval are nonlinear functions of a node's total activation (after noise and partial matching are taken into account). As we will show, this nonlinearity has an impact on how individual differences manifest themselves in our model predictions.

Working Memory in ACT-R

Basic Mechanisms and Representations in Working Memory

Before describing the mechanisms and representations of working memory in ACT-R, it is important to define working memory in terms of this theory. There are two ways to do so. One is to equate working memory with the *content* that is being maintained during processing (e.g., the elements representing the memory items in a working memory task). This content-oriented definition identifies working memory as a subset of the entire declarative memory. That is, working memory is not a special repository of information but just those declarative nodes that are highly activated because they have been stimulated from the environment and/or are strongly linked to the current goal (source activation). According to this definition, working memory mechanisms are just the mechanisms acting on declarative memory: learning, decay, and attentional activation.

The second way to define working memory emphasizes the *process* that enables memory elements to be concurrently maintained. This definition takes working memory as the propagation of source activation from the current goal. Defining ACT-R's working memory in these terms emphasizes the attentional activation mechanism that differentially activates items relevant to the current

---

[2] If declarative nodes were represented as feature vectors, the psychological distance between them would be a function of the overlap in their representations. Since declarative nodes are represented symbolically in ACT-R, this distance function is specified in the model description.

context. This process-oriented definition of working memory is complementary with the content-oriented one above: Nodes in the highly activated subset of declarative memory receive an important part of their activation from the process that spreads source activation. Note that other working memory researchers have similarly considered working memory as the union of content and process (e.g., Byrne, 1998; Cowan, Chapter 3, this volume).

Both definitions identify the basic mechanisms of working memory as the spreading of source activation (which primarily affects nodes strongly linked to the goal) and the general declarative mechanisms of base-level learning and decay (which affect all of declarative memory, of which working memory is a part). These mechanisms are always at work, influencing the accessibility of declarative knowledge and allowing for both context and learning/forgetting effects.[3]

With working memory defined, we can now address the issue of representation. Because working memory is a subset of all declarative memory, working memory representations are the same as those used for declarative nodes in general. Throughout declarative memory, however, different node structures (representations) are used for different kinds of information. For example, the arithmetic fact depicted in Figure 5.1a includes the features "addend1," "addend2," and "sum," whereas the memory-list item depicted later in Figure 5.8 incorporates the features "trial," "position," and "value." Each node incorporates its represented features in the linked structure. Similar items, such as addition facts "3 + 4 = 7" and "3 + 5 = 8," can thus be related in several ways: They can use the same node structure (both have links for addend1, addend2, and sum), they can have common elements (both include "three"), and they can have strong associative links ("3 + 4 = 7" and "3 + 5 = 8" may co-occur frequently). Note that it is also possible for different people (e.g., an expert vs. a novice) to represent the same object in different ways by encoding different features. Thus, a pair of nodes representing two items may be more or less similar for different people, both in terms of their representational structures and in terms of their strengths of association.

Such differences in representation influence processing in ACT-R. For example, the partial matching mechanism described above allows for interference among *similarly represented* items. Thus, confusions involving the retrieval of one node for another will tend to be limited to nodes of the same structure (e.g., misretrieving one arithmetic fact for another, or confusing one

---

[3] The learning/forgetting of base-level activation (Equation 1) allows for a variety of memory effects that are not the focus of this chapter. For example, familiar (highly practiced) declarative nodes will show slower decay than new nodes. Such differences have been observed and modeled with separate decay-rate parameters by Healy, Fendrich, Cunningham, and Till (1987). In the system we are describing, such a familiarity effect arises naturally from a single decay parameter: The more practiced an item, the more activation boosts that are combined to produce the item's total activation. Adding together more power-decay functions (each with a common decay rate) produces a combined function with slower decay.

word for another). Moreover, the greater the feature overlap between two items, the more likely such confusions are to occur. That is, confusions between phonologically similar words are more likely than confusions between phonologically dissimilar words, and confusions between related arithmetic facts are more likely than confusions between unrelated facts. Thus, interference effects arise mainly because of representational similarity. This implies that in dual-task situations where the two tasks require processing of similarly represented items, interference effects can substantially impair performance. Such effects have been found in several studies (e.g., Baddeley & Lieberman, 1980; Logie, 1986; Shah & Miyake, 1996).

The Nature of Working Memory Limitations

In ACT-R, working memory limitations are invoked by the constraint that source activation is limited and must be divided among the goal nodes, that is,

$$\Sigma_j W_j = W. \tag{6}$$

Here, W represents the total amount of attention focused on the current goal and W_j the share of source activation propagating from goal node j. Equation 6 implies that, for a fixed W, less source activation will be spread from each goal node the more goal nodes there are. Hence, in complex tasks (more goal nodes) there will be a smaller modulating effect of source activation on the accessibility of related declarative nodes.[4]

The share of source activation that is propagated from each goal node is spread among the different links emanating from that goal node. For example, in Figure 5.4, the source activation W_4 is spread to both add-fact$_i$ and add-fact$_k$. (In a complete model, there would be many more links.) Note that the link strengths S_{ji} are learned values that reflect the co-occurrence between nodes. As a default, the learned link strength S_{ji} is approximated by the expression $C–\log(n_j)$, with n_j as the number of nodes linked to node j. Thus, the more links emanating from a given goal node, the less source activation that is propagated along each link. Hence, for more memory-intensive tasks (i.e., more elements connected to each goal node), a smaller amount of source activation reaches any one linked node.

The key implication of a *limit* to source activation (W) is that the size of its modulating effect will be reduced in cases when source activation is divided among more goal nodes and spread among more links to declarative memory. Since relative amounts of total activation determine the latency and probability of retrievals (Equations 3 and 4), this reduction in the effect of source activation leads to degraded memory performance. Therefore, retrievals in

---

[4] For simplicity, we take source activation as divided evenly among the n nodes in the current goal: $W_j = \frac{W}{n}$. Thus, in Figure 5.4, $W_3 = W_4 = \frac{W}{2}$. Of course, an unequal division of W is possible.

complex, memory-loaded tasks will be less accurate and take longer than will retrievals in simpler tasks. This effect holds regardless of whether the memory load is part of a memory span task or part of a dual-task situation. We will show examples of each of these below.

In summary, ACT-R posits a limit in attentional resources (or source activation W) that leads to degraded memory retrieval in complex and memory-loaded tasks. The attentional limit is *not* a cap on total activation in the system but a cap on a particular kind of dynamic, attentional activation spreading from the goal. This attentional limit produces a limit in the degree to which goal-relevant items can be *differentially* activated. Such goal-based modulation of processing is similar to that proposed by O'Reilly, Braver, and Cohen (Chapter 11, this volume). Moreover, because this limitation affects the degree to which memory items can be differentially activated, it posits that *relative* activation levels are more important than absolute activation levels; thus, it is compatible with theories that attribute working memory limitations to inhibitory processes (e.g., Conway & Engle, 1994; Kane, Hasher, Stoltzfus, Zacks, & Connelly, 1994; Stoltzfus, Hasher, Zacks, Ulivi, & Goldstein, 1993; Zacks & Hasher, 1994).

The Control and Regulation of Working Memory

The primary mechanisms controlling working memory have already been delineated: (a) spreading source activation and (b) learning and decaying base-level activations. These mechanisms combine to produce the total activation levels of all declarative nodes (including those highly activated nodes that comprise working memory). Total activation, in turn, affects the accessibility of declarative nodes (Equations 3 and 4).

The main regulatory processes among these are the limit to source activation (W) and the decay of base-level activation. The limit on W constrains the degree to which goal-relevant nodes can be differentially activated relative to other nodes. Because this limitation specifies a fixed amount of source activation that must be shared and spread, there is a gradual degradation in memory performance as task complexity and memory demand increase (i.e., more complex tasks lead to thinner spreading of source activation, reducing its benefits). This implies that only a limited number of declarative nodes can be effectively differentiated (based on added source activation) from the remaining elements in declarative memory.

The decay of base-level activation, on the other hand, does not reflect a limitation in the amount of activation but rather in the duration of activation. This mechanism specifies that declarative nodes' activation (and hence general accessibility) will decrease as a power function of the time since they have been used (Equation 1). Therefore, nodes will tend to remain above threshold for only a limited amount of time. Like the spreading of source activation, this decay mechanism helps to keep working memory to a relatively small size.

Given these regulatory processes, there are two ways a node can be maintained in a highly activated state: (a) It can be part of the current goal and thus be in the focus of attention (e.g., when the concept "three" is activated by seeing a "3" in the environment),[5] (b) it can be strongly connected to one or more goal nodes and thus receive a large amount of source activation (e.g., when the fact "3 + 4 = 7" in memory is highly relevant to the goal).

The Relationship of Working Memory to Attention and Consciousness

Attention and our notion of working memory are closely related. As we have described above, working memory processing is heavily influenced by source activation, the "attentional energy" that is directed at the current goal and spread from the goal nodes. We view the limitations of working memory as stemming from limited attentional resources (Equation 6). Several of the tasks that we discuss and model in this chapter involve dual-task procedures in which attention must be divided among concurrent goals (e.g., reading and remembering). In our models of these dual-task situations, source activation is spread more thinly among a greater number of goal nodes – essentially dividing the attentional resource W between the two goals – leading to worse performance than under single-task conditions.

In lay terms, "attention" often refers to a dimension of motivation or alertness, suggesting that people can direct more or less of their attention to the current task. We have not modeled this kind of attention directing, but it could be modeled by varying the total amount of source activation or how it is shared among different components of the current goal. This is an interesting issue to explore in connection with how people strategically (vs. automatically) allocate attentional resources.

Relating working memory to consciousness is difficult. The most natural link under our framework is to consider those nodes with above-threshold activation as accessible to conscious awareness. Declarative nodes below this threshold still vary in total activation; this affects the processing required to bring them into awareness (cf. Reder & Gordon, 1997). For example, one's own name is so highly practiced, very little environmental stimulation can bring it into awareness (e.g., cocktail party effect). It is also possible to refer to our second definition of working memory – the spreading of source activation from the goal – and link consciousness to the ability to maintain a focus of attention that influences the processing of information.

---

[5] Note that in the current system, the current goal does not undergo decay. Thus, it is difficult to explain forgetting of the current goal in ACT-R. See the section on Biological Implementation for a generalization of ACT-R that handles this problem and makes connections to neural activation data.

The Unitary Versus Non-Unitary Nature of Working Memory

As implied above, the value of W impacts processing (i.e., retrieval proba-bilities and latencies) of all kinds of information. It represents a general resource that is used in any task that involves retrieval from declarative mem-ory. According to ACT-R, then, higher W will lead to better performance in any task, all else being equal. This leads to one of the hypotheses explored in our research: that the performance of an individual on one task is predictive of his or her performance on another task because both tasks tap into the same attentional resource W. This unitary hypothesis is similar to Engle, Kane, and Tuholski's (see Chapter 4, this volume); indeed, our model offers an information-processing account consistent with their analysis that supports a latent variable underlying working memory performance.

It is important to note, however, that all else is not always equal. For exam-ple, different situations may involve processing different kinds of declarative nodes (e.g., those representing spatial versus verbal information) and the interference among nodes across these situations may differ (see Basic Mechanisms section). Also, various tasks and subject populations may differ in terms of the base-level activation of the nodes involved, which can make W's effect on performance seem variable across tasks. For example, the latency of retrieval (Equation 3) is a nonlinear function of the sum of base-level and source activation: When base-level activations are high, the modu-lating effect of W is small and when base-level activations are low, W's effect is large. Finally, in many situations, participants' strategies for approaching a task may differ. These differences can affect the number and timing of retrievals and mask a common effect of W, especially if people choose strate-gies that compensate for their working memory capacity. This discussion highlights several of the sources of variability we try to reduce to study true differences in the limit to source activation. However, in most tasks, it is likely that both kinds of variability (domain-general and -specific) influence work-ing memory processes (cf. O'Reilly et al., Chapter 11, this volume).

It is interesting to contrast this view with other views that posit separate working memory capacities for different types of processes. For example, Shah and Miyake (1996) argue for separate verbal and spatial working memory capacities. Although it would be difficult to discriminate between models that specify unitary versus separate working memory pools, we prefer to posit a unitary working memory and ascribe individual differences in performance patterns across tasks to (a) different patterns of experience and (b) differences in buffer use. As discussed earlier, differences in the amount of practice at var-ious types of tasks (strength of productions), different strategies (sets of pro-ductions), and differences in knowledge representations (declarative nodes) may result in performance differences that vary with the type of task. These differences could produce performance differences across tasks even under a single working memory capacity.

Others have argued that more interference occurs within the same modality for dual tasks (Baddeley & Lieberman, 1980; Brooks, 1968; Logie, 1995) because of sharing of an input or processing buffer. Differences in modality-specific buffers may also account for some of the observed difference among individuals that has been taken as evidence for separate spatial and verbal working memory pools.

The Relationship of Working Memory to Long-Term Memory and Knowledge

As we noted before, working memory is not a special repository of information but rather a subset of declarative memory that is distinguished by higher activation levels. Otherwise, working memory elements are processed (e.g., they undergo learning and forgetting) just like any other node.

It is worth relating our view of working memory to the approach of Ericsson and Kintsch (1995) and Ericsson and Delaney (Chapter 8, this volume). We believe that their findings and our theoretical approach are compatible because learning processes play a large role in both. Their subject SF was trained to recall digit strings of over 80 digits. This superior digit span was achieved with a lot of training on recalling digits, practice at converting digits into running times (e.g., "826 is 8.26 seconds, an excellent 2 mile time"), and knowing ahead of time the length of the digit string so that the appropriate tree structure could be "loaded." Each of these processes was presumably learned and refined over SF's long training. For example, SF clearly had specialized, highly practiced procedures for recoding digits into running times (facilitated by the fact that he was an accomplished long-distance runner), special tree structures on which to hang these running times, and so on (see Chase & Ericsson, 1981, 1982 for more discussion). In contrast, SF was not able to recall letter strings that were at all exceptional in length. This speaks to the specificity of what SF learned and argues that his W was not altered, only his procedures and declarative knowledge.

The Biological Implementation of Working Memory

The question of how working memory is implemented in the brain is a difficult one: It requires bridging the gap between the abstract theoretical construct of working memory and the complex biological processes of the brain – neither of which is completely understood. Researchers have used three different approaches to attack this problem: (a) consider their working memory model analogous to the human brain and compare performance of both systems after specific impairments, (b) analyze the predictions of their model and look for these features in brain-imaging data, and (c) extend their model to refer to biological mechanisms and explore the model's performance. The first two approaches apply to the theory described in this chapter, so we will discuss them below. The third approach, exemplified by the work of O'Reilly et al. (Chapter 11, this volume), does not apply directly because ACT-R's processes have traditionally been described at a functional level rather than a biological one. (However, see Lebiere & Anderson, 1993, for a connectionist implementation of ACT-R.)

The first approach – comparing model performance to human performance when both have undergone some impairment – is relatively common in computational modeling (e.g., Plaut, 1996). This approach was applied to four ACT-R models developed by Kimberg and Farah (1993). The four models simulated the Stroop task, the Wisconsin Card Sorting Test, a context memory task, and a motor-sequencing task. These tasks were chosen for their variety and for the patterns of errors they evoke among frontal-lobe-damaged patients. Each model included the productions and interconnected declarative nodes required for performing the task. In its unimpaired form, each model performed with a high level of accuracy. However, when the strengths of the links between declarative nodes were reduced (representing relatively dispersed neurological damage), each model showed a level and kind of impairment akin to that exhibited among frontal-lobe-damaged patients. For example, the impaired motor-sequencing model performed inappropriate actions on each device (e.g., pulling instead of twisting a twister), and the impaired Stroop model exhibited greater interference from unattended stimulus features (it was slower to name the ink color of color-name words).

The impairment procedure applied to these models (weakening strengths of association) is closely related to reducing W, the source activation from the goal. Both "impairments" reduce the amount of source activation arriving at to-be-retrieved declarative nodes, thereby affecting retrieval performance. Since impairing the spreading activation process in a computational model produces effects similar to frontal lobe damage, the logic of this approach suggests that spreading source activation may have its counterpart in the human brain. It also suggests that working memory processes like spreading source activation are associated with frontal lobe function. Although this model-to-brain mapping is at an abstract level, it is consistent with the role of prefrontal cortex posited in the O'Reilly et al. model (Chapter 11, this volume).

The second approach to understanding the biological implementation of working memory involves comparing the predictions of a working memory model with data recorded from the brain. This approach does not speak directly to the mechanisms underlying working memory but can shed light on whether a proposed mechanism is consistent with observed changes in neural activation. Relating such data to models of working memory is a more recent approach (Cohen et al., 1994; Just, Carpenter, Keller, Eddy, & Thulborn, 1996; Lü, Williamson, & Kaufman, 1992a). For example, Lü, Williamson, and Kaufman have studied the habituation responses of various cortical (and subcortical) regions of the brain using event-related potential and magnetic source imaging techniques. One of their findings relevant to our work involves the response of two areas in the auditory cortex. In particular, they found that the event-related field response (100-ms component) for repeated tones shows an activation trace that decays with time after the presentation of the tone. They postulate that this trace (measured in terms of reduced responsiveness at increasingly short ISIs) reflects the neural availability of the tone for processing by working memory. Moreover, they have shown that the rate of decay varies considerably across individuals and relates to behavioral data. The shape of the decay they observed is well captured by an exponential function

$$e^{-(t - t_0)/\tau}, \tag{7}$$

where t is the current time, t_0 is the time of the tone's onset, and τ is the decay rate.

This neural activation function seems superficially similar to the ACT-R declarative learning mechanism, where nodes' base-level activations consist of accumulated power-decay functions. However, such a mapping suffers from the fact that the time course of decay studied by Lü et al. (1992a, b) was on a much shorter time scale (and fit by an exponential function). The more appropriate mapping we have found relates the amount of source activation W to the decay rate τ, assuming a slight extension to ACT-R's treatment of source activation. (See Appendix A.) The basic idea involves viewing the goal's source activation as a "leaky capacitor" (Sejnowsky, 1981) that needs to be continually pumped with source activation to maintain a fixed level W. That is, instead of W being automatically and instantaneously transferred to a new goal, source activation of the previous goal would gradually decline (à la Equation 7), and source activation of the new goal would gradually build to asymptote. In such a system, the total source activation across all goals (past and present) is a limited amount W that relates directly to the decay rate τ from Equation 7. It is noteworthy that Lü et al. (1992b) found individual differences in the decay rate τ for different subjects, just as we propose that differences in W will predict working memory differences among subjects.

This new view of W allocation helps explain why the brain might employ a limit to attentional resources such as attention or source activation. If attention could be allocated without limit (or, under our new generalization, if source activation did not decay), the system would not be able to focus differentially on the current goal. Not only would this make it difficult to distinguish the current goal from past goals, but goal-based modulation of declarative information would become ineffective with so many goals simultaneously activating so many declarative memory elements. This analysis suggests a certain computational efficiency to maintaining limited attentional resources and is similar to the analysis of Young and Lewis (Chapter 7, this volume) supporting functional limitations to working memory.

Table 5.2. *Critical Productions for Memory-Loaded Algebra Task*

Substitute for a:
IF   the goal is to solve an equation with *a* in it
*   and *f* is the first element of the memory list
THEN substitute *f* for *a*
Substitute for b:
IF   the goal is to solve an equation with *b* in it
*   and *s* is the second element of the memory list
THEN substitute *s* for *b*
Invert-transformation:
IF   the goal is to solve an equation *term1 op1 constant1* = *constant2*
**   and *op2* inverts *op1*
THEN transform equation to the form *term1* = *constant2 op2 constant1*
Collect-sum:
IF   the goal is to solve an equation that contains *c* + *d*
**   and *s* is the sum of *c* + *d*
THEN replace *c* + *d* by *s*

The Role of Working Memory in Complex Cognitive Activities

As mentioned above, ACT-R posits that memory performance is degraded in more complex tasks because the limited amount of source activation (W) must be shared among more elements. In this section, we exemplify this prediction in the context of a model of algebra problem solving. (See Anderson et al., 1996, for details.) This particular algebra task emphasizes working memory by incorporating a memory-load component. Specifically, in each trial the participant had to encode a digit list, hold the list in memory while solving an algebra problem, and then recall the digit list. The difficulty of both subtasks was manipulated over trials. For example, the digit span was either 2, 4, or 6 digits, and the algebra problems required either one or two transformations. Finally, the trials were divided into two types: those for which the algebra equation had all numeric constants (e.g., $3 \times - 8 = 7$) and those for which the equation required substituting digits from the digit span (e.g., $ax - b = 7$, where subjects had to substitute the first and second elements of the digit span for a and b, respectively, and then solve). The latter trial type was included to study working memory effects when the two subtasks required integrated processing.

Table 5.2 shows some production rules used in the model for this task. Notice that each asterisk (*) indicates retrieval from the memory list, and each double asterisk (**) indicates retrieval of an arithmetic/algebra fact. The probability and latency of these retrievals depends on the amount of source activation reaching the to-be-retrieved nodes. Figures 5.5a and 5.5b show that these amounts will differ between high-load and low-load trials. In Figure

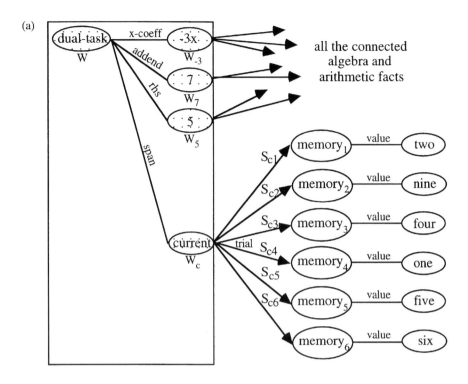

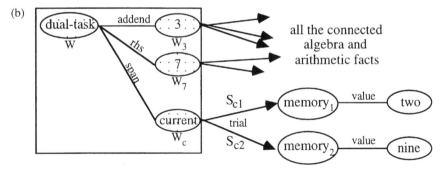

Figure 5.5. Goal and declarative memory for the algebra-memory dual task. (a) Representation of a trial with high-complexity algebra problem and high memory-load digit span. (b) Representation of a trial with low-complexity algebra problem and low memory-load digit span.

5.5a, very little source activation is reaching the relevant nodes in declarative memory. This is because there are many goal nodes (less source activation per goal node) and there are many links from these goal nodes to declarative memory (thinner spreading of each share of source activation). In contrast, in Figure 5.5b, fewer goal nodes are needed to represent the simpler algebra problem (more source activation per goal node) and there are fewer links from these nodes (better spreading of each share of source activation).

Because of these differences in source activation, the to-be-retrieved nodes will have less total activation on high-load trials than on low-load trials, which should lead to differences in probability and latency of recall. Notice that this prediction implies that manipulating the difficulty of one task should affect performance on that task as well as on the other task. For example, making the algebra equation more complex leads to smaller shares of source activation per goal node, thus leading to less source activation spreading to arithmetic facts and to memory items. Less source activation will make both arithmetic retrievals and memory span retrievals more error prone and slower. Moreover, making the algebra equation more complex increases the number of steps required to reach a solution. With more steps and slower retrievals, there will be a longer delay on high-load trials before the memory span can be recalled. That extra delay incurs greater decay for the memory digits, making their retrieval even more difficult. This shows that, given limited source activation, making one task more difficult can impair performance on both tasks.

Figure 5.6 shows some of the quantitative predictions of the model along with the corresponding observed results. Notice that both the model and participants take longer to solve the algebra problems when they are more complex, when they require substitution, and when the memory list is longer. In terms of string recall, accuracy suffers the longer the list and when the algebra problems are complex, but there is no reliable effect of substitution on memory.[6]

To generate predictions from this model, five free parameters were estimated. For the experiment shown in Figure 5.6, there were 48 data points in total to be fit, and the obtained goodness-of-fit statistic was $\chi^2(df = 43) = 79.3$. This value indicates a good fit (as can be seen), but there is significant residual variance not predicted. One possible source of that residual variance is unaccounted-for variation among participants in their working memory capacities. In the next section, we show how individual differences can be incorporated into the modeling framework described thus far and how doing so can improve overall model fits.

---

[6] The lack of an effect of substitution on memory span is probably due to the fact that the longer delay from making the substitution counteracts the extra practice of the first two digits when they are accessed for substitution.

(a)

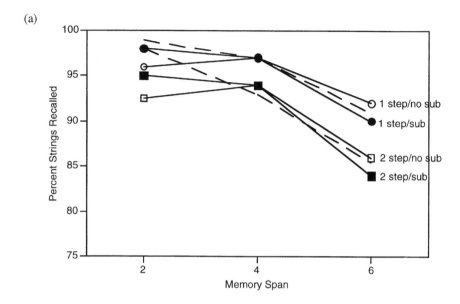

(b)

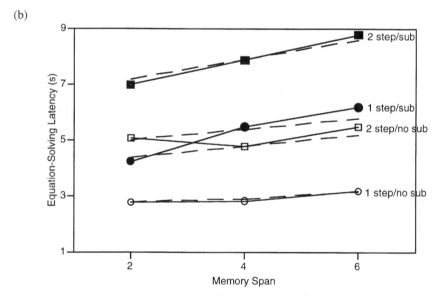

Figure 5.6. Selected (a) accuracy and (b) latency results, adapted with permission of Academic Press from Anderson, Reder, and Lebiere (1996). Solid lines are behavioral data, dashed lines are model predictions.

Modeling Working Memory Effects at the Individual Level

In this section, we describe some of the issues involved in modeling working memory effects at the individual subject level. We take W (the amount of source activation propagating from the goal) as the parameter reflecting individual differences in working memory. That is, in contrast to previous work (e.g., Anderson et al., 1996), which took W as a fixed limitation across subjects ($W \equiv 1$), we take W as a limitation that varies across the population ($W \sim \text{Normal}(1, \sigma^2)$). The results we present here are preliminary in nature but are encouraging with respect to our main hypothesis that varying the W parameter can capture individual differences in working memory performance. Our secondary hypothesis, based on the unitary nature of W in ACT-R, is that individual differences reflected in the W parameter will be similar across tasks and situations within the same individual. That is, we take an individual's W parameter to be relatively stable across time and tasks.[7] The topics discussed subsequently cover several issues associated with these hypotheses: theoretical issues (What are ACT-R's predictions under different values of W?), empirical issues (How can current research paradigms be adjusted to focus on individual differences caused by different working memory capacities and not by different strategies?), and modeling issues (How does variability in W impact model predictions?).

Theoretical Issues: Capturing Individual Differences in Working Memory

Just as varying the memory load of a task distributes source activation more or less thinly and leads ACT-R to predict differences in performance across task versions, varying the limit on source activation across individuals (for a fixed task) leads ACT-R to predict differences in performance across individuals. As described above, the more complex the task, the less source activation added to goal-relevant nodes, making them less likely to be retrieved. The same effect is obtained by keeping task complexity constant and decreasing the total amount of source activation (W) propagating from the goal. Thus, ACT-R predicts that people with lower attentional capacity W will have lower probability of retrieving goal-relevant nodes, all else equal. The value of W also has an effect on retrievals through the latency function (Equation 3). Here, when W is lower, goal-relevant nodes have less total activation, making their retrieval latencies longer. Longer latencies can have a secondary effect on other retrievals – they incur delayed processing of other information or less time for rehearsals, so other nodes' base-level activations will tend to be

---

[7] There may be moment-to-moment fluctuations of W within an individual (see section on Attention and Consciousness), but we are hypothesizing that the differences in W between individuals are potentially greater.

lower when their retrieval is attempted. These effects can accumulate across a task to produce markedly different behavior among subjects, as we will show.

It is noteworthy that our explanation of individual differences in working memory, though fundamentally based on the W parameter, also relies critically on the timing differences caused by differences in W. Thus, one view of our approach is that it provides a computational account of the processing-speed theory of age-related working memory differences (Salthouse, 1996). If the amount of attentional energy, W, decreases with age, then all retrieval latencies will be slower (not to mention somewhat more error prone) in older populations, making overall processing times slower. A related computational account of processing-speed theory by Byrne (1998) directly manipulates a rate parameter to produce differences between young and old populations. Our model, on the other hand, manipulates the parameter W thus indirectly affecting processing rate.

Other research suggests that decrements in performance among elderly subpopulations may be due to decrements in working memory capacity that are linked to inhibitory processes (Connelly & Hasher, 1993; Hasher & Zacks, 1988; Kane et al., 1994; Stoltzfus et al., 1993). Many of the effects seen in the elderly, especially under dual-task conditions, are reminiscent of problems associated with frontal-lobe-damaged patients. Postulating a lower value of W for individuals in either population might explain how these clinical behaviors arise. For example, smaller W can produce distractibility or inability to stay on task because less source activation propagates to goal-relevant items, making it easier for goal-irrelevant stimuli to capture attention.

Empirical Issues: Studying Individual Differences in Working Memory

The first experiment we report was designed to explore whether we could observe and model individual differences – subject-by-subject differences – in a dual-task memory experiment. We were specifically interested in capturing individual differences in working memory capacity. This meant that we had to be careful to design our experiment so as to minimize the introduction of other sources of individual differences. For instance, we sought to reduce between-subjects variability in motivation and on-taskedness by having an experimenter in the room to monitor each participant's progress. The main type of variability we sought to reduce, however, was *strategic variability*. We focused on designing the experiment so that subjects would tend to use the same strategy to perform the task. Building a model that matched this strategy would make the model more accurate and hence its parameter values (for both global and individual subject parameters) more interpretable.

The task we devised for this purpose is a variant of the digit working memory task developed by Oakhill and her colleagues (e.g., Yuill, Oakhill, & Parkin, 1989). It employs a dual-task procedure in that subjects had to read a sequence of digits aloud while maintaining in memory a selected subset of

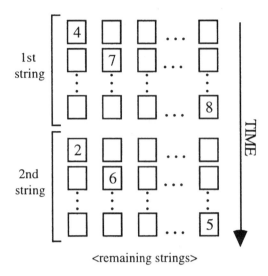

Figure 5.7. Time-based display of a trial in the digit working memory task.

those digits. Figure 5.7 shows the time-stepped presentation of a single trial. Digits were presented individually, appearing in one box and then disappearing before the next digit appeared in the next box. Subjects had to keep pace with the presentation rate by reading the digits aloud. (We used two presentation rates, 0.5 s and 0.7 s.) The rightmost digit in each string (8 and 5 in the figure) was to be remembered for later recall. These to-be-remembered digits were presented for double the presentation rate to allow for extra "memorizing" time; thus, the slower presentation rate offered more end-of-string time. After all the strings for a given trial were presented, subjects were prompted to recall the rightmost digits in the order they were presented. Recalling these string-final digits is analogous to recalling the sentence-final words in the Reading Span Task (Daneman & Carpenter, 1980).

This digit working memory task is distinguished from related working memory tasks in several ways. First, we maintained a precise digit-presentation rate via computer presentation. This reduced the variability from subjects choosing their own rates. Second, because our presentation rates were quite fast, variability owing to different rehearsal strategies was reduced – there was little time for any kind of rehearsal. Third, we varied the presentation rate to study its impact on memory performance. Note that a slower presentation rate increases the difficulty of the memory task by elongating the delay between storing and recalling the memory digits, but it leaves more time for additional processing of the memory digits. Fourth, we presented the different trial types in a random order. This eases the assumption that subjects come to each trial with an equal allocation of resources and eliminates potentially confounding time-based effects (e.g., learning, strategy change, boredom, fatigue). Finally, we included strict recall instructions for our task: The goal was to recall both the identity and position of each memory digit. Specifically, subjects' recall had to proceed once through the memory list without corrections or backtracking but with the possibility of skipping unknown digits. This procedure eliminated variability in recall order and reduced potential variability in recall strategies.

This task offers several options for manipulating task difficulty. A few that we have explored are (a) number of strings per trial (i.e., number of to-be-recalled digits), (b) number of digits to be read per string, and (c) interdigit presentation rate. Finally, to verify the similarity of different subjects' strategies in approaching this task, at the end of the experiment, we asked subjects to describe their approach to the task. A commonly reported strategy involved rehearsing memory digits at the end of each string after encoding the current to-be-remembered digit. We have incorporated this information into our model. More importantly for our study of individual differences, the frequency of this response suggests that subjects did not differ greatly in the strategies they applied to the task. Also, because of the simple nature of the items to be remembered and the fact that chunking strategies (i.e., encoding the digits into related groups) were so rare, it is reasonable to assume that undergraduate students would not differ greatly in their representations or their relevant knowledge about numbers. These arguments suggest that any memory differences to be found among subjects in this task would largely be a result of "architectural" differences in working memory capacity. At the very least, our procedure reduced other sources of variability more than is typically done.

Modeling Issues I: The Basic Model and Its Aggregate Predictions

The processes required to perform this task involve reading, storing, and recalling digits. Based on subjects' reports, it also appeared that people rehearsed digits (as time allowed) at the end of each string. We designed our model of the task to reflect all of these processes. Our model represents the two main goals of this task separately: reading digits and recalling digits. This corresponds to people switching between the goals as they process a single trial. Figure 5.8a depicts a goal to recall the digit in the first position of the current trial. Note that the representation of the corresponding memory digit (Figure 5.8b) is essentially the same; the only difference is that the value of the stored digit is included in the node structure.

These declarative structures are processed by productions that represent the different actions subjects perform in completing this task. Table 5.3 presents a list of some of the processes implemented by separate productions in our model. The "read" production applies whenever the goal is to read the digits and a digit is on the screen. After a digit has been read, if it is in the last position, the "store" production applies; this creates a new declarative node

(a)

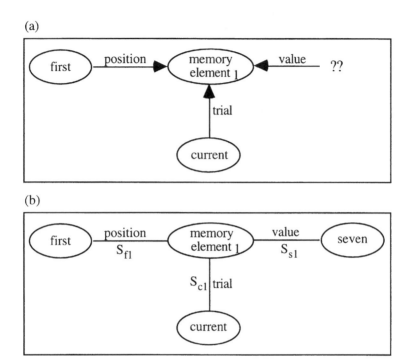

(b)

Figure 5.8. (a) A goal to recall the first digit in the digit working memory task. (b) The memory element for the first digit in the digit–working-memory task.

and endows that node with an initial boost of base-level activation. The "store" production also sets a subgoal to rehearse previous memory elements after the current digit is stored. Note that in our model, the production implementing rehearsal attempts to retrieve a particular memory digit. If successful, this retrieval gives a boost to the node's base-level activation, making the node more accessible subsequently (e.g., even easier to rehearse later). The probability of successful retrieval, however, depends on total activation, that is, if the target memory digit is highly activated relative to the others, it will likely be retrieved. Notice that a high value of W would produce high activation for the to-be-rehearsed digit, making rehearsals more likely to succeed and faster. The more successful rehearsals that fit into the time allowed at the end of each string, the greater total activations will be when the "recall" production attempts to retrieve the memory digits. This explains how different values of W can have impact on the amount of learning that goes on within a single trial.

Figure 5.9 shows that different values of W can also directly affect recall of the memory digits at the end of each trial. Here, the goal is to recall a digit for the first position of the current trial. The node representing this target mem-

---

Table 5.3. *Critical Productions for Digit Working Memory Task*

Read:
IF goal is to read a digit and digit d is on screen
THEN say digit d
Store:
IF goal is to read a digit and digit d is on screen and d is in last column and d has
been read
THEN store d and prepare to rehearse
Rehearse:
IF goal is to read a digit and digit d is in the position to be rehearsed
THEN update position to be rehearsed
Recall:
IF goal is to recall digit in position p of trial t and digit d "matches" but has not
been recalled
THEN say digit d

---

ory (memory element$_1$) receives source activation from both goal nodes "first" and "current," whereas other memory digits receive source activation only from the "current" goal node. This difference means that memory element$_1$ is receiving an additional $W_j \cdot S_{ji}$ units of source activation.[8] When either W_j or S_{ji} is smaller, this difference in activation will be reduced, and the relative ease and speed of retrieving the target memory element will be reduced, leading to poorer recall. As we described earlier, the link strength S_{ji} is smaller the more nodes linked to goal node j; thus, when the memory list is longer, the S_{ji}'s will be smaller and performance will be worse. Moreover, source activation W_j may differ among subjects. Therefore, subjects with a lower value of W will have a lower W_j, and hence show poorer recall performance. This effect will be even more pronounced on long lists, where the differential activation of target memory digits is the product of both a reduced W_j and a reduced S_{ji}.

To compute the model's predictions, we ran 22 simulations (one for each subject) under each of the task conditions used. These task conditions include all 16 possible combinations of the following factors: number of digits to be

---

[8] The activation of memory element$_1$ is also greater than that of the other memory elements because it exactly matches the current production's retrieval template (which involves the *first* element of the *current* trial). The other memory elements only partially match this template (they are not in the first position), so they compete for retrieval with an activation level reduced by the partial matching penalty (Equation 5). Because the mismatch penalty is smaller the greater the similarity between a candidate node and the retrieval template, this model produces similarity-based errors where similarity is a function of position in the recall string. Although we do not present them here, the pattern of positional errors produced by the model is very similar to that exhibited by subjects.

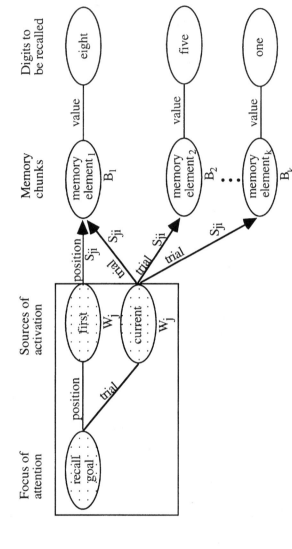

Figure 5.9. Goal and declarative memory representation for the digit working memory task.

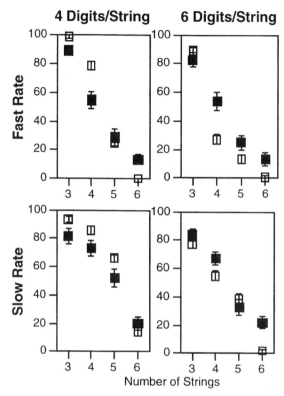

Figure 5.10. Aggregate data (solid boxes) and first-pass model predictions (open boxes) with standard error bars. The dependent measure on the ordinate is percentage of trials perfectly recalled.

recalled (3, 4, 5, or 6), number of digits per string (4 or 6), and presentation rate (0.5 s or 0.7 s). Since the main dependent measure of interest in this task is probability of recall, we computed the proportion of trials of a given type for which all the digits were recalled in the correct position (and averaged across simulations).

Figure 5.10 presents the model's predictions. These predictions are *not* based on an optimal fitting of the parameters: Most parameters were left at their default setting (e.g., $W = 1$), and two parameters, F and s, were adjusted slightly to produce predictions in the appropriate range. Also presented in Figure 5.10 are the aggregated results from 22 subjects who completed 64 trials each (four replications of each of the 16 trial types). Even without optimally tuned parameter values, these predictions show effects of the three main factors that are similar to those in the data. Specifically, our model predicts higher recall probabilities for trials with fewer strings (fewer to-be-recalled digits), for 4-digit strings over 6-digit strings, and for the slower presentation rate over the faster rate. The effect of number of strings is produced by the model because the fewer memory digits, the more source activation that gets spread along each link from a goal node to a declarative node. The effect of number of digits per string is produced by the model because fewer digits to be read shortens the delay between encoding and recall of the memory digits (i.e., base-level activation has had less time to decay). And, finally, the effect of presentation rate is produced by the model because the slower rate allows more rehearsals to be made at the end of each string. Presumably in our model this benefit of extra practice opportunities outweighs the disadvantage of slightly longer delays to recall. This advantage of the slower presentation rate observed in the data also supports subjects' self-report of doing extra rehearsals after each memory digit was presented. Our model would have predicted a disadvantage for the slower rate if rehearsals did not occur during this extra time.

This first-pass model fit is quite encouraging. Even without an optimized parameterization, the best-fitting line between the data and predictions is observed $= 0.71 \cdot$ predicted $+ 0.16$, $R^2 = .88$. Nevertheless, there are two deficiencies. First, it appears that the model tends to overpredict for the 4-digits-per-string trials and underpredict for the 6-digits-per-string trials, and second, the standard error bars for the model's predictions are consistently smaller than those for the data. To address these deficiencies, we next moved to incorporating individual differences into our model.

Modeling Issues II: Including Individual Differences in the Model

ADDING WORKING MEMORY DIFFERENCES TO THE MODEL. We proposed that the W parameter in our model, representing an attentional resource, would reflect individual differences in working memory. The model presented earlier, however, took W as fixed across all simulations. To incorporate individual differences in W in our model, we ran a different set of 22 simulations (one for each subject, as above), but this time each simulation was randomly assigned its own W value. (Each W was drawn from a Normal with mean 1.0 and standard deviation 0.25.) Here, the different simulations represented different subjects, each with its own limit to source activation. We maintained all other parameter settings, that is, *no* optimal parameter fitting.

Figure 5.11 shows the improved fit attained by the same model as in Figure 5.10 but with randomly varying W values. The best-fitting line between the observed data and these predictions is more similar to the line $y = x$ than before: observed $= 0.95 \cdot$ predicted $+ 0.02$, $R^2 = .92$. This reflects the fact that the average predictions of the model are now closer to the average observed accuracies. An important point to note here is that we did not fit each individual W parameter to a particular subject's data; rather, we drew the 22 W values randomly from a normal distribution. Thus, merely by adding variability to the input of our model via the W parameter, we obtained a better fit to the data. Another improvement in this second-pass model fit is that the stan-

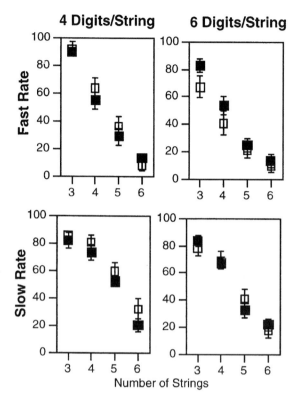

Figure 5.11. Aggregate data (solid boxes) and individual-differences model predictions (open boxes) with standard error bars. The ordinate in each plot is percentage of trials perfectly recalled.

dard-error bars of the predictions now appear similar in size to the error bars of the subjects. In contrast, the previous model did not exhibit enough variability in its predictions. In summary, these results show that by incorporating individual differences in our model, the mean level of the predictions changed as well as the standard error of those predictions. Such changes arose because of the nonlinearities in our model. In fact, adding variability to the input can have such effects in any nonlinear system.

FITTING INDIVIDUAL SUBJECT'S WORKING MEMORY DIFFERENCES. Although the foregoing model takes into account individual differences, the predictions portray only performance in the aggregate. It is possible that a model (even one that takes into account individual differences) can capture aggregate results but not be able to fit the data of any individual subjects. Thus, we next fit the parameter W to the data for each subject individually, keeping the other parameters fixed. Our model predicts that the higher an

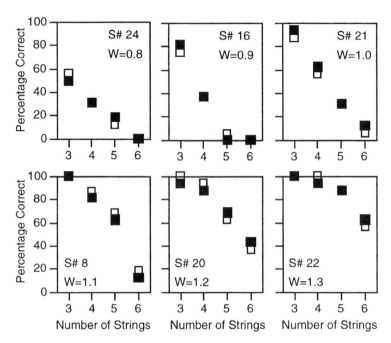

Figure 5.12. Individual participant data (solid boxes) and predictions (open boxes).

individual's attentional capacity W, the more likely correct retrievals will be. This influence of W on retrieval is twofold: (a) higher W values lead to faster retrieval latencies, which means that more rehearsals (learning) can be fit into a fixed amount of time, and (b) higher W values lead to the spreading of more source activation to memory elements that are strongly linked to the goal nodes, making those memory elements more accessible.

As Figure 5.12 shows, the model accounts well for individual subject's recall performance, even matching the shape of individual subject's data. In the figure we display the data only by number of strings to maintain a sufficient number of replications per data point. Although error bars are not plotted for the model predictions, activation noise leads to stochasticity in retrieval; even for a fixed value of W, the model's predictions vary somewhat from simulation to simulation. The six subjects in Figure 5.12 were chosen to represent the range of estimated W values; the model provided a good fit for all of the 22 subjects. Again, it is important to note that for these individual subject fits, the global parameters of the model were maintained at the same fixed (and not optimized) values. The only parameter we specially estimated for these fits was a particular W value for each subject.

It is interesting to note that this procedure led to a bell-shaped distribution of estimated W values for our sample (Figure 5.13): a few subjects were best fit

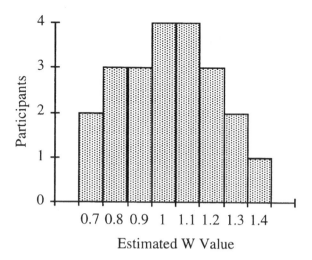

Figure 5.13. Histogram of number of participants with different estimated values for *W*.

by high or low *W*, and most subjects were fit by $W \sim 1$. Thus, these *W* estimates tell us something about the subject-to-subject variability in the quantity that *W* represents. Moreover, according to our model, each participant's *W* value represents a fixed quantity of source activation for that individual, which should be reflected across repeated performance of the same task and across performance in different tasks. We take up these issues of fixed *W* for each subject in the next two subsections.

Modeling Issues III: Modeling Performance Across Sessions

To begin to test our hypothesis that a subject's working memory capacity is fixed across time and tasks, we asked several subjects to perform the digit working memory task multiple times (each time with different stimuli). This allows us to measure the test–retest reliability of our paradigm and to evaluate how well our model – with a single *W* value per subject – can fit multisession data.

The declarative and procedural knowledge of the model is the same as that presented earlier. The one important difference from the previous treatment, however, is that here we are exploring the model's performance across multiple sessions. This means that we must consider the learning implications of getting practice at the task. In the general description of the ACT-R theory presented earlier, we focused exclusively on declarative learning mechanisms. However, repeating the digit working memory task with different stimuli does not allow for much benefit from declarative learning – nodes are not repeated or practiced across trials let alone sessions. The most reasonable kind of learning in which subjects likely engage as they repeat this task is *procedural learn-*

ing. In ACT-R, procedural learning involves the strengthening of productions with practice. This strengthening mechanism is analogous to the declarative learning mechanism; instead of increasing a node's base-level activation with each use, it involves increasing the strength of a given production with each use. As in declarative learning, these strength boosts decay with time since each use. Equation 8 specifies the strength of production p in terms of its uses at time lags t_k:

$$S_p = \log (\Sigma t_k^{-d}),\qquad\qquad(8)$$

Procedural learning has a similar effect to honing a useful tool: The more often the tool is used, the better it is used. That is, a production that has been used more frequently and more recently will require less time to do its processing. This allows us to extend the latency function of Equation 3 to describe the latency of retrieving declarative node i using production p:

$$T_{ip} = Fe^{-(S_p + A_i)},\qquad\qquad(9)$$

where S_p is the strength of the production and A_i is the total activation of the declarative node.

In terms of our digit working memory model, the basic prediction is that subjects will get faster at the processes involved in the task (e.g., doing rehearsals) as they gain experience. What implications does this have for memory performance? As we demonstrated, having more time for rehearsals leads to improved recall. Therefore, when subjects get faster because of procedural practice, they will have time for more rehearsals so greater declarative learning will produce an increase in their proportion of correct recalls. This prediction allows us to expect reliability of performance across repetitions of this task to be of a certain form: Subjects' recall scores will not necessarily hover at the same level across sessions but will tend to improve with practice.

To generate quantitative predictions regarding memory improvement across sessions, we analyzed our model in light of ACT-R's basic mechanisms to determine the effects of production practice on retrieval probabilities. By drawing on the ACT-R equations presented up to this point, we obtained the following approximation (see Appendix B for details):

$$\text{LogOdds}(i) = C + D \ln (i),\qquad\qquad(10)$$

where the equation refers to the log odds of correctly retrieving individual nodes at session i. When retrievals are plotted against session number on log–log coordinates, Equation 10 predicts a linear relationship between retrieval odds and session number. The value C in Equation 10 would be the y-intercept of that line; it is a constant related to the log odds of correct retrieval at session 1, which is a function of W as shown in the preceding model fits. Therefore, individual differences in W should lead to differences in the y-intercept of different subjects' retrieval functions. The value D, on the

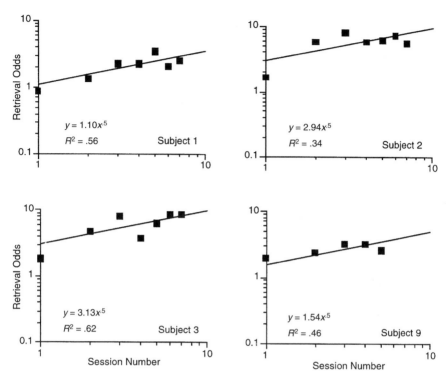

Figure 5.14. Individual subjects' average odds of retrieving memory digits, by session (in log-log coordinates).

other hand, represents the slope of the retrieval function in Equation 10; it is a constant related to the decay rate d. In all the models we have discussed, d was taken as fixed at 0.5 (the ACT-R default). Therefore, we would not expect differences in the slope of different subjects' retrieval function. This is consistent with other evidence that people do not differ in decay rates (e.g., Salthouse, 1994).

Figure 5.14 shows the data of four subjects who participated in five or more sessions. These data are plotted in log–log coordinates with odds of digit retrieval against session number. As the model predicted, for each subject, there is improvement across sessions. Moreover, the subjects differ in their session 1 retrieval performance, which is consistent with the predicted between-subject variability in W. The predictions of Equation 10 are represented by the solid line in each panel. These lines were fit with a common slope ($D = 0.5$) and estimated values for C. Because C is a function of an individual's W value, the different intercept values reflect our model's account of working memory differences in this task.

The main point of these individual-subject, multisession plots is to show that a single W value does not preclude improvement across sessions. Indeed, the fitted lines in Figure 5.14 are based on a stable W parameter for each individual and yet show improvement across sessions that is consistent with the data.[9] These results also suggest that it is helpful to view test–retest reliability and stability of individual differences in terms of a model of cognitive processing. In this way, learning effects can unfold naturally, and the model can provide mechanistic interpretations of both the stable components of behavior (e.g., relatively fixed W for each subject) and the variable ones (e.g., learning and practice effects).

Modeling Issues IV: Generalizing to Another Task

Thus far, we have shown that varying the amount of source activation (W) captures individual differences in a digit working memory task and that these differences appear stable across repeated sessions. One of the primary strengths of the ACT-R theory, however, is its broad applicability across different tasks. Therefore, in this section we show that varying the W parameter in a model of a different task produces the observed individual differences in that task as well. This supports the notion that W is general enough to account for memory differences across tasks. The next step then will be to explore the hypothesis that the same value for W predicts a given individual's performance on multiple tasks. Here, we describe our preliminary results on the way to that goal.

The task that we model has previously been studied in its exact form by Zbrodoff (1995) and others (Logan, 1988; Logan & Klapp, 1991; Rabinowitz & Goldberg, 1995). It is called an alpha-arithmetic task because the goal of each trial is to verify whether or not a given statement involving letters and numbers is true. For example, the statement A + 2 = C is true because C is two letters after A in the alphabet. Correspondingly, the statement A + 2 = D is false. In this task, a statement is presented, and the subject presses one of two keys to indicate whether the statement is true or false. Subjects' latency and accuracy are measured for each trial. We used stimuli from Zbrodoff's (1995) Experiment 1.[10] These include 12 different alpha-arithmetic statements, half true and half false, with numerical addends of 2, 3, and 4. During the experiment, the 12 unique statements were repeated (in random order) 48 times, giving subjects a chance to learn the facts associated with each.

Past results using this task suggest that subjects initially solve the problems by counting up from the initial letter a number of times specified by the numerical addend. More counts are required for problems with larger numer-

---

[9] Our procedural learning account of this memory improvement is also consistent with subjects' reports. When asked about their strategies after each session, participants tended to maintain the same basic store–rehearse–retrieve strategy mentioned earlier.

[10] We thank Jane Zbrodoff for sharing her experiment software with us.

Table 5.4. *Critical Productions for Alpha-Arithmetic Task*

Retrieve alpha-arithmetic
IF the goal is to analyze START + ADDEND = RESULT and the fact START +
ADDEND = RESULT has truth value X
THEN set a goal to respond X
Compute alpha-arithmetic
IF the goal is to analyze START + ADDEND = RESULT
THEN set a goal to compute START + ADDEND and compare with RESULT

ical addends, producing what is called the "problem-size effect": Latencies for
4-addend problems are greater than for 3-addend problems, which are greater
than for 2-addend problems. With practice, however, subjects gradually learn
the alpha-arithmetic facts required to solve the problems and thus no longer
need to count to verify each statement but can simply retrieve the relevant
fact. This retrieval phase is signaled by a reduction in the problem size effect
(i.e., the difference in latency across the 4-, 3-, and 2-addend problems
decreases or disappears because subjects are no longer counting up the alphabet).[11] The processes involved in this task are, for the most part, different
from those in the digit working memory task, and this alpha-arithmetic task
does not explicitly involve dual tasks. For our purposes, the task allows for the
study of working memory effects (and individual differences therein) in a relatively simple learning task.

Our model implements two productions for deciding whether the current
statement is true (Table 5.4): (a) a production to retrieve a relevant alpha-
arithmetic fact and (b) a production to initiate a sequence of steps for counting up the alphabet. The retrieval production will tend to be preferred,[12] but
if the retrieval attempt fails, the counting production will be initiated. Given
these two productions, performance is mainly driven by the activation of
alpha-arithmetic facts in declarative memory because these activations determine the probability and latency of retrieval (i.e., the first production).

Figure 5.15 displays a node structure corresponding to the fact "A + 3 = D is
true." Suppose this structure is already in declarative memory (i.e., the fact
has already been encountered and stored on a previous trial); it will have a
certain base-level activation. When the current goal involves processing the

---

[11] Notice, however, that in ACT-R retrieval latencies are a function of practice, so if the different sized problems occur with different frequencies, some problem-size effect is predicted to remain.

[12] Another related approach involves using the actual activation values of the problem representation to select among strategies, i.e., adopt a retrieval strategy if enough activation
from the elements of the problem intersect, but otherwise use a calculation strategy (see
Schunn, Reder, Nhouyvanisvong, Richards, & Stroffolino, 1997).

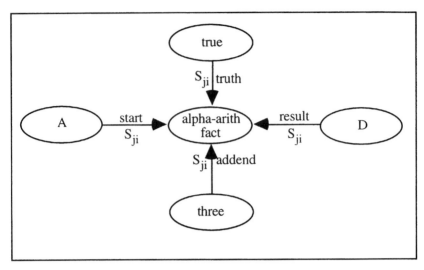

Figure 5.15. Node structure corresponding to the fact "A + 3 = D is true."

statement "A + 3 = D," the goal nodes "A," "three," and "D" will all spread source activation to this alpha-arithmetic fact, thereby increasing its total activation along all three links. This fact had been used only once many trials ago, and so its base-level activation would have decayed to a low value. These two components – received source activation and base-level activation – combine to determine a node's current accessibility.

As this model progresses through the alpha-arithmetic task, an important change occurs in its processing: Initially, it will tend to compute its response by counting (because the necessary alpha-arithmetic facts are not yet present or have very low base-level activations), and later (once these facts are present and have been practiced), the model will be able to consistently respond via retrieval. This general transition is consistent with aggregate results obtained for this task.

But what are the consequences of variation in W for this model? As in the digit working memory task, the higher W, the faster all retrievals will be and hence the shorter observed latencies will be. This effect applies both to the counting approach (because alphabet retrievals are required) and to the retrieval approach (because alpha-arithmetic fact retrievals are required). One prediction is that a person with a higher value for W will be faster overall than a person with a lower value of W. Recall from Equation 3 that latency is a power function of total activation. Thus, ACT-R predicts a linear relationship between log latencies and log number of node accesses (base-level activation component of total activation) and a shift in these lines for individual differences in W (source activation component). Figure 5.16a shows this relation-

(a)

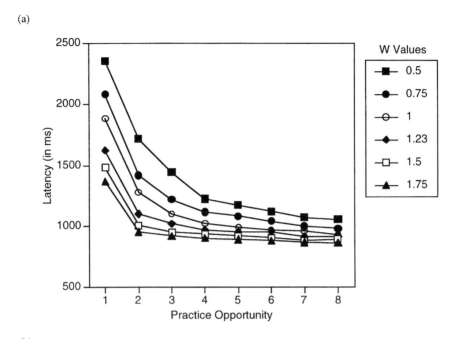

(b)

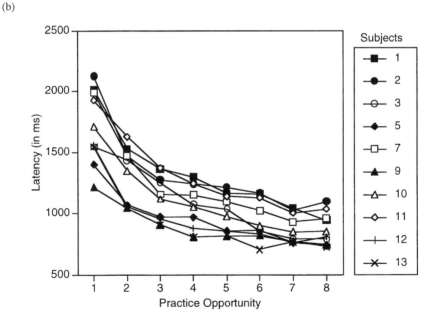

Figure 5.16. (a) Latency predictions for alpha-arithmetic as a function of node practice and W. (b) Observed practice effects for alpha-arithmetic experiment.

ship for several values of W. These values correspond quite well with the observed latencies for 10 different subjects (Figure 5.16b).

Another prediction of our model involves how quickly people will learn the alpha-arithmetic facts and thus make the transition from counting to retrieving. Recall that the higher W is, the more source activation will be propagated from the goal nodes to the alpha-arithmetic facts that are being learned throughout the course of the experiment. This makes the alpha-arithmetic facts more accessible than they would otherwise be with just their base-level activations alone. Therefore, an individual with high W will be more likely to retrieve a node with a certain base-level activation than will an individual with low W. This means that a person with high W will be able to retrieve the alpha-arithmetic facts earlier on in the experiment (when they have been less practiced) than will a person with a low W value. In terms of the two approaches for processing each trial, computation should phase out earlier for high-W subjects than for low-W subjects. We can gain an indirect measure of the relative amounts of computation and retrieval by inspecting the problem-size effect that the model produces in the first, second, and third blocks of the experiment. The problem-size effect here is measured as the average increase in trial latency per increase in numerical addend (i.e., how much slower is the response for +4 trials vs. +3 trials vs. +2 trials?). Figure 5.17a plots the model's problem-size effect for different values of W. Note that all the curves show a decrease in the problem-size effect, suggesting more retrieval and less computation. Moreover, the curves with high W (faster retrieval latencies) end up with very small problem-size effects, suggesting that there is almost no effect of addend size (and that retrieval is being used universally) in block 3. Figure 5.17b plots the corresponding observed data, with a separate curve for each subject, and shows similar effects. In summary, varying the W parameter in our model of this alpha-arithmetic task produces variations in performance (as measured by both latencies and problem-size effects) that correspond well to those exhibited across our sample.

Conclusions, Future Issues, and Speculations

We believe that the approach described here is a promising one. Table 5.5 gives a summary of our answers to the designated questions; however, to summarize more generally we list here what we take as some of our modeling accomplishments: (a) We developed several models in the ACT-R framework that produced working memory results similar to those exhibited by subjects. (b) We showed that varying the W parameter in those models improved model fits and produced a similar range of performance to that exhibited across subjects. (c) We fit individual simulation runs to individual subjects' data by estimating a single individual difference parameter, W. (d) Given the procedural learning mechanism built into the ACT-R framework, our models captured – with a stable W value for each individual – working memory

(a)

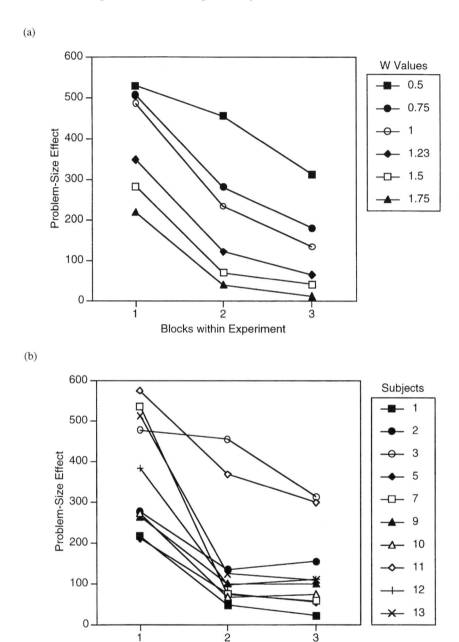

(b)

Figure 5.17. (a) Predicted and (b) observed problem-size effect in alpha-arithmetic task.

Table 5.5. *Summary of Answers to Designated Questions*

(1) Basic Mechanisms and Representations in Working Memory

Because working memory is conceived of as the highly activated subset of declarative memory, its representations are the same as those for declarative information. Declarative knowledge is represented as nodes in an interconnected network, with different types of information using different combinations of links (see Figure 5.1a). The basic mechanisms in working memory are (a) the spreading of source activation (a kind of "attentional energy") from the current goal to related nodes in declarative memory and (b) the learning and decay of declarative nodes' base-level activations. These two kinds of activation combine to determine a declarative node's accessibility: More highly activated nodes are more likely to be retrieved and tend to have shorter retrieval latencies.

(2) The Control and Regulation of Working Memory

The mechanisms described in answer 1 control the processing of information. Source activation propagating from the goal increases the total activation of goal-relevant nodes. This leads to context effects. However, there is an imposed limit to the amount of source activation focused on the goal, so this resource must be shared. The base-level activation of nodes reflects their accessibility independent of context. Base-level activation is not constrained by a fixed limit; it keeps accumulating the more a node is used. This leads to practice effects. However, base-level activation decays with time since each use, producing forgetting effects and sensitivity to time delays.

(3) The Unitary Versus Non-Unitary Nature of Working Memory

Because we conceive of working memory as the activated subset of declarative memory (i.e., it can be composed of all kinds of information and structures), it may be considered a non-unitary construct. On the other hand, ACT-R posits a limit to the source activation propagating from the current goal. This limited resource is fixed across all tasks, making working memory processing appear unitary. This common limit to source activation, however, is just one contributor to working memory performance; knowledge and strategy are other variables that influence performance.

(4) The Nature of Working Memory Limitations

Working memory limitations are imposed by the constraint that a limited amount of *source activation* (attentional energy) is directed from the current goal. This source activation must be shared among the elements of the goal (the more complex the goal, the smaller the shares) and then spread to neighboring nodes in declarative memory (the more neighbors, the smaller the subdivided amounts). This propagation of source activation to declarative memory serves to differentiate goal-relevant nodes from other nodes, making the former more accessible.

(5) The Role of Working Memory in Complex Cognitive Activities

The same working memory processes apply across all cognitive tasks. Because of the limit to source activation, more complex tasks produce greater sharing of that limited resource and hence lead to degraded performance. These effects of limited source activation apply in both dual-task situations and

Table 5.5, continued

memory-loaded situations. ACT-R models of a variety of complex cognitive tasks have provided good quantitative and qualitative fits to observed latencies and probabilities of recall.

(6) The Relationship of Working Memory to Long-Term Memory and Knowledge

Working memory is conceived of as the more activated subset of long-term memory. Working memory elements will tend to be those nodes in declarative memory that are strongly related to the current goal (i.e., those receiving extra source activation from the goal). Other nodes for which this is not true may still be in working memory, however, because of their high base-level activation (e.g., highly familiar concepts).

(7) The Relationship of Working Memory to Attention and Consciousness

A conception of working memory complementary to that in answer 6 emphasizes processes over contents. The primary working memory process is the spreading of source activation from the goal. This process represents the notion that attention is focused on elements of the goal that thereby modulate other information processing (e.g., retrieval). In this sense, we liken limited source activation to limited attentional resources. Working memory is related to consciousness in that elements of the goal and nodes in declarative memory are accessible to conscious awareness because of their heightened activation. Declarative nodes below this threshold of awareness can still vary in total activation; therefore, they vary in terms of the processing required to bring them into awareness.

(8) The Biological Implementation of Working Memory

Although connecting the theoretical construct of working memory to a biological implementation requires bridging a wide gap, neuropsychological and brain-imaging results suggest a biological implementation that is consistent with our theoretical position and computational models. First, damaging an ACT-R model's ability to spread source activation (an "ability" tightly linked to working memory and the W parameter) produced behavioral impairment similar to that of frontal-lobe patients (Kimberg & Farah, 1993). Second, brain-imaging data (Cohen et al., 1994) show that both context-sensitive processing and the maintenance of symbolic information produce activation in the prefrontal cortex. These brain functions have been modeled by a connectionist framework in which retrieval processes (represented as links between PFC and other brain areas) are modulated by the current goal (represented in the PFC). Third, brain-imaging studies have revealed individual differences in the parameters describing brain activation during working memory tasks. Mapping these results onto our framework suggests the goal-based processing (i.e., spreading of W) in our models describes brain functions associated with the PFC and the PFC's connection to other brain areas.

improvements across repeated sessions of the same task. (e) We showed preliminary simulations and data suggesting that these results generalize across tasks.

Clearly there is much more to do. Our next major goal is to explore the stability of W across tasks, that is, to explore whether the W parameter will predict individual differences for a given subject across tasks. This will test the hypothesis that W reflects a stable individual difference in working memory processes. Other research in this area suggests that the question is still an open one. Cases of both stability and change in individual differences across tasks have been found (e.g., Cantor & Engle, 1993; Shah & Miyake, 1996).

Our approach may help clarify these different results because it will explore individual differences in working memory in the context of computational models of cognitive processing. Our work has already shown that a complete cognitive model can clarify issues of test–retest reliability (by modeling test–retest effects in terms of procedural learning) and issues of individual differences (by incorporating variability in our modeling efforts and reducing important sources of strategic variability in our empirical efforts).

APPENDIX A

Take source activation of goal i at time T that has not been in focus since time t_i to be decaying according to the function $e^{-(T-t_i)/\tau}$ (Equation 7).

The sum of all such goals' source activations is bounded by

$$\int_0^T e^{-(T-t)/\tau}\,dt = e^{-T/\tau} \cdot \tau[e^{-T/\tau} -1] = \tau\,[1 - e^{-T/\tau}].$$

As the current time T increases, this expression goes to τ, which is to say the total amount of source activation in the system, with exponential decay rate τ upon goal switching, is capped by τ. In our framework, W represents that same cap, suggesting that our W parameter and Lü, Williamson, and Kaufman's (1992a,b) τ represent the same individual difference variable.

APPENDIX B

When practice opportunities are equally spaced, strength of production p, S_p, is approximated by $\ln\left[\dfrac{NL^{-d}}{1-d}\right]$, where N = number of practice opportunities, L = lifetime of the system, and d = decay rate. Let i = number of sessions and n = number of practice opportunities per session. Then, $S_{p,i} = S_0 + \ln\left[\dfrac{inL^{-d}}{1-d}\right]$, and the change in strength from session i to session $i+1$ is given by

$$S_{p,\Delta i} = S_{p,i+1} - S_{p,i} = \ln\left[\frac{(i+1)nL^{-d}}{1-d}\right] - \ln\left[\frac{inL^{-d}}{1-d}\right] = \ln\left[\frac{i+1}{i}\right].$$ (B1)

Using Equations 3 and B1, the ratio of latencies to retrieve node k with production p at session $i + 1$ to session i is

$$\frac{T_{k,p,i+1}}{T_{k,p,i}} = \frac{Fe^{-(A_{k,p}+S_{p,i+1})}}{Fe^{-(A_{k,p}+S_{p,i})}} = e^{-(S_{p,i+1}-S_{p,i})} = e^{-S_{p,\Delta i}} = e^{\ln\left[\frac{i+1}{i}\right]^{-1}} = \frac{i}{i+1}.$$

Let H_i = the average number of rehearsals per digit that are completed at session i. Then, $H_{i+1} = \dfrac{H_i(i+1)}{i}$, which can be used to determine the base-level activation of a node at sessions i and $i + 1$. Applying the production-strength learning approximation to base-level activation learning, the activation of node k is $\ln\left[\dfrac{NL^{-d}}{1-d}\right]$, where N = number of accesses of the node (rehearsals), L = lifetime of the system, and d = decay rate. Substituting H_i for N, we obtain

$$A_{k,p,i} = \ln\left[\frac{H_iL^{-d}}{1-d}\right] \text{ and } A_{k,p,i+1} = \ln\left[\frac{H_{i+1}L^{-d}}{1-d}\right] = \ln\left[\frac{H_i(i+1)L^{-d}}{i(1-d)}\right].$$

Using these activations in Equation 4 and converting to odds, we get $\text{Odds(retrieve}_{k,p}) = \dfrac{e^{A_{k,p}/s}}{e^{\tau}}$, with retrieval threshold τ as the competing node. From this, we derive the ratio for session $i + 1$ to i of the odds of retrieving node k with production p:

$$\frac{\text{Odds(retrieve}_{k,p,i+1})}{\text{Odds(retrieve}_{k,p,i})} = \frac{e^{\ln\left[\frac{H_i(i+1)^{1-d}L^{-d}}{i^{1-d}(1-d)}\right]^{\frac{1}{s}}}}{e^{\ln\left[\frac{H_iL^{-d}}{1-d}\right]^{\frac{1}{s}}}} = \left[\frac{i+1}{i}\right]^{\frac{1-d}{s}}.$$

By telescoping this odds ratio, we get $\text{Odds(retrieve}_i) = O_1 \cdot i^{\frac{1-d}{s}}$, where O_1 = Odds of retrieval at session 1, a function of W. Taking the log of both sides of this equation produces Equation 10 in the text, with $D = (1-d)/s$.

REFERENCES

Anderson, J. R. (1993). *Rules of the mind.* Hillsdale, NJ: Erlbaum.
Anderson, J. R., & Matessa, M. (1997). A production system theory of serial memory. *Psychological Review, 104,* 728–748.

Anderson, J. R., Reder, L. M., & Lebiere, C. (1996). Working memory: Activation limitations on retrieval. *Cognitive Psychology, 30,* 221–256.

Baddeley, A. D. (1986). *Working memory.* New York: Oxford University Press.

Baddeley, A. D., & Lieberman, K. (1980). Spatial working memory. In R. S. Nickerson (Ed.), *Attention and performance VIII* (pp. 521–539). Hillsdale, NJ: Erlbaum.

Brooks, L. R. (1968). Spatial and verbal components of the act of recall. *Canadian Journal of Psychology, 22,* 349–368.

Byrne, M. D. (1998). Taking a computational approach to aging: The SPAN theory of working memory. *Psychology and Aging, 13,* 309–322.

Cantor, J., & Engle, R. W. (1993). Working-memory capacity as long-term memory activation: An individual-differences approach. *Journal of Experimental Psychology: Learning, Memory, and Cognition, 19,* 1101–1114.

Caplan, D., Rochon, E., & Waters, G. S. (1992). Articulatory and phonological determinants of word length effects in span tasks. *Quarterly Journal of Experimental Psychology Human Experimental Psychology, 45A,* 177–192.

Chase, W. G., & Ericsson, K. A. (1981). Skilled memory. In J. R.. Anderson (Ed.), *Cognitive skills and their acquisition* (pp. 141–189). Hillsdale, NJ: Erlbaum.

Chase, W. G., & Ericsson, K. A. (1982). Skill and working memory. In G. H. Bower (Ed.), *The psychology of learning and motivation* (Vol. 16, pp. 1–58). New York: Academic Press.

Cohen, J. D., Forman, S. D., Braver, T. S., Casey, B. J., Servan-Schreiber, D., & Noll, D. C. (1994). Activation of prefrontal cortex in a nonspatial working memory task with functional MRI. *Human Brain Mapping, 1,* 293–304.

Connelly, S. L., & Hasher, L. (1993). Aging and the inhibition of spatial location. *Journal of Experimental Psychology: Human Perception & Performance, 19* (6), 1238–1250.

Conway, A. R. A., & Engle, R. W. (1994). Working memory and retrieval: A resource-dependent inhibition model. *Journal of Experimental Psychology: General, 123,* 354–373.

Daneman, M., & Carpenter, P. A. (1980). Individual differences in working memory and reading. *Journal of Verbal Learning and Verbal Behavior, 19,* 450–466.

Engle, R. W. (1994). Individual differences in memory and implications for learning. In R. J. Sternberg (Ed.), *Encyclopedia of intelligence.* New York: Macmillan.

Ericsson, K. A., & Kintsch, W. (1995). Long-term working memory. *Psychological Review, 102,* 211–245.

Hasher, L., & Zacks, R. T. (1988). Working memory, comprehension, and aging: A review and new view. In G. H. Bower (Ed.), *The psychology of learning and motivation: Advances in research and theory* (Vol. 22, pp. 193–225). San Diego: Academic Press.

Healy, A. F., Fendrich, D. W., Cunningham, T. F., & Till, R. E. (1987). Effects of cueing on short-term retention of order information. *Journal of Experimental Psychology: Learning, Memory, and Cognition, 13,* 413–425.

Just, M. A., & Carpenter, P. A. (1992). A capacity theory of comprehension: Individual differences in working memory. *Psychological Review, 99,* 122–149.

Just, M. A., Carpenter, P. A., Keller, T. A., Eddy, W. F., & Thulborn, K. R. (1996). Brain activation modulated by sentence comprehension. *Science, 274,* 114–116.

Kane, M. J., Hasher, L., Stoltzfus, E. R., Zacks, R. T., & Connelly, S. L. (1994). Inhibitory attentional mechanisms and aging. *Psychology & Aging, 9* (1) 103–112.

Kimberg, D. Y., & Farah, M. J. (1993). A unified account of cognitive impairments following frontal lobe damage: The role of working memory in complex, organized behavior. *Journal of Experimental Psychology: General, 122,* 411–428.

Lebiere, C., & Anderson, J. R. (1993). A connectionist implementation of the ACT-R production system. *Proceedings of the Fifteenth Conference of the Cognitive Science Society* (pp. 635–640). Hillsdale, NJ: Erlbaum.

Logan, G. D. (1988). Toward an instance theory of automatization. *Psychological Review, 95,* 492–527.

Logan, G. D., & Klapp, S. T. (1991). Automatizing alphabet arithmetic: I. Is extended practice necessary to produce automaticity? *Journal of Experimental Psychology: Learning, Memory, and Cognition, 17,* 179–195.

Logie, R. H. (1986). Visuo-spatial processing in working memory. *Quarterly Journal of Experimental Psychology, 38A,* 229–247.

Logie, R. H. (1995). *Visuo-spatial working memory.* Hove, UK: Erlbaum.

Lovett, M. C., & Anderson, J. R. (1996). History of success and current context in problem solving: Combined influences on operator selection. *Cognitive Psychology, 31,* 168–217.

Lü, Z.-L., Williamson, S. J., & Kaufman, L. (1992a). Behavioral lifetime of human auditory sensory memory predicted by physiological measures. *Science, 258,* 1668–1670.

Lü, Z.-L., Williamson, S. J., & Kaufman, L. (1992b). Human auditory primary and association cortex have differing lifetimes for activation traces. *Brain Research, 572,* 236–241.

Newell, A. (1990). *Unified theories of cognition.* Cambridge, MA: Harvard University Press.

Plaut, D. C. (1996). Relearning after damage in connectionist networks: Toward a theory of rehabilitation. *Brain and Language, 52,* 25–82.

Rabinowitz, M., & Goldberg, N. (1995). Evaluating the structure process hypothesis. In F. E. Weinert & W. Schneider (Eds.), *Memory performance and competencies: Issues in growth and development.* Hillsdale, NJ: Erlbaum.

Reder, L. M., & Gordon, J. S. (1997). Subliminal perception: Nothing special, cognitively speaking. In J. Cohen & J. Schooler (Eds.), *Cognitive and neuropsychological approaches to the study of consciousness* (pp. 125–134). Hillsdale, NJ: Erlbaum.

Salthouse, T. A. (1994). The nature of the influences of speed on adult age differences in cognition. *Developmental Psychology, 30,* 240–259.

Salthouse, T. A. (1996). The processing-speed theory of adult age differences in cognition. *Psychological Review, 103,* 403–428.

Schunn, C. D., Reder, L. M., Nhouyvanisvong, A., Richards, D. R., & Stroffolino, P. J. (1997). To calculate or not calculate: A source activation confusion (SAC) model of problem-familiarity's role in strategy selection. *Journal of Experimental Psychology: Learning, Memory, and Cognition, 23,* 1–27.

Sejnowski, T. J. (1981). Skeleton filters in the brain. In G. E. Hinton & J. A. Anderson (Eds.), *Parallel models of associative memory.* Hillsdale, NJ: Erlbaum.

Shah, P., & Miyake, A. (1996). The separability of working memory resources for spatial thinking and language processing: An individual differences approach. *Journal of Experimental Psychology: General, 125,* 4–27.

Stoltzfus, E. R., Hasher, L., Zacks, R. T., Ulivi, M. S., & Goldstein, D. (1993). Investigations of inhibition and interference in younger and older adults. *Journal of Gerontology, 48,* 179–188.

Waters, G. S., & Caplan, D. (1996). The measurement of verbal working memory capacity and its relation to reading comprehension. *Quarterly Journal of Experimental Psychology, 49A*, 51–79.

Yuill, N., Oakhill, J., & Parkin, A. (1989). Working memory, comprehension ability and the resolution of text anomaly. *British Journal of Psychology, 80*, 351–361.

Zacks, R. T., & Hasher, L. (1994). Directed ignoring: Inhibitory regulation of working memory. In D. Dagenbach & T. H. Carr (Eds.), *Inhibitory mechanisms in attention, memory, and language* (pp. 241–264). New York: Academic Press.

Zbrodoff, N. J. (1995). Why is 9 + 7 harder than 2 + 3? Strength and interference as explanations of the problem-size effect. *Memory & Cognition, 23*, 689–700.

6 Insights into Working Memory from the Perspective of the EPIC Architecture for Modeling Skilled Perceptual-Motor and Cognitive Human Performance

DAVID E. KIERAS, DAVID E. MEYER,

SHANE MUELLER, AND TRAVIS SEYMOUR

FIVE CENTRAL FEATURES OF THE THEORY

Computational modeling of human perceptual-motor and cognitive performance based on a comprehensive detailed information-processing architecture leads to new insights about the components of working memory. To illustrate how such insights can be achieved, a precise production-system model that uses verbal working memory for performing a serial memory span task through a strategic phonological loop has been constructed with the Executive-Process/Interactive-Control (EPIC) architecture of Kieras and Meyer. EPIC is characterized by five central features that may be compared and contrasted with those of other theoretical frameworks in this volume. These features include:

(1) Formal implementation with multiple component mechanisms for perceptual, cognitive, and motor information processing (cf. Barnard, Chapter 9; Lovett, Reder, & Lebiere, Chapter 5; Young & Lewis, Chapter 7; Schneider, Chapter 10).

(2) Representation of procedural knowledge in terms of a production system whose condition-action rules are all applied simultaneously and repeatedly during the cyclic operation of a central cognitive processor (cf. Lovett et al., Chapter 5; Young & Lewis, Chapter 7; O'Reilly, Braver, & Cohen, Chapter 11).

(3) Executive control procedures that schedule task activities efficiently and coordinate the use of limited-capacity peripheral perceptual-

This research was supported by grant N00014-92-J-1173 from the Cognitive Sciences Program of the Office of Naval Research. The authors thank members of the Brain, Cognition, and Action Laboratory (David Fencsik, Jennifer Glass, Leon Gmeindl, Cerita Jones, and Eric Schumacher) at the University of Michigan for helpful suggestions and criticisms. Many helpful comments from our colleagues, the editors, and other authors of the present book are also gratefully acknowledged.

motor processors (cf. Baddeley & Logie, Chapter 2; Cowan, Chapter 3; Engle, Tuholski, & Kane, Chapter 4).

(4) Explicit simulations that accurately account for quantitative behavioral data (cf. Lovett et al., Chapter 5; Young & Lewis, Chapter 7).

(5) Relatively parsimonious implementation (cf. Lovett et al., Chapter 5; Young & Lewis, Chapter 7; Schneider, Chapter 10; O'Reilly et al., Chapter 11).

During the past several years, we have been developing a comprehensive theoretical framework for symbolic computational modeling of skilled perceptual-motor and cognitive performance (Kieras & Meyer, 1994, 1995, 1997; Kieras, Wood, & Meyer, 1997; Meyer & Kieras, 1992, 1994, 1997a, 1997b, 1999). A principal objective of our research is to formulate precise, detailed, computational models of performance in realistic multiple-task situations such as aircraft-cockpit operation, air-traffic control, and human–computer interaction. Through such modeling, it may be possible to improve the designs of person–machine interfaces, the selection of personnel, and the content of training programs that will facilitate performance significantly.

Because cumulative scientific progress requires "starting simple" and gradually dealing with more and more complex phenomena, our research has focused initially on the performance of relatively elementary tasks. For example, we have spent considerable effort on modeling performance under the psychological refractory period (PRP) procedure, a basic dual-task paradigm that requires people to perform two discrete choice–reaction tasks concurrently. Some of our other related research has entailed modeling the concurrent performance of discrete choice–reaction and continuous visual–manual tracking tasks. In most (though not all) cases, the load imposed by these tasks on working memory has been light.[1] Thus, the components that mediate working memory in our theoretical framework have not required extensive elaboration yet. Nevertheless, it is clear that to thoroughly model the performance of complex tasks like aircraft-cockpit operation and air-traffic control, we must take the contributions and limitations of working memory more fully into account.

Such further treatment of working memory in the context of a practical computational-modeling project has much to recommend it. We have found previously that formulating computational models to account for substantial sets of empirical data can provide deep and surprising new insights about human information processing and major phenomena associated with it. On

---

[1] One important exception involves models that we have formulated to account for data collected by Ballas, Heitmeyer, and Perez (1992a, 1992b), who studied the concurrent performance of tactical-decision and visual-manual tracking tasks under conditions similar to those in aircraft cockpit operations, where an operator's global "situation awareness" plays a key role (cf. Graves, 1997; Gugerty, 1997).

occasion, such insights may directly contradict prevailing theoretical beliefs; for example, the belief that there is an immutable structural response-selection bottleneck in the human information-processing system (Pashler, 1994; Welford, 1967) has been refuted by some of our discoveries. Similarly, it may be anticipated that formulating more precise computational models for various diverse mechanisms of working memory will yield additional insights.

Toward this end, we take "working memory" to encompass the entire ensemble of temporary stored codes, knowledge representations, and procedures whereby information is maintained, updated, and applied for performing perceptual-motor and cognitive tasks. Our current definition is consistent with the seminal use of "working memory" by Miller, Galanter, and Pribram (1960), who pioneered the theoretical discussion of this term. Our definition is also, by and large, consistent with those of other contributors to the present volume.

More specifically, this chapter considers working memory from the perspective of a particular architecture for characterizing the human information-processing system. Such architectures are essential to construct because they provide theoretical foundations and sets of mechanisms for human cognition and action, through which veridical computational models of performance can be formulated for specific tasks. In accord with the proposals made by Anderson (1976) and by Laird, Rosenbloom, and Newell (1986), the construction of information-processing architectures has become acknowledged as a fundamental theoretical approach for cognitive science and experimental psychology (Newell, 1990). This approach synthesizes multiple basic concepts, subsuming a variety of "micro" models and mechanisms into a single coherent whole. When an information-processing architecture is implemented computationally, its implications and applicability can be explored rigorously. The progress of serious cognitive theorizing requires the development of more comprehensive and veridical architectures, as exemplified by several contributions to this volume (e.g., Lovett, Reder, & Lebiere, Chapter 5; Young & Lewis, Chapter 7; Schneider, Chapter 10).

In what follows, the *Executive-Process/Interactive-Control* (EPIC) architecture that we have constructed for modeling cognition and action is described and applied to address issues about working memory. EPIC incorporates many recent theoretical and empirical results concerning human performance in the form of a simulation software system. Using EPIC, a computational model can be formulated to represent procedures for performing a complex multimodal task with an explicit set of production rules. When an EPIC model is supplied with external task stimuli, it executes the procedures in whatever way the task requires, thereby emulating a human who performs the task, and generating predicted actions in simulated real time.

EPIC is an architecture devoted explicitly to constructing models of skilled performance; it is not yet a learning system per se, and so at this time has a different scope than do the theoretical frameworks of some other contributors (e.g., Young & Lewis, Chapter 7; Schneider, Chapter 10) to this volume. Instead, EPIC's current purpose is to characterize the perceptual and motor, as well as cognitive, constraints on people's ability to perform various tasks. Consistent with this purpose, the next section describes the components of the EPIC architecture. Then we introduce an instructive computational model based on EPIC to account for results from representative studies of verbal working memory.

The EPIC Architecture

Figure 6.1 outlines the overall organization of the component processors and memory stores in the EPIC architecture. At this level, EPIC resembles some previous theoretical frameworks for human information processing. Nevertheless, it constitutes a new synthesis of concepts and empirical results, being more comprehensive, detailed, and veridical than its predecessors.

We have designed EPIC to combine mechanisms for cognitive information processing and perceptual-motor activities with procedural task analyses of skilled performance. Our efforts complement production-system theories such as CCT (Bovair, Kieras, & Polson, 1990), ACT-R (Anderson, 1993; Lovett et al., Chapter 5, this volume), and Soar (Laird et al., 1986; Young & Lewis, Chapter 7, this volume). EPIC has a central cognitive processor surrounded by peripheral perceptual and motor processors. Applying EPIC to model the performance for a task requires specifying both the production-rule programming of the cognitive processor and the relevant operations of the perceptual and motor processors. When an EPIC model interacts with a simulated task environment, it produces an explicit sequence of overt serial and parallel actions required to perform the task, just as a human performer does. The procedural task analysis embodied in an EPIC model is general to a class of task scenarios (cf. John & Kieras, 1996).

The software for implementing EPIC is currently written in Common LISP. All EPIC models described in this chapter and elsewhere have actually been implemented and run to generate reported simulation results. EPIC really works![2]

The EPIC framework includes not only software modules for simulating a human performer, but also provisions for simulating interactions of the performer with external equipment. For example, the left side of Figure 6.1 shows a simulated task environment, where virtual devices such as a display screen and keyboard provide the "physical" interface to a simulated performer on the right. During simulations with EPIC, the task-environment software module assigns physical locations to the interface objects, and it

---

[2] Our simulation software and a technical description of EPIC are available at ftp.eecs.umich.edu/people/kieras/EPICarch.ps.

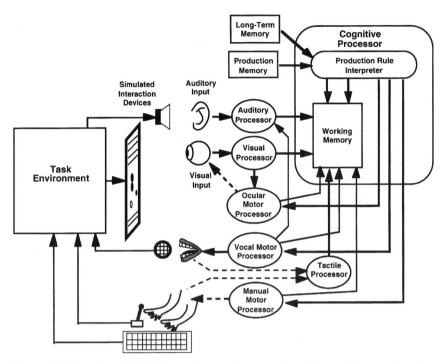

Figure 6.1. Overview of the EPIC architecture (adapted from Meyer & Kieras, 1997a).

generates simulated visual and auditory events in response to the simulated performer's behavior.

Within the EPIC architecture (Figure 6.1), information flows forward from peripheral sensors, through perceptual processors, to a cognitive processor (with a production-rule interpreter and working memory), whose outputs control motor processors that move peripheral effectors. The architecture also has multiple feedback pathways. Its degree of perceptual-motor development is substantially greater than found previously in other popular information-processing architectures such as the Model Human Processor (Card, Moran, & Newell, 1983), ACT-R (Anderson, 1993; Lovett et al., Chapter 5, this volume), and Soar (Laird et al., 1986; Newell, 1990; Young & Lewis, Chapter 7, this volume).

EPIC has separate perceptual processors with distinct temporal properties for several major sensory (e.g., visual, auditory, and tactile) modalities. There are also separate motor processors for several major motor (e.g., ocular, manual, and vocal) modalities. Feedback pathways from the motor processors and effectors to partitions of working memory help coordinate multiple-task performance.

The declarative/procedural distinction made by "ACT-class" architectures (e.g., Anderson, 1976, 1993; Lovett et al., Chapter 5, this volume) is embodied in EPIC with separate permanent memory stores for procedural knowledge (production rules) and declarative knowledge (propositions). EPIC's working memory contains all of the temporary information needed for and manipulated by a model's production rules, including control items such as task goals and sequencing indices, along with representations of received sensory inputs and selected motor outputs. These various types of information are stored in separate working memory partitions such as auditory working memory, visual working memory, the control store, and the tag store.

Under EPIC, there are three different types of numerical parameter: *standard*, *typical*, and *free*. The numerical values of standard parameters (e.g., the mean cycle duration of the cognitive processor) stay the same across all applications of the architecture. The numerical values of typical parameters (e.g., the time required to detect a visual stimulus) are derived from prior results in the literature on human performance (e.g., Atkinson, Hernstein, Lindzey, & Luce, 1988; Boff, Kaufman, & Thomas, 1986); we set them on an a priori basis before simulations with an EPIC model are run, but they may change across different task contexts. The numerical values of free parameters also may change across different task contexts; they are estimated iteratively by determining which values maximize the goodness-of-fit between simulated and empirical data. We hope that through further modeling experience, the free parameters in EPIC will become standard or typical ones, thereby increasing our models' predictive power. Nevertheless, even now, the predictive power of our models is substantial.

Perceptual Processors

EPIC has perceptual processors for the visual, auditory, and tactile sensory modalities. They are simple "pipelines" through which information feeds forward asynchronously in parallel. Each stimulus input to a perceptual processor may yield multiple symbolic outputs that are deposited in working memory as time passes. In addition, EPIC's tactile perceptual processor transmits feedback from effector organs to working memory. This can be important for coordinating performance of multiple tasks. Further details about EPIC's visual perceptual processor appear in Kieras and Meyer (1997). For now, we focus on the auditory perceptual processor, which is used extensively by the present EPIC computational model of verbal working memory.

AUDITORY PERCEPTUAL PROCESSOR. The auditory perceptual processor receives inputs from EPIC's ear and sends outputs to auditory working memory, where representations of stimulus sounds are stored. For example, when the auditory perceptual processor receives a short tone signal, it may first produce a symbolic item that corresponds to the onset of the tone (standard delay: 50 ms), then at a later time, an item that identifies the frequency of the tone (typical delay: 250ms), followed by an item that corresponds to the tone's offset (standard delay: 50 ms). Later, such items simply disappear from auditory working memory in an all-or-none manner after stochastic decay times whose magnitudes are consistent with typical durations of temporary stored auditory information (Balota & Duchek, 1986; Cowan, 1984; Cowan, Lichty, & Grove, 1990; Eriksen & Johnson, 1964; Watkins & Todres, 1980).

Following proposals by some previous investigators (e.g., Longoni, Richardson, & Aiello, 1993), the auditory perceptual processor codes external (overt) speech in the form of items for individual words and word sequences, which then go to auditory working memory just as coded information about tones does. We assume that specific amounts of time are required to identify individual words and to put their representations in working memory (typical delay: 150 ms). The auditory perceptual processor can also receive speech inputs from the vocal motor processor; such inputs, whose source is internal (covert), have a distinct code that differentiates them from speech inputs whose source is external (overt).

REPRESENTATION OF SERIAL ORDER. To represent the serial order of speech inputs, EPIC's auditory perceptual processor produces items that contain abstract symbolic tags pointing to the previous and to the next items of a sequence. Using these tags, a set of production rules can step through the stored items in auditory working memory for a series of spoken words, processing them one after another to complete a given task. Spoken items that come from external or internal sources are kept in separate source-specific sequential chains.

Of course, the format that we have chosen initially for representing the serial order of speech in EPIC is rather rudimentary and may require elaboration to explain or predict certain complex data. Nevertheless, there are precedents and virtues to recommend our chosen format (e.g., see Rumelhart & McClelland, 1986; Wicklegren, 1969). If and when the need arises, this format may be elaborated so that it accommodates hierarchical structures as well as sequential chaining (cf. Anderson & Matessa, 1997; Estes, 1972; Healy, 1974; Gordon & Meyer, 1987; Henson, Norris, Page, & Baddeley, 1996; Lashley, 1951; Shiffrin & Cook, 1978).

Cognitive Processor

EPIC's cognitive processor is programmed in terms of production rules and it uses the Parsimonious Production System (PPS) interpreter (Bovair et al., 1990). PPS production rules have the format (<rule-name> IF <condition> THEN <actions>). The rule condition refers only to the contents of the production-system working memory. The rule actions can add or delete items in working memory, and also send commands to the motor processors.

CYCLIC OPERATION. The cognitive processor operates cyclically, consistent with known periodicities of the human information-processing system (Callaway & Yeager, 1960; Kristofferson, 1967; Ray, 1990). At the start of each cycle, the contents of working memory are updated with new outputs from the perceptual processors and the actions of applicable rules on the preceding cycle. At the end of each cycle, commands are sent to the motor processors.

The cognitive-processor cycles are not synchronized with external stimulus and response events. Inputs from the perceptual processors are accessed only intermittently, when the production-system working memory is updated at the start of each cycle. The cognitive processor typically has a cycle time that is stochastic, with a mean of 50 ms (cf. Young & Lewis, Chapter 7, this volume; Newell, 1990). All other time parameters in the system are scaled proportionately with respect to the current randomly sampled cycle time. The variance of the cycle-time distribution is chosen to produce an approximately 20% coefficient of variation for simple reaction times, corresponding to typical observed values.

PRODUCTION-SYSTEM PARALLELISM. Most traditional production-system architectures let only one production rule be fired at a time, and only its actions are executed then (e.g., Anderson, 1976, 1993; Lovett et al., Chapter 5, this volume). Under these systems, when more than one rule has conditions that match the current contents of working memory, some kind of conflict-resolution mechanism must choose which rule to fire. Soar (Laird et al., 1986; Young & Lewis, Chapter 7, this volume) is perhaps the most complex case, in that its production rules only propose operators to apply, and many candidate operators can be proposed at once, but then a separate process must decide which particular candidate to apply.

In contrast, the Parsimonious Production System of EPIC's cognitive processor has a very simple policy: on each processing cycle, PPS fires all rules whose conditions match the current contents of working memory, and PPS executes all of their actions. Thus, EPIC models have true parallel cognitive processing at the production-rule level; multiple "threads" or processes can be represented with sets of rules such that they all run concurrently. Reaction-time data from basic multiple-task performance, which demonstrate the absence of a structural cognitive response-selection bottleneck, strongly support our assumptions about the cognitive processor (Meyer et al., 1995; Schumacher et al., 1997, 1998).

Our theoretical approach with respect to the nature of information-processing limitations is also a matter of scientific tactics: We make some radically simple assumptions and then explore their consequences. EPIC starts with obvious inherent limitations of human memory and perceptual-motor mechanisms; it incorporates other more elaborate and debatable constraints only when serious failures at accounting for empirical data compel us to do so. In part, such extreme parsimony differentiates us from other contributors to this volume (cf. Lovett et al., Chapter 5; Young & Lewis, Chapter 7; Schneider, Chapter 10; O'Reilly, Braver, & Cohen, Chapter 11). Perhaps because it forgoes elaborate incorrect assumptions, our approach has fared reasonably well thus far.

Working Memory

As mentioned already, the working memory for EPIC's cognitive processor does, of necessity, have several partitions. Taken together, their contents provide EPIC computational models with a basis for maintaining overall situation awareness under both laboratory conditions and real-world circumstances where "cognition in the wild" occurs (e.g., Graves, 1997; Gugerty, 1997).

MODAL WORKING MEMORY STORES. Three partitions of working memory are dedicated to specific perceptual modalities. These include visual, auditory, and tactile stores that contain information from the respective perceptual processors. Items persist there in an all-or-none manner for durations that depend on the types of information involved. EPIC also has a motor working memory that contains information about the current states of the motor processors.

PRODUCTION-SYSTEM MEMORY STORES. Two other partitions of working memory are production-system memory stores. These include a control store and a tag store. They contain information defined only in terms of the contents of production rules. By using them together with EPIC's modal working memory stores, motor processors, and perceptual processors, the cognitive processor may implement other working memory mechanisms such as a phonological loop (cf. Baddeley, 1986; Baddeley & Logie, Chapter 2, this volume).

Control Store. In the control store are items that represent current task goals and procedural steps for accomplishing them. Under PPS, such items are treated just like other types of information in working memory, and so they can be freely manipulated by rule actions. This is crucial for modeling multiple-task performance, because it enables the production rules of an executive process to coordinate the progress of task subprocesses.

The control store contains several types of item: (a) *goals*, which appear in the conditions of rules that accomplish a particular task; (b) *steps*, which cause rules to fire in a specific sequence; (c) *strategy items*, which enable or disable rules for implementing alternative versions of a task strategy; (d) *status items*, which represent the current states of various subprocesses, such as indicating what ones are now under way. Items in the control store have meaning only with respect to the production rules that test for, add, or delete them; they are not related by an "external semantics" to overt perceptual or motor events.

For now, the control store is assumed to have unlimited capacity and duration (cf. Lovett et al., Chapter 5, this volume). Thus, in practice, the number of items that it contains at any moment depends only on which task processes are being executed. The executive and task processes of our models typically delete control-store items whenever they are no longer needed. We await future theoretical and empirical results to determine whether the control store should have more constrained limits.

Tag Store. The tag store contains items that "label" other items in the modal (i.e., perceptual and motor) working memories. Such labeling assigns particular roles to modal working memory items referenced by the conditions and actions of production rules. For example, a production rule might update the tag store with a new tag for an object in visual working memory, labeling it as "the stimulus." This would specify which object is "the stimulus" to be checked subsequently when the conditions of other rules are tested for their truth values.

Under EPIC, each item in the tag store refers to only one item in a modal working memory store. The contents of a tag include only internal symbols; like control-store items, tags have no "external semantics." As for the control store, we likewise assume that the capacity and duration of the tag store are unlimited, and that executive or task processes delete tag items when they are no longer needed. Again we await future theoretical and empirical results to determine whether the tag store should have more constrained limits.

ILLUSTRATIVE PRODUCTION RULE. The following production rule illustrates some of EPIC's different possible working memory items and production-rule actions:

(EXAMPLE-RULE:

IF
((GOAL DESIGNATE TARGET)
(STRATEGY MAKE POKE IMMEDIATELY)
(STEP MAKE POKE-RESPONSE)
(TAG ?OBJECT IS STIMULUS)
(VISUAL ?OBJECT COLOR RED)
(NOT (VISUAL ??? SIZE LARGE))
(STATUS PERF-TACTICAL RESPONSE-PROCESS HAS EYE)
(MOTOR MANUAL PROCESSOR FREE))

THEN
((SEND-TO-MOTOR MANUAL PERFORM POKE (LEFT INDEX) ?OBJECT)
(ADDDB (GOAL WATCH-FOR DESIGNATION-EFFECT))
(DELDB (STEP MAKE POKE-RESPONSE))
(ADDDB (STEP WAIT-FOR WATCHING-DONE)))

The function of this rule is to touch a small red object on a display screen, designating it as a target by poking it with the left index finger. Embedded in the rule's condition are multiple expressions that must be true conjunctively with respect to the contents of working memory: here the goal (control-store item) is to designate a target; the strategy (control-store item) is to make the poke movement immediately; the current procedural step (control-store item) calls for making a poke movement; a certain visual object has been tagged as "the stimulus" (tag-store item); the tagged stimulus object (visual working memory item) is red; no large object is in view (i.e., visual working memory lacks any items about "large" objects); the process responsible for making the poke has a status (control-store item) that enables it to move EPIC's eye; and the state of the manual motor processor (control-store item) indicates that it is free to accept movement commands. If and when EPIC's various working memory partitions contain all requisite items for matching this rule's condition, then one of the rule's actions will command the manual motor processor to make a poke movement with the left index finger at the stimulus object. Also, the rule's other actions will establish a new subgoal (control-store item) to be accomplished next, delete the current step note, and add a note (control-store item) for the next step.

Motor Processors

EPIC has separate motor processors for moving the hands, eyes, and speech articulators. All of them operate simultaneously. To operate a motor processor, the cognitive processor sends it a command that contains the symbolic name for a desired type of movement and its relevant parameters. Then the motor processor produces a simulated overt movement of its effector, achieving the specified temporal and spatial characteristics for this movement. Many further details about movement representation, preparation, and execution by EPIC's ocular and manual motor processors appear in Kieras and Meyer (1997). For now, we focus on the vocal motor processor, because it is especially relevant to the present EPIC model of verbal working memory.

VOCAL MOTOR PROCESSOR. EPIC's vocal motor processor can produce either overt or covert spoken words, based on commands received from the cognitive processor, which provides symbolic information about the desired utterance's style and content. Each spoken word is then sent as an input to the auditory perceptual processor (Figure 6.1). For overt speech, we assume that actual sound production is delayed by about 100 ms after articulatory initiation and continues for an amount of time that depends on the number of syllables in each spoken word, as well as other relevant vocal parameters. Overt and covert speech are assumed to be produced motorically at essentially the same rate, consistent with empirical data (Landauer, 1962). During vocalization, an additional style parameter may specify intonation, acoustically marking each component word of a sequence as starting, continuing, or ending the sequence. A judicious combination of the vocal motor processor, auditory perceptual processor, and certain forms of working memory, operated through appropriate production-rule programming, may be used to construct EPIC models that have a plausible and precisely specified phonological-loop mechanism (cf. Baddeley & Logie, Chapter 2, this volume).

An EPIC Computational Model for Verbal Working Memory

The remainder of this chapter illustrates how EPIC can be applied for understanding and modeling human performance of tasks that involve intensive use of verbal working memory. For now, we focus on one prototypical case, the serial memory span task (Miller, 1956). In what follows, an EPIC computational model is presented to account quantitatively for representative data from this task and to reach new insights about how working memory works.

Our present EPIC model incorporates a phonological-loop mechanism that, in some but not all respects, resembles ones proposed by previous theorists (e.g., Atkinson & Shiffrin, 1968; Baddeley & Hitch, 1974; Baddeley & Logie, Chapter 2, this volume; Schweickert & Boruff, 1986; Sperling, 1967; Waugh & Norman, 1965).[3] For the sake of veracity and parsimony, we have implemented the phonological loop with EPIC's preexisting auditory working memory and vocal motor processor, which had been incorporated previously to model other types of real-time performance (e.g., Kieras et al., 1997). During covert verbal rehearsal, EPIC's vocal motor processor subvocalizes to-be-remembered items sequentially, relying on the chained representation format described earlier. This subvocalization creates representations of items in auditory working memory that disappear after a time, but that meanwhile can be used to vocalize the items again either covertly during further rehearsal, or overtly during final recall.

The total capacity of EPIC's phonological loop depends on the durations of items in auditory working memory and on the rate of subvocalization achieved with the vocal motor processor. This dependence is plausible because it stems from obviously required architectural constraints on human information processing. Consistent with our "minimalist" theoretical approach to architecture specification, we forgo making additional gratuitous, strong a priori assumptions about prevailing capacity limitations on working memory. Specifically, at present there is no assumed upper bound on the number of items that EPIC's auditory working memory may contain simultaneously. Nor does EPIC – unlike alternative theoretical frameworks – assume the existence of limited-capacity graded activation for items in its working memory stores (cf. Anderson & Matessa, 1997; Just, Carpenter, & Hemphill, 1996; also, in this volume, see Engle et al., Chapter 4; Lovett et al., Chapter 5; Schneider, Chapter 10; O'Reilly et al., Chapter 11).

Serial Memory Span Task

To facilitate the present theoretical endeavor, the version of the serial memory span task on which we focus now involves discrete trials with a

---

[3] We call the loop "phonological" to be consistent with terminology used by other authors (e.g., Baddeley & Logie, Chapter 2) in this volume. However, our use of this term is not meant to imply that the items in the loop have abstract phonological representations as defined by formal linguists (e.g., Akmajian, Demers, & Harnish, 1979). For present purposes, the items' representations may be more aptly called "auditory" and "articulatory." Thus, the mechanism described here may also be called an "articulatory loop," a term used frequently by past researchers (e.g., Baddeley et al., 1984; Burgess & Hitch, 1992; Gupta & MacWhinney, 1995). It remains an open question whether the items in the human articulatory loop have abstract "phonological" representations.

generic experimental design. This design has been a popular one (e.g., see Baddeley, Thomson, & Buchanan, 1975; Longoni et al., 1993; Standing, Bond, Smith, & Isley, 1980), and it typifies the studies whose empirical results are fit here with our EPIC model of verbal working memory. On each trial of these studies, a sequence of several (e.g., more than one but less than 10) words was presented auditorily at a constant moderate rate. After the last word of the sequence, which typically contained somewhere in the range of three to eight words, there was a recall signal, and a participant attempted to recall the presented words in their original order. Ample time (e.g., 15 s) was allowed for recall. Then a new trial began. For each trial, the presented words were drawn randomly from a small pool whose individual members were used repeatedly across trials but at most only once within a trial.[4] The participant's attempted recall on a trial was scored as being correct if and only if all of the presented words were recalled in their original order. The dependent variable was the percentage of trials on which correct recall occurred.

Under conditions similar or identical to these, it has been found that several independent variables affect percent correct recall systematically. The observed effects include the following:

SEQUENCE-LENGTH EFFECT. Longer word sequences (i.e., ones that contain more words) are less likely to be recalled correctly than are shorter sequences (e.g., Baddeley et al., 1975).

ARTICULATION-TIME EFFECT. Sequences that take more time to articulate are less likely to be recalled correctly than are sequences that take less time to articulate (e.g., Baddeley et al., 1975; Cowan et al., 1992; Gupta & MacWhinney, 1995; Longoni et al., 1993; Schweickert, Guentert, & Hersberger, 1990).

PHONOLOGICAL-SIMILARITY EFFECT. Sequences of phonologically similar words are less likely to be recalled correctly than are sequences of dissimilar words (e.g., Conrad & Hull, 1964; Longoni et al., 1993; Schweickert et al., 1990).

ARTICULATORY-SUPPRESSION EFFECT. Recall is less likely to be correct when participants perform a concurrent secondary task that precludes subvocal rehearsal than when they do not (e.g., Baddeley, Lewis, & Vallar, 1984; Levy, 1971; Longoni et al., 1993).

Our present EPIC model accounts quantitatively for such effects, using parsimonious plausible assumptions. In so doing, it yields instructive insights about the true properties of human auditory working memory, vocal motor processing, and the phonological loop. Insights about possible cognitive control strategies for performing the serial memory span task are also provided.

---

[4] This procedure for constructing the word sequences helps ensure that the task is performed simply on the basis of phonological-loop mechanisms rather than graded levels of activation in long-term memory, as some other theorists (e.g., Anderson & Matessa, 1997; Lovett et al., Chapter 5, this volume) have assumed.

Architectural Implementation of EPIC Model

Implementing our present EPIC model required relatively minor extensions to a previous version of the architecture (Kieras & Meyer, 1997). For this implementation, we gave EPIC's vocal motor processor a new subvocalization style with prosodic markers. Furthermore, a new motor-perceptual connection was introduced so that covert speech outputs could be sent from the vocal motor processor to the auditory perceptual processor, which recognized them and put their symbolic representations in auditory working memory. The auditory perceptual processor was also elaborated somewhat. As a result, it produced distinct codes for speech that came from internal and external sources, creating separate sequential chains of spoken items, depending on what the source was. This instantiation of source-specific coding in auditory working memory is consistent with empirical results from some prior behavioral (Cowan, 1984) and brain-imaging (e.g., Awh et al., 1996; Paulesu, Frith, & Frackowiak, 1993) studies.

Regarding auditory working memory, we also made six more assumptions: (1) No limit exists on the number of items stored there. (2) The loss or "decay" of a stored item is an all-or-none process. (3) Individual stored items have stochastically independent decay times. (4) Decay time has a lognormal distribution with two parameters, M, the median of the distribution, and s, the "spread" of the distribution.[5] (5) The values of M and s are affected by the stored items' phonological similarity and the type of source (external or internal) from which they come. (6) Information about serial order is contained in the stored items as supplementary tags that form an implicit "linked list" chain structure.

Several virtues of these assumptions should be mentioned. Although seemingly elaborate, they are essentially minimal ones required to account accurately for data from the serial memory span task. Results of past studies support some of them. Evidence for spontaneous decay of stored items in working memory has been reported (e.g., J. Reitman, 1974; cf. Shiffrin, 1973), consistent with Assumption 2. The probability of item decay increases as time passes (Brown, 1958), consistent with Assumption 4. Phonological similarity of stored items can shorten their decay times (Posner & Konick, 1966), consistent with Assumption 5. Linked-list chain structures may mediate vocal item-successor naming (Sternberg, 1969) and word-sequence production (Sternberg, Monsell, Knoll, & Wright, 1978), consistent with Assumption 6.

---

[5] The lognormal distribution is unimodal and positively skewed over the non-negative real numbers (Hastings & Peacock, 1975). These features are presumably ones that distributions of real decay times have. Parameterization with M and s facilitates implementing and interpreting effects caused by changes in the lognormal distribution's central tendency and dispersion.

Furthermore, the task strategy that our EPIC computational model uses to control its phonological loop for performing the serial memory span task can be justified on both theoretical and empirical grounds.

Strategy for the Serial Memory Span Task

As mentioned already, modeling the performance of any task with EPIC involves specifying a task strategy and representing it in terms of production rules. From formulating such specifications, we have found that the strategies needed for using a phonological loop to perform verbal memory tasks are surprisingly subtle and complex. This is because these tasks require the processing of new stimulus inputs to overlap temporally, in a coordinated fashion, with ongoing subvocal maintenance rehearsal of previously stored items.

For example, in performing the serial memory span task, each cycle of rehearsal presumably yields a fresh copy of an item chain, with recently received items being appended to an immediately prior chain of older items. Thus, the task strategy must juggle multiple individual items and multiple chains of items simultaneously in auditory working memory. Although EPIC's auditory perceptual processor can extend an item chain automatically as successive new inputs arrive, the task strategy still has to keep track of "where" its component processes are currently working in various parts of different subchains. The situation is further complicated by the fact that as time passes, items can disappear haphazardly from auditory working memory and task strategies must deal with the problem of lost items. Figure 6.2. shows how this complexity may be managed under at least some circumstances.

OVERALL TASK STRATEGY. The overall task strategy of our EPIC computational model for performing the serial memory span task is outlined in Figure 6.2. Here we assume that after a trial starts, several concurrent processes with complementary functions are executed. Together, using the aforementioned representational formats of EPIC's auditory perceptual processor, vocal motor processor, and auditory working memory, these processes orchestrate the construction, rehearsal, and recall of item chains built from items whose source is either external (overt auditory stimuli) or internal (covert subvocal rehearsal). Given that EPIC has inherent multiprocessing capabilities, each such process constitutes a *thread* of execution, running independently and simultaneously with other processes during the trial.

ITEM-CHAIN CONSTRUCTION PROCESSES. One of the assumed item-chain construction processes (upper left part of Figure 6.2) keeps track of an *add-chain* that contains new items received from the external stimulus source. This involves waiting for each successive external stimulus item to arrive in auditory working memory and then tagging it as a "new" item for the add-chain. Another item-chain construction process (upper right part of Figure 6.2) keeps track of a *rehearsal chain* that contains covert speech inputs produced by ongoing subvocal rehearsal. This involves waiting for each successive covert input and tagging it as a "new" item to be included in the next

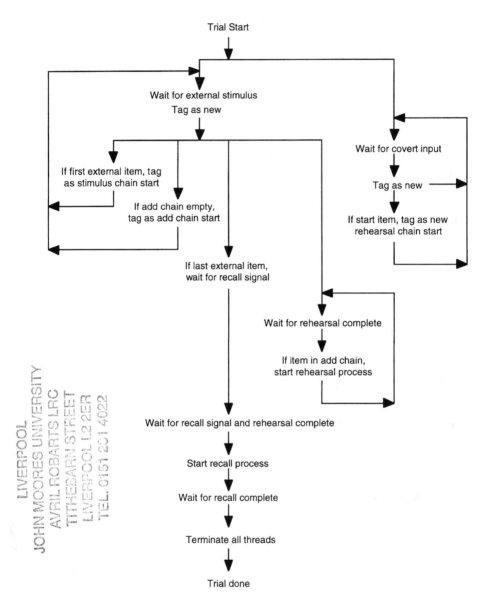

Figure 6.2. Flowchart of the overall task strategy used by the present EPIC model of verbal working memory for performing the serial memory span task. The task strategy includes concurrent processes for item-chain construction, subvocal rehearsal, and final recall.

cycle of rehearsal. The most recent copy of the rehearsal chain and the current contents of the add-chain then get used during the next rehearsal cycle.

REHEARSAL PROCESS. Under our present EPIC model, a cycle of rehearsal commences whenever either the first external stimulus item arrives in auditory working memory at the start of a trial, or an immediately preceding rehearsal cycle has been completed and the current add-chain contains some further external stimulus items that have not been rehearsed yet (see middle right part of Figure 6.2). If so, then the rehearsal process is assumed to go through the steps shown in Figure 6.3.

During a cycle of rehearsal, there are three consecutive phases. First, the rehearsal process checks whether an initial external stimulus item has arrived in auditory working memory. If so, then it is sent by the cognitive processor to the vocal motor processor, which subvocalizes the item and transmits its covert output to the auditory perceptual processor for recoding and storage in auditory working memory. Otherwise, each internal item in the most recent copy of the rehearsal chain is sent successively to the vocal motor processor and subvocalized once, with the resulting covert outputs again going to the auditory perceptual processor and auditory working memory for recoding and storage, respectively. Next, any external stimulus items in the current add-chain are sent successively to the vocal motor processor and subvocalized so that internal-item (covert speech) representations of them can be appended to an updated copy of the rehearsal chain.

Serial-order tags associated with the individual items of these chains are used by the cognitive processor to govern their order of subvocalization. A rehearsal cycle terminates when neither the current rehearsal chain nor the add-chain contains any more items to be subvocalized at the moment. For the next cycle of rehearsal, the aforementioned item-chain construction processes specify the new rehearsal chain in auditory working memory, tagging its starting item as "new" so that the cognitive processor can access it appropriately. Individual items and item chains that have been used during previous rehearsal cycles are tagged as "old" but remain in auditory working memory, disappearing haphazardly from there as time passes.

A major complexity caused by haphazard item decay is that the rehearsal process may fail occasionally and unpredictably. Such failures can occur at any moment during a rehearsal cycle if an item in the current rehearsal chain or add-chain happens to disappear from auditory working memory before it has been subvocalized. As a result, rehearsal would be disrupted. Recovery and graceful continuation after these disruptions require intervention by appropriate executive-control procedures of the task strategy.

RECALL PROCESSES. Successful performance of the serial memory span task also requires a set of final recall processes. We assume that recall starts after the last external stimulus item has been received, a recall signal has been detected, and any rehearsal cycle in progress has been completed (see bottom middle part of Figure 6.2). What happens thereafter involves one or the other

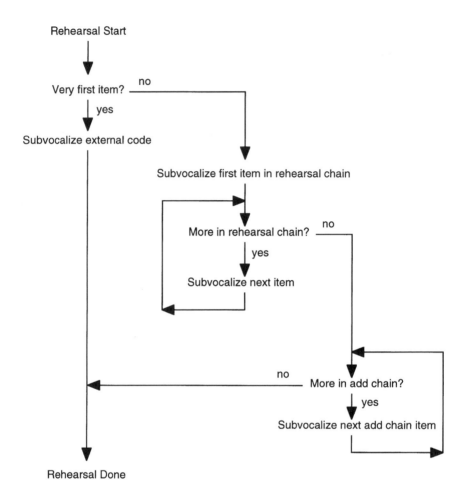

If required auditory item is missing at any point, clean up and exit.

Figure 6.3. Steps in one cycle of the rehearsal process used by the present EPIC model of verbal working memory for performing the serial memory span task (cf. Figure 6.2). A rehearsal cycle includes consecutive phases that, when need be, subvocalize the first external stimulus item on a trial, subvocalize each item of the current rehearsal chain in auditory working memory, and then subvocalize each item of the current add-chain.

of two recall processes shown, respectively, in the top and bottom panels of Figure 6.4, which enter the picture when either rehearsal has occurred previously during the trial or it has not. The latter option must be accommodated along with the former because on some trials, concurrent articulatory suppression or other ancillary distractions may preclude subvocal rehearsal.

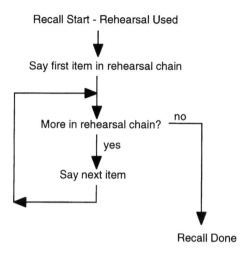

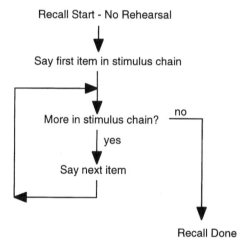

If required auditory item is missing at any point, clean up and exit.

Figure 6.4. The recall process used by the present EPIC model of verbal working memory for performing the serial memory span task (cf. Figure 6.2). The top panel shows steps in recall after prior rehearsal has occurred on a trial, and the bottom panel shows steps in recall if prior rehearsal has not occurred.

When rehearsal has occurred previously during the trial, the recall process attempts to vocalize every item in the most recent copy of the rehearsal chain (Figure 6.4, top panel). This vocalization proceeds by having the cognitive processor send the successive rehearsal-chain items one by one from auditory working memory to the vocal motor processor for overt output. As a result, correct recall will occur if, and only if, all of the originally presented items were incorporated into the most recent rehearsal chain and remain there (i.e., do not decay) throughout the recall process.

When no rehearsal has occurred previously during the trial, the recall process instead attempts to vocalize the stored chain of external-stimulus items that were input originally by the auditory perceptual processor to auditory working memory (Figure 6.4, bottom panel). This vocalization proceeds by having the cognitive processor send the successive stimulus-chain items one by one from auditory working memory to the vocal motor processor for overt output. As above, correct recall will occur if, and only if, all of these items are still present in auditory working memory and remain there (i.e., do not decay) throughout the recall process. Because items in the original stimulus chain have had more time to decay than do items in the most recent copy of a rehearsal chain, articulatory suppression or other factors that preclude subvocal rehearsal and thereby force use of the original stimulus chain may decrease the frequency of correct recall.

If recall based on either the rehearsal chain or original stimulus chain fails (e.g., because one or more relevant items have disappeared from auditory working memory), then the recall process cleans up and terminates, returning control to the overall task strategy. Our present EPIC model makes no attempt to guess the identities of missing items during recall or to produce them on the basis of residual information in auditory working memory. This restriction is justifiable for now because we focus exclusively on studies that scored performance as being correct if and only if the entire sequence of words presented on a trial was recalled in original order. Under such conditions, random and sophisticated guessing contribute negligibly little to obtained data.

Under other conditions, however, various types of supplementary guessing process may make substantial contributions, especially when credit is given for partially correct responses. Consequently, we have experimented with augmented EPIC models that incorporate such processes. These hold promise of accounting for patterns of data beyond those considered in this chapter (e.g., shapes of serial-position curves), but they are also much more complex, so we do not discuss them further here. Nevertheless, in the future, it will be important for both us and other theorists to develop these models more fully, because guessing strategies – rather than architectural mechanisms (e.g., residual graded activation levels; cf. Anderson & Matessa, 1997; also see Engle et al., Chapter 4, Lovett et al., Chapter 5, this volume) – may be primarily responsible for many ancillary phenomena observed during the performance of typical verbal working memory tasks.

Applications of EPIC Model

To test the present EPIC model, we have applied it in accounting for results from two representative studies with the serial memory span task.

The first of these is a classic study by Baddeley et al. (1975, Exp. 1). Empirical data from it are especially interesting and challenging because they embody large interactive effects of sequence length (number of items per sequence) and articulatory duration (time to vocalize a presented sequence). This interaction, together with other supplementary results, has led some investigators (e.g., Schweickert & Boruff, 1986) to infer that items stored in auditory working memory endure for only about 2 s.

The second study whose results are modeled here has been conducted by Longoni et al. (1993, Exp. 1). Its empirical data are interesting because they embody interactive effects of phonological similarity and articulatory suppression. These effects led Longoni et al. to infer that

the form of storage responsible for the (phonological similarity) effects must be functionally independent from the (subvocal rehearsal) processes that are manifested in the effect of (sequence) length. Indeed, the capacity of phonological storage seems to be a constant number of words, regardless of the number of phonemes or syllables that they contain, which suggests that the functional units of phonological storage are . . . discrete words rather than their constituent phonemes or syllables. (1993, pp. 13–14)

In what follows, we next discuss Longoni et al. and then Baddeley et al.

The Study of Longoni, Richardson, and Aiello

The generic version of the serial memory span task described earlier was used in the study by Longoni et al. (1993, Exp. 1).

EXPERIMENTAL DESIGN. On each trial, four auditory Italian words were presented successively to Italian speakers for subsequent recall in original order. During presentation of the word sequence and subsequent attempted recall, the participants either rehearsed the words covertly, or they performed a secondary articulatory-suppression task, which presumably precluded covert rehearsal. Subsequent recall attempts were produced in writing so that when required, articulatory suppression could continue throughout the trial.

Under both the articulatory-suppression and rehearsal conditions, some word sequences contained two-syllable words, whereas other word sequences contained four-syllable words. As measured by Longoni et al., the mean times that participants took to vocally articulate the sequences of four-syllable words were longer than those for the sequences of two-syllable words. Furthermore, the words in a sequence were either phonologically similar to or distinct from each other. Across trials, the phonological-similarity and articulation-time factors varied in a quasi-orthogonal manner. Four different pools of words were used to achieve this manipulation.

Overall, the experiment thus had a 2 (suppression/rehearsal) by 2 (short/long articulation time) by 2 (phonologically similar/distinct) factorial design. The inclusion of such multiple factors has important virtues. However, the absence of more than two levels within each factor also seriously limits the design's power.

EMPIRICAL RESULTS. The dark textured bars in the top and bottom panels of Figure 6.5 show the empirical results from Longoni et al.'s (1993, Exp. 1) study in terms of percent correct recall (i.e., percentages of trials on which participants recalled all words in correct order). All three independent variables had reliable main effects. Articulatory suppression, long articulation times, and phonological similarity each decreased percent correct recall substantially. Some reliable interactions also occurred. For example, the effect of articulation time was much less under the articulatory-suppression (rehearsal absent) condition than under the nonsuppression (rehearsal present) condition. In contrast, phonological similarity tended to magnify the articulation-time effect.

EPIC COMPUTATIONAL MODEL. In applying our EPIC computational model to account for these results, we decided that it was not necessary to simulate handwriting for final recall or to simulate articulatory suppression per se. Instead, we programmed the model's task strategy simply to suspend its rehearsal process (Figure 6.3) under the articulatory-suppression condition and to recall words orally by using the stored traces of items from either internal (subvocal rehearsal) or external (overt auditory stimuli) sources in auditory working memory, depending on whether or not rehearsal had taken place. This treatment makes the plausible assumptions that articulatory suppression completely precluded participants' subvocal rehearsal and that the model's vocal rate of recall approximately equaled participants' actual rate of written recall. Our simulation of performance by Longoni et al.'s participants therefore used their reported articulation rates as parameters.

To implement the simulation, we ran the model through Longoni et al.'s experimental procedure. In response, the model produced a sequence of correct and incorrect recall attempts. An iterative search was used to identify values of M and s, the parameters of the item decay-time distributions, that yielded maximally good fits between simulated and empirical results. Four pairs of M and s values were identified, including ones respectively associated with item codes for phonologically similar and distinct words from external (overt auditory stimuli) and internal (covert rehearsal) sources. In identifying these values, it was assumed that articulation time and articulatory suppression did not affect them.

SIMULATION RESULTS. The white bars in the top and bottom panels of Figure 6.5 show simulation results produced by the present EPIC model for Longoni et al. (1993, Exp. 1). We obtained an accurate quantitative account of the main effects and interactions caused by all three of Longoni et al.'s independent variables.

Table 6.1 shows our model's parameter values for the decay-time distributions as a function of the items' phonological similarity and source (external or internal). The mean decay times that yielded good fits to the empirical results were longer for phonologically distinct items and for items whose source was external. These two trends tended to be overadditive. In contrast,

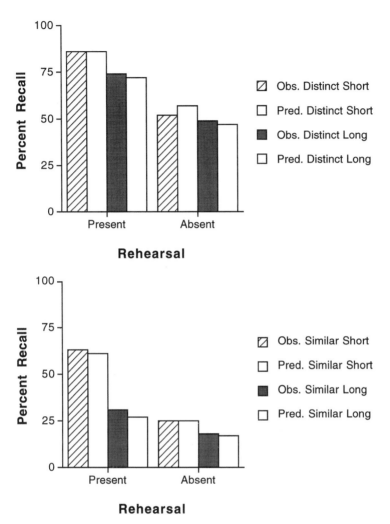

Figure 6.5. Empirical and simulation results for the study by Longoni, Richardson, and Aiello (1993, Exp. 1). Dark textured bars represent observed percentages of trials on which serial recall was perfectly correct as a function of short versus long word-sequence articulation time and articulatory suppression (rehearsal absent) versus non-suppression (rehearsal present). White bars adjacent to the right of the dark bars represent corresponding predicted percentages of trials on which serial recall was perfectly correct under the present EPIC model of verbal working memory. Top panel: Observed and predicted percentage correct recall with sequences of phonologically distinct words. Bottom panel: Observed and predicted percentage correct recall with sequences of phonologically similar words.

Table 6.1. *Parameter Values in EPIC Simulation for Study by Longoni et al. (1993)*

Source Type	Phonological Status	M (ms)	s
External	Similar	6,625	0.2
	Distinct	7,400	0.2
Internal	Similar	4,875	0.5
	Distinct	5,500	0.5

Note: M is the median of the lognormal decay-time distribution for items in auditory working memory; s is the distribution's spread parameter. The left two columns of the table indicate the characteristics of the stored items for which these parameter values were identified. The external source corresponds to overt auditory stimulation, and the internal source corresponds to covert vocal rehearsal.

the spread parameters of the decay-time distributions were less for items whose source was external, and they did not depend on phonological similarity.

THEORETICAL INTERPRETATION. There is a straightforward theoretical interpretation of these simulation results. Basically our EPIC model's assumptions may be correct! Elaborating the ideas of some previous theorists (e.g., Baddeley, 1986), the model provides a neat explanation of the articulatory-suppression effect. Performance is worse without rehearsal because only the original traces of external stimulus items are potentially available in auditory working memory to be recalled. However, following covert rehearsal, recall also may be based on traces of items generated internally through the model's phonological loop, because the rehearsal process generates fresh copies of them repeatedly.

The model likewise explains the interactive articulation-time and phonological-similarity effects. Item sequences that take more time to articulate are recalled less well because the rehearsal and recall processes proceed more slowly through them, and so items are more likely to be lost prematurely from auditory working memory. Phonologically similar items are recalled less well because their shorter decay times tend to preclude the rehearsal process from maintaining them. The articulation-time effect during rehearsal is greater for phonologically similar items because their shorter decay times make them disproportionately more likely to get lost during lengthy rehearsal cycles.

Concomitantly, the parameters of the decay-time distributions (Table 6.1) have an interesting interpretation. Given that different mean decay times were required for items that had external and internal sources, the present simulation suggests that source-specific coding does take place in human auditory working memory. This supports previous claims about multiple types of auditory working memory codes (Cowan, 1984). Likewise supported is the claim (Posner & Konick, 1966) that phonologically similar items decay more quickly than do distinct items.[6]

TECHNICAL LESSONS. Our work here also offers some instructive technical lessons. Although the goodness-of-fit produced by the present simulation was satisfactory, the data reported by Longoni et al. did not contain enough degrees of freedom for a completely convincing test. Fitting the EPIC model involved adjusting six parameters (Table 6.1), including four values of M and two values of s, whereas the data came from a 2-by-2-by-2 factorial design with only 8 df. This deficiency highlights a serious limitation of binary factorial designs. Although common in cognitive psychology, such designs are an "underpowered" source of data, because they yield only nominal-scale information about the effects of their independent variables. Future experimentation instead should use designs that have several levels per factor.

Yet despite these caveats, it would be mistaken to dismiss the initial success of the present EPIC model as trivial. Our simulation for Longoni et al.'s study was constrained by the model's architecture and task strategy. So even with six free decay-time parameters, there was not arbitrarily great freedom to fit the data. That the model accounted for the overall pattern of reported factor effects thus should be taken as an encouraging sign about the model's theoretical value. Further confirmation of this comes in our work with Baddeley et al.'s (1975, Exp. 1) study.

The Study of Baddeley, Thomson, and Buchanan

Fortunately, Baddeley et al.'s (1975, Exp. 1) classical study had an experimental design with ample power for a strong test of our EPIC model. This power stemmed from there being an independent variable that had several levels within it, namely, the number of words per sequence. After we adjusted the model's free parameters, numerous degrees of freedom remained in Baddeley et al.'s data to assess the model's goodness-of-fit carefully.

EXPERIMENTAL DESIGN. Baddeley et al.'s study used the generic serial memory span task described before. On each trial, either 4, 5, 6, 7, or 8 auditory English words were presented successively to participants for subsequent recall in original order. The participants always were allowed to rehearse; no articulatory suppression was required. Subsequent recall attempts were oral.

---

[6] Intriguingly, Longoni et al. (1993, Exp. 1) found that sequences of phonologically similar words took longer to articulate than did sequences of distinct words. At first blush, this finding seemed potentially sufficient to explain why the sequences of similar words were recalled less well. However, a preliminary simulation with our EPIC model revealed that by itself, the articulation-time difference between similar-word sequences and distinct-word sequences could not account entirely for the worse recall of the similar-word sequences. Fitting the data well also required there to be a difference between the mean decay times of similar and distinct words. Such a discovery illustrates the superiority of precise computational modeling over informal verbal theorizing for determining what conceptual constructs are truly necessary.

Within each sequence, the words took either relatively long or short times to articulate. Across trials, the number of words per sequence and the sequence's articulation time varied systematically. Overall, the experiment thus had a 5 (number of words per sequence) by 2 (short/long articulation time) factorial design. The sequences involving long articulation times were constructed from a pool of five-syllable words; a pool of one-syllable words was used to construct the sequences involving short articulation times.[7]

EMPIRICAL RESULTS. The dark textured bars in the top and bottom panels of Figure 6.6 show the empirical results from Baddeley et al.'s (1975, Exp. 1) study in terms of percent correct recall. Both independent variables had reliable main effects. As either the number of words per sequence or the sequence articulation time increased, percent correct recall decreased substantially. A reliable interaction also occurred between these effects. The number of words per sequence had a much greater effect for the sequences whose articulation times were long.

EPIC COMPUTATIONAL MODEL. To account for these empirical results, we ran our EPIC model through Baddeley et al.'s experimental procedure. In response, the model produced a sequence of correct and incorrect recall attempts. A single pair of mean and spread parameter values, identified by iterative search, was used for the item decay-time distributions: $M = 7500$ ms; $s = 0.2$.[8]

For the present simulation, we also needed to set the rates at which the words were vocalized in the sequences that had nominally "short" and "long" articulation times. Unfortunately, Baddeley et al. (1975, Exp. 1) did not report these rates. We therefore measured them ourselves by vocalizing representative word sequences at a crisp, comfortable pace of the sort typically used during covert rehearsal. The mean rates of vocalization for the sequences of words with long and short articulation times were measured respectively to be 804 ms and 419 ms per word. These rates were then used in our EPIC model.

SIMULATION RESULTS. The white bars in the top and bottom panels of Figure 6.6 show the simulation results produced by our model for Baddeley et al. (1975, Exp. 1). We obtained an accurate quantitative account of the main

---

[7] A confounding therefore existed here between number of syllables per word and articulation time. Nevertheless, more recent research by Baddeley and others, including us, has revealed that sequence articulation time per se is a crucial independent variable. This finding stands despite counterobjections by a few investigators (cf. Caplan, Rochon, & Waters, 1992).

[8] Because no articulatory suppression occurred in Baddeley et al.'s (1975, Exp. 1) study, it was not possible to accurately estimate different means and spreads for the decay times of items from external and internal sources. In this case, we therefore adopted the default assumption that these parameters did not differ as a function of the items' source. Also, we again assumed that sequence length and articulation rate did not affect them either. Thus, there were many fewer free parameters in our simulation for Baddeley et al. than in our simulation for Longoni et al.

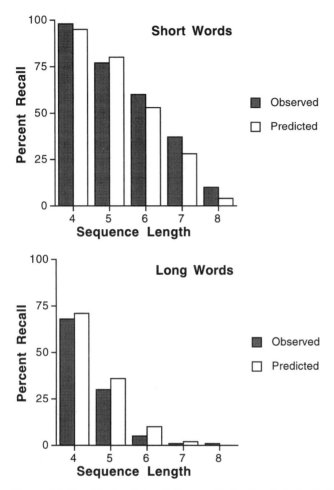

Figure 6.6. Empirical and simulation results for the study by Baddeley, Thomson, and Buchanan (1975, Exp. 1). Dark textured bars represent observed percentages of trials on which serial recall was perfectly correct as a function of sequence length (i.e., the number of words per sequence). White bars adjacent to the right of the dark bars represent corresponding predicted percentages of trials on which serial recall was perfectly correct under the present EPIC model of verbal working memory. Top panel: Observed and predicted percentage correct recall with sequences that contained short (one-syllable) words and had short articulation times. Bottom panel: Observed and predicted percentage correct recall with sequences that contained long (five-syllable) words and had long articulation times.

and interactive effects caused by both the sequence-length and articulation-time factors. This success occurred even though the present simulation used many fewer free parameters than there were degrees of freedom in the empirical results.

THEORETICAL INTERPRETATION. Our EPIC model fit well here because it aptly characterizes the complementary contributions of various item representations, covert subvocal rehearsal, and item decay in auditory working memory. To do so requires having precisely and veridically specified the task strategy through which the contents of auditory working memory are managed. It therefore appears that for the serial memory span task, we have successfully encompassed several auditory working memory mechanisms and arrived at a more complete correct description of the human phonological loop.

Substantive and Methodological Insights Concerning Verbal Working Memory

From our applications of EPIC to the data of Longoni et al. (1993, Exp. 1) and Baddeley et al. (1975, Exp. 1), several substantive and methodological insights concerning verbal working memory have been attained.

DURATION OF ITEMS IN AUDITORY WORKING MEMORY. In each simulation with the present EPIC model, the mean durations of auditory working memory items were two to four times greater than the 2 s claimed from some prior studies that have used the serial memory span task (e.g., Baddeley et al., 1975; Schweickert & Boruff, 1986). Instead, the item durations suggested by our modeling are more consistent with research on echoic and auditory memory that has used other types of paradigm, which point toward values around 10 s or greater (e.g., Balota & Duchek, 1986; Cowan, 1984; Cowan et al., 1990; Eriksen & Johnson, 1964; Watkins & Todres, 1980). What could account for this conflict? Perhaps previous theorists have neglected to consider how much executive control might lengthen the time consumed by covert rehearsal during sequence-presentation intervals when partial chains of memorized items are being constructed and elaborated by task-strategy procedures. If so, then they would not have realized that items in auditory working memory must endure for at least as long as such processes take, which – as our modeling shows – may be substantially longer than the time required to utter a sequence of items after it has been fully prepared. Attaining such realizations constitutes a strong incentive for seriously pursuing formal theoretical approaches.

SOURCE-DEPENDENT CODING. A second insight provided by the present work is that distinct codes are indeed used in auditory working memory for items that come from external (overt auditory stimulus) and internal (covert speech) sources. Specifically, we discovered that "imaginal" codes for internal-source items have shorter and more variable durations than do "literal" codes for external-source items (Table 6.1). This helps explain some of the complexity that has characterized the past literature on auditory memory (Cowan, 1984).

IMPORTANCE OF TASK STRATEGIES. Like our prior research in other task domains, the present research further demonstrates the crucial importance of precisely characterizing task strategies. For understanding working memory, this characterization is necessary even in seemingly simple cases like the serial memory span task. The executive control needed to perform this task is not trivial, involving several temporally overlapped threads of processing. Had we also chosen to model the sophisticated guessing processes that presumably contribute to partially correct recall attempts, the importance of task strategies would have been even more apparent. Future theorizing and experimentation about working memory therefore need to take task strategies much more seriously (cf. W. Reitman, 1970).

General Discussion

An important exercise for facilitating future research is to compare and contrast alternative theoretical frameworks being used currently to characterize human working memory. By doing so, commonalities among these frameworks may be identified, and as a result, theoretical integration may be fostered. Also, to the extent that there really are fundamental differences among frameworks, focusing on them may yield crucial empirical tests for determining which theories are most viable. Toward achieving these objectives, contributors to the present volume have been posed with eight designated questions. We are now in a position to answer them on the basis of EPIC.

Answers to Eight Designated Questions

Table 6.2 summarizes our answers to the eight designated questions.

Table 6.2. *Brief Summary of Answers to the Eight Designated Questions*

---

(1) **Basic Mechanisms and Representations in Working Memory**
Information is encoded symbolically and put in modal (e.g., auditory and visual) working memory stores by EPIC's perceptual and motor processors. Production rules in the cognitive processor, together with the perceptual-motor processors, are used to maintain and apply this information for task performance. The cognitive processor also uses production rules to maintain and apply symbolic information in the control and tag stores of working memory, which help direct the flow of processing.

(2) **The Control and Regulation of Working Memory**
EPIC has no general-purpose "central executive" separate from other architectural components. Rather, working memory is managed by task-specific executive control processes. With respect to the particular task(s) for which skilled performance is being modeled, executive control processes are specified in terms of production rules that update, maintain, and use the contents of working memory to complete the task(s) efficiently.

continued

Table 6.2, continued

---

(3) **The Unitary Versus Non-Unitary Nature of Working Memory**
Working memory in EPIC consists of multiple separable subcomponents. Some of these subserve the temporary storage and on-line use of symbolic declarative knowledge, such as perceptual (visual, auditory, tactile), motoric (ocular, manual, vocal), and procedural control (goals, task priorities, process status) information. Other subcomponents subserve the application of procedural (production rule) knowledge that implements executive and task processes. Interactions among these subcomponents occur through operations by EPIC's cognitive, perceptual, and motor processors.

(4) **The Nature of Working Memory Limitations**
The philosophy of modeling embodied in EPIC aspires to parsimonious and plausible assumptions about human information processing. Accordingly, the limits of EPIC's working memory capacity come mainly from two especially justifiable sources: finite processing speed and decay of symbolic codes in partitions of perceptual working memory. No limits have been set yet on the capacities of EPIC's stores for production rules and procedural control information. Furthermore, EPIC has no limited supply of a general resource such as activation capacity.

(5) **The Role of Working Memory in Complex Cognitive Activities**
EPIC's working memory components play multiple supporting roles in task performance. For processing of verbal information, contributions are made by auditory working memory, vocal-motor working memory, and a procedural control store. Similarly, visual working memory, ocular-motor working memory, and the procedural control store contribute to processing of visuospatial information. Functional task analyses based on EPIC reveal that even the simplest tasks require working memory and executive control to be performed successfully.

(6) **The Relationship of Working Memory to Long-Term Memory and Knowledge**
In EPIC, the partitions of working memory are structurally separate from LTM, but complement and interact with it. The production-rule store in EPIC's cognitive processor may be construed as a form of LTM for procedural knowledge. Given our objectives to date, EPIC's LTM for declarative knowledge has not been applied extensively yet to model skilled task performance. Nevertheless, it has the potential to represent and support the use of relevant symbolic knowledge structures as need be.

(7) **The Relationship of Working Memory to Attention and Consciousness**
In EPIC, "working memory" and "attention" refer to different theoretical constructs. Through judicious executive control and orienting of physical sensors, priority may be given to processing some external stimuli rather than others (i.e., "attention to perception"). Also, priority may be given to

---

Table 6.2, continued

producing some motor outputs rather than others (i.e., "attention to action"). This control is achieved by manipulating items in working memory (e.g., task goals) that determine which production rules are fired. The phenomenological experience called "consciousness" ordinarily plays no role in EPIC.

(8) The Biological Implementation of Working Memory
The theoretical assumptions embodied in EPIC are consistent with current findings from neuroscience about working memory. For example, EPIC emulates massively distributed parallelism of information processing and short-term storage through modular interactive mechanisms, as found in the human brain. Like those of the brain, EPIC's perceptual and motor mechanisms are treated as crucial subcomponents separate from and complementary to other cognitive mechanisms.

BASIC MECHANISMS AND REPRESENTATIONS IN WORKING MEMORY. Working memory in EPIC is mediated by a variety of specific mechanisms. The architecture's perceptual and motor processors encode information and put symbolic representations in modal working memory stores, such as auditory and visual working memory. These representations are accessed, maintained, and used for task performance by the cognitive processor, which applies sets of production rules to interact with the modal working memory stores and perceptual-motor processors. Applying its production rules, the cognitive processor also maintains and uses symbolic representations in the control and tag stores of working memory for directing the flow of processing.

For example, many of these mechanisms and representations contribute crucially to our EPIC model of performance in the serial memory span task. Sets of production rules in the cognitive processor, together with the auditory perceptual processor, auditory working memory, and vocal motor processor, implement the model's phonological loop. Coordinating item-chain construction, rehearsal, and recall processes under the model also requires manipulating items in the control and tag stores of the architecture's production-system working memory.

THE CONTROL AND REGULATION OF WORKING MEMORY. As the present model further illustrates, EPIC has no separate general-purpose "central executive" (cf. Baddeley & Logie, Chapter 2, this volume). Instead, the cognitive processor is programmed with specific sets of production rules to implement executive control processes (e.g., an overall task strategy) for performing particular tasks. These rules have the same format as other rules used in various individual subtasks (e.g., covert rehearsal and overt recall). A principal function of the executive control processes in EPIC is to coordinate progress on various subtasks so that they get completed correctly and efficiently. This involves managing the contents of EPIC's working memory control and tag stores with respect to task goals, step items, strategy items, status items, and tags, which govern when subtask processes are executed and what perceptual-motor resources are made available to them at each moment along the way.

THE UNITARY VERSUS NON-UNITARY NATURE OF WORKING MEMORY. Despite a deceptive impression that Figure 6.1 might create initially, by now it should be clear that working memory is not a single "construct," "place," or "box" in EPIC. Rather, EPIC's working memory has somewhat the same status as does the "self" in Buddhism (Bukkyo Dendo Kyokai, 1985); under various guises, it is at once both "everywhere" and "nowhere." More precisely, we conceive working memory to consist of multiple separable subcomponents. Some of these subserve the temporary storage and on-line use of declarative knowledge, such as perceptual (visual, auditory, tactile), motoric (ocular, manual, vocal), and procedural control (task goal, strategy item, status item) information. Other subcomponents subserve the application of procedural (production rule) knowledge that implements executive and task processes. Interactions among the various subcomponents of working memory occur through the operations of EPIC's cognitive processor.

The diverse and distributed multicomponent nature of working memory in EPIC is illustrated by our present model of performance for the serial memory span task. This model uses the architecture's auditory working memory, control store, and tag store to maintain complementary types of declarative knowledge during stimulus presentation, covert rehearsal, and overt recall. Implementation of these processes through the model's phonological loop also requires the cognitive processor to interact with the vocal motor processor and auditory perceptual processor.

THE NATURE OF WORKING MEMORY LIMITATIONS. EPIC is predicated on a philosophy of theory construction and performance modeling that aspires to make plausible parsimonious assumptions. Limits on EPIC's working memory capacity therefore come mainly from two especially justifiable sources: finite processing speed, and decay of symbolic representations in the modal (perceptual) working memory stores. We have set no limits yet on the capacities of EPIC's stores for production rules and procedural control information. Furthermore, EPIC has no limited supply of a general resource-like activation capacity. In these respects, our theoretical framework differs significantly from those of some other contributors to this volume (cf. Cowan, Chapter 3; Engle et al., Chapter 4; Lovett et al., Chapter 5).

The parsimony and plausibility to which we aspire in EPIC are exemplified by our present model for performance of the serial memory span task. According to it, percent correct recall depends simply on the rates of item decay in auditory working memory and on the rates at which chains of stored items can be constructed, rehearsed, and recalled during each trial. From prior research (e.g., Brown, 1958; J. Reitman, 1974; Sternberg et al.,

1978), we know that both of these basic limits probably exist. To the extent that the former (decay) rates are high and the latter (processing) rates are low, final recall will be poor. However, the rate of decay is not assumed to depend on the numerosity of the items in auditory working memory, nor are the processing rates – which stem from the cognitive processor's cycle time – assumed to depend on the numerosity of the production rules being used for task performance.

THE ROLE OF WORKING MEMORY IN COMPLEX COGNITIVE ACTIVITIES. Given our ultimate research objectives, we have constructed EPIC to be especially suited for modeling complex cognitive activities associated with skilled perceptual-motor performance in task situations such as aircraft-cockpit operation, air-traffic control, and speed-stressed human–computer interaction (Kieras & Meyer, 1997; Meyer & Kieras, 1999). In EPIC, some working memory components (e.g., control store and tag store) contribute especially to the executive control of task scheduling and to the allocation of perceptual-motor resources among various subtasks, which play crucial roles during realistic multiple-task performance. Complementing these contributions, other components – including EPIC's modal working memory stores – retain coded sensory and motor information that is needed for ongoing interactions with the physical environment.

Indeed, functional analyses based on EPIC reveal that to be performed successfully, even the simplest tasks require working memory and executive control (Meyer & Kieras, 1997a, 1997b). As our present model of performance in the serial memory span task illustrates, auditory working memory, vocal-motor working memory, the control store, and the tag store are all essential for processing elementary verbal information. Similarly, visual working memory, ocular-motor working memory, the control store, and the tag store are all essential for processing elementary visuospatial information. Presumably these mechanisms would be involved in more complex cognitive activities as well and may help constitute future models that we formulate to characterize realistic multiple-task performance.

THE RELATIONSHIP OF WORKING MEMORY TO LONG-TERM MEMORY AND KNOWLEDGE. EPIC's working memory is not simply an activated portion of long-term memory (cf. Cowan, Chapter 3, Engle et al., Chapter 4, Lovett et al., Chapter 5, this volume). Instead, various working memory partitions and temporary stores in our architecture are structurally separate from long-term memory. Nevertheless, their contents and those of long-term memory can interact through operations mediated by the cognitive processor.

EPIC's working memory provides a substrate for procedural skills to exploit available declarative knowledge during on-line task performance. The production-rule store in the cognitive processor may be construed as a form of long-term memory for procedural knowledge. Given our prevailing objectives, long-term memory for declarative knowledge has not been applied extensively yet in our modeling endeavors. This is evident, for example, from the present EPIC model of performance in the serial memory span task, where the organization and activation of declarative long-term memory play no explicit role. However, declarative long-term memory in EPIC has the potential to represent permanent symbolic knowledge structures and to support their use as need be. We envision that learning and practice may influence working memory limitations and functions beneficially by enhancing both the efficiency of procedural (production rule) knowledge and the efficacy of organized declarative (propositional) knowledge (cf. Lovett et al., Chapter 5; Young & Lewis, Chapter 7; Ericsson & Delaney, Chapter 8; Schneider, Chapter 10; O'Reilly et al., Chapter 11, this volume).

THE RELATIONSHIP OF WORKING MEMORY TO ATTENTION AND CON-SCIOUSNESS. How working memory relates to attention and consciousness is a complex and thorny issue with which cognitive psychologists have struggled at least since the time of William James (1890). The resolution of this issue hinges on the conceptual perspective that one has, and on the technical definitions that one adopts.

In EPIC, "working memory" and "attention" refer to different theoretical constructs. Through judicious executive control and orienting of physical sensors, EPIC computational models give priority to processing some external stimuli rather than others (i.e., "attention to perception"). Also, priority is given to producing some motor outputs rather than others (i.e., "attention to action"). This prioritization is achieved by manipulating items in the working-memory control store (e.g., task goals) that determine which production rules are fired. As a result, for example, eye movements to particularly interesting or important visual stimuli may be executed, and movements by one hand may be selected, prepared, and executed in preference to movements by the other hand. The new items that these activities cause to arrive in the modal working memory stores are the products of attention, but they are not attention itself. Furthermore, in other respects, working memory and covert attention are even more distinct under EPIC, because for reasons of theoretical parsimony, we have not yet incorporated covert attention shifting as part of the architecture's perceptual processors (cf. Schneider, Chapter 10, this volume).

Consistent with the latter conservatism, the phenomenological experience called "consciousness" ordinarily plays no role in EPIC. Unlike some daring philosophers of mind (e.g., Chalmers, 1996), we refrain from speculating here about how the architecture might yield this experience as an emergent property. No claims are made for now about whether our EPIC computational model of performance in the serial memory span task is conscious during the execution of its procedures!

THE BIOLOGICAL IMPLEMENTATION OF WORKING MEMORY. Although EPIC is an architecture for symbolic computational modeling of task performance, its assumptions are nonetheless compatible with implementation at biological and neural levels. This compatibility should not be surprising. As

Newell (1990) argued forcefully, principled symbolic computational modeling can be complementary – not antithetical – to biological and neural implementation. In fact, properties of human information processing at the neural level impose fundamental constraints that prospective architectures and symbolic computational models must take seriously and accommodate among their basic assumptions. By doing so, they enhance their empirical credibility and ultimate prospects for being implemented biologically. Conversely, biological and neural modeling may benefit from insights gained through symbolic computational modeling about the inherent functional characteristics of human information processing (e.g., see Schneider, Chapter 10, and O'Reilly et al., Chapter 11, this volume).

Among EPIC's assumptions that are relevant in these respects, we have made several concerning the distributed, quasi-modularized, semiautonomous, parallel nature of information processing. EPIC's perceptual, cognitive, and motor processors are assumed to operate simultaneously and asynchronously, just as parallel distributed processing in the brain does. The cyclicity of the cognitive processor's operations likewise mimic some of the brain's neural rhythms (Kristofferson, 1967; Ray, 1990). Various working memory stores in EPIC may have corresponding manifestations in the brain. For example, it is possible that the control and tag stores of working memory are implemented by anterior parts (frontal lobes) of the brain, whereas the modal working memory stores for visual, auditory, and other sensory information are implemented by posterior parts (e.g., temporal and parietal lobes). Some other contributors to this volume hold similar views (e.g., Schneider, Chapter 10; O'Reilly et al., Chapter 11).

These views are supported by recent evidence from brain-imaging experiments conducted on participants during their performance of representative working memory tasks (e.g., Awh et al., 1996; D'Esposito et al., 1995; Jonides et al., 1993; Paulesu et al., 1993). This evidence reveals that during such performance, multiple interconnected regions in the anterior and posterior parts of the brain are active, forming an apparent network of modules that subserve complementary functions, as we suggested above might be the case. The activation of these regions increases and decreases systematically, depending on exactly which functions are engaged by the prevailing task(s). Perhaps by collecting more such evidence in the context of new studies designed to test further hypotheses based on EPIC and other alternative information-processing architectures, progress can occur toward integrating theoretical frameworks like ours with the biological and neural domains.

Theoretical Caveats

Of course, more questions remain to be answered beyond the preceding designated eight. As presently formulated, our EPIC model does not directly accommodate all of the prominent factor effects that have been found during studies with the serial memory span task. For example, Brown and Hulme

(1995) have shown that performance of this task depends systematically on lexical and semantic properties of the items from which to-be-recalled sequences are constructed. Related findings like this have been reported by other investigators as well (e.g., Caplan, Rochon, & Waters, 1992; Gregg, Freedman, & Smith, 1989; Naveh-Benjamin & Ayres, 1986). Because of confoundings between sequence articulation times and other factors (e.g., see Wright, 1979), it is conceivable that our model can account for at least some of these results without resort to additional mechanisms. Nevertheless, a full, accurate account of them still may require augmenting the model with further contributions from declarative long-term memory.

Dealing with other results, such as ones concerning the putative separability of item and serial-order information (e.g., Estes, 1972; Healy, 1974; Shiffrin & Cook, 1978), also may require modifications or elaborations in terms of sophisticated guessing strategies and memory representations based on hierarchical structures.[9] Which modifications and elaborations are most appropriate presumably can be determined best through precise computational modeling rather than just informal verbal theorizing. Computational modeling helps resolve theoretical controversies!

Directions for Future Research

Furthermore, our future research with EPIC will focus especially on the role of working memory in realistic high-performance tasks. By doing so, we may gain additional insights about how working memory really works during "cognition in the wild." Also, insights may be gained about how to facilitate practical speed-stressed performance through new interface designs and modified task requirements.

For example, consider whether the usability of human–computer interfaces can be enhanced by augmenting them with capabilities for recognizing and responding to an operator's spoken commands. Concerning this issue, many computer technologists have become convinced that such augmentations would provide fantastic enhancements. However, there is some troublesome evidence that operating an interface by spoken commands actually interferes with the performance of verbally intensive tasks like text editing (Shneiderman, 1992). Such interference may occur too when task performance requires perceiving and classifying speech or other sounds as well as producing spoken commands. Could these disruptions stem from limitations of a phonological-loop mechanism on which operators rely during

---

[9] Because of the representation of serial order that our present model uses for items in auditory working memory, losing an item of a sequence involves losing some information about serial order. Clever guessing strategies could compensate for some of this loss. Also, consistent with results of some investigators (e.g., Healy, 1974), separate representations of item and order information are feasible in EPIC. However, for the sake of parsimony, we have not implemented them yet.

human–computer interaction? Perhaps we can answer this question more definitively by constructing future models of human–computer interaction that incorporate a phonological loop like the one in our present EPIC model of performance for the serial memory span task. From this endeavor, it then may be possible to predict more precisely when and how much particular interfaces that entail speech I/O will help or hinder task performance.

As another important example, consider tasks that require high performance in environments such as fighter aircraft cockpits, where overall situation awareness is crucial (Graves, 1997). There situation awareness presumably depends on working memory being filled with rich and ever-changing details about the current state of the prevailing task environment. Under these circumstances, if a fighter pilot loses situation awareness, the consequences easily can be fatal. Such losses may stem from excessive mental workload associated with the complex decisions, multiple-task coordination, and human–computer interaction that cockpit operations require. Thus, it is essential to understand how situation awareness can be fostered through improved system designs.

Yet the available theory regarding this matter has been distressingly vague (e.g., see O'Donnell & Eggemeier, 1986). We therefore hope that through future EPIC modeling of the perceptual, cognitive, and motor requirements in complicated cockpit operations, it will be possible to better characterize important aspects of situation awareness and mental workload, which could yield improved concepts and tools for designing cockpit systems. Of course, a key part of our anticipated endeavors will be to clarify and computationally represent the mechanisms of working memory in more detail.

REFERENCES

Akmajian, A., Demers, R. A., & Harnish, R. M. (1979). *Linguistics: An introduction to language and communication.* Cambridge, MA: MIT Press.
Anderson, J. R. (1976). *Language, memory, and thought.* Hillsdale, NJ: Erlbaum.
Anderson, J. R. (1993). *Rules of the mind.* Hillsdale, NJ: Erlbaum.
Anderson, J. R., & Matessa, M. (1997). A production system theory of serial memory. *Psychological Review, 104,* 728–748.
Atkinson, R. C., Hernstein, R. J., Lindzey, G., & Luce, R. D. (Eds.). (1988). *Stevens' handbook of experimental psychology* (2nd ed.). New York: Wiley.
Atkinson, R. C., & Shiffrin, R. M. (1968). Human memory: A proposed system and its control processes. In K. W. Spence (Ed.), *The psychology of learning and motivation* (Vol. 2, pp. 89–195). New York: Academic Press.
Awh, E., Jonides, J., Smith, E. E., Schumacher, E. H., Koeppe, R., & Katz, S. (1996). Dissociation of storage and rehearsal in verbal working memory: Evidence from PET. *Psychological Science, 7,* 25–31.
Baddeley, A. D. (1986). *Working memory.* New York: Oxford University Press.
Baddeley, A. D., & Hitch, G. J. (1974). Working memory. In G. H. Bower (Ed.), *The psychology of learning and motivation: Advances in research and theory* (Vol. 8, pp. 47–89). New York: Academic Press.

Baddeley, A. D., Lewis, V., & Vallar, G. (1984). Exploring the articulatory loop. *Quarterly Journal of Experimental Psychology, 36A,* 233–252.

Baddeley, A. D., Thomson, N., & Buchanan, M. (1975). Word length and the structure of short-term memory. *Journal of Verbal Learning and Verbal Behavior, 14,* 575–589.

Ballas, J. A., Heitmeyer, C. L., & Perez, M. A. (1992a). *Direct manipulation and intermittent automation in advanced cockpits* (Technical Report NRL/FR/5534–92–9375). Washington, DC: Naval Research Laboratory.

Ballas, J. A., Heitmeyer, C. L., & Perez, M. A. (1992b). Evaluating two aspects of direct manipulation in advanced cockpits. *Proceedings of the CHI'92 Conference on Human Factors in Computing Systems* (pp. 127–134). New York: ACM.

Balota, D. A., & Duchek, J. M. (1986). Voice specific information and the 20-second delayed-suffix effect. *Journal of Experimental Psychology: Learning, Memory, and Cognition, 12,* 509–516.

Boff, K. R., Kaufman, L., & Thomas, J. P. (Eds.). (1986). *Handbook of perception and human performance.* New York: Wiley.

Bovair, S., Kieras, D. E., & Polson, P. G. (1990). The acquisition and performance of text editing skill: A cognitive complexity analysis. *Human–Computer Interaction, 5,* 1–48.

Brown, G. D., & Hulme, C. (1995). Modeling item length effects in memory span: No rehearsal needed? *Journal of Memory and Language, 34,* 594–624.

Brown, J. (1958). Some tests of the decay theory of immediate memory. *Quarterly Journal of Experimental Psychology, 10,* 12–21.

Bukkyo Dendo Kyokai. (1985). *The teachings of Buddha.* Tokyo: Kosaido Printing Co.

Burgess, N., & Hitch, G. (1992). Toward a network model of the articulatory loop. *Journal of Memory and Language, 31,* 429–460.

Callaway, E., & Yeager, C. L. (1960). Relationship between reaction time and electroencephalographic alpha base. *Science, 132,* 1765–1766.

Caplan, D., Rochon, E., & Waters, G. S. (1992). Articulatory and phonological determinants of word length effects in span tasks. *Quarterly Journal of Experimental Psychology, 45A,* 177–192.

Card, S. K., Moran, T. P., & Newell, A. (1983). *The psychology of human–computer interaction.* Hillsdale, NJ: Erlbaum.

Chalmers, D. J. (1996). *The conscious mind.* New York: Oxford University Press.

Conrad, R., & Hull, A. J. (1964). Acoustic confusion in immediate memory. *British Journal of Psychology, 55,* 75–84.

Cowan, N. (1984). On short and long auditory stores. *Psychological Bulletin, 96,* 341–370.

Cowan, N., Day, L., Saults, J. S., Keller, T. A., Johnson, T., & Flores, L. (1992). The role of verbal output time in the effects of word length on immediate memory. *Journal of Memory and Language, 31,* 1–17.

Cowan, N., Lichty, W., & Grove, T. R. (1990). Properties of memory for unattended spoken syllables. *Journal of Experimental Psychology: Learning, Memory, and Cognition, 16,* 258–269.

D'Esposito, M., Detre, J., Alsop, D., Shin, R., Atlas, S., & Grossman, M. (1995). The neural basis of the central executive system of working memory. *Nature, 378,* 279–281.

Eriksen, C. W., & Johnson, H. J. (1964). Storage and decay characteristics of nonattended auditory stimuli. *Journal of Experimental Psychology, 68,* 28–36.

Estes, W. K. (1972). An associative basis for coding and organization in memory. In A. W. Melton & E. Martin (Eds.), *Coding processes in human memory* (pp. 161–190). Washington, DC: Winston.

Gordon, P. C., & Meyer, D. E. (1987). Control of serial order in rapidly spoken syllable sequences. *Journal of Memory and Language, 26,* 300–321.

Graves, K. (1997). Situational awareness in the tactical air environment. *CSERIAC Gateway, VII,* 12–13.

Gregg, V. H., Freedman, C. M., & Smith, D. K. (1989). Word frequency, articulatory suppression and memory span. *British Journal of Psychology, 80,* 363–374.

Gugerty, L. J. (1997). Situation awareness during driving: Explicit and implicit knowledge in dynamic spatial memory. *Journal of Experimental Psychology: Applied, 3,* 42–66.

Gupta, P., & MacWhinney, B. (1995). Is the articulatory loop articulatory or auditory? Reexamining the effects of concurrent articulation on immediate serial recall. *Journal of Memory and Language, 34,* 63–88.

Hastings, N. A. J., & Peacock, J. B. (1975). *Statistical distributions.* London: Butterworth.

Healy, A. F. (1974). Separating item from order information in short-term memory. *Journal of Verbal Learning and Verbal Behavior, 13,* 644–655.

Henson, R. N. A., Norris, D. G., Page, M. P. A., & Baddeley, A. D. (1996). Unchained memory: Error patterns rule out chaining models of immediate serial recall. *Quarterly Journal of Experimental Psychology, 49A,* 80–115.

James, W. (1890). *The principles of psychology.* New York: Holt.

John, B. E., & Kieras, D. E. (1996). The GOMS family of user interface analysis techniques: Comparison and contrast. *ACM Transactions on Computer–Human Interaction, 3,* 320–351.

Jonides, J., Smith, E. E., Koeppe, R. A., Awh, E., Minoshima, S., & Mintun, M. A. (1993). Spatial working memory in humans as revealed by PET. *Nature, 363,* 623–625.

Just, M. A., Carpenter, P. A., & Hemphill, D. D. (1996). Constraints on processing capacity: Architectural or implementational? In D. M. Steier & T. M. Mitchell (Eds.), *Mind matters: A tribute to Allen Newell* (pp. 141–178). Mahwah, NJ: Erlbaum.

Kieras, D. E., & Meyer, D. E. (1994). *The EPIC architecture for modeling human information-processing and performance: A brief introduction* (EPIC Report No.1, TR-94/ONR-EPIC-1). Ann Arbor: University of Michigan.

Kieras, D. E., & Meyer, D. E. (1995). Predicting human performance in dual-task tracking and decision making with computational models using the EPIC architecture. In D. S. Alberts, D. Buede, T. Clark, R. Hayes, J. Hofmann, W. Round, S. Starr, & W. Vaughan (Eds.), *Proceedings of the International Symposium on Command and Control Research and Technology* (pp. 314–325). Washington, DC: National Defense University.

Kieras, D. E., & Meyer, D. E. (1997). An overview of the EPIC architecture for cognition and performance with application to human–computer interaction. *Human–Computer Interaction, 12,* 391–438.

Kieras, D. E., Wood, S. D., & Meyer, D. E. (1997). Predictive engineering models based on the EPIC architecture for a multimodal high-performance human–computer interaction task. *ACM Transactions on Computer–Human Interaction, 4,* 230–275.

Kristofferson, A. B. (1967). Attention and psychophysical time. In A. F. Sanders (Ed.), *Attention and performance* (pp. 93–100). Amsterdam: North-Holland.

Laird, J., Rosenbloom, P., & Newell, A. (1986). *Universal subgoaling and chunking.* Boston: Kluwer Academic.

Landauer, T. K. (1962). The rate of implicit speech. *Perceptual and Motor Skills, 15,* 646.

Lashley, K. (1951). The problem of serial order in behavior. In L. A. Jeffress (Ed.), *Cerebral mechanisms in behavior* (pp. 112–131). New York: Wiley.

Levy, B. A. (1971). Role of articulation in auditory and visual short-term memory. *Journal of Verbal Learning and Verbal Behavior, 10,* 123–132.

Longoni, A. M., Richardson, A. T. E., & Aiello, A. (1993). Articulatory rehearsal and phonological storage in working memory. *Memory & Cognition, 21,* 11–22.

Meyer, D. E., & Kieras, D. E. (1992, November). *The PRP effect: Central bottleneck, perceptual-motor limitations, or task strategies?* Paper presented at the meeting of the Psychonomic Society, St. Louis, MO.

Meyer, D. E., & Kieras, D. E. (1994). *EPIC computational models of psychological refractory-period effects in human multiple-task performance* (EPIC Report No.2, TR-94/ONR-EPIC-2). Ann Arbor: University of Michigan.

Meyer, D. E., & Kieras, D. E. (1997a). A computational theory of executive cognitive processes and multiple-task performance: Part 1. Basic mechanisms. *Psychological Review, 104,* 3–65.

Meyer, D. E., & Kieras, D. E. (1997b). A computational theory of executive cognitive processes and multiple-task performance: Part 2. Accounts of psychological refractory-period phenomena. *Psychological Review, 104,* 749–791.

Meyer, D. E., & Kieras, D. E. (1999). Précis to a practical unified theory of cognition and action: Some lessons from computational modeling of human multiple-task performance. In D. Gopher & A. Koriat (Eds.), *Attention and performance XVII.* Cambridge, MA: MIT Press.

Meyer, D. E., Kieras, D. E., Lauber, E., Schumacher, E., Glass, J., Zubriggen, E., Gmeindl, L., & Apfelblat, D. (1995). Adaptive executive control: Flexible multiple-task performance without pervasive immutable response-selection bottlenecks. *Acta Psychologica, 90,* 163–190.

Miller, G. A. (1956). The magical number seven, plus or minus two: Some limits to our capacity for processing information. *Psychological Review, 63,* 81–97.

Miller, G. A., Galanter, E., & Pribram, K. H. (1960). *Plans and the structure of behavior.* New York: Holt.

Naveh-Benjamin, M., & Ayres, T. J. (1986). Digit span, reading rate, and linguistic relativity. *Quarterly Journal of Experimental Psychology, 38A,* 739–751.

Newell, A. (1990). *Unified theories of cognition.* Cambridge, MA: Harvard University Press.

O'Donnell, R. D., & Eggemeier, F. T. (1986). Workload assessment methodology. In K. R. Boff, L. Kaufman, & J. P. Thomas (Eds.), *Handbook of perception and human performance* (Vol.2). *Cognitive processes and performance* (pp. 42.1–42.49). New York: Wiley.

Pashler, H. (1994). Dual-task interference in simple tasks: Data and theory. *Psychological Bulletin, 116,* 220–244.

Paulesu, E., Frith, C. D., & Frackowiak, R. S. J. (1993). The neural correlates of the verbal component of working memory. *Nature, 362,* 342–345.

Posner, M. I., & Konick, A. F. (1966). On the role of interference in short-term memory. *Journal of Experimental Psychology, 72,* 221–231.

Ray, W. J. (1990). The electrocortical system. In J. T. Cacioppo & L. G. Tassinary (Eds.), *Principles of psychophysiology* (pp. 385–412). Cambridge, UK: Cambridge University Press.

Reitman, J. (1974). Without surreptitious rehearsal, information in short-term memory decays. *Journal of Verbal Learning and Verbal Behavior, 13*, 365–377.

Reitman, W. (1970). What does it take to remember? In D. A. Norman (Ed.), *Models of human memory* (pp. 470–509). New York: Academic Press.

Rumelhart, D. E., & McClelland, J. L. (1986). On learning the past tenses of English verbs. In J. L. McClelland & D. E. Rumelhart (Eds.), *Parallel distributed processing: Explorations in the microstructure of cognition* (Vol. 2). Cambridge, MA: MIT Press.

Schumacher, E. H., Lauber, E. J., Glass, J. M. B., Zurbriggen, E. L., Gmeindl, L., Kieras, D. E., & Meyer, D. E. (1998). Concurrent response-selection processes in dual-task performance: Evidence for adaptive executive control of task scheduling. *Journal of Experimental Psychology: Human Perception and Performance*, in press.

Schumacher, E. H., Seymour, T. L., Glass, J. M., Lauber, E. J., Kieras, D. E., & Meyer, D. E. (1997, November). *Virtually perfect time sharing in dual-task performance.* Paper presented at the meeting of the Psychonomic Society, Philadelphia, PA.

Schweickert, R., & Boruff, B. (1986). Short-term memory capacity: Magic number or magic spell? *Journal of Experimental Psychology: Learning, Memory, and Cognition, 12*, 419–425.

Schweickert, R., Guentert, L., & Hersberger, L. (1990). Phonological similarity, pronunciation rate, and memory span. *Psychological Science, 1*, 74–77.

Shiffrin, R. M. (1973). Information persistence in short-term memory. *Journal of Experimental Psychology, 100*, 39–49.

Shiffrin, R. M., & Cook, J. R. (1978). Short-term forgetting of item and order information. *Journal of Verbal Learning and Verbal Behavior, 17*, 189–218.

Shneiderman, B. (1992). *Designing the user interface* (2nd ed.). Reading, MA: Addison-Wesley.

Sperling, G. (1967). Successive approximations to a model for short-term memory. *Acta Psychologica, 27*, 285–292.

Standing, L., Bond, B., Smith, P., & Isely, C. (1980). Is the immediate memory span determined by subvocalization rate? *British Journal of Psychology, 71*, 525–539.

Sternberg, S. (1969). Memory-scanning: Mental processes revealed by reaction-time experiments. *American Scientist, 57*, 421–457.

Sternberg, S., Monsell, S., Knoll, R. L., & Wright, C. E. (1978). The latency and duration of rapid movement sequences: Comparisons of speech and typewriting. In G. E. Stelmach (Ed.), *Information processing in motor control* (pp. 117–152). New York: Academic Press.

Watkins, M. J., & Todres, A. K. (1980). Suffix effects manifest and concealed: Further evidence for a 20 second echo. *Journal of Verbal Learning and Verbal Behavior, 19*, 46–53.

Waugh, N. C., & Norman, D. A. (1965). Primary memory. *Psychological Review, 72*, 89–104.

Welford, A. T. (1967). Single channel operation in the brain. *Acta Psychologica, 27*, 5–22.

Wicklegren, W. A. (1969). Context-sensitive coding, associative memory, and serial order in (speech) behavior. *Psychological Review, 76*, 1–15.

Wright, C. E. (1979). Duration differences between rare and common words and their implications for the interpretation of word frequency effects. *Memory & Cognition, 7*, 411–419.

7   The Soar Cognitive Architecture and Human Working Memory

RICHARD M. YOUNG AND RICHARD L. LEWIS

FIVE CENTRAL FEATURES OF THE THEORY

From the viewpoint of the Soar cognitive architecture, the term *working memory* (WM) refers to the psychological mechanisms that maintain information retrieved or created during the performance of a task. The following are the five key points made in the chapter concerning Soar's treatment of human WM:

(1) Soar is not specifically a "model of WM," but rather a cognitive architecture of broad scope, which focuses on the functional capabilities needed for a memory system to support performance in a range of cognitive tasks. The functions of working memory are distributed across multiple components of the architecture, including the long-term production memory.

(2) Even in a cognitive architecture with an unbounded dynamic memory, WM limitations can arise on functional grounds. Where such functional accounts exist, they take theoretical priority over capacity-based explanations of WM phenomena.

(3) Soar does not currently include any capacity limits on its dynamic memory (SDM), but is compatible with certain such limitations. In particular, a constraint that SDM can hold at most two items of the same "type" (suitably defined) yields a coherent explanation for many psycholinguistic phenomena in the comprehension of sentences. This constraint is motivated by computational efficiency concerns and embodies the general principle of similarity-based interference (Baddeley & Logie, Chapter 2; Cowan, Chapter 3; Schneider, Chapter 10; and O'Reilly, Braver, & Cohen, Chapter 11, all in this volume).

(4) Soar emphasizes the role of learning in WM phenomena, even on tasks that experimentally are regarded as concerning just "performance." The moral is that WM cannot coherently be studied independently of long-term memory and while ignoring learning.

(5) Soar stresses the recognitional usage of information in long-term memory acquired as a by-product of earlier task performance. It therefore has close links to other approaches that emphasize the involvement of long-term memory in WM and may be able to offer

224

a computational process model for "long-term WM" (Ericsson & Delaney, Chapter 8, this volume).

In the Spring of 1987, Allen Newell delivered the William James lectures at Harvard University (Newell, 1990). He used the occasion to argue the case for striving toward theoretical unification in psychology, and to develop Soar, a new cognitive architecture, as the basis for a candidate unified theory. Soar had previously been presented as a problem-solving architecture for artificial intelligence (Laird, Newell, & Rosenbloom, 1987; Laird, Rosenbloom, & Newell, 1986). Since then, Soar, like the production system architectures from which it is derived (e.g., Newell & Simon, 1972), has been applied both within artificial intelligence as a vehicle for constructing knowledge-intensive systems and within psychology for the modeling of human cognition. Although more work has been done on the artificial intelligence side (e.g. Tambe et al., 1995), there has been a steady stream of work exploring how Soar offers state-of-the-art accounts of human empirical phenomena (Altmann, 1996; Altmann & John, in press; Howes & Young, 1996; Lewis, 1993, 1997a, 1997b; Miller & Laird, 1996; Polk & Newell, 1995; Wiesmeyer, 1992; Wiesmeyer & Laird, 1993).

Unlike smaller-scale theories in psychology, Soar is not shaped by the concerns of any single experimental area or paradigm. Soar therefore has no separate "memory mechanism" in the sense of components of the architecture aimed specifically at accounting for the results of experiments on human memory. Instead, the design of Soar is dominated by the functional considerations needed to exhibit general intelligence of human-like form (Newell, 1990). With regard to human memory, Soar's aim is not primarily to reproduce the findings of laboratory experiments, but to explain how memory works in the context of performing real, often complex, tasks. However, such an approach is useful even for the analysis of laboratory phenomena, because no psychological experiments test just memory. Instead, they all involve the entire cognitive system in the comprehension and performance of tasks.

The involvement of memory in complex cognitive tasks is, as Newell (1992) reminds us, an issue that memory theorists have largely neglected. In consequence, the "standard models" offered by most memory theorists are simply inadequate for explaining performance on cognitive tasks of any appreciable complexity. Decades of simulation work have shown that very small working memories – for example, those able to hold just a small number of items, say in the range 3 to 9 "chunks" or those holding 3 or 4 items in a "central executive" supplemented by phonological and similar loops – are simply incapable of supporting the performance of tasks such as problem solving or language processing (Broadbent, 1993). (For different reasons, similar doubts about the adequacy of the accounts of memory offered by mainstream cognitive psychology are expressed by other investigators, for example those concerned with studies of "practical memory" [e.g., Gruneberg, Morris, & Sykes, 1988] or with the importance of "ecological validity" [e.g., Neisser, 1982, 1985].)

In this chapter we therefore examine the various phenomena of human working memory (WM) from the viewpoint of a cognitive architecture of broad scope, which focuses on the functional capabilities needed for a memory system to support performance in a range of cognitive tasks. We argue for and demonstrate three points concerning the limitations of WM: (a) We show how the cognitive system, even with a limited-capacity short-term store, can handle complex tasks that require large quantities of information, by relying heavily on recognition-based long-term memory working in concert with the external environment. (b) We argue that limitations on WM arise even in purely functional cognitive systems built without preset capacity constraints, and hence that empirically demonstrated limitations of effective WM do not necessarily imply a capacity-constrained underlying memory system. (c) We show how a specific mechanism of similarity-based interference can act as a resource constraint on the cognitive system and offer a coherent account of a wide range of psycholinguistic phenomena.

Terminology

Before we proceed any further, we need to deal with a few points of terminology that are otherwise guaranteed to cause confusion.

First, the Soar architecture includes an internal declarative memory that holds information specific to the task in hand, including control information. As with most production system architectures, that memory is known as the "working memory." Because that memory is not necessarily to be taken as the counterpart of human working memory, we will refer to it as *Soar's dynamic memory*, abbreviated SDM. We will reserve the term *working memory* (WM) for the psychological construct. We explain the relation between the two in the next section.

Second, as we shall see, a central role is played by Soar's learning mechanism through which it acquires new production rules. In Soar, that process of acquiring new rules is called "chunking," and the new rules themselves are called "chunks." Because the term *chunk* is already widespread in the literature on human memory with a different (though related) meaning, we will again avoid the term in its specialized Soar sense, and simply talk about Soar's *learning* or *acquisition mechanism*, and refer to the new productions as *acquired rules*. These conventions should aid clarity within this chapter, but the reader who delves further will find that our usage is nonstandard with respect to the Soar research literature.[1]

---

[1] There is no primer or textbook for Soar, and Newell's (1990) book is now seriously out of date in several relevant respects. However, there is a user manual available (Congdon & Laird, 1995), and an on-line tutorial introduction to Soar for cognitive modeling (Ritter & Young, 1997). There is also a "gentle introduction" to Soar (Lehman, Laird, & Rosenbloom, 1998). Information about Soar can be found on the World Wide Web and is most conveniently accessed through the list of Frequently Asked Questions:

http://www.ccc.nottingham.ac.uk/pub/soar/nottingham/soar-faq.html

Third, we use the terms *production, rule,* and even *production rule* interchangeably and without distinction.

Finally, we discuss Soar here in terms of its most recent version, Soar7. The technical concepts in Soar7 differ considerably from those of earlier versions. For example, where Newell (1990) talks of goals (which have states) and subgoals (which also have states), in this chapter we talk simply of states and substates. The change has no psychological significance, but again the reader should be aware that most of the Soar literature employs an older terminology.

Basic Mechanisms and Representations in Working Memory, and the Control and Regulation of Working Memory

In order to identify those mechanisms in Soar that correspond to working memory, we must first provide a brief introduction to the Soar architecture. Next we will present a functional definition of working memory, abstracted from any particular mechanism that might realize it. We then describe how certain components of Soar realize the functions of working memory. The particular mapping we provide between Soar and human working memory is not the standard production system view, but we argue that it should hold for any *learning* production system.

Overview of Basic Soar Mechanisms

Soar is a cognitive architecture of broad scope, offered by Newell (1990) as a candidate "unified theory of cognition." Soar is best described at two levels, called the *problem space level* and the *symbol level.* At the problem space level, Soar casts all cognitive activity as transformations of *states* by *operators* within a state space. In a state space, there is a single *current state,* which encodes working information about the problem or situation being processed. Cognitive processing occurs by means of operators, which apply to the current state to yield a new current state. In straightforward cases, processing consists of a repeated cycle in which Soar first picks an operator and then applies it to transform the current state into a new one.

This abstract description of Soar is realized concretely at the symbol level. At this level, the states and current operators are stored in Soar's dynamic memory, SDM, as shown in Figure 7.1. All persistent knowledge – including knowledge of when to propose operators, how to choose them, and how to apply them – is encoded in production rules. Each production represents a content-addressed piece of knowledge, which is sensitive to a particular pattern of information in SDM, and when it detects that pattern proposes particular changes or additions to SDM. All productions that are satisfied, in other words, can find data in SDM to match their pattern, apply in parallel. Once all such rules have fired, their proposals are collected and the appropriate changes made to SDM. Usually, these changes will cause another set of productions to match, and the process continues.

Production Memory (LTM)

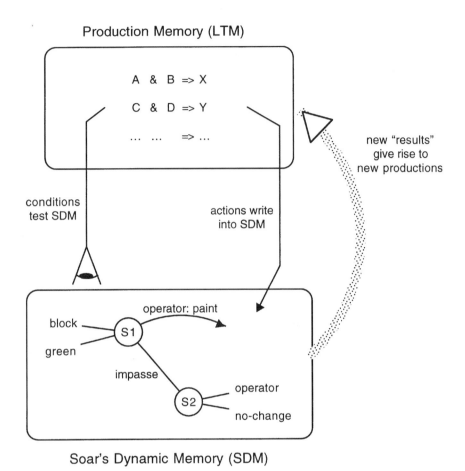

Figure 7.1. The main memories and processes in Soar.

At this level, Soar consists of two main memories: SDM, which declaratively holds dynamic information about the task at hand, and *production memory*, which holds persistent knowledge. Production memory is permanent. Once a rule is acquired, it is never lost (although there are ways in which it can be effectively masked or have its actions overruled).

Current versions of Soar employ a low-level, theoretically neutral representation of information in SDM, consisting of attribute–value pairs. Such a general-purpose representation can serve as a basis for building higher level constructs of the kind familiar in cognitive science, such as schemata, frames, and so on. However, the representation is theoretically weak and places little constraint on the form or content of information in SDM. Some work in Soar (e.g., Polk & Newell, 1995) has begun to explore the possibility of adopting a more constrained, theoretically stronger representation – specifically, that of "annotated models," inspired by the "mental models" of Johnson-Laird (1983). But the topic of representation remains an underdeveloped area for Soar.

Soar's "straightforward" processing described above, of repeatedly choosing an operator and applying it to the current state, can become blocked in various ways. For example, perhaps Soar knows of no operators to propose in the current state; or conversely, perhaps it proposes several but lacks the knowledge to choose between them; or perhaps it chooses an operator, but does not know how to apply it to the state. In these cases, Soar is said to encounter an *impasse*, where it is unable to proceed with its simple processing cycle. When this happens, Soar automatically sets up a new state (implicitly in a new state space), which is regarded as a substate to the state where the processing was blocked. The purpose of the substate is to trigger further processing (involving further implicit search of Soar's knowledge base) to retrieve information to resolve the impasse. For example, if the impasse arose because no operator was proposed, it can be resolved by finding a suitable operator. If the impasse arose because multiple operators were proposed, it can be resolved by finding knowledge to choose between them, and so on. Unsurprisingly, processing of the substate can itself encounter an impasse, which then leads to the setting up of a sub-substate, and so on. So at any time, Soar may have a whole hierarchy, or "stack," of spaces it is working in, each with its own current state and (possibly) operator.

Soar's Learning Mechanism

Because all knowledge in Soar is encoded as production rules held in production memory, learning – in the sense of adding new knowledge – consists of acquiring new productions. The mechanism for doing this is intimately tied in with the impasses just described.

Whenever processing in a substate leads to a change being made to the superstate, that change is called a *result*, and Soar automatically acquires a new production rule. Recall that a production has a *condition* side and an *action* side. The action side of the new production is, obviously, the result, that is, the change to the superstate. What should constitute appropriate conditions for the new production is less obvious. What Soar does is to use for the conditions all those items in SDM that (a) are part of the superstate, and (b) are causally implicated in the sequence of production firings that led to the result. Here, an item being "causally implicated" means, roughly, that one of the firing productions matches against it.

Suppose that A and B (and perhaps many other items) are part of the current state in SDM when an impasse occurs. In the processing of the substate, suppose that a production matches against A and adds X to the substate, another production matches against B and X and adds Y to the substate, and finally a third production matches against Y and adds the result R to the superstate. Then A and B, and only A and B, are both part of the superstate *and* matched against in the sequence of firings that leads to R, so they form the conditions, and Soar acquires a new production:

P1: $A \& B \Rightarrow R$.

In future, whenever A and B are both on a state in SDM, the new production will fire, adding R to the state. If R was sufficient to resolve the impasse, then the impasse will henceforth be avoided.

Working Memory in Soar

We have now described Soar completely enough to identify those mechanisms that correspond to working memory. But first, we must define clearly what we mean by *working memory*. Following the spirit of Miller, Galanter, and Pribram (1960), Baddeley and Hitch (1974), Just and Carpenter (1992), and others, we focus on the functional role of working memory in cognition. The following definition specifies that role independently of the mechanisms that realize it:

Working memory refers to those computational mechanisms that maintain and provide access to information created or retrieved during the performance of a task. Any computationally complete system must support such functionality, because computation is inherently a process that requires the temporary storage and manipulation of partial and intermediate products.

It should be clear that Soar's dynamic memory – its short-term declarative store – is precisely a component intended to serve the function of working memory. Indeed, that is why such components in productions systems are usually called "working memories." The traditional descriptions of Soar reinforce this identification by stating that the current "state" in the problem space is held in Soar's dynamic memory. Hence, it is natural to assume that the SDM directly corresponds to working memory.

However, making changes to SDM is not the only way that Soar can change state during the course of a task: The other way is for the content of the production rule memory itself to change, via Soar's learning mechanism. Because the rate of learning is a function of the rate of impasses, there are clearly some strong bounds on the rate at which the long-term memory (LTM) can encode new state changes. Nevertheless, for all but the simplest immediate reaction tasks, there is enough time (on the order of seconds) for Soar to encode some intermediate products in LTM and later retrieve that information during the task. In effect, the LTM can become part of the functional working memory system.

We can illustrate the idea by thinking of the declarative dynamic memory and the long-term production memory as being divided into four parts, according to the source and function of the constituent memory elements.

First, there are those memory elements that were created prior to the task and are not used in the task (constituting a small fraction of SDM, but a large portion – nearly all – of LTM). Second, there are those elements that were created prior to the task and *are* used in the task (constituting a small part of SDM, and some small fraction of LTM). In LTM, this part constitutes the preexisting skill for the task. Third, there are those elements that are both created and used during the task. This constitutes most of SDM, and again, a small fraction of LTM. *It is this third set of memory elements that plays the role of a working memory.* Finally, the fourth set consists of those elements created during the task, but not used.

This analysis leads to the inevitable conclusion that "working memory" in Soar consists of both SDM, in its familiar role, and also to some extent LTM, in its less familiar role of maintaining and retrieving intermediate products within a task. The components and processes of working memory, therefore, include both the short-term dynamic memory, the long-term memory, the matching of long-term productions to the dynamic memory, and the learning mechanism that gives rise to new productions. We will see this involvement of LTM in working memory spelled out in more detail in the next few sections.

Relation to Other Theories of Memory

The job of relating Soar's account of memory to others is spread throughout this chapter, but we make a start here with a first-cut comparison between what we have seen of Soar so far and other approaches.

We begin with the relatively easy topic of long-term memory. Most approaches to human memory impose a fairly clear-cut distinction between short-term and long-term memory (or memories). Soar is unequivocal in offering its production memory as the counterpart to human long-term memory. The various different kinds of aspects of long-term memory discussed in the literature – declarative, procedural, episodic, implicit, autobiographical – are not distinguished *structurally* in Soar. Differences among them would have to be reflected in the *content* of the knowledge in production memory (or perhaps, in some cases, in how that knowledge is used on different types of occasion). Soar's assumptions about the permanence of knowledge once acquired, and about its content-addressed, associative nature, place it near the mainstream of psychological theorizing and obviously share in a long tradition. Soar's long-term memory is, though, marked out by its structural uniformity and the leanness of its assumptions.

With regard to the part of working memory realized by SDM, Soar shares an evident family resemblance with other production system cognitive architectures, such as ACT (Anderson, 1983, 1993; Lovett, Reder, & Lebiere, Chapter 5, this volume) and CAPS (Just & Carpenter, 1992). Again, however, Soar's relative austerity is notable: Soar has no apparatus for rule strengths or activation levels or the like, and therefore has at least the potential for stronger theoretical accounts.

The comparison with models derived from experimental psychology is less straightforward. The sharp two-way division between permanent and ephemeral memories has obvious echoes of earlier ideas about "short-term" and "long-term" memory (e.g., Murdock, 1963) or "primary" and "secondary" memories (Atkinson & Shiffrin, 1968; Waugh & Norman, 1965) – and consequently, in the eyes of some memory psychologists, gives Soar an old-fashioned look. The most historically influential touchstones are probably the idea of a short-term memory for the temporary storage of information (e.g., Miller, 1956) and its later elaboration into a "working" memory for transient, task-relevant information, particularly under pressure of data from study of the immediate recall task and its variants (Baddeley, 1986; Baddeley & Hitch, 1974; Baddeley & Logie, Chapter 2, this volume). In relation to both of these, we need to repeat warnings we have already given in this chapter: Complex cognitive tasks simply *cannot* be performed with temporary storage of only 7 ± 2 items; Soar's SDM does not have an imposed capacity limit; and SDM should not be simplistically identified with the psychological notion of WM. To some extent, Soar can be seen as complementary to the main thrust of the last decade of WM work, since it focuses primarily on the so-called central executive concerning which WM researchers have, at least until recently (Baddeley, 1996), been so reticent.

Learning, Knowledge, and Long-Term Memory

The next two sections explore some of the surprisingly far-reaching implications of Soar's learning mechanism for human memory and learning. We first consider the unique theoretical role that learning has in cognitive models built in Soar, and then look at some examples of the mechanism in action. These examples lay the foundation for understanding precisely the role of Soar's learning and LTM in realizing working memory functions.

Where Do the Productions Come From?

We start this section with a brief look at a question often asked about a Soar model, namely, where do the productions come from?

One answer is, simply enough, that they are postulated by the theorist. In this, Soar differs not at all from any other kind of model. However, Soar offers also a second, less familiar, answer to the question of the origin of the production rules, which is that it learns them – or at least, some of them – for itself. An ideal cognitive model would learn all the relevant productions itself. Of course, in practice that is not possible. For a particular model, some handwritten rules have to be provided by the theorist as a starting point (although it is now quite common in Soar models for learned rules greatly to outnumber the handwritten ones, e.g., Altmann, 1996; Altmann & John, in press). The aim then is to provide, initially, only capabilities that it is reasonable to suppose a human subject has when he or she walks into the experimental situation. If a Soar model is able to interpret simple English sentences (Lewis, 1993), uses that ability to understand instructions (Huffman, 1994; Huffman & Laird, 1995), and by so doing acquires productions for performing a cognitive task (Lewis, Newell, & Polk, 1989), then those resulting productions have a stronger theoretical status than if they were simply written by hand, that is, "programmed" by the theorist. (Newell, 1990, refers to this methodology as one of "reducing the theorist's degrees of freedom.")

Rosemary's Baby

Consider the following situation. You know that Rosemary, a friend of yours married to Robert, has just had a baby, but you do not know whether it was a boy or a girl. You want to find out which it is, so that you can send Rosemary a congratulation card, buy a present, and generally be in a position to say the right things to Rosemary when you see her. You obviously cannot determine the sex of the baby by sitting down and *thinking* about it, so on the next suitable occasion you ask Robert, and he tells you that their baby is a girl. To learn this information means to remember it, so that in the future you will know the sex of Rosemary's baby without having to ask again. How can we model the cognitive (if not the social) aspects of this scenario in Soar?

The net effect of the learning process should be that whenever the Soar model wonders about the sex of Rosemary's baby, it retrieves the information that the baby is a girl. This means that the model needs, somehow, to acquire a production we can write as:

P2: what-is (sex-of, Rosemary's-baby) ⇒ girl.

An acquired rule of this form is described as a *recall* rule, because it serves to recall, that is, into SDM, an item of information which is known, that is, stored in production memory.

The question then is, How does the Soar model acquire that rule? One might imagine the following kind of route. In some state, Soar wants to know the sex of Rosemary's baby. It doesn't *know* the answer, that is, it doesn't yet have a production like P2, so there is an impasse and a substate is set up. The processing on the substate, to resolve the impasse, decides to go and ask Robert, and that subtask temporarily takes precedence in the main state over the primary task of finding the baby's sex. So Soar wanders off . . . and a little while later Robert tells Soar "It's a girl." With that information in hand, the substate can finish the task by marking "girl" on the superstate. That result, from a substate to a superstate, causes Soar to acquire a new production.

The trouble is that a Soar model operating along those lines acquires, not P2, but the somewhat different rule:

P3: what-is (sex-of, Rosemary's-baby) & answer=girl ⇒ girl.

P3 is the same as P2, except that it has the extra condition "answer=girl." That condition is included because in the processing that led to the result, some production must have matched against Robert's answer "It's a girl" in order for the right result to be found. The item "answer=girl" is therefore causally implicated in the result, and consequently included in the acquired rule.

The extra condition prevents P3 from doing the job we want. A production like P3 is known as a *circular recognition rule*. It cannot recall information, but it can recognize the answer in the sense that it fires when the right information is in SDM. But that still leaves us with the problem of explaining how the recall rule, P2, is acquired.

A Multistage Learning Model

To explain how P2 arises, we temporarily ignore the question of learning and focus instead on the task of obtaining the answer to the question "what-is (sex-of, Rosemary's-baby)." A Soar model has available to it four potential routes to the answer:

1. If Soar already has a rule like P2 that recalls the information, then it fires and the task is done. There will be no impasse.
2. If Soar happens to have the information already in SDM, then it is picked up and returned as the answer to the question.
3. Soar can generate the possible answers to the question (namely, "boy" and "girl"), and see if either of them triggers a recognition rule like P3. If so, that item is returned as the answer to the question.
4. Soar can seek the answer from an external source, such as by telephoning Robert and asking him.

These four routes are listed in order of increasing mental and (in the case of 4, physical) effort. Accordingly, it is rational for a Soar model to try the different routes in that order, with the easy ones first. The behavior of such a model, over a sequence of trials, is instructive. We assume initially that neither P2 nor P3 is present:

On the first trial, neither route 1 nor route 2 is applicable. Soar tries route 3, but fails because there is no recognition rule. It therefore adopts route 4, asks Robert for the information, and is told "It's a girl." With that information in SDM, route 2 can apply, so Soar picks up the reply and returns the answer "girl." We have already seen that the consequence of that behavior is that Soar acquires the recognition rule, P3.

On the second trial, again neither route 1 nor route 2 is applicable. Soar tries route 3, and asks itself in turn "boy?", "girl?". For the "girl" option, rule P3 fires, indicating that it recognizes "girl" as the answer it has previously seen. Soar can therefore return "girl" as the result. In so doing, it acquires a new rule, P2. This time, the unwanted extra condition is not included in the rule, because the Soar model has generated the answer itself (in a substate) instead of having to rely on its already being present in SDM. The "answer=girl" is therefore not this time causally implicated in the result, and does not appear in the rule conditions.

On the third trial, and subsequently, recall rule P2 fires, implementing route 1. The Soar model has therefore now "learned" the sex of Rosemary's baby.

A couple of features of this story about learning are worthy of comment. First, the model engages in no deliberate activity of "learning." Instead, the learning occurs as a side effect of doing the task, as a consequence of Soar's automatic mechanism for acquiring new rules. Second, this kind of learning is inherently multipass. The first trial is needed to acquire the recognition rule. The second trial makes use of the recognition rule to pick out the right answer from among those generated and leads to the acquisition of the recall rule. Only from the third trial onwards does the recall rule itself come into play. Third, the learning relies on a process of *generate and recognize*, in which the learner generates possible options and makes use of previously acquired knowledge to recognize which is right. This process has evident similarities to other generate-and-recognize models previously proposed for memory (e.g., Anderson & Bower, 1972; Bahrick, 1970; Kintsch, 1970).

Implications for Long-Term Memory

Although the model just presented is for a simple and somewhat contrived task, the approach and its characteristics generalize to a wide range of learning situations, basically those where crucial information has to be acquired for the task to be performed. (*Post-event learning*, where the learner has to remember the *outcome* of an action or event, is a little different in detail, but it shares the same generate-and-recognize basis.) Much of the work in Soar has dealt with the learning of instructions (Howes & Young, 1996; Huffman, 1994; Huffman & Laird, 1995), where the models exhibit a gradual progression from a performance that is initially externally based, that is, dependent on interpreting the externally presented instructions, through a stage of recognition-based learning, to a fully internalized and assimilated skill.

Vera, Lewis, and Lerch (1993) add an important ingredient to the story, by analyzing the kinds of situations that occur often in practice, in which the alternative answers are provided by the external environment and therefore do not have to be generated from the learner's internal, cognitive resources. In learning to use a bank automated teller machine (ATM), for example, the action at each step makes use of a specific external object: to press one of the labeled buttons, or type on the numeric keys, or insert a card into the card slot, and so on. To acquire the correct sequence, the learner needs to supply only the recognitional knowledge. As further discussed by Vera et al. (1993) and by Howes and Young (1996), Soar predicts that the skill acquired by the use of such external generators is strongly "situated" or "display based" (Larkin, 1989), in the sense that a person can perform the task fluently when in the task environment, but cannot produce the learned procedure – for example, by describing it – away from the situation. This inability is known to be characteristic of expert skill (Mayes, Draper, McGregor, & Oatley, 1988; Payne, 1991) and has been regarded as puzzling.

Howes and Young (1996, in press) review these findings and describe ways in which Soar's learning mechanism serves to constrain the kinds of models that can be acquired, thereby making architecturally based predictions about the corresponding human cognitive skill. In the area of learning to use interactive computer systems, the main differences in learnability between interfaces stem from the relative ease or difficulty of the generate part of the process. Howes and Young show that, in addition to the display-based nature of the learned skill, the learning mechanism predicts that, given certain common properties of the device, a display-based (e.g., menu) interface is necessarily easier to learn than a keyboard-based (e.g., command line) one; and that for keyboard-based devices, learning is necessarily easier with either meaningful (rather than meaningless) or mnemonic (rather than arbitrary) command names.

In this section we have examined some of the implications of Soar's learning mechanism for long-term memory, learning, and cognitive skill. The next section focuses more specifically on the consequences of that mechanism for WM.

Complex Cognitive Activities

Because Soar is constructed with the aim of providing the functional capabilities for an intelligent agent, it is on its home ground when being used to model memory and learning in complex cognitive activities. In this section we briefly describe three studies bearing on the role of WM in complex tasks. All three studies model situations where a human subject has to deal with large quantities of information relevant to the external situation. In all three cases, trying to hold that information in SDM is not a functionally adequate solution. Instead, these models make use of Soar's learning mechanism to hold the information in LTM, and perform the task with a bounded SDM. The picture that emerges from these studies is of how Soar's learning mechanism, and the strongly recognition-based processing it implies, provide an adequate basis for complex cognitive processing within a limited WM. These results are related to Ericsson and Kintsch's (1995) ideas about "long-term working memory."

Howes's Model of Recognition-Based Search

Howes (1993, 1994) describes a model, called Ayn, capable of searching and learning to navigate its way through large external spaces. It deals with an environment characterized as a set of *locations* connected by *paths*. It can deal with tasks such as finding its way through a hierarchical computer menu system or through the streets in an unfamiliar town center. In the former case, the locations are the possible menus and the paths are the choices from each menu. In the latter case, the locations are street intersections and the paths are the streets leading from each intersection.

Ayn works by exploiting the production rules acquired as a by-product of the process of dealing with locations and considering the choice of possible paths and then using them as the basis for a (long-term) recognitional memory. Each time Ayn encounters a location, it attempts to comprehend it, to see what clues (if any) it offers to the correct route. And each time Ayn considers a path, it sees if it has any basis for evaluating that move. Those processing steps lead to productions being acquired that, as with the example of Rosemary's baby in the previous section, can serve to recognize which locations or paths Ayn has seen before and which it has not. Ayn uses various heuristics that exploit the recognitional knowledge to improve its search. For example, if Ayn recognizes its goal as one that it has reached before, then it knows the goal can be reached by sticking to paths it has taken before, so it prefers paths it recognizes to those it does not. Over repeated trials, Ayn gradually improves its knowledge of the network to the point where it can navigate to familiar targets without error.

Because Ayn relies on recognitional knowledge, which is stored in Soar's production memory (corresponding to human LTM), it avoids making heavy demands upon SDM, and Ayn in fact will search a space of any size using an SDM of fixed capacity. Ayn minimizes the deliberate processing that has to be done to learn the network. Instead, as with the example of Rosemary's baby, Ayn makes recognitional use of knowledge acquired as a side effect of performing the main task.

Translated back into terms of human cognition, the Ayn model demonstrates how, even with a strictly limited short-term store, people can search an external space of indefinite size, by relying on recognitional use of knowledge acquired in LTM.

Altmann's Model of Episodic Memory for External Information

Altmann (1996; Altmann & John, in press; Altmann, Larkin, & John, 1995) analyzed and modeled the behavior of a skilled programmer working at a task of understanding and modifying a large computer program. She works primarily with a single window on a computer screen that, as she issues commands and requests new information at the bottom of the window, slides the older information up and eventually off the screen. At various points in her investigation, the programmer encounters items about which she knows she has previously seen some information, and she then retrieves that information for further processing by scrolling back through the display window. The interesting feature of this task is that the programmer is being presented with far more information and detail on the screen than she can possibly retain. Yet she manages to remember enough about the existence and location of relevant external information that she can find it again when she needs to, in order to dig deeper.

Altmann's model attempts to comprehend each new item of information that appears on the screen, although this comprehension can vary enormously in its depth and completeness. Each act of comprehension results in the acquisition of one or more new production rules, which include the salient features of the item being processed and a (very crude) indication of the circumstances in which the item appears. Such rules form effectively a (very simple) episodic trace of what has been seen. Even though only a tiny fraction of the content of the computer display is being captured in this way, these productions arising as a side effect of the comprehension can serve as recognitional knowledge. When the model encounters an item about which more information is needed, if one of these recognition rules fires, then Soar knows that it has seen the item before; and if the remembered context indicator differs from the current one, then Soar knows it must have seen the item earlier, and so can find it by scrolling back.

The implications of this model for human memory both reinforce and extend those we have seen from the previous examples. Once again, we have the idea of learning occurring as a side effect of processing, with heavily recognitional use being made of the production rules acquired as a by-product of that processing. In this case, the model shows how a human programmer can, within the constraints of a limited WM, make effective use of recognitional knowledge in LTM to index into and navigate around a large and growing display of external information.

Altmann and colleagues relate their results to the idea of long-term working memory (LT-WM) propounded by Ericsson and Kintsch (1995; Ericsson & Delaney, Chapter 8, this volume). Altmann's model shares with Ericsson and Kintsch's analysis the core suggestion that LTM be used to provide access to a larger set of information than can be carried in WM. Soar adds to LT-WM the twist that the relevant knowledge in LTM is primarily recognitional in character and serves to provide access to a potentially vast body of external information. Unlike the cases studied by Ericsson and Kintsch, Altmann's programmer does not put effort into the deliberate construction of retrieval cues for the information being memorized. Altmann and John (in press) ascribe this difference to the contrasting requirements of the tasks. Altmann's programmer encounters a huge amount of information, only a small part of which will ever be sought again, so there is no possibility of building specific retrieval structures. Instead, Altmann and John (in press) propose extending LT-WM with the idea of a ubiquitous "episodic LT-WM," which the cognitive architecture acquires passively and pervasively.

IDXL Model of Exploratory Search

Rieman, Young, and Howes (1996) describe a Soar model called IDXL, which performs the kind of exploratory search that experienced computer users engage in when asked to use an unfamiliar menu-driven application. IDXL accounts for many of the empirical phenomena observed with this kind of exploratory learning (Franzke, 1995; Rieman, 1994, 1996). Users typically cannot and do not go directly to the right menu item. Instead, they examine the menu headers, pull down and browse through some of the menus, focus on a few promising items, and may end up visiting the correct item several times, often for increasing durations, before finally choosing it.

IDXL pays attention to one item on the screen at a time, performing some processing on an item and then moving to an adjacent one. The processing of each item is done locally, with information being held in SDM about only the individual item being attended to. Each time an item is examined, a quantum of processing is performed to assess its relevance to the task being done, and this leads to a production being acquired to summarize the outcome of that assessment. Over multiple visits to an item, an increasingly detailed and reliable evaluation of the item is represented in the acquired rules. Those rules are also used recognitionally, for IDXL to know on each visit to an item what processing it has already received.

IDXL's implications for human memory agree substantially with those of the previous examples. IDXL shows how experienced users can explore a potentially large, externally presented space of possible actions with only a fixed-capacity WM, by storing information gathered during the exploration in LTM and using it recognitionally.

Limitations of Working Memory: Functional Limitations

In the previous section, we discussed three Soar models that perform complex cognitive tasks while operating within a limited working memory. That is only half the story (though a crucial half): We must now demonstrate how WM limitations might actually arise in Soar. In this section and the next, we present additional models that illustrate two theoretical points about WM limitations in Soar. First, there are several ways in Soar that phenomena attributed to limited WM may arise from the interaction of functionally motivated aspects of the architecture, without assuming any capacity constraints. Second, independent efficiency concerns in Soar lead us to posit a simple but severe representational constraint on SDM that is consistent with a well-known principle of human WM limitations, similarity-based interference. This constraint leads to detailed accounts of a number of psycholinguistic phenomena in sentence processing, while still allowing the complex task of comprehension to proceed.

Functional Limitations and Resource Limitations

The study of working memory is dominated by the topic of limitations. The majority of experimental studies demonstrate that people can hold a certain amount of information in WM, but no more, under such-and-such conditions. The most famous case, deriving from Miller's (1956) celebrated paper, is that of limited immediate memory capacity. Usually these limitations are seen as being due to underlying resource or implementational constraints. For example, the decay rate of the phonological loop (Baddeley & Logie, Chapter 2, this volume) is a hard constraint that presumably reflects properties of the neurobiological substrate. The same is true for models positing activation limits (Lovett, et al., Chapter 5, this volume) or limits of attentional span (Cowan, Chapter 3, this volume). The implicit assumption is that if the hardware of the brain had different properties – were somehow better designed – then we would be able to remember more, understand more complex language, think and learn faster, and so on.

The idea of resource constraints appears not to sit comfortably with Soar. It has no mechanisms of quantitative gradation, such as *activation level* or *trace strength*,[2] and attempts to impose a brute-force limitation on the size of SDM – to decide that it cannot hold more than seven items, say, or 17 – seem not to work well. This aspect makes many psychologists doubtful about Soar (e.g., the commentaries in Newell, 1992), but as we shall see it does not rule out the possibility that Soar can model and account for the psychological phenomena associated with limited WM.

Newell (1990) points to another possible source of performance limitations. He distinguishes between resource constraints and *functional limitations*, which can arise from the interaction of cognitive components motivated on purely functional grounds. In other words, they derive from considerations of the task an agent is trying to perform and what it has to do to perform it, without needing to appeal to properties of the implementational substrate. The existence of functional explanations of performance limitations is theoretically very important. If an explanation of a phenomenon can be offered on independently (and functionally) motivated grounds, then no further explanation need be sought in terms of implementational or resource constraints. In the following subsections we consider two examples of Soar models that exhibit such functional limitations.

Example 1: Performance Limitations and Individual Differences in Syllogistic Reasoning

It has long been known that certain forms of syllogistic reasoning are difficult for most people to perform. For example, the syllogism in (1) below is easy to solve correctly:

(1) All artists are beekeepers.
     All beekeepers are chemists.

     What (if anything) necessarily follows?

---

[2] However, that does not mean that Soar cannot account for certain graded phenomena. See, for example, Miller and Laird (1996).

It necessarily (and quite transparently) follows from the two premises that *all artists are chemists*. However, syllogisms such as (2) below are notoriously difficult to get right:

(2) No artists are beekeepers.
     Some beekeepers are chemists.

     What (if anything) necessarily follows?

The correct response to (2) is *some chemists are not artists*, though most subjects respond with *no artists are chemists, some artists are not chemists*, or *no chemists are artists*.

Why are certain forms of reasoning so difficult? Johnson-Laird (1983, 1988) has championed an approach to human reasoning that claims people (who are not trained in logic) approach such puzzles, and all kinds of everyday reasoning, by building and manipulating mental models of the situations described. A model is a representation containing elements that correspond directly to the individuals or objects in a situation. Models are to be contrasted with logic representations, which represent via a set of logical sentences or axioms and which are manipulated via proof procedures. The evidence Johnson-Laird garners in favor of the mental model theory is that reasoning difficulty is primarily a function of the number of models that must be constructed to solve a problem, not a function of the complexity of the logical proof (Johnson-Laird, 1988). The relation to working memory is that some reasoning tasks are difficult because they require the construction and maintenance of multiple models, which taxes a limited-capacity working memory.

Polk and Newell (1995) offer an alternative theory that also assumes people construct mental models in verbal reasoning tasks but does not assume that they construct multiple models. Polk and Newell argue that people solve verbal reasoning tasks, such as the three-term syllogisms exemplified above, by using their preexisting language skills. As a weak claim about a component process of reasoning, this is uncontroversial and undeniably true. But the theory makes a much stronger claim: Verbal reasoning is accomplished *exclusively* by existing comprehension and production skills, in particular, by comprehending and recomprehending the premises, that is, by building an initial single model and incrementally augmenting it. There are no special reasoning processes – not only are there no logical proof procedures, but there are also no special processes to support logical reasoning by constructing and manipulating multiple models.

The theory offered by Polk and Newell (1995) has a number of properties relevant to the question of functional constraints. First, the model is strongly functional. One sense of this claim is simply that the model performs the task, that is, it reads the two premises and attempts to draw a conclusion. The sense more directly relevant here is that the model is functional in that it draws on abilities, like language skills, that exist to provide the agent with certain functional capabilities (such as speaking, listening, reading) motivated independently of this particular task.

Second, subjects' difficulties with the task are explained as a consequence of this functional basis. Polk and Newell point out that although subjects' everyday language skills (e.g., of encoding and comprehension) can serve to perform the syllogism task, they are not perfectly adapted to that task, and so by themselves are not adequate for perfect performance. For example, the model resulting from language comprehension "is guaranteed to represent a situation in which that proposition is true. But, in general, . . . an annotated model may encode information that is not inherent in a proposition (and be unwarranted) or fail to encode information that is (and be incomplete)" (Polk & Newell, 1995). In this and similar ways, difficulties with the task are explained on the grounds of functional constraints without appeal to the notion of resource constraints.

Third, the model deals with individual differences. The model contains a number of qualitative parameters that determine such things as detailed aspects of how the premises are encoded, for example, whether or not a premise of the form *No X are Y* will be interpreted as also implying *No Y are X*. Different choices for the detailed structure generate a whole space of models, and Polk shows that different models in that space provide a good fit to different individuals. The fit to individual subjects is in fact at least as good as the subjects' test–retest fit to their own performance one week later. This parameterized model provides a highly successful account of individual differences, which makes no reference to resource constraints.

Example 2: Performance Limitations and Individual Differences in Ambiguity Resolution

We now turn to another aspect of verbal processing in which capacity limitations are implicated: ambiguity resolution in sentence comprehension. There is a long-standing and continuing controversy in psycholinguistics over the extent to which nonsyntactic factors can affect the initial structure assigned in parsing. Consider sentences (3) and (4), which contain a momentary ambiguity that is resolved later in the sentence:

(3) a. The defendant examined the courtroom.
    b. The defendant examined by the jury was upset.
----
(4) The evidence examined by the jury was suspicious.

The verb *examined* is ambiguous: It may be interpreted as the main verb (as in 3a) or as starting a relative clause (as in 3b and 4). Researchers have argued for a variety of factors that determine initial ambiguity resolution, ranging from purely structural properties (e.g., Ferreira & Clifton, 1986) to lexical semantics, lexical and structural frequencies, or referential properties (e.g.,

MacDonald, Pearlmutter, & Seidenberg, 1994). For example, the inanimacy of the subject (*evidence*) in (4) provides a cue that the verb *examined* should be interpreted as a relative clause, because that is the most plausible interpretation (inanimate objects usually do not examine things). Indeed, Trueswell, Tanenhans, and Garnsey (1994) and others have found that such semantic constraints can have a strong effect on ambiguity resolution.

Just and Carpenter (1992) added a novel twist to the debate, by demonstrating that ambiguity-resolution behavior is a function of individual differences as well as linguistic factors. In particular, they argued that the behavioral differences are due to differences in working memory capacity. People with high working memory capacity (high span) are able to appeal to nonsyntactic factors, such as the animacy features in (4), whereas people with low working memory capacity (low span) do not have the capacity to be sensitive to such factors. They found that low-span subjects performed in a modular fashion on material such as (4), whereas high-span subjects performed in an interactive fashion on identical material. Thus, they argue, modularity is not an all-or-none architectural issue, but a graded function of working memory limitations.

Lewis (1993) presents an alternative explanation of these individual differences that does not appeal to limited working memory capacity to account for the modular behavior of the low-span subjects. The explanation is derived from NL-Soar, a Soar model of language comprehension. In NL-Soar, local ambiguity manifests itself by the simultaneous proposal of multiple operators corresponding to the different interpretations. For example, in (3) and (4) above, at the verb *examined*, two operators are proposed: one corresponding to the main verb structure, the other corresponding to the relative clause structure. Ambiguity resolution then takes place by drawing on available search control knowledge. In the case of the ambiguity in (3) and (4), a search control production can test the proposed operators and the semantic content of the subject (e.g., *evidence*) and prefer the relative-clause operator in the appropriate contexts. Thus, NL-Soar can model the rapid, on-line effects of semantic context observed in the interactive studies (e.g., Trueswell et al., 1994) and in the high-span subjects of Just and Carpenter (1992).

However, nothing guarantees that such a search control production will be available. If the knowledge is present only through deliberate processing in substates, there may not be enough time to perform all the inferences necessary to make the right selection. Under press of time, there may be no alternative but to select one interpretation by some default preference. In such a case, NL-Soar behaves in a modular fashion because the required knowledge sources are not applied on-line.

Thus, like the explanation of individual differences in verbal reasoning discussed above, the NL-Soar theory attributes the individual differences in ambiguity-resolution behavior to differences in parsing skill. High-span subjects are not necessarily performing well because of their higher working memory capacity, but because they have been exposed to the appropriate linguistic material that led to the learning of specific, semantically sensitive ambiguity-resolution rules. (Lewis, 1993, describes how NL-Soar is in fact capable of learning such rules.)

Related Approaches

The focus on knowledge differences as an explanation of individual differences is shared by the long-term working memory approach of Ericsson and Delaney (Chapter 8, this volume) (see also Ericsson & Kintsch, 1995, which suggests a similar account of the Just & Carpenter data). Furthermore, the methodological approach of positing cognitive resource limitations only as a last resort is a prominent feature of the EPIC research (Kieras, Meyer, Mueller, & Seymour, Chapter 6, this volume). The point is that *some* (though not necessarily all) performance limitations may be a result of knowledge or skill differences and purely functional aspects of cognitive architecture. The novel aspects that the Soar theory adds include an account of how the relevant skill differences can actually arise as a function of experience and a precise explanation of how functional aspects of the architecture can lead to performance limitations.

Limitations of Working Memory: Resource Constraints

The previous sections demonstrated how performance limitations may arise in a functional model without assuming any resource or capacity constraints. Of course, this is not to deny that there are some kinds of hard resource constraints. We now consider one way of incorporating such constraints into Soar and apply the resulting theory to the domain of syntactic processing, again within the NL-Soar model discussed earlier. The constraint is motivated by efficiency concerns in Soar and yields a simple theory of capacity limitations that accounts for a wide range of cross-linguistic memory effects in parsing.

Efficient Representations in Working Memory

For syntactic parsing in NL-Soar, SDM keeps track of partial constituents as the sentence is incrementally structured. Recall from the overview of basic Soar mechanisms that SDM consists of a theoretically neutral attribute–value representation. The particular attributes and values used in parsing are incorporated from linguistic theory (in the case of NL-Soar, X-bar phrase structure [Chomsky, 1986], but for expository purposes here we adopt more traditional grammatical relations).

SDM is organized for parsing in the following way. Partial constituents are indexed by the syntactic relations that they may enter into with other constituents (e.g., subject of sentence, object of verb, and so on). SDM is divided into two parts: The *Heads* part indexes constituents by the syntactic relations they may assign. The *Dependents* part indexes constituents by the relations they may receive.

For example, when NL-Soar constructs the prepositional phrase *with the dog*, it must temporarily buffer the NP (noun phrase) *the dog* before creating the complete PP (preposition phrase). At that moment, the representation in SDM looks like:

(5) HEADS   prep-obj: [with]
     DEPENDENTS prep-obj: [the dog]
                        NP-modif: [with]
                        verb-obj: [the dog]

How should this representation in SDM be limited to ensure efficient processing? The answer comes from theoretical and empirical work on the computational complexity of the recognition match (Tambe, Newell, & Rosenbloom, 1990). This work has identified open, undiscriminated sets in SDM as the most significant source of match expense. An undiscriminated set is simply a set of elements indexed by a single relation or attribute. With such open sets, the recognition match becomes exponentially expensive and therefore psychologically and computationally implausible as the basis for efficient memory retrieval.

Such open sets can occur in any Soar model and, in practice, do lead to significant slowdowns in running the simulations. In NL-Soar, undiscriminated sets may be created when multiple constituents are indexed by a single syntactic relation. We can eliminate such open sets by limiting each relation to a small number of nodes. But how many?

It turns out that the minimum number required to parse any natural language is *two* (Lewis, 1996). Any less, and the system would be unable to parse basic structures that relate two propositions, such as sentential complements (*I think that John likes Mary*). We next consider the empirical implications of this severe capacity restriction, and then relate it back to general psychological theories of working memory.

Difficult Embeddings: The Classic Memory Effect in Parsing

The classic short-term memory effect in sentence comprehension is the difficulty of comprehending multiple center-embedded relative clauses (Miller & Chomsky, 1963). Single-embedded relative clauses such as (6) are quite comprehensible, but double center embeddings (7) cause severe difficulty:

(6) The cat that the bird chased ran away.
(7) The salmon that the man that the dog chased smoked fell.

Consider now how NL-Soar would parse these structures. To handle a structure such as (6), two noun phrases must be momentarily buffered as potential subjects waiting for their verbs:

(8) potential-subjects: [the cat], [the bird]

However, in (7), by the time *the dog* is read, three potential subjects must be buffered:

(9) potential-subjects: [the salmon], [the man], [the dog]

This exceeds the posited limit of two, and therefore the sentence cannot be parsed.

This simple model, with its uniform limit of two across all syntactic relations, accounts for a wide range of acceptable and unacceptable effects cross-linguistically. The type specificity of the limitation is crucial to the empirical success of the model. To see why, consider the comprehensible Japanese construction in (10) below (Lewis, 1993):

(10) John-wa   Bill-ni   Mary-ga   Sue-ni   Bob-o   syookai sita to   it-ta.
     John   Bill   Mary   Sue   Bob   introduced   said
     (John said to Bill that Mary introduced Bob to Sue.)

Although such sentences are surely complex, they do not cause the failure associated with (7), despite stacking up five NPs waiting for verbs. The crucial difference, of course, is that (10) requires maintaining no more than two NPs of any particular syntactic function: at most two subjects, two indirect objects, and a direct object.

Lewis (1993, 1996) presents the complete analysis of this and another four dozen or so constructions from six languages. The data in those papers illustrate the nature of the empirical constraints: a model of syntactic WM must account for the processing difficulty on structures such as (7), while still being powerful enough to handle other complex embeddings, such as (10), which speakers and listeners of a language find acceptable.

The Unifying Principle: Similarity-Based Interference

How does this model of syntactic working memory relate to existing psychological accounts of working memory or short-term memory? There is an important connection: The model gives rise to similarity-based interference, a key principle underlying other kinds of working memory. The effect is clearly seen from studies demonstrating *retroactive interference*, which occurs when a to-be-remembered stimulus is followed by a set of distracter items that the subject must attend to. The general finding is that distracter items similar in kind to the original stimulus cause forgetting, whereas dissimilar items are far less disruptive. For example, immediate memory for odor is disrupted by interpolated tasks involving odors, but is unaffected by a distracting verbal task such as counting backward (Walker & John, 1984). The broad categories for which such interference has been demonstrated include conceptual/semantic (Potter 1976), kinesthetic (Williams, Beaver, Spence, & Rundell, 1969), odor (Walker & John,

1984), sign language (Poizner, Bellugi, & Tweney, 1981), tone (Deutsch, 1970), verbal (Shiffrin, 1973; Waugh & Norman, 1965), and visual (Logie, Zucco, & Baddeley, 1990). What we are suggesting is that *syntactic* should be added to this list.

Such a suggestion is consistent with the demonstrations of within-category similarity-based interference in several different tasks and modalities, such as the *phonological similarity* effect in standard verbal STM tasks (Baddeley, 1966; Conrad, 1963) and corresponding effects in visual and sign language (Magnussen, Greenlee, Asplund, & Dyrnes, 1991; Poizner et al., 1981). We are claiming that there is also a "syntactic similarity effect," which shows up as difficulty with center embeddings. A consistent, emerging picture is one that characterizes working memory in terms of specific coding schemes, with severe limitations on the ability to represent items that are coded similarly.

Similarity-based interference, in one form or another, is part of a number of current theoretical frameworks, including Baddeley and Logie (Chapter 2, this volume), Cowan (Chapter 3, this volume), and O'Reilly, Braver, and Cohen (Chapter 11, this volume). Connectionist approaches such as that of O'Reilly et al. are particularly interesting in this respect, because network models exhibit similarity-based interference as an intrinsic property of their representation mechanisms.

Unitary Versus Non-Unitary Working Memory

As we have seen, Soar postulates a dynamic memory, SDM, which holds all the information in declarative form pertaining to the task in hand. As discussed in the previous section, however, although SDM is a single memory in regard to its function within the Soar architecture, the existence within it of different encodings and representations (arising from functional considerations) can give rise to what are effectively multiple memories. The processing of language, for example, involves information in specialized representations encoding syntactic and semantic relations between the various words, whereas the processing of, say, spatial information involves different, specialized representations for the spatial relationships between objects. To the extent that linguistic information is processed by production rules that are sensitive to linguistic data encoded in the linguistic representation and that produce further information in that representation, whereas spatial information is processed by rules sensitive to the spatial representation that produce further information in that representation, so the linguistic and the spatial data can be regarded as residing in different memories. These multiple memories may be active for the same task. For example, a person processing sentences asserting *A is to the left of B* and *C is to the right of B* may well have both a representation of the information reflecting its original linguistic structure and a more directly spatial encoding of the configuration being described.

Soar is neutral as to whether such functionally separable memories are or are not localized, that is, stored at different physical locations in the brain. Soar does, however, offer a couple of constraints on the extent to which the multiple memories can conform to an extreme version of modularity (Fodor, 1983). First is the observation that many tasks require transfer of information between and integration across the different representations. For example, to construct a spatial-like representation from sentences such as *A is to the left of B* requires rules that can translate information from one representation to the other and therefore "know about" both. The second constraint comes from the integrative nature of Soar's learning mechanism. Just as a Soar model of natural language processing acquires rules whose conditions combine lexical, syntactic, semantic, and pragmatic information (Lewis, 1993), so other tasks that involve deliberate processing (i.e., processing in a substate) of information held in different representations lead to the learning of rules that integrate over the different representations. There are therefore functional limits on just how independent the multiple memories can be.

Biological Considerations

The main way in which Soar contacts its implementational roots concerns timing. Newell (1990, 1992) employs a biologically based argument to identify the different time scales at which Soar operates. Newell uses the argument to squeeze the durations of Soar's processes between lower and upper bounds, in order to derive estimates such as the time taken to execute a cognitive operator uninterrupted by an impasse. For example, an increasing number of studies show that a figure of around 50 ms provides a consistent, good approximate fit to human performance across a variety of domains (e.g., Lewis, 1993; Wiesmeyer & Laird, 1993). This argument is of great theoretical importance, because it makes Soar the only major psychological theory to yield *absolute* (even though approximate) temporal predictions.

Beyond those temporal issues, Soar is largely neutral as to its biological implementation. Even the apparent commitment to using a production system is not an essential feature of Soar. The role of the existing production system is to provide Soar with a long-term, content-addressed associative memory. In principle, one could replace the production system by any other system for a content-addressed memory, such as one based on connectionist principles (Cho, Rosenbloom, & Dolan, 1991), and leave the architectural aspects of Soar intact. In practice, such a substitution is likely to lead to modifying the architecture in interesting ways.

The Relationship of Working Memory to Attention and Consciousness

From our perspective, *attention* and *consciousness* are very different issues, and we treat them separately.

Attention

According to Soar's viewpoint, *attention* is not a process separate from the rest of cognition, but rather a label for a collection of phenomena that emerge when a system with potential for a high degree of parallelism has to generate serial behavior. Whenever Soar has to deal with one object, or a small set of objects, out of the many that could be dealt with, then Soar is said to be *attending* to that object or set. As with so much else in Soar, attention is closely tied to the serial bottleneck imposed by the selection of one operator at a time. Suppose that Soar is holding three words in SDM, and the task is to check that each of them is the name of an animal. If we assume, as seems reasonable, that the relevant operators deal with only one word at a time, then Soar can propose in parallel three operators of type *check-for-animal-name*, one for each of the words. But the operators have to be selected and implemented serially, with the result that Soar "pays attention to" each word in turn. The Soar model most explicitly dealing with attentional phenomena is that of Wiesmeyer (1992; Wiesmeyer & Laird, 1993), in which a single model and set of assumptions provides a zero-parameter quantitative and qualitative fit to a range of phenomena in the psychology of covert visual attention.

Consciousness

The term *consciousness* has almost as many different meanings as there are commentators. Soar takes a stand mainly on one particular sense, that of conscious *awareness*. The natural way to read off a microtheory of awareness from the Soar architecture is functionally: Soar is aware of some item X if its behavior can be made to depend on X. Each item in SDM can potentially – given appropriate knowledge (i.e., production rules) – come to determine Soar's course of processing, and hence "enter awareness." In short, Soar is aware of the contents of SDM, which, as we have seen, is a subset of the contents of working memory. Whether or not it can produce a verbal report of those contents is another question, which depends on the representations involved, the cognitive demands of concurrent activity, and so on. Although one can imagine refinements to this position – for example, proposed but unselected operators probably remain outside of awareness, as perhaps do even selected operators – the approach seems viable, and indeed is very close to the position adopted by Ericsson and Simon (1980, 1984) in their treatment of the information available to someone in the context of a psychological experiment.

Conclusion

In this chapter we have considered working memory from the point of view of Soar, a broad cognitive architecture primarily motivated by functional concerns. At first blush, it was not clear that such an architecture would offer much to the theoretical study of working memory, because, in its original formulation, it did not incorporate any constraints on working memory capacity. However, the study of working memory from this functional point of view has provided answers to many of the designated questions, as summarized in Table 7.1. Soar's approach to issues of working memory has yielded three novel contributions:

(1) One of the distinctive contributions of Soar is to offer a detailed account of how complex human cognition can work even within a small working memory. There are now a number of Soar models that illustrate this point, and all rely on the same principle: Memory-demanding tasks are supported by relying on Soar's learning mechanism to produce a recognition memory during task performance. In most of the tasks studied so far, this recognition memory emerges as a by-product of normal task performance. The recognition memory is used reconstructively by relying on internally generated cues, or externally supplied (i.e., "situated") cues. These models go a long way toward helping resolve one of the troubling paradoxes about cog-

---

Table 7.1. *Brief Summary of Answers to the Eight Designated Questions*

(1) **Basic Mechanisms and Representations in Working Memory, and**

(2) **The Control and Regulation of Working Memory**

(These first two questions are answered together.) Soar is a cognitive architecture of broad scope, which focuses on the functional capabilities needed to support performance in a range of cognitive tasks. The Soar architecture has no separate "working memory mechanism" in the sense of components aimed specifically at accounting for memory phenomena. Soar is a production system architecture, with two main memories: a long-term production memory, storing permanent knowledge, and a dynamic memory that holds state information pertaining to the current task. The functions of working memory are distributed across both these memories. Processing occurs by cyclically choosing an operator to apply to the current state, thereby transforming it to a new state. Whenever that process is blocked, Soar sees an "impasse" and sets up a substate, processing of which is intended to produce information to allow processing of the original state to resume. New production rules are acquired whenever processing of a substate generates information for the original state.

(3) **The Unitary Versus Non-Unitary Nature of Working Memory**

Although Soar postulates a single dynamic memory, the existence of different encodings (arising from functional considerations) can give rise to what are effectively "multiple memories." Soar is neutral as to whether such functionally separable memories are localized in the brain. There is growing evidence that to extend Soar's correspondence to human memory, it may be necessary to supplement Soar's main dynamic memory with a number of short-term modality-specific stores, of which a phonological store is one.

Table 7.1, continued

(4) The Nature of Working Memory Limitations

We make two points. First, even in a cognitive architecture with an unbounded dynamic memory, working memory limitations can arise on functional grounds. Where such functional accounts exist, they render the usual kinds of resource-based explanations unnecessary. Second, Soar is compatible with certain kinds of capacity limitations. In particular, a constraint that dynamic memory can hold at most two items of the same "type" yields a coherent explanation for many psycholinguistic phenomena in sentence comprehension and embodies a general cognitive principle – similarity-based interference – operative across multiple kinds of working memory contents.

(5) The Role of Working Memory in Complex Cognitive Activities

Owing to its production system architecture, Soar is strong at modeling the performance of complex cognitive tasks. By making recognitional use of information in long-term memory acquired as a by-product of earlier task performance, Soar shows how tasks requiring search of a large problem space or the accumulation of large amounts of information can be performed within the constraints of a dynamic memory of bounded size.

(6) The Relationship of Working Memory to Long-Term Memory and Knowledge

Soar's working memory system *includes* long-term memory as one of its component mechanisms. Long-term memory serves the function of a working memory whenever it encodes, via learning, partial or intermediate products of computation in service of some task. Soar therefore has close links to other approaches that emphasize the involvement of long-term memory in working memory and may be able to offer a computational process model for Ericsson and Kintsch's "long-term working memory." The analysis shows that working memory cannot coherently be studied independent of long-term memory and while ignoring learning.

(7) The Relationship of Working Memory to Attention and Consciousness

Attentional phenomena are "real," but attention is not a separate "thing." Rather, it labels a collection of effects that emerge when a system with potential for a high degree of parallelism has to generate serial behavior. With regard to consciousness, Soar is "aware" of what it can respond to, that is, of the contents of its dynamic memory. Whether or not it can produce a verbal report of those contents depends on a variety of other factors.

(8) The Biological Implementation of Working Memory

Newell (1990) employs a biologically based argument to identify the different time scales at which Soar operates. This argument is of great theoretical importance, because it makes Soar the only major psychological theory to yield absolute (even though approximate) temporal predictions. Beyond that, Soar is neutral as to its biological implementation. In principle, one could replace the production system by any other implementation of a content-addressed associative memory, such as a connectionist network.

nitive models of complex tasks (particularly production system models): Most such models rely on implausibly large dynamic memories to support performance. The Soar models discussed in this chapter provide a concrete set of mechanisms that clearly demonstrate that such oversize memories are not needed. The resulting theory of performance has close ties to the ideas surrounding long-term working memory (Ericsson & Kintsch, 1995), provides a candidate set of mechanisms for realizing those ideas, and extends the relevant domains to any task requiring significant temporary memory storage – not just overlearned expert performance.

This is good news for both traditional working memory theorists concerned with capacity limitations and theorists concerned with complex task performance. For the former, it means that it may be possible to incorporate even severely limited models of working memory within a functional architecture; for the latter, it means that it should be possible to build new models (as well as reconstruct existing models) of complex cognition in such a way that the demands on working memory are minimal.

(2) The Soar models of reasoning and language demonstrate that some phenomena usually attributed to capacity limitations can arise from purely functional mechanisms or differences in knowledge or skill. In particular, we saw how Soar's control structure can yield performance limitations when it leads to the application of automatized skill in inappropriate situations. The Soar theory also includes an account of how certain skill differences may actually arise as a function of experience, providing an explanation of both the locus and the genesis of individual differences that might otherwise be assumed to be capacity based.

(3) Although Soar as originally formulated had no working memory capacity limits, concern for efficient processing (in particular, retrieval from the recognition memory) led to a constraint on SDM that yields similarity-based interference. In short, similarly coded items interfere more than dissimilar items. The application of this restriction to the domain of syntactic processing (along with an assumption about the severe limit on the number of similar linguistic items that can be maintained – the "magical number two") led to a simple model of difficult and acceptable embeddings that account for a wide range of processing effects across multiple languages. Similarity-based interference has been demonstrated in many different tasks and modalities. The various kinds of codings (phonological, visual, etc.) give rise to specialized memories, but these specializations emerge from, and are governed by, the same general cognitive principle.

By focusing on learning, long-term memory, and functionality, this story has strayed outside the traditional concerns of working memory research – but for good reasons. Though we are obviously in the early stages of this research, a couple of methodological lessons should be clear, even if particular theoretical aspects of Soar remain contentious. The first lesson is that we must be careful not to consider working memory in isolation from long-term memory: They are designed to work together (and with the external environment) in the performance of complex tasks. The second lesson is that we cannot separate learning from performance – even in what is conventionally regarded as pure "performance" tasks, learning can play an important role. Such lessons should not be cause for scientific pessimism because they defeat certain divide-and-conquer approaches to psychological investigation. Rather, they should encourage us to work harder on developing and empirically distinguishing precise unified architectures that explain how the different aspects of cognition work together.

REFERENCES

Altmann, E. M. (1996). *Episodic memory for external information.* Doctoral dissertation, Carnegie Mellon University, Pittsburgh, PA. CMU-CS-96-167.

Altmann, E. M., & John, B. E. (in press). Modeling episodic indexing of external information. *Cognitive Science.*

Altmann, E. M., Larkin, J. H., & John, B. E. (1995). Display navigation by an expert programmer: A preliminary model of memory. In I. R. Katz, R. Mack, & L. Marks (Eds.), *Proceedings of CHI'95: Human Factors in Computing Systems,* pp. (3–10). New York: ACM Press.

Anderson, J. R. (1983). *The architecture of cognition.* Cambridge, MA: Harvard University Press.

Anderson, J. R. (1993). *Rules of the mind.* Hillsdale, NJ: Erlbaum.

Anderson, J. R., & Bower, G. H. (1972). Recognition and retrieval processes in free recall. *Psychological Review, 79,* 97–123.

Atkinson, R. C., & Shiffrin, R. M. (1968). Human memory: A proposed system and its control processes. In K. W. Spence (Ed.), *The psychology of learning and motivation: Advances in research and theory* (Vol. 2, pp. 89–195). New York: Academic Press.

Baddeley, A. D. (1966). Short-term memory for word sequences as a function of acoustic, semantic, and formal similarity. *Quarterly Journal of Experimental Psychology, 18,* 362–365.

Baddeley, A. D. (1986). *Working memory.* New York: Oxford University Press.

Baddeley, A. D. (1996). Exploring the central executive. *Quarterly Journal of Experimental Psychology, 49A,* 5–28.

Baddeley, A. D., & Hitch, G. J. (1974). Working memory. In G. H. Bower (Ed.), *The psychology of learning and motivation: Advances in research and theory* (Vol. 8, pp. 47–89). New York: Academic Press.

Bahrick, H. P. (1970). Two-phase model for prompted recall. *Psychological Review, 77,* 215–222.

Broadbent, D. E. (1993). Comparison with human experiments. In D. E. Broadbent (Ed.), *The simulation of human intelligence.* Oxford, UK: Blackwell.

Cho, B., Rosenbloom, P. S., & Dolan, C. P. (1991). Neuro-Soar: A neural network architecture for goal-oriented behavior. In *Proceedings of the 13th Annual Conference of the Cognitive Science Society.* Chicago.

Chomsky, N. (1986). *Barriers.* Cambridge, MA: MIT Press.

Congdon, C. B., & Laird, J. E. (1995). *The Soar user's manual: Version 7.* Department of Electrical Engineering and Computer Science. Ann Arbor: University of Michigan.

Conrad, R. (1963). Acoustic confusions and memory span for words. *Nature, 197,* 1029–1030.

Deutsch, D. (1970). Tones and numbers. *Science, 168,* 1604–1605.

Ericsson, K. A., & Kintsch, W. (1995). Long-term working memory. *Psychological Review, 102,* 211–245.

Ericsson, K. A., & Simon, H. A. (1980). Verbal reports as data. *Psychological Review, 87,* 215–251.

Ericsson, K. A., & Simon, H. A. (1984). *Protocol analysis: Verbal reports as data.* Cambridge, MA: MIT Press.

Ferreira, F., & Clifton, C. (1986). The independence of syntactic processing. *Journal of Memory and Language, 25,* 348–368.

Fodor, J. A. (1983). *The modularity of mind.* Cambridge, MA: MIT Press.

Franzke, M. (1995). Turning research into practice: Characteristics of display-based interaction. In I. R. Katz, R. Mack, & L. Marks (Eds.), *Proceedings of CHI'95: Human Factors in Computing Systems* (pp. 421–428). New York: ACM Press.

Gruneberg, M. M., Morris, P. E., & Sykes, R. N. (Eds.). (1988). *Practical aspects of memory: Current research and issues. Vol. 4: Memory in everyday life.* New York: Wiley.

Howes, A. (1993). Recognition-based problem solving. *Proceedings of the Fifteenth Annual Meeting of the Cognitive Science Society* (pp. 551–556). Boulder, CO. Erlbaum.

Howes, A. (1994). A model of the acquisition of menu knowledge by exploration. In B. Adelson, S. Dumais, & J. R. Olson (Eds.), *Proceedings of CHI'94: Human Factors in Computing Systems* (pp. 445–451). New York: ACM Press.

Howes, A., & Young, R. M. (1996). Learning consistent, interactive and meaningful device methods: A computational model. *Cognitive Science, 20,* 301–356.

Howes, A., & Young, R. M. (1997). The role of cognitive architecture in modelling the user: Soar's learning mechanism. *Human–Computer Interaction, 12,* 311–343.

Huffman, S. B. (1994). *Instructable autonomous agents.* Doctoral dissertation, University of Michigan, Ann Arbor. Report CSE-TR-193-94.

Huffman, S. B., & Laird, J. E. (1995). Flexibly instructable agents. *Journal of Artificial Intelligence Research, 3,* 271–324.

Johnson-Laird, P. N. (1983). *Mental models.* Cambridge, MA: Harvard University Press.

Johnson-Laird, P. N. (1988). Reasoning by rule or model? *Proceedings of the Tenth Annual Conference of the Cognitive Science Society* (pp. 765–771). Montreal.

Just, M. A., & Carpenter, P. A. (1992). A capacity theory of comprehension: Individual differences in working memory. *Psychological Review, 99,* 122–149.

Kintsch, W. (1970). Models for free recall and recognition. In D. A. Norman (Ed.), *Models of human memory.* New York: Academic Press.

Laird, J. E., Newell, A., & Rosenbloom, P. S. (1987). Soar: An architecture for general intelligence. *Artificial Intelligence, 33,* 1–64.

Laird, J. E., Rosenbloom, P. S., & Newell, A. (1986). *Universal subgoaling and chunking: The automatic generation and learning of goal hierarchies.* Boston: Kluwer Academic.

Larkin, J. H. (1989). Display-based problem solving. In D. Klahr & K. Kotovsky (Eds.), *Complex information processing: The impact of Herbert A. Simon.* Hillsdale, NJ: Erlbaum.

Lehman, J. F., Laird, J. E., & Rosenbloom, P. S. (1998). A gentle introduction to Soar: An architecture for human cognition. In S. Sternberg & D. Scarborough (Eds.), *Invitation to cognitive science* (Vol. 4, pp. 211–253). Cambridge, MA: MIT Press.

Lewis, R. L. (1993). *An architecturally-based theory of human sentence comprehension.* Doctoral dissertation, Carnegie Mellon University, Pittsburgh, PA. CMU-CS-93-226.

Lewis, R. L. (1996). Interference in short-term memory: The magical number two (or three) in sentence processing. *Journal of Psycholinguistic Research, 25,* 93–115.

Lewis, R. L. (1997a). Leaping off the garden path: Reanalysis and limited repair parsing. In J. Fodor & F. Ferreira (Eds.), *Reanalysis in sentence processing.* Boston: Kluwer Academic.

Lewis, R. L. (1997b). Specifying architectures for language processing: Process, control, and memory in parsing and interpretation. In M. Crocker, M. Pickering, & C. Clifton (Eds.), *Architectures and mechanisms for language processing.* New York: Cambridge University Press.

Lewis, R. L., Newell, A., & Polk, T. (1989). Toward a Soar theory of taking instructions for immediate reasoning tasks. *Proceedings of the Eleventh Annual Conference of the Cognitive Science Society* (pp. 514–521). Ann Arbor, MI.

Logie, R., Zucco, G. M., & Baddeley, A. D. (1990). Interference with visual short-term memory. *Acta Psychologica, 75,* 55–74.

MacDonald, M., Pearlmutter, N., & Seidenberg, M. (1994). The lexical nature of syntactic ambiguity resolution. *Psychological Review, 101,* 676–703.

Magnussen, S., Greenlee, M. W., Asplund, R., & Dyrnes, S. (1991). Stimulus-specific mechanisms of visual short-term memory. *Vision Research, 31,* 1213–1219.

Mayes, J. T., Draper, S. W., McGregor, A. M., & Oatley, K. (1988). Information flow in a user interface: The effect of experience and context on the recall of MacWrite screens. In D. M. Jones & R. Winder (Eds.), *People and computers IV* (pp. 275–289). New York: Cambridge University Press.

Miller, C. S., & Laird, J. E. (1996). Accounting for graded performance within a discrete search framework. *Cognitive Science, 20,* 499–537.

Miller, G. A. (1956). The magic number seven, plus or minus two: Some limits on our capacity for processing information. *Psychological Review, 63,* 81–97.

Miller, G. A., & Chomsky, N. (1963). Finitary models of language users. In D. R. Luce, R. R. Bush, & E. Galanter (Eds.), *Handbook of mathematical psychology* (Vol. II). New York: Wiley.

Miller, G. A., Galanter, E., & Pribram, K. (1960). *Plans and the structure of behavior.* New York: Holt, Rinehart & Winston.

Murdock, B. B. (1963). Short-term memory and paired-associate learning. *Journal of Verbal Learning and Verbal Behavior, 2,* 320–328.

Neisser, U. (1982). *Memory observed: Remembering in natural contexts.* San Francisco: Freeman.

Neisser, U. (1985.) The role of theory in the ecological study of memory: Comment on Bruce. *Journal of Experimental Psychology: General, 114,* 272–276.

Newell, A. (1990). *Unified theories of cognition.* Cambridge, MA: Harvard University Press.

Newell, A. (1992). Précis of *Unified Theories of Cognition. Behavioral and Brain Sciences, 15,* 425–492.

Newell, A., & Simon, H. A. (1972). *Human problem solving.* Englewood Cliffs, NJ: Prentice-Hall.

Payne, S. J. (1991). Display-based action at the user interface. *International Journal of Man–Machine Studies, 35,* 275–289.

Poizner, H., Bellugi, U., & Tweney, R. D. (1981). Processing of formational, semantic, and iconic information in American Sign Language. *Journal of Experimental Psychology: Human Perception and Performance, 7,* 1146–1159.

Polk, T. A., & Newell, A. (1995). Deduction as verbal reasoning. *Psychological Review,* *102,* 533–566.

Potter, M. C. (1976). Short-term conceptual memory for pictures. *Journal of Experimental Psychology: Human Learning and Memory, 2,* 509–522.

Rieman, J. (1994). *Learning strategies and exploratory behavior of interactive computer users.* Doctoral dissertation, University of Colorado at Boulder. Technical Report: CU-CS-723-94.

Rieman, J. (1996). A field study of exploratory learning strategies. *ACM Transactions on Computer–Human Interaction, 3,* 189–218.

Rieman, J., Young, R. M., & Howes, A. (1996). A dual-space model of iteratively deepening exploratory learning. *International Journal of Human–Computer Studies, 44,* 743–775.

Ritter, F. E., & Young, R. M. (1997). *Psychological Soar tutorial* [On line]. Available: http://www. psychology.nottingham.ac.uk/staff/ritter/pst.html.

Shiffrin, R. M. (1973). Information persistence in short-term memory. *Journal of Experimental Psychology, 100,* 39–49.

Tambe, M., Johnson, W. L., Jones, R. M., Koss, F., Laird, J. E., Rosenbloom, P. S., & Schwamb, K. (1995). Intelligent agents for interactive simulation environments. *AI Magazine, 16,* 15–40.

Tambe, M., Newell, A., & Rosenbloom, P. S. (1990). The problem of expensive chunks and its solution by restricting expressiveness. *Machine Learning, 5,* 299–348.

Trueswell, J. C., Tanenhaus, M. K., & Garnsey, S. M. (1994). Semantic influences in parsing: Use of thematic role information in syntactic ambiguity resolution. *Journal of Memory and Language, 33,* 285–318.

Vera, A. H., Lewis, R. L., & Lerch, F. J. (1993). Situated decision-making and recognition-based learning: Applying symbolic theories to interactive tasks. *Proceedings of the 15th Annual Conference of the Cognitive Science Society* (pp. 84–95). Boulder, CO: Erlbaum.

Walker, H. A., & John, E. E. (1984). Interference and facilitation in short-term memory for odors. *Perception & Psychophysics, 36,* 508–514.

Waugh, N. C., & Norman, D. A. (1965). Primary memory. *Psychological Review, 72,* 89–104.

Wiesmeyer, M. D. (1992). *An operator-based model of human covert visual attention.* Doctoral dissertation, University of Michigan.

Wiesmeyer, M., & Laird, J. E. (1993). NOVA, covert attention explored through unified theories of cognition. In *Proceedings of the Fifteenth Annual Conference of the Cognitive Science Society* (pp. 102–107). Boulder, CO: Erlbaum.

Williams, H. L., Beaver, W. S., Spence, M. T., & Rundell, O. H. (1969). Digital and kinesthetic memory with interpolated information processing. *Journal of Experimental Psychology, 80,* 530–536.

8 Long-Term Working Memory as an Alternative to Capacity Models of Working Memory in Everyday Skilled Performance

K. ANDERS ERICSSON AND PETER F. DELANEY

FIVE CENTRAL FEATURES OF THE THEORY

(1) We define working memory in terms of its function, namely maintaining efficient selective access to information that is needed to complete a given task. This function can be achieved in everyday skilled performance by a wide range of different mechanisms. In contrast, traditional short-term working memory employs only a small subset of those alternatives.

(2) The amount of information that can be maintained in accessible form in working memory for a specific task is not limited by a fixed capacity. As part of the extended skill acquisition necessary to attain very high levels of performance, experts acquire knowledge and skills to rapidly encode information in long-term memory such that the information can be efficiently accessed with retrieval cues (long-term working memory or LT-WM) whenever it is later needed to complete the task. Similar acquired mechanisms mediate the large working memory in skilled everyday performance.

(3) LT-WM is mediated by associative recall from long-term memory, and to function reliably it provides different types of mechanisms for overcoming the problems of interference resulting from repeated associations to related retrieval cues.

(4) LT-WM reflects a complex skill acquired to meet the particular demands of future accessibility for information with tasks within a particular domain of expertise. Domain-relevant skills, knowledge, and procedures for the task are so tightly integrated into the skills for encoding of information that the traditional assumption of a strict separation between memory, knowledge, and procedures is not valid for skilled performance.

(5) Different methods of maintaining access to memories through LT-WM exist even within the same domain, including access based on temporal recency cues, on association to explicit retrieval structures, or on associations to elaborated cognitive structures generated dur-

257

ing learning. Furthermore, the detailed structure of LT-WM may differ across individuals because their available representations, knowledge, and preferred strategies differ.

As interest in working memory has grown, more and more researchers are using the term *working memory* in their discussions of their findings and models. It is thus becoming increasingly important that we reach a consensus on what working memory really is. Only then can we proceed to compare and contrast various detailed models of its function and mediating mechanisms. Every psychologist has an intuitive idea of what working memory is, but virtually all of them would be very hard pressed to clearly define the term and distinguish it clearly from other related terms. One potential solution to this confusion could be to ask experts to define their models of working memory by their model's relations to more basic constructs, such as short-term memory, long-term memory, and attention. However, it is rather humbling to see the controversies that still surround the appropriate definition and characterization of those supposedly basic terms. For example, even the fruitfulness of distinguishing between short-term and long-term stores (cf. Crowder, 1993) and of viewing automaticity as release of attentional capacity (Logan, 1988, 1991) are legitimately contested. Hence, defining models of working memory in terms of other similarly controversial and diffuse theoretical constructs is unlikely to reduce confusion and may even increase it. Another potential solution to the search for a definition of working memory would be to capitalize on the recent breakthroughs in biology, particularly in the study of the nervous system. It is now possible to record correlates of the neural activity of the different parts of the brain during cognitive processes. The temporal and spatial resolution of these records is steadily improving, and soon we may have a sequence of detailed snapshots of a single brain. Scientists have already demonstrated that the activation of certain brain regions can be consistently related to engagement in some types of activities. However, the problem with using these results to clarify what we mean by working memory is that the search is still in progress – we are using our psychological knowledge about what types of cognitive processes are involved while performing a task to understand the function of brain regions, rather than using our knowledge of brain region functions to assess what processes are involved in a psychological task. O'Reilly, Braver, and Cohen (Chapter 11, this volume) show how the emerging knowledge of anatomical and functional characteristics of different brain regions will be essential to identify plausible implementations of working memory in the brain. Nevertheless, at least in the near future, research on brain activity is unlikely to supply the decisive set of evidence that defines the structure of working memory in complex cognitive tasks.

In times of rapidly changing theoretical conceptions, one should look for a consensus based on reproducible empirical phenomena. The history of science is replete with conflicts over the theoretical accounts of empirical phenomena, but it is rarer that the empirical observations and facts themselves are disagreed over. Hence, we should begin by seeking agreement that some particular empirical phenomena reflect the general concept of working memory (cf. Cowan, Chapter 3, this volume). Once we have succeeded in reaching such an agreement, it becomes possible to compare and contrast different theoretical models' accounts of the corresponding empirical evidence from the laboratory and everyday life. It is very easy to find everyday activities and human performance that would require mediation of working memory. In fact, working memory is so central to human cognition that it is hard to find activities where it is not involved.

Many recent attempts to define working memory make use of example tasks that place large, salient demands on storage in working memory. Baddeley (1992, p. 638), in his entry on working memory in *The Encyclopedia of Learning and Memory*, gives a prototypical instance of working memory. Baddeley asks readers to calculate how much change they would get back if they gave a $10 bill to cover the cost of three bottles of mineral water at $1.80 a bottle. Baddeley (1992, p. 638) says that "in order to work this out you almost certainly need to hold the results of your initial calculations while performing other operations, storing interim results for which you have no need once the answer was reached." Unlike many other tasks, the main challenge here is the difficulty of maintaining the results of calculations made on the way to the solution. There are many other tasks that are known for placing large demands on working memory, such as multiplying a pair of three-digit numbers mentally. The entry on working memory in *The Encyclopedia of Psychology* by Reisberg (1994) presents detailed examples of the memory demands involved in planning and while comprehending text. We believe that there is a high degree of consensus that the tasks and activities just described present greater demands than average on working memory. Consequently, it would make sense that empirical studies of performance on those tasks should significantly advance our understanding of the mechanisms of working memory for those tasks whatever mechanisms are supported by the emerging empirical evidence.

In a 1992 paper, one of the most influential researchers in the study of working memory, Alan Baddeley, chose to use a more narrow definition of working memory as "a system that provides *temporary* storage of information that is being used in such complex activities as reasoning, comprehending and learning" (emphasis added). The inclusion of the additional requirement of temporary storage in the definition of working memory is problematic because there is no accepted term for alternative mechanisms meeting the same functional requirements. In more recent work, Baddeley and Logie (e.g., Chapter 2, this volume) have instead proposed a more comprehensive view of working memory based around a central executive system that manages memory performance, thereby leaving open the possibility of other types of storage, such as storage in long-term memory. In the following, we will use

Ericsson and Kintsch's (1995) terminology, where the temporary storage in working memory proposed by Baddeley (1992) is called short-term working memory (ST-WM), distinguishing it from other possible types of working memory, such as maintained access to information in long-term working memory (LT-WM). In fact, we will advocate the broadest possible description of working memory and its possible mechanisms. At the most general level, the essence of the concept of working memory (or that part of memory that works) is that only a minute fraction of all the knowledge, skills, and information stored in subjects' vast long-term memory is influencing the subjects' behavior and thought processes at a specific instant of time. Hence, the phenomenon of working memory includes *all those mechanisms that maintain selective access to the information and the procedures that are necessary for a subject to complete one or more specific concurrent tasks.* By adopting this broad description of working memory, we are now in a position to compare and contrast more specific mechanisms and conceptions and their distinctive research approaches within a common framework.

Three General Approaches to the Study of Working Memory

The ultimate goal of the scientific study of working memory is to provide an understanding of its role in all types of activities in everyday life (see Figure 8.1). However, the context of everyday life is typically so complex that most researchers believe that observation and analysis alone are unlikely to allow us to extract generalizable insights into the structure of working memory. Some type of systematic study is necessary, and approaches differ primarily in which type of phenomena they try to reproduce under controlled laboratory conditions. The most salient difference between approaches is their views on knowledge and complex skills. In Figure 8.1, at one extreme we have placed research on basic processes, because this research attempts to minimize the influence of experience and complex knowledge on some observed performance. At the other extreme, we have placed expert performance in specific domains of expertise, where the research actively seeks out the highest degree of complexity of knowledge and skill as well as the largest amounts of relevant experience. In the middle we have placed the diverse category of skilled everyday activities, corresponding to an intermediate level of experience and complexity of knowledge and skill.

We will distinguish three different approaches to the study of working memory. Each of these is intended to explain working memory in all of these diverse contexts, but its research program focuses primarily on performance on one of the three types of tasks shown in Figure 8.1. The first one, which we will call the *basic-capacity approach,* is based on the assumption that all cognitive activity draws on a set of common mechanisms and basic capacities. Given that these basic capacities are involved in every cognitive activity, the preferred strategy for studying them is to identify the simplest tasks that allow

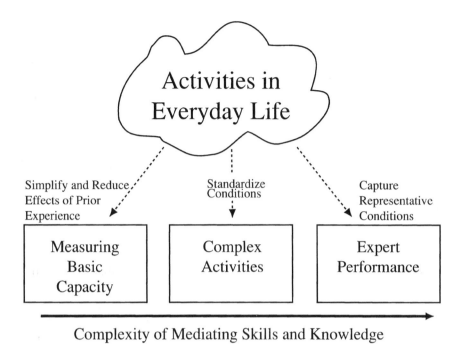

Figure 8.1. Three laboratory-based approaches to the study of working memory for skilled everyday activities.

us to measure the capacities under laboratory conditions that are uncontaminated by experience and acquired skills.

An alternative approach employs complex tasks eliciting everyday activities such as reasoning and comprehension. Once representative tasks have been identified and associated performance can be reliably reproduced in the laboratory, the involvement of working memory can be examined with experimental methods. The primary technique allows the experimenter to selectively interfere with information maintained in various hypothetical components of the subjects' working memory. By examining the differential effects on performance from the various types of interference, the experimenter can draw inferences about the degree of usage of the corresponding store during an activity. Given that this approach focuses only on transiently stored information and how this form of storage can be disrupted by experimental methods, we will refer to this approach as the *transient-storage approach*.

The appeal of both the basic-capacity and the transient-storage approaches is that they are able to assess the role of general memory capacities without having to describe the knowledge and acquired skills mediating complex activities. However, to truly understand the detailed mechanisms involved in working memory, one would like to analyze the specific intermediate products that individuals generate during complex activities. We will later show that it is possible to collect information on the sequence of intermediate products generated during a subject's performance and to evaluate theories with respect to their ability to reproduce these intermediate products. If researchers had the opportunity to describe the processes mediating the performance of any subject on any activity in everyday life, then it is likely that they would search for a performance where a very large amount of information is maintained in working memory. Once performance with exceptional working memory has been identified in everyday life, it is possible to design tasks to capture this reproducible complex performance in the laboratory. If one selects individuals who have reached their expert performance after years or decades of sustained efforts to improve, one could argue that their performance reflects nearly maximal adaptation to working memory demands (see Figure 8.1). Advocates of this *expert-performance approach* argue that the mechanisms mediating exceptional working memory may reveal something about the general structure of mechanisms that support working memory in skilled everyday activities (Ericsson & Charness, 1994).

In the following, we will briefly review the findings of each of these three approaches (basic-capacity, transient-storage, and expert-performance) in turn with respect to their research on working memory.

The Basic-Capacity Approach

Ebbinghaus's (1885) laboratory study of memory is generally viewed as the starting point of modern scientific psychology. Ebbinghaus believed that recall of events in everyday life was primarily influenced by the individuals' interest, level of attention, relevant knowledge, and experience. To study memory under controlled conditions in the laboratory, Ebbinghaus designed a task where the subjects[1] should direct their complete attention to a sequence of presented stimuli. For the stimulus material he selected nonsense syllables (e.g., XIG, BIF) because he wanted to observe the formation of basic associations between the syllables with minimal influence of experience and knowledge. Furthermore, he presented the syllables at a fast rate to further minimize the risk that the subjects would still have time to access their prior knowledge. The general thesis was that by careful design of a laboratory task with rapid sequential presentation of "meaningless" information, experimenters could constrain subjects to rely only on their basic memory capacity and their basic processes of association. Ebbinghaus's (1885) general laws of memory and forgetting were confirmed by subsequent replications with a wide range of other materials, typically lists of arbitrary words or digits. However, the rate of mem-

---

[1] Ebbinghaus served as his own only subject in his original work. However, Ebbinghaus believed that any subject would exhibit the same performance if tested under comparable conditions.

orization on these arbitrary lists was remarkably slow and subjects required many exposures to each stimulus before it was committed to memory. The total time to successfully store an association in long-term memory (LTM) was later estimated at between 5 and 10 s (Simon, 1974).

The next major advance concerned measuring the basic capacity of short-term memory (STM). In his classic review, George Miller (1956) found that the maximum number of items that subjects could recall immediately after a rapid sequential presentation (memory span) differed dramatically depending on the type of material presented. When arbitrary lists of letters were presented, subjects could recall around 6 or 7. When the letters formed words, however, they could remember 6 or 7 words, or the equivalent of 20 to 40 different letters. According to Miller, the capacity of STM was remarkably stable across materials when defined in terms of familiar patterns (chunks) and corresponded to around seven. Chase and Simon (1973) extended this account to explain chess experts' superior memory for chess positions. When actual chess games were briefly presented, the best experts could reproduce the entire chess position (around 25 chess pieces) in terms of meaningful patterns or clusters of chess pieces (chunks). For boards of randomly arranged chess pieces that lacked such patterns, their recall was limited to around 5 pieces. This is no better than the recall performance of novice chess players for normal chess positions. More generally, experts exhibit clearly superior memory for representative stimuli from their domain but not for randomly rearranged versions of the same stimuli in a wide range of different domains.[2] In sum, the assumption that the capacity of STM can be described in terms of a fixed number of independent patterns (chunks) has had, and still has, a major impact on theories and simulation models of human thinking. Furthermore, individual differences in the capacity of STM have been proposed as a possible explanation for general differences in observed performance across different types of tasks (Newell & Simon, 1972).

Consistent with the assumption of stable individual differences in the capacity of STM, individuals' memory spans for different types of materials are highly correlated, and factor analyses suggest that a single factor can explain the memory span performance (Carroll, 1993). Laboratory studies have identified rehearsal as the principal mechanism underlying memory span (maximal STM capacity) and shown that individual differences in the speed of articulation of the material are sufficient to explain most of the differences in memory span (Baddeley, 1986).

In spite of the solid evidence for stable individual differences in STM capacity (generalizable across many types of rehearsable information), a num-

---

[2] Recent reviews (Ericsson & Lehmann, 1996; Gobet & Simon, 1996a) show that the pattern of results is a little bit more complex. Experts can recall more than novices even for randomly rearranged versions of stimuli, but the absolute differences are typically an order of magnitude smaller.

ber of findings raise doubt that those measures reflect a general basic memory capacity that constrains working memory in more complex activities in everyday life. The most devastating finding for that hypothesis is that the memory span of normal adults is only weakly correlated with performance in skilled everyday activities[3] such as text comprehension (Daneman & Merikle, 1996) and regular work performance (Verive & McDaniel, 1996). Additionally, some individuals with brain damage show normal performance on complex tasks, such as text comprehension, even when they have severely impaired immediate memory performance (Martin, 1993). Finally, performance on the tests of immediate memory for a particular type of material can be dramatically improved, even by 1,000%, with practice (Chase & Ericsson, 1982; Ericsson, 1985; Kliegl, Smith, Heckhausen, & Baltes, 1987; Wenger & Payne, 1995). Taken together these pieces of evidence raise considerable doubts that the capacity of STM, as measured by memory span, limits or determines performance on representative complex activities.

Another challenge to the conception of a general working memory capacity concerns how much of the capacity of STM is available as working memory during the execution of a task involving reasoning and comprehension (rather than just the recall of the presented information). When subjects perform such tasks, Broadbent (1975) argued, the reliable working memory capacity available for storage of information appears to be far below the magical number seven and closer to three or four chunks. This estimate of free general capacity is so low that it seems difficult to construct models of cognitive processes within those processing constraints unless one proposes additional activity-specific resources. Furthermore, the conception of working memory implies the possibility of a trade-off between resources for processing and storage. Arguably, individual differences in available working memory capacity could in part be due to a differential need for working memory for control processing; more able individuals require less, thus providing a larger available portion of working memory for storage. The most influential proposal for measurement of free capacity during processing was given by Daneman and Carpenter (1980), whose reading span test measured subjects' capacity to manipulate and maintain unrelated words in working memory during comprehension of a series of sentences. This and other tests assessing available working memory capacity during the execution of a very complex skilled activity are designed using principles very different from the basic-capacity approach. They are, however, closely related to those procedures advocated by the transient-storage approach, to which we will now turn.

---

[3] It is a matter of controversy whether the observed modest correlations between memory span and performance reflect individual differences in capacity. The available evidence (Dempster, 1981) appears to be more consistent with an account in terms of a third factor, namely differences in knowledge and quality of representations of symbol systems, such as numbers, which in turn influence both memory span and performance. For a dissenting view, see Engle, Kane, and Tuholski (Chapter 4, this volume).

The Transient-Storage Approach

By studying working memory during skilled everyday activities, it is possible to eliminate the problematic step of first measuring the basic general capacity in "pure" form with a laboratory task. The central hypothesis of this approach is that typical performance requires temporary storage of information in general systems of limited capacity and that it is possible to design experimental procedures to selectively interfere with storage in those systems. In his seminal book, Baddeley (1986) described the three general components of short-term working memory. The central component was the central executive, but its temporary storage could be extended by two slave systems, the phonological loop and visuospatial sketchpad.[4] For each slave system, simple activities were identified that would interfere with storage in one but not the other system, neatly demonstrating their independence. For example, if subjects had to concurrently chant "hiya, hiya" while performing a task, such as reading a text, then the chanting would occupy the articulatory mechanism and thus disable temporary storage in the phonological loop. Another general procedure proposed by Baddeley and Hitch (1974) involved presenting subjects with information to be remembered just before the start of the target activity and then requiring that the subject be able to recall it upon completion of the activity. This procedure was designed to preload working memory, because if working memory capacity is a general resource then the available working memory capacity for the target task should be reduced by the same amount. The results from a large body of studies using the interference approach are rather consistent (Baddeley, 1986; Baddeley & Logie, Chapter 2, this volume) and show that performance on laboratory tasks eliciting complex cognitive activities, such as reasoning, do exhibit interference but the degree of interference is much smaller than would have been expected from the theoretical view of general working memory capacity. For the tasks most closely representative of skilled everyday activities, such as text comprehension, the interference effects are difficult to detect unless the number of preloaded items exceeds the limit for reliable working-memory capacity of 3 or 4 items. Similarly, Engle, Kane, and Tuholski (Chapter 4, this volume) show that manipulating the difficulty of a primary task such as mental arithmetic has remarkably small effects on a concurrent memory task. Studies attempting to interfere with temporary storage during expert performance, especially performance believed to require extensive working memory, have found essentially no reliable effects (Ericsson & Kintsch, 1995). Hence, most forms of skilled and expert performance in everyday life do not seem to critically depend on temporary storage in the two slave systems.

---

[4] Note, though, that Baddeley and Logie (Chapter 2, this volume) no longer allow storage in the central executive, which is now exclusively reserved for control processing.

An extension of the interference approach allows us to ask to what extent working memory during skilled and expert performance is mediated *by temporary storage of any kind.* If temporary storage is implicated, it ought to be possible to disrupt an ongoing task by forcing subjects to switch to a different working memory–demanding task before they finish. Once the subjects are allowed to resume the original activity, all the transiently stored information associated with the original task would be lost. Examining the effects of such interruptions on tasks once they are resumed provides a general method for assessing the amount of information in temporary storage. In their review of the effects of complete interruptions on skilled and expert performance, Ericsson and Kintsch (1995) found that, surprisingly, the performance was essentially unimpaired. Hence, the role of temporary storage in skilled and expert performance appears to be very limited. For example, subjects were able to read texts without decrements in comprehension when they had to engage in a completely unrelated task interspersed between the reading of some of the sentences in the text (Fischer & Glanzer, 1986; Glanzer & Nolan, 1986). The only reliable effect of brief interruptions was that subjects took a little longer to read the first sentence following the interruption – 250 to 450 ms. For longer interruptions (about 30 s), reading times for the first sentence increased by between 1200 and 1800 ms (Fischer & Glanzer, 1986). In another example, Charness (1976) showed that chess masters' superior recall of briefly presented chess positions is only slightly impaired when they had to engage in one of many unrelated, attention-demanding activities like calculating a running total of random digits. However, the latency to start the recall of the chess pieces is increased by the interruption.

In sum, experimental studies of skilled and expert performance find very limited effects of various types of interruptions and concurrent interference. This suggests that information essential for completion of tasks is not maintained primarily in temporary storage, at least for the types of skilled performance studied to date. Interruptions do not appear to influence storage of information, but rather its accessibility as indicated by the longer processing times observed at the resumption of the main activity after an interruption.

Changing the Primary Basis of Working Memory from Transient Storage to Skilled Access

Theories of working memory based on transient activation of information in LTM cannot explain how a subject could resume an activity once the information in working memory was irretrievably lost; that is, the information cannot be distinguished from all the other information in LTM, because it does not have a higher level of activation. When a skilled activity can be interrupted and then be successfully resumed later, it strongly suggests that the cognitive state just prior to the interruption can be regenerated – at least in all important respects – at the time that the activity is subsequently resumed. Ericsson and Kintsch (1995) proposed that the information associated with the regenerated state had been stored in LTM. In support of that hypothesis, they cited evidence for substantial incidental memory among experts for information concerning completed tasks. The stable incidental memory, as well as intentional memory for the task-relevant information at the completion of a collection of tasks, suggests that experts store information for working memory in LTM. Furthermore, the finding that resumption of an activity takes additional time is consistent with a hypothesis of the regeneration of the original state in terms of reestablished access to the associated information by reactivation of the relevant retrieval cues. In fact, the subjects would have to reinstate all the information even about the task and their current strategies and methods. Consistent with this need for reinstatement, Fischer and Glanzer (1986) found that the time necessary to resume the original task increased the more dissimilar the interrupting task and the original task were.

Building on the work on skilled memory of Chase and Ericsson (1982; Ericsson & Chase, 1982), Ericsson and Kintsch (1995) proposed the existence of a "long-term working memory" (LT-WM). According to them, individuals may become able to encode relevant information into LTM in such a manner that the information can be efficiently retrieved from LTM whenever it is subsequently needed. This ability is attained through the acquisition of specific skills ("memory skills") that control the way information is encoded in LTM and the way that selective access to the encoded information can be maintained. Although Cowan (Chapter 3, this volume) points to the similarity between LT-WM and virtual short-term memory (Cowan, 1995), there are several important differences between the two proposals. According to our reading, Cowan (1995) was primarily arguing that *retrieval* from long-term memory can in some cases "mimic the functioning of short-term memory" (p. 111). In particular, subjects can generate contextual retrieval cues that speed up retrieval from long-term memory in a manner similar to the spontaneous benefits of higher activation for retrieval from STM (Cowan, 1995, pp. 108, 132). In contrast, LT-WM offers a complete proposal for how subjects can acquire domain-specific working memory by acquiring skills to encode task-relevant information in LTM in such a manner that they can access it efficiently on demand during subsequent processing. When Ericsson and Kintsch (1995) proposed LT-WM, the primary controversy was not whether the accessibility of information retrieved from LTM could mimic that of STM – the prime concern in virtual STM – but rather whether it was possible with training to be able to rapidly encode information in LTM in a manner that successfully anticipates future retrieval demands during a specific task-related activity.

Memory is often likened to a filing system. When new information (documents) arrives, some of it is discarded and the rest is filed into folders based on content.[5] Filed information is indexed so that it can be found based on

---

[5] Although most people file only a single copy, it is possible to make several copies of something and file them in all relevant locations. Alternatively, one can file written notes indicating where other relevant pieces of information are filed.

topic or by searching through the most recently added items in a folder. For this system to work, information must be accurately indexed at filing time, which in turn requires accurate anticipation of the conditions under which it will later be used. When pieces of information are encountered, their relevance is (should be) monitored and appropriate associative updates with related tasks and plans are (should be) made at the time of the original exposure. Often, incoming information is directly integrated into a complex structure that is being generated in LTM, as in text comprehension. The methods for encoding and subsequent retrieval from LTM are consistent with a large body of knowledge about storage, retrieval, and interference in LTM, and the encodings and their subsequent retrieval can be viewed as deliberate efforts to capitalize on the encoding-specificity principle (Tulving & Thompson, 1973). In sum, depending on the specific working memory demands of the particular skilled activity, generated pieces of information are encoded associatively to elements in preexisting cognitive structures or integrated with other information into new structures or both. As long as elements of these structures remain activated in ST-WM, the subject retains access to the information, although the access may be indirect. When the subjects are forced to interrupt the performance of a task, activation decreases but the structures remain intact in LTM.[6] Upon resuming, the subjects can reinstate the relevant structures, most likely by first initiating the task-related strategies and then accessing associated structures.

On a general level, LT-WM is an integral part of the skilled procedures for performing the tasks in the associated domain of activity. In the same way that cognitive processes mediating skilled performance are acquired to meet the demands of the activity, so are the processes and retrieval structures that allow maintained access to all the relevant information. Given that the working memory demands differ among activities, so will the structure and the specific mechanisms of LT-WM. For example, some activities require keeping a large amount of information accessible for extended periods of time, as when playing several games of blindfold chess simultaneously. Other activities require the ability to manipulate one rapidly changing intermediate product, such as mentally adding long lists of large numbers with a mental abacus. Many other tasks require that experts do more than simply store information; they must plan or synthesize large amounts of information at once (Ericsson & Lehmann, 1996). Advanced chess players, for example, plan out the consequences of long sequences of exchanges in their minds prior to deciding on their next move. Medical experts reason about information about their patients to allow them to evaluate alternative diagnoses and select the most

---

[6] In those cases where temporal information is used to distinguish the most recently associated piece of information to a retrieval cue, an interruption will increase the effects of proactive interference and this might disable a successful reinstatement of all relevant information (see Ericsson & Kintsch, 1995).

appropriate one. Hence, a skill-based theory of working memory proposes how different types of working memory demands could be met by different types of mechanisms and how these mechanisms can be acquired as integral parts of the skilled performance.

The Expert-Performance Approach: Methods for Studying Exceptional Working Memory in Skilled and Expert Performance

The hypothesized tight coordination between the skilled procedures for executing a task and the methods for encoding and storage of intermediate products presents a fundamental challenge to psychological scientists. It is no longer possible to isolate the critical components of working memory without first considering their functional context in the corresponding skilled activities. Likewise, the information in LT-WM will be associatively connected to a great deal of preexisting knowledge in LTM. Many psychological scientists would argue that describing the structure of the cognitive processes employed during a skilled task, including the encoding and storage of information to be maintained in LTM, is a futile endeavor. Especially with traditional measures and experimental methods, these processes are simply too complex. When someone proposes to study skilled and expert working memory in everyday life, additional methodological issues emerge. Given that our goal is to understand working memory in these naturally occurring activities as well as the related phenomena of exceptional working memory reproduced in the laboratory, we will first briefly describe a successful approach addressing these methodological issues.

In everyday life, individual differences in skilled performance and LT-WM appear to be primarily attributable to a gradual adaptation to increased performance demands through skill acquisition. If we want to understand the limits of adaptation and attained skill, it is reasonable to search in everyday life for the highest levels of performance recorded and thus by implication the most extensive adaptation to stable task conditions. In our society, experts exhibit the highest level of performance and they do so in a highly reproducible fashion. Recent research on expert performance in many different domains has shown that it is possible to identify collections of tasks that can be administered under controlled laboratory conditions and still capture the essential aspects of the experts' superior performance (Ericsson & Smith, 1991). For example, the ability to consistently select the best next move for unfamiliar chess positions is the single best correlate of chess-playing ability as measured by results from participation in chess tournaments (De Groot, 1946/1978; Ericsson & Lehmann, 1996). Most significantly, the experts' superior performance can be repeatedly reproduced in the laboratory by sampling and presenting different tasks on different trials and even different sessions. When the laboratory tasks faithfully represent the natural conditions of performance in the domain, then one would not expect changes in performance of the experts owing to learning, because these experts have already invested years and even decades of deliberate practice to attain their highest level of performance (Ericsson & Lehmann, 1996). For our current purposes, the most important conclusion is that it is possible to reliably reproduce the large differences in performance between experts and less skilled performers under controlled conditions – the largest observable among healthy adults. Furthermore, the hallmarks of expert performance are very high accuracy, remarkable consistency, and frequently blinding speed. These features make it a very attractive scientific phenomenon for experimental analysis.

The complexity and the cognitive nature of the processes mediating the superior expert performance rules out the possibility of directly observing how the correct responses are generated. The cognitive processes have to be inferred using information from the structure of the task combined with observable behavior and indicators of the processes. Any specific task given to an expert or subject can be submitted to a task analysis, where the scientists logically analyze the presented information that has to be considered and the necessary knowledge along with essential inferences that would have to be made to consistently generate the correct response to that particular task (Ericsson & Oliver, 1988; Newell & Simon, 1972). By considering what kind of related knowledge and skills subjects might bring to the task, it is often possible to propose alternative models for how they produced the correct answer step by step. The complexity of expert performance makes such a task analysis difficult to complete and even more difficult to communicate to nonexperts, so instead let us illustrate this type of analysis for Baddeley's (1992) water-bottle problem. The correct answer could be generated by multiplying $1.80 by 3 and obtaining $5.40 ((3*0.8 = 2.40) + 3*1), which when subtracted from $10 yields an answer of $4.60 in change. Alternatively, a subject could add $1.80 to $1.80 (= $3.60) and add $1.80 to get $5.40 and then subtract that from $10. Yet another possible way is to subtract $1.80 three times from $10 to yield the following sequence of intermediate products: $8.20, $6.40, and $4.60. Each of these different possible solution methods or strategies can be described by a corresponding sequence of processing steps with associated states explicating the intermediate products and the information that has to be maintained to generate the answer.

Conceptions of the mechanisms of thinking differ greatly between philosophers and different theories of cognition. Ever since Aristotle, though, complex cognitive activities like thinking have uncontroversially been described as a sequence of thoughts (Ericsson & Crutcher, 1991). We can describe thinking in terms of a sequence of stable, often reportable, states (thoughts) separated by nonreportable transient activities involving pattern recognition, perception, and memory retrieval (Ericsson & Simon, 1993). Following Ericsson and Kintsch (1995), we will consider only the sequence of stable states (thoughts). Such a sequence of intermediate products has been illustrated in the top line of Figure 8.2.

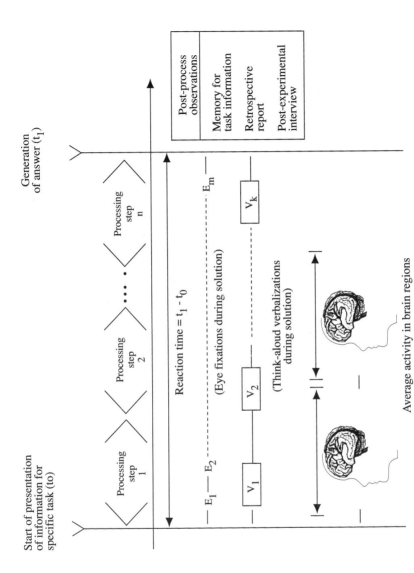

Figure 8.2. Different types of observations relevant to the sequence of thoughts mediating the successful production of the correct answer for a task.

Between the time a subject sees the problem description (t_0 in Figure 8.2) and when he gives the correct answer (t_1 in Figure 8.2), there are many potentially observable indicators of the underlying cognitive processes. The most commonly studied is the latency or time required to generate the answer. Under the assumption that the intermediate products are generated in sequence, the total time reflects the number of such component processing steps. However, from a small number of latencies it is impossible to infer the detailed strategy or solution method used. More information about individual solution processes is obtained by recordings of eye fixations and concurrent verbal reports. Although many alternative strategies yield distinctive predictions for the sequence by which subjects look at different pieces of information, the eye fixations cannot reveal what the subjects recall from memory nor think about independent of their immediate perceptions. The best method to monitor subjects' thinking is to instruct them to "think aloud," or in other words verbalize their current thoughts. When subjects are given standardized instructions and warm-ups, there is currently no evidence that "thinking aloud" alters the structure of their thinking as reflected in changes of accuracy of solutions. For some types of tasks, however, subjects' solution times increased somewhat because verbally expressing one's thoughts requires some time (Ericsson & Simon, 1993). Figure 8.2 also lists other related methods that are used to gather information about the subjects' thoughts while generating a solution, such as asking them to give an immediate retrospective report on what they can explicitly remember thinking during the trial. Finally, there are a number of physiological measures, such as EEG and images of neural activity in the brain. Drawing on Ericsson and Simon's (1993) recent review, we argue that verbal reports are the most informative valid indicator of sequences of thoughts on the task. For example, if a subject working on the water-bottle problem reported intermediate products, such as "8.20, 6.40, and 4.60," only one of the hypothesized solution methods could account for the subject's verbalization of those particular thoughts. In the following we will show that verbal reports provide us with sufficient information to produce hypotheses about the mechanisms that mediate the superior performance of specific experts and how these hypotheses have been confirmed by experiments that were designed specifically for each skilled subject (Ericsson, 1988). The concern that the superior performance of experts would be almost completely automated without any reportable intermediate thoughts has been shown to be unfounded by recent reviews (Ericsson & Lehmann, 1996; Ericsson & Simon, 1993). In fact, the locus of superiority in many types of expert performance concerns differences related to ability to plan, reason, and predict – tasks that place large demands on working memory.

The Acquisition and Use of Exceptional Working Memory

The expert-performance approach to working memory involves the search for phenomena in everyday life that appear to display the largest individual

Table 8.1 *Characteristic Differences Between the Digit Span Performance of Untrained Subjects and That of the Trained Digit Span Experts*

Property	Untrained S's	Digit Span Experts
Digit span at a rate of 1 digit/s	4–10	20–100
Correlation with spans for other rehearsable materials	Medium to high	Low/near zero
Effects of different presentation rates (3 digit/s to 0.3 digit/s)	Essentially none	Large effects
Postsession recall of digits	Very poor	Very good – often 90%+ recall

differences in working memory capacity. A good way to select the most amazing working memory feats is to ask ourselves to list what types of performance people are willing to pay to go and see. This list would include mental multiplication of large numbers, blindfold chess, and the ability to quickly memorize long sequences of digits. Of these, perhaps the simplest is the immediate recall of numbers (digit span). Since this task emerged as the most common measure of general basic memory capacity and of the phonological loop, it also provides us with a good way of comparing the three approaches we have discussed side by side. This is also the first domain where the dramatic effects of practice were directly observed in the laboratory. We will briefly review this work, discussing studies of individuals with alleged exceptional memory. We will then show how the same general types of mechanisms found originally in the context of immediate memory for digits mediate other types of expert performance with large demands for working memory.

THE DEVELOPMENT OF MEMORY SKILLS IN THE DIGIT SPAN TASK. When Chase and Ericsson (1981; Ericsson, Chase, & Faloon, 1980) became interested in the possibility of expanding STM (ST-WM) through practice, it was natural for them to select the digit span task for the reasons we have already discussed. They found that with repeated testing (practice), their subjects were able to dramatically improve their performance on the digit span task. After 50 hr of practice, all four subjects attained digit spans of 20 or more digits, and with additional practice two subjects attained spans over 80 digits (Chase & Ericsson, 1982; Ericsson, 1988; Staszewski, 1988).

If we considered only their performance on the task, it would be difficult to demonstrate that the digit span experts used qualitatively different mechanisms after practice as compared to before. However, when we consider the characteristics listed in Table 8.1, we find that the skilled performance shows marked qualitative differences. The trained subjects rely on storage in LTM and are able, during postsession recall, to reproduce most of the 200 to 300 digits presented during the trials of the session. Furthermore, trained subjects are sensitive to differences in presentation rate, and the elevated digit span performance is not associated with superior recall of other materials. These results show that qualitatively different processes can mediate performance on a task designed to measure a basic capacity.

The subjects' retrospective reports on their thought processes during the memory trials provided the primary evidence for changes in the subjects' encoding processes during the gradual increases in digit span performance across sessions. These reports showed that for the first few practice sessions, subjects rehearsed the digits, often in a grouped format, in a fashion similar to that observed for other untrained subjects. Eventually, the trained subjects started to deliberately associate the digits in the first group with their own preexisting knowledge. For example, "408" might be encoded as a time for running the mile – "8 seconds away from a 4-minute mile." After encoding the digits in the first group, they moved their attention to subsequent digits in the presented list, thus waiting to retrieve the initially encoded digit group until the recall period. With further practice, subjects were able to successfully encode several digit groups in a list, and by associating different spatial locations with each, they could later retrieve them in the correct order; for example, three-digit groups might be labeled as the one on the left, the middle one, and the rightmost one. At about this time, Chase and Ericsson (1981) designed an experiment to test the implications of one subject's (initials SF) verbally reported mnemonic encodings as running times for races. In one condition, they constructed lists consisting of three-digit groups that SF couldn't encode as running times; for example, "498" does not make sense as a mile time: "4 minutes and 98 seconds for a mile." They found that SF's performance on such lists was reduced to a level approaching his original digit span. However, some time after this experiment SF added new mnemonic encoding categories, and would have encoded "498" as an age "49. 8 – almost 50 years old." After further improvement, SF added a new layer of organization to his spatial structure for organizing retrieval cues associated with groups for a digit sequence of a given length – SF's retrieval structure for a 30-digit list is illustrated in Figure 8.3.

The validity of the reported retrieval structures has been demonstrated by a number of analyses of the temporal structure of the recall of the digit sequence, where pauses mark the transitions between groups (Ericsson et al., 1980; Richman, Staszewski, & Simon, 1995; Staszewski, 1988). However, the most distinctive evidence comes from studies of the ability to retrieve specific groups within the retrieval structure using cued recall. After a 30-digit sequence had been recalled, the experimenter would point to a specific location in a schematic diagram of the retrieval structure (similar to Figure 8.3) and ask the subject to recall the corresponding group or the groups preceding it, as fast as possible. Subjects could perform both these tasks and the inverse

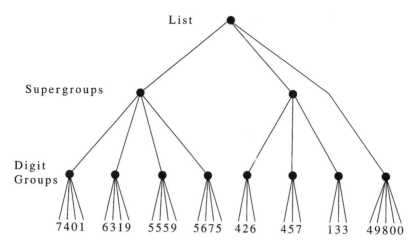

Figure 8.3. An illustration of the organization of the retrieval structure used by SF to encode lists of 30 digits.

task, pointing to where in the retrieval structure a given group of digits was stored, efficiently and accurately.

If, however, the same retrieval cues are repeatedly associated with different digit groups on different trials, subjects should have problems always retrieving only the most recently associated group. Ericsson and Kintsch (1995) reviewed the extensive evidence for this type of proactive interference, especially for the digit span experts, and discussed two general methods for overcoming that influence. First, the most recently stored item linked to an associate can, under some conditions, be distinguished on the basis of its temporal context (Baddeley & Hitch, 1993; see also Schneider's [Chapter 10, this volume] proposal for storage based on rapidly changing connection weights). Retrieval based primarily on recency appears to be particularly effective for the short storage times used in, for example, the frequent updating of partial sums during mental addition.

Alternatively, proactive interference from prior associations to retrieval cues can be minimized by generating unique, meaningful associations between the mnemonic encodings of digit groups (see Figure 8.4).[7] For example, the subject might encode that two adjacent digit groups are running times for the mile and that the first running time is slower than the following

---

[7] This account differs in several important ways from that proposed by Richman et al. (1995). The most salient difference with respect to Figure 8.4 is that Richman et al. argue that single digits can be associated with cues in the retrieval structure, whereas Chase and Ericsson (1982) and Ericsson and Kintsch (1995) claimed that each digit group had to be encoded semantically in LTM prior to associations to the retrieval structure and other encoded digit groups.

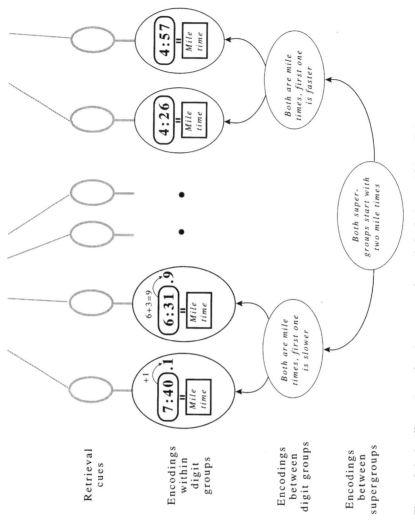

Figure 8.4. An illustration of various types of encoded relations within a digit group, between digit groups, and between supergroups.

one. The same subject might even encode associations at higher hierarchical levels, as in "the first supergroup contains two mile times followed by two ages, whereas the next supergroup consisted primarily of running times for the marathon and the 2-mile" (see Chase & Ericsson, 1982, and Staszewski, 1990, for actual examples). In this second method, the subject actively generates part of a structure that can augment encodings to cues in the retrieval structure. The subject could even generate a complete structure, exemplified in the use of the "story mnemonic" (Bower, 1972) and in text comprehension (Ericsson & Kintsch, 1995).

COMPARISON OF MEMORY EXPERTS WITH TRAINED SUBJECTS. The 10-fold increases in immediate memory for rapidly presented digits are not associated with increases in a general capacity of ST-WM (see Table 8.1). Instead, acquired memory skills allow efficient encoding of information in LTM and effective access to those items when they are needed to perform the task. We know that these skills are not automatically acquired as a consequence of experience with the task. Neither are they a direct consequence of years of experience with numbers or mental calculation; the digit spans of the world's best mental calculators are only about 15 digits (Ericsson, 1985).

The approach of searching for individuals with alleged exceptional memory should help us find those individuals with large generalized memory capacity, if they exist. Regardless of the benefits of extensive practice, an innately superior general memory capacity would be a significant advantage. Significantly, however, reviews of exceptional memory (Ericsson, 1985, 1988) show that the structure of "exceptional" subjects' performance is consistent with that of trained subjects, and that both types of subjects prefer to encode groups of 3 or 4 digits during rapid sequential presentation. When the digit span experts (Chase & Ericsson, 1981, 1982) used groups of 5 or 6 digits for the very last group of a list, the experts always used rehearsal to maintain the digits until these digits could be recoded as an association between a couple of different encodings. Similarly, the mathematics professor Rückle had a preference for 6-digit groups, but they were associations between two 3-digit groups often involving relations between numbers, such as that 451 and 697 are both multiples of 41 (Müller, 1911).

CAPACITY OF DIGIT SPAN EXPERTS AND SPECIFICITY OF THEIR MEMORY SKILLS. Exceptional digit span performance does not reflect increases in the basic capacity of ST-WM, and any description of the performance in terms of capacity is misleading. The "capacity" will in fact be influenced by many factors, among them the amount of time available to form associations and the type of recall required of the subjects. No single value for the "capacity" accurately describes the working memory resources available to these individuals; the "capacity" is a function of the particular characteristics of the encountered test situation.

Acquired memory skills are more adaptable than commonly thought and can mediate superior performance in a wide range of situations. For example,

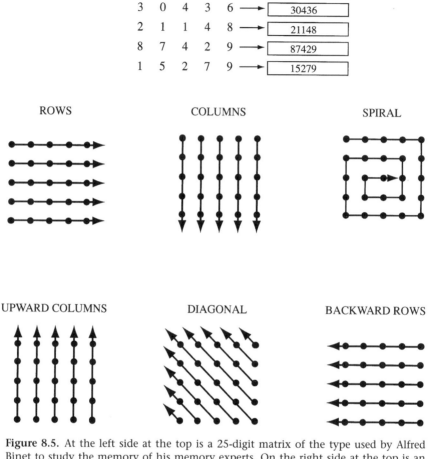

Figure 8.5. At the left side at the top is a 25-digit matrix of the type used by Alfred Binet to study the memory of his memory experts. On the right side at the top is an illustration of how experts and novices memorized this matrix as a series of digit groups with one group for each row. Binet asked his subjects to repeat the whole memorized matrix in the various orders shown as fast as they could.

without any specific training, the digit span experts were able to memorize matrices of digits like the one shown in Figure 8.5 and to retrieve the digits according to all of the prescribed orders of recall in a manner comparable to individuals with alleged exceptional memory. Detailed analyses (Ericsson & Chase, 1982) showed that all subjects, both trained and "exceptional," appear to encode each row of the matrix as a digit group, making recall by rows much faster than recall by columns (see Figure 8.5).

Several sources of evidence suggest that one source of such flexibility is the dynamic way that subjects apply their skills at the time of encoding. Subjects are not restricted to recognizing the exact patterns, such as particular running times, that are stored in their memories. Rather, new encodings based on such knowledge can be generated for individual digit groups (Ericsson & Chase, 1982). For example, in encoding "4237" SF was unable to distinguish it from other running times around 4 minutes and 20 seconds without using additional encodings relating the final two digits to the first two – in this particular case, "3 follows 2" and "4 + 3 = 7." Furthermore, during the encoding of just-presented digit groups, the subjects occasionally reported that they automatically retrieved similar digit groups that had been encoded in memory on prior trials in the same session. The retrieved digit group would share at least the first two digits and the same mnemonic category with the group being encoded. In further support of the strong association between the first couple of digits and the last digit of a group, Chase and Ericsson (1981) showed that SF could recall the last digit in a presented group with a probe like "423_ " virtually instantaneously, whereas a probe like "_237" would take 5 to 10 s and would normally involve self-generating the digits from 0 to 9 to see which one of the digits led to recognition.

Flexibility is still limited in this task and others by the availability of semantic cues and facility at manipulating those cues. Sometimes it is not the semantic structures themselves but access to those structures in the context of the domain that limits performance, as in the case of SF's difficulties encoding digit groups that did not make sense as running times, which only abated when he learned to use other familiar numbers such as ages during encoding (Chase & Ericsson, 1981). However, in other cases, even if one could train subjects to follow the same strategies for encoding information into LTM, individual differences in knowledge and, more generally, the structure and content of semantic memory would produce differences in memory performance. For example, when subjects have extensive (expert) knowledge about words, such as "quarterback" for football experts, then they can associate arbitrary words to those domain-relevant words better than for other words outside of their domain of expertise (Bellezza & Buck, 1988), presumably because of the experts' more elaborate and stable semantic representation of the concepts from their domain of expertise, which facilitate both storage of associations with new words and retrieval of those memory traces.

Long-Term Working Memory for Planning and Reasoning

It would be a serious mistake to focus on the mnemonic encodings and the hierarchical retrieval structure in the memory skills for digits as the essential elements of LT-WM. In fact, the mnemonic encoding is really a necessary crutch to allow the subjects to access their rich semantic memory containing patterns and knowledge for running times that permits them to encode digit groups and associations between them. Hence, if we were primarily interested in potential of LT-WM we should have changed the memory task so that it matched as closely as possible their prior knowledge and experience of memorizing sequences of running times for the same running distance, for example, presenting sequences of representative running times for immediate recall.

When our subjects were confronted with the unfamiliar task of memorizing digits in the laboratory, they searched around for existing knowledge and skills that they could use as building blocks in their acquired exceptional memory skill. In contrast, when subjects acquire skills under normal conditions, they acquire LT-WM as an integrated part of skill. The specific implementation of LT-WM will differ with the retrieval demands of the task and the subjects' existing semantic representations (Ericsson & Kintsch, 1995), and so no single example of LT-WM will suffice to show the entire range of potential mechanisms. Although it is beyond the scope of this chapter to detail all of the representations that have been observed, we will discuss a few theoretically interesting cases that illuminate other issues in working memory.

In most everyday activities such as cooking a meal, driving to a location, and reading a text, an experienced individual knows how to select the relevant information and encode it in LT-WM. With sufficient practice, one can reliably anticipate future relevance of information with its future usage to integrate selection, encoding, and subsequent retrieval into the acquired skill. However, there are cases in which even experts cannot fully anticipate the future use of encountered information. For example, when a doctor encounters a patient with a number of specific symptoms, when most of them suggest a single common diagnosis, it would be very efficient to encode the matching symptoms and the connecting associations to the diagnosis in LT-WM. Unfortunately, encoding only the matching symptoms in this way would make it nearly impossible for the doctor to revise the diagnosis in light of conflicting evidence encountered later. A skilled doctor, then, has to acquire a working memory representation that encodes the reported symptoms in such a way as to allow reasoning about all the relevant aspects of the symptoms in the context of several different diagnoses in an unbiased and invariant manner. One of the best examples of the difficulty of reinterpreting information already encoded in LTM is found for memory of visual figures (Finke, 1989; Reed, 1974). When subjects encode the star (see the left panel of Figure 8.6), they typically encode it in memory as two juxtaposed triangles. When they are later asked to judge from memory whether the presented figure contains a parallelogram, they are unable to generate a match because of the inconsistent patterns used in their original memory encoding. When the figure is perceptually available, though, alternative encodings can be generated – at least after some effort.

Similarly, any other effective representation for planning or evaluation should minimize the need for interpretation-biased semantic encoding of the information to be considered. The advantages of encoding items in memory

SOME POSSIBLE
MEMORY ENCODINGS

PRESENTED

Figure 8.6. On the left, a figure presented briefly to subjects. On the right, some alternative ways to encode the figure in memory with the most common one at the top.

using related patterns may be insufficient to offset the constraints imposed by the structure on the generation of alternative interpretations. Let us discuss the evidence from chess on the acquisition of LT-WM to support the possibility of exploring alternative courses of action through planning.

CHESS. Studies of how very skilled chess players generate superior moves for chess positions show that they rapidly "perceive" some alternative moves and then engage in planning and search to select the best one, or even to discover new and better moves (De Groot, 1946/1978). Although better chess players can recognize good moves without planning, if necessary (Calderwood, Klein, & Crandall, 1988; Gobet & Simon, 1996b), it is also true that when they have the time, searching reduces errors and improves the quality of their final move (Saariluoma, 1990, 1992; Gobet & Simon, 1996b). Even the world-class chess players studied by de Groot (1946/1978) would occasionally discover better moves by searching and planning.

If chess experts encoded chess positions solely in terms of familiar configurations (chunks), it would be quite difficult for them to explore the consequences of arbitrary combinations of moves. This would therefore hamper their ability to discover new moves and reinterpret situations. Therefore, for planning to be effective, it must allow the expert to encode and freely explore mentally generated chess positions for unbiased evaluation of weaknesses and promising move sequences.

Ericsson and Oliver (Ericsson & Staszewski, 1989) proposed that chess experts have acquired a retrieval structure representing the 64 locations of a chess board to supplement the pattern-based meaningful encodings of the chess position. In support of this hypothesis, they found that a chess master could rapidly retrieve information about the contents of individual locations and clusters of adjacent locations for a memorized chess position. More recently, Saariluoma (1989) found that chess masters were still able to commit a chess position to memory even when it was not displayed all at once in the traditional visual format. Saariluoma (1989) presented the chess position sequentially to his subjects as a list of all individual pieces with their respective locations on the chess board. Under these conditions, chess masters were able to recall most of the information in both regular chess positions and randomly arranged versions, provided that the presentation rate was sufficiently slow. In the beginning of this type of memory trial, the location of the initially presented chess pieces must be encoded virtually exclusively by direct association to the retrieval structure, because there are no opportunities for relational encodings with other chess pieces. Once more chess pieces have been presented, then opportunities for relational encodings emerge. Even for random positions, it is often possible to discover meaningful relations between presented pieces that share spatial relations. In a couple of experiments, Saariluoma (1989) showed that chess masters' superior memory for regular chess positions was due to the meaningful integration and storage of the entire chess positions in LTM, whereas recall of random positions seemed to reflect primarily associations to the retrieval structure that would be highly susceptible to retroactive interference.

The development of both the ability to store chess positions in LTM and the ability to plan several moves ahead parallels the increases in general chess-playing skill, at least up to the level of chess experts (Charness, 1989). Highly skilled chess players exhibit some amazing related skills. These chess players can recall much information from a rapid presentation of up to nine different chess positions (Cooke, Atlas, Lane, & Berger, 1993; Gobet & Simon, 1996c). They are also capable of playing blindfold chess – without a perceptually available chessboard – at a level not far below their normal strength (Holding, 1985; Karpov, 1995; Koltanowski, 1985). Saariluoma (1991) demonstrated that a grandmaster could, under blindfold conditions, maintain the chess positions for 10 simultaneous chess games in memory with virtually no errors. At the same time, these individuals' memory for randomly rearranged chess positions after a brief presentation is limited to around five pieces, or roughly the level of recall of normal chess positions by beginners at chess (Gobet & Simon, 1996a).

As with digit span experts, these specialized skills and the associated LT-WM do not appear as an inevitable consequence of extensive chess playing and tournament play. Rather, their acquisition is closely associated with the amount of deliberate study of chess alone (Charness, Krampe, & Mayr, 1996). From interviews with chess masters, Ericsson, Krampe, and Tesch-Römer (1993) found that aspiring chess players spent up to 4 h a day studying published chess games by world-class players. They would try to predict the next move made by the masters, and if a different move was predicted, then they would try to identify the reasons for the master's move by extensive planning and evaluation. Hence, the observed LT-WM of chess masters appears to be a slow adaptation to the demands of this and related forms of planning over years or even decades of deliberate practice.

Conclusions

The structure of acquired working memory mechanisms varies dramatically across domains because they are acquired to meet the specific working memory demands of different activities. Our ability to adapt to retrieval demands and thereby circumvent the usual limits introduced by ST-WM mechanisms does not imply that there are no constraints on working memory. The unique constraints that emerge center around the semantic structure of the domain and how information should be encoded and indexed to allow efficient access of all aspects relevant to the skilled activity. Furthermore, expert performers acquire flexible representations (LT-WM) to support planning, reasoning, and self-monitoring of their performance to allow them to adapt rapidly to changes in situational demands as well as keep improving their performance throughout their careers (Ericsson, 1996; Ericsson & Lehmann, 1996). The difficulty of acquiring these representations through deliberate practice provides a plausible explanation for the need for 10 years of preparation before achieving the highest level of performance in many domains (Simon & Chase, 1973; Ericsson et al., 1993).

Toward an Integrated Perspective on Working Memory

Our brief review of different approaches to the study of working memory suggests a few, we hope relatively uncontroversial, conclusions – at least if we constrain ourselves to skilled and expert activities. First, it is possible to reliably measure individual differences in transient working memory capacity (ST-WM), but these differences appear to be almost unrelated to performance in everyday skilled activities for adults in the normal range of intellectual functioning. Second, concurrent tasks that interfere with information stored in ST-WM decrease performance on some complex laboratory tasks, but the interference from similar procedures on many types of expert performance has been negligible.[8] Finally, studies of the cognitive processes mediating exceptional working memory show that working memory in these activities is primarily mediated by skilled access to LT-WM rather than to ST-WM. In fact, in these skilled activities the encountered information is semantically encoded and immediately related to other presented information as well as elements of the structures of the skilled activities. Under those conditions, the number of independent chunks or structures maintained in ST-WM is no longer a meaningful concept.

In this section we will try to integrate the evidence on working memory for unfamiliar and skilled activities by reviewing research attempting to trace the cognitive processes involved in tasks measuring basic capacity of memory and in tasks measuring reserve capacity while performing a familiar task. In our discussion we will propose ways that the behavioral evidence cited in support of individual difference in attention and transient working memory capacity could be explained within the theoretical framework of LT-WM.

Working Memory in the Performance of Laboratory Tasks

Why don't the individual differences in basic working memory capacity measured in the laboratory play a more significant role in skilled activities in everyday life? When the subjects have to confront tasks with arbitrary information, they adopt special methods, such as mnemonic encoding and rehearsal, rather than rely on some truly basic memory capacity. Even scientists contemporary with Ebbinghaus immediately criticized his claim that only basic processes were involved and presented evidence for grouping, spatial encoding of location, and mnemonic associations to knowledge (see Woodworth, 1938, for an excellent review). Subsequent research reviewed by

---

[8] When we exclude skills that rely on temporal cues to distinguish the most recently encoded association as in mental calculation and abacus calculation (Ericsson & Kintsch, 1995).

Montague (1972) dispelled the belief in the "nonsense" syllable and showed large differences in the rated meaningfulness of such syllables, which in turn predicted the speed of memorization. The ratings were closely related to verbal reports of mnemonic encoding with natural language mediators, such as ZYQ → "not sick," XAJ → "XAJerate," and MIB → "MIBery" (by analogy to misery) (Miller, Galanter, & Pribram, 1960).

Based on our review of expert performance, we found that neither mnemonic encoding nor rehearsal is typically useful in skilled everyday activities. The main problem with both methods is that the encoding of the presented information is not semantically appropriate for the performance of the task at hand. When information has been encoded phonologically or with an unrelated mnemonic, a desired piece of relevant information cannot be accessed by a semantic cue,[9] which forces the subject to search for the information sequentially. A striking example of useless mnemonic encodings is provided by a student training her memory for briefly presented chess positions (Ericsson & Harris, 1990). The student had essentially no knowledge of chess, but within 50 h she was able to match chess experts' recall of regular chess positions by encoding configurations of chess pieces with mnemonics; for example, noticing that a pawn chain looks like a familiar object. This memory skill would be worthless to a skilled chess player because it doesn't provide effective access to information about attack/defense relations necessary for both planning and reasoning about chess positions. The small number of documented examples of expert performers actually using mnemonics or rehearsal is consistent with the usefulness of the phonological loop as a temporary buffer for presented information prior to task-appropriate encodings (cf. Ericsson & Polson, 1988) and with the effectiveness of unrelated mnemonic encodings for the sole purpose of storage in contexts with massive interference (cf. storage during mental multiplication: Chase & Ericsson, 1982; Dansereau, 1969). These observations suggest that people don't rely on ST-WM and rehearsal in skilled everyday activities involving comprehension and semantic encodings – with only a small number of exceptions.

Why is the use of mnemonic encoding and especially rehearsal so common in laboratory studies when it is so rare in everyday life? Research on concept formation, problem solving, and decision making also uses unfamiliar tasks to be able to study general basic processes without the influence of specific knowledge and related experience. The general approach has been to design the simplest tasks possible that would produce the associated behavioral phenomena in their most general and pure form. To attain maximal generalizability, experimenters use abstract or arbitrary variables and present all logically

---

[9] Research on the speed and accuracy of recognition is not very relevant to working memory because the issue that is critical for successful performance concerns the efficient retrieval of desired information at the appropriate processing stages. In contrast, tests of recognition present the item to the subject, thus eliminating the problem of retrieving it.

possible combinations of stimulus values. For example, early work on concept formation asked subjects to infer logical rules from a long series of positive and negative instances of general features, such as a red large circle, a blue small triangle, and a green small square. Under such conditions subjects encounter large amounts of proactive interference from previously seen instances and are thus virtually unable to remember specific instances. Consequently, they adopt a strategy of maintaining their hypothesis by rehearsal. The similarity of states and tasks in studies of problem solving and decision making also frequently produce proactive interference, leading many subjects to maintain only a small amount of information by rehearsal (Kintsch & Ericsson, 1996).

In sum, the traditional bias toward explaining most of variance in performance by reference to individual differences in basic working memory capacity is inconsistent with current empirical evidence. Even for unfamiliar activities in which subjects lack relevant knowledge and extensive experience to acquire LT-WM, they rely on general mechanisms such as rehearsal and actively encode information with patterns and remote mnemonic associations to their prior knowledge. Future theories of working memory need to consider evidence from process tracing and should consider a broader range of potential mechanisms for working memory in performance whether it concerns highly skilled activities or behavior on an unfamiliar task encountered for the first time.

Individual Differences in Working Memory and Their Implications for Performance

Most architectures that implement simulation models of skilled performance clearly distinguish the storage of the general procedures for completing the task (production rules) from the transient storage of information (ST-WM) – but see Young and Lewis (Chapter 7, this volume) and Kieras, Meyer, Mueller, and Seymour (Chapter 6, this volume) for interesting exceptions. Furthermore, within these general architectures it is generally assumed that working memory capacity (ST-WM) has a fixed capacity but that the amount of working memory capacity will likely differ between individuals (Just & Carpenter, 1992; Shah & Miyake, 1996; also see Lovett, Reder, & Lebiere, Chapter 5, this volume). The standard method for measuring individuals' capacity engages the subjects in a representative task in the corresponding domain to assess their "spare working memory capacity," as exemplified by the reading span task (Daneman & Carpenter, 1980). Under these test conditions the subjects' ability to maintain additional information would have to reflect ST-WM capacity, essentially by default, as long as storage in LTM was excluded as impossible on theoretical grounds. However, recent empirical demonstrations of storage in LTM and LT-WM allow us to question the inference that the reading span task and other related tasks necessarily measure ST-WM and even take issue with the modal view of a strict separation between strategy/productions and working memory capacity.

How do subjects simultaneously maintain information, such as a sequence of words, while they perform a different task, as in, for example, the reading span test? It is at least theoretically possible that the to-be-remembered words are maintained by the activation they received automatically at presentation without any additional intentional efforts to encode the presented words in the reading span test. However, research by Engle, Cantor, and Carullo (1992) shows that subjects, especially high-IQ subjects, allocate their attention strategically toward the presented words when they are instructed to remember them. We, furthermore, propose that subjects encode and store the presented words at the time of presentation as elaborations of other information stored in LT-WM during the performance of the primary task, such as the meaning of the presented sentences, or by generating meaningful associations to previously presented words, or by some combination of different types of associations. This hypothesis of storage in LTM is consistent with evidence from experimental studies of performance on the reading span test (see Ericsson & Kintsch, 1995, for a brief review) and the participants' verbal reports of their active encoding operations (Daneman & Carpenter, 1980). Within the LT-WM account, individual differences in "spare working memory capacity" would then primarily reflect differences in ability to encode efficiently the presented words in LTM along with appropriate associations to allow subsequent retrieval at recall.

The LT-WM account of individual differences in the reading span test and other similar tests is attractive and parsimonious. It explains the test performance with reference to the same types of mechanisms that mediate LT-WM during normal representative activities, such as reading texts. In their review of text comprehension, Ericsson and Kintsch (1995) found that the evidence was consistent with the generation of new integrated structures in LTM where sustained access to relevant information was attained with retrieval cues. Individual differences in comprehension were found to depend on the availability of at least two factors to maintain appropriate access to relevant information (cf. situation model), namely appropriate encoding skills and relevant knowledge for efficient storage. Early studies indicated that knowledge was the primary factor influencing comprehension of texts in restricted domains of expertise, such as baseball and soccer (for a review, see Ericsson & Kintsch, 1995). However, more recent studies (Adams, Bell, & Perfetti, 1995; Schneider, Bjorklund, & Maier-Brüker, 1996; Singer & Ritchot, 1996) show effects of both knowledge and encoding skills (verbal ability). This makes sense, because it is not only domain-specific knowledge that is relevant. General knowledge about language, such as vocabulary, different senses of words, and available syntactical constructions, reflected in the subjects' semantic memory also influences the quality of comprehension and the constructed representations in LT-WM (Ericsson & Kintsch, 1995). In fact, if the measure of "spare working memory capacity" primarily reflects differences in the amount of relevant knowledge and the structure of the mediating representations and skills, then this hypothesis alone may well provide a parsimonious account of the main findings: the large correlations with different performance in a broad category of tasks sharing the same type of mental representations and LT-WM, such as tasks involving language or spatial processing (Just & Carpenter, 1992; Shah & Miyake, 1996), as well as the surprisingly low correlations with other types of performance in the same general domain (Carpenter, Miyake, & Just, 1994) that would not share the same representations and LT-WM.

In conclusion, any comprehensive theory of working memory needs to able to account for WM in the full range of human activities shown in Figure 8.1. At one extreme we have the participation in laboratory tasks that have been deliberately designed to minimize the relevance of past experience and knowledge. At the other extreme we have the international level of performance by experts in various domains of expertise. Clearly, we need to describe how individuals' performance is incrementally improved from the level of the beginner to that of the international expert. The evidence we reviewed suggests that the traditional view of expert performance as a mere accumulation of knowledge and automatization of production rules within an information-processing system with invariant basic capacities is wrong. Indeed, Ericsson and Lehmann (1996) found in their review that experts' memory for task-relevant processing increases with increased performance, rather than decreasing as the automatization view would predict. The review also showed that experts had acquired memory skills to represent and evaluate complex plans for future courses of action that also allowed them to monitor their performance and to reason and reflect on how they can improve it. LT-WM provides one account of how experts could increase the amount and quality of information they can consider while engaging in representative activities from their domain. Theories of working memory in skilled activities need to develop more comprehensive mechanisms than they typically do. In fact, Engle et al.'s (Chapter 4, this volume) claim that our framework cannot explain individual differences in concurrent memory performance once the difficulty of the primary task (mental arithmetic) is held constant across subjects presumes that the methods used by more-skilled subjects are simply faster, less resource-demanding versions of those used by less-skilled subjects. In contrast, we argue for the need to consider the acquisition of qualitatively different mediating mechanisms, such as LT-WM.

At the same time we need to propose theoretical accounts for how individuals are able to successfully engage in unfamiliar or infrequently encountered activities when they lack the acquired specific skills and knowledge to support working memory. In such cases they must rely on more general methods and generalizable encodings that Baddeley and Logie (Chapter 2, this volume) have so carefully described. Furthermore, individuals would need to rely on general types of working memory mechanisms as they initially acquire their skills and LT-WM, as well as when they subsequently refine the quality of their encodings and semantic representations. Only by integrating the theoretical perspectives can one attain a comprehensive account of working memory in all types of human activities.

Concluding Remarks

We have summarized our position in Table 8.2 to facilitate comparison with other theoretical models. Unlike many other definitions of working memory, our recommended definition is sufficiently general to encompass all types of mechanisms that provide selective access to a very small number of cognitive structures and procedures necessary to complete a task and to distinguish these structures from the massive amount of other information and knowledge stored in any individual's LTM. In our brief historical overview, we showed how pioneering researchers have explored more restricted aspects of this general phenomenon, and we demonstrated how different approaches to the study of working memory were guided by intuitive ideas about the major underlying mechanisms. First came Ebbinghaus's efforts to study general processes and basic capacities with "nonsense" material, allowing him to disregard all the knowledge and accumulated experience in the subjects' LTM. Then the information-processing models explicated all the knowledge and procedures necessary to complete the task in LTM and assumed initially a single distinct STM with a fixed capacity as transient storage for intermediate results. Within the last couple of decades, investigators have come to view working memory as a more diverse system (Baddeley, 1986) in which transient storage corresponds to the minute portion of LTM that is activated at a given time (Shiffrin, 1976).

Today, the primary models of working memory provide accounts for storage of intermediate results (ST-WM) in terms of transient activation because storage in LTM was prematurely precluded on theoretical grounds (Ericsson & Kintsch, 1995). The notion of LT-WM takes a few more steps toward our broader definition of WM. First, it outlines the restricted conditions under which subjects can meet the demands for working memory through storage and sustained access to information in LTM. Second, it questions the strict distinction between procedures (cf. production rules) and storage of information and proposes how storage in LT-WM can be attained by an integration of procedures and working memory in LTM (see also Kieras et al., Chapter 6, this volume; O'Reilly et al., Chapter 11, this volume). The latter finding of the close integration between storage and procedures in skilled activities raises the issue of how selective access to the relevant procedures for performing the task is accomplished – an issue that needs to be considered in future research.

The most important implication of viewing working memory as acquired skills is not the rejection of fixed constraints on basic capacity but its affirmative proposal for *alternative constraints* in terms of the acquisition of prerequisite structures necessary for efficient encoding and sustained access to relevant information during skilled activities. These new constraints are theo-

Table 8.2. *Answers to Designated Questions*

(1) Basic Mechanisms and Representations in Working Memory
To complete any task subjects need to maintain selective access to relevant
procedures and presented, retrieved, and generated information by distinguishing that information from the vast amount of other knowledge and procedures stored in LTM. Our definition of working memory includes all
different mechanisms that allow subjects to control and selectively access relevant information during the sequence of stable cognitive states. In particular, subjects can maintain access to information in skilled activities by
encoding it in LTM in such a way that it can efficiently be retrieved from
LTM whenever it is subsequently needed for the task.

(2) The Control and Regulation of Working Memory
As part of the acquisition of skilled performance in a task domain, people
acquire a set of skills (LT-WM) that enable them to anticipate the retrieval
demands for information in that task environment and then to store the
relevant information in a fashion that allows its access with appropriate
cues. Many different types of methods for encoding/retrieval are possible,
such as access based on temporal recency cues, on associations to explicit
retrieval structures, and on associations to generated elaborated cognitive
structures. In unfamiliar laboratory tasks subjects lack the acquired skills
and knowledge and tend to rely on general-purpose methods for maintenance of information in working memory such as phonemic rehearsal and
mnemonic encoding in LTM.

(3) The Unitary Versus Non-Unitary Nature of Working Memory
In skilled activities, working memory in the form of LT-WM is acquired to
meet the specific retrieval demands of the particular tasks involved in the
activity, which are primarily semantic in nature and therefore are usually useful only in those tasks (that is, LT-WM is typically domain specific). However,
some representations that support planning cannot be completely semantically encoded because reinterpretation would be impeded by such an encoding. Instead, they are supplemented with hierarchical and spatial retrieval
structures that could potentially be adapted for use in other activities. When
more semantically appropriate working memory methods are unavailable, as
in the case of unfamiliar laboratory tasks, individuals might instead rely on
more general – but not universally applicable – methods such as phonemic
rehearsal or mnemonic encoding in LTM. Results that have been taken to
indicate specific capacities for particular types of material may actually indicate that different processes are relevant to the task rather than that the
underlying cognitive machinery relies on separate capacity-based systems.

(4) The Nature of Working Memory Limitations
There is no universal capacity limit for how much information can be kept
accessible during the performance of a specific task. During the development
of the skilled performance for a task domain, the mechanisms mediating
encoding and retrieval with LT-WM are acquired to meet the retrieval

Table 8.2, continued

demands of the domain. Furthermore, demands for higher levels of performance lead to deliberate efforts to refine representations with associated improvements of working memory in support of monitoring, planning, and evaluation of performance. For unfamiliar laboratory tasks the limits of working memory will reflect the limits of the remaining applicable methods such as phonemic rehearsal, chunking, and mnemonic encoding in LTM.

(5) **The Role of Working Memory in Complex Cognitive Activities**
Long-term working memory is the theoretical generalization of analyses of expert performance in many different task domains that are known to have unusually high demands of working memory. Ericsson and Kintsch (1995) showed that the same types of mechanisms of working memory mediate skilled activities in everyday life.

(6) **The Relationship of Working Memory to Long-Term Memory and Knowledge**
Working memory during skilled performance reflects an aspect of complex skills specifically acquired to meet the particular demands of future accessibility for information for tasks within a particular domain of expertise. Domain-relevant skills, knowledge, and procedures for the task are so tightly integrated into the skills for encoding of information that the traditional separation among memory, knowledge, and procedures cannot be meaningfully made. However, skilled activities involving planning and reasoning require representations that allow systematic exploration of possibilities and in which the initial semantic encoding has to be restricted to allow more independent evaluation and reinterpretation of information.

(7) **The Relationship of Working Memory to Attention and Consciousness**
Information in the subjects' attention is only a small special subset of the information that they are able to keep selectively accessible for further processing during skilled performance (cf. Cowan, Chapter 3, this volume). Concurrent verbal reports and think-aloud protocols provide the most informative data on the particular sequence of attended information and heeded thoughts during a specific subject's performance for the task.

(8) **The Biological Implementation of Working Memory**
The acquired nature of LT-WM, its dependence on storage in LTM, and its tight integration with semantic memory and the specific strategies for completing tasks in the domain will make efforts to localize working memory difficult. However, skilled activities involving spatially based retrieval structures may well rely on particular subsystems of the brain that could be identified (cf. O'Reilly et al., Chapter 11, this volume). The more general mechanisms for working memory for unfamiliar tasks and information are likely to be much more closely linked to specific subsystems (cf. Baddeley & Logie, Chapter 2, this volume).

retically powerful enough to explain both the complex representations used by experts to plan, reason, and evaluate alternative future actions and at the same time the struggling efforts by the same subjects to solve unfamiliar tasks in the laboratory. They also provide new conceptual tools for discussing a broader range of mechanisms mediating selective access to both procedures and relevant information not seriously considered by most earlier computational theories of ST-WM. The traditional conception of working memory as "temporary storage of intermediate results" led investigators to focus on the stable application of procedures in well-defined tasks disregarding the initial phase when subjects warm up and select their strategies. Given the arbitrary nature of most laboratory tasks, it is very unlikely that subjects can simply retrieve and apply a preexisting well-entrenched procedure. Hence, during the instructional and warm-up phases of experiments and psychometric tests, subjects must retrieve and integrate relevant procedures and skills to attain an accurate and efficient test performance. An analysis of these early phases of the generation of integrated strategies for unfamiliar tasks will allow us to assess the structure of these constructed strategies and how they are maintained in working memory – that is, how selective access to these specific strategies as opposed to the vast number of other procedures in LTM is maintained. An analysis of these phases will be critical to an understanding of how more-proficient subjects are consistently able to generate more-efficient strategies than less-proficient ones (Bjorklund & Schneider, 1996; Bors & MacLeod, 1996; Just & Carpenter, 1985). From our perspective, it would be interesting to explore the characteristics of the planning representations that allow the more-able students to retrieve and assemble superior strategies to examine potential similarities to mechanisms and representations uncovered from the study of expert performers. We believe that collecting process traces for single subjects across a series of different tasks will offer especially rich evidence on the selection and active maintenance of procedures and their associated LT-WM. For example, future accounts of working memory must provide explanations for subjects' ability to efficiently resume earlier activities after very demanding interactions with an intervening task. In sum, the real promise of LT-WM becomes apparent when we consider the full range of general phenomena of working memory that have to be accounted for by any complete model of performance on laboratory tasks. Whereas the traditional models of ST-WM could not easily be extended toward such complete accounts, we believe that the mechanisms of LT-WM can account for the ability to selectively maintain access to large bodies of information that are essential to perform adaptively under both laboratory and everyday conditions.

Although LT-WM was initially developed to account for expert and skilled performance, we have tried to extend its mechanisms to account for working memory in many everyday activities. In accordance with that view, limits on performance would not reflect invariant basic constraints on working memory capacity but rather the interaction between the representations, the procedures, and the knowledge that together constitute the skill. Regardless of whether the specific mechanisms proposed by LT-WM need to be replaced or extended, our proposal will raise new issues about the nature of individual differences and the relationship between novice and skilled performance.

REFERENCES

Adams, B. C., Bell, L. C., & Perfetti, C. A. (1995). A trading relationship between reading skill and domain knowledge in children's text comprehension. *Discourse Processes, 20,* 307–323.

Baddeley, A. D. (1986). *Working memory.* New York: Oxford University Press.

Baddeley, A. D. (1992). Working memory. In L. R. Squire (Ed.), *The encyclopedia of learning and memory.* New York: Macmillan.

Baddeley, A. D., & Hitch, G. J. (1974). Working memory. In G. H. Bower (Ed.), *The psychology of learning and motivation: Advances in research and theory* (Vol. 8, pp. 47–89). New York: Academic Press.

Baddeley, A. D., & Hitch, G. J. (1993). The recency effect: Implicit learning with explicit retrieval? *Memory & Cognition, 21,* 146–155.

Bellezza, F. S., & Buck, D. K. (1988). Expert knowledge as mnemonic cues. *Applied Cognitive Psychology, 2,* 147–162.

Bjorklund, D. F., & Schneider, W. (1996). The interaction of knowledge, aptitude, and strategies in children's memory performance. *Advances in Child Development and Behavior, 26,* 59–89.

Bors, D. A., & MacLeod, C. M.(1996). Individual differences in memory. In E. L. Bjork & R. A. Bjork (Eds.), *Memory* (pp. 411–441). San Diego: Academic Press.

Bower, G. H. (1972). Mental imagery and associative learning. In L. W. Gregg (Ed.), *Cognition in learning and memory* (pp. 51–88). New York: Wiley.

Broadbent, D. E. (1975). The magic number seven after fifteen years. In A. Kennedy & A. Wilkes (Eds.), *Studies in long-term memory* (pp. 3–18). London: Wiley.

Calderwood, R., Klein, G. A., & Crandall, B. W. (1988). Time pressure, skill, and move quality in chess. *American Journal of Psychology, 101,* 481–493.

Carpenter, P. A., Miyake, A., & Just, M. A. (1994). Working memory constraints in comprehension: Evidence from individual differences, aphasia, and aging. In M. A. Gernsbacher (Ed.), *Handbook of psycholinguistics* (pp. 1075–1122). San Diego: Academic Press.

Carroll, J. B. (1993). *Human cognitive abilities: A survey of factor-analytic studies.* New York: Cambridge University Press.

Charness, N. (1976). Memory for chess positions: Resistance to interference. *Journal of Experimental Psychology: Human Learning and Memory, 2,* 641–653.

Charness, N. (1989). Expertise in chess and bridge. In D. Klahr & K. Kotovsky (Eds.), *Complex information processing: The impact of Herbert A. Simon* (pp. 183–208). Hillsdale, NJ: Erlbaum.

Charness, N., Krampe, R., & Mayr, U. (1996). The role of practice and coaching in entrepreneurial skill domains: An international comparison of life-span chess skill acquisition. In K. A. Ericsson (Ed.), *The road to excellence: The acquisition of expert performance in the arts and sciences, sports, and games* (pp. 51–80). Mahwah, NJ: Erlbaum.

Chase, W. G., & Ericsson, K. A. (1981). Skilled memory. In J. R. Anderson (Ed.), *Cognitive skills and their acquisition* (pp. 141–189). Hillsdale, NJ: Erlbaum.

Chase, W. G., & Ericsson, K. A. (1982). Skill and working memory. In G. H. Bower (Ed.), *The psychology of learning and motivation* (Vol. 16, pp. 1–58). New York: Academic Press.

Chase, W. G., & Simon, H. A. (1973). Perception in chess. *Cognitive Psychology, 4*, 55–81.

Cooke, N. J., Atlas, R. S., Lane, D. M., & Berger, R. C. (1993). Role of high-level knowledge in memory for chess positions. *American Journal of Psychology, 106*, 321–351.

Cowan, N. (1995). *Attention and memory: An integrated framework*. New York: Oxford University Press.

Crowder, R. G. (1993). Short-term memory: Where do we stand? *Memory & Cognition, 21*, 142–145.

Daneman, M., & Carpenter, P. A. (1980). Individual differences in working memory and reading. *Journal of Verbal Learning and Verbal Behavior, 19*, 450–466.

Daneman, M., & Merikle, P. M. (1996). Working memory and language comprehension: A meta-analysis. *Psychonomic Bulletin & Review, 3*, 422–433.

Dansereau, D. F. (1969). An information processing model of mental multiplication. *Dissertation Abstracts International, 30*, 1916B (University Microfilms No. 69–15746).

de Groot, A. (1978). *Thought and choice in chess*. The Hague: Mouton. (Original work published 1946.)

Dempster, F. N. (1981). Memory span: Sources of individual and developmental differences. *Psychological Bulletin, 89*, 63–100.

Ebbinghaus, H. (1964/1885). *Memory: A contribution to experimental psychology* (H. A. Ruger & C. E. Bussenius, Trans.). New York: Dover. (Original work published 1885.)

Engle, R. W., Cantor, J., & Carullo, J. J. (1992). Individual differences in working memory and comprehension: A test of four hypotheses. *Journal of Experimental Psychology: Learning, Memory, and Cognition, 18*, 972–992.

Ericsson, K. A. (1985). Memory skill. *Canadian Journal of Psychology, 39*, 188–231.

Ericsson, K. A. (1988). Analysis of memory performance in terms of memory skill. In R. J. Sternberg (Ed.), *Advances in the psychology of human intelligence* (Vol. 5, pp. 137–179). Hillsdale, NJ: Erlbaum.

Ericsson, K. A. (1996). The acquisition of expert performance: An introduction to some of the issues. In K. A. Ericsson (Ed.), *The road to excellence: The acquisition of expert performance in the arts and sciences, sports, and games* (pp. 1–50). Mahwah, NJ: Erlbaum.

Ericsson, K. A., & Charness, N. (1994). Expert performance: Its structure and acquisition. *American Psychologist, 49*, 725–747.

Ericsson, K. A., & Chase, W. G. (1982). Exceptional memory. *American Scientist, 70*, 607–615.

Ericsson, K. A., Chase, W. G., & Faloon, S. (1980). Acquisition of a memory skill. *Science, 208*, 1181–1182.

Ericsson, K. A., & Crutcher, R. J. (1991). Introspection and verbal reports on cognitive processes – two approaches to the study of thinking: A response to Howe. *New Ideas in Psychology, 9*, 57–71.

Ericsson, K. A., & Harris, M. S. (1990). *Expert chess memory without chess knowledge: A training study*. Poster presented at the 31st Annual Meeting of the Psychonomic Society, New Orleans, LA.

Ericsson, K. A., & Kintsch, W. (1995). Long-term working memory. *Psychological Review, 102,* 211–245.

Ericsson, K. A., Krampe, R. Th., & Tesch-Römer, C. (1993). The role of deliberate practice in the acquisition of expert performance. *Psychological Review, 100,* 363–406.

Ericsson, K. A., & Lehmann, A. C. (1996). Expert and exceptional performance: Evidence for maximal adaptations to task constraints. *Annual Review of Psychology, 47,* 273–305.

Ericsson, K. A., & Oliver, W. (1988). Methodology for laboratory research on thinking: Task selection, collection of observations, and data analysis. In R. J. Sternberg & E. E. Smith (Eds.), *The psychology of human thought* (pp. 392–428). New York: Cambridge University Press.

Ericsson, K. A., & Polson, P. G. (1988). A cognitive analysis of exceptional memory for restaurant orders. In M. T. H. Chi, R. Glaser, & M. J. Farr (Eds.), *The nature of expertise* (pp. 23–70). Hillsdale, NJ: Erlbaum.

Ericsson, K. A., & Simon, H. A. (1993). *Protocol analysis: Verbal reports as data* (Rev. ed.). Cambridge, MA: MIT Press.

Ericsson, K. A., & Smith, J. (1991). Prospects and limits of the empirical study of expertise: An introduction. In K. A. Ericsson & J. Smith (Eds.), *Toward a general theory of expertise: Prospects and limits* (pp. 1–38). New York: Cambridge University Press.

Ericsson, K. A., & Staszewski, J. (1989). Skilled memory and expertise: Mechanisms of exceptional performance. In D. Klahr & K. Kotovsky (Eds.), *Complex information processing: The impact of Herbert A. Simon* (pp. 235–267). Hillsdale, NJ: Erlbaum.

Finke, R. A. (1989). *Principles of mental imagery.* Cambridge, MA: MIT Press.

Fischer, B., & Glanzer, M. (1986). Short-term storage and the processing of cohesion during reading. *Quarterly Journal of Experimental Psychology, 38A,* 431–460.

Glanzer, M., & Nolan, S. D. (1986). Memory mechanisms in text comprehension. In G. H. Bower (Ed.), *The psychology of learning and motivation* (pp. 275–317). New York: Academic Press.

Gobet, F., & Simon, H. A. (1996b). The roles of recognition processes and look-ahead search in time-constrained expert problem-solving: Evidence from grand-master-level chess. *Psychological Science, 7,* 52–55.

Gobet, F., & Simon, H. A. (1996a). Recall of rapidly presented random chess positions is a function of skill. *Psychonomic Bulletin & Review, 3,* 159–163.

Gobet, F. & Simon, H. A. (1996c). Templates in chess memory: A mechanism for recalling several boards. *Cognitive Psychology, 31,* 1–40.

Holding, D. H. (1985). *The psychology of chess skill.* Hillsdale, NJ: Erlbaum.

Just, M. A., & Carpenter, P. A. (1985). Cognitive coordinate systems: Accounts of mental rotation and individual differences in spatial ability. *Psychological Review, 92,* 137–172.

Just, M. A., & Carpenter, P. A. (1992). A capacity theory of comprehension: Individual differences in working memory. *Psychological Review, 99,* 122–149.

Karpov, A. (1995). Grandmaster musings. *Chess Life.* November, pp. 32–33.

Kintsch, W., & Ericsson, K. A. (1996). Die kognitive Funktion des Gedächtnisses. In D. Albert & K. H. Stapf (Eds.), *Enzyklopädie der Psychologie, Themenbereich C: Theorien und Forschung, Serie II: Kognition, Band 4: Gedächtnis, Kapitel 8* (pp. 541–601). Göttingen, Germany: Hofgrefe.

Kliegl, R., Smith, J., Heckhausen, J., & Baltes, P. B. (1987). Mnemonic training for the acquisition of skilled digit memory. *Cognition and Instruction, 4,* 203–223.

Koltanowski, G. (1985). *In the dark.* Corapolis, PA: Chess Enterprises.

Logan, G. D. (1988). Toward an instance theory of automatization. *Psychological Review, 95,* 492-527.

Logan, G. D. (1991). Automaticity and memory. In W. E. Hockley & S. Lewandowsky (Eds.), *Relating theory and data: Essays on human memory in honor of Bennet B. Murdock* (pp. 347–366). Hillsdale, NJ: Erlbaum.

Martin, R. C. (1993). Short-term memory and sentence processing: Evidence from neuropsychology. *Memory & Cognition, 21,* 176–183.

Miller, G. A. (1956). The magical number seven, plus or minus two: Some limits of our capacity for processing information. *Psychological Review, 63,* 81–97.

Miller, G. A., Galanter, E., & Pribram, K. H. (1960). *Plans and the structure of behavior.* New York: Holt.

Montague, W. E. (1972). Elaborative strategies in verbal learning and memory. In G. H. Bower (Ed.), *The psychology of learning and motivation* (Vol. 6, pp. 225–302). New York: Academic Press.

Müller, G. E. (1911). Zur Analyse der Gedächtnistätigkeit und des Vorstellungsverlaufes: Teil I [Toward analyses of memory and imagery: Part I]. *Zeitschrift für Psychologie, Ergänzungs Band, 5.*

Newell, A., & Simon, H. A. (1972). *Human problem solving.* Englewood Cliffs, NJ: Prentice-Hall.

Reed, S. K. (1974). Structural descriptions and the limitations of visual images. *Memory & Cognition, 2,* 329–336.

Reisberg, D. (1994). Working memory. In R. J. Corsini (Ed.), *Encyclopedia of psychology* (Vol. 3, pp. 586–587). New York: Wiley.

Richman, H., Staszewski, J. J., & Simon, H. A. (1995). Simulation of expert memory using EPAM IV. *Psychological Review, 102,* 305–330.

Saariluoma, P. (1989). Chess players' recall of auditorily presented chess positions. *European Journal of Cognitive Psychology, 1,* 309–320.

Saariluoma, P. (1990). Apperception and restructuring in chess players' problem solving. In K. J. Gilhooly, M. T. G. Keene, & G. Erdos (Eds.), *Lines of thought: Reflections on the psychology of thinking* (Vol. 2, pp. 41–57). London: Wiley.

Saariluoma, P. (1992). Error in chess: The apperception-restructuring view. *Psychological Research, 54,* 17–26.

Schneider, W., Bjorklund, D. F., & Maier-Brückner, W. (1996). The effects of expertise and IQ on children's memory: When knowledge is, and when it is not enough. *International Journal of Behavioral Development 19,* 773–796.

Shah, P., & Miyake, A. (1996). The separability of working memory resources for spatial thinking and language processing: An individual differences approach. *Journal of Experimental Psychology: General, 125,* 4–27.

Shiffrin, R. M. (1976). Capacity limitations in information processing, attention and memory. In W. K. Estes (Ed.), *Handbook of learning and cognitive processes: Attention and memory* (Vol. 4, pp. 177–236). Hillsdale, NJ: Erlbaum.

Simon, H. A. (1974). How big is a chunk? *Science, 183,* 482–488.

Simon, H. A., & Chase, W. G. (1973). The mind's eye in chess. In W. G. Chase (Ed.), *Visual information processing* (pp. 215–281). New York: Academic Press.

Singer, M., & Ritchot, K. F. M. (1996). The role of working memory capacity and knowledge access in text inference processing. *Memory & Cognition, 24,* 733–743.

Staszewski, J. J. (1988). The psychological reality of retrieval structures: An investigation of expert knowledge. *Dissertation Abstracts International, 48,* 2126B.

Staszewski, J. J. (1990). Exceptional memory: The influence of practice and knowledge on development of elaborative encoding strategies. In W. Schneider & F. Weinert (Eds.), *Interactions among aptitudes, strategies, and knowledge in cognitive performance* (pp. 252–285). New York: Springer-Verlag.

Tulving, E., & Thompson, D. M. (1973). Encoding specificity and retrieval processing in episodic memory. *Psychological Review, 80,* 352–373.

Verive, J. M., & McDaniel, M. A. (1996). Short-term memory tests in personnel selection: Low adverse impact and high validity. *Intelligence, 23,* 15–32.

Wenger, M. J., & Payne, D. G. (1995). On the acquisition of mnemonic skill: Application of skilled memory theory. *Journal of Experimental Psychology: Applied, 1,* 194–215.

Woodworth, R. S. (1938). *Experimental psychology.* New York: Holt, Rinehart & Winston.

9 Interacting Cognitive Subsystems

Modeling Working Memory Phenomena Within a Multiprocessor Architecture

PHILIP J. BARNARD

FIVE CENTRAL FEATURES OF THE THEORY

(1) The cognitive mechanisms underlying working memory performance involve multiple processes and types of mental representation.

(2) The detailed properties of performance depend on the configuration of specific processes needed to accomplish the task and the specific types of memory records they access and use in executing the task.

(3) There are no specific capacity limitations on what is stored at any particular level of mental representation. Capacity limitation arises out of restrictions on the interfunctioning of processes within a wider system.

(4) The use of memory records requires the generation or revival of a description of the content to be accessed. This can also functionally constrain performance.

(5) There is no unified "central executive" component; central executive functions are themselves accomplished by processing interactions among subsystems.

The dominant approach to formulating theory within experimental psychology is to develop models of restricted scope and capability. Individual models strive to predict properties of behavior in tasks that are assumed to tap specific mental faculties such as visual perception, language, problem solving, emotion, memory, or motor skills. It is taken for granted that moving toward an understanding of the complete mental mechanism is rather like solving a jigsaw puzzle. Ultimately a complete picture should emerge as local theories become validated and as segments of increasing size emerge and are themselves pieced together. One problem with this approach is the very complexity of the interrelationships between the various mental faculties. All too often theories founder because they do not readily extend beyond the specific behavioral context for which they were originally designed.

An alternative approach is initially to develop a theory of broad scope, focused on the "design" of the complete mental mechanism. The medium-term objective would be to address precisely those questions of the macro-organization of the mental mechanism about which local theories have little to offer. Such a macro-theory should be designed from the outset to incorporate sufficient resources to enable it to address problems across normally distinct conceptual domains such as visual perception, language, and so on. The obvious risk with this kind of approach is the potential for introducing a vast number of unwarranted or untested assumptions that, when deployed in an ad hoc manner, will enable the "theory" to explain everything. If we are to proceed along this path, then some tractable means needs to be found for framing system-level assumptions and for controlling the way in which they are elaborated to provide accounts and predictions at increasing levels of detail for specific behaviors. In spite of the risks, it is this latter path that will be adopted here.

Interacting Cognitive Subsystems (ICS) is a theoretical framework that specifies the component resources of the "complete" mental mechanism (Barnard, 1985; Teasdale & Barnard, 1993). At a systemic level it defines what the resources are, how they are organized, what they do, and how they interoperate. To control the potential problem of rapid proliferation of unwarranted assumptions, a layered approach is adopted. The "core" theory assumes an architecture composed of nine subsystems. These all share an identical internal structure involving three basic resources: processes that change the form in which information is represented; an image record that preserves past input to the subsystem; and a process that simply copies information into that record. The presence of specific processes that change the representation of information implies that they take an input and produce an output. Outputs, of course, must be in a form that can be interpreted by another subsystem or by an effector mechanism. The processes within subsystems thus effectively define the patterns of information flow that are possible among subsystems.

From this point of departure, theory development can proceed by making a relatively small number of basic assumptions concerning information flow and mental representation. Because all subsystems have identical form, it can be assumed that their operation is governed by the same principles. They differ only in the content of their inputs and outputs. Clearly, any explanation of experimental phenomena or real-world behavior will require further assumptions about the form and content of those inputs and outputs. Given the nature of the architecture, it is not hard to constrain and layer the introduction and evaluation of these additional assumptions. All types of mental representation can be assumed to have a common form in which "basic units" are constructed out of "constituent elements" and have a "superordinate structure." The form and content of representations will then be intimately related to information flow. Where a subsystem receives information from the outputs of several other subsystems, the basic units of representation will themselves be a product of composing constituents from different sources. Explanations can then be developed by moving from simple principles of flow and representation to the dynamics of information-processing activity throughout the architecture. Any additional assumptions should not only map onto specific behaviors. Their wider effectiveness can be evaluated for both internal consistency and breadth of application. They should help us to understand how and why very different phenomena are related and furnish them with a common basis of explanation.

This introductory sketch already invokes constraints on what follows in terms of a model of working memory. "Working memory" is not, in and of itself, a basic construct within the overall framework. The theoretical resources at our disposal are processes that construct representations, image records that preserve past inputs, and processes that change the representation of information. The fact that these resources are replicated over nine subsystems within a wider architecture quite clearly determines the types of answers that will be offered to the eight questions serving here to support a comparison of alternative models. ICS must account for performance in working memory tasks on the basis of multiple resources rather than a unitary construct. The overall control and regulation of the wider system must itself occur through the dynamic interactions between processes and the different types of representation they can access. Equally, working memory limitations must arise from these self-same representations and process interactions. Any additional assumptions that expand the common core should serve to make it very clear how the phenomena of working memory relate to other tasks such as language understanding, attention, consciousness, perceptual motor control, or the role of long-term memory.

The chapter is organized into two parts. The first describes the basic mechanisms and representations of the ICS framework in a series of stages. The architecture will be introduced first in outline form, together with a basic description of the types of information handled by each subsystem. The internal organization of subsystem resources and the core principles governing their operation are then defined. The full architecture is subsequently elaborated, followed by concrete illustrations of the wider patterns of information flow that it permits. The theoretical description concludes with a characterization of four general classes of constraint, defined at a systemic rather than process level, on the workings of the whole architecture. The second part addresses the eight questions covered in all the chapters in this volume; it includes a brief overview of some current research driven by the approach, and concludes with a summary of the answers to the key questions.

Basic Mechanisms in ICS

ICS is a distributed, multiprocessor architecture encompassing sensory, central, and effector processing activity (Figure 9.1). The architecture specifies three sensory subsystems specialized for handling information derived from

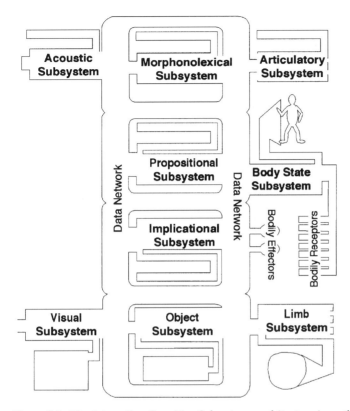

Figure 9.1. The Interacting Cognitive Subsystems architecture in outline.

visual, auditory, and body state sources. Two effector subsystems deal with the control of skeletal action (Limb) and speech output (articulatory). There are four central subsystems. Two of these handle abstract structural descriptions of auditory/verbal information and of visuospatial information. These are referred to as the morphonolexical (MPL) and object subsystems. The two remaining central subsystems are specialized to process rather different types of meaning. One handles meaning at a level that specifies reference to objects, actions, events, and experiences in terms of their semantic identity, their properties, and their interrelationships. This is referred to as the propositional subsystem. The second type of meaning is more abstract and schematic. Its content integrates the products of processing propositional meaning with information derived from the wider patterning of all sensory inputs, including cross-modal regularities in, for example, tone of voice, facial expression, and body state information. This type of semantics is referred to as implicational meaning. Propositional meaning can usefully be thought of as specific, "cold," and "rational," whereas implicational meaning is both generic and potentially "affect related." The nine types of representation can be thought of as superordinate organizations of basic units constructed from constituents in different mental "codes" whose dimensions are summarized in Table 9.1.

Figure 9.1 illustrates a key distinction between sensory, central, and effector subsystems. Sensory subsystems take as input information derived directly from the external world by sense-specific transducers. Effector subsystems take inputs from other subsystems and map their outputs in the form of motor instructions to the relevant musculatures. Central subsystems interact. They take inputs from other subsystems and produce outputs that can be used by other subsystems. To avoid many overlapping direct connections, this is captured by the convention of having the central subsystems contained within a "data network" and the sensory and effector ones outside it. It is important that the data network *not* be understood literally as a general communication link of specific capacity over which "packets" of information are transmitted.

The Internal Architecture of All Subsystems

All subsystems share a common internal structure (Figure 9.2). Information in the defining code of the subsystem is mapped onto an input array. A subsystem contains a number of processes that can operate in parallel on the information on the input array. First, a "copy" process transfers incoming information to the image record. In doing so, it creates a representation of input over time, and the record preserves images of all input received. Acting in parallel with the copy process are two or more processes that transform incoming information into outputs in different mental codes. For example, were this to be the acoustic subsystem, one transformation (e.g., X to Y) might take the full sensory details of speech sounds and transform them into the morphonolexical code, a more abstract structural description of the underlying speech information. In parallel, another process (e.g., X to Z) might detect other dimensions in voice patterning and transform these directly into implicational code signifying a more generic property such as "agitation."

The operation of the processes and image records is governed by a number of simple information-processing principles:

- Any one transformation process can transform only a single coherent stream of information at any one time.

For example, if two people were to be speaking at the same time, the process in the acoustic subsystem that creates a morphonolexical representation would be able to transform only one of them.

- The copy process is an unselective identity transformation. Given an input in X, it produces an output in X, and hence all information on the input array would be copied to the image record.

Table 9.1. *The Types of Information Handled by Each Subsystem within the Architecture (From Teasdale & Barnard, 1993, copyright © 1993, reprinted by permission of Psychology Press Limited, Hove, UK)*

Peripheral Subsystems

(a) Sensory

  (1) Acoustic (AC): Sound frequency (pitch), timbre, intensity, etc. Subjectively, what we 'hear in the world'.

  (2) Visual (VIS): Light wavelength (hue), brightness over visual space, etc. Subjectively, what we 'see in the world' as patterns of shapes and colours.

  (3) Body State (BS): Type of stimulation (e.g., cutaneous pressure, temperature, olfactory, muscle tension), its location, intensity, etc. Subjectively, bodily sensations of pressure, pain, positions of parts of the body, as well as tastes and smells, etc.

(b) Effector

  (4) Articulatory (ART): Force, target positions and timing of articulatory musculatures (e.g., place of articulation). Subjectively, our experience of subvocal speech output.

  (5) Limb (LIM): Force, target positions and timing of skeletal musculatures. Subjectively, 'mental' physical movement.

Central Subsystems

(c) Structural

  (6) Morphonolexical (MPL): An abstract structural description of entities and relationships in sound space. Dominated by speech forms, where it conveys a surface structure description of the identity of words, their status, order and the form of boundaries between them. Subjectively, what we 'hear in the head', our mental 'voice'.

  (7) Object (OBJ): An abstract structural description of entities and relationships in visual space, conveying the attributes and identity of structurally integrated visual objects, their relative positions and dynamic characteristics. Subjectively, our 'visual imagery'.

(d) Meaning

  (8) Propositional (PROP): A description of entities and relationships in semantic space conveying the attributes and identities of underlying referents and the nature of relationships among them. Subjectively, specific semantic relationships ('knowing that').

  (9) Implicational (IMPLIC): An abstract description of human existential space, abstracted over both sensory and propositional input, and conveying ideational and affective content: *schematic models* of experience. Subjectively, 'senses' of knowing (e.g., 'familiarity' or 'causal relatedness' of ideas), or of affect (e.g., apprehension, desire).

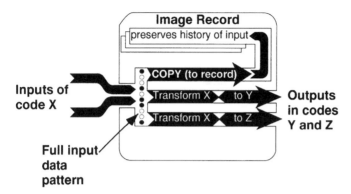

Figure 9.2. The internal structure of each subsystem (after Teasdale & Barnard, 1993). Adapted by permission of Psychology Press Limited, Hove, UK.

For example, if two people were to be speaking at the same time, an acoustic representation of both would be copied into the image record of the acoustic subsystem.

• A transformation process is rate limited. It can produce an output in real time only if the rate at which information is arriving lies within the limiting rate of output code production.

For example, presentation of seven compressed auditory digits at a rate of 10 a second would exceed the rate at which the acoustic to morphonolexical transformation could function. Because the copy process does not require change, its rate limits would be greater.

The idea that information arriving at a subsystem is copied into the image record has two powerful properties that can be capitalized on when developing accounts of learning and memory. First, it means that a subsystem can represent information before being able to transform it. Thus, an infant can represent speech sounds before it knows how to transform them into phonology. Second, it provides the basis for the use of past experience. Both learning and memory are supported within a subsystem by a configural principle:

• A transformation process can disengage from processing information on the input array and reconfigure to access the representation of the most recent input to the image record. At any given time only one process in a subsystem can access its image record.

This principle creates a mode of operation in which a single transformation process effectively operates in series with the copy process to "buffer" the processing of incoming information (Figure 9.3a). There is a vital difference

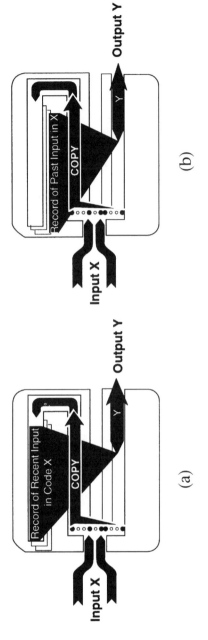

Figure 9.3. (a) Buffered processing (Teasdale & Barnard, 1993). Copyright, 1993, reprinted by permission of Psychology Press Limited, Hove, UK. (b) Reuse of past input.

between the buffered processing mode and the "direct" mode of processing shown earlier in Figure 9.2. In direct processing the activity of transforming one mental code into another is based on the moment-to-moment dynamic changes in the information arriving, in real time, on the input array of the subsystem. In the buffered processing mode, a process transforming one mental code into another is using a representation with an extra dimension of encoding – an extent over time. The transformation can be based on the structuring of the constituent elements and basic units within a larger representation, rather than relying on moment-to-moment transitions on the input array. If a word is presented in a noisy background, the noise can mask part of the speech signal. Under these circumstances, the transformation of acoustic information into its underlying morphonolexical constituents could prove problematic in direct mode. However, by switching to buffered mode, the transformation can take into account other information within the extended representation, which has just been copied into the image record, to constrain and support the generation of an output. In this respect, the buffered mode of operation is a more robust basis for a process to compute an output.

Buffered processing is one type of "immediate" bridge to past experience. In buffered mode, a process is using a representation of the record's most recent input. Figure 9.3b shows the transformation process configured not to the "front plane" of the image record, but to its "rear plane." This indicates that a record of prior, as opposed to the most recent, input is being used as a basis for generating an output. It is not helpful to think of the record resource as either "a tape recorder" or a "filing system" for distinct representations. It is better thought of as a process that acts as a pattern-completion mechanism. Given an input in the form of a description, it produces a representation on the "rear plane" of a record of past input in code X. The overall approach adopted is very much like the records and descriptions framework of Norman and Bobrow (1979).

This theoretical view of the basic mechanisms of memory carries with it a number of important consequences. Representations are not literally "retrieved." Rather, a process reconfigures to use the representation generated on "the back plane" of Figure 9.3b. This representation, also in code X, is *reused* by the transformation process to produce an output in code Y. For example, if at some point I process the sentence "Michael is in the kitchen," a semantic representation of this fact will be copied into the image record of the propositional subsystem. If I am later asked the question "Who is in the kitchen?", a semantic description $<x?>$ <location> <kitchen> would be mapped onto the image record of the propositional subsystem and a semantic representation of <Michael> <location> <kitchen> would be generated by pattern completion on the "rear plane" of the record resource. The process that transforms meaning into surface structure form (propositional to morphonolexical) can then reuse the pattern-completed relationship between referent and location to generate a verbal answer "Mike is in the kitchen."

A process can thus operate in three modes, distinguished by the source of the information used as input to drive the transformation: the input array (direct processing, Figure 9.2); the front plane of the record resource (buffered processing of a current representation, Figure 9.3a); and the rear plane of the record resource (the reuse of a representation of past experience, Figure 9.3b).

Technically, the product of a process accessing a past memory stored in code X is a "new" representation in the output code Y. It is in this sense that representations are *reused* rather than *retrieved* or *recovered*. As with buffered processing, the products of a process operating on a representation of past input are represented only at the down-line subsystem that handles the information output by the process. This form of reuse has two inherently "reconstructive" aspects – within the pattern-completion mechanism of the image record and within what happens when the record so completed is transformed for output. Although the memory substrate is a local resource associated with a particular subsystem, the consequences are systemic rather than local – the reuse of a stored representation can have an effect only if the products of the process are used by a subsequent subsystem or motor process.

Within the ICS framework, two specific mechanisms are proposed to govern the reuse of representations from an image record (Barnard, 1985). One mechanism, the principle of revival, is entirely local to a subsystem's operation: A transformation process can internally "revive" a description, access the image record, and reproduce an output. The other mechanism involves a description being generated by a process elsewhere, with the description being taken as fresh input and mapped onto the image record. In both mechanisms access is mediated through the internal operation of the transformation processes themselves, not through the copy process. In either case, some information exchange among subsystems is essential in the generation of descriptions, in the use of subsystem output, or both. In consequence, theoretical explanations of the active maintenance of mental representations in the context of working memory tasks, and of the control and regulation of those tasks, will require analysis of system-level constraints on mental activity across the wider architecture. Similarly, both mechanisms can play a role in system-wide activity to support long- as well as short-term memory.

The Complete Architecture

The basic principles of information flow, the reuse of stored records, and the different types of mental representation have now been defined. The principles were not individually justified as they were introduced. Many of the core assumptions can be traced back to past theory and evidence (see Barnard, 1985; Teasdale & Barnard, 1993). For example, the basic assumption that any one process can handle only a single stream of data at any one time is directly inherited from Broadbent (1958), whereas the idea that there

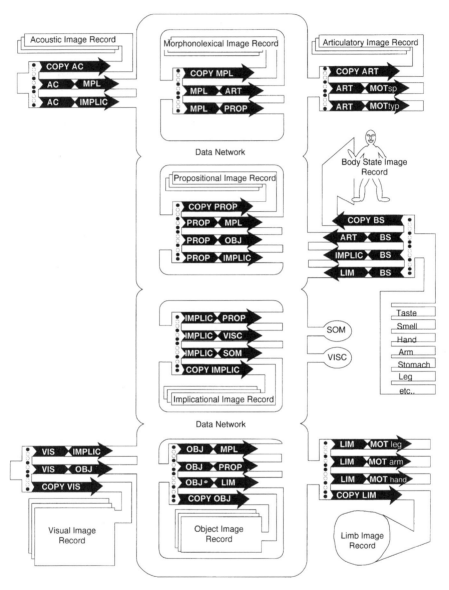

Figure 9.4. An overall view of the ICS architecture, showing the main transformation processes within each subsystem (Teasdale & Barnard, 1993). Copyright, 1993, reprinted by permission of Psychology Press Limited, Hove, UK.

are different levels of mental representation, each of which has a constituency and superordinate structure, is pervasive in cognitive psychology. What the ICS framework adds is the idea that such assumptions can be generalized and brought together within a unified explanatory framework. A set of relatively simple basic resources rapidly becomes a richly interconnected and complex system. Figure 9.4 now elaborates the architecture by including specific processes identified in terms of their inputs and outputs. These processes are sufficient to support analyses of the tasks that dominate experimentation on cognitive phenomena. The structures on the right center of this diagram are intended to capture "effects in the body." Thus, it is assumed that specific processes in the implicational subsystem control patterns of visceral (VISC) and somatic (SOM) responses. Effects here can be picked up together with other bodily sensations from specific regions and mapped into the body state subsystem.

Figure 9.5 dissolves away the individual processes and highlights some of the major flow patterns made possible within the system. This diagram further illustrates how flow is constrained from the sensory to central subsystems, and from the central subsystems to the effector subsystems. It also indicates a general pattern of rich, but nonetheless constrained, interactions among the central subsystems. These subsystems receive multiple inputs and hence the mental coding of constituents, their combination into basic units of central representation, and their superordinate organization will be derived from multiple sources. The general idea that representation and flow are intimately intertwined is made concrete through this illustration.[1]

System-Level Constraints on the Operation of the ICS Architecture

Within the overall ICS framework, it should be possible to call upon a relatively small number of additional assumptions to provide principled accounts of the phenomena associated with working memory tasks. These additional assumptions can be developed by considering four classes of constraint operating at a systemic level rather than at the level of individual subsystems. They are the "configurations" of processes involved in task performance; the "procedural knowledge" embodied within specific processes; the "record content" created and used by them; and the way in which the overall mechanism is "dynamically controlled and coordinated" over time.

---

[1] Thinking about the way information flows through a subsystem and among subsystems can be greatly helped by viewing dynamic animations of the operation of the architecture. Animations of basic principles and selected WM tasks can be downloaded from one of two internet sites for ICS:

http://www.mrc-cbu.cam.ac.uk/personal/phil.barnard/ics/
http://www.shef.ac.uk/~pc1jm/ics/

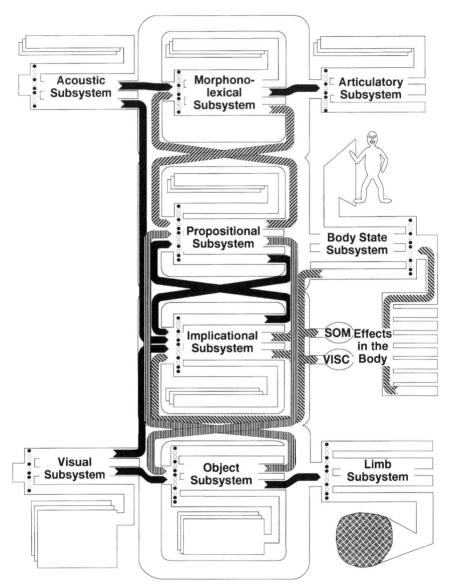

Figure 9.5. Illustrative patterns of information flow (Teasdale & Barnard, 1993). Copyright, 1993, reprinted by permission of Psychology Press Limited, Hove, UK.

Configurations and Procedural Knowledge

Performance will be constrained by the configuration of processes required to support a task. Performance on a visuospatial tracking task will call into play a different configuration of processes, and their associated image records, than the understanding or production of language. Performance will be also constrained by the procedural knowledge embodied in the full set of transformation processes within those configurations. Procedural knowledge is defined as the underlying capability to transform one representation into another. So, for example, an individual who has never learned the French language may well be able (via AC to MPL in the acoustic subsystem) to generate a representation of the surface structure of what has been said, but would lack the capability to generate much in the way of propositional representation of its meaning (via the MPL to PROP process in the morphonolexical subsystem). In much the same way, short-term memory (STM) tasks often make use of nonsense syllables, digits, or letters. Representations of such material would be copied into the image records of those subsystems that encode surface form (e.g., in morphonolexical or articulatory codes), but would not lead to much by way of a coherently structured propositional representation. Equally, parallel routes (e.g., via AC to IMPLIC or VIS to IMPLIC::IMPLIC to PROP)[2] might support some generic inference or guessing. Such inferences might represent properties such as the presence "nonsense" or "numerosity" in the input stream and, for example, prevent 12 items being recalled when only six are presented.

Record Content

Performance will be constrained by the task-related material that is copied into and stored within image records. The information so preserved depends on exactly what task-related material was actively being transformed by processes within the overall configuration at the time when the to-be-recalled information was encountered. The architecture itself obviously allows for the possibility that multiple records of the same material will be created and laid down. The properties of overt recall will, in turn, depend on the nature of the representations used in the period of recall and their particular form of encoding (see Table 9.1). In principle, this enables the framework to capture many different strategies for recall. In practice, the tasks of experimental psychology are usually sufficiently well constrained so as to limit the way in which the record resources can effectively be used to meet the task demands.

Dynamic Control and Coordination

The only resources defined within the ICS architecture are processes and records of information. There is no homunculus or central executive that determines what happens across the entire mechanism. Everything depends on how "local capabilities" are able to meet task requirements.

For a task such as walking along a path, the relevant configuration may involve three processes in the subsystems shown within the lower segment of

---

[2] The symbol :: is used to indicate the sequencing of processes within a configuration. It can be "understood" as transfer over the data network from the output of one subsystem to the input array of the next subsystem. Other abbreviations are defined in Table 9.1.

Figures 9.4 and 9.5 (VIS to OBJ::OBJ to LIM::LIM to MOTlegs). So long as these processes embody the "procedural knowledge" to handle the information dependencies, the configuration should be able to operate quite automatically, with self-regulatory feedback being provided both by the flow of constantly updating visual information and by a proprioceptive flow from the body state subsystem back to the limb subsystem. So long as the environmental dependencies remain straightforward, this subconfiguration can operate independently of other processes. When climbing up a difficult mountain track, the dependencies may become rather more complex, and "decisions" may need to be made about where to place a foot. Under such circumstances, the system can be dynamically reconfigured in the very short term so that properties of the local ground topography are represented centrally (e.g., via VIS to OBJ::OBJ to PROP:: PROP to IMPLIC) and foot placing explicitly evaluated via an interchange between propositional and implicational subsystems (::PROP to IMPLIC::IMPLIC to PROP::). The outcome of such processing can then be fed back to the object subsystem (via PROP to OBJ). The products of central processing can thus be integrated with the flow of information through the more peripheral configuration, at the second stage within the VIS to OBJ::OBJ to LIM::LIM to MOTlegs sequence, to accomplish "centrally determined" modulation of foot placement.

The operation of the ICS architecture is thus regarded as dynamically self-controlling via the representations passed among the various subsystems. Processing exchanges between propositional and implicational meaning, and the two image records available for their use, lie at the heart of the framework's approach to central executive functioning. This particular interaction pattern has been referred to as the "central engine" of cognition (Barnard & Teasdale, 1991; Teasdale & Barnard, 1993). Though the concept of a central executive connotes a mechanism for making a series of discrete decisions among options or scheduling them, the concept of an engine is more suggestive of a continuously operating source of ideational content, propelling the thematic evolution of thought and any "inferences" associated with it. In their use of central processes, the tasks of experimental psychology are no different from any other more naturally occurring experience. The experimental instructions will be interpreted, a record of "what to do" will be laid down in the image record of the propositional subsystem, and relevant schematic models will be invoked as implicational representations. Reciprocal exchanges between the propositional and implicational subsystems will control and regulate the flow of information to and from the more peripheral subsystems.

Approximate Models of Cognitive Activity

Although the four system-level constraints on the functioning of the ICS architecture will be used relatively informally in this chapter, the concepts have been elaborated in considerable technical detail elsewhere (e.g., Barnard & May, 1993) and used to develop three generations of expert systems. These rule systems generate approximate models that describe properties of mental activity in terms of configurations, procedural knowledge, record content, and dynamic control. The property descriptions of mental activity throughout the system are then used to predict characteristics of overt behavior in complex practical tasks (e.g., Barnard, Wilson, & MacLean, 1988). In marked contrast to other approaches, such models are neither simulations of an architecture's operation (e.g., Lovett, Reder, & Lebiere, Chapter 5; Kieras, Meyer, Mueller, & Seymour, Chapter 6; Young & Lewis, Chapter 7; all in this volume), nor are the assumed maintenance and control mechanisms directly linked to underlying brain subsystems (cf. O'Reilly, Braver, & Cohen, Chapter 11, this volume). Rather, an explicit representation of mental activity is used to support ways of reasoning about human mentation and behavior. To further this aim, several of the basic principles have also been specified in axiomatic form, using deontic extensions of modal action logic. The basic functioning of computer systems can be formalized in exactly the same type of logic, as can constraints on the interaction between a user and a computer. The axiomatic specifications can then support prediction via a *formal mathematical proof* that the behavior of the combined user–computer system should exhibit particular properties, for example, in the use of advanced graphical and multimodal computer interfaces (e.g., see Duke, Barnard, Duce, & May, 1995).

Definition of Working Memory

Technically, there can be no formal definition of working memory, because it is not a core construct within ICS. The properties of performance on working memory tasks must be attributed to process-mediated interactions among multiple subsystems of cognition. Processes within each subsystem have access to a repertoire of representations of its past inputs stored within image records. Explanations of individual working memory phenomena must therefore be generated and evaluated by considering how configurations of specific processes, the procedural knowledge embodied within them, and their use of record contents influence the dynamic control and coordination of the mechanism over time. To avoid confusion in the analysis of immediate recall, the term *short-term memory* tended to be used to refer to the tasks, while the term *short-term storage* was assigned to the theoretical entities on which explanations were based. In seeking to address the eight basic issues concerning the nature of working memory, the following sections use the term *working memory* to describe the tasks, with the processes and memory records of the ICS architecture being taken as the basis for theoretical explanation.

ICS and the Performance of Working Memory Tasks

Basic Mechanisms and Representations

Traditional theories of short-term storage were often cast within the metaphor of a Von Neumann computer architecture: a single central processor supported by short- (RAM) and long-term stores (disk). Specific theories of working memory were introduced largely because this early body of theory could not readily accommodate observed variation in capacity (e.g., Craik & Lockhart, 1972), because hypothesized structural relationships between short- and long-term stores could not be sustained (e.g., Warrington & Shallice, 1969), or because they could not readily account for the pattern of performance in more complex tasks involving dual demands (e.g., Baddeley & Hitch, 1974). ICS reinvokes the idea of specific connections and flow between component resources and multiple stores preserving information in different codes (e.g., Murray, 1968). In doing so, it makes use of a range of really quite detailed ideas about how modern multiprocessor architectures can be made to work.

As a multiprocessor architecture, ICS shares some properties with the position advocated by Schneider (Chapter 10, this volume). However, by making extensive use of process interactions, it is perhaps most closely related to the Baddeley and Logie (Chapter 2, this volume) position. The ICS framework differs in that it postulates specific underlying processes and representations within each component. It invokes no general-purpose resources such as "contention scheduling" or a "supervisory attentional system" (Baddeley, 1990; Shallice, 1988) within the central executive component. All defined resources have a specific function motivated within a wider design for the complete mental mechanism.

The design of the overall architecture (see Figure 9.4) means that the MPL record, which preserves surface structure form, can be addressed by the products of semantic processing (via PROP to MPL) and that any products regenerated as a consequence can be fed back to the propositional subsystem. From here they can be evaluated semantically and schematically in relation to the task demands by processing exchanges between the propositional and implicational subsystems. In effect, this forms a "phonological loop" that can intersect with the central engine of cognition that fulfills executive functions (Figure 9.6).

Because the high-level principles are generic, exactly the same considerations and arguments govern the processing of information in those subsystems specialized for the processing of visuospatial information. The image records of the visual and limb subsystems have the same kind of addressing constraints as the acoustic and articulatory subsystems, whereas the object subsystem functions in an analogous fashion to the MPL subsystem. The difference lies not in their functioning, but in the types of information to which they have access. Thus, the equivalent of Baddeley's (1986) visuospatial sketchpad, and indeed a wider treatment of internally generated "visual imagery," is shown in Figure 9.7.

The key configural building blocks for ICS accounts of performance in working memory paradigms are three intersecting processing loops: a reciprocal interaction between the propositional and morphonolexical subsystems (see Figure 9.6); a reciprocal interaction between the propositional and object

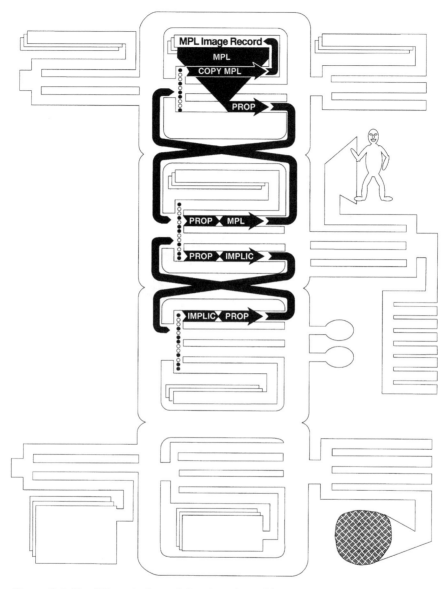

Figure 9.6. The ICS equivalent of the phonological loop (Teasdale & Barnard, 1993). Copyright, 1993, reprinted by permission of Psychology Press Limited, Hove, UK.

subsystems (see Figure 9.7); and a reciprocal interaction between the propositional and implicational subsystems (in both figures). These loops interconnect four fundamentally different types of information and their associated memory records. The general relationship between ICS and the Baddeley and

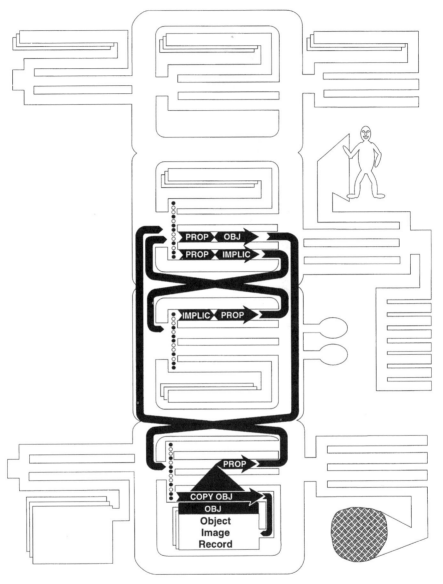

Figure 9.7. The ICS equivalent of the visuospatial sketchpad (Teasdale & Barnard, 1993). Copyright, 1993, reprinted by permission of Psychology Press Limited, Hove, UK.

Logie model (Chapter 2, this volume) is depicted in Figure 9.8. Other components do need to be added to these basic configurations to meet the demands of specific tasks. For example, the processing of written words requires a cross modal transformation from OBJ to MPL, whereas a process in the articulatory

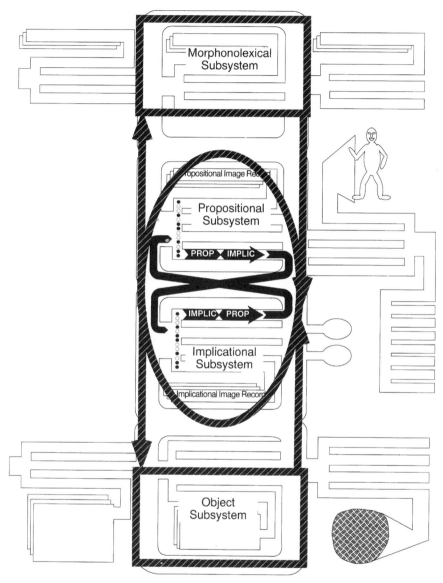

Figure 9.8. The relationship between ICS and the working memory framework originating with Baddeley and Hitch (1974) and Baddeley and Logie (Chapter 2, this volume).

subsystem accomplishes subvocal rehearsal. Nonetheless, the principal mental activity underlying most working memory tasks is carried out by processes within the four central subsystems and calls on the representations preserved in their image records.

When fulfilling their executive functions in complex tasks, specific propositional and implicational processes within the central engine play distinct roles. The propositional subsystem generates input to the implicational subsystem and is also responsible for seriating or otherwise organizing the underlying content of thought into linguistic or spatial codes. In effect, it acts as the central engine's gateway to, and from, surface structure form. It is the propositional arm that "controls" the framework's equivalent of the phonological loop (see Figure 9.6) and visuospatial sketchpad (see Figure 9.7). In addition to generating new propositional content from schematic models, the "implicational arm" of the central engine is associated with wider synthesis of the products of sensory and conceptual information and mediates the central experience of affect. The incorporation of a specific role for affect at this level of representation marks another key distinction between the ICS approach and the type of central executive resources assumed by Baddeley and Logie, and indeed most other contributors to this volume.

Within the flow of information from the propositional subsystem to the implicational subsystem, specific semantic detail is discarded. At the implicational level, the products of propositional processing can be integrated with other immediate products of processing environmental patterns or body states (Figure 9.9). The schematic models so formed can in turn be used to generate new propositions as indicated by the cross-hatched data flow in Figure 9.9. Suppose a sentence such as "John saw Carol drop her mother's delicate Meissen plate onto the hard kitchen floor" is spoken by a child who could have been present at the event and who has a slightly nervous expression and tone of voice. Although not depicted in the figure, the strictly "lexical information" would have been processed through the acoustic and morphonolexical subsystems to deliver a basic propositional representation of the referents and their interrelationships. The process that now transforms this into an implicational representation may add substance by generating a wider model encompassing additional generic features, not present in its literal meaning, such as "possible radical change of physical object state." When combined with equally generic features such as the speaker's expression and tone of voice, content something like "something unfortunate has happened" might be added in as well. The inverse process (IMPLIC to PROP) might then quite reasonably generate a propositional representation derived from this input incorporating explicit reference to the likelihood that the plate broke.

Successive cycles might access relevant propositional records, perhaps referencing the knowledge that this antique was left to the mother by her grandfather and invoking other schematic properties, such as the attribution of blame or potential feelings of loss on the part of the owner. During these cycles, were the listener to realize that his or her job might now be to "explain" this event to the mother, other processes in the implicational subsystem (see Figure 9.9) might then initiate a facial wince (IMPLIC to SOM) or

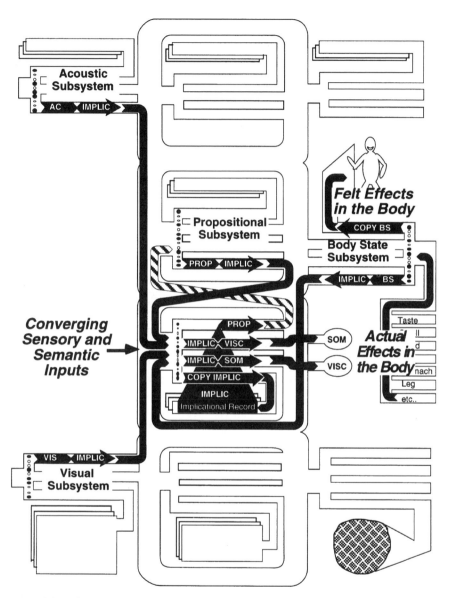

Figure 9.9. Information integration at the implicational subsystem (Teasdale & Barnard, 1993). Copyright, 1993, reprinted by permission of Psychology Press Limited, Hove, UK.

a flutter of physical anxiety (IMPLIC to VISC), which when fed back to the center (via a flow from BODY STATE to IMPLIC) would add a general sense of apprehension to the evolving schematic model for the event. In a manner directly analogous to shifts in visual attention, propositional and implicational processing undergoes successive shifts of topic, from the people involved in the event, through the effects on the hypothetical mother, to the self-related problem of explaining the unfortunate happening to a significant other. As with other aspects of the functioning of the ICS architecture, changes in the "focus of attention," as well as the use of memory records, can be analyzed in basically the same technical manner at all levels within the wider system to provide "explanations" of complex cognitive activities.

It now needs to be demonstrated that the basic mechanisms and representations of ICS can be used to provide accounts of a range of working memory phenomena. The accounts should be internally consistent and make economic reuse of the general principles of information representation and flow.

ICS and the Performance of Working Memory Tasks

In classic serial recall, subjects must recall item and order information. From an ICS perspective, interpretation of the experimental instructions would initially provide a propositional representation of these task demands. Following practice, strategies and tactics to govern processing activity would also be implicitly represented within an abstract implicational model for task execution. During auditory presentation of a list of digits, the incoming information would be encoded using the configurations for language comprehension and production. Specifically, the list items would be transformed from the acoustic subsystem through the morphonolexical subsystem to the propositional subsystem, with image records being laid down by the action of the copy process in each one. In parallel, a separate morphonolexical process can recode information into an articulatory representation which, in turn, is automatically copied into the image record of this effector subsystem. The speech effector process (ART to MOTspeech) can internally switch to buffered mode (Figure 9.3a) and, via the principle of revival, rehearse those items that fall within the scope of the articulatory representation.

As the list presentation terminates, the central engine interrelates perceptual (e.g., the absence of an item on the rhythmic beat) and task representations to initiate recall. Items being cumulatively rehearsed by the articulatory mechanism might be output initially, and then the digit represented as the initial basic unit of the propositional representation of the list can be used to generate a description (via PROP to MPL) for an externally driven access to the MPL image record. This would most probably yield products that overlapped with items already recalled, so the items reused might again be fed back to the propositional subsystem and checked for redundancy of output before any further material is passed through to the articulatory subsystem for overt recall. As this pattern unfolds, the central engine might call on propositional and implicational knowledge of the item set to "guess" what item might go in which of the unfilled positions.

Variation in the structure and content of list materials should influence recall systematically. The following examples are brief reworkings of previous arguments describing how ICS might deliver detailed explanations of the phenomena of serial recall (Barnard, 1985). The proposed mechanism of articulatory rehearsal should be subject to constraints associated with the constituency of the basic articulatory units: The more constituents, the fewer the number of basic units that fall within the scope of the rehearsal mechanism. Occupying the rehearsal mechanism with a subsidiary task like articulatory suppression should remove any advantage accruing to short words. This is consistent with evidence that word length effects are abolished when suppression is performed through *both* presentation and recall (Baddeley, Lewis, & Vallar, 1984). Multiple representation within ICS implies that recall can still be mediated by the recovery of item and order information from the MPL image record and passed through the articulatory subsystem for written recall via the process ART to MOTwriting. The subvocal suppression task can be supported by a parallel process operating in buffered mode – ART to MOTspeech. Under such circumstances output should reflect, not articulatory properties, but the encoding of basic units of MPL code, such as lexical stems and bound morphemes.

Serial position effects can also be directly linked to other factors limiting or supporting representation and reuse of memory records. Within ICS, cross-modal recoding of lexical material is carried out by a process in the object subsystem (OBJ to MPL). For visually presented words, this transformation would not be on a speech-time base. According to the rate-limitation principle, transformation processes within the MPL subsystem could not work in the direct mode shown earlier in Figure 9.2. The input would nevertheless be copied into the MPL image record from where it can be processed in buffered mode (see Figure 9.3a) to overcome the rate limitation. The MPL to ART process passing items on for articulatory rehearsal and the MPL to PROP process transforming the same input for semantic representation could not both enter the buffered mode of operation simultaneously. For both to make use of the input, dynamic control would have to become rather more complex, with "oscillations" between two configural patterns. This would imply that there should be an advantage throughout the list for auditory presentation where such oscillation would not be necessary. Following on from the arguments in the previous paragraph, this advantage should be clearly apparent only under conditions of articulatory suppression (e.g., see Barnard, 1985, for a reanalysis of data from Baddeley, Thomson, & Buchanan, 1975).

Since lipread material is visually presented, but on a speech-time base, its processing should follow the same general pattern as auditorily presented material. Indeed, lipreading produces serial position curves very similar to auditorily presented lists, including full "auditory suffix effects" not present with written material (e.g., see Campbell & Dodd, 1980; Spoehr & Corin, 1978). This provides an alternative explanation of crucial modality effects without recourse to a mechanism of precategorical acoustic storage previously used to explain the effects of auditory suffixes (Crowder & Morton, 1969).

This is important for internal consistency – the ICS architecture does not support a direct flow of information from the central subsystems "back to" the acoustic subsystem.

With digit lists semantic relationships are usually absent, particularly when the design precludes repetition and increasing or decreasing number sequences. The propositional representation would lack meaningful superordinate structure. Only the semantic constituents, marking features such as magnitude and parity, would be available to generate descriptions to support reuse of representations. Where task environments permit more elaborate semantic encoding, the basic units and superordinate structures of propositional representation would be of greater utility. Naturally, where the material to be recalled involves sentences, text, or other meaningful life events, it would be propositional and implicational levels of representation whose access and reuse would govern the properties of overt recall.

In this respect ICS bears some similarity to the levels of processing approach (Craik & Lockhart, 1972), which originally argued that "shallow" processing led to a less durable basis for recall than "deeper," more elaborate encoding. The more specific view presented here, concerning types of encoding and the regulation of the wider mechanism, provides an explicit basis for avoiding potential circularity in the definition of "depth." It also accommodates evidence that tasks with apparently differing degrees of "depth" do not always map directly onto the extent of recall (e.g., see Baddeley, 1978). Those tasks traditionally regarded as "shallow" involve characteristics such as judging whether or not words were written in upper- or lowercase, or making rhyming judgments or phoneme monitoring. Very evidently, these tasks would make active use of the surface structure representations of the object and morphonolexical subsystems. According to the principles of transformation, such information would normally be discarded when propositional representations are formed in normal reading or auditory verbal comprehension.

In the case of phoneme monitoring, the repertoire of procedural knowledge within the MPL to PROP transformation would have developed primarily to recode surface structure form into referential meaning and propositional relationships, with the identity of the phonemes being discarded in the process. Accordingly, additional exchanges between the propositional and MPL subsystems would be required to identify the constituent phoneme. In addition, exchanges within the central engine would be required to evaluate the products of the more surface exchanges in relation to the task demands. In short, recall in certain shallow tasks may be poor, not only because they rely on representations of surface form, but because they can be extremely demanding of those resources that fulfill central executive functions. If they are "busy" working out how to meet the task demands, then they will be generating and evaluating very different representations of meaning than if they had been interpreting the substance of the input itself. Depth of processing effects should reflect, not only the nature of the representations and the degree of semantic elaboration, but also the nature of the information-processing demand placed on the central engine at both presentation and recall (Morris, Bransford, & Franks, 1977).

There is thus a clear connection between depth of processing effects and the performance of tasks that would be regarded as very demanding of central executive resources. The generation of random sequences of letters or numbers is regarded as just such a task (e.g., see Baddeley, 1966, 1990). The whole point of developing processes that transform representations is to capture *regularities* in the world of information patterns. "Randomness," almost by definition, is an abstract concept that captures the absence of such regularities. The task of producing such sequences would place heavy demands on the processing loop between both propositional and implicational subsystems as well as the loop between the propositional and MPL subsystems.

The generation task might start by framing initial propositional reference to two numbers (e.g., "5" then "7"). Since this representation does not inherently capture either their surface form or their order, the information would have to be mapped to the MPL subsystem, where an "ordered" image of the two digits would be created. This would then be fed back to the propositional level where the incoming information might quite automatically lead to the PROP to IMPLIC::IMPLIC to PROP cycle processing "increase" and, through this, adding reference to a new item "9." This in turn would once again be mapped out to the MPL level providing the surface form of "five, seven, nine." When yet again fed back to the central engine, further cycles might now infer features of schematic "regularity," because it is a sequence of ascending magnitude made up of numbers with odd parity. It would therefore be evaluated as "discrepant" with the task demands and yet further cycles would be required to deliver a means of accomplishing randomness – perhaps accessing a propositional image of the tactic of "go low magnitude and even parity." This might then result in the generation and surface realization of "two" to replace the "nine." When the sequence "five, seven, two" is fed back to the central engine for further evaluation, it would be accepted as "random" and passed through all stages of output to overt articulation.

Exactly the same fundamental approach would be taken in the provision of accounts of tasks involving visuospatial manipulations such as the classic mental rotation task of Shepard and Metzler (1971) or of Brooks's (1967) task in which subjects are instructed sequentially to place digits in the squares of a 4 × 4 spatial matrix. The alternative version of this task was to remember a sequence of nonsense instructions with the same verbal surface structure. In the first case, the task demands would most naturally be met using the ICS framework's equivalent of the visuospatial sketchpad (see Figure 9.7), whereas the nonsense version would be more likely to be supported using verbal codes (see Figure 9.6).

Mental images in object code are either created from the products of sensory processing (VIS to OBJ), or by the propositional subsystem (via PROP to

OBJ). Just as the MPL subsystem acts as a gateway mediating both input and output to the central engine, so the object subsystem fulfills the equivalent role in visuospatial tasks. In the dynamic control of these tasks the transformation processes within the object subsystem, like those in any other subsystem, can "do" only one thing at a time, and hence dual tasks that place demands on the same resources could be accomplished only if the configural pattern of control oscillates so that the same resources can be deployed to process different streams of data. The effects of this on times and errors would vary according to the task. A single illustration can support the general point. Baddeley, Grant, Wight, and Thomson (1975) combined the basic Brooks task with a visuospatial tracking task. This required subjects to follow the circular motion of a visual target with a stylus. This task should require regular intervention of central processes into the visuospatial configuration. When the tasks were performed alone, subjects made only an occasional error on both the nonsense and spatial versions of the Brooks task. When combined with tracking, the level of errors on the nonsense version of the task was unaffected. There was, however, massive interference in the visuospatial version of the matrix task, with the number of errors rising substantially. Such a pattern would be entirely consistent with the view that both tasks require the propositional–spatial loop (::PROP to OBJ::OBJ to PROP::) and that central engine resources cannot readily coordinate and control the two information streams effectively.

The Control and Regulation of Working Memory

The general picture to emerge from the specific illustrations is one of a self-controlling system whose component parts dynamically reconfigure to draw in different process and different record structures according to the current-information-processing demand of the task. Technically, all processes and all records are regarded as of equal importance. At a local level, what a particular process "does" is determined by its inputs, and its outputs determine what other subsystems do. If a particular process produces an output, it is passed to another subsystem or effector mechanism. If a subsystem is involved within the configuration, then all input is copied to, and represented within, its image record. Because a transformation process can handle only one stream of data at a time, not all information represented in the image record is necessarily used. At a more systemic level, if all the transformation processes within a configuration are fully capable of handling the input–output mappings, then that configuration may well be able to operate as a sequence of automatic or autonomous processes. When the input–output mappings are not fully proceduralized, when the contingencies are complex or, for example, in potentially dangerous settings, processes within the central engine are brought into the configuration and effectively exert control over data flow among the other subsystems. Even this central form of control ultimately boils down to inputs and outputs and the available repertoire of image records. Information discrepancies and the buffering of information reflect two interrelated facets of control and regulation.

Within the overall pattern of self-regulation a crucial role is played by informational discrepancies. This was alluded to in the discussion of random number generation, where "regularity" was described as "discrepant" with the propositional representation of the task demands. Information discrepancies not only help to drive the evolution of central thought patterns, they also act as a forcing function on learning within the transformation processes. Thus, if a novel "word" is heard, it can deliver an MPL encoding but not a propositional encoding. The "system" would then need to resolve this rather different, but nonetheless related, "discrepancy" by establishing a new mapping within the MPL to PROP transformation. Early on in development, this might involve adding to the underlying coding scheme at either level. Later on, once the underlying coding scheme is fully evolved, the updating would require linking up existing "constituents" into new basic units and establishing what output to generate. The greater the repertoires of fully established input–output mappings making up the procedural knowledge of processes within a configuration, the less complex the overall coordination and control of the architecture becomes. At around 12 months of age, central engine resources may have difficulty coordinating the control of standing or walking while listening to a parent. Rather later in life, the important informational discrepancies may be between implicational schematic models of the "self" and some more ideal model. As explored in detail by Teasdale and Barnard (1993), this may cause cycles of central engine operation to become "interlocked" with information fed back from the body state subsystem. The representations processed through the three loops are dominated by negative thoughts, memories, and their associated verbal and visual imagery. In this sense, unipolar depression can be regarded as a dysfunction in the control and regulation of the very mechanisms underlying performance in working memory tasks.

The buffering of incoming information within a subsystem also plays a key role in the regulation of data flow *and* learning. When outputs cannot be generated on the basis of moment-to-moment transitions in the patterns of information on the input array to a subsystem, the immediate "local" difficulty may be handled by switching to the buffered mode. In essence, this has the effect of mapping a representation in one subsystem onto the input array of another. Most obviously in the case of central subsystems, reciprocal flows can then support pattern completion, or the forging of longer term connections between the two levels of representation. For example, a partial specification of a word heard in noise (AC to MPL) may get completed as a result of "top down" predictive feedback based on the wider semantic context (PROP to MPL). The buffering of a process also subserves an associated function at a systemic level by providing a locus of flow control. It is conjectured that only one process within a configuration can be buffered at a given moment and that the rate of data flow through the entire configuration then becomes "locked onto" and coordinated around a rate determined by that process. This idea is elaborated subsequently in the context of the discussion of attention and consciousness.

The Unitary Versus Non-Unitary Nature of Working Memory

It is very evident that the ICS framework approaches its accounts of working memory phenomena in a non-unitary fashion. The resources of the theory (transformation processes, copy processes, and image records) are organized within higher order theoretical units (subsystems using different types of information), which can themselves have various superordinate organizations imposed to characterize their processing activity (configurations).

The Nature of Working Memory Limitations

All limitations on performance must be traced back to the operation of specific processes, either directly transforming information arriving at a subsystem or transforming representations of current or past experience. So, for example, the ability of a particular process to "revive" a description and access its memory record is, according to the model, limited to the reprocessing of the basic units within a superordinate structure that has itself just been processed. The consequences of such access obviously depend on the type of representation involved. Exactly what falls within the scope of revival at an articulatory level will differ from what falls within the scope of revival for MPL, object, propositional, and implicational representations. The consequences of the reuse of information in a particular representation also depend on how the products of that reuse are dealt with within the overall configuration currently supporting cognitive activity.

Working memory tasks characteristically involve the construction and reuse of multiple records of stimulus material and of the task demands. Most "real" limitations are best viewed at the systemic level of analysis. Overall performance is constrained by the configuration of processes; by the capability of individual processes to transform information; by the specific memory records available for use in a task context; and by the way the overall mechanism is dynamically controlled during different phases of task execution. As indicated in the earlier illustrations of specific working memory phenomena, our ability to recall or otherwise evaluate information depends on what type of representation can most usefully be accessed to resolve the demands of the current task. The execution of some tasks relied on alternative representations of surface form, whereas others relied on representations of meaning. Equally, limitations arise from representations, preserved within the central engine, of how to do the task itself. At this level, alternative strategies will limit performance in different ways. Young children's ability to "do" serial recall will improve at the point at which they develop central representations and models for the control and regulation of articulatory rehearsal (e.g., Chi, 1978).

Other advanced forms of control and regulation are well illustrated in the phenomena discussed by Ericsson and Delaney (Chapter 8, this volume). Yet other limitations derive from the fact that a particular process can do only one thing at a time. To meet specific task demands fully, a particular process may need to switch between the processing of different "streams" of information. Any such configural oscillations will restrict the ability of that process to revive recent representations.

The wider picture is not one of performance delimited by a simple list of specific capacities, but rather a picture in which the fundamental limitation lies in the capacity of the entire architecture to reconfigure dynamically and use all its representational and processing resources to best advantage.

The Role of Working Memory in Complex Cognitive Activities

Many of the developments of the ICS framework were motivated by applied concerns – a need to develop a body of theory that could be used to deal with complex tasks in the real world (e.g., see Barnard, 1987, 1991). It was a design requirement of the architecture that it be capable of interrelating as many different facets of mental life as possible in a simple, yet approximate form, while being as consistent as possible with the implications of our laboratory findings.

The explanations of the phenomena associated with working memory tasks offered earlier all relied on a dynamic exchange of representations among the central subsystems within the ICS architecture. Such central exchanges were partially dependent on information originally passed to them from the sensory subsystems, whereas the products of central exchanges controlled overt behavior via flows to the effector subsystems. Within this kind of analysis, the performance of all kinds of complex tasks – including the interpretation of visually perceived actions and events, as well as language understanding, implicit inference, problem solving, or even the impact of emotion on memory and cognition – will all draw on the same basic set of underlying central resources. Complex cognitive tasks do not depend on a unitary "working memory." Rather, human performance observed in working memory research is itself viewed as a representative product of one type of complex cognitive task.

Indeed, analyses of laboratory phenomena from working memory research, including serial position effects, modality effects, grouping effects, suffix effects, word length effects, articulatory suppression effects, and the effects of irrelevant speech, were originally used to motivate the basic form and content of the ICS architecture (Barnard, 1985). Both its extensibility and its practical utility have subsequently been explored in other representative forms of complex tasks. As a part of a larger project aimed at formulating and testing a theory of depression (Barnard & Teasdale, 1991; Teasdale & Barnard, 1993), the framework has been applied quite extensively to effects of mood on memory. Practical tasks to which the framework has been applied include vocabulary learning in human–computer interaction (Barnard, Hammond, MacLean, & Morton, 1982); the learning of complex sequences of command actions (Barnard, 1987; Barnard & Hammond, 1982; Barnard, MacLean, & Hammond, 1984); visual search in icon arrays and more complex structures on computer displays (May, Barnard, & Blandford, 1993; May & Barnard, 1995; May, Scott, & Barnard, 1995); and the use of multimodal computer interfaces (Barnard & May, 1995).

The Relationship of Working Memory to Long-Term Memory and Knowledge

"Knowledge" is captured within ICS as (a) the repertoires of record content preserved in each subsystem; and (b) the "procedural knowledge" enabling processes to transform one type of representation into another.

It may have been tempting for the reader to infer that the mechanism of process buffering, as well as the principle of revival, could usefully be associated with short-term storage capability distributed across the wider system. It may have been equally tempting to equate the reuse of records following external addressing with "long-term storage." Such a direct conceptual equation would represent something of an oversimplification. The image records do inherently embody a repertoire of long-term representations of past experience. Similarly, the buffering process and revival mechanism "maintain" information within the relatively short term as "active task records" (Barnard & May, 1993). Like short-term recall, retrieval from long-term memory is best thought of at the systemic level. Most long-term recall tasks would be seen as relying on interactions between propositional processes, implicational processes, and the image records on which they depend. The principles governing the reuse of these records in tasks such as long-term memory for text are nonetheless exactly the same as those involved in tasks involving shorter term retention demands.

Just as short-term recall depends on the properties of the more peripheral subsystems and the superordinate structures, basic units and constituent elements of their representations, so long-term recall should be governed by application of these contrasts, but this time within the operation of the central engine itself. In a relatively recent applied study (Eldridge, Barnard, & Bekerian, 1994), we sought to examine autobiographical memories of daily work. In an attempt to establish properties of their "schematic models," a group of office workers was asked to describe a "typical" day at work. Protocols were analyzed to determine how many different "basic work activities" were present, and structure diagrams were drawn to reflect their superordinate organization. The number of different activities was taken as an index of the degree of elaboration in an individual's underlying schematic model of their work. Some subjects doing very similar jobs showed quite different degrees of schematic elaboration.

Subjects were also asked to recall what they had done yesterday and what they had done on the same day during the previous week. Unsurprisingly, people recalled more activities from yesterday's work than they did from the same day on the week before. The recall of yesterday's activities was dominated by atypical activities not reported in their schema for a typical day. After a week's interval, the atypical activities dropped substantially, leaving slightly more "typical" than atypical content and, on other grounds, the recall had a more schematic quality. Most important, there was a strong relationship between the amount of recall for last week's activities and the elaboration of the model of daily work. People who had more-elaborated representations of their day's work recalled considerably more activities than those with less-elaborated representations. There was no evidence of such a relationship in the recall of yesterday's activities – by autobiographical memory standards a relatively short-term retention interval. This pattern of data is quite consistent with the general theoretical position that the content of schematic models is used to generate a description to address propositional records. The more complex descriptions yield more in the way of recovered propositional content.

The Relationship of Working Memory to Attention and Consciousness

The ICS approach to attention and consciousness has projections onto individual processes, representations, and configurations of processes within the wider system.

The concept of attention is directly related both to the selection of a particular "stream" of information and to how representations are thematically handled across a wider configuration. At a local level, process operation is selective. When more than one stream of information is arriving at a subsystem, a single process may operate on, or "attend to," only one of them. What constitutes "a stream" will depend on the form in which the incoming information is encoded. It may be one among many voices, a local region of visual space, or a particular stream of ideas in the central engine. A given process is not only selecting input, it is building a representation about something in particular, which is being output for use elsewhere in the system. At a wider configural level, peripheral processes may be "locked onto" a particular voice while processes within the central engine are, in turn, "attending to" some aspect of the meaning of what has been said. However, the propositional subsystem can receive information from the MPL subsystem, from the implicational subsystem, and from the object subsystem (see Figure 9.5). In language understanding, input from the object subsystem is, for example, used to resolve deictic reference, as might occur when pointing to something while saying "pick *that* up" (Barnard, May, & Salber, 1996). From moment to moment, the process transforming propositional meaning into implicational meaning may itself be "attending to" any one of these streams or, where the information from different sources is coherently related, to a stream that effectively "blends" their content. At a configural level "attended information" is composed of a set of related representations being sequentially created throughout the system.

ICS assumes that the operation of those processes that transform information from one code to another is unavailable to consciousness. Our phenomenological awareness of what is being attended to is related to the construction of representations and the manner in which they are processed (cf. Marcel, 1983). The basic operation of the "copy" process within a given subsystem involves constructing a representation in the "here and now." ICS directly links general phenomenological awareness to the action of the copy processes. What we are aware of in the here and now is the creation of representations throughout the system. I am concurrently broadly aware of the visual information on the computer screen, the sound of its disk, the touch of the keyboard, and what I am trying to write about. However, from moment to moment the status of the different representations within conscious awareness alters, with one form of information being more "focal" than others.

The mode of "buffered" processing shown earlier in Figure 9.3a is associated with focal awareness of information in the specific representation whose processing is buffered. The mode of buffered processing plays a vital role in the regulation of activity within system-wide configurations. In any multiprocessor system, the interoperation of processes must be coordinated. For example, the rate of data flow across the component processes within a configuration will, within limits, need to be synchronized. A plausible means of achieving this would be to assume that within any one independently coherent configuration, only one process can be buffered at a given time and that this implicitly provides a locus of flow control. Enhanced awareness would occur because the products of buffered processing would be propagated, and effectively "attended to," throughout the configuration. At each stage, information being copied into the image records of subsequent subsystems would be related to the representation being buffered. If the locus of the buffer is changed, the new state of the configuration can be linked to a different quality of experience. So, for example, when watching a movie, I can "switch" between paying attention to the high-frequency "hiss" in the fricatives of the speech (buffer at AC to MPL); I can concentrate on the rhymes in what is being said (buffer at MPL to PROP); I can simply pay close attention to the meaning of what is being said (buffer at PROP to IMPLIC); or I could be struck by a vivid pattern of coloring (buffer at VIS to OBJ), overwhelmed by emotion (buffer at IMPLIC to PROP), or experience acute physical discomfort from the cinema seating (buffer at BODY STATE to IMPLIC).

The theory assumes that only one process at a time can be buffered within a coherent configuration of interacting processes. Given that there can be more than one independent configuration active at a time in those dual tasks not subject to mutual interference, this would imply that focal awareness is, at a systemic level, not a unitary construct. One configuration of processes may be generating verbal thoughts while another is controlling the propulsion of a bicycle, each configuration having its own locus of control. The line of argument would then suggest that it would be possible to be simultaneously focally aware of *both* the pressure pattern in the feet pushing on the

Symbolic transformation of information in code X into code Y.

If {B & A & T} then {"BAT"}
Code X   Code Y

Concurrent "connectionist" transformation of information in code X into both code Y and code Z.

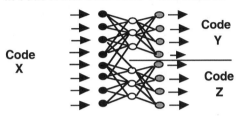

Figure 9.10. Two forms of hypothetical implementation for processes that transform information from code *X* into codes *Y* or *Z*.

pedals *and*, for example, verbal thoughts. However, the fact that only one of the two configurations can be connected up to the central engine would effectively allow for rather different experiential qualities to be associated with the two "foci." Only the consequences of one stream would be accompanied by multiple "overlays" of representations of meaning. This form of analysis is not only intellectually engaging; it also suggests that reports about experiential quality can themselves be a source of evidence concerning the configurations underlying performance in working memory tasks (e.g., see Teasdale & Barnard, 1993).

The Biological Implementation of Working Memory

ICS is a system level model from which we can reason about behavior without necessarily needing reference to a lower level implementation. The basic units in the model are processes that can simply be regarded as a function. Given an input, it produces an output. Provided that the theory develops an increasingly detailed specification of the function, it can be used to reason about behavioral consequences. It would matter little to the theory itself whether the underlying mechanics were to be implemented within a symbolic production system, a subsymbolic connectionist network, or some hybrid. Figure 9.10 depicts two hypothetical realizations of the function mapping from one code to another. Although such implementations of local phenomena might be instructive, simulation of the complete mechanism would currently be absurd – it would require a huge range of detailed assumptions about exactly how each form of mental representation was encoded, about the massive repertoire of experiential records, and about any associated variation across individuals. Few of these assumptions could be fully warranted from the empirical phenomena we know about. It would be far more productive in the medium term to develop more abstract theoretical methods for rendering the theoretical reasoning explicit and automating them for task domains such as working memory (e.g., see Barnard et al., 1988; Duke et al., 1995).

Higher level mappings between brain and cognition can still be of high utility. Indeed, much of the reasoning that went into the design of the ICS architecture was based on neuropsychological analyses of functions exhibiting double dissociations (e.g., see Shallice, 1988). In the context of a comparison of models of working memory, the discussion can be limited to memory capabilities. It has been known for a long time that patients exist whose short-term memory functioning is substantially impaired. Their long-term memory functioning is nonetheless intact, as to a great extent is their ability to comprehend language (e.g., Warrington & Shallice, 1969). Similarly, amnesic patients can have grossly impaired long-term memory and a relatively intact short-term memory (e.g., see Baddeley, 1990). They too tend to have intact ability to understand and produce language. This general pattern was used to motivate the parallel organization of the copy process and transformation processes within a subsystem. It was also used as a basis for arguing that the image records were required for "learning" new mappings within a transformation process (Barnard, 1985). Once the new mappings are learned, the direct mode of recoding can proceed without necessarily requiring use of the associated image record. Language understanding and production could remain intact in the absence of a supporting record – particularly when the wider system furnished some redundancy via multiple levels of encoding. Loss of the ability to "copy" different sorts of record should be associated both with specific deficits in recall and deficits in the ability to learn new mappings.

Thus, neurological loss of the copy MPL process should impair short-term recall and prevent the acquisition of new mappings – a pattern certainly exhibited in the patient PV studied by Baddeley, Papagno, and Vallar (1988). Similarly, loss of the copy PROP process should impair performance on tasks supported by referential meaning and abolish the individual's ability to learn new "facts" – again a characteristic feature of anterograde amnesia. Within the ICS architecture, as specified here, loss of a copy process does not prevent external addressing of the image record, a feature that would be wholly consistent in anterograde amnesia with a preserved ability to recall propositional records laid down before onset of the amnesic condition. Exactly the same arguments would apply to the loss of the copy IMPLIC process, except here it would be the ability to copy new implicational images that would be impaired, along with the capability to generate new generic schematic models to support mappings to propositional meaning. Patients with certain forms of damage to the frontal lobes are quite capable of performing familiar tasks without much apparent impairment, but can exhibit rather generic deficits in their ability to cope with very novel tasks (again, see Shallice, 1988). Patients exhibiting all these deficits are nonetheless capable of understanding and producing language, and the configural resources needed for this capability are organized in parallel throughout the ICS architecture. The architecture accommodates key features of both what is impaired and functions that remain unimpaired.

Given the increasing availability of brain-scanning technologies, it would be tempting to set out to map the processes of the ICS architecture onto areas known to be activated in different tasks. The component processes of the configurations involved in language understanding and production could conceivably map directly into activation in brain areas known to underpin language processing. Equally, those configurations supporting the successive interpretation of visual streams in perceptual interpretation and those processing visual streams through to the control of limb movement might just map directly onto the dorsal and ventral routes, proposed at a brain level, to support such tasks (e.g., Goodale, Milner, Jacobson, & Carey, 1991; Goodale & Milner 1992). Likewise, operation of the processes making up the three reciprocal loops forming the ICS equivalent of the central executive, the phonological loop, and the visuospatial sketchpad could be evident in "pictures" of brain activity in working memory in action (e.g., Paulesu, Frith, & Frackowiak, 1993; Smith & Jonides, 1997). Given some of the arguments advanced in the previous paragraph, the activation of frontal regions might well be taken as indicative of the operation of implicational processes or their use of image records.

However, there is no necessary reason to suppose that functional architecture maps topographically onto specific brain regions. The underlying neurons that make up the copy processes, the image records that they service, and the processes of transformation do not necessarily have to all be in the same physical location. Indeed, the hypothetical connectionist view depicted in Figure 9.10 might readily suggest that the neurons underlying a particular process could actually "be" in very different places. The processes that transform information map inputs onto outputs in different codes. The theoretical logic would suggest that a particular subsystem's "output" is not mediated by a separate integrated "output layer" within that subsystem itself but is topographically part of the *input* layer of the down-line subsystem that actually uses the code so produced.

Some Current Research on Central Executive Functioning

Our current research is primarily concerned with central executive function. The objective is to develop a more detailed, theoretical specification of implicational representations, of the processing of informational "discrepancies" within the central engine, and of other properties of the interaction between schematic and propositional content. Much of this research is examining the role of the central engine in the development, maintenance of, and recovery from depressive states (Teasdale, Taylor, Cooper, Hayhurst, & Paykel, 1995;

Barnard, Scott, & Murray, 1996). Other work on the mental processing of "numbers" is more closely related to classic working-memory tasks and will be used as a final illustration of the ICS approach.

The mental processing of numbers represents a cognitive "domain" in which most people are unlikely to have very elaborated implicational models. In a series of studies (Scott, Barnard, & May, 1995), we examined the interplay between externally defined "propositional" constraints, derived from task instructions, and the internal "schematic" constraints derived from implicational models of large numbers. To tap central executive function, we ensured that the task was both novel and unpracticed, and that the task domain was itself unexpected. We asked very large numbers of subjects a simple question requiring them to generate a large number in between two bounds, for example, "Please can you give me a number between one million and ten million." We asked over thirteen hundred subjects a total of 11 variants of this type of question – altering the propositional content, while keeping the range essentially the same (Please can you give me a number between one million and nine million, nine hundred and ninety-nine thousand, nine hundred and ninety-nine; Please can you give me a random number between one million and ten million; and so on). The key results can be summarized reasonably succinctly. Although there were some nine million possible answers, we found that what subjects actually did could be captured in a very small number of strategies. The numbers generated were classified according to their thematic structure. For large numbers the "subject" of the representation is the first element that normally signifies the magnitude range – in this case, the number of millions. The "predicate" is any numeric elaboration in the lower ranges of thousands or hundreds and units. The data indicated that subjects were marking magnitude, parity, and numeric elaboration quite systematically in their responses. Particular generic features also appeared to recur in specific combinations. These combinations were taken as indexing properties of their schematic representations of number. The alterations to the propositional content of the questions were obviously designed to highlight rather different schematic properties, and such changes could clearly be related to often quite dramatic shifts in the patterns of numbers generated.

Rather surprisingly, many subjects made errors. Depending on the condition, between 6% and 24% of the subjects answered with a number that was either below the lower boundary or above the upper boundary specified in the question. In making their errors they appeared to have focused their "conceptual" attention on a subset of task-relevant features. The number "errors" were composed according to the same schematic combinations as the correct responses. Central engine operation had either failed faithfully to represent the task demands at a propositional level or had failed to evaluate the ideational content of their output in relation to a faithful representation before "engaging the mouth." There is some evidence that frontal-lobe-damaged patients with "dysexecutive syndrome" routinely make errors of a very similar kind (Shallice & Evans, 1978). When asked to make numeric estimates of the height of a well-known building, they tend to produce answers that lie well outside the range of answers produced by normal controls. In this respect, we may accidentally have stumbled on a way of exploring the properties of dysfunction in the control and coordination of the central engine – but in a "normal" population.

Conclusion

This chapter has described one approach to developing a macro-theory of the organization and functioning of the complete mental mechanism, Interacting Cognitive Subsystems. It then sought to illustrate how ICS could be applied to the analysis and explanation of performance in working memory tasks. The illustrations and discussion of underlying principles were framed by the eight key questions serving to support a comparison of alternative models – in terms of the way that they approach the active maintenance of representations and the executive control of task performance. The answers to these questions are now summarized in Table 9.2. Because working memory is not, in itself, a core construct of the theory, the answers are framed in terms of the types of processes and representations of ICS.

Table 9.2. *A Summary of the ICS Position on the Issues Discussed Under Each of the Eight Headings Serving to Support the Comparison of Alternative Models*

(1) **Basic Mechanisms and Representations in Working Memory**
Performance in working memory tasks is viewed as supported by three basic types of information processing resource: processes that change the representation of information, memory records, and processes that change incoming information to those memory records. These three resources are combined into subsystems that themselves interact within a wider system. There are nine different types of mental representations, each associated with a specific subsystem and each of which can contribute to performance in working memory tasks.

(2) **The Control and Regulation of Working Memory**
The ICS architecture is viewed as a mechanism that is regulated and controlled by the exchanges of information among subsystems. There is no homunculus or central executive. However, key aspects of executive functioning are fulfilled by processing exchanges involving propositional and implicational meaning.

(3) **The Unitary Versus Non-Unitary Nature of Working Memory**
Because many processes and types of representations are called into play in the execution of working memory tasks, ICS very clearly presents an extreme form of the non-unitary position.

continued

Table 9.2, continued

(4) The Nature of Working Memory Limitations
All limitations on performance must be traced back to the operation of specific processes either directly transforming information arriving at a subsystem or transforming representations of current or past experience. However, most real limitations arise at the systemic level of analysis. The fundamental limitation lies in the capacity of the entire architecture to reconfigure dynamically and use all its representational and processing resources to best advantage in a specific task context.

(5) The Role of Working Memory in Complex Cognitive Activities
The ICS architecture encompasses all types of sensory, central, and effector processing activity. It was actually designed to support the successive development of explanations of performance across a broad range of complex tasks. The self-same processes and representations, together with their principles of operation, can be used as a basis for explaining working memory performance in exactly the same way that they are used to deal with any other complex task.

(6) The Relationship of Working Memory to Long-Term Memory and Knowledge
"Knowledge" is captured within the repertoires of record content preserved in each subsystem, and within repertoires of "procedural knowledge" enabling processes to transform one type of representation into another. Performance in long- and short-term recall is mediated by processes acting on records. Whereas those representations usually called into play in working memory tasks involve surface properties of verbal or spatial form, those that most usefully support long-term recall are representations of propositional and implicational meaning.

(7) The Relationship of Working Memory to Attention and Consciousness
Attention is linked to the selection, by a process, of a "stream" of information. What is currently "being attended to" includes a consideration of how the "streams" are used to produce representations throughout a configuration. General conscious awareness is linked to those "copy" processes that are actively creating representations. Focal awareness is associated with the particular process that is configured for buffered processing and thereby acting as the locus of control for processing activity within the wider configuration.

(8) The Biological Implementation of Working Memory
ICS is an architecture specified at a functional level of analysis. To develop explanations of cognitive behavior, no reference to underlying brain mechanisms or implementation is required. Key aspects of the model are nonetheless consistent with evidence from brain-damaged patients, and the potential exists to explore possible relationships between different patterns of mental activity and the activation of specific brain regions.

REFERENCES

Baddeley, A. D. (1966). The capacity for generating information by randomization. *Quarterly Journal of Experimental Psychology, 18,*119–129.

Baddeley, A. D. (1978). The trouble with levels: A re-examination of Craik & Lockhart's framework for memory research. *Psychological Review, 85,* 139–152.

Baddeley, A. D. (1986). *Working memory.* New York: Oxford University Press.

Baddeley, A. D. (1990). *Human memory: Theory and practice.* Hove, UK: Erlbaum.

Baddeley, A. D., & Hitch, G. J. (1974). Working memory. In G. H. Bower (Ed.), *The psychology of learning and motivation: Advances in research and theory* (Vol. 8, pp. 47–89). New York: Academic Press.

Baddeley, A. D., Grant, S., Wight, E., & Thomson, N. (1975). Imagery and visual working memory. In P. M. A. Rabbitt & S. Dornic (Eds.), *Attention and performance V* (pp. 295–317). London: Erlbaum.

Baddeley, A. D., Lewis, V. J., & Vallar, G. (1984). Exploring the articulatory loop. *Quarterly Journal of Experimental Psychology, 36,* 233–252.

Baddeley, A. D., Papagno, C., & Vallar, G. (1988). When long-term learning depends on short-term storage. *Journal of Memory and Language, 27,* 586–595.

Baddeley, A. D., Thomson, N., & Buchanan, M. (1975). Word length and the structure of short-term memory. *Journal of Verbal Learning and Verbal Behavior, 14,* 575–589.

Barnard, P. J. (1985). Interacting cognitive subsystems: A psycholinguistic approach to short term memory. In A. Ellis (Ed.), *Progress in the psychology of language* (Vol. 2, pp. 197–258). London: Erlbaum.

Barnard, P. J. (1987). Cognitive resources and the learning of human-computer dialogues. In J. M. Carroll (Ed.), *Interfacing thought: Cognitive aspects of human–computer interaction* (pp. 112–158). Cambridge, MA: MIT Press.

Barnard, P. J. (1991). Bridging between basic theories and the artefacts of human-computer interaction. In J. M. Carroll (Ed.), *Designing interaction: Psychology at the human–computer interface* (pp. 103–127). Cambridge, UK: Cambridge University Press.

Barnard, P., & Hammond, N. V. (1982). Usability and its multiple determination for the occasional user of interactive systems. In M. B. Williams (Ed.), *Pathways to the information society* (pp. 543–548). Amsterdam: North Holland.

Barnard, P. J., Hammond, N. V., MacLean, A., & Morton, J. (1982). Learning and remembering interactive commands in a text-editing task. *Behaviour and Information Technology, 1,* 347–358.

Barnard, P. J., MacLean, A., & Hammond, N. V. (1984). User representations of ordered sequences of command operations. In B. Shackel (Ed.), *Proceedings of Interact '84: First IFIP conference on human–computer interaction* (Vol. 1, pp. 434–438). London: IEE.

Barnard, P. J., & May, J. (1993). Cognitive modelling for user requirements. In P. Byerley, P. Barnard, & J. May (Eds.), *Computers, communication and usability: Design issues, research and methods for integrated services* (pp. 101–146). Amsterdam: North Holland.

Barnard, P. J., & May, J. (1995). Interactions with advanced graphical interfaces and the deployment of latent human knowledge. In F. Paterno (Ed.), *The design specification and verification of interactive systems* (pp. 15–49). Berlin: Springer Verlag.

Barnard, P. J., May, J., & Salber, D. (1996). Deixis and points of view in media spaces: An empirical gesture. *Behaviour and Information Technology, 15,* 37–50.

Barnard, P. J., Scott, S. K., & Murray, L. (1996). *Depression, early experience and the development of schematic models of the self.* Paper presented at the Summer Meeting of the Experimental Psychology Society, Cambridge, UK.

Barnard, P. J., & Teasdale, J. D. (1991). Interacting cognitive subsystems: A systemic approach to cognitive-affective interaction and change. *Cognition and Emotion, 5,* 1–39.

Barnard, P. J., Wilson, M., & MacLean, A. (1988). Approximate modelling of cognitive activity with an expert system: A theory based strategy for developing an interactive design tool. *The Computer Journal, 31,* 445–456.

Broadbent, D. E. (1958). *Perception and communication.* London: Pergammon.

Brooks, L. R. (1967). The suppression of visualisation by reading. *Quarterly Journal of Experimental Psychology, 19,* 189–299.

Campbell, R., & Dodd, B. (1980). Hearing by eye. *Quarterly Journal of Experimental Psychology, 32,* 85–99.

Chi, M. T. H. (1978). Knowledge structure and memory development. In R. S. Siegler, (Ed.), *Children's thinking: What develops?* Hillsdale, NJ: Erlbaum.

Craik, F. I. M., & Lockhart, R. S. (1972). Levels of processing: A framework for memory research. *Journal of Verbal Learning and Verbal Behavior, 11,* 671–684.

Crowder, R. G., & Morton, J. (1969). Precategorical acoustic storage (PAS). *Perception & Psychophysics, 5,* 365–373.

Duke, D. J., Barnard, P. J., Duce, D. A., & May, J. (1995). Systematic development of the human interface. *APSEC '95: Second Asia-Pacific Software Engineering Conference* (pp. 313–321). Los Alamitos: IEEE Computer Society Press.

Eldridge, M., Barnard, P. J., & Bekerian, D. (1994). Autobiographical memory and daily schemas at work. *Memory, 2,* 51–74.

Goodale, M. A., & Milner, A. D. (1992). Separate visual pathways for perception and action. *Trends in Neurosciences, 15,* 20–25.

Goodale, M. A., Milner, A. D., Jacobson, K. S., & Carey, D. P. (1991). A neurological dissociation between perceiving objects and grasping them. *Nature, 349,* 154–156.

Marcel, A. (1983). Conscious and unconscious perception: An approach to the relations between phenomenal experience and perceptual processes. *Cognitive Psychology, 15,* 197–237.

May J., & Barnard, P. J. (1995). The case for supportive evaluation during design. *Interacting with Computers, 7,* 115–143.

May, J., Barnard, P. J., & Blandford, A. (1993). Using structural descriptions of interfaces to automate the modelling of user cognition. *User Modelling and User-Adapted Interaction, 3,* 27–64.

May, J., Scott, S., & Barnard, P. J. (1995). *Structuring displays: A psychological guide.* Eurographics Tutorial Notes Series. Geneva: EACG.

Morris, C. D., Bransford, J. D., & Franks, J. J. (1977). Levels of processing versus transfer appropriate processing. *Journal of Verbal Learning and Verbal Behavior, 16,* 519–533.

Murray, D. (1968). Articulation and acoustic confusability in short-term memory. *Journal of Experimental Psychology, 78,* 679–684.

Norman, D. A., & Bobrow, D. (1979). Descriptions: An intermediate stage in memory retrieval. *Cognitive Psychology, 11,* 107–123.

Paulesu, E., Frith, C .D., & Frackowiak, R. S. J. (1993). The neural correlates of the verbal component of working memory. *Nature, 362*, 342–344.

Scott, S. K., Barnard P. J., & May, J. (1995). *Specifying executive function in random generation tasks.* Paper presented at the Cognitive Section Meeting of the British Psychological Society, Bristol, UK.

Shallice, T. (1988). *From neuropsychology to mental structure.* New York: Cambridge University Press.

Shallice, T., & Evans, M. E. (1978). The involvement of the frontal lobes in cognitive estimation. *Cortex, 4*, 294–303.

Shepard, R. N., & Metzler, J. (1971). Mental rotation of three dimensional objects. *Science, 171*, 701–703.

Smith, E. E., & Jonides, J. (1997). Working memory: A view from neuroimaging. *Cognitive Psychology, 33*, 5–42.

Spoehr, K., & Corin, W. (1978). The stimulus suffix effect as a memory coding phenomenon. *Memory & Cognition, 6*, 583–589.

Teasdale, J. D., & Barnard, P. J. (1993). *Affect, cognition and change: Re-modelling depressive thought.* Hove, UK: Erlbaum.

Teasdale, J. D., Taylor, M. J., Cooper, Z., Hayhurst, H., & Paykel, E. S. (1995). Depressive thinking: Shifts in construct accessibility or in schematic mental models? *Journal of Abnormal Psychology, 104*, 500–507.

Warrington, E., & Shallice, T. (1969). The selective impairment of verbal short-term memory. *Brain, 92*, 885–896.

10 Working Memory in a Multilevel Hybrid Connectionist Control Architecture (CAP2)

WALTER SCHNEIDER

FIVE CENTRAL FEATURES OF THE THEORY

In a connectionist control network, working memory is implemented via short-term activation and connection changes that support cognitive operations. The CAP2 approach is a model of skilled processing and learning. When applied to working memory the model instantiates multiple forms and mechanisms of working memory. The major features are:

(1) Memory and processing occur in a multilayered hierarchy of modular processors with limited interactions and a single executive modulating activity. The CAP2 micro- and macrostructural characteristics and temporal expectations show parallels in cortical architecture and activation patterns.

(2) Memory takes the form of activation vectors in modules, fast and slowly changing connection weights within and between modules with different activation, interference, and decay effects.

(3) The control and regulation of working memory is performed by a hierarchical control structure of an executive using activity and priority reports from the network of modules and input of messages on the inner loop to monitor and modulate message traffic.

(4) The executive is a limited sequential processing network that can execute the production system–like sequential operations, which are particularly critical in learning new tasks and maintaining temporary variable information that is not coded in consistent association patterns in the modular network. The executive has local memory to maintain variable bindings and sequential procedures to control the network to perform cognitive tasks.

(5) Skilled performance involves automatic module-to-module transmissions that can perform consistent associative mappings with little loading of the executive.

This work was supported in part by NIH Grant 1-R01 HD32395-03A1 and Naval Research Grant N00014-91-J-1708. The brain activation work cited was done in conjunction with Jason Chein and Jeff Shrager.

Working memory is an important concept in psychology albeit vaguely defined. In this chapter, working memory shall be defined as short-term activation and connection changes that support maintenance, planning, and the organization of cognitive operations in the performance of short-term tasks (minutes). Working memory has many components depending on its form (activation or weights), its parameters (decay rate, learning rate), its knowledge specialization (visual perception, goal planning), and its connection pathways (including loops supporting reactivation). Over the years, working memory has made a transition from the concept of a temporary buffer of information (as in the short-term store of Atkinson & Shiffrin, 1968) to multiple processors (Baddeley, 1986) and distributed networks of processing (Rumelhart, McClelland, & the PDP Research Group, 1986).

This chapter provides an interpretation of working memory based on biological, information-processing, and behavioral constraints. The chapter interrelates previously published themes, which include the distinction between controlled and automatic processing (Schneider & Shiffrin, 1977), the role of a multileveled connectionist control structure in working memory (Schneider & Detweiler, 1987), the use of that control structure to enable learning by instruction (Schneider & Oliver, 1991), attentional control (Shedden & Schneider, 1990, 1991), and the role of consciousness in the effective control of processing (Schneider & Pimm-Smith, 1997). Topics include (a) a brief review of physiological themes and mechanisms underlying working memory; (b) a detailed description of the CAP2 (Controlled Automatic Processing version 2); (c) some brief brain-imaging results about the changes that occur as skill is acquired; and (d) the conclusion with a discussion of the specific working memory questions, as well as a commentary about the other models presented in this volume.

CAP2 Model Summary

We will begin by characterizing the CAP2 architecture in summary form, which will be expanded in the next section. This chapter applies the CAP2 architecture to issues of working memory. The architecture is a series of connectionist simulations of both associative and symbolic processing. The microstructure includes thousands of cortical modules that involve an input layer of connectionist units with autoassociative feedback and an output layer. Each module outputs scalar report signals to an executive controller. These reports characterize the priority and activity of the vector within the module. These modules receive three control signals from the executive that influence the within-module feedback, output gain, and a global reinforcement signal. The macroscale includes modules organized into levels, and levels organized into regions with the regions communicating on an innerloop. The executive is a connectionist sequential net that controls information flow and executes sequential procedures to accomplish goal-based problem solving. The executive is not "aware" of messages except those that are transmitted on the innerloop. The CAP2 computational model quantitatively predicts why novice performance must be serial, and how initial learning can be fast but results in slow, serial, effortful, fragile performance. As the model practices on consistent component tasks, automatic component processes develop that can operate with minimal executive control and lead to fast, parallel, low-effort processing.

Physiological Perspectives on the Architecture for Cognitive Processing

Working memory operates in the brain to perform computational functions that produce behavioral results. The CAP2 architecture is built on a foundation of biological mechanisms that are at least physiologically inspired. These have been simplified in connectionist simulations and applied to interpreting behavioral phenomena including working memory.

CAP2 seeks to use biology to suggest a framework for the cognitive architecture. Modeling generally uses task constraints (e.g., EPIC, Kieras, Meyer, Mueller, & Seymour, Chapter 6, this volume), computational constraints (e.g., Soar, Young, & Lewis, Chapter 7, this volume), or biological architectural constraints. Biology provides not only rich concepts that suggest different and powerful metaphors, but also excellent models for processing with a different style of computing than often is present in computational optimization constraints. For example, the computer model provided the concepts of a general short-term-store (STS) and long-term-store (LTS), which is based on computer RAM and disk storage (e.g., Atkinson & Shiffrin, 1968). This suggested a false independence of content in STS and LTS. In contrast, the biological perspective of connection weights and activation suggests a much more integrated and interactive STS and LTS. The biology model provides specific mechanisms such as how attentional control and memory change signaling occur physiologically (see subsequent discussion). Churchland and Sejnowski (1992) provide a book-length discussion of neurophysiological constraints of cognitive function plus a good review of neuroscience and computational issues for understanding these concepts in cognition.

The structure of the brain provides several scales of organization and interconnection. The cortex appears to be composed of a *hierarchy of processing modules* (Martin, 1988; Felleman & Van Essen, 1991; Szentagothai, 1975) and the CAP2 architecture assumes that processing is performed within this hierarchy of modules. These modules have specialized functions and are composed of *columns* of cells that process a related function (e.g., processing lines of a given orientation for a given portion of the visual field). Each column contains large numbers of cells (e.g., 40,000 in a column) and the columns are further organized into modules that share similar input and output functions (see Martin, 1988). For example, the first visual area is V1, which is composed of hundreds of columns (Van Essen & Anderson, 1990). In vision there are an estimated 32 regions that are visually driven (Felleman & Van Essen, 1991). There are a large number of modules, perhaps in the range of a hundred thousand,[1] and there are likely to be 500 to 1000 *cortical areas*. These areas are organized into *cortical regions* (e.g., vision, motor output) in which the modules are interconnected and have a predominantly within-hierarchy pattern of connections (Felleman & Van Essen, 1991).

There are different characteristics of connection patterns between modules and the four classes of projections. The two classes of major projections from a module are *feed-forward* and *feed-backward*. For example, the visual area V2 has large projections forward in the processing hierarchy to V4 and from V2 backward down to V1. These are characterized by the many fibers that project to multiple modules in the neighboring regions. Within a module there is a layering of cell types that can be visually identified as discrete changes in the makeup of cells, typically in six layers of cortex. For example, new inputs come into cells primarily in layer 4. The feed-forward projections tend to originate from the superficial layers (2, 3) and project to the layer 4 area in the ascending module. Feedback layers originate either above or below layer 4 and project back down, avoiding layer 4 (Felleman & Van Essen, 1991). These connections are dense enough to convey detailed information (e.g., specific features to recognize a letter). The third class of projections is *point-to-point control*. This involves small numbers of deep, layer 5 or 6 pyramidal cells projecting subcortically to specific nuclei with return projections from those nuclei. These projections involve a small number of fibers relative to the feed-forward projections that may provide control signals (e.g., attention) rather than information signals. The fourth class of projections involves *broadcast* projections in which small nuclei project to broad areas of cortex. Projections from the locus ceruleus and the ventral tegmentum area (Schultz, Apicella, & Ljungberg, 1993) project to large regions of cortex, including multiple lobes. These broadcast connections are too few to convey detailed content informa-

---

[1] The model uses physiological data to provide "order of magnitude" estimates of the number of modules involved. An estimate of the number of modules would relate to the number of cortical hypercolumns (Szentagothai, 1975), which are about a square millimeter in size. The human cortex has an estimated 250,000 mm² of surface area, suggesting 250,000 modules. The number of levels may be estimated by the Felleman and Van Essen (1991) visual system data, estimating the average size of visual areas in the monkey, and relating that size to the equivalent sizes in the human, and then dividing the human cortex number by the estimated size of a level (250,000 mm² divided by 170 mm² and assuming an average of 2 replications of an area, for 735 levels). The number of regions would include the basic input and output modalities and internal representational systems (e.g., object vision, location, audition, semantic memory, motor output, context), perhaps in the range of 10 to 30. For discussion purposes in this text, the exact numbers are not critical but the relative order of magnitude provides a perspective of the number of modules that need to be controlled.

tion but are well situated to convey arousal tuning and perhaps reinforcement signals during learning.

There are potentially hundreds of thousands of inputs that must be routed to converge on individual points in the cortex (e.g., a human can be instructed to attend to hundreds of visual or auditory locations and have a stimulus at a given location activate a single finger movement). To facilitate this convergence, there are structures that *coordinate communications* between modules. The major components of these circuits include areas of the anterior and posterior attentional systems, which include cortical and subcortical regions (Goldman-Rakic, 1988; Mesulam, 1990; Schneider, Pimm-Smith, & Worden, 1994).

Brain-imaging data support a view that cortical processing involves the differential use of cortical areas and changes in the cortical function with practice (Raichle et al., 1994). For example, our brain-imaging subjects learn simple tasks such as entering phone numbers. Subjects show a dramatic reduction in the amount of cortical activity as they move from novice to skilled performers.

CAP2 Cognitive Architecture

The basic components of the Controlled and Automatic Processing Version 2 (CAP2) architecture simulates cognitive processing in a hierarchical network of connectionist modules that captures the themes presented previously. CAP2 provides a configurable architecture in which control signals alter the signal paths within the architecture, thus enabling a wide variety of cognitive operations. The architecture is composed of neuron-like units organized into modules that are organized in levels. The modules have control signals that both monitor and manage the processing that accomplishes goal-directed activities.

The basic components of the architecture are illustrated in Figures 10.1 to 10.3. Processing occurs within a module, between modules, and between the executive control system and the modules. To understand the model's connectivity, it is helpful to conceptualize how the network might process a string of characters in reading a word. Information is coded in the form of a vector of units that is transmitted from level to level. For example, the letter "T" might be coded as having the features of upper horizontal and middle vertical bars with a conjunction.

The *module microstructure* (Figure 10.1) involves two layers of units and five control signals. The biological candidates for these modules are the cortical columns seen throughout the cortex. The vector of activity inputs on an *input layer* of units, which project back to themselves (autoassociative connection) as well as to a set of output units. A biological candidate for a large number of these units is the layer 4 granular cells (White, 1989). The autoassociative connections clean up and categorize the signal (see J. A. Anderson, 1983), and

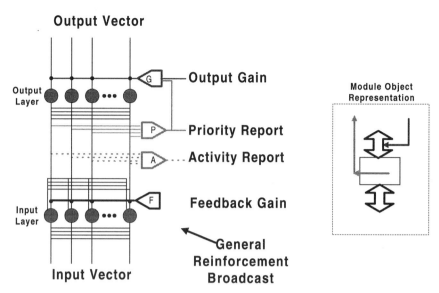

Figure 10.1. Microstructure of a CAP2 module. An input vector of activation enters the module (from below) as the result of the activity of a set of input neurons. The activity passes through a connection matrix that reflects prior learning and evokes a new activation pattern in the input layer. The input layer then activates the output layer through a second connection matrix. An autoassociative layer connects the input layer units back to themselves, thus providing feedback gain. The module output is controlled by a feedback gain that determines the autoassociative feedback and output gain that controls the transmission to other modules. There are two output report units that signal the activity of the module (the summed activity of the input layer) and the priority report (the associated priority of the message for the output transmission). The priority report also has a local impact on the output gain, which allows the module to output even in the absence of an executive input if a high-priority signal is present. There is also a general reinforcement signal that is broadcast to all the modules and triggers the module to change the connection weights. The figure on the right shows a small version of a module and illustrates the flow of the message vectors and the report and control signals. This smaller representation of a module is used in Figure 10.2.

the *output layer* of units sends a vector of activation to other modules. The vector transmission of information occurs in three sets of units. The activated output units from the previous module's output layer project to the input layer on the next module, which in turn outputs to that module's output layer, which outputs to the next module. The three layers of processing involve input, intermediate, and output layers, all of which are common in connectionist models. The intermediate or hidden layers enable complex pattern association (see Rumelhart, Hinton, & Williams, 1986). This module has both control input and output report signals.

There are two input control signals that influence module activity. The *input feedback* increases the feedback between units in the input layer. This increase of the feedback can be thought of as a multiplying of all the input layer units by a scalar constant. This multiplication causes greater autoassociation and coarser categorization of the input (J. A. Anderson, 1983) as well as latching of the signal (Shedden & Schneider, 1990). For example, at low input feedback, all of the features must be present to detect an object, whereas at high feedback gain, a few critical features can result in perception of the object (e.g., recognition of an object as a snake only when color, shape, and size match the prototype during the day, but at night a subset of features such as a curving line can trigger false recognition). Modulating the input feedback allows the network to dynamically alter the match criterion (e.g., when an ambiguous input occurs, the input feedback can increase until it matches a recognized memory).

The second input module control signal is the *output gain,* which determines attentional selection. The output gain is a scalar multiplication of all the output units. The output gain control is the principal mechanism of attentional control. When one attends to the left ear in a dichotic listening experiment and ignores the right ear, the relative gain is like turning up the volume (scalar multiplication of the signal) on the left ear and turning down the volume on the right ear. The biological candidate for this function is the chandelier-cell inhibitory neurons that contact upper level pyramidal cells as they make feed-forward connections (DeFelipe, Hendry, Jones, & Schmechel, 1985). This provides an attenuation gate of the information from the module. Single-unit recordings of attentional filtering suggest that attention can reduce the magnitude of single-unit activity (see Luck, Chelazzi, Hillyard, & Desimone, 1997). The biological candidate for the output control signals is the subcortical control signals from intralaminar nuclei of the thalamus.

There are two module *output report* signals that provide the controller with information to guide selection and detect memory match and recognition. The first is an *activity report,* which provides a metric of activity in the module (e.g., measures of the number of active units [see Shedden & Schneider, 1991]). This provides a basis for determining the activity in a unit and indirectly provides the degree of match between inputs to the unit. The activity report enables the controller to optimize the search to include only active channels. The controller can limit search to only those channels that have activity (e.g., attend to the ear that has a signal and ignore the other). In visual search experiments subjects can skip blank channels (e.g., searching randomly two out of four channels at a speed no slower than searching two specified channels; Shiffrin & Schneider, 1977), suggesting that activity controls selection.

The second module output report is the *priority report,* which determines which active channels are the most important (e.g., attend to the ear in which you heard your name and ignore the other ear even if the other ear input is louder than the channel with your name, the "cocktail party effect"). The priority report is a result from an association of the input vector to the priority (a learned priority) signal for that vector. Important stimuli (e.g., your name) get a high priority and are likely to be attended to. If the priority report is sufficiently high, it will result in an output from a module even in the absence of automatic gain input to the module.

Deep pyramidal neurons are a biological candidate for report cells. These neurons connect to intralaminar thalamic nuclei and do not appear to be gated (White, 1989). For the controller to determine what modules to gate (via output gain), it must receive report signals that are not gated. With separate report signals, unattended channels (with low output) could still make the controller aware of the existence of an important message, which the controller could later output by increasing the output gain for the module. The need to communicate control and report signals between the controller and the modules would produce a point-to-point connection pattern that is seen between cortical areas and subcortical structures in the thalamus (see White, 1989).

The final module control signal is a *reinforcement signal* that is broadly transmitted to all modules with a broadcast type of connection pattern. This causes a change in the connection weights within and between the modules. The broad projections from the locus ceruleus and the ventral tegmentum are potential biological candidates for this signal. For example, the ventral tegmentum area is active when the animal is learning a new contingency (Schultz et al., 1993).

The *macrolevel structure* of CAP2 involves a network of the aforementioned modules with a control structure to modulate communications within the system. The modules are organized into a lattice (see Figure 10.2) with multiple levels and multiple modules in each level. This is analogous to the structure of the visual areas (e.g., V1, V2, V4). The levels are organized into regions (e.g., vision, motor output) and each module within a region connects to multiple modules above and below it. The network can be dynamically reconfigured to perform different tasks. By reducing gain, a module can be effectively removed from processing. For instance, by reducing feedback, input signals can be allowed to decay, but by increasing feedback the input can be latched and new inputs blocked. In addition to the modules and the vector connections between modules, there is an executive control structure that manages transmissions between modules. The report and control signals provide the executive information to determine which modules have messages to transmit. Message vectors are transmitted between modules within layers. The top level of each region is interconnected with other top-layer modules on a circuit referred to as the *innerloop* (Schneider & Detweiler, 1987). The innerloop of modules allows cross-area transmissions (e.g., vision to motor output).

The macrolevel structure enables the model to perform a variety of important information-processing operations. These include the chunking of infor-

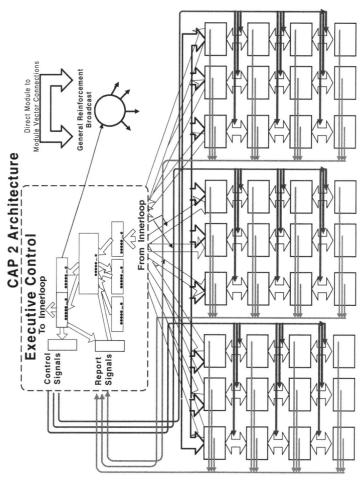

Figure 10.2. Macrostructure of CAP2 network showing three regions with four levels in each region. The central executive monitors the activity and priority reports of all the modules and the messages of the upper set of innerloop modules. The executive also controls the attentional gating and feedback of the modules in the network. The general reinforcement signal (upper right) is a signal transmitted to all the modules.

mation to combine several inputs (either sequential or spatial) into a higher level code and coding item-order effects (see Schneider & Detweiler, 1987).

A *central executive* monitors and controls network activity. It is very important that the executive does not suffer from the "homunculus problem" (e.g., all the complexity is passed on to the executive without reduction in the decision-making requirements). In CAP2, the executive has the complex task of managing the activity of potentially thousands of modules. Much of the complexity present in the modules must be reduced to enable the executive to make decisions regarding the full network. For example, the executive does not see the messages within or between modules at lower levels. However, the executive can detect the priority and activity reports of those modules. This reduces the data of a particular vector within a module to the scalar activity and priority report (e.g., a pattern of a 10,000-element vector of neural activities would be conveyed to the executive as two scalar values). The compression of information at the module level allows a simplistic executive to moderate network communication. For example, to determine which module will be next attended to, a winner-take-all connectionist circuit (Feldman & Ballard, 1982) could pick the most active or highest priority module, and then the output gain on that module could be increased to transmit the high-priority message. Such a network could moderate the message traffic of hundreds of modules so that only a small number of modules transmit at a time (thus limiting interference problems).

The central executive has a variety of functions that can explain limitations and capabilities of human cognition. In the following text eight core functions are detailed. It should be kept in mind that the performance of a single task may involve use of all of these functions to accomplish the task.

Comparing Information

The first function is to *compare information*. The module can compare information (e.g., if two letters have a name match "aA"). The degree of a match resulting from the input of two vectors into a module can be determined by monitoring the activity report. Figure 10.3 shows the mean and standard deviation of activity reports that occur as a result of the additive effects of two vectors on a module (see Shedden & Schneider, 1991). In the simulation, the match represented inputting two vectors that were assumed to be semantically related (for related items half of the vector elements matched the prototype for the category). The addition of two vectors provides a metric of the degree of correlation of those vectors (see Schneider & Detweiler, 1987; Shedden & Schneider, 1991).

The CAP2 activity report comparison can explain a paradox in human behavioral literature. Given that the brain has 10 billion neurons, why must humans serially compare letters even after extended practice of varied mapping stimuli (see Schneider & Shiffrin, 1977)? In a simulation, Shedden and Schneider (1991) examined the potential accuracy for serial and parallel com-

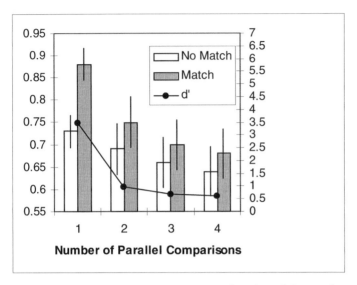

Figure 10.3. Activity-report monitoring as a function of the number of items used in the comparison. This shows the effect of comparing one display item to 1, 2, 3, or 4 memory items by adding the vectors and using the metric of the euclidean length of the added vector. (The vectors from the same category shared half the vector feature elements from the prototype category vector.) The bars show the average activity and standard deviation as a function of the number of comparisons for the Match and No Match conditions, the length ranging from 0.55 to 0.95 activity (left axis). The line shows the *d'* with the axis on the right. (Adapted from Shedden & Schneider, 1991.)

parisons based on the activity report. Figure 10.3 shows the results. The *d'* was 3.6 (1% error) for serial comparisons and reduced to *d'* of 0.98 (14% error) for two parallel comparisons and *d'* of 0.57 (29% error) with four comparisons. For an activity-based judgment there is a need to make the comparisons serially even though their vectors involve parallel activation of potentially thousands of units.

Attending to High-Priority Messages and Automatic Transmission

A second central executive function is to *attend to high-priority messages* so that the outputs can reach the other modules in the network (see Gupta & Schneider, 1991). The priority mechanism provides the mechanism that supports the development of automatic processing, enabling consistently attended-to information to be output from a module automatically.

In CAP2 a module can prioritize information and enable automatic processing. A connectionist simulation of priority-report learning predicts reaction time speedup in search tasks. The reinforcement signal increased the magnitude of the priority signal when the module had recently output a vector after a match and decreased the magnitude after a trial without a match

(Gupta & Schneider, 1991). Figure 10.4A shows the development of priority reports during training. The initial priority of a vector is neutral (0). In a search trial, the subject compares visual stimuli to a set of memory items and responds when there is a match (e.g., Schneider & Shiffrin, 1977). On a match trial, the last stimulus that the subject attended was output through a series of modules followed by the response. In CAP2 a successful response generates a global reinforcement signal. It is important to conceptualize the events that occur in a module across time. For a module containing the stimulus, the module outputs its vector and shortly thereafter the module receives a reinforcement signal. In CAP2 the sequence of transmission followed by a reinforcement signal results in an increase in priority for the message within the module. This has been simulated (Gupta & Schneider, 1991) by having the reinforcement signal increase the activity of the priority units and then change the connection weights between the input vector and the more activated priority units. For a stimulus that is a consistent target, this results in a gradually increased priority over time (see Figure 10.4A, Consistent Target line). In CAP2 once the priority is above the *automatic transmission threshold,* the model will output the vector even in the absence of executive control processing. The ability of modules to do automatic transmissions allows the network to execute long chains of associations as long as the stimuli are consistently attended to and the input–output mappings are consistent across trials.

The degree of consistency determines the priority of vectors within a module as practice proceeds. In CAP2, on a trial where a stimulus does not result in a reinforcement signal, the priority decreases. For a module that transmitted a nonmatching stimulus, the sequence would be that the module outputs a vector followed by a period without a reinforcement signal being received. In the simulation (Gupta & Schneider, 1991) the priority units receive a negative bias after transmission. In the absence of the reinforcement signal, the association of the input vector to the negatively biased priority units reduces the priority over time. In Figure 10.4A the consistent distractor line shows that decrease. If a stimulus alters between being a target and a distractor, the priority will randomly move up and down over trials (see Figure 10.4A varied target/distractor).

In CAP2 the consistent target-comparisons events trigger priority learning that enables within-module automatic transmission of a vector. The resulting processing becomes fast and parallel with little increase in the number of memory or display comparisons (Gupta & Schneider, 1991, see Figure 10.4B). The model predicts how automatic processing develops with consistent practice, as is seen in the human literature (Shiffrin, 1988). As a module consistently outputs the same message following the same input message, the module learns the input to the output association. If the priority of the message is high enough, the message will be automatically transmitted without the need for executive input to increase the gain of the output units. If the

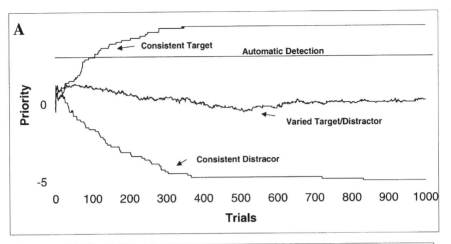

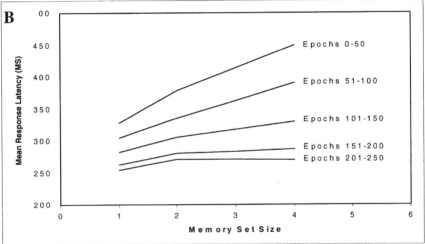

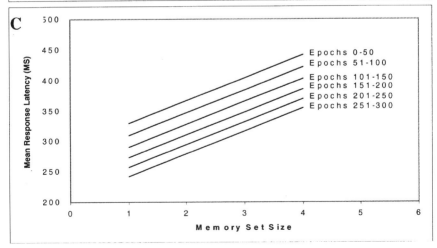

Figure 10.4. Priority learning simulation results. (A) Priority for a consistent target (upper line), consistent distractor (lower line), and the varied target/distractor (middle line). The automatic detection line indicates the point at which the module outputs the vector automatically. (B) Simulated consistent search shows the decline in the memory set size effect with practice. (C) Simulated varied mapping showing the linear slope effect after extended practice. (Adapted from Gupta & Schneider, 1991.)

mapping is not consistent, the priority report cannot be used to separate targets from distractors and the executive must continue to do slow serial comparisons even after extended practice (see Figure 10.4C).

Buffering Information

The third executive function is to manage the *buffering of information* by latching data for short periods of time or delaying the transmission of the data without loss of information. The buffering of information is integral to cognitive processing and to the components of working memory. The feedback connections on the input layer allow the module to accept a short burst of information and maintain that information even if the input data are removed (see Shedden & Schneider, 1990, Fig. 4). Such buffering and latching of inputs is a common component of complex computational devices and enables asynchronous operation between subsystems. The duration of buffering in the module may be a constant for a given region (e.g., maintaining the input vector for up to one second). The executive's function is to serialize module outputs to minimize the cross-talk between modules owing to concurrent transmission. Having a buffer allows delaying transmission, enabling multiplexing to reduce interference between message transmissions.

Configuring the Module Network

A fourth function is *configuring the module network* to process a particular task (see Schneider & Oliver, 1991). For example, if you were to read out the letters of "word" backward as "d-r-o-w," the modules would be configured to accept the four letters in four visual modules and then alter attention to sequentially scan the letters in reverse order. The configuration is based on the goal state of the executive (see later discussion) and the priority and activity reports in the network. If a message comes into a module, the executive becomes aware of the need to evaluate the information based on the activity and priority report. If, however, other network traffic has higher priority, the executive can increase the feedback of the reporting module to buffer the message (see Shedden & Schneider, 1990), thus allowing the network to use asynchronous transmission. As the priority and activity reports decay, the executive "forgets" about information in the network, and it is unlikely that the information will be communicated to other modules in the network.

Building New Associations

The fifth executive function is to *build new associations* during learning. There are three components to this: (a) placing the proper associations in the critical modules; (b) causing an input to occur to a target module before the critical output; and (c) triggering a learning event to cause a connection change. For example, during a search experiment the subject is instructed to push the left index finger whenever an "animal" word is presented (see Schneider & Fisk, 1984). Verbal instructions could load the "index finger response" into a motor module. The input of a word (e.g., "bear") would be transmitted to see if it matched the vector of "animal" in its semantic activity (see Shedden & Schneider, 1991), and upon a match would then release the motor "index finger" response. If it is assumed that the executive also sent out a global reinforcement signal, then the motor response module would encounter the sequence of vector input "animal," and vector output "index finger," and the global reinforcement signal. In CAP2 the global reinforcement signal causes modules that experienced a recent vector in–out event to modify connection weights, thus allowing the input to evoke the output. This allows rapid acquisition of arbitrary associations that can vastly speed up learning relative to shaping-based methods of acquiring initial skills (see Schneider & Oliver, 1991). The executive can use verbal instructions and set up comparison and response operations to provide the fast acquisition of complex input–output mappings.

Goal-based Executive Operations

The sixth executive function is to perform *goal-based operations.* Schneider and Oliver (1991) used a connectionist sequential net to control the network (see Figure 10.5). The sequential net successfully executed multistep programs as a series of associations to accomplish goals (e.g., prediction of digital logic output). These programs are very similar to the goal-based problem-solving operations in ACT-R (J. R. Anderson, 1983; Lovett, Reder, & Lebiere, Chapter 5, this volume) and Soar (Young & Lewis, Chapter 7, this volume). The sequential rule net performed operations such as "compare," "attend," and "load" and received input of the activity reports that had arguments that addressed particular modules (see Figure 5.7 as well as Table 5.1 in Schneider & Oliver, 1991). The executive could also transmit declarative vectors to modules, which then provided intermediate states for the learning of modules in the general network. In the simulations of the hybrid architecture of a sequential net controlling a lattice of modules, learning occurred at a very fast rate (i.e., 120 trials to learn a six-gate digital logic task), which was much faster than a typical connectionist learning (10,835 trials). In principle, this type of architecture could perform the types of problem-solving activities associated with production system models (e.g., Soar and ACT-R).

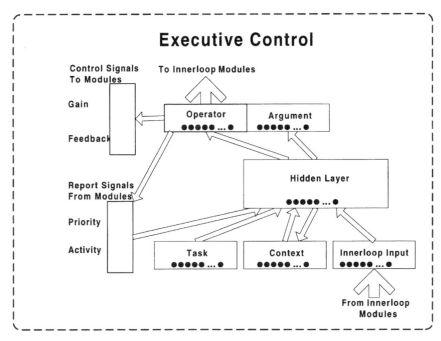

Figure 10.5. Connectionist representation of the executive sequential rule network. The network sequences operations to perform cognitive tasks. Vectors in the network encode the current task. The context vector encodes the activation of hidden units to enable sequential operations. The executive receives priority and activity signals for the module matrix. The innerloop modules project to the innerloop vector input and the operator vector projects to the innerloop modules. The sequential net can execute sequences of operations to control the information flow in the network (see Schneider & Oliver, 1991).

Monitoring Message Content to Sequence Goal Operations

In the course of simulations with CAP2, it became apparent that the executive could perform more specific goal-based problem-solving operations if it was provided access to some of the messages and had local memory that was not shared with the modules that it controlled. Early versions of CAP2 were too limited to account for the specificity of human goal-seeking behavior and the ability of humans to maintain a mental state in the face of interruptions.

To accomplish specific goals, the executive must have access to some of the messages in the network. The differentiation of the goal-seeking behavior, based solely on priority and activity reports, is quite impoverished and is limited to differentiation of the modules in the processing system. Assuming there is an order of magnitude of a thousand processing levels, the activity and priority system could accomplish only broad goals instead of goals that are specific (e.g., seek "food" but not seek "chocolate-covered almonds").

With only activity awareness, the controller would be limited to accomplishing a module-based goal such as "reduce the activity of the eating module," which presumably would be more active during a period of hunger. To satisfy a specific goal, the executive must have access to the specific messages as well as their priorities. To avoid the homunculus problem, it is critical to keep the controller from monitoring all the messages in the network. Schneider and Pimm-Smith (1997) proposed that the controller does have *access to the innerloop messages* – that is, that there is a module on the innerloop that receives input from any of the modules that are transmitting on the innerloop and that the controller could use that data to control goal-based behavior. Such limited awareness of messages matches the developing evidence that conscious awareness is limited to a higher level of information coding (e.g., we can make orientation judgments of high spatial frequency information available at V1 without the ability to consciously perceive the visual grating [see Crick & Koch, 1995]).

Context Memory Enabling Return to Previous Tasks

To provide a processing system that is robust to interruptions, it is beneficial to have a *context memory* that can be used to reinstate messages on the innerloop. A serious problem for any architecture that maintains only temporary information in dynamic activity is that if a message uses the module that contained information, the short-term information is lost. Humans show interruption effects in a short-term memory task such as remembering a list of words (Peterson & Peterson, 1959); however, when performing complex tasks, such as truck delivery scheduling, performance is only slightly effected by loading tasks (Klapp, Marshburn, & Lester, 1983). To provide robustness in CAP2, we added a context module that used fast weights to store the messages on the innerloop (Schneider & Detweiler, 1987). The fast weights allowed the system to associate the messages on the innerloop with the current context. If an interruption occurred clearing modules, the executive could reestablish the content of the innerloop by evoking the context and using the associations to modules in the innerloop, thus reactivating the previous messages. Because the innerloop learning occurs through fast connection weight change, the learning can become effective in a single association, but it suffers from severe retroactive interference and hence cannot function as a good permanent memory system. The use of fast weights to store context memory is very similar to the interpretations of hippocampal storage of temporary information (O'Reilly, Braver, & Cohen, Chapter 11, this volume).

A Model of Skill Acquisition

The CAP2 model is intended to be a model of human performance and skill acquisition rather than a specific model of working memory. Its core phenomenon is how the model can learn to perform a complex task. Performance goes through five overlapping phases as skill is acquired (see Schneider & Detweiler, 1987; Schneider & Oliver, 1991). For simple search tasks, subjects typically require several hundred trials to make the transition through the five phases of skill acquisition. Phase I (e.g., trials 1 to 10 in a simple search task) involves the executive performing the task by encoding instructions into an interpretive sequence of steps the executive can perform. This sequence will be run in the sequential net that will load modules with critical codes and monitor modules to detect if the inputs satisfy the conditions that will warrant releasing one of the verbally specified responses. During this early phase, interruptions cause task failure. In phase II (e.g., trials 5 to 50), the context-storage mechanism has developed that enables reloading of the innerloop messages. Controlled processing is still needed, but if an interruption occurs, the subject can deal with the interrupting task, reevoke the context of the innerloop, and subsequently switch back to the task after interruption. In phase III (e.g., trials 21 to 150) associations from the goal state acquire enough strength to load working memory without the use of the context storage. In phase IV (e.g., after trial 100) there is a substantial reduction on the controlled processing resources as the associations between the goal state and the input evoke the response state. In phase V (after about 200 trials/rule) the modules develop automatic processing so that the message is transmitted even in the absence of controlled processing input if the input–output mappings and attending are consistent.

The use of working memory varies depending on the task and phases of skill acquisition. The combination of context storage and controlled process comparison enables the network to accurately perform novel tasks after only a few trials. With practice the system modifies the long-term memory associations so that automatic processing develops, enabling fast and accurate as well as low-resource processing.

Brain Imaging of Executive Dropout with Practice

The CAP2 model predicts that as skill is acquired for consistent tasks there is a substantial drop of executive operations. This was tested in a brain-imaging experiment using functional magnetic resonance imaging (fMRI). Subjects learned a phone number task in which they associated a six-digit phone number with one of four names (e.g., "Mike is 323-132"). This was contrasted with a fixed motor response (e.g., "press 123-123") requiring little learning. Subjects also learned to associate faces to color team identifications (e.g., three similar female faces are assigned to the red team, green team, and blue team respectively). Figure 10.6 shows an image of cortical activity in a study contrasting novel (3 min of practice) versus well-learned (5 h of practice on four phone numbers and six faces with single- and dual-task training) execution of the tasks. What was found was that early practice involved over 20 regions in frontal, parietal, and cingulate cortex that dropped out in the prac-

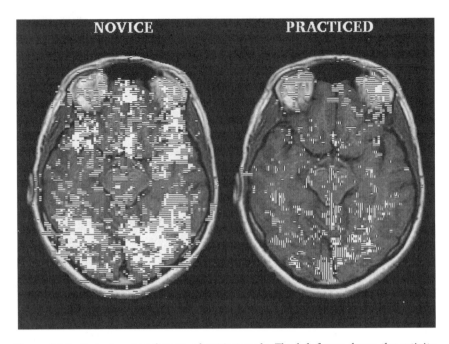

Figure 10.6. Brain-imaging data in a learning study. The left figure shows the activity early in learning the task, the right after extended practice. This is a maximum-projection image of the full brain superimposed on an axial structural image. There are three types of activation shown. Activation by the face-learning task (vertical lines), phone task (horizontal lines), and both tasks (white). Note the large areas of activity on the left (novice performance) relative to the areas on the right (practiced performance). For the novice performer, most of the activation is common to both the face and phone tasks (white areas). These areas are likely to include common executive control areas used in initial task acquisition. The right image shows the activity after the tasks are well learned. After practice there is relatively little activation and almost no overlap between the two tasks. The lack of overlap indicates disjoint areas of skilled performance. Ignore the lined/white areas over the eye region at the top of the image because since these represent eye movement artifacts.

ticed state. There was an 80% reduction in the amount of brain activation for the skilled performer. We also compared the areas of activity in a phone and face learning task and found high overlap in the areas that dropped out. This indicates common learning structures involved in learning two different tasks (e.g., the phone number task involved sequential output, chunking, and verbal coding; the face-learning task was a simple association of the face to a color name with minimal verbal coding). The many areas that are common and drop out as skill is acquired suggest that there is a network of executive functions that are involved in mediating the task, processing the feedback, and modifying memory that is not required for skilled performance. These executive areas appear to overlap areas associated with working memory (Cohen et al., 1997; O'Reilly et al., Chapter 11, this volume).

Applying CAP2 to Issues of Working Memory

The CAP2 model has many forms of memory working together to produce a variety of working memory phenomena. The remainder of this chapter will directly address the eight designated questions of this volume and relate the mechanisms to other conceptualizations of working memory. The summary of the answers to the questions is provided in Table 10.1.

Basic Mechanisms and Representations in Working Memory

In CAP2 memory is instantiated as activation patterns and connection weights. Working memory is the result of activation patterns, feedback latching of data, and context memory instantiated in terms of fast weight change units that associate information on the innerloop to the context. The activation memory rapidly decays (within seconds) without additional coding. The buffer memory can maintain signals as long as the feedback signal is high. This buffer memory typically maintains vectors for a second or two. The context memory allows retrieval of the context for a period of minutes to hours. Inside the executive there is also a sequential net that includes memory for the current goal-state that provides memory on the order of minutes. Different regions code different types of information (e.g., auditory, visual, and motor output).

The general approach of a hybrid connectionist/control architecture has similarity to symbolic and connectionist models of working memory. The subgoal problem-solving activity of the executive processing functions similarly to the interpretive execution of productions in ACT-R (J. R. Anderson, 1983; Lovett et al., Chapter 5, this volume). The use of production-like condition action rules is similar to Soar (Young & Lewis, Chapter 7, this volume), EPIC (Kieras et al., Chapter 6, this volume), and ACT-R. The use of fast weights for innerloop context storage parallels the models of the hippocampal storage of temporary information (O'Reilly et al., Chapter 11, this volume).

The expectation that there is a variety of specialized peripheral processors in CAP2 parallels the ICS (Barnard, Chapter 9, this volume) and EPIC models (Kieras et al., Chapter 6, this volume). The CAP2 architecture contains similarities and differences relative to the Baddeley and Logie (Chapter 2, this volume) view. Both models assume that there is a specialized central executive as well as peripheral processors. Baddeley and Logie present detailed results that support two specialized processors: the phonological loop and the visuospatial sketchpad. In CAP2 there is an expectation of multiple peripheral processors that encode special types of data. The CAP2 model has not been elaborated to account for the specialization of the peripheral processors, but the modular storage mechanism in CAP2 does illustrate the acoustic similar-

Table 10.1. *CAP2 Answers to Designated Questions for Models of Working Memory*

(1) Basic Mechanisms and Representations in Working Memory

Memory is stored in activation patterns across cells (vectors of activation) and in short-term connection weights. There are multiple forms of working memory with different decay rates including activation memory (seconds), buffer memory (seconds), context memory in fast weights to maintain state information with temporal-based retrieval (minutes), and planning goal-state memory (minutes). Different regions code different types of information (e.g., visual imagery versus motor program). There are multiple forms of memory, which include activity within a module, priority report to the executive, control signals from the executive, and sequential activation in a recurrent net in the executive. The particular areas code different information with different interference, decay, and refresh ability.

(2) The Control and Regulation of Working Memory

Control is performed by a hierarchical control structure with both regional and central control. Network communication is controlled by executive modulation of control signals for output gain and input feedback. The output gain is the basic mechanism of selective attention. There is a central control executive that can engage in the complex planning and execution of attentional control programs, thereby allowing skill acquisition (e.g., digital logic). Control operations depend on the task and can include complex logical operations. The basic operations are setting gain, feedback, monitoring activity and priority reports, sending specific messages or a reinforcement signal, and monitoring activity in the innerloop.

(3) The Unitary Versus Non-Unitary Nature of Working Memory

Working memory has multiple forms (e.g., short-term weights, control, data, context, and goal memory; see the answers to Question 1). The memories interact based on the attentional routing circuits that are set up via attention and feedback control. The central control structure has local memory, local planning, and limited monitoring ability.

(4) The Nature of Working Memory Limitations

The limitations of working memory are related to communication cross-talk interference, storage limitations (number of regions), and severe executive control limitations as well as connection-learning interference effects. Different constraints apply to different memories. Interference for buffered memory depends on the similarity of related codes, the number of units, and the difficulty of control operations (e.g., forward versus reverse digit span). Buffering is sensitive to the interference and similarity of the data. Interference is a major limitation in learning owing to a connectionist's faster learning producing larger retroactive forgetting. Multiple learning rates allow the advantages of slow and fast learning.

(5) The Role of Working Memory in Complex Cognitive Operations and Skill Acquisition

The multiple forms of working memory interact to enable complex cognition. The executive sequential net allows interpretive execution of complex tasks. The limitations of vector comparisons require serial processing of the

Table 10.1, continued

novice performer. The use of the sequential net allows the executive to load control programs that enable instructable/verbally controllable learning. Language is interpreted as an important role of a between-person transfer method to convey basic control structure and limited data information between individuals. To enable the executive plan and process control operations, there is a need for the executive to have separate control and data memory that is not part of the module architecture that is being controlled. As expertise develops, the need for executive control reduces for consistent task components. The executive is still necessary to maintain temporary variable information (e.g., previous digit in memory N-back last; see Chapter 11, this volume) or for difficult judgment decisions (e.g., near threshold).

(6) **The Relationship of Working Memory to Long-Term Memory and Knowledge**
Long-term memory is the connection weights (including bias on individual units) in the system. Working memory is always the result of the interaction of an activation vector activating a connection matrix, which in turn activates a new vector at another level of processing. Through the development of automatic processing, many of the working memory control limitations can be reduced.

(7) **The Relationship of Working Memory to Attention and Consciousness**
Attention and working memory are interactive, each having marked impact on the operations of the other. Attention and memory are different. Attention serves the role of gating information, and memory involves maintenance and the association of information. Consciousness includes monitoring the message traffic in the network, planning, and executing control operations. Consciousness has available only a subset of the data (i.e., innerloop codes) and is the basis for innerloop vector monitoring of information and the execution of goal-based operations. It is also central to between-person verbal communication of attentional control strategies.

(8) **The Biological Implementations of Working Memory**
The CAP2 model seeks to use biological architecture to provide structural characteristics of the model. The basic module is assumed and relates cortical hypercolumns with the cortical layers that implement the input layer and output layer of the model. The control of attentional gating and feedback is assumed to occur via specialized cell types within cortical modules (e.g., attentional gating via chandelier cells). Executive control is assumed to occur via parietal and frontal activation and modulate cortical activity through connections that pass through the thalamus. Context state information is maintained via the hippocampus with fast connection weight change. Early learning occurs in a network of frontal, parietal, and cingulate cortex that is common across tasks and drops out as skill is acquired. Global reinforcement signals are output from subcortical structures (e.g., locus ceruleus and ventral tegmentum) that trigger within-module changes in connection matrices and priority coding.

ity effects in short-term memory (Conrad, 1964) and would be expected to produce a rehearsal loop storage that is similar to the EPIC implementation (Kieras et al., Chapter 6, this volume). CAP2's use of an executive, focusing of attention, and the development of automaticity are themes also seen in the Cowan model (1995; Chapter 3, this volume).

The model diverges from the related models by assuming a specific structure of the executive and the pivotal role of monitoring activity and priority reports from modules. The priority report in CAP2 involves each module characterizing the importance of the message it has to send and subsequently sending a scalar priority signal to the attention system. Humans and animals are attracted to critical events (e.g., loud noise as in thunder; see Yantis & Johnson, 1990) and at least momentarily pause as a result of such events. The priority mechanism is instantiated by a tagging code in EPIC and by a priority code in Soar. ACT-R does not have a priority mechanism and hence it is unable to account for attentional interruption phenomena. It should be noted that the priority system is not limited to input cue-coding. Internal events (e.g., memory retrievals) and output events (e.g., expecting an extra stair) also cause interruptions. In CAP2 the priority coding of modules is the major method of information compression used by the executive to enable the management of the complex interactions in the network.

The Control and Regulation of Working Memory

CAP2 deals explicitly with the control and regulation of network communications and learning and hence the control of working memory. Control is performed by a hierarchical control structure that includes the control of modules within a level, between levels within a region, and between regions. A reasonable hierarchical method of dealing with control would be for each level to identify the highest priority message, each region to identify the highest priority level, and the central executive to identify the highest priority region. The priority reports by the modules substantially influence what is attended to. The executive can exert control by giving priority to the output requests of one of the module regions, which would bias the effect of the priority scheduling (e.g., if the task demands ignoring auditory input and attending to visual input, a low-priority request from a visual module could be executed before a high-priority request from an auditory module). If there are structures that can produce a loop (module A outputs to B, which outputs to A), a rehearsal loop could be established to maintain a code (as in the phonological loop mechanism in EPIC).

The regulation of communication is based on the control of the output gain that determines the strength of the message vector transmitted out of the module. By controlling the feedback within a module, the executive can latch signals to maintain information over brief periods of time, thereby enabling them to hold a message until other network communications are complete. The sequential net in the central executive monitors the priority and activity levels of messages in the network. Winner-take-all connection networks can identify the highest priority message that will be transmitted. Control routines, which are based on goal-states, can bias the order of re-sponding to priority requests.

Executive control includes setting the gain and feedback in a module as well as determining which module to monitor (e.g., determining to monitor the degree of match by assessing the activity report of the physical-match or name-match level module). The control actions include setting the gain to transmit messages, setting the feedback to latch messages, and sending mes-sages to innerloop modules (see Schneider & Oliver, 1991).

The executive also controls memory modification by determining when to send a general reinforcement signal. By controlling when vectors output in the network and when reinforcement signals are sent, the executive deter-mines what will be associated and when (e.g., change in slow weights within and between modules and change in fast weights between the innerloop and the context).

The executive programs are implemented as a goal-based program that operates in a sequential connectionist network. These programs can be rapidly altered to allow task switching and time multiplexing. The ability to rapidly alter the executive program (see Schneider & Oliver, 1991) contrasts with the slow learning of priority codes within modules (see Gupta & Schneider, 1991) and the typical slow learning in connectionist models. In humans, the control programs can be loaded by verbal instruction, enabling rapid acquisition of control tasks that can influence learning and performance.

The goal-based control of this model is similar to the production sys-tem–based models (e.g., ACT-R, Soar, EPIC). The regulation of information is similar to the ICS model (Barnard, Chapter 9, this volume). In contrast to ICS, CAP2 models an executive that has a global view of the information requests from the entire network (though not the content of the messages).

The Unitary Versus Non-Unitary Nature of Working Memory

In CAP2 working memory has multiple forms and locations. There are per-haps a thousand levels in the system, each with separate modules that can buffer information. This allows systems to operate independently and allows extensive dual-task operations for at least highly skilled automatic behaviors that do not require substantial executive control. Memory is coded in terms of activation, short-term weight change, context memory, goal memory, and control subroutines. Portions of the network can operate without outputting to other portions of the network. This limiting of communications within the network provides the foundation to develop specialized peripheral processors such as the phonological loop and visuospatial sketchpad in the Baddeley and Logie models (Chapter 2, this volume). Rehearsal loops can be established to maintain information (as in ACT-R and EPIC).

The multiple forms of memory provide robustness to the system and enable parallel processing. The existence of the context storage in the inner-loop allows the system to recover the activation of the innerloop after an interruption might clear the system. In CAP2 the executive has local memory that is not shared with the rest of the network. This is important because the executive can then engage in the planning and evaluation of behaviors without disrupting or being disrupted by automatic behaviors that are operating in the data network. The lack of interconnections between regions allows the regions to process in parallel without interference. The non-unitary nature of working memory has the advantage of allowing parallel processing at the expense of some functions that are performed without information derived from other parts of the network unless the information is conveyed by messages transmitted on the innerloop.

The Nature of Working Memory Limitations

The CAP2 model has many components, each with limitations. A module can store only one vector message at a time (see Shedden & Schneider, 1990). There are thousands of modules, but because they each contain specialized information, one cannot substitute one module for another unless they are of related types.

Most of the limitations in the system are interference based rather than directly energy based. It is assumed that all the modules have a sufficient energy capacity to transmit simultaneously for extended periods of time. The computational reason for not transmitting in parallel is that the transmission of multiple messages in the same channel is inefficient relative to serializing the transmissions (owing to intermessage interference in the channel). To use an analogy, during a meeting, most humans have the energy capacity to output messages at a high energy level (e.g., yell) for extended periods of time. However, owing to the interference produced, it is generally more information efficient to transmit serially (i.e., being recognized and speaking individually). If two regions do not communicate to a common target region, they can transmit in parallel without interference (e.g., inputting a visual input for one word while typing the keys of the previous word). As more messages are input into a module there is greater interference. If one message is somewhat weak relative to the others in the module, its influence is greatly reduced (e.g., a 10% advantage in the relative strength of a signal can produce a shift recognition from chance to perfect; Shedden & Schneider, 1990). In control of the network communications it is critical to balance the need to transmit messages with the need to minimize intermessage interference.

One of the major factors that reduce interference is the buffering of messages and delay of their transmission. Each module can buffer a message that is within it. If a message transmission is short relative to the time until the information is needed, it can be buffered and the effective capacity can be greatly increased (e.g., if transmission can occur in 200 ms and can be maintained for

800 ms, the effective capacity to store could increase fourfold). This is consistent with the data on the readout of sensory iconic store (Sperling, 1960); however, buffering produces a limitation. Because a module can maintain only one message at a time, buffering a previous message limits the ability of new messages to enter the module (see Shedden & Schneider, 1990). Hence, it is likely that the feedback within a module would normally hold for only a short period of time past the presentation of a stimulus (e.g., in the second range), which in turn produces a limitation. The module can buffer input, but it should limit the duration of buffering the input to keep from blocking future input. This holding period may vary between regions. Rehearsal might be added by having a set of modules with a long hold to maintain the auditory signal as in the Baddeley and Logie model (Chapter 2, this volume).

There are interference limitations in the memory weight change. As the rate constant for connectionist learning changes, the speed of learning new patterns increases; however, the forgetting of the old patterns is also increased (see Schneider & Detweiler, 1988; Sharkey & Sharkey, 1995). It is useful to have both fast and slow learning. The learning between the context and the innerloop is a fast learning system and very useful to acquire the representation in a few trials that will allow the system to recover from interruptions. However, this type of learning is of little value the following day. The learning of input–output associations is slower on the order of tens of trials, but is evident the following day. The learning of the priority acquisition seems to be very slow and increases over hundreds of trials. This has the advantage of providing a very long duration code but the inability to alter it rapidly.

The executive is a major limitation to the processing in the network. CAP2 has only one executive, which controls potentially thousands of modules with a simple sequential net that has a substantial cycle time to change tasks (on the order of 100 ms). Executive control can focus on a set of modules that control attentional gating, monitoring activity, and priority reports. However, while the executive controls modules in one region of the network, it cannot control other modules. When the task of the executive is more difficult and requires more operations, it reduces the ability of the executive to maintain information in the network (e.g., difference between forward and backward digit span).

Transmissions that occur automatically are not limited by executive functions. To the extent that modules operate automatically (e.g., the priority code is high enough to cause output of the message from a module without executive assistance), large numbers of modules could transmit in chains of input–output transmissions with little or no executive impact except by setting the goal-state (e.g., jogging while the executive is solving an unrelated task). The automatic processes have limits in that a module can code only a single message and multiple transmissions to a given module can cause local interference. However, levels and regions can operate in parallel as long as there are no local collisions of messages.

This model has common features found in most of the models presented in this volume. There is a limited executive in the models of Baddeley and Logie (Chapter 2), Cowan (Chapter 3), Engle et al. (Chapter 4), EPIC (Chapter 6), and ICS (Chapter 9). The role of interference is important in nearly all of the models. Although the ICS model does not have an "executive," Barnard (Chapter 9, Table 9.2) states that "the fundamental limitation lies in the capacity of the entire architecture to dynamically reconfigure and use all its representational and processing resources to best advantage in a specific task context." In CAP2 the role of the executive is to reconfigure the network for dynamic processing. The multiple-speed learning rates are central to the O'Reilly et al. (Chapter 11) model. The model contrasts with other models that assume there is a common limited activation pool (e.g., Lovett et al., Chapter 5). In CAP2 each module has sufficient power to transmit any message. However, the module operates under the rule to remain quiet unless it either has a high-priority message or the executive has provided permission (allocated gain) to transmit the message. The limitation is that the executive coordinates the activity. It should be noted that if a message is automatically transmitted (i.e., owing to a high-priority tag), processing occurs without being directly limited by executive resources.

The Role of Working Memory in Complex Cognitive Activities and Skill Acquisition

The CAP2 model addresses how skills are acquired and in particular how the slow, controlled, effortful, serial processing of the novice is transformed into the fast, parallel, low-effort, and automatic processing of the expert (see Gupta & Schneider, 1991; Schneider & Detweiler, 1987; Schneider & Oliver, 1991). The novice performance is critically limited by the program in the executive sequential net sequencing through steps of altering gains, monitoring reports, and performing actions based on those reports.

In the simulation of learning to predict digital gates (Schneider & Oliver, 1991), the sequential net learned a set of rules to load modules, control module outputs, and monitor the activity and priority reports of specific modules. The sequential nature of the rules can be coded into language and expressed so that an expert human can interpret his or her control program, convert it into a string of words, and thus communicate it to a novice human. The program is a sequence of rules such as "Look at the input points of the gate," "Compare them to see if they are on," "If all are on then the output is on . . ." In a small number of trials (e.g., 20) the sequential network learns the control operations to perform the task. Performance during this early stage is slow, serial, and effortful. Because there is only one controller, other tasks that require the controller must be either delayed or time shared.

As the modules repeatedly execute input–output transmissions under executive control, the modules learn the input–output associations and the priority of the message (see Gupta & Schneider, 1991). After sufficient consistent practice the module can categorize an input and associate the output and priority report. If the priority is high enough, the module can output the message without the need for executive gain allocation. Long chains of such automatic actions can take place.

During early practice the multiple types of working memory may be highly taxed. In this case the subject needs to remember the context and general task state (fast weights on innerloop); remember the executive program (fast weights in the executive sequential net); and maintain information in modules that will be compared and the correct response(s) contingent on the results of the comparison. This is required even for a simple task (e.g., face naming; see Figure 10.6) in which fMRI studies show that many cortical areas are activated.

The executive load of the expert performer depends on the nature of the task. When the task is consistent, the input can evoke a chain of automatic transmissions with minimal working memory load (i.e., loading only the specific modules in the input–output stream and potentially interrupting the executive processes if the priority is high). There may be minimal use of working memory. The reductions in activation in Figure 10.6 illustrate the expected large-scale dropout of areas of the expert compared to the novice activation patterns.

Working memory is used in skilled performance to track inconsistent variable information, alter strategies, and deal with threshold situations. In inconsistent tasks in which the variables are always changing, working memory is required to maintain the variable bindings of the process (e.g., as in varied mapping search; Figure 10.4C). Many skilled tasks require working memory to maintain intermediate results (e.g., multicolumn addition), set varying strategy goals (e.g., the shifting from a fatiguing opponent to playing a fast game in a tennis match), or deal with difficult threshold judgment cases (e.g., when there is a darkening in a radiological image of a tumor).

The CAP2 approach to skill acquisition and skilled performance has parallels in the Soar and ACT-R skill-acquisition methods. In the process of skill acquisition, Soar uses domain-general problem-solving methods to accomplish the task and then chunks the specific elements into condition-action rules that are applied when the conditions are active in working memory (Newell, 1990; Young & Lewis, Chapter 7, this volume). The chunking mechanism is similar to the input–output mapping that occurs within a module in CAP2, although in the CAP2 version the association is limited to only those inputs and outputs received by a given module. Hence chunking is limited only to a part of the information network. This explains why simple associations, such as learning to output a negation of a gate, may never produce a new chunk that removes that stage (see Carlson, Sullivan, & Schneider, 1989). Soar learns by building ever-more-complex chunks to reduce the number of chunks that fire. CAP2 builds automatic transmissions for consistent actions, thus eliminating the need for executive processing. In CAP2 most of the learning time is not involved in acquiring a chunk, but in strengthening the input–output association and the priority learning (Schneider & Oliver, 1991). The strengthening of input–output association in CAP2 modules is similar to the strengthening activity that occurs in ACT-R (Lovett et al., Chapter 5, this volume). CAP2's executive can alter enabling conditions (e.g., change gain on a critical module) that alter task priorities. EPIC (Kieras et al., Chapter 6, this volume) has similar enabling operations. The inability to produce strong chunks when the input–output mappings are inconsistent limits the input–output associations in CAP2 and similarly limits the chunking operations in Soar and ACT-R. CAP2 views the memory as less unitary than do ACT-R and Soar. This is because each model sees only a very small percentage of the messages in the network. ACT-R produces a somewhat similar effect of having variable types that influence subsets of the productions.

The Relationship of Working Memory to Long-Term Memory and Knowledge

In CAP2, long-term memory is involved in connection weights that determine the module input–output associations, priority tags, and executive sequential processing routines. Note that there are many connection matrices in the network: within modules (for autoassociate feedback); between modules (for encoding and translation, with both feed-forward and feedback connections); within the executive sequential net (for executing sequential procedures); between the executive and the innerloop modules (for activating codes and context learning); and from the executive to the innerloop. The working memories (activation within modules and executive, and fast weights on the innerloop) activate codes in modules and hence are always influenced by long-term memory. It is somewhat inappropriate to think of working memory as a subset of long-term memory. Working memory is generally a result of an activation vector (working memory) multiplied by a connection matrix (long-term memory) producing a new activation vector (working memory). It is not simply a proper subset of long-term memory but rather a dynamic, productive activation that can activate new never-before generated patterns (e.g., create an image of a flying stapler). The connection weights are changed with practice. The model is a connectionist model as in O'Reilly et al. (Chapter 11, this volume). Production system models (e.g., ACT-R, 3CAPS) generally use long-term memory to produce activation in working memory in a manner analogous to the connectionist approach, although not as generative because the input of different codes cannot be simply added as in connectionist models.

The Relationship of Working Memory to Attention and Consciousness

CAP2 as a model of attention has some interesting perspectives on the role of consciousness. The ability to alter output gains in the network is a model of attentional control (Schneider & Detweiler, 1987; Shedden & Schneider, 1990, 1991; Shiffrin & Schneider, 1977). The limitations of the small number of modules that the executive can manage at any time determine the limited nature of attention and predict the slow serial behavior of the novice when dealing with varied information. Note that attention and memory serve different functions. Attention generally gates information through the network and monitors the activity and priority of the resulting transmissions. The information that is gated is the result of the active vector (working memory), long-term memory (connection matrix), and attention (scalar multiplication of the activation vector).

The role of working memory and consciousness represents an important extension to the CAP2 architecture. The executive originally implemented was "unconscious," that is, it received input only from the priority and activity reports in the network (Schneider & Oliver, 1991) but no message vectors. This minimized the homunculus problem, but only allowed the executive to solve very broad goals that were represented at the coarse grain of the labeled priority lines from the various modules in the system (e.g., satisfy hunger but not locate chocolate-covered almonds). In Schneider and Pimm-Smith (1997), the information-processing value of consciousness was directly addressed. They discussed the benefits and costs of the executive being "conscious" of module messages, that is, the receipt of vector messages from modules in the network. A "message aware" executive could execute goal-based problem solving that would activate a particular code in the innerloop rather than a particular module in the network. To keep the executive from falling into the homunculus trap of having to process all the messages, the CAP2 executive can receive messages from the modules only at the innerloop. This means that much of the richness of the lower level modules is unavailable to the executive unless it is coded in the upper level codes (e.g., the visual system can detect thousands of hue differences, but the typical person verbally codes fewer than 10). The executive can also transmit messages on the innerloop so that its messages can load modules as well. This proves very helpful for modules to learn intermediate states, which greatly speeds learning (Schneider & Oliver, 1991).

To enable parallel processing, it is important to limit the "awareness" of modules in the network to the conscious state. We suggested (Schneider & Pimm-Smith, 1997) that only the innerloop modules were directly aware of the vectors from the executive and that lower level modules could have their codes influenced by the upper level codes via feedback connections. Through the feedback connections the consciousness could influence lower level activity. The limited awareness of modules of conscious codes contrasts with models that assume that the contents of consciousness are broadcast globally to all the modules in the network (see Baars, 1988). Because any global message transmission would interfere with all transmissions in the entire network, it would be very disruptive to broadcast the consciousness message to all modules. By limiting the broadcast to the innerloop, most of the network can operate with minimal interference unless the conscious vector has strong feedback connections down to a module.

In CAP2 consciousness plays an important role in enabling verbal instruction and learning. The central executive operates by sequentially monitoring and modulating network activity. If an organism could learn to output a symbol stream for each action of the executive (e.g., language), and that stream could be encoded by a second organism, the species could do instructed learning. Instructed learning can be orders of magnitude faster than simple connectionist associative learning (see discussion in Schneider & Oliver, 1991), which would provide the species enormous survival value for a social animal.

CAP2 proposes that consciousness is a very reduced subset of the working memory. Consciousness is the sequence of messages that go between the executive and innerloop. Working memory includes far more information (activations throughout the modules and in the executive, and fast weights). Although CAP2 uses consciousness to guide goal behavior as in ACT-R, EPIC, and Soar, it assumes that consciousness is much more limited because the cost of global communications of the contents of consciousness is so high.

The Biological Implementation of Working Memory

The goal of the CAP2 architecture is to relate biological, behavioral, and computational constraints. All of the components are implemented in a biologically inspired, feasible form. The model's basic structure, modules, levels, regions, transmission of message vectors, and scalar control signals are all consistent with the organizational themes in cortical processing (see DeFelipe et al., 1985; Felleman & Van Essen, 1991; Martin, 1988; White, 1989). The work on hippocampal storage and fast weights (McClelland, McNaughton, & O'Reilly, 1995; O'Reilly et al., Chapter 11, this volume) is consistent with the proposed innerloop fast weight learning. The model's predictions of cortical control circuits are consistent with the frontal and parietal control areas for attention and working memory (Goldman-Rakic, 1988; Mesulam, 1990; O'Reilly et al., Chapter 11, this volume). The dropout of these areas during learning (Figure 10.6) is consistent with the theoretical proposal of an executive control structure that is highly taxed during learning and is far less active in skilled processing. The CAP2 prediction of a global broadcast reinforcement signal is consistent with the observed projection and the timing of activity from subcortical pathways (see Schultz et al., 1993). The within-module predictions of CAP2 are consistent with cortical physiology. The gating of pyramidal cell output by chandelier cells is a biological candidate for the expected multiplicative gating of module output (DeFelipe et al., 1985). The lower level ungated pyramidal cells on a cortical column that project subcortically (e.g., intralaminar nuclei of the thalamus; White, 1989) are a biological candidate for the report cells. The within-module connections provide feedback that could buffer a signal (Martin, 1988). The neurophysiological data on neglect (Halligan & Marshall, 1994; Mesulam, 1990) show a syndrome consistent with the loss of priority information in which individuals do not attend to major parts of the visual field even though tests reveal that they can perceive information in the neglected field.

CAP2 has parallels to Cowan's work as well as that of Baddeley and Logie. The CAP2 macrolevel expectations are similar to those that O'Reilly et al. (Chapter 11, this volume) model in terms of the role of prefrontal cortex, hippocampal learning, and global broadcast or reinforcement signals. CAP2 differs from the O'Reilly et al. model in that scalar attention multiplication occurs throughout the systems rather than primarily into and out of the frontal cortex. CAP2 does predict that there should be a method of scaling the input to the executive as in the O'Reilly et al. model. The model suggests that there will be specialized cortical regions that could support the phonological loop and visuospatial sketchpad (Baddeley & Logie, Chapter 2, this volume), but does not detail the nature of the slave processors. The model predicts a central executive as in Baddeley and Logie (Chapter 2, this volume), Cowan (Chapter 3, this volume), and Engle, Kane, and Tuholski (Chapter 4, this volume).

The predictions of CAP2 are similar to the Cowan model (1995; Chapter 3, this volume, see Figure 3.9). CAP2's modules with feedback can implement Cowan's sensory store cell assemblies. Automatic processing output in the modules implements Cowan's automatic operations. As Cowan predicts, CAP2 expects the automatic activation to "diffuse" throughout the network. CAP2 expects executive function and the "conscious" monitoring of messages to occur in learning new tasks. The brain-imaging results show substantial activation in frontal and parietal cortex. Cowan divides these functions and attributes the consciousness to inferior parietal areas and the executive functions to prefrontal cortex. Both Cowan's and the CAP2 model provide a special role of projections to and from the thalamus relating to attentional control (the signaling of the need for attention as well as potential control). Cowan uses global broadcast signals (from locus ceruleus) to orient attention. In CAP2 such signals can influence the global attention state; however, the primary interpretation of those signals is to initiate learning within modules.

Concluding Observations

Working memory is a central, useful, and vague construct of cognitive function. It is a result of many mechanisms that achieve the robust and powerful computation that humans perform. Table 10.1 provides a summary of the answers to the specific questions based on the CAP2 modeling. I expect we will come to understand a cognitive architecture for working memory as an architecture for skill acquisition and performance. In building simulations of learning and skill acquisition, we have had to employ concepts that are common in working memory (buffers, fast weights). This volume presents many models of working memory that differ in terms of the diagrams and implementation details. However, I am struck by the commonality of the models at the deep structure level. There are common themes represented in most of the models, which show an important convergence of concepts. We have clear expectations as to divisions of the executive, when it should operate, how it influences processing, and how the network might be specialized. In the years ahead, this will prove a solid foundation of computational and behavioral concepts that can merge with the biological constraints from the micro- (neural) and macro- (brain-imaging) scale to identify the structure, function, and detailed mechanisms of working memory.

REFERENCES

Anderson, J. A. (1983). Cognitive and psychological computation with neural models. *IEEE, Transactions on systems, man, and cybernetics,* SMC-13, 799–815.

Anderson, J. R. (1983). *The architecture of cognition.* Cambridge, MA: Harvard University Press.

Atkinson, R. C., & Shiffrin, R. M. (1968). Human memory: A proposed system and its control processes. In K. W. Spence & J. T. Spence (Eds.), *The psychology of learning and motivation: Advances in research and theory* (Vol. 2, pp. 89–195). New York: Academic Press.

Baars, B. J. (1988). *A cognitive theory of consciousness.* New York: Cambridge University Press.

Baddeley, A. D. (1986). *Working memory.* New York: Oxford University Press.

Carlson, R. A., Sullivan, M. A., & Schneider, W. (1989). Practice and working memory effects in building procedural skill. *Journal of Experimental Psychology: Learning, Memory, and Cognition, 15,* 517–526.

Churchland, P. S., & Sejnowski, T. J. (1992). *The computational brain.* Cambridge, MA: MIT Press.

Cohen, J. D., Perlstein, W. M., Braver, T. S., Nystrom, L. E., Jonides, J., Smith, E. E., & Noll, D. C. (1997). Temporal dynamics of brain activity during a working memory task. *Nature, 386,* 604–608.

Conrad, R. (1964). Acoustic confusions in immediate memory. *British Journal of Psychology, 55,* 75–84.

Cowan, N. (1995). *Attention and memory: An integrated framework.* New York: Oxford University Press.

Crick, F., & Koch, C. (1995). Are we aware of neural activity in primary visual cortex? *Nature, 375,* 121–123.

DeFelipe, J., Hendry, S. H., Jones, E. G., & Schmechel, D. (1985). Variability in the terminations of GABAergic chandelier cell axons on initial segments of pyramidal cell axons in the monkey sensory-motor cortex. *Journal of Computational Neurology, 231,* 364–384.

Feldman, J. A., & Ballard, D. H. (1982). Connectionist models and their properties. *Cognitive Science, 6,* 205–254.

Felleman, D. J., & Van Essen, D. C. (1991). Distributed hierarchical processing in the primate cerebral cortex. *Cerebral Cortex, 1,* 1–46.

Goldman-Rakic, P. S. (1988). Topography of cognition: Parallel distributed networks in primate association cortex. *Annual Review of Neuroscience, 11*, 137–156.

Gupta, P., & Schneider, W. (1991). Attention, automaticity, and priority learning. *Proceedings of the Thirteenth Annual Conference of the Cognitive Science Society* (pp. 534–539). Hillsdale, NJ: Erlbaum.

Halligan, P. W., & Marshall, J. C. (Eds.) (1994). *Spatial neglect: Position papers on theory and practice.* Hove, UK: Erlbaum.

Klapp, S. T., Marshburn, E. A., & Lester, P. T. (1983). Short-term memory does not involve the "working memory" of information processing: The demise of a common assumption. *Journal of Experimental Psychology: General, 11*, 240–264.

Luck, S. J., Chelazzi, L., Hillyard, S. A., & Desimone, R. (1997). Neural mechanisms of spatial selective attention in areas V1, V2, and V4 of macaque visual cortex. *Journal of Neurophysiology, 77*, 24–42.

Martin, K. A. (1988). The Wellcome prize lecture: From single cells to simple circuits in the cerebral cortex. *Quarterly Journal of Experimental Physiology, 73*, 637–702.

McClelland, J. L., McNaughton, B. L., & O'Reilly, R. C. (1995). Why there are complementary learning systems in the hippocampus and neocortex: Insights from the successes and failures of connectionist models of learning and memory. *Psychological Review, 102*, 419–457.

Mesulam, M. M. (1990). Large-scale neurocognitive networks and distributed processing of attention, language, and memory. *Annals of Neurology, 28*, 597–613.

Newell, A. (1990). *Unified theories of cognition.* Cambridge, MA: Harvard University Press.

Peterson, L. R., & Peterson, J. J. (1959). Short-term retention of individual verbal items. *Journal of Experimental Psychology, 58*, 193–198.

Raichle, M. E., Fiez, J. A., Videen, T. O., MacLeod, A. M., Pardo, J. V., Fox, P. T., & Petersen, S. E. (1994). Practice-related changes in human brain functional anatomy during nonmotor learning. *Cerebral Cortex, 4*, 8–26.

Rumelhart, D. E., Hinton, G. E., & Williams, R. J. (1986). Learning internal representation by error propagation. In D. E. Rumelhart & J. L. McClelland (Eds.), *Parallel distributed processing* (pp. 318–364). Cambridge, MA: MIT Press.

Rumelhart, D. E., McClelland, J. L., & the PDP Research Group. (1986). *Parallel distributed processing: Explorations in the microstructure of cognition. Vol. 1. Foundations.* Cambridge, MA: MIT Press.

Schneider, W., & Detweiler, M. (1987). A connectionist/control architecture for working memory. In G. H. Bower (Ed.), *The psychology of learning and motivation* (Vol. 21, pp. 54–119). New York: Academic Press.

Schneider, W., & Detweiler, M. (1988). The role of practice in dual-task performance: Toward workload modeling in a connectionist/control architecture. *Human Factors, 30*, 539–566.

Schneider, W., & Fisk, A. D. (1984). Automatic category search and its transfer. *Journal of Experimental Psychology: Learning, Memory, and Cognition, 10*, 115.

Schneider, W., & Oliver, W. L. (1991). An instructable connectionist/control architecture: Using rule-based instructions to accomplish connectionist learning in a human time scale. In K. Van Lehn (Ed.), *Architectures for intelligence: The 22nd Carnegie Mellon symposium on cognition* (pp. 113–145). Hillsdale, NJ: Erlbaum.

Schneider, W., & Pimm-Smith, M. (1997). Consciousness as a message aware control mechanism to modulate cognitive processing. In J. Cohen & J. Schooler (Eds.),

Scientific approaches to consciousness: The 25th Carnegie Symposium on Cognition (pp. 65–80). Mahwah, NJ: Erlbaum.

Schneider, W., Pimm-Smith, M., & Worden, M. (1994). The neurobiology of attention and automaticity. *Current Opinion in Neurobiology, 4,* 177–182.

Schneider, W., & Shiffrin, R. M. (1977). Controlled and automatic human information processing: I. Detection, search, and attention. *Psychological Review, 84,* 1–66.

Schultz, W., Apicella, P., & Ljungberg, T. (1993). Responses of monkey dopamine neurons to rewards and conditioned stimuli during successive steps of learning a delayed response task. *Journal of Neuroscience, 13,* 900–913.

Sharkey, N. E., & Sharkey, A. J. C. (1995). An analysis of catastrophic interference. *Journal of Neural Computing, Artificial Intelligence and Cognitive Research, 7,* 301–329.

Shedden, J. M., & Schneider, W. (1990). A connectionist model of attentional enhancement and signal buffering. *Proceedings of the Twelfth Annual Conference of the Cognitive Science Society* (pp. 566–573). Hillsdale, NJ: Erlbaum.

Shedden, J. M., & Schneider, W. (1991). A connectionist simulation of attention and vector comparison: The need for serial processing in parallel hardware. *Proceedings of the Thirteenth Annual Conference of the Cognitive Science Society* (pp. 546–551). Hillsdale, NJ: Erlbaum.

Shiffrin, R. M. (1988). Attention. In R. C. Atkinson, R. J. Herrnstein, G. Lindzey, & R. D. Luce (Eds.), *Stevens' handbook of experimental psychology* (pp. 739–811). New York: Wiley.

Shiffrin, R. M., & Schneider, W. (1977). Controlled and automatic human information processing: II: Perceptual learning, automatic attending, and a general theory. *Psychological Review, 84,* 127–190.

Sperling, G. (1960). The information available in brief visual presentations. *Psychological Monographs, 74* (Whole No. 498).

Szentagothai, J. (1975). The "module-concept" in cerebral cortex architecture. *Brain Research, 95,* 475–496.

Van Essen, D. C., & Anderson, C. H. (1990). Information processing strategies and pathways in the primate retina and visual cortex. In S. F. Zornetzer, J. L. Davis, & C. Lau (Eds.), *An introduction to neural and electronic networks.* San Diego: Academic Press.

White, E. L. (1989). *Cortical circuits: Synaptic organization of the cerebral cortex: Structure, function, and theory.* Boston: Brikhauser.

Yantis, S., & Johnson, D. N. (1990). Mechanisms of attentional priority. *Journal of Experimental Psychology: Human Perception and Performance, 16,* 812–825.

11 A Biologically Based Computational Model of Working Memory

RANDALL C. O'REILLY, TODD S. BRAVER, AND
JONATHAN D. COHEN

FIVE CENTRAL FEATURES OF THE MODEL

We define working memory as controlled processing involving active maintenance and/or rapid learning, where controlled processing is an emergent property of the dynamic interactions of multiple brain systems, but the prefrontal cortex (PFC) and hippocampus (HCMP) are especially influential owing to their specialized processing abilities and their privileged locations within the processing hierarchy (both the PFC and HCMP are well connected with a wide range of brain areas, allowing them to influence behavior at a global level). The specific features of our model include:

(1) A PFC specialized for active maintenance of internal contextual information that is dynamically updated and self-regulated, allowing it to bias (control) ongoing processing according to maintained information (e.g., goals, instructions, partial products).

(2) An HCMP specialized for rapid learning of arbitrary information, which can be recalled in the service of controlled processing, whereas the posterior perceptual and motor cortex (PMC) exhibits slow, long-term learning that can efficiently represent accumulated knowledge and skills.

(3) Control that emerges from interacting systems (PFC, HCMP, and PMC).

(4) Dimensions that define continua of specialization in different brain systems: for example, robust active maintenance, fast versus slow learning.

(5) Integration of biological and computational principles.

We would like to thank Andrew Conway, Peter Dayan, Yuko Munakata, Ken Norman, Mike Wolfe, and all of the symposium participants for useful comments. We were supported by NIH Grant MH47566-06, and R.O. was also supported by a McDonnell Pew Postdoctoral Fellowship at MIT in the Department of Brain and Cognitive Science.

Working memory is an intuitively appealing theoretical construct – perhaps deceptively so. It has proven difficult for the field to converge on a fully satisfying, mechanistically explicit account of what exactly working memory is and how it fits into a larger model of cognition (hence the motivation for this volume). Existing theoretical models of working memory can be traced to ideas based on a traditional computer-like mental architecture, where processing is centralized and long-term memory is essentially passive. In this context, it makes sense to have RAM or cache-like working memory buffers dedicated to temporarily storing items that are needed during processing by the *central executive* (Baddeley, 1986). Alternative processing architectures have been proposed, within both the computational and psychological literatures (Anderson, 1983; Newell, 1990), in which working memory is defined functionally – as the activated component of long-term memory representations – rather than structurally as a dedicated component of the system. However, these typically include a structural distinction between processing and memory. None of these architectures seems to correspond closely to the architecture of the brain, in which processing and memory functions are typically distributed within and performed by the same neural substrate (Rumelhart & McClelland, 1986).

We believe that considering how working memory function might be implemented in the brain provides a unique perspective that is informative with regard to both the psychological and biological mechanisms involved. This is what we attempt to do in this chapter, by providing a biologically based computational model of working memory. Our goal is not only to provide an account that is neurobiologically plausible, but also one that is mechanistically explicit and that can be implemented in computer simulations of specific cognitive tasks. We share this goal with others in this volume who have also committed their theories to mechanistically explicit models, at both the symbolic (Lovett, Reder, & Lebiere, Chapter 5; Kieras, Meyer, Mueller, & Seymour, Chapter 6; Young & Lewis, Chapter 7, all this volume) and neural (Schneider, Chapter 10, this volume) levels.

It is possible to identify a core set of information-processing requirements for many working memory tasks: (a) Task instructions and/or stimuli must be encoded in such a form that they can either be actively maintained over time, and/or learned rapidly and stored offline for subsequent recall, (b) The active maintenance must be both dynamic and robust, so that information can be selectively maintained, flexibly updated, protected from interference, and held for arbitrary (although relatively short) durations, (c) The maintained information must be able to rapidly and continually influence (bias) subsequent processing or action selection. (d) The rapid learning must avoid the problem of interference to keep even relatively similar types of information distinct. In addition to these specifications for an *active-memory* system and a *rapid-learning* system, we think that the working memory construct is generally associated with tasks that require *controlled processing*, which governs the updating and maintenance of active memory and the storage and retrieval of rapidly learned information in a strategic or task-relevant manner. This is consistent with the original association of working memory with central executive–like functions. Taken together, these functional aspects of working memory provide a basic set of constraints for our biologically based model.

Our approach involves two interrelated threads. The first is a focus on the functional dimensions along which different brain systems appear to have specialized and the processing trade-offs that result as a consequence of these specializations. The second is a set of computational models in which we have implemented these functional specializations as explicit mechanisms. Through simulations, we have endeavored to show how the interactions of these specialized brain systems can account for specific patterns of behavioral performance on a wide range of cognitive tasks. We have postulated that prefrontal cortex (PFC), hippocampus (HCMP), and posterior and motor cortex (PMC) represent three extremes of specialization along different functional dimensions important for working memory: sensory and motor processing based on inference and generalization (PMC); dynamic and robust active memory (PFC); and rapid learning of arbitrary information (HCMP). Because each of these specializations involves trade-offs, it is only through interactions between these systems that the brain can fulfill the information-processing requirements of working memory tasks.

As an example of how these components work together, consider a simple real-world task that involves contributions from these different brain systems. Imagine you are looking for some information (the name of a college friend's child) contained in an e-mail message you received a year ago and have stored in one of your many message folders. You can remember several things about that e-mail, such as who sent it (a good friend who knows the college friend) and what else was happening at around that time (you had just returned from a conference in Paris), but you don't remember the subject line or where you filed it. This information about the e-mail is retrieved from the HCMP system, which was able to bind together the individual features of the memory and store it as a unique event or episode. Once recalled, these features must be used to guide the process of searching through the folders and e-mail messages. We think that this happens by maintaining representations of these features in an active state in the PFC, which is able to keep them active for the duration of the search and protect them from being dislodged from active memory by all the other information you read. Meanwhile the basic abilities of reading information and issuing appropriate commands within the e-mail system are subserved by well-learned representations within the PMC, guided by representations held active in PFC.

Once initiated, the search requires the updating of items in active memory (college friend's name, good friend's name, Paris conference) and its interaction with information encountered in the search. For example, when you list all of the folders, you select a small subset as most probable. This requires an interaction between the items in active memory (PFC), long-term knowledge about the meanings of the folders (PMC), and specific information about what was filed into them (HCMP). The result is the activation of a new set of items in active memory, containing the names of the new set of folders to search. You may first decide to look in a folder that will contain an e-mail telling you exactly when your conference was, which will help narrow the search. As you do this, you may keep that date in active memory and not maintain the conference information. Thus, the items in active memory are updated (activated and deactivated) as needed by the task at hand. Finally, you iterate through the folders and e-mail messages, matching their date and sender information with those maintained in active memory, until the correct e-mail is found.

All of this happened as a result of strategic, controlled processing, involving the activation and updating of goals (the overall search) and subgoals (e.g., finding the specific date). The maintenance and updating of goals, like that of the other active memory items, is dependent on specialized mechanisms in the PFC system. Thus, the PFC system plays a dominant role in both active memory and controlled processing, which are two central components of the working memory construct. However, other systems can play equally central roles. For example, if you were interrupted in your search by a phone call, then you might not retain all the pertinent information in active memory ("Now, where was I?"). The HCMP system can fill in the missing information by frequently (and rapidly) storing snapshots of the currently active representations across much of the cortex, which can then be recalled after an interruption to pick up where you left off. Thus, working memory functionality can be accomplished by multiple brain systems, though the specialized active memory system of the PFC remains a central one.

We have studied a simple working memory task based on the continuous performance test (CPT), which involves searching for target letters in a continuous stream of stimuli (typically letters). For example, in the AX version of the CPT (AX-CPT), the target is the letter X, but only if it immediately follows the letter A. Thus, the X alone is inherently ambiguous, in that it is a nontarget if preceded by anything other than an A. Like the e-mail search task, this requires the dynamic updating and maintenance of active memory representations (e.g., the current stimulus must be maintained to perform correctly on the subsequent one), which makes this a working memory task. Active maintenance is even more important for a more demanding version of this task called the N-*back*, in which any letter can be a target if it is identical to the one occurring N trials previously (where N is prespecified and is typically 1, 2, or 3). Thus, more items need to be maintained simultaneously, and across intervening stimuli. The N-back also requires updating the working memory representations after each trial, to keep track of the order of the last N letters.

There are several other relevant demands of this task. For example, upon receiving the task instructions, subjects must rapidly learn the otherwise arbitrary association between the letters A and X. We assume that this is carried out by the HCMP. Of course, subjects must also be able to encode each stimulus and execute the appropriate response, which we assume is carried out by PMC. Together, the rapid association of the cue with the correct response to the target (HCMP), the active maintenance of information provided by the specific cue presented in each trial (PFC), and the use of that information to guide the response (PMC), constitute a simple form of working memory function. In Figure 11.1, we present a computational model of performance in this task that illustrates our theory regarding the functional roles of PFC, PMC, and HCMP. We have implemented components of this model and demonstrated that it can account for detailed aspects of normal behavior in the AX-CPT, as well as that of patients with schizophrenia who are thought to suffer from PFC dysfunction (Braver, Cohen, & McClelland, 1997a; Braver, Cohen, & Servan-Schreiber, 1995; Cohen, Braver, & O'Reilly, 1996).

In the model, the PMC layer of the network performs stimulus identification and response generation. Thus, in panel a, when the A stimulus is presented, an unequivocal nontarget response (here mapped onto the right hand, but counterbalanced in empirical studies) is generated. However, the PFC is also activated by this A stimulus, because it serves as a cue for a possible subsequent target X stimulus. During the delay period shown in panel b, the PFC maintains its representation in an active state. This PFC representation encodes the information that the prior stimulus was a cue, and thus that if an X comes next, a target (left-hand) response should be made. When the X stimulus is then presented (panel c), the PFC-maintained active memory biases processing in the PMC in favor of the interpretation of the X as a target, leading to a target (left-hand) response. We think that the HCMP would also play an important role in performing this task, especially in early trials, by virtue of its ability to rapidly learn associations between the appropriate stimuli (e.g., A in the PMC and "left-to-X" in the PFC) based on instructions and to provide a link between these until direct cortical connections have been strengthened. However, we have not yet implemented this important component of working memory in this model (see Figure 11.1).

In the following sections, we first elaborate our theory of working memory in terms of a more comprehensive view of how information is processed within neural systems. Although we believe it is important that our theory is based on mechanistic models of cognitive function whose behavior can be compared with empirical data, a detailed consideration of individual models or empirical studies is beyond the scope of this chapter. Furthermore, many of the features of our theory have not yet been implemented and remain a challenge for future work. Thus, our objective in this chapter is to provide a high-

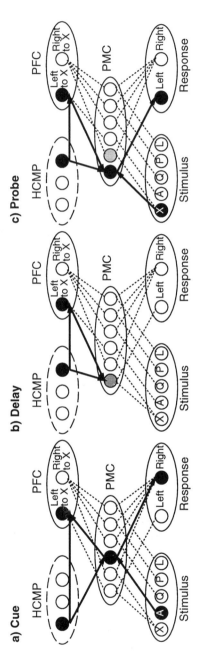

Figure 11.1. Neural network model of the AX-CPT task, showing roles of PMC (posterior and motor cortex), PFC (prefrontal cortex), and HCMP (hippocampus and related structures; not actually implemented in our models yet). Activation is shown by black units, and the weights between such units are highlighted to emphasize the flow of information through the network. Lateral inhibition exists within each of the layers. (a) The cue stimulus *A* is presented, resulting in the activation of a PFC representation for "Respond with left (target) hand if an *X* comes next." (b) During the delay, the PFC representation is actively maintained, providing top-down support for the target interpretation of the *X* stimulus. (c) When the *X* comes, it results in a target (left) response (whereas a nontarget [right] response would have occurred without the top-down PFC activation during the delay period). In early trials, the HCMP provides appropriate activation to various task components, as a result of its ability for rapid learning.

level overview of our theory and to show how it addresses the theoretical questions posed for this volume.

A Biologically Based Computational Model of Cognition

Our model of working memory is a unified one in that the same underlying computational principles are used throughout. We and others have relied on these computational principles in previous work to address issues regarding cognitive function and behavioral performance in many other task domains, including ones involving response competition, classical conditioning, and covert spatial attention. Moreover, the functional specializations that we postulate for different brain systems emerge as different parametric variations within this unified framework, giving rise to a continuum of specialization along these dimensions. The basic computational mechanisms are relatively simple, including standard parallel-distributed-processing (PDP) ideas (McClelland, 1993; Rumelhart & McClelland, 1986; Seidenberg, 1993), the most relevant being:

The *brain* uses *parallel, distributed processing* involving many relatively simple elements (neurons or neural assemblies), each of which is capable of performing local processing and memory, and which are grouped into systems.

Systems are composed of groups of related elements that subserve a similar set of processing functions. Systems may be defined anatomically (by patterns of connectivity) and/or functionally (by specialization of representation or function).

Specialization arises from parametric variations in properties possessed by all elements in the brain (e.g., patterns of connectivity, time constants, regulation by neuromodulatory systems). Parameter variations occur along continuous dimensions, and thus subsystem specialization can be a graded phenomenon.

Knowledge is encoded in the synaptic connection strengths (*weights*) between neurons, which typically change slowly compared with the time course of processing. This means that neurons have relatively stable (*dedicated*) representations over time.

Cognition results from *activation propagation* through interconnected networks of neurons. Activity is required to directly influence ongoing processing.

Learning occurs by *modifying weights* as a function of activity (which can convey *error* and *reward* feedback information from the environment).

Memory is achieved either by the relatively short-term persistence of activation patterns (*active memory*) or longer lasting weight modifications (*weight-based memory*).

Representations are *distributed* over many neurons and brain systems, and at many different levels of abstraction and contextualization.

Inhibition between representations exists at all levels, both within and possibly between systems, and increases as a (nonlinear) function of the number of active representations. This results in *attention* phenomena and has important computational benefits by enforcing relatively *sparse* levels of activation.

Recurrence (bidirectional connectivity) exists among the elements within a system and between systems, allowing for *interactive* bottom-up and top-down processing, *constraint satisfaction* settling, and the communication of error signals for learning.

A central feature of this framework, as outlined above, is that different brain systems are specialized for different functions. To characterize these specializations (and understand why they may have arisen), we focus on basic trade-offs that exist within this computational framework (e.g., activity- vs. weight-based storage, or rapid learning vs. extraction of regularities). These trade-offs lead to specialization, because a homogeneous system would require compromises to be made, whereas specialized systems working together can provide the benefits of each end of the trade-off without requiring compromise. This analysis has led to the following set of coincident biological and functional specializations, which are also summarized in Figure 11.2 and Table 11.1:

Posterior perceptual and motor cortex (PMC) The PMC optimizes knowledge-dependent *inference* capabilities, which depend on dense interconnectivity, highly distributed representations, and slow *integrative* learning (i.e., integrating over individual learning episodes) to obtain good estimates of the important structural/statistical properties of the world, upon which inferences are based (McClelland, McNaughton, & O'Reilly, 1995). Similarity-based overlap among distributed representations is important for enabling generalization from prior experience to new situations. These systems perform sensory/motor and more abstract, multimodal processing in a hierarchical but highly interconnected fashion, resulting in the ability to perceive and act in the world in accordance with its salient and reliable properties. We take this to be the canonical type of neural computation in the cortex and view the other systems in reference to it.

Prefrontal cortex (PFC) The PFC optimizes *active memory* via restricted recurrent excitatory connectivity and an active gating mechanism (discussed subsequently). This results in the ability to (a) flexibly update internal representations, (b) maintain these over time and in the face of interference and, (c) by propagation of activation from these representations, bias PMC processing in a task-appropriate manner. PFC is specialized because there is a fundamental trade-off between the ability to actively sustain representations (in the absence of enduring input or the presence of distracting information) and the presence of dense interconnectivity underlying distributed

HCMP

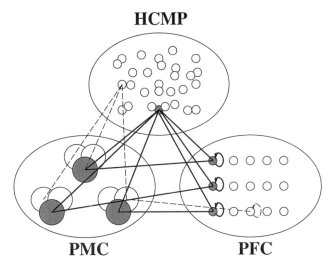

PMC   PFC

Figure 11.2. Diagram of key properties of the three principal brain systems. Active representations are shown in gray; highly overlapping circles are distributed representations; nonoverlapping are isolated; in between are separated. Weights between active units are shown in solid lines; those of nonactive units in dashed. Three active feature values along three separate "dimensions" (e.g., modalities) are represented. PMC representations are distributed and embedded in specialized (e.g., modality-specific) processing systems. PFC representations are isolated from each other, and combinatorial, with separate active units representing each feature value. Unlike other systems, PFC units are capable of robust self-maintenance, as indicated by the recurrent connections. HCMP representations are sparse, separated (but still distributed), and conjunctive, so that only a single representation is active at a time, corresponding to the conjunction of all active features.

(overlapping) representations such as in the PMC (Cohen et al., 1996). As a result, the individual self-maintaining representations in PFC must be relatively *isolated* from each other (as opposed to distributed). They can thus be activated *combinatorially* with less mutual interference or contradiction, allowing for flexible and rapid updating. Because they sit high in the cortical representational hierarchy, they are less embedded and more globally accessible and influential. Because they are actively maintained and strongly influence cognition, only a relatively small number of representations can typically be concurrently active in the PFC at a given time for coherent cognition to result. Thus, inhibitory attentional mechanisms play an important role in PFC, as well as for understanding the origin of capacity constraints.

Hippocampus and related structures (HCMP) The HCMP optimizes rapid learning of arbitrary information in weight-based memories. This permits the binding of elements of a novel association, including representations in

Table 11.1. *Critical Parameterizations of the Three Systems*

System	Function	Internal Relation	External Relation	Act Capacity	Learn Rate
PMC	Inference processing	Distributed, overlapping	Embedded	Many	Slow
PFC	Maintenance, control	Isolated, combinatorial	Global	Few	Slow
HCMP	Rapid learning	Separated, conjunctive	Context sensitive	One	Fast

Note: Function specifies the function optimized by this system. *Internal relation* indicates how representations within each system relate to each other. *External relation* indicates how representations relate to other systems. *Act capacity* indicates how many representations can be active at any given time. *Learn rate* indicates characteristic rate of learning. See text for fuller description.

PFC and PMC, providing a mechanism for temporary storage of arbitrary current states for later retrieval. There is a trade-off between such rapid learning of arbitrary information without interfering with prior learning (retroactive interference) and the ability to develop accurate estimates of underlying statistical structure (McClelland et al., 1995). To avoid interference, learning in the HCMP uses *pattern separation* (i.e., individual episodes of learning are separated from each other), as opposed to the integration characteristic of PMC. This separation process requires *sparse, conjunctive* representations, in which all the elements contribute interactively (not separably) to specifying a given representation (O'Reilly & McClelland, 1994). This conjunctivity is the opposite of the combinatorial PFC, in which the elements contribute separably. Conjunctivity leads to *context-specific* and *episodic* memories, which bind together the elements of a context or episode. This also implies that there is a single HCMP representation (consisting of many active neurons) corresponding to an entire pattern of activity in the cortex. Because only one HCMP representation can be active at any time, reactivation is necessary to extract information from multiple such representations.

Although there are undoubtedly many other important specialized brain systems, we think that these three provide central and critical contributions to working memory function. However, brainstem neuromodulatory systems, such as dopamine and norepinephrine, play an important supporting role in our theory, as a result of their capacity to modulate cortical processing according to reward, punishment, and affective states. In particular, as we discuss further below, we have hypothesized that dopamine activity plays a critical role in working memory function, by regulating active maintenance in PFC (Cohen & Servan-Schreiber, 1992; Cohen et al., 1996).

It should also be emphasized that the foregoing are relatively broad characterizations of large brain systems, which (especially in the case of the neocortical systems) may have subsystems with different levels of conformance to these generalizations. Further, there may be other important differences between these systems that are not reflected in our account. Nevertheless, these generalizations are consistent with a large corpus of empirical data and ideas from other theorists (e.g., Fuster, 1989; Goldman-Rakic, 1987; Shallice, 1982; Squire, 1992). Finally, we note that there are still important portions of this account that have not yet been implemented in computational models, and the sufficiency of these ideas to perform complex cognitive tasks, especially those involving extended sequential behavior, remains untested at present. Nevertheless, encouraging progress has been made in implementing and testing models of some of the more basic functions we have described, such as the active maintenance function of PFC and the binding function of hippocampus (see Cohen et al., 1996; Cohen & O'Reilly, 1996; McClelland et al., 1995, for reviews).

In what follows, we will elaborate the ways in which these brain systems interact to produce controlled processing and working memory and make more clear their relationship to other constructs such as consciousness and active memory. We will then focus on a set of important issues surrounding the operation of the PFC active memory system, followed by an application of these ideas to understanding some standard working memory tasks. This then provides a sufficient set of principles to address the theoretical questions posed in this volume.

Controlled Processing and Brain System Interactions

We consider controlled processing to be an important aspect of our theory of working memory. This has classically been described in contrast with *automatic processing* (Posner & Snyder, 1975; Shiffrin & Schneider, 1977), and has been thought to involve a limited-capacity attentional system. However, more recent theories have suggested that a continuum may exist between controlled and automatic processing (Cohen, Dunbar, & McClelland, 1990; Kahneman & Treisman, 1984), and we concur with this view. Thus, working memory also varies along this same continuum. In particular, we have conceptualized controlled processing as the ability to flexibly adapt behavior to the demands of particular tasks, favoring the processing of task-relevant information over other sources of competing information and mediating task-relevant behavior over habitual or otherwise prepotent responses. In our models this is operationalized as the use and updating of actively maintained representations in PFC to bias subsequent processing and action selection within

PMC in a task-appropriate manner. For example, in the AX-CPT model described earlier, the context representation actively maintained in PFC is able to exert control over processing by biasing the response made to an ambiguous probe stimulus.

Though it is tempting to equate controlled processing with theoretical constructs such as a central executive (Gathercole, 1994; Shiffrin & Schneider, 1977), there are critical differences in the assumptions and character of these mechanisms that have important consequences for our model of working memory. Perhaps the most important difference between our notion of controlled processing and theories that posit a central executive is that we view controlled processing as emerging from the interactions of several brain systems, rather than the operation of a single, unitary CPU-like construct. We believe that our interactive, decentralized view is more consistent with the graded aspect of controlled processing, as well as the character of neural architectures. However, aspects of our theory are compatible with other models. For example, Shallice (1982) has proposed a theory of frontal function, as well as the operation of a central executive, in terms of a supervisory attentional system (SAS). He describes this using a production system architecture, in which the SAS is responsible for maintaining goal states in working memory, to coordinate the firing of productions involved in complex behaviors. This is similar to the role of goal stacks and working memory in ACT (Anderson, 1983; Lovett et al., Chapter 5, this volume). Similarly, our theory of working memory and controlled processing depends critically on actively maintained representations (in PFC). This central role for active maintenance in achieving controlled processing contrasts with a view in which active maintenance and executive control are strictly segregated (Baddeley & Logie, Chapter 2, this volume).

We consider controlled processing to arise from the interplay between PFC *biasing* and HCMP *binding* (Cohen & O'Reilly, 1996). Figure 11.3 illustrates the central ideas of this account, which is based on the functional characterizations of the PFC and HCMP as described earlier. According to this view, the degree to which controlled processing is engaged by a task is determined by the extent to which either or both of the following conditions exist:

• Sustained, weakly learned (i.e., relatively infrequent), or coordinated processing is required.
• Novel information must be rapidly stored and accessed.

Since the PFC can bias processing in the rest of the system, sustained activity of representations in PFC can produce a focus of activity among representations in PMC needed to perform a given task. This can be used to support representations in PMC over temporally extended periods (e.g., in delayed response tasks), and/or weakly learned representations that might otherwise

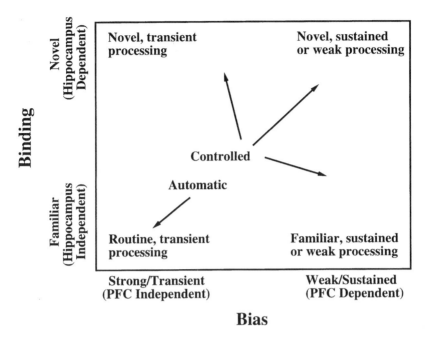

Bias

Figure 11.3. Ways in which the HCMP and PFC contribute to the automatic vs. controlled processing distinction (after Cohen & O'Reilly, 1996). Bias is provided by the PFC and can be used to perform sustained processing, can facilitate the processing of weakly learned (i.e., relatively infrequent) tasks, and can serve to coordinate processing across different systems. Binding is provided by the HCMP and can be used to rapidly learn and store the information necessary to perform novel tasks or processing. Controlled processing can involve either or both of these contributions, whereas automatic processing can be performed independent of them.

be dominated by stronger ones (e.g., in the Stroop task, where highly practiced word-reading dominates relatively infrequent color naming; Cohen et al., 1990). This function of PFC corresponds closely to Engle, Kane, and Tuholski's (Chapter 4, this volume) notion of controlled attention and to Cowan's (Chapter 3, this volume) notion of focus of attention. In contrast, the HCMP contributes the ability to learn new information rapidly and without interference, binding together task-relevant information (e.g., task instructions, particular combinations of stimuli, intermediate states of problem solutions) in such a form that it can be retrieved at appropriate junctures during task performance. This may be relevant for Ericsson and Delaney's (Chapter 8, this volume) notion of long-term working memory and Young and Lewis' (Chapter 7, this volume) production learning mechanism, as well as Moscovitch and Winocur's (1992) notion of "working-with-memory." We propose that the combination of these two functions (PFC biasing and HCMP binding) can account for the distinction between controlled and automatic processing. On this account, automatic processing is what occurs via activation propagation through intrinsic PMC connectivity, whereas controlled processing reflects the additional constraints on the flow of activity brought to bear by the PFC and/or HCMP.

Activation Propagation and Multiple-Constraint Satisfaction

Though some aspects of behavior can be understood in terms of relatively local processes within the brain, we assume that, under most circumstances, behavior is determined by a rich and dynamic set of interactions involving the widespread propagation of activation to multiple, distributed brain systems. Although the detailed outcome of such processing in a particular case may be difficult, if not ultimately impossible, to describe, its general character can be understood in terms of *multiple-constraint satisfaction*: The activation state that results from this propagation of information over weighted neuronal connections is likely to be one that satisfies various constraints, including those imposed by three critical components: (a) external stimuli; (b) sustained activity in PFC; and (c) recalled information from the HCMP. Thus, representations in PFC and HCMP act as "control signals," insofar as these influence the flow of activity and thereby shape the constraint-satisfaction process that is taking place in the rest of the brain. Furthermore, their activation states are themselves influenced by similar constraint-satisfaction mechanisms based on activations from the PMC (though a presumed gating mechanism in the PFC can make it more or less susceptible to this "bottom-up" influence; see subsequent discussion). All of these constraints are mediated by the synaptic connections between neurons, which are adapted through experience in such a way as to result in better activation states in similar situations in the future. Thus, much of the real work being done in our model (and our avoidance of a homunculus or otherwise unspecified central executive mechanisms when we discuss controlled processing), lies in these activation dynamics and their tuning as a function of experience. Computational models are essential in demonstrating the efficacy of these mechanisms, which may otherwise appear to have mysterious properties.

Accessibility and Consciousness

In our model, one of the dimensions along which brain systems differ is in the extent to which their representations are globally accessible to a wide range of other brain systems, as opposed to being embedded within more specific processing systems and less globally accessible. We view this difference as arising principally from a system's relative position within an overall hierarchy of abstractness of representations. This hierarchy is defined by how far removed a system is from direct sensory input or motor output. Systems supporting high-level, more-abstract representations are more centrally located with respect to the overall network connectivity, resulting in greater accessibility. Accordingly, because both the PFC and HCMP are at the top of the hierarchy (Fuster, 1989; Squire, Shimamura, & Amaral, 1989), they are more influential and accessible than subsystems within PMC. Like the other dimensions along which these systems are specialized, we view this as a graded continuum, and not as an all-or-nothing distinction. Furthermore, we assume that the PMC has rich "lateral" connectivity between subsystems at the same general level of abstraction (at least beyond the first few levels of sensory or motor processing). Nevertheless, the PFC and HCMP assume a position of greater accessibility, and therefore greater influence, relative to other systems.

Accessibility has many implications that relate to issues of conscious awareness as well as psychological distinctions like *explicit* versus *implicit* or *declarative* versus *procedural*. We view the contents of conscious experience as reflecting the results of global constraint-satisfaction processing throughout the brain, with those systems or representations that are most influential or constraining on this process having greater conscious salience (cf. Kinsbourne, 1997). In general, this means that highly accessible and influential systems like PFC and HCMP will tend to dominate conscious experience over the more embedded subsystems of the PMC. Consequently, these systems are most clearly associated with notions of explicit or declarative processing, whereas the PMC and subcortical systems are associated with implicit or procedural processing. We endorse this distinction, but add the important caveats that PFC and HCMP are participants in an extended interactive system and that, once again, such distinctions should be considered along a continuum. Thus, our theory is not compatible with strong assumptions about informationally encapsulated modules (Fodor, 1983; Moscovitch & Winocur, 1992).

Active Memory Versus Working Memory

In our model, we use the term *active memory* to refer to information that is represented as a pattern of activity (neuronal spiking) across a set of units (neural assembly) that persists over some (possibly brief) time interval. We view working memory as relying on active memory, by virtue of the need to rapidly and frequently access stored information over short intervals and use this information to bias processing in an ongoing way in other parts of the system. However, the HCMP, because it is capable of rapidly forming novel associations and retrieving these in task-relevant contexts, is also useful for working memory. Conversely, we do not assume that actively maintained representations are invoked exclusively within the context of working memory. Sustained activity can occur and play a role in automatic processing as well. For example, it is not difficult to imagine that relatively automatic tasks such as typing would require persistent active representations, and sustained activity has indeed been observed in areas outside of PFC (Miller & Desimone, 1994). We assume that actively maintained representations participate in working memory function only under conditions of controlled processing –

that is, when sustained activity is the result of representations currently being actively maintained in the PFC or retrieved by the HCMP. This corresponds directly to the distinctions, proposed by Cowan (Chapter 3, this volume) and Engle et al. (Chapter 4, this volume), between controlled or focused attention and other sources of activation and attentional effects.

Regulation of Active Memory

It has long been known from electrophysiological recordings in monkeys that PFC neurons remain active over delays between a stimulus and a contingent response (Fuster & Alexander, 1971). Furthermore, though such sustained activity has been observed in areas outside of PFC, it appears that PFC activity is robust to interference from processing intervening distractor stimuli, whereas activity within the PMC is not (Miller, Erikson, & Desimone, 1996; Cohen et al., 1997). Although the precise mechanisms responsible for active maintenance in PFC are not yet known, one likely mechanism is strong recurrent excitation. If groups of PFC neurons are strongly interconnected with each other, then strong mutual excitation will lead to both sustained activity and some ability to resist interference. This idea has been developed in a number of computational models of PFC function (Dehaene & Changeux, 1989; Zipser, Kehoe, Littlewort, & Fuster, 1993). However, we believe that this simple model is inadequate to account for both robust active maintenance and the kind of rapid and flexible updating necessary for complex cognitive tasks.

The underlying problem reflects a basic trade-off – to the extent that units are made impervious to interference (i.e., by making the recurrent excitatory connections stronger), this also prevents them from being updated (i.e., new representations activated and existing ones deactivated). Conversely, weaker excitatory connectivity will make units more sensitive to inputs and capable of rapid updating, but will not enable them to be sustained in the face of interference. To circumvent this trade-off, we think that the PFC has taken advantage of midbrain neuromodulatory systems, which can provide a *gating* mechanism for controlling maintenance. When the gate is opened, the PFC representations are sensitive to their inputs and capable of rapid updating. When the gate is closed, the PFC representations are protected from interference. Such a gating mechanism can augment the computational power of recurrent networks (Hochreiter & Schmidhuber, 1997), and we have hypothesized that dopamine (DA) implements this gating function in PFC, based on a substantial amount of biological data (Cohen et al., 1996).

Thus, we propose that the midbrain DA nuclei (the ventral tegmental area, VTA), under control of descending cortical projections, enable the PFC to actively regulate the updating of its representations by controlling the release of DA in a strategic manner. Specifically, we propose that the afferent connections into the PFC from other brain systems are usually relatively weak compared to stronger local excitation, but that DA enhances the strength of these afferents[1] at times when updating is necessary. This would predict that the VTA should exhibit phasic firing at those times when the PFC needs to be updated. Schultz, Apicella, and Ljungberg (1993) have found that, indeed, the VTA exhibits transient, stimulus-locked activity in response to stimuli that predicted subsequent meaningful events (e.g., reward or other cues that then predict reward). Further, we argue that this role of DA as a gating mechanism is synergistic with its widely discussed role in reward-based learning (Montague, Dayan, & Sejnowski, 1996). As will be discussed further in the final discussion section, this learning helps us to avoid the need to postulate a homunculus-like mechanism for controlled processing.

General Nature of Active Memory Representations

Our theory places several important demands on the nature of representations within the PFC, in addition to the rapidly updatable yet robust active maintenance discussed before. In general, we view the PFC's role in controlled processing as imposing a sustained, task-relevant, top-down bias on processing in the PMC. Thus, in complex cognitive activities, the PFC should be constantly activating and deactivating representations that can bias a large number of combinations of PMC representations, while sustaining a coherent and focused thread of processing. This means that the PFC needs a vast repertoire of representations that can be activated on demand, and these representations need to be connected with the PMC in appropriate ways. Further, there must be some way of linking together sequences of representations in a coherent way.

Our initial approach toward understanding PFC representations has been dominated by an interesting coincidence between the previously mentioned functional characterization of the PFC and a consequence of an active maintenance mechanism based on recurrent excitation. Distributed representations, which are thought to be characteristic of the PMC, are problematic for this kind of active maintenance mechanism, because they rely critically on afferent input to select the appropriate subset of distributed components to be activated. In the absence of this afferent selection (e.g., during a delay period), recurrent excitation among the components will spread inappropriately and result in the loss of the original activity pattern. This is illustrated in Figure 11.4, in which a distributed representation is used to encode three different items, which each share two out of three total features. If these distributions have the strong recurrent excitatory connections necessary for active maintenance, then it will be difficult to keep a unique subset of two features active without also activating the third: Activation will spread to the third unit via the connections necessary to maintain it in other circumstances. The alternative (shown in panel b) is to use *isolated* representations, which maintain only themselves. However, what is missing from these isolated representations is

---

[1] In addition, it appears that inhibitory connections are also enhanced, which would provide a means of deactivating existing representations.

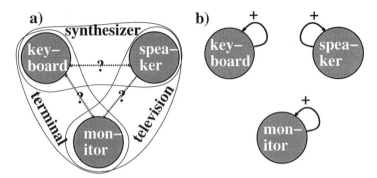

Figure 11.4. Illustration of difficulties with active maintenance via recurrent excitation with distributed representations. (a) No value of the excitatory weights will enable an appropriate subset of two features to be maintained, without also activating the third. (b) If representations are made independent, then maintenance is no problem, but semantic relatedness of the features is lost. One could also just maintain the higher-level items (i.e., synthesizer, terminal, and television).

the rich interconnectivity that encodes knowledge about the relationships between the features, which could be used for performing the knowledge-dependent inference that we think is characteristic of the PMC. We obtain theoretical leverage from this basic trade-off, which can be avoided by having two specialized systems (PMC and PFC).

The idea that PFC representations are relatively isolated from each other has important functional consequences beyond the active maintenance of information. For example, to achieve flexibility and generativity, PFC representations must be useful in novel contexts and combinations. Thus, individual PFC representations should not interfere much with each other so that they can be more easily and meaningfully combined – this is just what one would expect from relatively isolated representations. We think that learning in the PFC is slow and integrative like the rest of the cortex, so that this gradual learning taking place over many years of human development produces a rich and diverse palette of relatively independent PFC representational components, which eventually enable the kinds of flexible problem-solving skills that are uniquely characteristic of adult human cognition.

This view of PFC representations can be usefully compared with that of human language. In terms of basic representational elements, language contains words, which have a relatively fixed meaning and can be combined in a huge number of different ways to express different (and sometimes novel) ideas. Words represent things at many different levels of abstraction and concreteness, and complicated or particularly detailed ideas can be expressed by combinations of words. We think that similar properties hold for PFC representations, and indeed that a substantial subset of PFC representations do correspond with word-like concepts. However, we emphasize that word meanings have highly distributed representations across multiple brain systems (Damasio, Grabowski, Tranel, Hichwa, & Damasio, 1996), and also that the PFC undoubtedly has many nonverbal representations. Nevertheless, it may be that the PFC component of a word's representation approaches most closely the notion of a discrete, symbol-like entity.

Taking this language idea one step further, it may provide useful insights into the kinds of updating and sequential linking that PFC representations need to undergo during processing. For example, language is organized at many different levels of temporal structure, from short phrases, through longer sentences to paragraphs, passages, and so on. These levels are mutually constraining, with phrases adding together to build higher-level meaning and this accumulated meaning biasing the interpretation of lower-level phrases. This same interactive hierarchical structure, present during problem solving and other complex cognitive activities, is critical for understanding the dynamics of PFC processing. We think that all of these different levels of representation can be active simultaneously, mutually constraining each other. Further, it is possible that the posterior–anterior dimension of the PFC may be organized roughly according to level of abstraction (and correspondingly, temporal duration). For example, there is evidence that the most anterior area of PFC, the frontal pole, is activated only in more complicated problem-solving tasks (Baker et al., 1996), and that posterior PFC receives most of the projections from PMC, and then projects to more anterior regions (Barbas & Pandya, 1987, 1989). Finally, this notion of increasingly abstract levels of plan or internal task context is consistent with the progression from posterior to anterior seen within the motor and premotor areas of the frontal cortex (Rizzolatti, Luppino, & Matelli, 1996).

Specialization of Active Memory Representations

An important issue both within the working memory literature and with regard to theories of PFC function is that of specialization along functional and/or representational dimensions. For example, Baddeley (1986) proposed that there are two separate working memory buffers: a *phonological loop* and a *visuospatial sketchpad*, which might itself be subdividable into object and spatial components. It has been proposed that this functional specialization reflects an underlying specialization in the brain systems subserving the different buffer systems (Gathercole, 1994). For example, there may be specific brain systems subserving verbal rehearsal (e.g., Broca's area and/or angular gyrus). There is also a well-recognized segregation of processing of object and spatial information into ventral (temporal) and dorsal (parietal) streams within the PMC (Ungerleider & Mishkin, 1982) that may correspond to the two subdivisions of Baddeley's visuospatial sketchpad. At a somewhat more general level, Shah and Miyake (1996) have found evidence consistent with the idea of separable spatial and verbal capacities.

Specialization may also play a role in PFC organization and function. Arguments in the literature have centered around two dimensions along which PFC may be organized: functional and content-based. However, we argue that it is difficult to draw a clean distinction between function and content. Indeed, a basic principle of neural networks is that processing and knowledge (content) are intimately intertwined. For example, the functional distinction between memory (in the dorsolateral PFC) and inhibition (in the orbital areas; Diamond, 1990; Fuster, 1989), could also be explained by a content-based distinction in terms of the representation of affective, appetitive, and social information in the orbital areas, which might be more frequently associated with the need for behavioral inhibition. Similarly, the functional dissociation between manipulation (in dorsalateral areas) and maintenance (in ventrolateral areas; Petrides, 1996) may be confounded with the need to represent sequential-order information in most tasks that involve manipulation. To further complicate the issue, one type of functional specialization can often give rise to other apparent functional specializations. For example, we have argued that the memory and inhibitory functions ascribed to PFC may both reflect the operation of a single mechanism (i.e., inhibition can result from maintained top-down activation of representations that then inhibit other competing possibilities via lateral inhibition; Cohen & Servan-Schreiber, 1992; Cohen et al., 1996).

Given these problems, we find it more useful to think in terms of the computational motivations described before to understand how the PFC is specialized (i.e., in terms of the trade-off between active maintenance and distributed representations). Thus, we support the idea that the PFC is specialized for the function of active maintenance. Consequently, representations within the PFC must be organized by the content of the representations that are maintained. A number of neurophysiological studies have suggested a content-based organization that reflects an anterior extension of the organization found in the PMC, with dorsal regions representing spatial information (Funahashi, Bruce, & Goldman-Rakic, 1993) and more ventral regions representing object or pattern information (Wilson, O'Scalaidhe, & Goldman-Rakic, 1993). Other content dimensions have also been suggested, such as sequential-order information (Barone & Joseph, 1989) and "dry" cognitive versus affective, appetitive, and/or social information (Cohen & Smith, 1997). However, the data do not consistently support any of these ideas. For example, Rao, Rainer, and Miller (1997) have recorded more complex patterns of organization in neurophysiological studies, with significant degrees of overlap and multimodality of representations. Recent findings within the human neuroimaging literature are also confusing, because early reports that indicated distinctions in the areas activated by verbal versus object and verbal versus spatial information (e.g., Smith, Jonides, & Koeppe, 1996) have not been reliably replicated (as reported in a number of recent conference proceedings and in unpublished data from our lab).

In light of these data, we suggest that the PFC may be organized according to more abstract, more multimodal, and less intuitive dimensions than have been considered to date (i.e., that do not correspond simply to sensory modalities or dimensions). This seems likely, given the relatively high-level position of the PFC in the processing hierarchy (see previous discussion), which would give it highly processed multimodal inputs. Further, this type of input may interact with the learning mechanisms and other constraints on the development of representations within PFC. For example, we have shown that task demands and training parameters (i.e., blocked vs. interleaved exposure) can play an important role in determining whether a simulated PFC develops uni- or multimodal representations of object and spatial information (Braver & Cohen, 1995).

Example Working Memory Tasks

Earlier, we provided an example of how the mechanisms we have proposed are engaged in a simple working memory task (the AX-CPT). Here, we consider how they may come into play in two tasks that are commonly used to measure working memory capacity and contrast them with ones that are thought *not* to involve working memory. The verbal working memory span task (Daneman & Carpenter, 1980) involves reading aloud a set of sentences and remembering the final words from each sentence for later recall. Thus, these final words must be maintained in the face of subsequent processing, which makes this task heavily dependent on the robust PFC active maintenance mechanisms. A spatial version of this task (Shah & Miyake, 1996) involves identifying letters presented at different non-upright orientations as being either normal or mirror-reversed, which appears to require some amount of mental rotation to the upright orientation, while remembering the orientations of the letters for later recall. This mental rotation requires the driving of PMC-based visual transformations (learned over extensive experience seeing visual transformations such as rotation, translation, etc.) in a task-relevant manner, presumably via actively maintained PFC top-down biasing. Further, the orientation information must be maintained in the face of subsequent processing of the same kinds of information, which again requires robust PFC active maintenance.

These working memory span tasks have been contrasted with others that are not considered to involve working memory. For example, the verbal working memory span task has been compared with a simple digit span task, which presumably requires only active maintenance, but not controlled processing. Behaviorally, the verbal working memory span task is better correlated with other putative verbal working memory tasks that also involve controlled processing, compared to this simple digit span task (Daneman & Merikle, 1996). The other half of this argument has been made in the case of a spatial equivalent of the digit span task (which involved remembering the orientations of a set of arrows), which was significantly correlated with a simple visual-processing task, whereas the spatial working memory span measure was not (Shah & Miyake, 1996). See Engle et al. (Chapter 4, this volume) for a more detailed discussion of this issue and other relevant experimental results.

Another example, involving the use of the HCMP system, is the comprehension of extended written passages. Because of limited capacity in the PFC active memory system, it is likely that some of the representations activated by the comprehension of prior paragraphs are encoded only within the HCMP and must be recalled as necessary during later processing (e.g., when encountering a reference like, "this would be impossible, given Ms. Smith's condition," which refers to previously introduced information that may not have remained active in the PFC). The idea is that this later reference can be used to trigger recall of the previous information from the HCMP, perhaps with the addition of some strategic activation of other relevant information that has persisted in the PFC (e.g., the fact that Ms. Smith lives in Kansas). A successful recall of this information will result in the activation of appropriate representations within the PFC and PMC, which combined with the current text results in comprehension (e.g., Ms. Smith was hit by a tornado and can't come into work for an important meeting). In contrast with theories that draw a strong distinction between active memory and HCMP weight-based memories (e.g., Moscovitch & Winocur, 1992), we think that a typical cognitive task analysis may not distinguish between these types of memory in many situations, making the generic working memory label more appropriate for both. Finally, Young and Lewis (Chapter 7, this volume) present what appears to be a roughly similar role for rapid learning in their theory of working memory, and Ericsson and Delaney (Chapter 8, this volume) describe relatively long-lasting working memory representations that would seem to involve the HCMP (as well as the effects of extensive experience on underlying cortical representations).

Answers to Theoretical Questions

This section summarizes our answers to a set of eight basic questions about our theory of working memory. The questions are summarized by the section headers, and Table 11.2 provides a concise summary of our answers to these questions.

Basic Mechanisms and Representations in Working Memory

Active maintenance (for which the PFC is specialized), rapid learning (for which the HCMP is specialized), and controlled processing (biasing and binding based on these) are the basic mechanisms of working memory in our account. Controlled processing emerges from the interactions between all three primary brain systems (PFC, HCMP, PMC), but is most strongly influenced by the PFC and HCMP. For purposes of comparison, we describe our

Table 11.2. *Summary of Our Answers to the Eight Designated Questions*

(1) **Basic Mechanisms and Representations in Working Memory**
The basic mechanisms of active memory and rapid learning via controlled processing are implemented by the prefrontal cortex (PFC), hippocampus and related structures (HCMP), and the posterior perceptual and motor cortex (PMC). Representations, distributed throughout the system, are encoded by controlled activation, maintained by robust PFC mechanisms and weight-based HCMP learning, and retrieved in the case of HCMP by controlled activation of cues. Verbal and perhaps spatial and/or numerical representations are especially useful ways of encoding.

(2) **The Control and Regulation of Working Memory**
Working memory is not separated from control, because controlled processing and active memory are intimately related. Control is also not centralized, emerging instead from interactions between different brain systems. PFC plays an important role owing to its robust maintenance capabilities, flexible and rapid updating of representations, and position at the top of the cortical processing hierarchy (with HCMP).

(3) **The Unitary Versus Non-Unitary Nature of Working Memory**
Working memory is not unitary: It consists of active memory and rapid learning and controlled processing and is distributed over several brain systems. The common use of controlled processing mechanisms may contribute a unitary-like component to performance.

(4) **The Nature of Working Memory Limitations**
There are two mechanisms: inhibition and interference. PFC has greater inhibition to promote coherent processing, and thus lower capacity. Capacity has domain-specific and general components (see Question 3), and corresponding experience and genetic bases. Capacity is highly dependent on amount and type of controlled processing necessary, as well as efficiency of underlying representations learned over experience.

(5) **The Role of Working Memory in Complex Cognitive Activities**
Working memory is critical, because complex congnitive activities are defined by the involvement of controlled processing and require active memory/rapid learning to maintain intermediate results. Distributed brain systems are involved as relevant in particular tasks, with more common involvement of PFC and HCMP.

(6) **The Relationship of Working Memory to Long-Term Memory and Knowledge**
Working memory is largely just the active portion of long-term memory, which is itself distributed over many brain areas. More globally accessible systems and those that provide particularly useful representations (e.g., language) are more likely to be involved in working memory, leading to a bias

continued

Table 11.2, continued

toward declarative or explicit representations instead of implicit or procedural ones.

(7) **The Relationship of Working Memory to Attention and
Consciousness**
Working memory is the subset of representations attended to by virtue of
controlled processing. Attention also refers to a constraining mechanism
(inhibition) and can be influenced by automatic processing. Consciousness
reflects the global constraint-satisfaction process, which is disproportionately
influenced by controlled processing systems. Thus, the content of conscious
experience is likely to reflect that of working memory.

(8) **The Biological Implementation of Working Memory**
Our model is based on biology, including neural-level properties like activation, inhibition, and learning, and a computational account of specialized
brain system function, including the PFC, HCMP, and PMC. A large amount
of empirical data from patients, neuroimaging, neurophysiology, and animal
studies is consistent with our model.

basic mechanisms in terms of standard memory terminology of encoding,
maintenance, and retrieval.

Encoding Owing to slow learning, the cortical systems (PFC and PMC) have relatively stable representational capability. Thus, encoding in these systems
relies on the selection and activation (via constraint-satisfaction processing
operating over experience-tuned weights) of those preexisting representations that are most relevant in a particular context. In the HCMP, encoding
involves the rapid binding together of a novel conjunction of the representations active in the rest of the brain. An important influence on this
process, and a critical component of controlled processing, is the strategic
activation (under the influence of the PFC) of representations that influence HCMP encoding in task-appropriate ways (e.g., activating distinctive
features during elaborative encoding in a memory task).

Maintenance Only the PFC is thought to be capable of sustaining activity over
longer delays and in the face of other potentially interfering stimuli or processing. However, under conditions of shorter delays and the absence of
interference, PMC can exhibit sustained active memories (Miller et al.,
1996). We include in our definition of the PFC the frontal language areas
that have been shown to be active in neuroimaging studies involving
active memory as discussed earlier. For example, considerable evidence
supports the idea that maintenance in this system is implemented by a
phonological loop (Baddeley, 1986; Baddeley & Logie, Chapter 2, this vol-

ume), which may involve more highly specialized mechanisms than those hypothesized to exist in other areas of PFC. We do not think that the HCMP maintains information in an active form, but rather through rapid weight changes made during encoding. These weight-based HCMP memories can persist over much longer intervals than active memories (cf. Ericsson & Delaney, Chapter 8, this volume).

Retrieval For active memories, retrieval is not an issue, but for HCMP weight-based memories, retrieval typically requires multiple cues to trigger a particular hippocampal memory (owing to its conjunctive nature). As with encoding, the strategic activation of such cues constitutes an important part of controlled processing.

As for the nature of the representations in our model of working memory, we have characterized the distinctive properties of representations in each of the three main brain systems (see Table 11.1 and Figure 11.2). However, because we do not adhere to a buffer-based or any other distinct substrate view of working memory, this question is difficult to address. Essentially, the space of possible different representations for working memory is as large as the space of all representations in the neocortex and hippocampus, because any such representation could be activated in a controlled manner, thus satisfying our definition of working memory. However, we think that brain systems specialized for language may provide an exceptionally powerful and general-purpose representational system for encoding arbitrary information and are likely to be used to encode even superficially nonverbal information. Similarly, it may also be that abstract spatial and/or numerical representations are useful for encoding relational and perhaps temporal information.

The Control and Regulation of Working Memory

In our theory, control results from the biasing function of the PFC and the binding function of the HCMP. These systems, in turn, are regulated by each other, the PMC, and ascending brainstem neuromodulatory systems. Thus, control and regulation are interactive and distributed phenomena that involve all parts of the system. Though these interactions are necessarily complex, it is possible to identify characteristic contributions made by each component of the system. The PFC plays a dominant role in controlled processing by virtue of its characteristic features: its ability to maintain activation over time; the flexible and rapid updating of representations owing to their combinatorial and active nature; and its position high in the cortical processing hierarchy. Note that unlike models that separate control (e.g., a central executive) from active storage (e.g., buffers), active maintenance plays a central role in control in our model.

Representations within the PFC are themselves subject to the influence of processing within the PMC and HCMP, by way of specialized control mechanisms that regulate access to the PFC. As described earlier, we suggest that the midbrain dopamine (DA) system provides an active gating of PFC representations, controlling when they can be updated and protecting them from interference otherwise. We think that the PFC, together with the PMC and possibly the HCMP, controls the firing of the DA gating signal, through descending projections. Furthermore, we assume that these projections are subject to learning, so that the PFC and PMC can learn how to control the gating signal through experience.

The Unitary Versus Non-Unitary Nature of Working Memory

We take the view that working memory is not a unitary construct – instead we suggest that it is the combination of active memory, rapid learning, and emergent controlled processing operating over distributed brain systems. Instead of the moving of information from long-term memory into and out of working memory buffers, we think that information is distributed in a relatively stable configuration throughout the cortex and that working memory amounts to the controlled activation of these representations. As we noted at the outset, this view shares some similarities with the view of working memory offered by production-system accounts (e.g., ACT, Anderson, 1983; Lovett et al., Chapter 5, this volume). However, it does not include the structural distinction between declarative and procedural knowledge assumed by such accounts.

This non-unitary view is consistent with findings like those of Shah and Miyake (1996), who found no significant correlation between an individual's verbal and spatial working memory capacities. We would further predict that working memory capacity will vary along a variety of dimensions, depending on the quality of the relevant PMC and PFC representations developed over experience (cf. Ericsson & Delaney, Chapter 8, this volume). However, working memory is also affected by more domain-general, controlled processing mechanisms (such as those supported by brainstem neuromodulatory systems), so that some characteristics of working memory function might exhibit more unitary-like features (cf. Engle et al., Chapter 4, this volume). Thus, the actual performance of a given subject, under a given set of task conditions, will depend on a combination of both domain-specific and more general factors.

The Nature of Working Memory Limitations

The presence of capacity limitations seems to be one of the few points about which there is consensus in the working memory literature. Despite this agreement, there is relatively little discussion of why such limitations exist. Are these the unfortunate by-product of fundamental limitations in the underlying mechanisms (e.g., insufficient metabolic resources to sustain additional mental activity), or do they reflect some more interesting computational constraint? We adhere to the latter view. We believe that capacity limitations in working memory reflect a trade-off between two competing factors: the accessibility and widespread influence of PFC representations – necessary to implement its biasing function as a mechanism of control – and the need to constrain the extent of activation throughout the PMC, to avoid "runaway" activity and promote focused and coherent processing. We assume that this trade-off is managed by inhibitory mechanisms that constrain spreading activation and prevent the runaway activity that would otherwise result from the positive feedback loops within the cortex. This is particularly important in the PFC, because of its widespread and influential projections to the rest of the brain. We have begun to explore this possibility in explicit computational modeling work (Usher & Cohen, 1997). This account emphasizes the potential benefits of what otherwise might appear to be arbitrary limitations (cf. Lovett et al., Chapter 5, this volume). Note that Young and Lewis (Chapter 7, this volume) and Schneider (Chapter 10, this volume) present functional motivations similar to our own.

As we stated before, we think there are both domain-specific and more general contributions to working memory function. Similarly, there are likely to be both experience-dependent and genetically based contributions. Further, it is likely that there are interactions between these factors. For example, extensive experience will produce a rich and powerful set of domain-specific representations that support the ability to encode more domain-specific information both in active memory and via rapid learning in the HCMP. However, this is unlikely to affect more general factors (e.g., neuromodulatory function or the overall level of inhibition within the PFC). This is consistent with the general lack of cross-domain transfer from experience-based working memory capacity enhancements as discussed in Ericsson and Delaney (Chapter 8, this volume) and with the relatively domain-general limitations observed by Engle et al. (Chapter 4, this volume).

The role of experience-based learning (which is an important component of our overall model) in enhancing domain-specific working memory capacity can be illustrated by considering the following phases of experience:

Novel phase HCMP is required to store and recall novel task-relevant information, so that capacity is dominated by the constraint of having only one HCMP representation active at a time, with significant controlled processing required to orchestrate the use of this information with ongoing task processing. This is like the first time one tries to drive a car, at which time complete attention is required, everything happens in slow serial order, and many mistakes are made.

Weak phase PFC is required to bias the weak PMC representations underlying task performance, so that capacity is dominated by the relatively more constrained PFC. Thus, it is difficult to perform multiple tasks during this phase or to maintain other items in active memory. This is like the period after several times of driving, when one still has to devote full attention to the task (i.e., use PFC to coordinate behavior), but the basic operations are reasonably familiar and some can be performed in parallel.

Expert phase Weights within the PMC have been tuned to the point that automatic processing is capable of accomplishing the task. Since the PMC representations are relatively more embedded, they can happily coexist with activity in other areas of PMC, resulting in high capacity. This is the case with expert drivers, who can carry on conversations more effectively than novices while driving. Note that slow improvements within this phase occur with continued practice, resulting in experience-based differences in strength and sophistication of underlying representations, which contribute to individual differences in capacity and performance. This is true in the PFC as well, where fewer active representations need be maintained if a more concise (e.g., "chunked") representation has been learned over experience.

The Role of Working Memory in Complex Cognitive Activities

Complex cognitive activities involve controlled processing and thus, by our definition, involve working memory. According to our account of the roles of the PFC (biasing) and HCMP (binding), controlled processing occurs under conditions of temporally extended and/or novel tasks and in cases that require coordinated processing among multiple systems. Typically, complex tasks involve the temporally extended coordination of multiple steps of processing, often in novel combinations and situations, and the storage of intermediate products of computation, subgoals, and so on. Active memory together with the controlled encoding and retrieval of HCMP memories can be used to retain the intermediate results of these processing steps for subsequent use.

We have yet to apply our model to specific complex tasks, because we have yet to produce satisfactory implementations of the entire set of neural systems that would be required. Our overarching goal in developing such models is the ability to account for complex task performance without resorting to a homunculus of one form or another. Although many accounts of executive control remain purely verbal and are obviously susceptible to the homunculus problem, even mechanistically explicit accounts of complex task performance in production-system architectures (e.g., Young & Lewis, Chapter 7, this volume; Lovett et al., Chapter 5, this volume) have a hidden homunculus in the form of the researcher who builds in all the appropriate productions to enable the system to solve the task. As we discuss in greater detail subsequently, our current modeling efforts are focused on developing learning mechanisms that would give rise to a rich and diverse palette of PFC representations (and corresponding PMC subsystems), which should be capable of performing complex tasks without resorting to a homunculus of any form.

The Relationship of Working Memory to Long-Term Memory and Knowledge

We view working memory as being the active portion of long-term memory, where long-term memory refers to the entire network of knowledge distributed throughout the cortex, HCMP, and other brain systems. As noted earlier, this is similar to production-system theories of working memory (such as ACT; Anderson, 1983; Lovett et al., Chapter 5, this volume). However, we also specify that the term *working memory* applies only to those representations that are activated as a result of controlled processing. Thus, it is possible to have active representations that exist outside of working memory (cf. Cowan, Chapter 3, this volume; Engle et al., Chapter 4, this volume, for similar views). Because of this intimate relationship between working memory and long-term memory, we expect working memory to be heavily influenced by learning in the long-term memory system (see the discussion in the capacity section above and Ericsson & Delaney, Chapter 8, this volume).

We do not think that all components of long-term memory are equally likely to be represented in working memory. As discussed previously, language provides a particularly useful means of encoding arbitrary information and is thus heavily involved in working memory. In contrast, more embedded, low-level sensory and motor processing is less likely to come under the influence of controlled processing and is not typically considered to be involved in working memory. Thus, the general level of accessibility associated with a given brain system is correlated with the extent to which it is likely to be involved in working memory. As discussed earlier, this means that more *declarative* or *explicit* long-term knowledge is likely to be involved in working memory, whereas *implicit* or *procedural* knowledge is more associated with automatic processing.

The Relationship of Working Memory to Attention and Consciousness

Working memory, attention, and consciousness are clearly related in important ways. We view the underlying constraint that gives rise to attention as resulting from the influence of competition between representations, implemented by inhibitory interneurons throughout the cortex (and possibly also by subcortical mechanisms in the thalamus and basal ganglia). This inhibition provides a mechanism that causes some things to be ignored while others are attended to and is a critical aspect of attention that is not strictly part of working memory. However, assuming this constraint, controlled processing plays an important role in determining what is active in a given context (and via competition and inhibition, also what is ignored). Thus, working memory and attention are related in that they are both defined in part by the mechanisms that determine what is activated in a particular context.

Consciousness is also related to both working memory and attention. As stated previously, we view conscious experience as reflecting the outcome of global constraint-satisfaction processing, with salience a function of the degree of influence over this process attributable to a given representation. Thus, systems that are globally accessible like the PFC and HCMP are also highly influential and thus likely to dominate conscious experience. This means that the controlled processing–based activation (attention) mediated by these systems is most relevant for consciousness and that the contents of conscious experience are likely to reflect that of working memory as we have defined it (see also previous section and Kinsbourne, 1997).

The Biological Implementation of Working Memory

Our model is based largely on biological data, and its neural implementation has been described both in terms of basic properties such as activation, inhibition, and learning, and in terms of the interactions of the specialized brain systems described earlier (PFC, HCMP, PMC). By virtue of these biological foundations, there is a wealth of data that are consistent with our model, from anatomy and physiology to neuroimaging and neuropsychological work. We will review just some of the most relevant data here.

With respect to the involvement of the PFC in working memory tasks, our lab has focused on neuroimaging and schizophrenic patient performance on the AX-CPT task described in the introduction. By making the target A-X sequence very frequent (80%), and the delay between stimuli longer (5 s), we predicted that schizophrenic patients suffering an impairment of PFC function would make a relatively large number of false alarms to B-X sequences (where B is any non-A stimulus) owing to a failure of PFC-mediated working memory for the prior stimulus. This was confirmed, with unmedicated schizophrenic patients showing the predicted increase in false alarms, whereas medicated schizophrenics and control subjects did not (Servan-Schreiber, Cohen, & Steingard, 1997). In addition, neuroimaging of healthy subjects performing the AX-CPT showed that PFC increased activity with increases in delay interval (Barch et al., 1997). Neuroimaging during N-back performance revealed that PFC activity also increases with working memory load (Braver et al., 1997b) and is sustained across the entire delay period (Cohen et al., 1997). These data together with other consistent findings from monkey neurophysiology (e.g., Fuster, 1989; Miller et al., 1996) and frontally damaged patients (e.g., Damasio, 1985) support the idea that the PFC is critically important for working memory. Also, Engle et al. (Chapter 4, this volume) discuss the importance of the PFC in working memory.

With respect to the role of the HCMP in working memory, it has long been known that the HCMP is critical for learning new information (Scoville & Milner, 1957; see McClelland et al., 1995; Squire, 1992, for recent reviews). Recent neuroimaging data suggest that the controlled encoding and retrieval of information in the HCMP depends on interactions between the PFC and the HCMP (Tulving, Kapur, Craik, Moscovitch, & Houle, 1994). Further, patients with frontal lesions show impaired ability to perform strategic encoding and retrieval on standard memory tests (Gershberg & Shimamura, 1995). All of this is consistent with our view that PFC and HCMP interactions are important for the controlled processing of memory storage and retrieval, which can be used as a nonactive form of working memory.

Recent Developments and Current Challenges

Our theory of working memory represents an attempt to understand this construct in terms of a set of biologically based, computational mechanisms. This has resulted in a novel set of functional principles that explain many of the same phenomena as traditional working memory constructs, but in a manner that contrasts with existing theoretical ideas in important ways. Our existing computational work has instantiated and validated a number of aspects of our theory, including the graded nature of controlled processing (Cohen et al., 1990); the ability of PFC representations to bias subsequent processing (Cohen & Servan-Schreiber, 1992); the role of PFC in active maintenance (Braver et al., 1995); and the role of the HCMP in rapid learning (O'Reilly & McClelland, 1994; O'Reilly, Norman, & McClelland, 1998). However, we have not yet implemented a computational model that captures all of our ideas regarding working memory and controlled processing. Moreover, there are a number of important issues raised by our overall model that have not been properly addressed in our prior work and that form the current focus of our research.

These unresolved issues can be described at two general levels of analysis – one level involves the development of better models of each of the individual brain systems that play a role in our overall model (PMC, PFC, HCMP), and the other level involves characterizing the nature of interactions between these systems. Obviously, the latter effort depends critically on the success of the former, which is where we have been primarily focused. Underlying the entire endeavor are issues of the computational sufficiency of the proposed mechanisms for learning and performing temporally extended controlled-processing tasks.

Models of the PMC, PFC, and HCMP

Because it represents the canonical form of cortical processing, our model of the PMC lies at the foundation of the other models. We have recently made important advances in characterizing the nature of processing and learning in cortex and now have a computational framework (called *Leabra*; O'Reilly, 1996a, 1996b) that contains all of the basic mechanisms and properties required by our model. In particular, the Leabra framework combines recurrence, inhibition, and integrated error-driven and Hebbian learning mechanisms in a simple, principled, robust, and biologically plausible manner. Though these properties have been implemented separately in different models before, Leabra integrates them into a unified, coherent framework. Our model of the HCMP system is relatively well developed conceptually (McClelland et al., 1995), and parts of it have been modeled at a very detailed level (O'Reilly & McClelland, 1994). Recently, we have created a complete HCMP model using the Leabra framework (O'Reilly et al., 1998) and have modeled the recollective contribution to many of the basic recognition memory phenomena (list length, list strength, etc.).

It is the PFC that has received most of our recent theoretical attention, building on previous work that establishes a basic framework for understanding the computational role of PFC in controlled processing. There are two primary threads: (a) the role of a dopamine (DA) mediated active gating mechanism as described previously; and (b) the nature of PFC representations necessary to accomplish controlled processing in complex tasks. We have recently implemented a DA-like gating mechanism in a computational model of PFC and shown that it can successfully account for all of the phenomena accounted for by our previous models, while making new predictions based on the phasic nature of the DA gate (Braver et al., 1997a). This model is being extended to more complex tasks that will better test the gating mechanism by requiring both rapid updating and sustained maintenance in the face of interference. Our current work on the PFC representations is investigating the trade-off between distributed representations and active maintenance as a function of different task demands.

Reward-Based Learning, Goals, and the PFC

One of the most important unresolved challenges to models of working memory (and cognition more generally) is specifying the mechanistic basis of executive control (controlled processing) in a way that does not resort to a homunculus. Though we have provided a general characterization of our view of how controlled processing emerges from constraint satisfaction and the specialized properties of the PFC and HCMP, actually showing that this works in real tasks remains a challenge. We think that the solution to this problem requires a powerful learning mechanism capable of developing something like the "productions" that underlie the performance of complex cognitive tasks (thus avoiding the hidden homunculus of the researcher who builds in the appropriate productions for each task). The following is one set of ideas regarding the nature of this learning mechanism, which emerges from a synthesis of our basic ideas about a DA-based mechanism for active gating and the nature of the representations in the PFC.

These ideas can be motivated by thinking about the essential difference between human cognition and that of even our closest primate relatives. It is obvious that language, abstraction, problem solving, and tool use are important behavioral differences. However, we suggest that these may all be facilitated by the ability to internalize, abstract, and chain together representations of reward (and punishment). In short, the real difference between humans and other primates may be that we can establish elaborate systems of internalized reward that motivate us to learn and engage in these more abstract behaviors, whereas other primates, who can learn impressively complex and abstract tasks, must nevertheless be constantly motivated by external forces (e.g., food, juice) to do so. Thus, instead of being a "pure" cognitive system divorced from all emotional or motivational concerns, the PFC may instead be centrally involved in the dirty business of motivation, emotion, pleasure, and pain (Bechara, Tranel, Damasio, & Damasio, 1996; Davidson & Sutton, 1995).

This observation proves tantalizing in the context of our ideas about the role of dopamine (DA) in the PFC. In particular, if the critical specialization of the PFC is that it has taken control over the DA system to regulate its own active maintenance function, then it is also in a position to take over and internalize the deployment of DA-mediated reinforcement. It is well known that DA plays a critical role in reinforcement-based learning (Schultz et al., 1993; Montague et al., 1996). If the activation of PFC representations corresponds essentially to goals that are maintained in an active and relatively protected state in the absence of DA firing, then the act of satisfying a goal should simultaneously result in reinforcement and gating (i.e., the deactivation of that goal representation and the opportunity to activate a subsequent one). The firing of DA under PFC control would provide both, and the influence of this DA signal on learning should result in more effective elicitation and efficient execution of that goal in the future.

Further, we have argued previously that the PFC has the capacity for the simultaneous representation of many levels of temporal extent and abstraction, which would be needed to account for the goal structures underlying complex human cognition. Because reward is under the descending control of the PFC itself, the need for external reward is reduced, allowing for the development of elaborate means (intervening goals) to accomplish remote and abstract ends. In contrast, other animals depend to a much greater extent on constant external input to drive the DA reward system and thus cannot build these elaborate internal goal structures.

There are many different ways in which the internalized control of DA could be implemented in the PFC, but unfortunately little is known about the relevant biological details. Thus, we are using computational models to determine the relative advantages and disadvantages of different implementations. Another important implementational issue has to do with learning on the basis of actively maintained, isolated representations like those in the PFC, which have a more discrete, binary character and thus do not appear to be amenable to the types of gradient-based learning mechanisms that work so well in the distributed, graded representations characteristic of the PMC. The specializations of the PFC will likely require specialized learning mechanisms, which are the focus of our current research.

Conclusion

In summary, our overall model of the brain system's underlying working memory, including the PMC, PFC, and HCMP, is still under construction, but we have a broad and compelling blueprint for future exploration. This model provides many examples in which computational principles (e.g., basic tradeoffs) are used to understand biological properties, in ways that, though consistent with existing ideas in many cases, can achieve a new level of synthesis and clarity. We hope that this approach will continue to prove useful, despite the inevitable revision of many of the specific ideas proposed herein.

REFERENCES

Anderson, J. R. (1983). *The architecture of cognition*. Cambridge, MA: Harvard University Press.

Baddeley, A. D. (1986). *Working memory*. New York: Oxford University Press.

Baker, S. C., Rogers, R. D., Owen, A. M., Frith, C. D., Dolan, R. J., Frackowiak, R. S. J., & Robbins, T. W. (1996). Neural systems engaged by planning: A PET study of the Tower of London task. *Neuropsychologia, 34*, 515–526.

Barbas, H., & Pandya, D. N. (1987). Architecture and frontal cortical connections of the premotor cortex (area 6) in the rhesus monkey. *Journal of Comparative Neurology, 256*, 211–228.

Barbas, H., & Pandya, D. N. (1989). Architecture of intrinsic connections of the prefrontal cortex in the rhesus monkey. *Journal of Comparative Neurology, 286*, 353–375.

Barch, D. M., Braver, T. S., Nystrom, L. E., Forman, S. D., Noll, D. C., & Cohen, J. D. (1997). Dissociating working memory from effort in human prefrontal cortex. *Neuropsychologia, 35*, 1373–1380.

Barone, P., & Joseph, J. P. (1989). Prefrontal cortex and spatial sequencing in macaque monkey. *Experimental Brain Research, 78*, 447–464.

Bechara, A., Tranel, D., Damasio, H., & Damasio, A. R. (1996). Failure to respond autonomically to anticipated future outcomes following damage to prefrontal cortex. *Cerebral Cortex, 6*, 215–225.

Braver, T. S., & Cohen, J. D. (1995). A model of the development of object and spatial working memory representations in prefrontal cortex. *Cognitive Neuroscience Abstracts, 2*, 95.

Braver, T. S., Cohen, J. D., & McClelland, J. L. (1997a). An integrated computational model of dopamine function in reinforcement learning and working memory. *Society for Neuroscience Abstracts, 23*, 775.

Braver, T. S., Cohen, J. D., Nystrom, L. E., Jonides, J., Smith, E. E., & Noll, D. C. (1997b). A parametric study of frontal cortex involvement in human working memory. *NeuroImage, 5*, 49–62.

Braver, T. S., Cohen, J. D., & Servan-Schreiber, D. (1995). A computational model of prefrontal cortex function. In D. S. Touretzky, G. Tesauro, & T. K. Leen (Eds.), *Advances in neural information processing systems* (pp. 141–148). Cambridge, MA: MIT Press.

Cohen, J. D., Braver, T. S., & O'Reilly, R. C. (1996). A computational approach to prefrontal cortex, cognitive control, and schizophrenia: Recent developments and current challenges. *Philosophical Transactions of the Royal Society of London: Series B (Biological Sciences), 351*, 1515–1527.

Cohen, J. D., Dunbar, K., & McClelland, J. L. (1990). On the control of automatic processes: A parallel distributed processing model of the Stroop effect. *Psychological Review, 97*, 332–361.

Cohen, J. D., & O'Reilly, R. C. (1996). A preliminary theory of the interactions between prefrontal cortex and hippocampus that contribute to planning and prospective memory. In M. Brandimonte, G. O. Einstein, & M. A. McDaniel (Eds.), *Prospective memory: Theory and applications* (pp. 267–295). Mahwah, NJ: Erlbaum.

Cohen, J. D., Perlstein, W. M., Braver, T. S., Nystrom, L. E., Jonides, J., Smith, E. E., & Noll, D. C. (1997). Temporal dynamics of brain activity during a working memory task. *Nature, 386,* 604–608.

Cohen, J. D., & Servan-Schreiber, D. (1992). Context, cortex, and dopamine: A connectionist approach to behavior and biology in schizophrenia. *Psychological Review, 99,* 45–77.

Cohen, J. D., & Smith, E. E. (1997). Response to Owen A. M., Tuning in to the temporal dynamics of brain activation using functional magnetic resonance imaging (fMRI). *Trends in Cognitive Sciences, 1,* 124.

Damasio, A. R. (1985). The frontal lobes. In K. M. Heilman & E. Valenstein (Eds.), *Clinical neuropsychology* (pp. 339–375). New York: Oxford University Press.

Damasio, H., Grabowski, T. J., Tranel, D., Hichwa, R. D., & Damasio, A. R. (1996). A neural basis for lexical retrieval. *Nature, 380,* 499–505.

Daneman, M., & Carpenter, P. A. (1980). Individual differences in working memory and reading. *Journal of Verbal Learning and Verbal Behavior, 19,* 450–466.

Daneman, M., & Merikle, P. (1996). Working memory and language comprehension: A meta-analysis. *Psychonomic Bulletin & Review, 3,* 422–433.

Davidson, R. J., & Sutton, S. K. (1995). Affective neuroscience: The emergence of a discipline. *Current Opinion in Neurobiology, 5,* 217–224.

Dehaene, S., & Changeux, J. P. (1989). A simple model of prefrontal cortex function in delayed-response tasks. *Journal of Cognitive Neuroscience, 1,* 244–261.

Diamond, A. (1990). The development and neural bases of memory functions as indexed by the A-not-B task: Evidence for dependence on dorsolateral prefrontal cortex. In A. Diamond (Ed.), *The development and neural bases of higher cognitive functions* (pp. 267–317). New York: New York Academy of Science Press.

Fodor, J. (1983). *The modularity of mind.* Cambridge, MA: MIT Press.

Funahashi, S., Bruce, C. J., & Goldman-Rakic, P. S. (1993). Dorsolateral prefrontal lesions and oculomotor delayed-response performance: Evidence for mnemonic "scotomas." *Journal of Neuroscience, 13,* 1479–1497.

Fuster, J. M. (1989). *The prefrontal cortex: Anatomy, physiology and neuropsychology of the frontal lobe* (2nd ed.). New York: Raven Press.

Fuster, J. M., & Alexander, G. E. (1971). Neuron activity related to short-term memory. *Science, 173,* 652–654.

Gathercole, S. E. (1994). Neuropsychology and working memory: A review. *Neuropsychology, 8,* 494–505.

Gershberg, F. B., & Shimamura, A. P. (1995). Impaired use of organizational strategies in free recall following frontal lobe damage. *Neuropsychologia, 33,* 1305–1333.

Goldman-Rakic, P. S. (1987). Circuitry of primate prefrontal cortex and regulation of behavior by representational memory. In F. Plum (Ed.), *Handbook of physiology: The nervous system* (Vol. 5, pp. 373–417). Bethesda, MD: American Physiological Society.

Hochreiter, S., & Schmidhuber, J. (1997). Long short term memory. *Neural Computation, 9,* 1735–1780.

Kahneman, D., & Treisman, A. (1984). Changing views of attention and automaticity. In R. Parasuraman & D. R. Davies (Eds.), *Varieties of attention* (pp. 29–61). New York: Academic Press.

Kinsbourne, M. (1997). What qualifies a representation for a role in consciousness? In J. D. Cohen & J. W. Schooler (Eds.), *Scientific approaches to consciousness* (pp. 335–355). Mahwah, NJ: Erlbaum.

McClelland, J. L. (1993). The GRAIN model: A framework for modeling the dynamics of information processing. In D. E. Meyer & S. Kornblum (Eds.), *Attention and performance XIV: Synergies in experimental psychology, artificial intelligence, and cognitive neuroscience* (pp. 655–688). Cambridge, MA: MIT Press.

McClelland, J. L., McNaughton, B. L., & O'Reilly, R. C. (1995). Why there are complementary learning systems in the hippocampus and neocortex: Insights from the successes and failures of connectionist models of learning and memory. *Psychological Review, 102,* 419–457.

Miller, E. K., & Desimone, R. (1994). Parallel neuronal mechanisms for short-term memory. *Science, 263,* 520–522.

Miller, E. K., Erickson, C. A., & Desimone, R. (1996). Neural mechanisms of visual working memory in prefrontal cortex of the macaque. *Journal of Neuroscience, 16,* 5154–5167.

Montague, P. R., Dayan, P., & Sejnowski, T. J. (1996). A framework for mesencephalic dopamine systems based on predictive Hebbian learning. *Journal of Neuroscience, 16,* 1936–1947.

Moscovitch, M., & Winocur, G. (1992). The neuropsychology of memory and aging. In T. A. Salthouse & F. I. M. Craik (Eds.), *The handbook of aging and cognition* (pp. 315–372). Hillsdale, NJ: Erlbaum.

Newell, A. (1990). *Unified theories of cognition.* Cambridge, MA: Harvard University Press.

O'Reilly, R. C. (1996a). Biologically plausible error-driven learning using local activation differences: The generalized recirculation algorithm. *Neural Computation, 8,* 895–938.

O'Reilly, R. C. (1996b). *The Leabra model of neural interactions and learning in the neocortex.* Unpublished doctoral dissertation, Carnegie Mellon University, Pittsburgh, PA.

O'Reilly, R. C., & McClelland, J. L. (1994). Hippocampal conjunctive encoding, storage, and recall: Avoiding a tradeoff. *Hippocampus, 4,* 661–682.

O'Reilly, R. C., Norman, K. A., & McClelland, J. L. (1998). A hippocampal model of recognition memory. In M. I. Jordan (Ed.), *Advances in neural information processing systems 10.* Cambridge, MA: MIT Press.

Petrides, M. E. (1996). Specialized systems for the processing of mnemonic information within the primate frontal cortex. *Philosophical Transactions of the Royal Society of London, Series B, 351,* 1455–1462.

Posner, M. I., & Snyder, C. R. R. (1975). Attention and cognitive control. In R. L. Solso (Ed.), *Information processing and cognition* (pp. 55–85). Hillsdale, NJ: Erlbaum.

Rao, S. C., Rainer, G., & Miller, E. K. (1997). Integration of what and where in the primate prefrontal cortex. *Science, 276,* 821–824.

Rizzolatti, G., Luppino, G., & Matelli, M. (1996). The classic supplementary motor area is formed by two independent areas. *Advances in Neurology, 70,* 45–56.

Rumelhart, D. E., & McClelland, J. L. (1986). On learning the past tenses of English verbs. In J. L. McClelland, D. E. Rumelhart, & PDP Research Group (Eds.), *Parallel distributed processing. Vol. 2: Psychological and biological models* (pp. 216–271). Cambridge, MA: MIT Press.

Schultz, W., Apicella, P., & Ljungberg, T. (1993). Responses of monkey dopamine neurons to reward and conditioned stimuli during successive steps of learning a delayed response task. *Journal of Neuroscience, 13*, 900–913.

Scoville, W. B., & Milner, B. (1957). Loss of recent memory after bilateral hippocampal lesions. *Journal of Neurology, Neurosurgery, and Psychiatry, 20*, 11–21.

Seidenberg, M. (1993). Connectionist models and cognitive theory. *Psychological Science, 4*, 228–235.

Servan-Schreiber, D., Cohen, J. D., & Steingard, S. (1997). Schizophrenic performance in a variant of the CPT-AX: A test of theoretical predictions concerning the processing of context. *Archives of General Psychiatry, 53*, 1105–1113.

Shah, P., & Miyake, A. (1996). The separability of working memory resources for spatial thinking and language processing: An individual differences approach. *Journal of Experimental Psychology: General, 125*, 4–27.

Shallice, T. (1982). Specific impairments of planning. *Philosophical Transactions of the Royal Society of London, 298*, 199–209.

Shiffrin, R. M., & Schneider, W. (1977). Controlled and automatic human information processing: II. Perceptual learning, automatic attending, and a general theory. *Psychological Review, 84*, 127–190.

Smith, E. E., Jonides, J., & Koeppe, R. A. (1996). Dissociating verbal and spatial working memory using PET. *Cerebral Cortex, 6*, 11–20.

Squire, L. R. (1992). Memory and the hippocampus: A synthesis from findings with rats, monkeys, and humans. *Psychological Review, 99*, 195–231.

Squire, L. R., Shimamura, A. P., & Amaral, D. G. (1989). Memory and the hippocampus. In J. H. Byrne & W. O. Berry (Eds.), *Neural models of plasticity: Experimental and theoretical approaches.* San Diego: Academic Press.

Tulving, E., Kapur, S., Craik, F. I. M., Moscovitch, M., & Houle, S. (1994). Hemispheric encoding/retrieval asymmetry in episodic memory: Positron emission tomography findings. *Proceedings of the National Academy of Sciences, USA, 91*, 2016–2020.

Ungerleider, L. G., & Mishkin, M. (1982). Two cortical visual systems. In D. J. Ingle, M. A. Goodale, & R. J. W. Mansfield (Eds.), *The analysis of visual behavior.* Cambridge, MA: MIT Press.

Usher, M., & Cohen, J. D. (1997). Interference-based capacity limitations in active memory. *Abstracts of the Psychonomics Society, 2*, 11.

Wilson, F. A. W., O'Scalaidhe, S. P., & Goldman-Rakic, P. S. (1993). Dissociation of object and spatial processing domains in primate prefrontal cortex. *Science, 260*, 1955–1957.

Zipser, D., Kehoe, B., Littlewort, G., & Fuster, J. (1993). A spiking network model of short-term active memory. *Journal of Neuroscience, 13*, 3406–3420.

12 Models of Working Memory

Eight Questions and Some General Issues

WALTER KINTSCH, ALICE F. HEALY,
MARY HEGARTY, BRUCE F. PENNINGTON, AND
TIMOTHY A. SALTHOUSE

What have we learned about working memory from the 10 models described in this volume (Chapters 2 to 11)? What answers have these models provided for each of the eight questions raised by the editors (Shah & Miyake, Chapter 1), and how do these answers relate to one another? Do seemingly different answers given to the same question really reflect some fundamental differences between the models, or should they be regarded as a difference in emphasis? More generally, how well have these models, as a whole, addressed each of the eight designated questions? Although the answers to these questions can ultimately be obtained by a critical reading of the chapters themselves and careful reflections on these theoretical issues, we hope to help readers with this task by providing systematic, issue-by-issue comparisons among the models of working memory covered in this volume.[1] To this end, we will first analyze and comment on the answers provided by the contributors for each of the designated questions. We will then raise and discuss some general issues that transcend the specific questions.

We would like to thank Alan Baddeley, Marsha Lovett, Peter Polson, Sashank Varma, and Alexander Witzki for comments and suggestions.

[1] This chapter is based on the discussions at the "Models of Working Memory" symposium (July, 1997). Initially, the discussions were led by Healy (for Questions 1 and 6), Hegarty (for Questions 3 and 5), Pennington (for Questions 2 and 8), and Salthouse (for Questions 4 and 7). Kintsch was responsible for general discussion at the symposium and served as the coordinator of this chapter. The editors of this volume (Miyake and Shah) also actively participated in the rewriting and editing process to make the chapter coherent as a whole.

Analyses of the Answers Provided to the Eight Designated Theoretical Questions

Question 1: Basic Mechanisms and Representations in Working Memory

The first question asked the contributors to outline their view of three mechanisms that provide a basis for working memory processes – the encoding, maintenance, and retrieval mechanisms. The question also asked the contributors to specify their assumptions about the nature of working memory representations.

ENCODING. The issue of encoding has received relatively little attention in the present set of chapters, presumably because it would have more to do with perception, rather than working memory per se. This is particularly true of the computational models of working memory, which tend to focus on "central" cognitive processes and skip over perceptual (as well as motor) processes. A notable exception for this trend is the EPIC model (Kieras, Meyer, Mueller, & Seymour, Chapter 6), which has a relatively well-developed interface between "perception" and "cognition," but, here too, encoding is not a major issue. Perhaps the most elaborate account of the encoding mechanism comes from Cowan (Chapter 3). According to Cowan, encoding of information in working memory consists of activating the composite of appropriate features in long-term memory (LTM), a view that seems to be endorsed by several contributors (e.g., Engle, Kane, & Tuholski, Chapter 4; O'Reilly, Braver, & Cohen, Chapter 11). Not denying this standard view (which is more closely related to what they call short-term working memory or ST-WM), Ericsson and Delaney's (Chapter 8) long-term working memory (LT-WM) framework offers a different account of encoding, suggesting that experts' information retrieval is faster and more successful because they can efficiently construct a robust retrieval structure during the initial processing of the stimuli.

MAINTENANCE. The maintenance question is fundamental to a model of working memory, but the only mechanism discussed in some detail is that of verbal rehearsal (e.g., Baddeley & Logie, Chapter 2; Cowan, Chapter 3; Kieras et al., Chapter 6; Barnard, Chapter 9). Here, there seems to be some general consensus about how the verbal rehearsal is performed, but the details have yet to be specified. Kieras et al. offer a promising new mechanistic account of the rehearsal process in this respect. The models that do not explicitly include rehearsal mechanisms tend to have some account of how working memory elements or representations are kept active, but this activation-maintenance mechanism is, in most cases, addressed only indirectly. Activation maintenance has a lot to do with the nature of working memory limitations, the focus of Question 4.

RETRIEVAL. In contrast to encoding, the retrieval question touches on the essence of working memory because of the common assumption that information "in" working memory is directly and effortlessly retrievable. In fact, information in LTM that is active and readily available defines the concept of working memory in some models in this volume (e.g., Cowan, Chapter 3; Engle et al., Chapter 4), although other models go further by proposing that the speed or accuracy of retrieval is a function of the activation level of the target item (e.g., Lovett, Reder, & Lebiere, Chapter 5). Again, Ericsson and Delaney's (Chapter 8) notion of LT-WM is unique in this regard. Although it is commonly assumed that retrieval from ST-WM is not cue dependent, retrieval of information from LT-WM is crucially dependent on the availability of appropriate retrieval cues.

REPRESENTATIONS. This issue is closely linked to the question of the unitary versus non-unitary nature of working memory (Question 3), a source of controversy in the literature. Although the discussion is sometimes vague and indirect, most chapters address the representation question in some detail.

Baddeley's (1986) classic formulation in terms of different domain-specific "slave" systems provides a conceptual basis for the representational issue. As discussed in Chapter 2, Baddeley and Logie clearly postulate different codes or formats for information held in the phonological loop and in the visuospatial sketchpad. They also suggest the existence of different codes within the sketchpad, separating the visual component (the visual cache) from the spatial component (the inner scribe).

Several models build on the Baddeley–Logie conceptualization by postulating other modality-specific codes or representations. Barnard (Chapter 9) and Schneider (Chapter 10), for example, explicitly postulate multiple subsystems or submodules that operate on different codes, but the number of the subsystems postulated is far greater than in the Baddeley–Logie model. Barnard's ICS architecture, for example, includes nine separable subsystems (see Figure 9.1 in Chapter 9), whereas Schneider's hierarchically organized CAP2 system postulates at least eight modules at the macrostructure level (e.g., visual, auditory, speech, lexical, semantic, motor, mood, context; Schneider & Detweiler, 1987) and "hundreds of thousands" of cortical submodules at the microstructure level. Despite the number of subsystems postulated in these models, Barnard and Schneider both argue that these different subsystems share the same internal structure and are governed by the same processing principles.

Cowan's (Chapter 3) and Kieras et al.'s (Chapter 6) models are also similar to Barnard's and Schneider's models in that they assume different domain-specific codes (or "partitions" in the case of EPIC) in working memory (e.g., tactile, motor, and body state). Unlike Barnard and Schneider (as well as Baddeley and Logie), however, they do not explicitly postulate physically separable subsystems. Kieras et al., for example, explicitly point out that their modality-specific partitioning of working memory is not "hardwired" in EPIC. Cowan essentially makes the same argument as Kieras et al., but also points out that various types of codes all have similar properties (e.g., decay rate) and, hence, emphasizes the similarities, rather than the differences, among different codes. Although the overall appearance is rather different, O'Reilly et al.'s (Chapter 11) model is similar to these models. Despite their explicit rejection of the notion of separate storage buffers, O'Reilly et al. postulate the existence of domain-specific representations on the basis of known functional specialization in the brain. Domain-specific representations are supported by different regions of the posterior perceptual and motor cortex, which are specialized for various perceptuomotor and cognitive processes.

Although these models explicitly incorporate the notion of multiple codes or representations, other models take a more neutral attitude toward the representational issue (Engle et al., Chapter 4; Lovett et al., Chapter 5; Young & Lewis, Chapter 7; Ericsson & Delaney, Chapter 8). Ericsson and Delaney are not particularly concerned with specifying the nature of codes in ST-WM, because they believe that most forms of skilled and expert performance in everyday life do not critically depend on ST-WM per se. Engle et al. (Chapter 4) and Lovett et al. (Chapter 5) are both concerned with ST-WM, but their emphasis is on the apparent unitary characteristic of working memory. They both acknowledge that some domain specificity exists, but no particular details are provided in terms of specific codes or formats. For example, Lovett et al. describe an ACT-R model of serial memory (Anderson & Matessa, 1997) that would seem to apply equivalently to serial lists defined in terms of temporal or spatial orders, despite earlier experimental evidence (e.g., Healy, 1975; Healy, Cunningham, Gesi, Till, & Bourne, 1991) that temporal and spatial orders rely on different codes or representations. Similarly, Young and Lewis note that current versions of Soar employ a low-level, theoretically neutral representation of information in Soar's dynamic memory, consisting of attribute–value pairs. Although Soar postulates a single dynamic memory at this point, nothing in the architecture prevents the inclusion of different types of representations or modality-specific buffers. Indeed, their emphasis on "similarity-based interference" as a basis of capacity limitations seems to be consistent with the need for different codes or representations.

As this review makes clear, there seem to be no major disagreements among the models in this volume regarding the representational issue. Although some models are neutral with respect to this issue, none of them positively denies the existence of different codes or representations. There is much less direct discussion of encoding, maintenance, and retrieval mechanisms, but one could say that there are no major disagreements there, either. This lack of major disagreements is rather surprising, but we suspect that it reflects, at least in part, the lack of precise specification of these issues in the present set of models. There was a lot of handwaving in the descriptions of these issues in the chapters, and deciphering and inferring exactly what their positions are was not always straightforward. We would argue that the basic mechanisms and representations issue has not yet been handled satisfactorily. The most empirically verified model still seems to be that of Baddeley and

Logie (Chapter 2). It is a good starting point, but, as is clear from our review, it cannot be the whole story. Just what the rest of the story is, however, is only implied in the chapters discussed here, not fully developed.

Question 2: The Control and Regulation of Working Memory

The second question asked whether a central control structure, such as the central executive, is necessary to explain control functions of working memory and, if not, how control and regulation arise without such a central structure. This topic immediately raises the problem of the homunculus in a paradoxical way. We use the construct of working memory to refer to the dynamic control and coordination of processing and storage that take place during the performance of complex cognitive tasks, but speaking of the control and regulation of working memory implies yet a higher rung in the hierarchy. Who or what could be controlling or regulating working memory? How well did the models in this volume address this homunculus problem? Although the answers provided in the chapters clearly represent a significant advance, a critical reading makes it clear that it is not easy to get the homunculus out of working memory.

Several models in this volume, for example, explicitly postulate a central control mechanism (e.g., Baddeley & Logie, Chapter 2; Cowan, Chapter 3; Engle et al., Chapter 4). These chapters attempt to go beyond the notion of a structurally separate, unitary controller by specifying the subfunctions of this central control mechanism (Baddeley & Logie) or identifying some brain regions that may play a crucial role for executive control (Engle et al.). Such specification, however, does not necessarily resolve the homunculus problem, unless it leads to a detailed account of how these subfunctions work together as a whole to control and regulate our behavior and how these crucial brain regions perform executive functions.

Production-system models do not postulate such obviously homunculus-like constructs (e.g., Lovett et al., Chapter 5; Kieras et al., Chapter 6; Young & Lewis, Chapter 7), hence seemingly resolving the problem. One could argue, however, that a homunculus is hiding behind more subtle mechanisms intrinsic to production-system architectures themselves. For example, the cognitive processing in ACT-R (Lovett et al.) is goal driven, but how do these goals get formed in the first place? As for EPIC (Kieras et al.), how do the productions that perform "executive" processes get created? Where do sequential "tags" come from? One crucial feature of Soar (Young & Lewis) is impasse-driven learning, but who or what detects the impasse and creates a new problem space? Although it is not a production-system model, a similar argument can be made for Ericsson and Delaney's (Chapter 8) model. Their notion of LT-WM emphasizes the importance of retrieval structures in experts' working memory performance, but who or what comes up with and encodes retrieval structures appropriate for the incoming stimuli?

Perhaps closest to avoiding the problem of the homunculus are those models that produce autocontrol or self-regulation of some sort, but, here too, one could locate a homunculus-like element if one reads their descriptions carefully. For example, Barnard (Chapter 9) argues that self-regulation arises through reciprocal exchanges among the subsystems of his ICS architecture, but, in his account of attention, he introduces the notion of "focus of attention," without a clear explanation of how the "focus of attention" can emerge from interacting subsystems and how it can be shifted. Schneider's CAP2 model (Chapter 10) has both regional and central control. The priority signals passed from individual modules to the inner loop serve as an important component of this control process. It is still somewhat unclear, however, how modules determine their *current* priority. They could have learned about usual priorities through modifying internal connections, but what if they are processing something that is of high priority to a current goal but that lacks a high learned priority? Finally, O'Reilly et al. (Chapter 11) offer a fairly detailed account of how autocontrol might naturally arise through dynamic interactions among different brain regions, but they have yet to implement their intriguing idea in an explicit, full-scale computational model and demonstrate that their account indeed completely resolves the homunculus problem. An actual, full-scale implementation of their model might reveal some homunculus-like construct, just as the other computational models in this volume have.

Given this difficulty of eliminating homunculus-like constructs, two questions arise. The first is, Why is there such a strong need to include some sort of explicit or implicit control mechanisms? Are these control mechanisms required by real computational constraints, or by the folk psychological sense of agency? We bring up folk psychology not to be disparaging, but to highlight how pervasive and useful the attribution of agency is in human cognition, as Dennett (1987) argues in his book *The Intentional Stance*. According to him, human beings and other animals are only virtual agents. Our intentions all derive from the simple and nonintentional fact that organic molecules that can copy themselves are more likely to persist than those that cannot. We are elaborate machines whose goal is to facilitate this copying. Both evolution and development have shaped our brains so that we usually provide a convincing simulation, both to ourselves and to others, of an agent. These points of Dennett's are important because, by saying that our agency is "virtual," we may be able to invert our usual bias, which is to find behavior typical of an agent commonplace and deviations from agency surprising or not believable. We argue that we should focus more theoretical attention on deviations from agency (such as action slips, multiple personality disorder, autism, and hallucinations and delusions) because they could shed light on how the virtual agent is simulated and on how the control and regulation of working memory is ordinarily achieved.

The second, harder question is how we get control and regulation of working memory (and our behavior) without an explicit executive or control structure or mechanism. What makes this question difficult is that it is essentially the body–mind problem: How can the mind arise from a physical mechanism? Unless we resort to dualism, the control and regulation of working memory must be an emergent property of a complex physical system. As discussed above, some of the computational models in this volume are relatively successful in this regard. Indeed, shifting the level of discourse from the verbal to the modeling domain represents real progress, especially if we can be sure that our models solve the control problem, and not just avoid it. A computational model that starts out with a given goal or specific rules for executive control mechanisms merely steps around the homunculus problem but does not solve it. We have, however, seen here a number of attempts that go beyond that, where goal setting and control are as much part of the system as encoding and retrieval. It is the success of those attempts, represented in this volume, that promise an eventual solution to this age-old and recalcitrant problem.

Question 3: The Unitary Versus Non-Unitary Nature of Working Memory

The third question concerns the unitary versus non-unitary nature of working memory. As discussed in the section on Question 1 (see the "Representations" subsection), all of the chapters in this volume admit (explicitly or implicitly) the possibility of domain-specific codes or representations in working memory, but there are some striking differences in focus among the 10 models. In what way are these models different? Are these differences fundamentally incompatible with one another?

In our analysis, there are three major dimensions along which the 10 models differ from one another. First, there is some disagreement on the *number* of different domain-specific codes or representational systems that are explicitly incorporated in the models. For example, without denying domain-specific representations or codes, Engle et al. (Chapter 4) and Lovett et al. (Chapter 5) emphasize the domain-general aspects of working memory. Baddeley and Logie (Chapter 2) explicitly incorporate domain-specific systems for only phonological and visual-spatial information, whereas others explicitly incorporate a broader range of modality-specific codes (e.g., Kieras et al., Chapter 6; Barnard, Chapter 9; Schneider, Chapter 10). Second, the models differ in their account of the *source(s)* of domain-specificity effects. Some models, for example, account for domain specificity primarily in terms of peripheral domain-specific subsystems (e.g., Baddeley & Logie, Chapter 2; Barnard, Chapter 9), whereas other models do so primarily in terms of domain-specific knowledge or skills (e.g., Young & Lewis, Chapter 7; Ericsson & Delaney, Chapter 8). Finally, the models (particularly those that postulate multiple subcomponents or subsystems) also differ in the *types of distinctions* on which their fractionations are based. Some of the major distinctions made by the theories in this volume include the information code (e.g., spatial, phonological, or propositional codes), the modality in which that information is processed (e.g., visual, auditory, haptic), the brain systems that are involved in processing the information (e.g., prefrontal cortex, hippocampus), the type of knowledge (e.g., declarative, procedural), and the domain of processing (e.g., chess, algebra, language).

On further examination, however, many of these apparent inconsistencies can be seen as reflecting differences in emphasis and definition, rather than fundamental disagreements among the contributors. This difference in focus is apparent in considering the scope of the models of working memory. For example, the theorists who focus primarily on linguistic and/or numerical tasks – tasks that emphasize verbal–numerical aspects of working memory (but not visuospatial) – tend to emphasize domain-general aspects of working memory in their theoretical accounts (Engle et al., Chapter 4; Lovett et al., Chapter 5). In contrast, other theorists who examine how working memory is involved in skilled performance of complex everyday tasks tend to emphasize the role of knowledge and skills to account for domain-specificity effects (e.g., Young & Lewis, Chapter 7; Ericsson & Delaney, Chapter 8). Furthermore, theorists such as Kieras et al. (Chapter 6) and Barnard (Chapter 9) recognize the importance of perceptuomotor and emotional processes in complex cognition and attempt to include these factors in their models. Such differences in research focus might explain the seemingly disparate answers to the unitary versus non-unitary issue among the models. In addition, apparent differences in the types of subcomponents proposed by different models may be somewhat deceptive in the sense that they could essentially refer to similar concepts. For example, because verbal information is often coded phonologically, the phonological component (defined by a representational code) in one model could be the same as the verbal component (defined by a domain) in another model. It is important for researchers to study the relations between some of these distinctions and to be precise in their definition of just what distinguishes a working memory component.

Given this state of affairs, there is clearly a need to define a set of criteria that should be met before we postulate the existence of a subcomponent in working memory. The contributors to this volume have used a number of empirical criteria including dual-task studies (e.g., Baddeley & Logie, Chapter 2), correlational studies (e.g., Engle et al., Chapter 4), studies of highly skilled individuals (e.g., Ericsson & Delaney, Chapter 8), and cognitive neuroscience studies using either neuroimaging techniques (e.g., Smith & Jonides, 1997) or behavioral analyses of cognitive deficits exhibited by brain-damaged patients (e.g., Baddeley & Logie, Chapter 2). Although each of these methodologies has yielded important insights into the nature of the working memory system, they are also limited in some respects: These methodologies cannot differentiate between models that define subsystems in terms of storage buffers, specialized processes, or pools of resources. Consider, for example, a case in which a researcher found a task that (a) was significantly impaired by spatial tapping (a typical spatial interference task) but not by articulatory suppression (a typical phonological interference task); (b) was highly correlated with spatial-ability measures, but not with verbal-ability measures; and (c) was impaired by lesions of the parietal cortex, but not by lesions of the language-related areas (e.g., Broca's and Wernicke's areas). The researcher would probably be justified in claiming that this task employs a spatial subcomponent of working memory. However, the empirical evidence would not enable him or her to make any claims about whether this spatial subcomponent was a storage buffer, a set of procedures specialized for processing spatial information, or a pool of "neural resources" that could be shared among spatial information processing and storage. Therefore, it might not be possible to characterize the precise nature of working memory components on the basis of empirical evidence alone.

In summary, the existing models of working memory differ in scope, with more unitary theorists considering a relatively narrower scope of working memory phenomena. In general, however, there is limited support for a completely unitary view of working memory, and most theorists postulate multiple subsystems within working memory (or some other mechanisms that are domain specific in nature), although they disagree about the characterizations of the subsystems. To advance our understanding of working memory, we need to agree on the scope of the construct of working memory and the criteria for establishing the existence or nonexistence of additional subcomponents. In the interests of parsimony, it is desirable that additional subcomponents of working memory are postulated only when there is evidence for dissociations between subsystems on the basis of several different methodologies. Finally, it is also important that we examine the relations among the distinctions made in existing working memory theories (e.g., subsystems defined in terms of domains, codes, or modalities) so that we have a clearer idea of how different models of working memory relate to one another.

Question 4: The Nature of Working Memory Limitations

One of the most salient aspects of human cognition is its limitations, and in recent years working memory and attention have been postulated to be responsible for at least some of these limitations. It is therefore critical to try to understand the nature of the constraints responsible for those limits, an issue raised by the fourth designated question.

The chapters in this volume each provide interesting answers to this question. As Miyake and Shah argue in Chapter 13, all the contributors seem to admit that there is no single, all-encompassing capacity-limiting factor for working memory (despite the fact that a few models seem to emphasize a single factor of their preference over others). Despite this global-level agree-

Table 12.1. *Sources of Working Memory Limitations Discussed in Different Chapters of This Volume and Other Recent Publications*

Information decay (e.g., Baddeley & Logie, Chapter 2; Cowan, Chapter 3; Kieras et al., Chapter 6)

Efficiency of controlled attention or executive mechanisms (Baddeley & Logie, Chapter 2; Engle et al., Chapter 4)

Limits in the availability of activation (Lovett et al., Chapter 5; Just & Carpenter, 1992)

Limits in processing speed or efficiency (Kieras et al., Chapter 6; Barnard, Chapter 9; Salthouse, 1996)

Lack of skill or knowledge for efficient encoding and retrieval (Young & Lewis, Chapter 7; Ericsson & Delaney, Chapter 8)

(Similarity-based) interference (Baddeley & Logie, Chapter 2; Young & Lewis, Chapter 7; O'Reilly et al., Chapter 11)

Lack of inhibitory control (Engle et al., Chapter 4; O'Reilly et al., Chapter 11; Zacks & Hasher, 1994)

Limitations in communications and interactions among different subsystems or subcomponents (Barnard, Chapter 9; Schneider, Chapter 10)

---

ment, however, there is no clear consensus, at a more microlevel of analysis, as to the specific mechanisms that constrain the capacity of working memory. The specific capacity-limiting factors discussed in this volume are indeed wide ranging. Table 12.1 provides a list of most (if not all) sources of working memory limitations mentioned in this volume and some other recent publications. This list may give readers a rather chaotic picture of our understanding of the nature of working memory limitations, but the positions of the different chapters can be classified and summarized according to several different dimensions.

SCOPE. First, the limitations could be universal or could vary across individuals. An example of the former is that no one can remember the license plates of all the cars in the parking lot of a shopping mall. An example of the latter is that some people may have difficulty remembering one license plate, whereas other people may be able to remember as many as 10. In general, limitations that are universal include computational and architectural constraints that are unavoidable and therefore presumably ·applicable to everyone, with some clear examples being the perceptual and motor limitations assumed by Kieras et al. (Chapter 6) and the cross-talk limitations assumed by Barnard (Chapter 9). Those limitations that are sources of individual differences are based on characteristics of the individual and may be more closely related to knowledge and skill (Ericsson & Delaney, Chapter 8), although the specific computational and architectural limitations could also vary across people (Engle et al., Chapter 4; Lovett et al., Chapter 5).

INHERENT VERSUS EMERGENT LIMITATIONS. The distinction that seems the most fundamental in classifying the models presented in this volume is whether working memory limitations reflect the fundamental limitations of the underlying cognitive system per se or whether they are an emergent property of the system, something that naturally arises as a consequence of dynamic interactions that take place within the cognitive system.[2] Some models emphasize the former perspective, each emphasizing a specific hard-wired constraint of some sort in their theoretical account (e.g., Engle et al., Chapter 4; Lovett et al., Chapter 5). In contrast, some models consider working memory limitations from the latter, emergent-property perspective (e.g., Young & Lewis, Chapter 7; Barnard, Chapter 9; Schneider, Chapter 10; O'Reilly et al., Chapter 11). Other models appear to be somewhere in between these two extremes in the sense that they tend to postulate multiple hard-wired constraints (e.g., decay rate, processing speed) that together determine the capacity of working memory (e.g., Baddeley & Logie, Chapter 2; Cowan, Chapter 3; Kieras et al., Chapter 6).

MODIFIABILITY. Limitations can also vary with respect to their permanence or invariance over time. One possibility is that the limitations reflect relatively invariant, possibly "innate" characteristics of the individual, somewhat analogous to an individual's height, and that they are nearly always operative. In our reading of the chapters, none of the constructs postulated corresponds to this characterization in a strict sense, though one could argue that Ericsson and Delaney's (Chapter 8) characterization of ST-WM (not LT-WM) may come closest. An alternative possibility is that either the nature or the magnitude of the limitations might vary with experience or skill and possibly with development in either the child or adult portion of the life span. Clearly, skill-based or knowledge-based models of working memory fall into this category (e.g., Young & Lewis, Chapter 7; Ericsson & Delaney, Chapter 8; Schneider, Chapter 10; O'Reilly et al., Chapter 11). Constructs postulated in some models (e.g., Engle et al.'s "controlled attention ability," Chapter 4; Lovett et al.'s W parameter, Chapter 5) seem to be somewhere in between these extremes. Although these authors are likely to argue that these constructs strongly reflect some inherent characteristics of the individual and are nearly always operative, they are also likely to argue that they can vary as a function of some biological changes such as those associated with aging.

FUNCTIONALITY. Another dimension that could distinguish different models concerns the functionality of working memory limitations. That is, a limitation of working memory could be viewed as a mistake or as a type of design

---

[2] Although certainly not identical conceptually, this dimension could also be considered in terms of the ease of specifying the source or nature of the constraints (or identifiability). Some limitations could be transparent or explicit (such as the total amount of source activation), whereas other limitations could be opaque or implicit, perhaps because of a large number of processes interacting in a complex manner with no single critical parameter.

flaw because of an assumption that an optimum system would have no limitations. In contrast, one could also view the limitation as having some functional significance. The models that focus on individual differences and demonstrate the advantage of larger-capacity participants over smaller-capacity participants in various cognitive functions could (but may not necessarily) be interpreted as representing the former perspective (e.g., Engle et al., Chapter 4; Lovett et al., Chapter 5), whereas the O'Reilly et al. model (Chapter 11) explicitly articulates the latter perspective. In general, this interesting and potentially useful dimension is not clearly represented in this volume (see Miyake & Shah, Chapter 13, for further discussion of the functionality of working memory limitations).

These considerations suggest that, even though the specific capacity-limiting factors postulated in different models seem to be radically different from one another, the models tend to fall into two general clusters: the cluster that includes Engle et al. (Chapter 4) and Lovett et al. (Chapter 5) on the one hand, and the cluster that includes Young and Lewis (Chapter 7), Barnard (Chapter 9), Schneider (Chapter 10), and O'Reilly et al. (Chapter 11) on the other hand. Whether these two clusters of working memory models are fundamentally incompatible or, rather, simply reflect different theoretical emphases (perhaps owing to the limited range of working memory phenomena explored by each model) is an open question at this moment.

At the level of specific capacity-limiting factors, it is reasonable to conclude that no proposal can be considered more plausible or convincing than others at this time. One problem is that each model tends to adopt a small number of capacity-limiting factors, without demonstrating that other possible capacity-limiting factors do not work. A more systematic exploration of the possible space of working memory limitations may be a useful research strategy with this issue.

Question 5: The Role of Working Memory in Complex Cognitive Activities

As is clear from the reading of the chapters, many contributors have defined working memory as temporary maintenance of task-relevant information *in the service of complex cognition*. Although they agree that we should understand the functions of working memory in the context of complex cognition, they appear to agree less on what they mean by complex cognition. Table 12.2 lists examples of "complex" cognitive tasks discussed in the 10 theory chapters. As the list suggests, many of the tasks that have been characterized as "complex" by the authors in this volume might be considered relatively simple, such as the word span task. Although it can be argued that word span is complex in the sense that multiple different coding strategies can be employed in carrying out this task (e.g., Kieras et al., Chapter 6), it is clearly less complex than such tasks as discourse comprehension, interacting with multimedia computer interfaces, and flying an airplane. Although it might be

---

Table 12.2. *Examples of "Complex" Cognitive Tasks Discussed in Chapters 2 to 11*

Immediate serial recall of digits and words (Baddeley & Logie, Chapter 2; Cowan, Chapter 3; Kieras et al., Chapter 6; Ericsson & Delaney, Chapter 8)

Continuous performance test (AX-CPT and *N*-back tasks) (O'Reilly et al., Chapter 11)

Sentence comprehension (Young & Lewis, Chapter 7)

Mental arithmetic (Baddeley & Logie, Chapter 2)

Algebra problem solving (Lovett et al., Chapter 5)

Working memory span tasks (reading span, operation span, etc.) (Baddeley & Logie, Chapter 2; Engle et al., Chapter 4; Lovett, et al., Chapter 5)

Syllogistic reasoning (Baddeley & Logie, Chapter 2; Young & Lewis, Chapter 7)

Random number generation (Baddeley & Logie, Chapter 2; Barnard, Chapter 9)

Raven's Progressive Matrices Test (Engle et al., Chapter 4)

Chess playing (Ericsson & Delaney, Chapter 8)

Understanding and modifying a large computer program (Young & Lewis, Chapter 5)

---

advantageous at early stages of theory development to study tasks at the less complex end of the continuum, we cannot expect the models of working memory developed in the context of tasks such as digit or word span to necessarily scale up to models of tasks such as language comprehension and decision making. There is a danger of underestimating the capacity and flexibility of the working memory system if we do not take account of the memory demands of the complete range of complex cognition, especially if the tasks fit only one or two of the criterion characteristics of complex cognition proposed in this volume. The criteria for "complex" cognition mentioned in at least one chapter are as follows.

TASKS THAT REQUIRE CONTROLLED PROCESSING. Several chapters (e.g., Engle et al., Chapter 4; Schneider, Chapter 10; O'Reilly et al., Chapter 11) characterized complex cognition as involving *controlled* processing. A related characteristic is task novelty, because novel tasks require controlled rather than automatic processing. An example is the *N*-back task, discussed by O'Reilly et al. (Chapter 11), in which participants must respond whenever an item in a continuous stream is the same as the item exactly *N*-items (any small number) preceding it. Although this task clearly involves cognitive control, the response choices that must be made are quite simple and the amount of to-be-maintained information relatively small.

TASKS REQUIRING THE COORDINATION OF MULTIPLE STEPS OF PROCESSING. Another characteristic of many complex cognitive tasks, such as mental arithmetic and algebra problem solving (Baddeley & Logie, Chapter 2; Lovett et al., Chapter 5), is the coordination of multiple steps of processing. For example, in the classic Tower of Hanoi task, the solver must complete a sequence of moves or steps to solve the problem. At each stage, there are several legal moves that can be made, and successful solution of the problem requires planning and executing a sequence of moves according to a strategy, such as the goal-recursion strategy. Although some of the tasks listed in Table 12.2 fit this characteristic, they tend to be those that require a relatively small number of steps.

TASKS THAT REQUIRE MULTIPLE COMPONENTS OF THE WORKING MEMORY SYSTEM. Many complex cognitive tasks require the coordination of multiple components or functions of the system. For example, some chapters in this volume argued that performance on complex span tasks (e.g., the reading or operation span test) involves the coordination of the slave systems and the central executive in Baddeley and Logie's terms (Chapter 2) and short-term memory (STM) and controlled attention in Engle et al.'s terms (Chapter 4). Dual-task performance (Baddeley & Logie) is another "complex" task situation that requires the coordination of multiple components. Many real-world tasks, such as comprehension of text accompanied by diagrams and use of multimodal computer interfaces, also involve the coordination of different working memory subcomponents and, in that sense, studying dual-task performance in the laboratory might be beneficial for our understanding of the role of working memory in real-world tasks.

A distinction can be made, however, between dual-task situations and these real-world tasks. In dual-task studies, the different subcomponents are typically competing with each other, whereas in many real-world tasks, different components are collaborating. For example, in understanding a text-and-diagram description of a machine, people must carry out several different kinds of cognitive processes, such as comprehending the text, interpreting the diagram, resolving co-reference between the text and diagram, and imagining the movement of the machine (Narayanan & Hegarty, 1998). All of these cognitive processes collaborate toward the common goal of understanding how the machine works. Thus, an account of the role of working memory in complex cognition should also specify how the subcomponents of working memory share information and collaborate, and not just how they compete with each other.

TASKS THAT INVOLVE A LARGE AMOUNT OF INFORMATION THAT EXCEEDS TYPICAL WORKING MEMORY LIMITATIONS. Ericsson and Delaney (Chapter 8) have pointed out that many skilled everyday activities require the maintenance and later retrieval of a large amount of information usually considered beyond the capacity of ST-WM. From a traditional viewpoint, ST-WM has been said to maintain a limited number of chunks, such as 7 plus or minus 2 chunks (Miller, 1956) or 2 to 4 chunks (Cowan, Chapter 3; Young & Lewis, Chapter 7). Although the validity of characterizing working memory limitations from the perspective of a discrete number of chunks can be debated, it seems to be reasonably obvious that accounts of complex cognition must include an account of how ST-WM is augmented in the performance of complex cognitive tasks.

One way in which ST-WM is augmented is via LT-WM (Young & Lewis, Chapter 7; Ericsson & Delaney, Chapter 8; O'Reilly et al., Chapter 11). Another way, which has received relatively little attention by the contributors to this volume, is by external memory (Hegarty & Steinhoff, 1997; Hutchins, 1995a). Although it is obvious that an individual's ST-WM is often augmented by external displays (e.g., various displays in a cockpit) or external memory systems (e.g., reference books), we usually do not have a good understanding of the interplay between internal and external representations in these tasks. One possibility is that there are parallels between LT-WM and external stores. In the case of LT-WM, experts develop sophisticated indexing and retrieval structures that allow them to rapidly access task-relevant information in their LTM. Similarly, reading a reference book might enable one to construct a mental index of the important information in the book, which in turn enables one to access frequently needed information without having to fully represent that information internally (see Miyake & Shah, Chapter 13, for further discussion of the importance of external memory in working memory research).

In summary, although there is general agreement that working memory should be studied in the context of real-world, complex cognition, many of the tasks currently being studied by working memory researchers are quite simple and artificial and cannot really be considered "cognition in the wild" (Hutchins, 1995b). Although there is no general agreement on their definition, complex cognitive tasks can be characterized as being under cognitive control, involving multiple steps of processing, involving multiple components of the memory system, and requiring fast access to large amounts of information. In the interests of understanding the full range of capacities of human working memory, it is important that we do not stop short in studying tasks that have just one of these properties, but ultimately try to understand the operation of working memory in tasks that possess several or all of these properties.

Question 6: The Relationship of Working Memory to Long-Term Memory and Knowledge

As outlined in the introductory chapter (Shah & Miyake, Chapter 1), the traditional view of human memory (e.g., Atkinson & Shiffrin, 1968) is built around the assumption that STM and LTM are structurally separate storage systems. Although this traditional conception is a familiar one, it has been controversial (Crowder, 1982; Healy & McNamara, 1996). In addition, working memory is a concept that goes beyond the storage-oriented concept of STM. The sixth designated question, thus, asked the contributors to outline how working memory and LTM relate to each other. Although none of the models in this volume argue for a strict structural separation between working memory and LTM, there are some differences in the way they explain the relationship between the two.

Following the traditional conception, some models postulate a clear distinction between working memory and LTM, although the distinction is not necessarily structural in nature (e.g., Baddeley & Logie, Chapter 2; Kieras et al., Chapter 6; Schneider, Chapter 10). Baddeley and Logie, for example, admit that there is considerable evidence for the contribution of long-term knowledge to performance in working memory tasks, but, on the basis of theoretical considerations and neuropsychological evidence, they also argue that working memory and LTM must be separate and serve different functions. Baddeley and Logie propose that the notion of "fast" versus "slow" weights in neural network systems might provide a useful basis for considering the relationship between working memory and LTM. This view echoes that of Schneider, whose connectionist control architecture (CAP2) actually incorporates a similar notion.[3] The distinction between working memory and LTM is more structural in nature in Kieras et al.'s EPIC architecture. They also argue, however, that this structural separation does not necessarily imply that working memory is characterized as a separate "box" within EPIC, because it actively interacts with LTM.

In contrast to these models, a few models postulate a more continuous relationship between working memory and LTM, namely that working memory is an activated portion of LTM, a view originally proposed by Norman (1968) (e.g., Cowan, Chapter 3; Engle et al., Chapter 4; Lovett et al., Chapter 5; O'Reilly et al., Chapter 11). For example, according to Cowan, working memory includes information activated from LTM – not just the active information in the "focus of attention" (of which an individual is consciously aware), but also activated memory outside of attention or conscious awareness. Engle et al. hold a similar view, but their notion of working memory consists of LTM units activated above threshold and what they call "controlled attention." Analogously, O'Reilly et al. argue that working memory consists largely of the representations activated from LTM and also emphasize, like Engle et al., that their notion of working memory applies to the activated information as a result of controlled processing. In the ACT-R model of Lovett et al., working memory is viewed as a subset of declarative memory, those declarative chunks that are highly activated because they have been recently encoded or rehearsed and are linked to the current goal.

Barnard's (Chapter 9) model seems to be rather different from these two classes of theoretical proposals. His ICS model does not postulate a clear dis-

---

[3] This view is also somewhat analogous to the distinction between a short-term store (STS) and a long-term store (LTS) parameter made in a variant of the perturbation model developed by Estes (1972, 1997). A series of STM experiments using the distractor paradigm (e.g., Cunningham, Healy, Till, Fendrich, & Dimitry, 1993; Healy, Fendrich, Cunningham, & Till, 1987) indicates the perturbation model was able to fit the data only when both the STS and LTS parameters were included, suggesting the necessity of separating STM and LTM.

tinction between working memory and LTM at either the structural level or the functional level. Rather, it essentially adopts Craik and Lockhart's (1972) "levels-of-processing" perspective and attempts to explain differences between working memory and LTM phenomena in terms of differences in the types of processes or representations (or "image records") that are often implicated when performing short-term and long-term recall (e.g., surface properties of more peripheral subsystems vs. representations concerning propositional and implicational meanings, respectively).

This classification indicates that there are some important differences in the way these models prefer to characterize the relationship between working memory and LTM, but how fundamental are these differences? We do not deny the existence of some fundamentally incompatible claims at the level of specific proposals; for example, EPIC's structural distinction between working memory and LTM (Kieras et al., Chapter 6) does not sit well with ICS's position (Barnard, Chapter 9). At a more global level of analysis, however, we believe that these differences may be more apparent than real. The main reason for this assessment is that most (if not all) models explicitly acknowledge the close relationship between working memory and LTM, regardless of whether they emphasize the distinction or the continuity between the two constructs.

For example, consider Young and Lewis's (Chapter 7) and Ericsson and Delaney's (Chapter 8) theoretical proposals. Some aspects of these proposals could be interpreted as supporting a "structural" distinction between working memory and LTM (i.e., the distinction between Soar's dynamic memory and production memory and the distinction between ST-WM and LTM, respectively). The relationship between working memory and LTM is much more complex in these models, however. From the perspective of skilled and expert performance, Ericsson and Delaney argue that working memory includes not just the content of ST-WM, but also part of LTM that functions as if it were elements "in" ST-WM. Young and Lewis essentially make the same claim. These two theoretical perspectives illustrate that postulating some sort of distinction between working memory and LTM does not necessarily mean that one's influence on the other has to be limited.

In fact, other models in this volume also explicitly acknowledge that complex everyday tasks (e.g., reading comprehension) as well as some simple laboratory tasks (e.g., immediate serial recall of words and digits) implicate the contribution of long-term knowledge and skills (Baddeley & Logie, Chapter 2; Cowan, Chapter 3; Engle et al., Chapter 4; Lovett et al., Chapter 5; Schneider, Chapter 10; O'Reilly et al., Chapter 11). This view is shared regardless of whether the model emphasizes the functional separation between working memory and LTM (Baddeley & Logie; Schneider) or the continuous relationship between the two (Cowan; Engle et al.; Lovett et al.; O'Reilly et al.). For example, Cowan argues that information not in an activated state can serve as if it were "in" working memory if there are cues in working memory that point to it and thereby facilitate its later retrieval. This use of long-term knowledge – referred to as "virtual short-term memory" by Cowan – resembles the notion of LT-WM. O'Reilly et al.'s biologically based model (Chapter 11) – another model that postulates that working memory consists of an activated portion of LTM – also incorporates a mechanism that can serve a function analogous to LT-WM. In addition to these theoretical proposals, empirical evidence pointing to the contribution of long-term knowledge and skills in working memory tasks is also abundant (e.g., Kutinsky & Healy, 1998). Such wide acknowledgment of the difficulty of separating out the effects of (short-term) working memory and long-term knowledge and skills suggests that the differences among the models may not be as fundamental as they initially sound.

Question 7: The Relationship of Working Memory to Attention and Consciousness

Working memory and attention are related because both refer to control of information, and both are postulated to have limits with respect to how much information can be controlled (or processed). But what is the actual relationship between working memory and attention and between both of these constructs and consciousness? Do these terms refer to exactly the same construct? Or are they somehow separate from each other (either partially or completely)? If the constructs are distinct, how do they interact with each other? These issues were the major focus of the seventh designated question.

WORKING MEMORY AND ATTENTION. Many chapters in this volume argue that working memory and attention are closely related. "Attention," however, is a concept that has many different facets (e.g., Parasuraman & Davies, 1984), and most chapters tend to single out one specific aspect of attention in their account. Those specific aspects can be classified into two general categories: *selective control* and *mental energy* or *resources*.

First, several chapters in this volume focused on selective-control functions of attention as an important link between working memory and attention. Their answers, however, seem to center around at least two different aspects of selective control. Some models, for example, point out that attention (or, more specifically, selective attention) determines which sensory information gets encoded into working memory, which motor output gets executed, and which mentally represented information gets attended to (e.g., Cowan, Chapter 3; Kieras et al., Chapter 6; Ericsson & Delaney, Chapter 8; Schneider, Chapter 10). At least two of these models (Kieras et al. and Schneider) tend to view attention and working memory as serving *separate* functions, though they closely interact with each other. Other models emphasize a higher level control and regulation of cognitive and perceptuomotor processing (e.g., Baddeley & Logie, Chapter 2; Engle et al., Chapter 4; O'Reilly et al., Chapter 11). These models tend to view such attentional control functions as an essential *part* or *subset* of a larger working memory system. This viewpoint is particularly clearly articulated by Engle et al., who argue that working memory can be considered STM plus "controlled attention." Although Cowan (Chapter 3) does not elaborate much about the nature of such higher level regulatory control mechanisms, his model also seems to assume that attention may be a subset of working memory in the sense that working memory includes information outside the focus of attention as well as information within the focus of attention.

Another facet of attention represented in this volume is the notion of attention as mental energy or resources (Just & Carpenter, 1992; Kahneman, 1973). Engle, for example, used to consider working memory capacity from the perspective of attentional resources (e.g., Engle, Cantor, & Carullo, 1992), though he has recently abandoned that view (Engle et al., Chapter 4). Lovett et al.'s ACT-R model of working memory (Chapter 5) also adopts this perspective, linking their source activation parameter (W) to limited attentional resources. In these models, the same entity – activation – limits both attention and working memory. In that specific sense, one could argue that Lovett et al.'s proposal may come closest to equating attention and working memory, although their notion of working memory certainly encompasses more than just a limited amount of source activation.

These two classes of models are not necessarily incompatible with each other. For example, although the mental energy metaphor of attention is highly salient in Lovett et al.'s description (Chapter 5), their source activation essentially can serve as the modulator of cognitive processing by keeping task-relevant information (e.g., goals and subgoals) active in working memory. In this respect, the distinction between the two classes of models should be considered complementary, rather than fundamentally incompatible.

It is worth noting that, although they do not explicitly discuss the relationship between attention and working memory, Young and Lewis (Chapter 7) take the position that attention is an emergent property of the underlying cognitive architecture (see also O'Reilly et al., Chapter 11). This "effect" view of attention has been gaining support recently, particularly from the perspective of cognitive neuroscience (e.g., Allport, 1993; Desimone & Duncan, 1995). It may thus be beneficial to explore the relationship between working memory and attention from the perspective of how each phenomenon emerges as a result of complex and dynamic interactions among the underlying subsystems or processes.

WORKING MEMORY AND CONSCIOUS AWARENESS. How might consciousness or conscious awareness be related to working memory? Although this question is addressed only briefly and indirectly in many chapters, some chapters provided intriguing ideas and useful distinctions.

Although there is a temptation to equate working memory to consciousness, such a simple equation of working memory and consciousness may not be warranted. Indeed, while acknowledging that consciousness and working memory are highly related, many chapters in this volume argue for a subset relationship, namely that only a subset of information that is actively maintained is also that which one is aware or conscious of (e.g. Cowan, Chapter 3; Lovett et al., Chapter 5; Young & Lewis, Chapter 7; Ericsson & Delaney, Chapter 8; Barnard, Chapter 9; O'Reilly et al., Chapter 11). Another important reason for not equating working memory to consciousness is that there can be profound disruptions in working memory without disrupting consciousness. Damage to the prefrontal cortex, for example, tends to disrupt working memory or executive functions and impairs the "virtual agent" we mentioned earlier, in that goal-directed behavior is disrupted (Duncan, Emslie, Williams, Johnson, & Freer, 1996). Prefrontal lesions, however, typically leave consciousness – phenomenological awareness – intact. At the same time, it is possible for lesions elsewhere to disrupt phenomenological awareness. Right parietal lesions, for example, can produce unilateral neglect, which is a disturbance of conscious awareness, as Cowan (Chapter 3) pointed out. Brainstem lesions can produce coma, which is a profound disturbance of consciousness as well as the regulation of sleep. Both trauma and drugs can also alter consciousness. Traditionally, neurologists have distinguished delirium – an alteration in the level of consciousness characterized by extreme excitement, disordered speech, and hallucinations – from dementia – a disruption in rationality. These dissociations between working memory and consciousness suggest that there may be some separability between those constructs.

One way to reconcile the apparent close relationship between working memory and consciousness on the one hand and the neuropsychological dissociation between working memory (at least its executive functions) and consciousness on the other hand is to recognize that there are at least two meanings of the term "consciousness" (though the specific fractionation of consciousness is currently an issue of debate). Block (1995), for example, differentiates between the notion of *phenomenal consciousness*, which he defines as the subjective experience of being in a state, from *access consciousness*, which he defines as "availability for use in reasoning and rationally guiding speech and action" (p. 227). Furthermore, he argues that most cognitive theories of consciousness (e.g., Andrade, 1993; Baars, 1988) refer to access consciousness. Churchland (1995) also focused on this second sense of consciousness in proposing seven dimensions of consciousness, which include: (a) it involves STM; (b) it is independent of sensory inputs; (c) it displays steerable attention; (d) it has the capacity for alternative explanations of complex or ambiguous data; (e) it disappears in deep sleep; (f) it reappears in an altered form in dreaming; and (g) it integrates the experiences of the different senses into a single unified experience. It is striking how closely his seven dimensions resemble the characteristics of working memory.

Indeed, it is this sense of *access* consciousness to which the contributors to this volume generally refer when they propose that consciousness may be a subset of that information that is actively maintained or that which is *accessible*. The issue of the relationship of working memory to the first sense of consciousness is less clear, and the neuropsychological dissociations discussed earlier suggest that there may not be a strong relationship. Two ideas presented in this volume, however, indicate that there may be some relationship between working memory and phenomenal consciousness. Baddeley and Logie (Chapter 2), for example, briefly mention some recent research suggesting that one type of phenomenal consciousness, the subjective experience of the vividness of mental images, may also be related to working memory (Baddeley & Andrade, 1998). Also, the two levels of consciousness in Barnard's model (Chapter 9), for example, seem to be analogous to the two senses of consciousness: the copy image record (which is similar to diffuse phenomenal awareness) and the system location of the attentional focus (which is similar to access consciousness). Thus, although the accounts of the relationship between working memory and consciousness presented in this volume are highly speculative, an attempt to examine and specify the relationship between the two is important and may even be crucial for our understanding of each construct.

Question 8: The Biological Implementation of Working Memory

Working memory is one of the most active areas of research inquiry in the new blossoming field of cognitive neuroscience. An exploration of the neural basis of working memory has been done at different levels of analysis, ranging from behavioral studies of brain-damaged patients, through neuroimaging (e.g., PET, fMRI) and electrophysiological (e.g., ERP) studies, to neuron-level or even cellular-level studies. The eighth designated question, thus, asked the contributors to address (a) how such neuroscience data relate to their own model of working memory and (b) how their model may be implemented in the brain. Although some chapters had little to say on this eighth question, many chapters incorporated, in one way or another, recent cognitive neuroscience findings to back up their claims, thus addressing the first part of the biological-implementation question. The chapters differ, however, in the role neuroscience evidence has played in theory development.

Obviously, neuroscience findings have played an essential role in Schneider's (Chapter 10) and O'Reilly et al.'s (Chapter 11) models in that they are both built around cognitive neuroscience findings and the principles of neural information processing. The Baddeley–Logie model (Chapter 2) also seems to have had a fruitful relationship with neuropsychology (i.e., behavioral studies of brain-damaged patients). Since its conception, the model has provided a useful framework to explore interesting patterns of selective sparing and impairments observed among brain-damaged patients (and, more recently, brain activation data from neuroimaging studies; see Smith & Jonides, 1997), and a set of neuropsychological dissociations, in turn, have led to some significant modifications (particularly, fractionation) of different subcomponents in the model (for a review, see Gathercole, 1994).

Other models seem to be less closely tied to neuroscience findings than the three models discussed before. However, recent neuropsychological and neuroimaging studies of attention and executive function have clearly served as a major source of inspiration for Engle et al.'s "controlled attention" framework (Chapter 4). Similarly, event-related brain potentials (ERP) studies using the so-called mismatch negativity as an index (e.g., Cowan, Winkler, Teder, & Näätänen, 1993) have also provided important evidence for Cowan's model (Chapter 3). Although his model can be viewed as a sophisticated extension of a traditional information-processing model (like Broadbent's, 1958), Cowan also speculates on the mapping between each component of his model and the underlying neural substrates. Even some of the symbolic models that are proposed purely at the cognitive level, such as ACT-R (Lovett et al., Chapter 5) and 3CAPS (Just & Carpenter, 1992), have also provided a basis for explaining some neuropsychological findings (e.g., Haarmann, Just, & Carpenter, 1997; Kimberg & Farah, 1993).

These chapters unanimously agree that one central function of working memory, namely, executive control, is associated strongly, if not exclusively, with the prefrontal cortex. Although some contributors are somewhat skeptical (e.g., Ericsson & Delaney, Chapter 8), another general agreement is that cognitive neuroscience evidence provides useful constraints on the cognitive models of working memory. Despite these points of consensus (and a lot of excitement about recent progress in the cognitive neuroscience of working memory), detailed mechanisms have yet to be worked out (see Miyake & Shah, Chapter 13, for further discussions on this issue). In addition, with some notable exceptions (particularly, Schneider, Chapter 10; O'Reilly et al., Chapter 11), the broad-scope cognitive models of working memory in this volume have not yet been integrated well enough with neuroscience findings to provide a detailed account of the second part of this eighth designated question, namely, the actual implementation of working memory in the brain.

LOCALIZATION OF WORKING MEMORY IN THE BRAIN. When we attempt to specify the neural basis of working memory, one key issue has to do with the localization of specific functions in the brain. As many chapters in this volume emphasized, however, working memory is a complex system consisting of multiple subcomponents. Some contributors went further and argued that it may even be better conceptualized as an emergent property arising from the dynamic interactions among these subcomponents (e.g., Cowan, Chapter 3; Young & Lewis, Chapter 7; Barnard, Chapter 9; Schneider, Chapter 10; O'Reilly et al., Chapter 11). Given this increasingly popular characterization of working memory, does it really make sense to specify its neural basis by attempting to localize it in the brain, as some (but not all) neuroimaging studies seem to do? We believe we should be extremely cautious in such attempts, a point also made explicit in some chapters (e.g., Baddeley & Logie, Chapter 2; Engle et al., Chapter 4; Schneider, Chapter 10).

Although localization has recently become popular in cognitive neuroscience (especially given the power of the new imaging technologies such as PET and fMRI), it is useful to recall that debates over localization of function have recurred throughout the history of neuropsychology. A core axis of this recurring debate is holism versus reductionism. In the past, the holistic side of the debate made telling criticisms. For instance, shortly after Broca's famous discovery, Hughlings Jackson (cited by Head, 1926, p. 50) commented in 1864: "To locate the damage which destroys speech and to localize speech are two different things." Similarly, Lashley (1929, p. 162) offered a prescient warning for modern cognitive neuropsychology: "Localization as an explanatory principle can progress in only one way: by the demonstration of correspondences between ever more restricted anatomical divisions and smaller units of behavior until some ultimate anatomical and behavioristic elements are reached . . . ." Nonetheless, holism lost adherents because it lacked a concrete alternative proposal to localizationist accounts.[4]

Holistic reservations about localization inferences from lesion studies apply equally to functional neuroimaging studies of normal subjects, so these reservations should be considered as we evaluate PET or fMRI studies that purport to localize components of working memory. In essence, the holistic critique holds that both lesion and neuroimaging methods are inductive and circular in their attempt to localize cognitive components. These methods presuppose that independent cognitive components exist and then use dissociations or subtractions to localize them (Poeppel, 1996; Van Orden & Paap, 1997). Inductive methods cannot validate their own underlying assumptions, however. Thus, lesion studies will inevitably find correlations between given cognitive tasks and particular brain locations, as will functional neuroimaging studies, but these correlations do not confirm the assumption of independent cognitive components that underlies each method.

If current cognitive models of working memory stress that it is a system-level, emergent property that arises from dynamic interactions, it seems peculiar to revert to an (implicit) noninteractive cognitive theory to study the neural basis of working memory. Even Fodor (1983), who believed that the modular aspects of cognition might be localizable, seriously doubted that so-called central aspects of cognition could be localized, just because central cognition requires complete interaction. He argued that everything that one knows should be available as a constraint on what one believes – and, as working memory theorists might add, on what actions one selects (Pennington, 1994).

---

[4] This situation has changed, however, with the advent of connectionist models, which can produce dissociations (even double dissociations) within fully interactive networks (Plaut, 1995).

In summary, we still have a long way to go to fully understand the neural basis of working memory, but the emerging synergies between cognitive psychology and cognitive neuroscience make us optimistic about the possibility of developing models of working memory that are solid at both cognitive and biological/neural levels.

General Theoretical Issues

Evaluation of the Common-Question Approach to Theory Comparisons

Having analyzed the models of working memory represented in this volume in terms of the eight designated questions, we must now ask ourselves what we might have missed and whether these eight questions were the right ones. One might argue that the approach we and the editors have taken is misguided. The editors' idea was to create a common basis for comparisons among models of working memory by asking each contributor to address the same set of important theoretical questions. In some cases, however, this comparison was not entirely satisfactory because the answers to some of the questions were not directly derivable from the models under discussion and were made simply by informal argument (or even handwaving), rather than by referring to specific aspects of the models.

Alternatively, one might think that a more complete and satisfying comparison of the models could be obtained by asking everyone to address the same set of data and do so in a rigorous fashion. Toward this end, one could use a standard experimental paradigm and data set as a test bed. For instance, one set of data may come from a study of immediate serial recall of words with or without articulatory suppression. Another set of data may come from a study of individual differences in syllogistic reasoning performance among college students who differ in their working memory span scores. Our comparison among models would be based on how (i.e., the specific mechanisms and processes) each model accounts for such a data set that includes key working memory findings. Our relative evaluations of the different models could be based on their relative degrees of success in this endeavor.

Although such a strategy has a lot of merit, its applicability to the current set of models might be rather limited, unfortunately. The phenomena studied under the rubric of working memory are far too diverse to enable well-focused, detailed comparisons of these 10 different models (see Table 12.2 for the range of tasks discussed in this volume). There is probably no single experiment or phenomenon that would provide a fair test for all 10 models under discussion – not even a set of half a dozen such experiments would do the job, at least for now. We have discussed this problem in our analysis of the answers to Question 5 – even when we limit our focus to complex cognitive activities involving working memory, it is rather difficult to identify a common core in terms of the phenomena under consideration. Different theorists and experimenters are interested in different empirical phenomena and, indeed, rightfully so – an artificial narrowing of focus could only hurt the vitality of the research on working memory. Thus, as a general strategy for a comparison of the 10 models covered in this volume, this approach is limited and seems to provide no viable alternative to the eight-question approach adopted here.

Nonetheless, we would like to emphasize that, to the extent that direct experimental face-offs among models are possible, they should certainly be encouraged. Obviously, such comparisons would be very informative, and much more could be and should be done in this respect than has heretofore been attempted. Indeed, detailed data-driven comparisons seem to be quite possible (or even desirable) for different subsets of the models in this volume that focus on similar empirical phenomena.

Are there major issues in working memory research that are not adequately addressed by the eight questions that framed our discussion? We have not found any major omissions. It seems to us that significant progress has been made in the study of different aspects of working memory, both in the accumulation of empirical research results and in the construction of models that provide a basis for theoretical interpretations of the empirical data. This progress appears to be well characterized by the eight dimensions implied by our list of questions, although not all of these dimensions are equivalent: Some specify research issues and problems for future research, whereas others characterize approaches and research areas.

Two of the questions do not address specific problems or issues in the study of working memory, but research areas and/or methods: how working memory functions in complex cognitive processes (Question 5) and how working memory is implemented biologically (Question 8). We expect a great deal of work in both of these areas in the near future and are highly optimistic that this work will significantly advance our understanding of working memory. Until recently, most of what we know about working memory has come from studies of the serial recall of word lists and the like. Such studies will certainly retain their importance in working memory research (Gathercole, 1996; see also Baddeley & Logie, Chapter 2; Cowan, Chapter 3; Kieras et al., Chapter 6), but, as laboratory research extends to understanding and thinking, our conception of working memory will be enriched and expanded. New issues that simply do not arise in the serial recall of word lists will become important – not at the expense of the old ones, but in addition to them. Similarly, as our understanding of the biological underpinnings of working memory improves, our whole conception of the parts and components of the working memory system may change. New biological constraints will alter our views, not by slighting the old, familiar behavioral constraints on which our models have been based almost exclusively up to now, but by revealing new constellations that we could not see before.

Synergies Between Computational Models and Verbal-Conceptual Models

Although the chapters in this volume all deal with models of working memory, they do so in two contrasting ways: in some cases, as broad conceptual frameworks, and, in others, as explicit computational models. In the former case, the emphasis is often on the empirical work, and the function of the model is to integrate the empirical results. One can attack such formulations as fuzzy and incomplete, but their authors would respond that fuzziness and incompleteness are to be preferred when our knowledge does not reach further. In contrast, the computational-modeling approach is perforce more explicit, formal, and complete and is associated with well-known advantages: It enforces systematicity and consistency, draws attention to gaps in the research evidence, and permits one to derive the formal implications of the model, which may contain some surprises and new discoveries. These advantages are usually obtained at some risk, however. As Kieras et al. (Chapter 6) argue, premature modeling can be sterile when too many unsupported assumptions have to be made, resulting in an illusory systematicity and completeness.

Proponents of these two approaches often treat each other with distrust or even hostility. The chapters here show that such an attitude is not necessary and that a productive interchange between these two camps is entirely possible. Indeed, the fact that such an interchange was easily and quite naturally established was one of the most positive features of the companion symposium on which the present book is based. Such synergies between the two approaches are clearly reflected in the rich set of cross-references of similar, compatible ideas and proposals between computational modeling chapters and conceptual-framework chapters. Clearly, both approaches have their strengths, and both can make important contributions. A systematic, formal account is surely where our field must eventually be headed – but, in the meantime, a more flexible, informal approach can often be highly effective.

Working Memory as a System

Working memory research has grown out of the research on STM, which has a relatively long history. It started in the United States with some acute observations on primary and secondary memory by William James in 1890. At about the same time, STM was actively investigated in the laboratories of Georg Elias Müller, Hermann Ebbinghaus, and Wilhelm Wundt in Germany. Neither of these beginnings proved to be lasting, however. It took the invention of a new experimental procedure to revive interest in the STM concept – the Brown–Peterson distractor procedure (Brown, 1958; Peterson & Peterson, 1959). In consequence, research on STM exploded and became an inextricable component of the cognitive revolution. In more recent years, we have seen the extinction of the STM concept and its replacement by working memory.

The primary mover in that changeover was Alan Baddeley. By replacing STM with the multicomponent working memory system, Baddeley transformed the way we look at STM in fundamental ways. The old STM was essentially a box in an information flow diagram, whereas working memory is a system combining memory storage and processing.

Baddeley's move was a brilliant one, but his decision to name the new system working memory in analogy to STM has been a continuing source of trouble. Although the notion that working memory is supposed to be a processing system is a relatively familiar one, the old thought schemata are all too powerful and people have a hard time adhering to the system view of working memory. The name "working memory" is part of the problem. It emphasizes "memory" (by analogy to STM), but memory storage is only a part of working memory, and the lesser part, indeed. What Baddeley named the central executive is its central aspect, which has more to do with attention and control and less with memory per se. Baddeley was aware of this dilemma from the very beginning (see Baddeley, 1993), but could not think of a better name than "working memory" (and neither can we now). "Working memory" is a little bit like false advertising; we, as memory researchers, know better, but our audience – psychologists as well as lay public – is easily misled into thinking of working memory as an entity like liver, or LTM, for that matter.

For working memory researchers, working memory is a system – not exclusively, or even primarily, a memory store. Every single chapter in this book reinforces this point. Baddeley and Logie (Chapter 2) discuss extensively how working memory is implicated in various cognitive tasks (such as language comprehension, mental arithmetic, and syllogistic reasoning) – not about memory per se. Cowan (Chapter 3) defines working memory as any process that maintains information about any task – which means that we should study the process; there is no claim of a general working memory common to all or many tasks. Engle et al. (Chapter 4) specifically comment that working memory capacity is not about memory but about "controlled attention." Ericsson and Delaney (Chapter 8) are concerned with the interaction between retrieval structures in LTM and cues in STM – LT-WM is the result of this interaction. As we turn to the production-system models, working memory is not a hardwired, structural entity of the model (Lovett et al., Chapter 5; Kieras et al., Chapter 6; Young & Lewis, Chapter 7). Moreover, the capacity limitations of working memory arise in EPIC (Kieras et al.) and Soar (Young & Lewis) not from any structural features of the model, but from existing functional constraints. These models can account well for specific working memory phenomena – not by postulating a working memory, but by using components already available in the system. For Barnard (Chapter 9) and Schneider (Chapter 10), working memory is an emergent phenomenon that arises at the system level from the interplay of other components of the model – buffers, decay effects, feedback loops, and so on. Similarly, O'Reilly et al. (Chapter 11) describe how working memory phenomena arise from the interaction of various brain areas. There is no working memory at the basic level in these models – working memory emerges at the system level.

Despite its emergent nature, "working memory" is still a convenient label and will continue to be useful in psychology. It is a term with a great deal of face validity and ecological validity, it is easy to explain to the users of our theories, and it is useful in applications. But we should remember that working memory is not only about memory but at least as much about processes, and that it is best viewed as a system-level concept rather than a basic component of psychological or biological models.

REFERENCES

Allport, A. (1993). Attention and control: Have we been asking the wrong questions? A critical review of twenty-five years. In D. E. Meyer & S. Kornblum (Eds.), *Attention and performance XIV: Synergies in experimental psychology, artificial intelligence, and cognitive neuroscience* (pp. 183–218). Cambridge, MA: MIT Press.

Anderson, J. R., & Matessa, M. (1997). A production system theory of serial memory. *Psychological Review, 104*, 728–748.

Andrade, J. (1993). Consciousness: Current views. In J. G. Jones (Ed.), *Depth of anesthesia.* New York: Little, Brown.

Atkinson, R. C., & Shiffrin, R. M. (1968). Human memory: A proposed system and its control processes. In K. W. Spence & J. T. Spence (Eds.), *The psychology of learning and motivation: Advances in research theory* (Vol. 2, pp. 89–195). New York: Academic Press.

Baars, B. J. (1988). *A cognitive theory of consciousness.* New York: Cambridge University Press.

Baddeley, A. D. (1986). *Working memory.* New York: Oxford University Press.

Baddeley, A. D. (1993). Working memory or working attention? In A. D. Baddeley & L. Weiskrantz (Eds.), *Attention: Selection, awareness, and control. A tribute to Donald Broadbent* (pp. 152–170). New York: Oxford University Press.

Baddeley, A. D. & Andrade, J. (1998). Working memory and consciousness: An empirical approach. In M. A. Conway, S. E. Gathercole, & C. Cornoldi (Eds.), *Theories of memory II* (pp. 1–23). Hove, UK: Psychology Press.

Block, N. (1995). On a confusion about a function of consciousness. *Behavioral and Brain Sciences, 18*, 227–287.

Broadbent, D. E. (1958). *Perception and communication.* London: Pergamon Press.

Brown, J. (1958). Some tests of the decay theory of immediate memory. *Quarterly Journal of Experimental Psychology, 10*, 12–21.

Churchland, P.M. (1995). *The engine of reason, the seat of the soul.* Cambridge, MA: MIT Press.

Cowan, N., Winkler, I., Teder, W., & Näätänen, R. (1993). Memory prerequisites of the mismatch negativity in the auditory event-related potential (ERP). *Journal of Experimental Psychology: Learning, Memory, and Cognition, 19*, 909–921.

Craik, F. I. M., & Lockhart, R. S. (1972). Levels of processing: A framework for memory research. *Journal of Verbal Learning and Verbal Behavior, 11*, 671–684.

Crowder, R. G. (1982). The demise of short-term memory. *Acta Psychologica, 50*, 291–323.

Cunningham, T. F., Healy, A. F., Till, R. E., Fendrich, D. W., & Dimitry, C. (1993). Is there really very rapid forgetting from primary memory?: The role of expectancy and item importance in recall. *Memory & Cognition, 21*, 671–688.

Dennett, D. C. (1987). *The intentional stance.* Cambridge, MA: MIT Press.

Desimone, R., & Duncan, J. (1995). Neural mechanisms of selective visual attention. *Annual Review of Neuroscience, 18*, 192–222.

Duncan, J., Emslie, H., Williams, P., Johnson, R., & Freer, C. (1996). Intelligence and the frontal lobe: The organization of goal-directed behavior. *Cognitive Psychology, 30*, 257–303.

Engle, R. W., Cantor, J., & Carullo, J. J. (1992). Individual differences in working memory and comprehension: A test of four hypotheses. *Journal of Experimental Psychology: Learning, Memory, and Cognition, 18*, 972–992.

Estes, W. K. (1972). An associative basis for coding and organization in memory. In A. W. Melton & E. Martin (Eds.), *Coding processes in human memory* (pp. 161–190). New York: Halsted Press.

Estes, W. K. (1997). Processes of memory loss, recovery, and distortion. *Psychological Review, 104*, 148–169.

Fodor, J. A. (1983). *The modularity of mind.* Cambridge, MA: MIT Press.

Gathercole, S. E. (1994). Neuropsychology and working memory: A review. *Neuropsychology, 8*, 494–505.

Gathercole, S. E. (Ed.). (1996). *Models of short-term memory.* Hove, UK: Psychology Press.

Haarmann, H. J., Just, M. A., & Carpenter, P. A. (1997). Aphasic sentence comprehension as a resource deficit: A computational approach. *Brain and Language, 59*, 76–120.

Head, H. (1926). *Aphasia and kindred disorders of speech.* Cambridge, UK: Cambridge University Press.

Healy, A. F. (1975). Coding of temporal-spatial patterns in short-term memory. *Journal of Verbal Learning and Verbal Behavior, 14*, 481–495.

Healy, A. F., Cunningham, T. F., Gesi, A. T., Till, R. E., & Bourne, L. E. (1991). Comparing short-term recall of item, temporal, and spatial information in children and adults. In W. E. Hockley & S. Lewandowsky (Eds.), *Relating theory and data: Essays on human memory in honor of Bennet B. Murdock* (pp. 127–154). Hillsdale, NJ: Erlbaum.

Healy, A. F., Fendrich, D. W., Cunningham, T. F., & Till, R. E. (1987). Effects of cuing on short-term retention of order information. *Journal of Experimental Psychology: Learning, Memory, and Cognition, 13*, 413–425.

Healy, A. F., & McNamara, D. S. (1996). Verbal learning and memory: Does the modal model still work? *Annual Review of Psychology, 47*, 143–172.

Hegarty, M., & Steinhoff, K. (1997). Individual differences in use of diagrams as external memory in mechanical reasoning. *Learning and Individual Differences, 9*, 19–42.

Hutchins, E. (1995a). How a cockpit remembers its speed. *Cognitive Science, 19*, 265–288.

Hutchins, E. (1995b). *Cognition in the wild.* Cambridge, MA: MIT Press.

Just, M. A., & Carpenter, P. A. (1992). A capacity theory of comprehension: Individual differences in working memory. *Psychological Review, 99*, 122–149.

Kahneman, D. (1973). *Attention and effort.* Englewood Cliffs, NJ: Prentice-Hall.

Kimberg, D. Y., & Farah, M. J. (1993). A unified account of cognitive impairments following frontal lobe damage: The role of working memory in complex, organized behavior. *Journal of Experimental Psychology: General, 122,* 411–428.

Kutinsky, J., & Healy, A. F. (1998). *The effects of articulatory suppression and imagery level on immediate serial recall.* Manuscript submitted for publication.

Lashley, K. S. (1929). *Brain mechanisms and intelligence.* Chicago: University of Chicago Press.

Miller, G. A. (1956). The magical number seven, plus or minus two: Some limits on our capacity for processing information. *Psychological Review, 63,* 81–97.

Narayanan, N. H., & Hegarty, M. (1998). On designing comprehensible interactive hypermedia manuals. *International Journal of Human–Computer Studies, 48.* 267–301.

Norman, D. A. (1968). Toward a theory of memory and attention. *Psychological Review, 75,* 522–536.

Parasuraman, R., & Davies, D. R. (Eds.). (1984). *Varieties of attention.* New York: Academic Press.

Pennington, B. F. (1994). The working memory function of the prefrontal cortices: Implications for developmental and individual differences in cognition. In M. M. Haith, J. B. Benson, R. J. Roberts, & B. F. Pennington (Eds.), *The development of future-oriented processes* (pp. 243–289). Chicago: University of Chicago Press.

Peterson, L. R., & Peterson, M. J. (1959). Short-term retention of individual verbal items. *Journal of Experimental Psychology, 58,* 193–198.

Plaut, D. (1995). Double dissociation without modularity: Evidence from connectionist neuropsychology. *Journal of Clinical and Experimental Neuropsychology, 17,* 291–321.

Poeppel, D. (1996). What genetics can and cannot learn from PET studies of phonology. In M. L. Rice (Ed.), *Toward a genetics of language.* Mahwah, NJ: Erlbaum.

Salthouse, T. A. (1996). The processing-speed theory of adult age differences in cognition. *Psychological Review, 103,* 403–428.

Schneider, W., & Detweiler, M. (1987). A connectionist/control architecture for working memory. In G. H. Bower (Ed.), *The psychology of learning and motivation* (Vol. 21, pp. 54–119). New York: Academic Press.

Smith, E. E., & Jonides, J. (1997). Working memory: A view from neuroimaging. *Cognitive Psychology, 33,* 5–42.

Van Orden, G. C., & Paap, K. R. (1997). Functional neuroimages fail to discover pieces of mind in the parts of the brain. *Philosophy of Science, 64,* 585–594.

Zacks, R. T., & Hasher, L. (1994). Directed ignoring: Inhibitory regulation of working memory. In D. Dagenbach & T. H. Carr (Eds.), *Inhibitory processes in attention, memory, and language* (pp. 241–264). San Diego: Academic Press.

13 Toward Unified Theories of Working Memory

Emerging General Consensus, Unresolved Theoretical Issues, and Future Research Directions

AKIRA MIYAKE AND PRITI SHAH

This final chapter starts where the previous chapter left off (Kintsch, Healy, Hegarty, Pennington, & Salthouse, Chapter 12). The main goal of the current chapter is to offer some thoughts we have about the *future* directions of working memory research. In particular, we present our own view of where the field stands and where it may be going in the belief that such reflection on the "big picture" is something this field needs.

The organization of the chapter is as follows. We will first present six points of general theoretical consensus that appear to be emerging among the models of working memory included in this volume. Despite this global-level agreement about the nature of working memory, there are some important disagreements among different models. Thus, we will next point out some unresolved theoretical issues for each of the eight designated questions. In the last section, we will outline several issues that have not yet received much attention in the current models of working memory, but we believe will become increasingly important for future empirical and theoretical investigations.

General Theoretical Consensus About the Nature of Working Memory

At the beginning of Chapter 1, we quoted H. J. Eysenck's (1986) rather pessimistic remark about psychometric theories of intelligence[1] and pointed out that some people would probably feel the same way about working memory:

We would like to thank the following people for providing comments on earlier versions of this chapter: Alan Baddeley, Philip Barnard, Andrew Conway, Nelson Cowan, Naomi Friedman, Arthur Graesser, Reid Hastie, James Hoeffner, Janice Keenan, Daniel Kimberg, Walter Kintsch, Marsha Lovett, William Marks, David Meyer, Randall O'Reilly, Peter Polson, Satoru Saito, and Sashank Varma.

[1] To repeat the quote here, Eysenck's remark was: "Discussions concerning the theory, nature, and measurement of intelligence historically have resulted more in disagreement than in agreement, more in smoke than in illumination" (H. J. Eysenck, 1986, p. 1).

There are many different models of working memory out there, but they all seem so different that it is difficult to see how they relate to one another. We tended to agree with this assessment when we started to organize the companion symposium in the fall of 1995. The models that we knew about at that time – most of them are included in this volume – looked so different from one another that we even feared that discussions at the symposium might turn into a battle royal (metaphorically speaking, of course)! Certainly, the scope of each model is quite different, and important disagreements divide the opinions of the contributors of this volume.

Despite this somewhat confusing state of affairs at a microlevel of analysis, we are convinced that Eysenck's remark does not apply to models of working memory. At a more macrolevel analysis, all of the seemingly disparate models in this volume have a lot in common. When the editors and the contributors of this volume got together in July 1997, we were all pleasantly surprised that there was more agreement than disagreement as to the fundamental nature of working memory. The extensive cross-references included in each chapter were intended not only to point out some similar (or sometimes contrasting) proposals made in other models but also to communicate our excitement about the commonalities that seem to unify different models of working memory.

In this section, we outline our analysis of the emerging general consensus among the models included in this volume (Chapters 2 to 11). Specifically, we offer six common themes that run across all 10 models. Although the ideas behind the six common themes have been around for a while, we did not know how widely these ideas had been accepted until extensive discussions at the symposium.

Theme 1: Working Memory Is Not a Structurally Separate Box or Place in the Mind or the Brain

The contributors of this volume all agree that working memory should not be considered a separate "box" for short-term storage that is structurally distinct from other memory or cognitive systems. As Kintsch et al. (Chapter 12) pointed out, all the models reinforce (either implicitly or explicitly) the point that the traditional view of short-term memory (STM) or working memory as a special "place" that stores a limited amount of information no longer holds at either the cognitive level or the neural level.

At the cognitive level, essentially all the models in this volume view working memory from one or both of two interrelated perspectives, namely, a functional perspective and/or a content-oriented perspective (a point made by Lovett, Reder, & Lebiere, Chapter 5). Some models in this volume characterize working memory from a functional perspective, in terms of its functions, processes, or mechanisms that subserve complex cognitive activities. Other models view working memory from a more content-oriented perspective, arguing that activated elements in long-term memory (LTM) constitute working memory, at least in part. *None* of the models portrays working memory from a purely structural point of view, as a special "place" in the mind. One concept that may be mistakenly identified as a structurally separate storage "place" is the notion of the two slave systems postulated in Baddeley and Logie's (Chapter 2) model, which they argue must be somewhat separable from LTM so that novel information can still be represented and maintained in those subsystems. Despite this separability argument, however, Baddeley and Logie do not reject the notion that working memory consists of an activated portion of LTM; rather, they accept that notion simply as part of the story and propose extra mechanisms (e.g., fast weights vs. slow weights) that could make the slave systems somewhat functionally separable from LTM. Another theoretical proposal that needs to be interpreted cautiously is EPIC's structural separation between "partitions" of working memory and LTM (Kieras, Meyer, Mueller, & Seymour, Chapter 6). As Kieras et al. explicitly point out, EPIC's working memory cannot be considered a separate "box" or "place," because EPIC's partitioning of working memory is not hardwired, and working memory elements dynamically interact with LTM.

At the neural level, the models in this volume do not endorse a strict structural view of working memory either. Instead of postulating a single location (or a small number of locations) in the brain that is specifically dedicated to the temporary storage of information, the current models adopt a more complex view of the biological implementation of working memory. The agreement is that various brain areas, including the prefrontal cortex (PFC), work together to produce working memory phenomena. This point is important because recent neuroimaging studies of working memory seem to be frequently misinterpreted as attempts to localize the special "site(s)" or "box(es)" in the brain specialized for temporary storage, rather than as attempts to elucidate the complex and distributed neural circuits or systems that, as a whole, dynamically contribute to working memory processes. O'Reilly, Braver, and Cohen (Chapter 11), for example, outlined one way to view such dynamic coordination among different brain regions. Other chapters also explicitly pointed out the danger of simply mapping working memory to a restricted area (or areas) of the brain (Baddeley & Logie, Chapter 2; Engle, Kane, & Tuholski, Chapter 4).

Although this theme may be obvious to some readers, we would like to stress its importance because the "box" or "place" metaphor of working memory is still prevalent. The phrase "working memory," by association with the earlier concept of STM, seems to trigger the view that it is a structurally separate box and that, to be "in" working memory,[2] information must be literally transferred to that special place in the mind or brain. Reacting to this still-prevalent traditional conception, some researchers have criticized working

---

[2] It is unfortunate that the common phrase "*in* working memory" strongly implies the "box" or "place" interpretation of working memory.

memory research by arguing that there is no such "thing" called working memory. They also tend to dismiss the results from recent neuroimaging studies because, to them, such studies seem almost like a search for the "Holy Grail." The chapters in this volume make it clear that such common complaints about working memory research are off the mark. These criticisms may be appropriate for the strict structural view of working memory, but the current models of working memory no longer hold such a view (at least those in this volume).

If we borrow the expression from the title of Crowder's (1982) influential critique of STM, we might be justified to conclude that this volume marks the "demise" of the "box" or "place" metaphor of working memory.

Theme 2: Working Memory's Maintenance Function Is in the Service of Complex Cognition

The chapters in this volume unanimously endorse the view that the maintenance function of working memory is an active process closely tied to, or even inextricably intertwined with, cognitive processes. In other words, working memory is not for "memorizing" per se, but, rather, it is in the service of complex cognitive activities, such as language processing, visuospatial thinking, reasoning and problem solving, and decision making.

This close link between working memory and cognition is not a new concept. In fact, as we pointed out in Chapter 1 (Shah & Miyake), it served as one of the major driving forces behind the theoretical development of working memory (Baddeley & Hitch, 1974). We believe, however, that this point deserves to be included here, partly because the level of consensus is so strong and partly because the most frequently used example to illustrate the function of working memory (or STM) in introductory textbooks is still that of temporarily memorizing an unfamiliar phone number, a task that highlights the "memory" part, rather than the "working" part, of working memory.

In addition, there is one more important – and maybe even surprising – reason why this apparently obvious point is chosen as one of the six emerging themes: Several chapters in this volume put forth an argument that even phonological working memory (or the phonological loop), seemingly specialized for simple retention of speech-based information (such as phone numbers), may also have evolved in the service of complex cognition. For example, Baddeley and Logie (Chapter 2) suggested that the phonological loop system may have developed to serve as a device for learning and acquiring language, one of the most complex and sophisticated cognitive abilities humans have (for more details, see Baddeley, Gathercole, & Papagno, 1998; Ellis & Sinclair, 1996). In addition, O'Reilly et al. (Chapter 11) suggest that inner speech, mediated by the phonological aspect of working memory, may serve as a particularly useful medium for thinking (see also Carlson, 1997, for elaboration of this idea). Moreover, as both Kieras et al. (Chapter 6) and Barnard (Chapter 9) argued, the phonological loop could also be construed as an emergent property of dynamic interactions of different, already existing perceptual and motor systems (e.g., an articulatory system, an auditory system), whose functional or evolutionary significance is more obvious. Thus, even a seemingly simple subsystem like the phonological loop may be more deeply rooted in complex cognitive activities than once thought.

We believe that current models of working memory have overcome another focus of Crowder's (1982) critique of the concept of STM – the lack of a close relationship to the rest of cognition. Moreover, they also suggest that it may be time to abandon the common practice of viewing the phonological loop as a "temporary memory" or "rehearsal" device in the service of pure temporary memorization (similar arguments might hold for other peripheral subsystems like the visuospatial sketchpad).

Theme 3: Executive Control Is Integral to Working Memory Functions

A third general point of consensus is closely related to the second theme we just considered. Working memory is not really about "memory" per se; it is also about "control" and "regulation" of our cognitive action. Of course, this point itself is not big news. Since its initial conception, the Baddeley and Hitch (1974) model has had a component dedicated to executive control, namely the central executive. Even the "modal" model of Atkinson and Shiffrin (1968) was equipped with control processes, albeit only for the sake of memorizing. What makes this third theme worth including here is the contributors' new interest in specifying exactly what these executive control mechanisms are.

This new interest in executive control starts with the Baddeley–Logie model (Chapter 2). Although the central executive component of their model was once called "the area of residual ignorance" (Baddeley, 1986, p. 225), it is now a major focus of their research, which attempts to fractionate the system into specific subcomponents or subfunctions (Baddeley, 1996a, 1998). Cowan's (Chapter 3) and Engle et al.'s (Chapter 4) views are similar to Baddeley and Logie's in that both approach the control and regulation issue from the perspective of attention. Cowan elaborates on how voluntary and involuntary mechanisms of the central executive interact to control and regulate "the focus of attention." Engle et al. propose that "controlled attention" is an essential component of working memory and presents a series of ingenious studies to demonstrate that "controlled attention" is what crucially mediates the correlation between working memory spans and complex cognitive tasks.

The three production-system models in this volume (Lovett et al., Chapter 5; Kieras et al., Chapter 6; Young & Lewis, Chapter 7) do not postulate specific control mechanisms, but, in all cases, the control and regulation of working memory contents and cognitive behavior emerge naturally as a consequence of the dynamic interaction between productions and working memory elements. Kieras et al.'s approach is noteworthy here because of its emphasis on strategies as a central component of executive control processes (Meyer &

Kieras, 1997). Although not a production-system model, Ericsson and Delaney's (Chapter 8) proposal also echoes that of Kieras et al. in that they view skilled, strategic processing and encoding of information as a key to successful later retrieval in complex everyday tasks.

The remaining three models (Barnard, Chapter 9; Schneider, Chapter 10; O'Reilly et al., Chapter 11) are similar to the production-system models in that they also view executive control as an emergent property. However, they differ from the production-system models in that they all emphasize the dynamic interaction among the subcomponents or submodules of the cognitive system, rather than the interaction between production rules and working memory elements. These models each offer a unique account of executive control mechanisms. More specifically, Barnard discusses how Baddeley and Logie's (Chapter 2) central executive – or the "central engine" in Barnard's terminology – can be implemented within his distributed architecture. Schneider proposes a more hierarchical control mechanism, involving control at both local and central levels. O'Reilly et al. discuss how the interaction among different brain systems – the posterior perceptual and motor cortex, the hippocampus, and, most importantly, the PFC – may lead to executive control of behavior.

Although the approaches to the control and regulation issue taken by the contributors are rather diverse, it is clear that the field has passed the stage at which the executive control component was essentially "a useful ragbag to contain all the phenomena that cannot be readily accounted for otherwise" (Baddeley & Logie, Chapter 2, p. 39). Together with a recent surge of new research on and interest in executive function (e.g., Lyon & Krasnegor, 1996; Rabbitt, 1997a), the approaches to the control and regulation issue outlined in this volume hold promise for someday resolving the homunculus problem.

Theme 4: Capacity Limits Reflect Multiple Factors and May Even Be an Emergent Property of the Cognitive System

The fourth point of general consensus is that the limits of working memory capacity reflect multiple factors, rather than a single, all-encompassing factor. As Kintsch et al. commented in Chapter 12, all the chapters explicitly mention at least two contributing factors (see Table 12.1 for the list of capacity-constraining factors postulated in this volume). Some contributors even argue that the capacity limits of working memory are simply an emergent property of the underlying cognitive system (Young & Lewis, Chapter 7; Barnard, Chapter 9; Schneider, Chapter 10; O'Reilly et al., Chapter 11). It is important to note that even the theorists who emphasize one capacity-constraining factor over others (e.g., Engle et al., Chapter 4; Lovett et al., Chapter 5) explicitly acknowledge that other factors (e.g., skills, strategies) can influence an individual's working memory capacity.

This multiple-constraint notion makes a lot of sense to us, but it was nonetheless somewhat of a surprise because of the way this working memory limitation issue is typically portrayed in the literature. Despite Newell's (1973) cautions, a common practice in examining the nature of working memory limitations and the source of individual variation is to postulate two (or more) competing hypotheses and pit them against each other in experiments (Platt, 1964), as we briefly pointed out in Chapter 1 (Shah & Miyake). A related problem in theoretical articles is that the claims of a competing theory are often oversimplified (for example, by claiming that the other theory postulates only one type of limitation, despite the fact that this other theory may acknowledge the role of other factors) to create a straw man. It almost seems that research on the nature of working memory limitations centers around an implicit assumption that there is only one correct capacity-limiting factor. Thus, the explicit mention of multiple capacity-limiting factors in all the chapters pleasantly surprised us.

We believe that this agreement is important because it forces a refocusing of the research endeavor on working memory limitations. The common practice of pitting one account of capacity limitations against another makes sense if there is only one capacity-limiting factor operating. However, if everybody agrees that multiple factors exist, the dichotomous approach does not make much sense; rather, the key issue is to identify which factors are operating under what circumstances and to specify how these different factors jointly contribute to the overall capacity limitation, as we elaborate further in a later section. Although the specific capacity-limiting factors explicitly acknowledged in each chapter are radically different (e.g. information-decay, limits in speed of processing, lack of knowledge, similarity-based interference), we nonetheless declare here the demise of the prevalent implicit assumption that working memory limitations reflect a single mechanism.

Theme 5: A Completely Unitary, Domain-General View of Working Memory Does Not Hold

The fifth point of general consensus is closely related to the fourth one – working memory is not completely unitary, and any comprehensive theory of working memory should be able to account for some domain-specific effects reported in the literature. Although some models emphasize the unitary aspects of working memory, none of the models in this volume defends the position that working memory is entirely unitary. Even Engle et al. (Chapter 4), who also emphasize the unitary nature of what they call "controlled attention," explicitly admit that "In truth, [. . .] the working memory/attention system is probably neither entirely unitary nor entirely separable into domain-specific systems" (p. 125) (for similar arguments, see also O'Reilly et al., Chapter 11; Moscovitch & Umiltà, 1990).

In our view, this point is closely related to Theme 4 for two reasons. First, just like the capacity limitation issue, the unitary versus non-unitary issue has so far been addressed in the literature in a simplistic dichotomous fashion (we ourselves are guilty in this regard; Shah & Miyake, 1996). Second, at least one of the multiple capacity-limiting factors explicitly acknowledged in each chapter is primarily domain specific in nature (e.g., similarity-based interference, long-term knowledge, skills), and this trend clearly reflects the necessity to accommodate some domain-specific effects of working memory found in the literature. Lovett et al. (Chapter 5), for example, emphasize the limit on domain-general source activation (*W*) as a central capacity-limiting factor, but they also acknowledge the possible contribution of knowledge and skills to working memory performance as well as the existence of domain-specific buffers (see also Engle et al., Chapter 4, for similar arguments).

Thus, we hereby declare the bankruptcy of a completely unitary view of working memory. Like the capacity-limitation issue we considered previously, the rejection of a simple dichotomous view means that the key theoretical question we should address also needs to change. Rather than debating whether working memory is unitary or not, the key issue may be to specify the source(s) of domain-specific effects found in both experimental (e.g., dual-task) studies and correlational studies. If one postulates a domain-general factor, another key issue is to specify the extent to which the domain-general and domain-specific factors, respectively, contribute to constraining working memory performance.

Theme 6: Long-Term Knowledge Plays an Integral Role in Working Memory Performance

The last point of emerging consensus is that long-term knowledge and skills play an integral role in working memory performance and, hence, that working memory cannot be understood without considering these factors. This point was rather surprising to us, because, when we planned this volume, our impression was that the contribution of long-term knowledge and skills was generally not well appreciated or at least not emphasized in the existing models of working memory. To the best of our knowledge, Ericsson and Kintsch's (1995) then brand-new "long-term working memory" (LT-WM) article was the only theoretical proposal exclusively dedicated to this issue.

In contrast to our original expectation, however, many contributors to this volume other than Ericsson and Delaney (Chapter 8) either enthusiastically or cautiously endorse the LT-WM proposal (most notably, Baddeley & Logie, Chapter 2; Cowan, Chapter 3; Young & Lewis, Chapter 7; O'Reilly et al., Chapter 11). For example, Young and Lewis discuss how Soar's performance in complex cognitive tasks can exhibit LT-WM phenomena. From a more cognitive neuroscience perspective, O'Reilly et al. discuss how the interactions between the hippocampus (creation and storage of retrieval structures) and the PFC (controlled encoding and retrieval as well as active maintenance of retrieval cues) could account for LT-WM phenomena.

The contribution of long-term knowledge to working memory performance is also explicitly acknowledged even for simpler, laboratory tasks like the immediate serial recall of words (Baddeley & Logie, Chapter 2; Cowan, Chapter 3). Cowan, for example, proposes the notion of "virtual short-term memory" – an LTM that, along with other factors (such as temporal distinctiveness), could make some memory representations more easily retrievable (Cowan, 1995). Although the precise mechanism underlying this virtual STM has yet to be specified, Cowan's proposal nonetheless highlights the integral role of LTM and knowledge in working memory performance.

It is important to point out that even the models that do not give long-term knowledge and skills a central status in their theoretical accounts (Engle et al., Chapter 4; Lovett et al., Chapter 5) also acknowledge that such factors play a role in working memory tasks. Although these models put much less emphasis on the knowledge and skills factor, such differences may simply reflect a difference in scope and emphasis. As Ericsson and Delaney (Chapter 8) argue, models like Engle et al.'s and Lovett et al.'s may primarily capture people's performance on relatively novel tasks to which prior knowledge and skills cannot contribute much, whereas models like Ericsson and Delaney's and Young and Lewis's (Chapter 7) primarily capture highly skilled performance on everyday tasks.

What Is Working Memory?

Having considered the six themes of general consensus, we can now return to the question that we first brought up in Chapter 1, "What is working memory, anyway?" We would argue that the six themes directly speak to this question, at least by characterizing what working memory is, what working memory is not, and what working memory is for. Based on these themes, as well as the particular definitions of working memory provided by the contributors in their chapters (see Table 13.1), we would like to propose the following, all-encompassing definition of working memory:

Working memory is those mechanisms or processes that are involved in the control, regulation, and active maintenance of task-relevant information in the service of complex cognition, including novel as well as familiar, skilled tasks. It consists of a set of processes and mechanisms and is not a fixed "place" or "box" in the cognitive architecture. It is not a completely unitary system in the sense that it involves multiple representational codes and/or different subsystems. Its capacity limits reflect multiple factors and may even be an emergent property of the multiple processes and mechanisms involved. Working memory is closely linked to LTM, and its contents consist primarily of currently activated LTM representations, but can also extend to LTM memory representations that are closely linked to activated retrieval cues and, hence, can be quickly reactivated.

This definition captures all six points of general consensus that unify the models of working memory in this volume and thus provides a reasonable answer to the frequently asked embarrassing question, "What is working memory, anyway?" Moreover, being able to pull many common themes out of 10 different models clearly suggests that H. J. Eysenck's (1986) characterization of intelligence theories does not apply to working memory research.

Table 13.1. *The Definition of Working Memory Offered by Each Theory Chapter of This Volume*

Chapter 2 (Baddeley & Logie)

"[W]orking memory . . . comprises those functional components of cognition that allow humans to comprehend and mentally represent their immediate environment, to retain information about their immediate past experience, to support the acquisition of new knowledge, to solve problems, and to formulate, relate, and act on current goals" (pp. 28–29).

Chapter 3 (Cowan)

"[W]orking memory refers to cognitive processes that retain information in an unusually accessible state, suitable for carrying out any task with a mental component. . . . The mnemonic functions preserving information that can be used to do the necessary work collectively make up working memory. This is a functional definition in that any processing mechanisms contributing to the desired outcome, which is the temporary availability of information, are said to participate in the working memory system" (pp. 62–63).

Chapter 4 (Engle, Kane, & Tuholski)

"We think of 'working memory' as a system consisting of (a) a store in the form of long-term memory traces active above threshold, (b) processes for achieving and maintaining that activation, and (c) controlled attention" (p. 104).

Chapter 5 (Lovett, Reder, & Lebiere)

"[From a functional perspective, working memory is] the *process* that enables memory elements to be concurrently maintained. This definition takes working memory as the propagation of source activation from the current goal" (p. 143). "[From a content-oriented perspective, working memory is] the content that is being maintained during processing (e.g., the elements representing the memory items in a working memory task). This content-oriented definition identifies working memory as a subset of the entire declarative memory. That is, working memory is not a special repository of information but just those declarative nodes that are highly activated . . ." (p. 143).

Chapter 6 (Kieras, Meyer, Mueller, & Seymour)

"[W]e take 'working memory' to encompass the entire ensemble of temporary stored codes, knowledge representations, and procedures whereby information is maintained, updated, and applied for performing perceptual-motor and cognitive tasks" (p. 185).

Chapter 7 (Young & Lewis)

"*Working memory* refers to those computational mechanisms that maintain and provide access to information created or retrieved during the performance of a task. Any computationally complete system must support such functionality, because computation is inherently a process that requires the temporary storage and manipulation of partial and intermediate products" (p. 230).

continued

Table 13.1, continued

Chapter 8 (Ericsson & Delaney)
"[W]e will advocate the broadest possible description of working memory and its possible mechanisms. At the most general level, the essence of the concept of working memory (or that part of memory that works) is that only a minute fraction of all the knowledge, skills, and information stored in subjects' vast long-term memory is influencing the subjects' behavior and thought processes at a specific instant of time. Hence, the phenomenon of working memory includes *all those mechanisms that maintain selective access to the information and the procedures that are necessary for a subject to complete one or more specific concurrent tasks"* (p. 260).

Chapter 9 (Barnard)
"Working memory per se is not a core construct in the ICS framework. The properties of performance on working memory tasks are attributed to process-mediated interactions among multiple subsystems of cognition. Processes within each subsystem have access to a repertoire of representations of its past inputs stored in the form of image records" (personal communication).

Chapter 10 (Schneider)
"[W]orking memory shall be defined as short-term activation and connection changes that support maintenance, planning, and the organization of cognitive operations in the performance of short-term tasks (minutes). Working memory has many components depending on its form (activation or weights), its parameters (decay rate, learning rate), its knowledge specialization (visual perception, goal planning), and its connection pathways (including loops supporting reactivation)" (p. 341).

Chapter 11 (O'Reilly, Braver, & Cohen)
"We define working memory as controlled processing involving active maintenance and/or rapid learning, where controlled processing is an emergent property of the dynamic interactions of multiple brain systems . . ." (p.375).

Even though they may appear rather disparate on the surface, the models of working memory are actually more in agreement than in disagreement, more in illumination than in smoke.

Unresolved Theoretical Issues for the Eight Designated Questions

Although we find it exciting and encouraging to see the emergence of such general agreements about the fundamental nature of working memory at a global level, the glass is only half full. At a more microlevel of analysis, there are many disagreements and unresolved issues. In other words, the foregoing definition serves only as a starting point for further explorations of working memory and development of more comprehensive, explicitly specified models and theories.

In this section, we outline our view of how we can go about filling the empty half of the glass. More specifically, we point out some of the unresolved theoretical issues (including major disagreements) that have become clear to us in the process of making issue-by-issue comparisons of the 10 models of working memory and development of more comprehensive explicitly specified models and theories. We also outline our prescription of how to address these unresolved issues in future research.

Question 1: Basic Mechanisms and Representations in Working Memory

In Chapter 12, Kintsch et al. pointed out that the issue of basic mechanisms (encoding, maintenance, and retrieval) and representational formats is not satisfactorily handled by the chapters in this volume. We essentially agree with this assessment, but in our view the problem reflects a characteristic trade-off between computational and noncomputational models. Specifically, noncomputational models tend to offer accounts of basic mechanisms and representations based on (or consistent with) empirical findings, but their accounts are sometimes quite vague. In contrast, computational models have the potential of providing more detailed specifications of the basic mechanisms and representations, but they often include seemingly arbitrary assumptions that lack a strong empirical basis.

One promising approach to circumventing this dilemma, suggested by Kieras et al. (Chapter 6), is to create explicit computational models and evaluate how well they can make precise *quantitative* predictions about the effects of *parametric* manipulations of some relevant factor. In addition, we advocate combining this approach with the "competitive argumentation" technique (VanLehn, Brown, & Greeno, 1984) – pitting different models (or different versions of the same model) with different assumptions about the basic mechanisms and representations against one another to see which model or version fits the data best. Such an approach takes advantage of the precision of the computational approach and the empirical strength of the noncomputational approach to specify basic mechanisms.

In retrospect, we realize that one major reason why many chapters in this volume did not directly address the answers to Question 1 in terms of the concepts used to frame that question – encoding, maintenance, retrieval, and representation format – is that those issues have been explored primarily in the context of STM research, focusing on pure memory processes, rather than memory processes that operate in the service of complex cognition. Given this reason, the lack of clear, well-focused discussion of the basic mechanism and representation issue is totally understandable. Nonetheless, we find it an important task to precisely characterize exactly how the encoding, maintenance, and retrieval of task-relevant information take place within the context of specific complex cognitive tasks.

Recent research has already begun to move in that direction. For example, Engle and his colleagues (Conway & Engle, 1994; Rosen & Engle, 1997) recently examined the mechanisms of the retrieval process from a working memory perspective (Engle et al., Chapter 4). The LT-WM account (Ericsson & Kintsch, 1995) has also provided a useful framework to examine the encoding and retrieval processes implicated in skilled everyday activities (Ericsson & Delaney, Chapter 8). Moreover, as we argue later in this chapter, expanding the scope of working memory research to encompass the role of external representations and actions provides a new way to examine the encoding, maintenance, and retrieval issues in the context of complex cognition (Ballard, Hayhoe, Pook, & Rao, 1997; Carlson, Wenger, & Sullivan, 1993).

Question 2: The Control and Regulation of Working Memory

The chapters in this volume all recognize the importance of precisely specifying the control and regulatory mechanisms of working memory (Theme 3). However, serious attempts have begun only recently, and there are a number of important unresolved issues. We point out two here.

One issue concerns a specification of the relationship between the active maintenance and executive control functions of working memory. The models in this volume offer two different characterizations of this issue. Some chapters explicitly advocate segregating these two functions. For example, in their chapter, Baddeley and Logie (Chapter 2) argue that their current conceptualization of working memory no longer attributes any storage capabilities to the once-almighty central executive. Engle et al. (Chapter 4) make the same argument by proposing that working memory is STM (maintenance) plus "controlled attention" (executive control). In contrast, other chapters argue for a more intertwined relationship between maintenance and executive control. According to Lovett et al. (Chapter 5), for example, the maintenance of working memory elements (such as goals) is essential for appropriate control and regulation of cognitive behavior to arise. A similar argument applies to O'Reilly et al.'s account (Chapter 11). One important research question, thus, is to evaluate the degree to which the maintenance function and the executive control functions of working memory are separable.

Another unresolved issue concerns a precise specification of different executive control functions and their interrelationship. As some chapters pointed out (Baddeley & Logie, Chapter 2; Engle et al., Chapter 4), attempts to classify and examine different executive functions have begun recently (e.g., Baddeley, 1996a, in press; see also Schneider, Chapter 10). Some of the most often mentioned executive functions include (a) switching attention between multiple tasks and mental sets (Rogers & Monsell, 1995); (b) active inhibition or suppression of prepotent responses or irrelevant information (Roberts, Hager, & Heron, 1994); (c) monitoring and updating of the content of working memory (Van der Linden, Bredart, & Beerten, 1994); (d) temporal tagging and contextual coding of incoming information (Jonides & Smith, 1997); and

(e) planning and sequencing of intended actions (Ward & Allport, 1997). Although the detailed specification of each of these executive functions is an important task, an equally important question is how these presumed executive functions relate to one another. Are these functions somewhat independent? Or is it the case that they are closely related functions and even reflect a common underlying mechanism?

Various approaches can be taken to address this issue. One approach may be to computationally investigate whether separate mechanisms need to be postulated to account for task performance considered to implicate different executive functions (Kimberg & Farah, 1993). Another approach may be to perform a latent-variable analysis (Engle, Tuholski, Laughlin, & Conway, in press; see also Engle et al., Chapter 4) of different postulated executive functions. Most individual-differences studies of executive functions conducted so far have focused on zero-order correlations among various so-called frontal tasks (such as the Wisconsin Card Sorting Task and the verbal fluency task), without detailed analyses of what executive functions and what other nonexecutive functions (e.g., visual analysis, verbal processing) each "frontal task" specifically taps. The problem with such studies is that it is not completely clear whether the often-reported lack of correlation among these "frontal tasks" truly reflects the independence of different executive functions (Duncan, Johnson, Swales, & Freer, 1997; Rabbitt, 1997b). Instead, it is quite possible that major differences in nonexecutive processing requirements have simply masked the existence of some underlying commonalities among the chosen "frontal tasks." Thus, carefully selecting multiple tasks that specifically tap the target executive functions and examining the relationships among them at the level of latent variables may be a more powerful approach.

Question 3: The Unitary Versus Non-Unitary Nature of Working Memory

As we discussed earlier, the general consensus that a completely unitary model of working memory does not hold (Theme 5) requires a major reframing of the unitary versus non-unitary issue, because it no longer makes sense to decide, in a dichotomous fashion, whether working memory is unitary or not. A more interesting question is how the effects of domain-specificity should be accounted for. The possible sources for domain specificity mentioned in this volume include (a) domain-specific subsystems or storage buffers; (b) similarity-based interference; (c) domain-specific knowledge, skills, and strategies; and (d) domain-specific processing speed. We believe that future research should determine the relative contribution of these factors to different types of domain-specific effects reported in the literature.

One type of domain-specific effect, for example, concerns the results from dual-task studies using different secondary tasks, such as articulatory suppression and spatial tapping, which have been shown to exert remarkably domain-specific influence (Baddeley & Logie, Chapter 2). Another type of domain-specific effect concerns the correlational dissociations found between complex working memory span measures such as reading span and spatial span (Daneman & Tardif, 1987; Shah & Miyake, 1996). It is quite likely that different factors contribute differentially to various types of domain-specific effects of working memory found in the literature, and the important task is to specify which of these factors underlie each of these effects.

Although it is difficult to completely tease apart the effects of the afore-mentioned factors, some of the factors are amenable to specific manipulations (e.g., extended practice, specific instructions as to the strategy to use) or to correlational (or latent variables) analyses. As for the correlational dissociations, one way to investigate the underlying factors may be to conduct behavioral genetics studies, which attempt to decouple the role of genetic and environmental (shared vs. nonshared) factors by examining special populations such as identical and nonidentical twins and children in adoptive families[3] (e.g., Plomin, Fulker, Corley, & DeFries, 1997). If the domain specificity of working memory is mainly owing to differences in experience (such as skills and knowledge), then the separability effect should strongly reflect environmental factors. Of course, one difficulty with behavioral genetics methods is that because genetic and environmental factors influence each other, partitioning of variance into different factors is not necessarily clear-cut. Nevertheless, a demonstration of substantial environmental influences for the separability of, say, reading and spatial spans among college students may point to a major contribution of the knowledge and skills factor to such correlational dissociations.

Question 4: The Nature of Working Memory Limitations

The general consensus that there are multiple capacity-limiting factors (Theme 4) also shifts the focus of research on the nature of working memory limitations. As we argued before, pitting one factor against another in a dichotomous manner to determine which factor can provide the best account of the data no longer makes much sense. Rather, we believe that an important research question is to specify the relative importance of different capacity-limiting factors for each target population and for each type of task. One likely possibility is that the nature of working memory constraints varies as a function of the novelty and/or complexity of the task (Ericsson & Delaney, Chapter 8). Another possibility is that different capacity-limiting factors may be more important to account for age-related changes in working memory

---

[3] Behavioral genetics methods have recently been applied successfully to demonstrate the genetic contribution to the functioning of phonological STM (Bishop, North, & Donlan, 1996; Wadsworth, DeFries, Fulker, Olson, & Pennington, 1995).

during adulthood than to account for individual differences in working memory among college students. For example, processing speed might be a more important factor (i.e., in terms of the amount of variance it can account for) in age-related changes in working memory than in individual differences among college students. Although it is highly possible that some common factor may play an important role across different populations and across different types of tasks, its level of contribution is unlikely to be uniform. We thus would like to emphasize that future attempts to specify the nature of working memory limitations or the individual differences thereof should be highly precise as to the tasks or populations under investigation.

The likely importance of multiple capacity-limiting mechanisms brings up another unresolved issue. In general, different capacity-limiting mechanisms are unlikely to be completely independent of each other; indeed, they (or at least some of them) are likely to be related to one another. For example, at least as far as cognitive aging is concerned, the two often mentioned sources of age-related differences in working memory – efficiency of inhibitory mechanisms and processing speed – are closely related to each other in the sense that they share a lot of common variance (Salthouse & Meinz, 1995). The question is what such a relationship indicates. Is it the case that slower processing speed somehow leads to less-efficient inhibition processes, as Salthouse and Meinz (1995) seem to suggest? Alternatively, can inefficient inhibition lead to slower processing speed? Or is there a third underlying factor that influences both processing speed and inhibition?

This issue may be rather difficult to resolve on a purely empirical basis, and we believe that computational explorations might be particularly beneficial. Within the context of a specific cognitive architecture, one can explore how one or a small number of constraining mechanisms might naturally affect other capacity-constraining factors. For example, in the 3CAPS framework (Just & Carpenter, 1992), the postulated limit in the total amount of activation can put constraints on two other often-mentioned sources of capacity limits – slower processing speed and/or faster decay of information. Currently, the accounts of the sources of working memory limitations seem somewhat chaotic at a microlevel of analysis, but such systematic computational explorations of the relationships among different capacity-constraining factors may help synthesize the seemingly disparate claims.

Question 5: The Role of Working Memory in Complex Cognitive Activities

Although we are generally impressed with the research progress made on the issue of the role of working memory in complex cognitive activities, we submit two specific issues as important future research agendas for Question 5.

First, as Kintsch et al. (Chapter 12) briefly pointed out, it is important to examine how different subsystems of working memory work together as a whole. Most previous research addressing the role of working memory in complex cognition has focused on tasks primarily implicating one particular subsystem or aspect of working memory within a single domain (e.g., language processing, visuospatial processing). Although we recognize the potential benefit of focusing on one subsystem or domain at a time, the performance of many everyday cognitive activities (e.g., watching a television show, comprehending an illustrated text) requires the involvement of multiple different subsystems (or at least different codes, representations, and/or types of processes). Thus, elucidating how these different subsystems work together as a whole in integrating and coordinating multiple sources of information might be one fruitful research direction.

Second, it also seems important to take a closer look at the two methodological tools that have guided much research on the role of working memory in complex cognition – dual-task performance and complex working memory span tasks. Although both the dual-task approach and the individual-differences approach have made important contributions in the field (Shah & Miyake, Chapter 1), there seems to be no clear agreement as to how people perform two or more tasks simultaneously or as to what working memory span tasks really measure.

As for dual-task performance, since the heyday of resource theories of attention in the late 1970s and the early 1980s (Navon & Gopher, 1979; Norman & Bobrow, 1975; Wickens, 1984), not much theoretical work has been done to characterize dual-task performance, particularly with respect to exactly *how* people manage to coordinate multiple tasks simultaneously. As briefly mentioned by Kieras et al. (Chapter 6), recent accounts of a relatively simple dual-task situation, called the psychological refractory period (PRP) phenomenon, disagree as to whether the interference effect reflects a response selection bottleneck (Pashler, 1994) or task-specific strategies (Meyer & Kieras, 1997). Explanations of more-complex dual-task situations are also controversial. According to the traditional explanation, a fixed amount of flexibly deployable "attentional resources" must be divided between the two different tasks, supporting the simultaneous execution of both (Kahneman, 1973). In contrast, a more recent explanation argues that one can pay attention to only one task at a time and, hence, that dual-task performance essentially involves the rapid switching back and forth of attention between the two tasks (Pashler, 1992). Given that dual-task performance is a signature working memory task, resolving such seemingly contradictory claims about dual-task performance and developing a coherent, mechanistic account of exactly how people handle dual-task situations is an important goal.[4]

---

[4] In this context, we should also note that specifying exactly what the random number (or letter) generation task really taps is an important task. Despite the prevalent use of this task as a secondary task that disrupts central executive functioning (see Baddeley & Logie, Chapter 2), its underlying processes and task demand have only begun to be examined in detail (e.g., Towse, 1998; Towse & Valentine, 1997; Vandierendonck, De Vooght, & Van der Goten, 1998).

As for working memory span tasks, several chapters in this volume propose different explanations of what they really measure and why they are often good predictors of complex cognitive tasks. Engle et al. (Chapter 4), for example, propose that working memory span tasks measure the STM capacity plus one's "controlled attention" ability, particularly the ability to switch attention between processing and storage requirements (see Baddeley & Logie, Chapter 2, for a similar claim). They further add that it is this "controlled attention" ability that is responsible for the correlation between working memory span tasks and fluid intelligence tasks. In contrast, Ericsson and Delaney (Chapter 8) argue that individual differences in span tasks reflect differences in encoding and retrieval skills, more specifically, the ability to encode in, and retrieve to-be-recalled items from, LTM. Both of these accounts are yet different from other existing accounts (e.g., Stoltzfus, Hasher, & Zacks, 1996; Towse, Hitch, & Hutton, 1998; Waters & Caplan, 1996), including the original proposal by Daneman and Carpenter (1980) that performance on working memory span tasks reflects the amount of residual resources that can be allocated for storage purposes after processing. To the extent that much of the individual-differences research is built on these working memory tasks, it is essential to evaluate these claims – while keeping in mind that they are not necessarily mutually incompatible – and precisely specify what working memory spans really measure and where their predictive powers come from.

Question 6: The Relationship of Working Memory to Long-Term Memory and Knowledge

Although answers to the sixth designated question provide a major source of two common themes (Themes 1 and 6), the precise mechanisms by which long-term knowledge and skills contribute to working memory performance are not necessarily clear. Consider, for example, Cowan's (Chapter 3) proposal of the notion of "virtual STM," which seems on the surface quite similar to Ericsson and Kintsch's LT-WM. Ericsson and Delaney (Chapter 8), however, argue that some important differences exist between virtual STM and LT-WM (Chapter 8, p. 267), and we agree. Although both notions can be applied to the immediate serial recall paradigm, LT-WM involves much more elaborate encoding (i.e., deliberate, skilled creation of retrieval structures), as in the case of expert digit recall performance, whereas virtual STM does not seem to involve such deliberate encoding.

Even within the LT-WM account, we see some differences between its explanation of memorization tasks such as expert digit recall and of more complex, cognitive tasks such as discourse comprehension. In the case of expert digit recall, the underlying retrieval structures are quite clear and well specified, and the creation and encoding of such structures undoubtedly involve deliberate use of acquired skills and strategies. In contrast, discourse comprehension does not seem to involve exactly the same types of processes. Although readers are constructing mental structures or representations of the

text during comprehension (Kintsch, 1998), the construction of such structures is certainly not as deliberate as in the case of expert digit recall, nor are
they likely to be as nicely structured as the ones created by expert
mnemonists during the encoding of digits (see Figure 8.3 in Chapter 8). Thus,
it is not completely clear to us whether the identical mechanism can account
for both types of LT-WM phenomena.

To further complicate the situation, the LT-WM account presented by
Ericsson and Delaney (Chapter 8) may not be the only way to account for
various LT-WM phenomena (e.g., readers being able to go back to the text
quickly after a lengthy interruption). Activation-based models like ACT-R
(Lovett et al., Chapter 5) and 3CAPS (Just & Carpenter, 1992), for example,
can accommodate many of these findings relatively easily in terms of working memory elements (WME) whose activation levels are under the threshold value (hence, technically not "in" working memory), but are not
completely zero, either. If one assumes that the underlying activation function is a nonlinear, sigmoid function (e.g., Lovett et al., Chapter 5; Cohen,
Dunbar, & McClelland, 1990), then one could argue that a WME with a just-
below-threshold level of activation could easily get reactivated and become
available "in" working memory (e.g., Baddeley & Hitch, 1993), once related
concepts or cues are presented and provide an activation "boost" via spreading activation (or any other mechanisms postulated in the architecture).
Although this activation–based account involves an extra assumption about
the activation-decay function, it can serve as a basis for explaining the LT-
WM phenomena without postulating a distinction between short-term working memory (ST-WM) and LTM.

Given that there are multiple ways of accounting for the contribution of
long-term knowledge and skills (see also the accounts provided by Young &
Lewis, Chapter 7; O'Reilly et al., Chapter 11), the challenge is to more precisely specify the mechanisms that operate under different task situations
and conditions. If different accounts based on mutually incompatible
assumptions can explain the same types of processes, then going beyond the
sufficiency argument seems to be in order. If different accounts reflect differences in perspectives and are, hence, complementary to one another, an
important task will be to examine the relationships among the postulated
mechanisms. One possibility is that the three types of phenomena demonstrating the close relationship between working memory and LTM we discussed here – Cowan's virtual STM account as applied to immediate serial
recall, Ericsson and Kintsch's (1995) LT-WM account as applied to discourse
comprehension and applied to expert digit recall performance – may be on a
continuum (particularly in terms of the deliberateness of the encoding
process and the well-structuredness of the resulting retrieval structure), with
virtual STM on the one end of the continuum, expert digit recall on the other
end, and discourse comprehension somewhere in the middle.

Question 7: The Relationship of Working Memory to Attention and Consciousness

Whereas there seems to be clear emerging consensus regarding Question 6, the same cannot be said about Question 7. Some chapters in this volume provided interesting discussions on this topic (particularly on the relationship between working memory and attention), but, somewhat ironically, it is clearly a theoretical issue that has not received much "attention" from current models of working memory. Other than the already well-accepted point that working memory, attention, and consciousness are closely related to one another, we do not see any new emerging consensus that runs across all 10 models covered in this volume.

In our analysis, the set of answers to Question 7 provided in this volume is quite analogous to the clichéd metaphor of several blind persons touching different parts of an elephant, trying to describe to one another what it is like. Although the characterization of the relationship among working memory, attention, and consciousness offered in each chapter is certainly reasonable, it seems to be telling only part of the story, a rather small fraction. In the case of attention, the chapters focused on different aspects of attention and elaborated how the aspect of their choice may relate to their conceptualization of working memory. Although this analogy is less appropriate in the case of consciousness, Kintsch et al. (Chapter 12) pointed out the possibility of at least two different types of consciousness related to working memory in different ways. We believe that the field needs to go beyond this situation and develop a more comprehensive account of the relationships among the three constructs in question.

In our view, the most efficient way of moving toward that goal may be to explicitly acknowledge that both attention and consciousness are not completely unitary constructs and are associated with different functions and properties. As we argued earlier (Themes 4 and 5), the models of working memory in this volume are in unanimous agreement in regard to the multifaceted nature of working memory. Given the available evidence (for a review, see Allport, 1993; Styles, 1997), it also makes sense to us to consider both attention and consciousness multifaceted and then start systematically mapping the relationships between aspects of working memory and those of attention or consciousness.

The field of attention has already provided some useful distinctions that could be related to some ideas discussed in this volume. Posner and his colleagues (Posner & Peterson, 1990; Posner & Raichle, 1994), for example, introduced a distinction between the posterior attention network (or the network for visual orienting) and the anterior attention network (or the executive attention network). In Chapter 4, Engle et al. discussed the anterior attention system, which involves the anterior cingulate gyrus, a brain region that is located in the center of the brain and has a close connection to the dorsolateral portion of PFC. Baddeley's (1993) notion of "working attention" can also be mapped onto Posner's anterior portion of attention. In contrast, some chapters emphasized the role of attention as determining which sensory information enters into working memory (Cowan, Chapter 3; Kieras et al., Chapter 6; Schneider, Chapter 10). Clearly, this aspect of attention, when limited to visual information, is more closely related to Posner's posterior attention network, which primarily implicates the parietal lobes. Although not mentioned in this volume, this posterior attention network may also be related to the maintenance or rehearsal mechanisms of spatial information (Awh & Jonides, 1998), one of the basic mechanisms that has not yet been sufficiently worked out.

Of course, this global-level distinction of Posner's is not the only classification scheme currently available, and there are other interesting classification schemes that might be useful to map out the relationship between attention and working memory (Allport, 1993; Pashler, 1997; Stuss, Shallice, Alexander, & Picton, 1995). As the brief example based on Posner's scheme illustrates, however, this type of systematic mapping between specific aspects of working memory and those of attention may be an efficient approach to developing a comprehensive model of the relationship between working memory and attention that goes beyond the currently somewhat fragmentary situation. Although classifications of consciousness are highly controversial, a similar approach might also be applicable to the specification of the relationship between working memory and consciousness (see Kintsch et al., Chapter 12, for more detailed discussions on the relationship between working memory and consciousness).

Question 8: The Biological Implementation of Working Memory

Although there has been significant progress in understanding the neural basis of working memory, one specific controversial issue that needs to be addressed in future research concerns the organization of the PFC, particularly the dorsolateral PFC. As O'Reilly et al. (Chapter 11) briefly mentioned, the debate concerns whether the dorsolateral PFC is organized in terms of content (domains) or functions (processes). Based on their elegant single-cell recording and lesioning work in nonhuman primates, Goldman-Rakic and her colleagues argue that the dorsolateral PFC includes regions specialized, at least to some degree, for specific types or domains of information, such as objects, locations, and so on (Goldman-Rakic, 1995; see also Courtney, Petit, Maisog, Ungerleider, & Haxby, 1998). In contrast, some researchers argue instead that the PFC may be organized in terms of the nature of the processing or operations performed, rather than the content or domain of information being processed (Fuster, 1995; Petrides, 1995).

Indeed, recent meta-analytic reviews of functional neuroimaging studies from humans seem to be more in line with the function-specific organization hypothesis (D'Esposito, Aguirre, Zarahn, Ballard, & Shin, 1998; Owen, 1997). Also, a recent single-cell recording study has shown that only some cells in the dorsolateral PFC play specialized roles and that other cells are more multipurpose and are sensitive to different contents of information (Rao, Rainer, & Miller, 1997). These findings suggest that at least an extreme domain-specific view of the dorsolateral PFC organization may not hold (we also suspect that an extreme version of the function-specific view may not hold, either). As O'Reilly et al. (Chapter 11) indicate, however, the nature of the underlying dimensions is currently unclear, and further research on this issue is likely to have important implications for the organization of working memory.

In addition to this specific unresolved issue, we would like to raise two more general issues regarding future cognitive neuroscience research on working memory. First, even more than cognitive psychological studies of working memory, cognitive neuroscience studies tend to focus on one highly specific aspect of working memory at a time, using rather simple experimental tasks. This general tendency is quite understandable, and there is nothing inherently wrong with the approach, particularly at this early stage. However, we would like to see more cognitive neuroscience studies that illuminate how different regions of the brain dynamically work together as a whole to enable the performance of complex cognitive tasks. D'Esposito and his colleagues' recent (1995) fMRI work is an excellent example of this exciting new line of research. In this study, D'Esposito et al. (1995) examined patterns of brain activation while participants were performing a spatial task (mental rotation) and a verbal task (semantic verification) concurrently. The key finding of the study is that, when the two tasks are performed simultaneously, the dorsolateral PFC is activated (as well as parts of the brain regions implicated in the performance of the spatial and verbal tasks), even though neither of the tasks activates that particular area by itself. This result suggests that some sort of executive control processes, in which the PFC seems to play an important role, are implicated in coordination of multiple tasks simultaneously.

Second, different levels of analyses used in the cognitive neuroscience studies of working memory need to be bridged and synthesized. Although there are many interesting studies that have potentially important implications for models of working memory, it is not necessarily clear (at least to many cognitive psychologists) how individual findings from different levels of analysis fit together (e.g., cellular-level analysis vs. systems-level analysis). We hope to see more integration and synthesis of neuroscience findings from different levels of analysis so that the implications of not only systems-level but also cellular-level and neurotransmitter-level findings for models of working memory can be more fully appreciated (Fuster's, 1997, recent synthesis of the frontal lobe functions is one example). We consider this a crucially important step for one of the major goals of current working memory research – namely, more fully integrating cognitive psychological and cognitive neuroscience models of working memory.

Other Future Directions for Working Memory Research

The previous section pointed out some of the unresolved theoretical issues that need to be addressed in future research for each of the eight designated questions. Although those questions covered a wide range of theoretical issues, there are several important topics that we believe will become increasingly important, but that have not been adequately addressed so far by the models in this volume. These topics, discussed in this section, are presented in the spirit of Baddeley's (1996b) recent remark, "[working memory] sits at the intersection of research on memory with that of perception and action, and its future would seem to depend at least in part on its continuing capacity to integrate with the surrounding fields" (p. 22). Systematic explorations of these virtually uncharted territories will further expand the horizons of current models of working memory and, hence, assure working memory research a continuing role as "a microcosm of the field of cognition" (Haberlandt, 1997, p. 213).

Functional Significance of Limited Working Memory

Although the nature of working memory limitations has been one of the central research issues in this field, one important question that has received surprisingly little attention so far is the functional (or evolutionary) significance of working memory limitations: Why is our working memory capacity limited in the first place? This question presents an interesting paradox because, as numerous individual-differences studies have demonstrated (Engle et al., Chapter 4), individuals with larger working memory capacities are almost always better off than those with smaller capacities in performing various complex cognitive tasks. If a large working memory capacity is a preferable – or arguably, an adaptive – attribute, then why should it be so limited?

One possibility is that it reflects some sort of evolutionary fluke and does not have much functional significance. Indeed, Anderson (1990) expressed such a view, speculating that "short-term memory limitations do not have a rational explanation" and may "reflect the human trapped on some local optimum of evolution" (pp. 91–92).

It may also be the case, however, that there are some interesting functional or computational reasons for the limitations of working memory. One such reason, mentioned briefly by Lovett et al. (Chapter 5) as well as O'Reilly et al. (Chapter 11), is that the limitation may serve to help prevent too much activity in the brain and keep the ongoing cognitive processes well-focused and coherent (see also Glenberg, 1997, for a related argument). Another argument supporting the functional benefits of working memory limitations arises from synchronous oscillation models of "binding" (Halford, Wilson, & Phillips, 1998; Hummel & Holyoak, 1997; Shastri & Ajjanagadde, 1993). According to these accounts, binding of different attributes of an item takes place by synchronous firing of relevant attributes of an item; computationally, it is assumed that only one item and its attributes can be simultaneously activated so that unwanted cross-talk or interference can be avoided. This limitation, in turn, may lead to a limit in working memory, because the number of items that can be oscillated between is ultimately constrained by oscillation and neuron firing rates. These functional and computational reasons for working memory limitations are interesting proposals that seem to be particularly suited for rigorous computational exploration.

Another possible reason, which has recently gained some empirical support, is that limitations in working memory may facilitate certain types of learning. In particular, recent evidence suggests that severely restricted working memory may be particularly beneficial for detecting subtle yet important probabilistic regularities in the environment, an ability crucially important for language acquisition. A computer simulation study (Elman, 1993), for example, has shown that a recurrent connectionist network eventually fails to learn complex grammatical rules if the model is equipped with adultlike capacity from the onset. The network, however, is capable of learning the complex rules fully if it is initially "handicapped" with a limited working memory and gradually "matures" into an adultlike capacity. Similarly, another recent theoretical analysis (Kareev, 1995) proposes that a limited "window size" increases the probability of detecting meaningful yet subtle covariations present in the input, a point that was empirically supported in two recent experiments, in which a smaller working memory capacity promoted more accurate judgments of covariation present in the stimulus (Kareev, Lieberman, & Lev, 1997).

These findings are particularly intriguing from the perspective of a recent demonstration (Saffran, Aslin, & Newport, 1996) that 8-month-old infants can competently extract statistical relationships between neighboring speech sounds from only 2 minutes of exposure to the tape-recorded stimuli. As Newport's (1990) "less is more" hypothesis suggests, it may indeed be the case that limited working memory capacity is advantageous (or even necessary) for native-level attainment of linguistic competence by children.

The reason why the functional significance of capacity limitations has received little attention may be that, other than speculating on what could have possibly happened during the course of evolution, there were no obvious ways to address the question empirically. We believe that the methodologies illustrated here – computational modeling and empirically documenting cognitive tasks or situations in which less is more (i.e., a smaller working memory capacity is more advantageous than a larger capacity) – should help our understanding of this important yet so far neglected question.

External Memory, External Action, and Working Memory

In their chapter, Ericsson and Delaney (Chapter 8) proposed the LT-WM framework as an account of how long-term knowledge and skills can supplement or help overcome the severe capacity limits associated with what they call ST-WM. As briefly pointed out by Kintsch et al. (Chapter 12), however, another important yet neglected way to supplement or overcome limitations in ST-WM concerns the use of external representations and external actions. Despite the fact that the use of external memory aids is ubiquitous in everyday life (e.g., using paper and pencil to solve arithmetic problems, drawing diagrams to solve syllogistic reasoning problems) and that the role of external representations and actions in cognition is an important topic in cognitive science (Hutchins, 1995; Larkin & Simon, 1987; Suchman, 1987), all the chapters in this volume focused almost exclusively on internal processes and representations. We believe that it is time to extend our notion of working memory one step further and incorporate the role of external representations and actions into theoretical accounts of working memory.

We suspect that the role of external representations in complex cognition has been neglected by working memory researchers primarily because external memory has been viewed as a simple memory aid, something that eliminates or at least greatly reduces internal memory load. This prevalent view is too simplistic, however. During the performance of many (if not all) complex everyday cognitive tasks, the processing of external information and internal information needs to interact dynamically, going back and forth between information distributed across the internal mind and the external world (Zhang, 1997). Working memory, we would argue, may serve as the important interface between external representations and internal representations.

Indeed, subtle changes in external representations can exert a powerful effect on a task's demand and, consequently, an individual's performance on that task. Zhang and Norman (1994), for example, recently investigated the role of external representations, using various isomorphs of the Tower of Hanoi puzzle. In a series of experiments, they manipulated the number of puzzle rules that were required to be internally remembered and those that could easily be inferred from the external representation of the task itself and, hence, did not need to be remembered. The main finding of these experiments was that, when more rules were externally represented, problem solving was faster and more accurate, suggesting that processing internally represented rules poses a heavy demand on working memory and, hence, makes other crucial problem-solving processes (such as planning and goal management) suffer.

In addition to external representations, external actions can also influence working memory in interesting ways. A classic demonstration of this point comes from a study by Reisberg, Rappaport, and O'Shaughnessy (1984), which showed that digit span can be extended by combining the use of the phonological loop (via typical articulatory rehearsal) and the use of what they termed the "finger loop" (simultaneous serial tapping of fingers to which each digit is assigned). A more recent demonstration concerns Kirsh and Maglio's (1994) study of how people play a popular interactive video game called "Tetris," which requires rotating and appropriately placing continuously falling simple geometric shapes. Kirsh and Maglio's interesting observation is that, while playing this game, players usually make a lot of seemingly unnecessary moves, physically rotating each piece constantly as they fall, rather than mentally rotating it. These moves seem superfluous from the traditional view that physical actions are meant to create new physical states that advance one toward a goal, but these actions make perfect sense if they are viewed as *epistemic actions* – "physical actions that make mental computations easier, faster, or more reliable" (Kirsh & Maglio, 1994, pp. 513–514). By physically rotating the falling shapes, players can avoid demanding mental rotation processes and thereby reduce their mental computational load, which in turn allows them to focus on other crucial aspects of the game.[5]

These demonstrations of the effects of external representations and external actions on performance on complex cognitive tasks suggest that an exploration of the role of external representations and actions from the perspective of working memory might be a fruitful research avenue. In particular, specifying how external representations and actions contribute to the active maintenance of information in internal working memory or the reduction of an internal computational load is an important task. Another research agenda of central importance to models of working memory is to provide a more precise characterization of the dynamic interplay between external and internal representations. Such an interplay requires a host of executive control mechanisms, including "allocating and switching attention between internal and external representations, integrating internal and external information, and coordinating perceptual and cognitive operations" (Zhang, 1997, p. 186). Although few in number, recent studies of executive control mechanisms that interface perception and cognition (Ballard et al., 1997; Carlson et al., 1993; Hayhoe, Bensinger, & Ballard, 1998) have begun to enrich our understanding of working memory as well as promote a better understanding of problem solving and other complex cognitive tasks that involve external representations.

It is important to point out that an exploration of the role of external representations and external actions does not necessarily invalidate the notion of internal working memory, unlike what some critics might claim. Donald (1991), for example, recently argued that "[internal or what he calls biological] working memory is too transient, too vulnerable to distraction, and too limited in capacity to manage a major cognitive project that may eventually result in theoretic products" (p. 331) and that, once external representations are taken

---

[5] The use of external actions (or "epistemic actions") to supplement or help overcome limited working memory is prevalent in everyday lives. For example, when there is no access to paper and pencil, many people use their finger and palm for relatively complex mental calculations, a strategy that seems to help them retain intermediate products of their mental computations. Similarly, novice chess players often find it useful to physically move a chess piece to ponder the possible consequences of their next move.

into account, "the role of biological 'working memory' is not at all clear" (p. 332). In our view, Donald (1991) severely underestimates the importance of internal or biological working memory, particularly given how durable and robust it can be when knowledge and skills can contribute to it (Ericsson & Delaney, Chapter 8). Far from invalidating the notion of internal working memory, studies of external memory, external representations, and external actions should enrich our understanding of internal working memory.

Additional Factors Influencing Working Memory and Their Underlying Mechanisms

One popular line of research in the field examines the sources of individual differences in working memory, but most studies conducted so far on this topic have focused on interindividual variation among college students. Recent empirical research, however, has identified a host of developmental, neurological, neuropharmacological, and emotional factors that modulate not only interindividual but also intraindividual variation in working memory capacity. We believe further research is necessary to understand why and how these additional capacity-limiting factors influence working memory and then to broaden the scope of models of working memory by incorporating these factors. In this subsection, we briefly list some of the factors that have been examined, along with some pointers to recent empirical articles that outline the nature of the effects and provide a review of previous research on that topic.

DEVELOPMENTAL FACTORS. As for early development, age-related increase in children's working memory has been documented from the perspective of neo-Piagetian (Halford et al., 1998; see also Engle et al., Chapter 4) and information-processing approaches (Cowan, 1997; see also Cowan, Chapter 3). At the other end of the developmental spectrum, a series of recent studies have identified a set of factors – such as processing speed (Byrne, 1998; Salthouse, 1996), efficiency of inhibition (Stoltzfus et al., 1996; Zacks & Hasher, 1997), and a subtle decline in perceptual ability (Pichora-Fuller, Schneider, & Daneman, 1995) – that may be mediating a well-documented age-related decline in working memory capacity.

NEUROLOGICAL FACTORS. Brain pathologies, whether acquired or developmental, can also have a profound influence on working memory performance. Table 13.2 lists a wide range of acquired and developmental disorders for which some sort of working memory deficits are suspected or reported. The nature of the working memory deficits in these populations, however, seems to vary from disorder to disorder. Children with specific language impairments, for example, have problems in phonological working memory, whereas that aspect of working memory is usually relatively spared in patients with Alzheimer's disease.

NEUROPHARMACOLOGICAL FACTORS. Neuropharmacological factors can also influence working memory capacity. Consistent with O'Reilly et al.'s

---

Table 13.2. *Acquired and Developmental Disorders Associated with Some Form of Working Memory and Executive Deficits (with Recent Publications Documenting the Nature of the Deficits)*

Acquired Pathologies

Aphasia (e.g., Caspari, Parkinson, LaPointe, & Katz, 1998; Miyake, Carpenter, & Just, 1994; Murray, Holland, & Beeson, 1997)

Frontal-lobe impairments (e.g., Baddeley, Della Sala, Papagno, & Spinnler, 1997)

Traumatic brain injury (e.g., Duncan, Johnson, Swales, & Freer, 1997; McDowell, D'Esposito, & Whyte, 1997)

Alzheimer's disease (e.g., Brugger, Monsch, Salmon, & Butters, 1996; Morris, 1994)

Parkinson's disease (e.g., Owen, Iddon, Hodges, Summers, & Robbins, 1997)

Multiple sclerosis (e.g., Arnetet et al., 1997)

Alcoholism (e.g., Rapeli, Service, Salin, & Holopainen, 1997)

Schizophrenia (e.g., Sullivan, Shear, Zipursky, Sagar, & Pfefferbaum, 1997)

Developmental Pathologies

Specific language impairment (Montgomery, 1995; Weismer, 1996)

Fragile X syndrome (e.g., Mazzocco, Hagerman, Cronister-Silverman, & Pennington, 1992)

Phenylketonuria (PKU) (e.g., Welsh, Pennington, Ozonoff, Rouse, & McCabe, 1990)

Hydrocephalus (e.g., Fletcher et al., 1996)

High-functioning autism (e.g., Bennetto, Pennington, & Rogers, 1996)

Attention deficit hyperactivity disorder (ADHD) (e.g., Barkley, 1997)

(Chapter 11) claim about the potential role of dopamine in working memory performance, recent studies have shown that the pharmacological manipulation of brain dopamine concentration (using dopamine receptor agonists like bromocriptine or antagonists like haloperidol) can modulate an individual's performance on various working memory tasks in interesting ways (e.g., Kimberg, D'Esposito, & Farah, 1997; Luciana & Collins, 1997).

EMOTIONAL FACTORS. A host of emotional factors can also modulate an individual's performance on working memory tasks. The best documented is anxiety (particularly, test anxiety), which seems to have a negative impact on working memory performance (M. W. Eysenck & Calvo, 1992), especially on tasks that are verbal, but not visuospatial, in nature (Markham & Darke, 1991). (See also Ashcraft, Kirk, & Hopko, in press, for the effects of mathematics anxiety.) Positive mood (Oaksford, Morris, Grainger, & Williams, 1996) and smoking urges (Zwaan & Truitt, 1998) are two other emotional factors that have recently been shown to influence working memory functioning.

It is important to point out that, with the exception of cognitive development and aging, empirical studies of these capacity-modulating factors have just begun. Thus, the nature and extent of the influence on working memory associated with each brain pathology, each drug, and each emotional factor has not been well specified yet. For example, it is not completely clear what aspects of working memory (e.g., active maintenance and/or executive control; verbal, visuospatial, and/or numerical) are influenced by each factor. There are also reports of seemingly conflicting results (particularly for the effects of different neuropharmacological factors and emotional factors), pointing to the complexity and multifaceted nature of the effects. Certainly, a more systematic documentation of the working memory effects for each factor is needed.

Nonetheless, we believe that extending the scope of working memory models to include these capacity-modulating factors will become increasingly important for several reasons. First, the fact that these diverse factors somehow all influence working memory itself presents a major theoretical challenge. Any comprehensive model of working memory must eventually be able to explain why that is indeed the case. Second, an attempt to figure out the mechanism(s) underlying each of these factors provides a useful test bed for models of working memory. In particular, such an attempt is likely to help delimit the explanatory scope or power of different theoretical constructs – for example, examining the applicability of the W parameter in the ACT-R framework (Lovett et al., Chapter 5) to different types of intraindividual or interindividual differences may help define more sharply what it can do and cannot do. The same argument holds for the knowledge and skills account strongly advocated by Young and Lewis (Chapter 7) and Ericsson and Delaney (Chapter 8). Moreover, models of working memory are likely to provide an important theoretical basis for the empirical studies of these factors themselves. Thus, a closer rapprochement between theoretical models of working memory and empirical studies of these capacity-limiting factors is likely to mutually illuminate each other.

Emotion, Working Memory, and Executive Control

The effects of emotional factors (e.g., anxiety, mood, smoking urges) on intraindividual differences in working memory suggest another promising research direction, namely, the relationship among emotion, working memory, and executive control. As is clear from the reading of Chapters 2 to 11, most empirical studies and theoretical models of working memory have focused on the active processing and maintenance of emotionally neutral information (Barnard's ICS architecture, discussed in Chapter 9, is a major exception; see also Schneider, Chapter 10; O'Reilly et al., Chapter 11). As indicated by recent neuroanatomical findings, however, there may be a much closer connection between emotion and working memory than is currently appreciated (A. R. Damasio, 1994; Kosslyn & Koenig, 1992/1995; LeDoux, 1996; Rolls, 1996), and an exploration of the relationship of emotion to working memory and executive control may become increasingly important in the future.

Indeed, the PFC, which constitutes an integral part of the working memory circuitry in the brain (Engle et al., Chapter 4; O'Reilly et al., Chapter 11), is closely connected with some brain structures known for their role in the processing of emotions. One such emotion-related neural substrate is the amygdala, a subcortical structure closely associated with the feeling of fear (LeDoux, 1996). Although the amygdala sends relatively sparse connections to the lateral portion of PFC, it sends strong connections to the orbital portion of the PFC, part of which (specifically, the ventromedial portion) was damaged in the cases of famous frontal-lobe patients – Phineas Gage (Damasio, Grabowski, Frank, Galaburda, & Damasio, 1994) and EVR or "Eliott" (A. R. Damasio, 1994) – who demonstrated severe "dysexecutive" problems in everyday planning and decision making. In addition, the amygdala also sends strong connections to the anterior cingulate cortex, which constitutes an integral part of the "anterior attention" system or the "executive attention" network (Posner & Peterson, 1990; see also Engle et al., Chapter 4). These projections from the amygdala to prefrontal regions highlight the possibility that emotion may exert an important influence on working memory and executive control.

In addition to these neuroanatomical reasons, there are also several important cognitive-level reasons why we believe the scope of models of working memory needs to be extended to include the processing and regulation of emotional information. First, just as working memory may serve as an interface between perception and cognition (or external and internal representations), it may also serve as an interface between emotion and cognition. Indeed, in his recent book *The Emotional Brain*, LeDoux (1996) identifies "how emotional information comes to be represented in working memory" (p. 282) as a crucial question for the cognitive neuroscience of emotion, because it allows researchers to address emotion in a concrete mechanistic manner (i.e., in a manner analogous to the way we address verbal and visuospatial information) and may eventually help them tackle the bigger, more difficult question of how conscious feelings of emotions come about.

Second, extending the scope of working memory models to encompass emotion may also be a key to better understanding the mechanisms of executive control and eventually resolving the "homunculus" problem (O'Reilly et al., Chapter 11). For example, A. R. Damasio (1994) recently put forth an intriguing argument that emotion may play an integral role in controlling and regulating cognitive activities. In any complex decision-making or reasoning context, there are a myriad of possible choices of action, possibly too many to explicitly consider without exceeding limits of working memory or attention. Fortunately, some options are associated with negative emotions or feelings because of previous experience and, when these options come to mind, one may have a fleeting negative reaction or "gut feeling." This negative reaction is what Damasio (1994) calls a "somatic marker," formed and stored in the ventromedial portion of the PFC. According to Damasio, somatic markers allow one to immediately and unconsciously reject choices of action associated with those negative "gut feelings," thus reducing the number of possible courses of action (or "problem space") that must be attended to and consciously considered and making the decision-making process significantly faster and more efficient.

Recent studies using a gambling paradigm yielded evidence consistent with this "somatic marker" hypothesis (Bechara, Damasio, Tranel, & Damasio, 1997; Bechara, Tranel, Damasio, & Damasio, 1996). In these studies, normal participants showed anticipatory skin conductance responses (SCRs) before choosing cards from risky decks, suggesting they had unconscious awareness of risk, but patients with damage to the ventromedial PFC were found not to show these SCRs, suggesting that one source of their deficits might be an inability to form negative emotional associations with options that have negative consequences. Albeit highly controversial, A. R. Damasio's (1994) hypothesis provides an intriguing account of how emotions might play an integral role in executive control of behavior.

Currently, emotion and cognition are treated as completely separate topics in psychology, as reflected by the fact that, out of 16 cognitive psychology textbooks we own, only one (M. W. Eysenck & Keane, 1995) includes a chapter specifically dedicated to the issue of the cognition–emotion relationship. An exploration of the relationship between emotion, working memory, and executive control may help bring studies of cognition and studies of emotion into closer alignment with each other.

More Competitive Argumentation and Further Theoretical Synthesis

We would like to end our discussion of future research directions by emphasizing again the importance of competitive argumentation and theoretical synthesis in the studies of working memory. As we outlined in Chapter 1 (Shah & Miyake), it was actually one of the major reasons why we originally decided to edit this volume. We believe that the systematic, issue-by-issue comparison of the 10 models of working memory offered in this volume successfully elucidate several important general agreements that seem to be emerging in the field, along with some major disagreements and unresolved issues that need to be addressed in future research. Although the differences in theoretical scope did not necessarily allow us to directly compare all 10 models on all eight dimensions covered by the designated questions, we nonetheless believe that this volume, as a whole, offers some useful crystallization of what theoretical ideas and proposals are merely complementary and, hence, need to be synthesized and integrated and what theoretical ideas and proposals are mutually incompatible and, hence, need to be empirically tested in future research.

Now it is time to move forward and start rigorously testing competing, mutually incompatible claims through competitive argumentation as well as actively synthesizing mutually compatible ideas within a coherent framework toward the larger goal of a unified theory of working memory. Given the enormously wide range of issues and topics that working memory encompasses, it is probably not surprising that a comprehensive theory of working memory is actually something akin to a unified theory of cognition. Although we still have a long way to go, the general consensus that seems to be emerging across different models of working memory represented in this volume makes us cautiously optimistic about the possibility of eventually being able to develop such a theory.

Concluding Remarks

Theoretical conceptions of working memory have changed dramatically during the past 30 years or so. Although the traditional notion of STM is still prevalent, the 10 models represented in this volume make us realize how much progress the field has made since the proposal of the highly influential modal model of human memory (Atkinson & Shiffrin, 1968). We were particularly struck by the research progress made in the field when we recently reread the classic book *Models of Human Memory* (Norman, 1970), on which the main title of this volume is based. Although the Norman (1970) book is a collection of various models of human memory in general, not necessarily models of working memory or STM per se, the main theme that runs through all the models in that volume (perhaps except Feigenbaum's, 1970, EPAM model) is the metatheoretical notion that "memory" is for "memorizing." The types of phenomena that these models focused on were so far removed from other domains of cognition that, in his final overview chapter, Reitman (1970) cautioned that "the simplifications involved in producing these memory models and data typically are quite severe, raising questions about their relevance to everyday memory phenomena, particularly those of interest to the student of thinking" (p. 473). In contrast, the distinction between "memory" and "thinking" is now no longer clear and, as we argued above, one of the major themes that run across the models of working memory in the current volume is, rather, that the "memory" function of working memory is in the service of complex cognition.

The Norman (1970) book was published when the limitations of the modal model of human memory had begun to become obvious. Although the details differed from model to model, many models included in the Norman volume were essentially variations of the modal model and, hence, their claims about STM became quickly obsolete, particularly after Baddeley and Hitch (1974) proposed a more processing-oriented, multicomponent model of working memory only four years after the publication of the book.

The notion of working memory is currently going through rapid changes. As we document in this volume, the models of working memory have begun to specify the once-neglected executive control mechanisms. The integral role that long-term knowledge and skills play in working memory performance has not necessarily been widely recognized at least until quite recently, but many models now explicitly acknowledge its contribution. As we suggested earlier, an exploration of the interaction between external and internal memory representations will further extend the scope of working memory research and is likely to change the theoretical scene of the field. Moreover, we now know much more about the neural basis of working memory than we did 10 years ago, and advances in neuroscience methods and technologies will no doubt yield new results and findings that fundamentally challenge the current conceptions of working memory.

Given such rapid changes in this field, we invite readers to speculate whether the same fate that overtook the Norman (1970) volume – serving as a midwife to a revolution – awaits the current volume and the models of working memory presented here. It is quite possible that some major reconceptualization of the current notion of working memory will take place and will replace it with a totally new concept. Another possibility is that future research will successfully specify different functions and subsystems of working memory to the extent that an umbrella term like "working memory" or the "central executive" may no longer be necessary. Regardless of what fate befalls this volume, however, we hope that the theoretical ideas that the contributors of this volume so eloquently and sometimes even passionately put forth in their respective chapters will inspire further systematic research and theorizing on working memory and eventually lead to better, more comprehensive models of working memory.

REFERENCES

Allport, A. (1993). Attention and control: Have we been asking the wrong questions: A critical review of twenty-five years. In D. E. Meyer & S. Kornblum (Eds.), *Attention and performance XIV: Synergies in experimental psychology, artificial intelligence, and cognitive neuroscience*. Cambridge, MA: MIT Press.
Anderson, J. R. (1990). *The adaptive character of thought*. Hillsdale, NJ: Erlbaum.
Arnetet, P. A., Rao, S. M., Grafman, J., Bernardin, L., Luchetta, T., Binder, J. R., Lobeck, L. (1997). Executive functions in multiple sclerosis: An analysis of temporal ordering, semantic encoding, and planning abilities. *Neuropsychology, 11*, 535–544.
Ashcraft, M. H., Kirk, E. P., & Hopko, D. (in press). On the cognitive consequences of mathematics anxiety. In C. Dolan (Ed.), *The development of mathematical skills*. Hove, UK: Psychology Press.
Atkinson, R. C., & Shiffrin, R. M. (1968). Human memory: A proposed system and its control processes. In K. W. Spence & J. T. Spence (Eds.), *The psychology of learning and motivation: Advances in research and theory* (Vol. 2, pp. 89–195). New York: Academic Press.
Awh, E., & Jonides, J. (1998). Spatial selective attention and spatial working memory. In R. Parasuraman (Ed.), *The attentive brain* (pp. 353–380). Cambridge, MA: MIT Press.

Baddeley, A. D. (1986). *Working memory*. New York: Oxford University Press.

Baddeley, A. D. (1993). Working memory or working attention? In A. D. Baddeley & L. Weiskrantz (Eds.), *Attention: Selection, awareness, and control. A tribute to Donald Broadbent* (pp. 152–170). New York: Oxford University Press.

Baddeley, A. D. (1996a). Exploring the central executive. *Quarterly Journal of Experimental Psychology, 49A*, 5–28.

Baddeley, A. D. (1996b). The concept of working memory. In S. E. Gathercole (Ed.), *Models of short-term memory* (pp. 1–27). Hove, UK: Psychology Press.

Baddeley, A. D. (1998). The central executive: A concept and some misconceptions. *Journal of the International Neuropsychological Society, 4*, 523–526.

Baddeley, A. D., Della Sala, S., Papagno, C., & Spinnler, H. (1997). Dual-task performance in dysexecutive and nondysexecutive patients with a frontal lesion. *Neuropsychology, 11*, 187–194.

Baddeley, A. D., Gathercole, S. E., & Papagno, C. (1998). The phonological loop as a language learning device. *Psychological Review, 105*, 158–173.

Baddeley, A. D., & Hitch, G. J. (1974). Working memory. In G. H. Bower (Ed.), *The psychology of learning and motivation: Advances in research and theory* (Vol. 8, pp. 47–89). New York: Academic Press.

Baddeley, A. D., & Hitch, G. J. (1993). The recency effect: Implicit learning with explicit retrieval? *Memory & Cognition, 21*, 146–155

Ballard, D. H., Hayhoe, M. M., Pook, P. K., & Rao, R. P. N. (1997). Deictic codes for the embodiment of cognition. *Behavioral and Brain Sciences, 20*, 723–767.

Barkley, R. A. (1997). Behavioral inhibition, sustained attention, and executive functions: Constructing a unifying theory of ADHD. *Psychological Bulletin, 121*, 65–94.

Bechara, A., Damasio, H., Tranel, D., & Damasio, A. R. (1997). Deciding advantageously before knowing the advantageous strategy. *Science, 275*, 1293–1294

Bechara, A., Tranel, D., Damasio, H., & Damasio, A. R. (1996). Failure to respond autonomically to anticipated future outcomes following damage to prefrontal cortex. *Cerebral Cortex, 6*, 215–225.

Bennetto, L., Pennington, B. F., & Rogers, S. J. (1996). Intact and impaired memory functions in autism. *Child Development, 67*, 1816–1835.

Bishop, D. V. M., North, T., & Donlan, C. (1996). Nonword repetition as a phenotypic marker for inherited language impairment: Evidence from a twin study. *Journal of Child Psychology and Child Psychiatry, 37*, 391–404.

Brugger, P., Monsch, A. U., Salmon, D. P., & Butters, N. (1996). Random number generation in dementia of the Alzheimer type: A test of frontal executive functions. *Neuropsychologia, 34*, 97–103.

Byrne, M. D. (1998). Taking a computational approach to aging: The SPAN theory of working memory. *Psychology and Aging, 13*, 309–322.

Carlson, R. A. (1997). *Experienced cognition*. Mahwah, NJ: Erlbaum.

Carlson, R. A., Wenger, J. L., & Sullivan, M. A. (1993). Coordinating information from perception and working memory. *Journal of Experimental Psychology: Human Perception and Performance, 19*, 531–548.

Caspari, I., Parkinson, S. R., LaPointe, L. L., & Katz, R. C. (1998). Working memory and aphasia. *Brain and Cognition, 37*, 205–223.

Cohen, J. D., Dunbar, K., & McClelland, J. L. (1990). On the control of automatic processes: A parallel distributed processing model of the Stroop effect. *Psychological Review, 97*, 332–361.

Conway, A. R. A., & Engle, R. W. (1994). Working memory and retrieval: A resource-dependent inhibition model. *Journal of Experimental Psychology: General, 123,* 354–373.

Courtney, S. M., Petit, L., Maisog, J. M., Ungerleider, L. G., & Haxby, J. V. (1998). An area specialized for spatial working memory in human frontal cortex. *Science, 279,* 1347–1350.

Cowan, N. (1995). *Attention and memory: An integrated framework.* New York: Oxford University Press.

Cowan, N. (1997). The development of working memory. In N. Cowan (Ed.), *The development of memory in childhood* (pp. 163–199). Hove, UK: Psychology Press.

Crowder, R. G. (1982). The demise of short-term memory. *Acta Psychologica, 50,* 291–323.

Damasio, A. R. (1994). *Descartes' error: Emotion, reason, and the human brain.* New York: Grosset/Putnam.

Damasio, H., Grabowski, T. J., Frank, R., Galaburda, A. M., & Damasio, A. R. (1994). The return of Phineas Gage: Clues about the brain from the skull of a famous patient. *Science, 264,* 1102–1105.

Daneman, M., & Carpenter, P. A. (1980). Individual differences in working memory and reading. *Journal of Verbal Learning and Verbal Behavior, 19,* 450–466.

Daneman, M., & Tardif, T. (1987). Working memory and reading skill reexamined. In M. Coltheart (Ed.), *Attention and performance XII: The psychology of reading* (pp. 491–508). Hillsdale, NJ: Erlbaum.

D'Esposito, M., Aguirre, G. K., Zarahn, E., Ballard, D., & Shin, R. K. (1998). Functional MRI studies of spatial and non-spatial working memory. *Cognitive Brain Research, 7,* 1–13.

D'Esposito, M., Detre, J. A., Alsop, D. C., Shin, R. K., Atlas, S., & Grossman, M. (1995). The neural basis of the central executive system of working memory. *Nature, 378,* 279–281.

Donald, M. (1991). *Origins of the modern mind: Three stages in the evolution of culture and cognition.* Cambridge, MA: Harvard University Press.

Duncan, J., Johnson, R., Swales, M., & Freer, C. (1997). Frontal lobe deficits after head injury: Unity and diversity of function. *Cognitive Neuropsychology, 14,* 713–741.

Ellis, N. C., & Sinclair, S. G. (1996). Working memory in the acquisition of vocabulary and syntax: Putting language in good order. *Quarterly Journal of Experimental Psychology, 49A,* 234–250.

Elman, J. L. (1993). Learning and development in neural networks: The importance of starting small. *Cognition, 48,* 71–99.

Engle, R. W., Tuholski, S. W., Laughlin, J. E., & Conway, A. R. A. (in press). Working memory, short-term memory, and general fluid intelligence: A latent variable approach. *Journal of Experimental Psychology: General.*

Ericsson, K. A., & Kintsch, W. (1995). Long-term working memory. *Psychological Review, 102,* 211–245.

Eysenck, H. J. (1986). The theory of intelligence and the psychophysiology of cognition. In R. J. Sternberg (Ed.), *Advances in the psychology of human intelligence* (Vol. 3, pp. 1–34). Hillsdale, NJ: Erlbaum.

Eysenck, M. W., & Calvo, M. G. (1992). Anxiety and performance: The processing efficiency theory. *Cognition and Emotion, 6,* 409–434.

Eysenck, M. W., & Keane, M. T. (1995). *Cognitive psychology: A student's handbook.* Hove, UK: Erlbaum.

Feigenbaum, E. A. (1970). Information processing and memory. In D. A. Norman (Ed.), *Models of human memory* (pp. 451–468). New York: Academic Press.

Fletcher, J. M., Brookshire, B. L., Landry, S. H., Bohan, T. P., Davidson, K. C., Francis, D. J., Levin, H. S., Brandt, M. E., & Kramer, L. A. (1996). Attentional skills and executive functions in children with early hydrocephalus. *Developmental Neuropsychology, 12,* 53–76.

Fuster, J. M. (1995). *Memory in the cerebral cortex: An empirical approach to neural networks in the human and nonhuman primate.* Cambridge, MA: MIT Press.

Fuster, J. M. (1997). *The prefrontal cortex: Anatomy, physiology, and neuropsychology of the frontal lobe* (3rd ed.). Philadelphia: Lippincott–Raven.

Glenberg, A. M. (1997). What memory is for. *Behavioral and Brain Sciences, 20,* 1–55.

Goldman-Rakic, P. S. (1995). Architecture of the prefrontal cortex and the central executive. *Annals of the New York Academy of Sciences, 769,* 71–83.

Haberlandt, K. (1997). *Cognitive psychology* (2nd ed.). Boston: Allyn & Bacon.

Halford, G. S., Wilson, W. H., & Phillips, S. (1998). Processing capacity defined by relational complexity: Implications for comparative, developmental, and cognitive psychology. *Behavioral and Brain Sciences, 21,* 803–864.

Hayhoe, M. M., Bensinger, D. G., & Ballard, D. H. (1998). Task constraints in visual working memory. *Vision Research, 38,* 125–137.

Hummel, J. E., & Holyoak, K. J. (1997). Distributed representations of structure: A theory of analogical access and mapping. *Psychological Review, 104,* 427–466.

Hutchins, E. (1995). *Cognition in the wild.* Cambridge, MA: MIT Press.

Jonides, J., & Smith, E. E. (1997). The architecture of working memory. In M. D. Rugg (Ed.), *Cognitive neuroscience* (pp. 243–276). Cambridge, MA: MIT Press.

Just, M. A., & Carpenter, P. A. (1992). A capacity theory of comprehension: Individual differences in working memory. *Psychological Review, 99,* 122–149.

Kahneman, D. (1973). *Attention and effort.* Englewood Cliffs, NJ: Prentice-Hall.

Kareev, Y. (1995). Through a narrow window: Working memory capacity and the detection of covariation. *Cognition, 56,* 263–269.

Kareev, Y., Lieberman, I., & Lev, M. (1997). Through a narrow window: Sample size and the perception of correlation. *Journal of Experimental Psychology: General, 126,* 278–287.

Kimberg, D. Y., D'Esposito, M., & Farah, M. J. (1997). Effects of bromocriptine on human subjects depend on working memory capacity. *NeuroReport, 8,* 3581–3585.

Kimberg, D. Y., & Farah, M. J. (1993). A unified account of cognitive impairments following frontal lobe damage: The role of working memory in complex, organized behavior. *Journal of Experimental Psychology: General, 122,* 411–428.

Kintsch, W. (1998). *Comprehension: A paradigm for cognition.* New York: Cambridge University Press.

Kirsh, D., & Maglio, P. (1994). On distinguishing epistemic from pragmatic action. *Cognitive Science, 18,* 513–550.

Kosslyn, S. M., & Koenig, O. (1992/1995). *Wet mind: The new cognitive neuroscience.* New York: Free Press.

Larkin, J. H., & Simon, H. A. (1987). Why a diagram is (sometimes) worth ten thousand words. *Cognitive Science, 11,* 65–99.

LeDoux, J. (1996). *The emotional brain: The mysterious underpinnings of emotional life.* New York: Simon & Schuster.

Luciana, M., & Collins, P. F. (1997). Dopaminergic modulation of working memory for spatial but not object cues in normal humans. *Journal of Cognitive Neuroscience, 9,* 330–347.

Lyon, G. R., & Krasnegor, N. A. (Eds.). (1996). *Attention, memory, and executive function.* Baltimore: Brookes.

Markham, R., & Darke, S. (1991). The effects of anxiety on verbal and spatial task performance. *Australian Journal of Psychology, 43,* 107–111.

Mazzocco, M. M., Hagerman, R. J., Cronister-Silverman, A., & Pennington, B. (1992). Specific frontal lobe deficits among women with the fragile X gene. *Journal of the American Academy of Child and Adolescent Psychiatry, 31,* 1141–1148.

McDowell, S., D'Esposito, M., & Whyte, J. (1997). Working memory impairments in traumatic brain injury: Evidence from a dual-task paradigm. *Neuropsychologia, 35,* 1341–1353.

Meyer, D. E., & Kieras, D. E. (1997). A computational theory of executive cognitive processes and multiple-task performance: II. Accounts of psychological refractory-period phenomena. *Psychological Review, 104,* 749–791.

Miyake, A., Carpenter, P. A., & Just, M. A., (1994). A capacity approach to syntactic comprehension disorders: Making normal adults perform like aphasic patients. *Cognitive Neuropsychology, 11,* 671–717.

Montgomery, J. W. (1995). Sentence comprehension in children with specific language impairment: The role of phonological working memory. *Journal of Speech and Hearing Research, 38,* 187–199.

Morris, R. (1994). Working memory in Alzheimer's disease. *Neuropsychology, 8,* 545–554.

Moscovitch, M., & Umiltà, C. (1990). Modularity and neuropsychology: Modules and central processes in attention and memory. In M. F. Schwartz (Ed.), *Modular deficits in Alzheimer-type dementia* (pp. 1–59). Cambridge, MA: MIT Press.

Murray, L. L., Holland, A. L., & Beeson, P. M. (1997). Grammaticality judgments of mildly aphasic individuals under dual-task conditions. *Aphasiology, 11,* 993–1106.

Navon, D., & Gopher, D. (1979). On the economy of the human processing system. *Psychological Review, 86,* 214–255.

Newell, A. (1973). You can't play 20 questions with nature and win: Projective comments on the papers of this symposium. In W. G. Chase (Ed.), *Visual information processing* (pp. 283–308). New York: Academic Press.

Newport, E. L. (1990). Maturational constraints on language learning. *Cognitive Science, 14,* 11–28.

Norman, D. A. (Ed.). (1970). *Models of human memory.* New York: Academic Press.

Norman, D. A., & Bobrow, D. J. (1975). On data-limited and resource-limited processes. *Cognitive Psychology, 7,* 44–64.

Oaksford, M., Morris, F., Grainger, B., & Williams, J. M. G. (1996). Mood, reasoning, and central executive processes. *Journal of Experimental Psychology: Learning, Memory, and Cognition, 22,* 476–492.

Owen, A. M. (1997). The functional organization of working memory processes within human lateral frontal cortex: The contribution of functional neuroimaging. *European Journal of Neuroscience, 9,* 1329–1339.

Owen, A. M., Iddon, J. L., Hodges, J. R., Summers, B. A., & Robbins, T. W. (1997). Spatial and non-spatial working memory at different stages of Parkinson's disease. *Neuropsychologia, 35,* 519–532.

Pashler, H. (1992). Attentional limitations in doing two tasks at the same time. *Current Directions in Psychological Science, 1,* 44–48.

Pashler, H. (1994). Dual-task interference in simple tasks: Data and theory. *Psychological Bulletin, 116,* 220–244.

Pashler, H. E. (1997). *The psychology of attention.* Cambridge, MA: MIT Press.

Petrides, M. (1995). Functional organization of the human frontal cortex for mnemonic processing: Evidence from neuroimaging studies. *Annals of the New York Academy of Sciences, 769,* 85–96.

Pichora-Fuller, M. K., Schneider, B. A., & Daneman, M. (1995). How young and old adults listen to and remember speech in noise. *Journal of the Acoustical Society of America, 97,* 593–608.

Platt, J. R. (1964). Strong inference. *Science, 146,* 347–353.

Plomin, R., Fulker, D. W., Corley, R., & DeFries, J. C. (1997). Nature, nurture, and cognitive development from 1 to 16 years: A parent–offspring adoption study. *Psychological Science, 8,* 442–447.

Posner, M., & Peterson, S. (1990). The attention system of the human brain. *Annual Review of Neuroscience, 13,* 25–42.

Posner, M. I., & Raichle, M. E. (1994). *Images of mind.* New York: Scientific American Books.

Rabbitt, P. (Ed.). (1997a). *Methodology of frontal and executive function.* Hove, UK: Psychology Press.

Rabbitt, P. (1997b). Introduction: Methodologies and models in the study of executive function. In P. Rabbitt (Ed.), *Methodology of frontal and executive function* (pp. 1–38). Hove, UK: Psychology Press.

Rao, S. C., Rainer, G., & Miller, E. (1997). Integration of what and where in the primate prefrontal cortex. *Science, 276,* 821–824.

Rapeli, P., Service, E., Salin, P., & Holapainen, A. (1997). A dissociation between simple and complex span impairment in alcoholics. *Memory, 5,* 741–762.

Reisberg, D., Rappaport, I., & O'Shaughnessy, M. (1984). The limits of working memory: The digit digit-span. *Journal of Experimental Psychology: Learning, Memory, and Cognition, 10,* 203–221.

Reitman, W. (1970). What does it take to remember? In D. A. Norman (Ed.), *Models of human memory* (pp. 470–508). New York: Academic Press.

Roberts, R. J., Hager, L. D., & Heron, C. (1994). Prefrontal cognitive processes: Working memory and inhibition in the antisaccade task. *Journal of Experimental Psychology: General, 123,* 374–393.

Rogers, R. D., & Monsell, S. (1995). Costs of a predictable switch between simple cognitive tasks. *Journal of Experimental Psychology: General, 124,* 207–231.

Rolls, E. T. (1996). The orbitofrontal cortex. *Philosophical Transactions of the Royal Society of London, 351,* 1433–1444.

Rosen, V. M., & Engle, R. W. (1997). The role of working memory capacity in retrieval. *Journal of Experimental Psychology: General, 126,* 211–227.

Saffran, J. R., Aslin, R. N., & Newport, E. L. (1996). Statistical learning by 8-month-old infants. *Science, 274,* 1926–1928.

Salthouse, T. A. (1996). The processing-speed theory of adult age differences in cognition. *Psychological Review, 103*, 403–428.

Salthouse, T., & Meinz, E. J. (1995). Aging, inhibition, working memory, and speed. *Journals of Gerontology: Psychological Sciences, 50B*, P297–P306.

Shah, P., & Miyake, A. (1996). The separability of working memory resources for spatial thinking and language processing: An individual differences approach. *Journal of Experimental Psychology: General, 125*, 4–27.

Shastri, L., & Ajjanagadde, V. (1993). From simple associations to systematic reasoning: A connectionist representation of rules, variables, and dynamic bindings using temporal synchrony. *Behavioral and Brain Sciences, 16*, 417–494.

Stoltzfus, E. R., Hasher, L., & Zacks, R. T. (1996). Working memory and aging: Current status of the inhibitory view. In J. T. E. Richardson, R. W. Engle, L. Hasher, R. H. Logie, E. R. Stoltzfus, & R. T. Zacks (Eds.), *Working memory and human cognition* (pp. 66–88). New York: Oxford University Press.

Stuss, D. T., Shallice, T., Alexander, M. P., & Picton, T. W. (1995). Structure and functions of the human prefrontal cortex. *Annals of the New York Academy of Sciences, 769*, 191–211.

Styles, E. A. (1997). *The psychology of attention*. Hove, UK: Psychology Press.

Suchman, L. (1987). *Plans and situated actions: The problem of human-machine communication*. New York: Cambridge University Press.

Sullivan, E. V., Shear, P. K., Zipursky, R. B., Sager, H. J., & Pfefferbaum, A. (1997). Patterns of content, contextual, and working memory impairments in schizophrenia and nonamnesic alcoholism. *Neuropsychology, 11*, 195–206.

Towse, J. N. (1998). On random generation and the central executive of working memory. *British Journal of Psychology, 89*, 77–101.

Towse, J. N., Hitch, G. J., & Hutton, U. (1998). A reevaluation of working memory capacity in children. *Journal of Memory and Language, 39*, 195–217.

Towse, J. N., & Valentine, J. D. (1997). Random generation of numbers: A search for underlying processes. *European Journal of Cognitive Psychology, 9*, 381–400.

Van der Linden, M., Bredart, S., & Beerten, A. (1994). Age-related differences in updating working memory. *British Journal of Psychology, 85*, 145–152.

Vandierendonck, A., De Vooght, G., & Van der Goten, K. (1998). Interfering with the central executive by means of a random interval repetition task. *Quarterly Journal of Experimental Psychology, 51A*, 197–218.

VanLehn, K., Brown, J. S., & Greeno, J. (1984). Competitive argumentation in computational theories of cognition. In W. Kintsch, J. R. Miller, & P. G. Polson (Eds.), *Methods and tactics in cognitive science* (pp. 235–262). Hillsdale, NJ: Erlbaum.

Wadsworth, S. J., DeFries, J. C., Fulker, D. W., Olson, R. K., & Pennington, B. F. (1995). Reading performance and verbal short-term memory: A twin study of reciprocal causation. *Intelligence, 20*, 145–167.

Ward, G., & Allport, A. (1997). Planning and problem-solving using the five-disc Tower of London task. *Quarterly Journal of Experimental Psychology, 50A*, 49–78.

Waters, G. S., & Caplan, D. (1996). The measurement of verbal working memory capacity and its relation to reading comprehension. *Quarterly Journal of Experimental Psychology, 49A*, 51–79.

Weismer, S. E. (1996). Capacity limitations in working memory: The impact of lexical and morphological learning by children with language impairment. *Topics in Language Disorders, 17*, 33–44.

Welsh, M. C., Pennington, B. F., Ozonoff, S., Rouse, B., & McCabe, X. (1990). Neuropsychology of early-treated phenylketonuria: Specific executive function deficits. *Child Development, 61,* 1697–1713.

Wickens, C. D. (1984). Processing resources in attention. In R. Parasuraman & D. R. Davies (Eds.), *Varieties of attention* (pp. 63–102). New York: Academic Press.

Zacks, R. T., & Hasher, L. (1997). Cognitive gerontology and attentional inhibition: A reply to Burke and McDowd. *Journal of Gerontology: Psychological Sciences, 52B,* P274-P283.

Zhang, J. (1997). The nature of external representations in problem solving. *Cognitive Science, 21,* 179–217.

Zhang, J., & Norman, D. A. (1994). Representations in distributed cognitive tasks. *Cognitive Science, 18,* 87–122.

Zwaan, R. A., & Truitt, T. P. (1998). Smoking urges affect language processing. *Experimental and Clinical Psychopharmacology, 6,* 325–330.

Author Index

Note: The notations *n*, *t*, and *f* refer to citations in footnotes, tables, and figure captions, respectively.

Subject Index

The subject index is organized in two sections. The first section is a special index designed to facilitate comparisons of the working memory theories represented in the volume. It provides pointers to the pages in the text that are most relevant to the respective designated theoretical questions (see Table 1.1, pp. 5–6); there may be other parts of the text that also refer to the issues raised in those questions (particularly Chapters 4 and 8, which address the designated questions in a more distributed manner than other chapters).

The second section is a regular subject index that picks up more specific terms used in each chapter. Whenever an entry in the regular subject index refers to one or more of the designated questions, see also the corresponding entries in the first section.

Index for the Eight Designated Questions

Note: The numbers in parentheses designate the chapter numbers; for example, 6–7(1) means pp. 6–7 of Chapter 1.

Index for Technical Terms and Concepts

Note: The notations *n, t,* and *f* mean the occurrence of the designated terms in footnotes, tables, and figure captions, respectively.